ROMANTICISM AND CONSCIOUSNESS

Essays in Criticism

ROMANTICISM

～ AND ～

CONSCIOUSNESS

Essays in Criticism

Edited by

HAROLD BLOOM

YALE UNIVERSITY

W · W · NORTON & COMPANY

New York · London

W. W. Norton & Company, Inc., 500 Fifth Avenue, New York, N.Y. 10110

Copyright © 1970 by W. W. Norton & Company, Inc.

ISBN 0-393-09954-7

Library of Congress Catalog Card No. 75-117446

PRINTED IN THE UNITED STATES OF AMERICA

2 3 4 5 6 7 8 9 0

Contents

v

Part Four *The Major Poets*

Preface

Freud, meditating upon the three powers—art, philosophy, religion—that might dispute the basic position of psychoanalysis, declined to regard the aesthetic opponent as serious:

> Art is almost always harmless and beneficent; it does not seek to be anything but an illusion. Except for a few people who are spoken of as being 'possessed' by art, it makes no attempt at invading the realm of reality.

In the context of Romanticism, Freud's statement is hardly adequate, though its confidence is appealing. Romanticism inescapably enters the realms of the reality principle, and students of the Romantic poets struggle with imaginative works that indeed seek to be anything but an illusion. This anthology collects what are in my judgment the best commentaries on the major intellectual issues created by Romanticism in its invasion of what Freud termed reality's realm.

As there are individual introductions to each of the four sections of this book, and since the volume's first essay was conceived as a thematic introduction to all that follows, this preface confines itself to explaining the book's organization. The first section, "Nature and Consciousness," collects exploratory studies of Romantic self-consciousness, for increasingly the advanced criticism of Romanticism has identified this area as the most central in our attempt to define our own relation to these poets. The second, "Nature and Revolution," brings together a group of essays definitively tracing the close effect of the French Revolution upon Romanticism. The third section, "Nature and Literary Form," attempts to establish the factors responsible for Romantic innovations in aesthetic theory and practice. The last section, "The Major Poets," supplements theoretical and historical studies with detailed criticism of the six major English Romantic poets.

Though some of the essays in this volume are advanced, their difficulty is always inevitable, and belongs to the proper study of these poets. The student and reader who persists will be rewarded by finding himself in these poets, by the aid of these scholars and critics, "more truly and more strange."

Harold Bloom

PART ONE

Nature and Consciousness

Subjectivity or self-consciousness is the salient problem of Romanticism, at least for modern readers, who tend to station themselves in regard to the Romantics depending on how relevant or adequate they judge the dialectic of consciousness and imagination to be. The essays in this section map the Romantics' myth of consciousness, starting with Samuel H. Monk's classic account of the greatest theoretician of the sublime mode, Edmund Burke, who has a unique relation to Romanticism. As a conservative political prophet, Burke led the British intellectual reaction against the French Revolution, but Burke's conservatism was as Romantic as Blake's or Shelley's radicalism, emphasizing as it did a longing for romance virtues in society, and a myth of societal bond transcending the cycles of mutability. The essay by Alfred Cobban in the next section examines this aspect of Burke; here Monk discusses Burke's significance as a literary aesthetician, whose conception of the sublime is fundamental to all Romantic quests, even for Blake, who insisted on his contempt for Burke's aesthetics as well as for his politics. Blake hated Burke's insistence on the "obscurity" of the Sublime, but may have insisted upon misunderstanding Burke's emphasis.

Burke's understanding that the mere description of nature is inadequate to express the soul's exaltation or terror in confronting the Sublime is related to the brief but profound chapter which I have excerpted from Owen Barfield's *Saving the Appearances, a Study in Idolatry*. Barfield is a historian of human consciousness, who, in this remarkable book, traces and deplores our loss of "participation," the awareness "of an extra-sensory link between the percipient and the representations." The progressive loss of the sense of participation, over the centuries, results in an idolatry of memory-images. In Barfield's view, Romanticism arose as an iconoclastic movement, seeking to smash the idols and return men to an original participation in phenomena.

This Romantic iconoclasm is explored in the essay by Geoffrey H. Hartman, but here the dream of original participation is set aside, with the critic's careful assumption that the divisions of self-consciousness are inevitable for the Romantic and modern mind. Excessive subjectivity is considered as a necessary stage in the mind's growth toward a more humanized imagination, marking the essay as a modern version of Wordsworthianism. The subsequent essay, drawn from J. H. Van den Berg's *Metabletica*, a brilliant phenomenological theory of a historical psychology, is a contrary statement to Hartman's, for it insists (convincingly to me) that the Romantic (and Freudian) estrangement from nature and other selves was and is unnecessary.

The two remaining essays in this section, by Paul de Man and W. K. Wimsatt, Jr., move the discussion to the imagistic edge of consciousness, and illuminate the structure of Romantic imagery in contrary but complementary ways. De Man, more powerfully than any other critic, emphasizes the Romantic renunciation of the natural object, and enhances our awareness of the intentional separation between consciousness and nature in Romantic vision. Wimsatt, in his justly celebrated essay, defines the radical difference from the past that characterizes Romantic nature imagery, with its importation of tenor into vehicle, a microcosmic instance of the Romantic longing (despite knowing better) for unity. It may be noted that Burke (as expounded by Monk), Hartman, and de Man tend to line up in one tradition, emphasizing the necessary disjunction between nature and consciousness, while Barfield, Van den Berg, and Wimsatt fit together in a contrary tradition (a less Romantic one), setting a higher value on a union or reconciliation between nature and consciousness.

HAROLD BLOOM

The Internalization of Quest-Romance †

Freud, in an essay written sixty years ago on the relation of the poet to daydreaming, made the surmise that all aesthetic pleasure is forepleasure, an "incitement premium" or narcissistic fantasy. The deepest satisfactions of literature, in this view, come from a release of tensions in the psyche. That Freud had found, as almost always, either part of the truth or at least a way to it, is clear enough, even if a student of Blake or Wordsworth finds, as probably he must, this Freudian view to be partial, reductive, and a kind of mirror image of the imagination's truth. The deepest satisfactions of reading Blake or Wordsworth come from the realization of new ranges of tensions in the mind, but Blake and Wordsworth both believed, in different ways, that the pleasures of poetry were only forepleasures, in the sense that poems, finally, were scaffoldings for a more imaginative vision, and not ends in themselves. I think that what Blake and Wordsworth do for their readers, or can do, is closely related to what Freud does or can do for his, which is to provide both a map of the mind and a profound faith that the map can be put to a saving use. Not that the uses agree, or that the maps quite agree either, but the enterprise is a humanizing one in all three of these discoverers. The humanisms do not agree either; Blake's is apocalyptic, Freud's is naturalistic, and Wordsworth's is—sometimes sublimely, sometimes uneasily—blended of elements that dominate in the other two.

Freud thought that even romance, with its elements of play, probably commenced in some actual experience whose "strong impression on the writer had stirred up a memory of an earlier experience, generally belonging to childhood, which then arouses a wish that finds a fulfillment in the work in question, and in which elements of the recent event and the old memory should be discernible." Though this is a brilliant and comprehensive thought, it seems inadequate to the complexity of romance, particularly in the period during which romance as a genre, however displaced, became again the dominant form, which is to say the age of Romanticism.

† First published in *The Yale Review*, Vol. LVIII, No. 4 (Summer, 1969). Copyright © 1969 by Harold Bloom.

For English-speaking readers, this age may be defined as extending from the childhood of Blake and Wordsworth to the present moment. Convenience dictates that we distinguish the High Romantic period proper, during which the half-dozen major English poets did their work, from the generations that have come after them, but the distinction is difficult to justify critically.

Freud's embryonic theory of romance contains within it the potential for an adequate account of Romanticism, particularly if we interpret his "memory of an earlier experience" to mean also the recall of an earlier insight, or yearning, that may not have been experiential. The immortal longings of the child, rather variously interpreted by Freud, Blake, and Wordsworth, may not be at the roots of romance, historically speaking, since those roots go back to a psychology very different from ours, but they do seem to be at the sources of the mid-eighteenth-century revival of a romance consciousness, out of which nineteenth-century Romanticism largely came.

J. H. Van den Berg, whose introduction to a historical psychology I find crucial to an understanding of Romanticism, thinks that Rousseau "was the first to view the child as a child, and to stop treating the child as an adult." Van den Berg, as a doctor, does not think this was necessarily an advance: "Ever since Rousseau the child has been keeping its distance. This process of the child and adult growing away from each other began in the eighteenth century. It was then that the period of adolescence came into existence." Granting that Van den Berg is broadly correct (he at least attempts to explain an apparent historical modulation in consciousness that few historians of culture care to confront), then we are presented with another in a series of phenomena, clustering around Rousseau and his age, in which the major change from the Enlightenment to Romanticism manifested itself. Some of these are analyzed in this volume, by Barfield, Van den Berg, and Frye in particular, not so much as changes in consciousness, but as changes in figuration. Changes in consciousness are of course very rare and no major synthesizer has come forth as yet, from any discipline, to demonstrate to us whether Romanticism marks a genuine change in consciousness or not. From the Freudian viewpoint, Romanticism is an "illusory therapy" (I take the phrase from Philip Rieff), or what Freud himself specifically termed an "erotic illusion." The dialectics of Romanticism, to the Freudians, are mistaken or inadequate, because the dialectics are sought in Schiller or Heine or in German Romantic philosophy down to Nietzsche, rather than in Blake or the English Romantics after him. Blake and Coleridge do not set intellect and passion against one another, any more than they arrive at the Freudian simplicity of the endless conflict between Eros and Thanatos. Possibly because of the clear associations between Jung and German Romanticism, it has been too easy for Freudian intellectuals to confound Romanticism with various modes of irrationalism. Though much contemporary scholarship attempts to study English and continental Romanticism as a unified phenomenon, it can be argued that the English Romantics tend to lose more than they gain by such study.

Behind continental Romanticism there lay very little in the way of a congenial native tradition of major poets writing in an ancestral mode, particularly when compared to the English Romantic heritage of Spenser, Shakespeare, and Milton. What allies Blake and Wordsworth, Shelley and Keats, is their strong mutual conviction that they are reviving the true English tradition of poetry, which they thought had vanished after the death of Milton, and had reappeared in diminished form, mostly after the death of Pope, in admirable but doomed poets like Chatterton, Cowper, and Collins, victims of circumstance and of the false dawn of Sensibility. It is in this highly individual sense that English Romanticism legitimately can be called, as traditionally it has been, a revival of romance. More than a revival, it is an internalization of romance, particularly of the quest variety, an internalization made for more than therapeutic purposes, because made in the name of a humanizing hope that approaches apocalyptic intensity. The poet takes the patterns of quest-romance and transposes them into his own imaginative life, so that the entire rhythm of the quest is heard again in the movement of the poet himself from poem to poem.

M. H. Abrams, in an essay included in this volume, brilliantly traces these patterns of what he calls "the apocalypse of imagination." As he shows, historically they all stem directly from English reactions to the French Revolution, or to the intellectual currents that had flowed into the Revolution. Psychologically, they stem from the child's vision of a more titanic universe that the English Romantics were so reluctant to abandon. If adolescence was a Romantic or Rousseauistic phenomenon of consciousness, its concomitant was the very secular sense of being twice-born that is first discussed in the fourth chapter of *Émile*, and then beautifully developed by Shelley in his visionary account of Rousseau's second birth, in the concluding movement of *The Triumph of Life*. The pains of psychic maturation become, for Shelley, the potentially saving though usually destructive crisis in which the imagination confronts its choice of either sustaining its own integrity, or yielding to the illusive beauty of nature.

The movement of quest-romance, before its internalization by the High Romantics, was from nature to redeemed nature, the sanction of redemption being the gift of some external spiritual authority, sometimes magical. The Romantic movement is from nature to the imagination's freedom (sometimes a reluctant freedom), and the imagination's freedom is frequently purgatorial, redemptive in direction but destructive of the social self. The high cost of Romantic internalization, that is, of finding paradises within a renovated man, shows itself in the arena of self-consciousness. The quest is to widen consciousness as well as to intensify it, but the quest is shadowed by a spirit that tends to narrow consciousness to an acute preoccupation with self. This shadow of imagination is solipsism, what Shelley calls the Spirit of Solitude or *Alastor*, the avenging daimon who is a baffled residue of the self, determined to be compensated for its loss of natural assurance, for having been awakened from the merely given condition that to Shelley, as to Blake, was but the sleep of death-in-life. Blake calls this spirit of solitude a Spectre, or the genuine Satan, the Thanatos or death instinct in every natural man. One of the essays by Geoffrey H. Hartman in this volume concerns the Romantic search for an anti-self-consciousness, a way out of the morass of inwardness. Modernist poetry in English organized itself, to an excessive extent, as a supposed revolt against Romanticism, in the mistaken hope of escaping this inwardness (though it was unconscious that this was its prime motive).

Modernist poets learned better, as their best work, the last phases of W. B. Yeats and Wallace Stevens, abundantly shows, but criticism until recently was tardy in catching up, and lingering misapprehensions about the Romantics still abide. Thus, Irving Howe, in an otherwise acute essay on literary modernism, says of the Romantic poets that "they do not surrender the wish to discover in the universe a network of spiritual meaning which, however precariously, can enclose their selves." This is simply not true of Blake or Wordsworth or Shelley or Keats, nor is the statement of Marius Bewley's that Howe quotes approvingly, that the Romantics' central desire is "to merge oneself with what is greater than oneself." Indeed, both statements are excellent guides to what the major Romantics regarded as human defeat or a living death, as the despairing surrender of the imagination's autonomy. Since neither Howe nor Bewley is writing as an enemy of the Romantics, it is evident that we still need to clear our minds of Eliotic cant on this subject.

Paul de Man terms this phenomenon the post-Romantic dilemma, observing that every fresh attempt of Modernism to go beyond Romanticism ends in the gradual realization of the Romantics' continued priority. Modern poetry, in English, is the invention of Blake and of Wordsworth, and I do not know of a long poem written in English since which is either as legitimately difficult or as rewardingly profound as *Jerusalem* or *The Prelude*. Nor can I find a modern lyric, however happily ignorant its writer, which develops beyond or surmounts its debt to Wordsworth's great trinity of *Tintern Abbey, Resolution and Independence,* and the *Intimations of Immortality* ode. The dreadful paradox of Wordsworth's greatness is that his uncanny originality, still the most astonishing break with tradition in the language, has been so influential that we have lost sight of its audacity and its arbitrariness. In this, Wordsworth strongly resembles Freud, who rightly compared his own intellectual revolution to those of Copernicus and Darwin. Van den Berg quietly sees "Freud, in the desperation of the moment, turning away from the present, where the cause of his patients' illnesses was located, to the past; and thus making them suffer from the past and making our existence akin to their suffering. It was not necessary." Is Van den Berg right? The question is as crucial for Wordsworth and Romanticism as it is for Freud and psychoanalysis. The most searching critique of Romanticism that I know is Van den Berg's critique of Freud, particularly the description of "The Subject and his Landscape" included in this anthology:

> Ultimately the enigma of grief is the libido's inclination toward exterior things. What prompts the libido to leave the inner self? In 1914 Freud asked himself this question—the essential question of his psychology, and the essential question of the psychology of the twentieth century. His answer ended the process of interiorization. It is: the libido leaves the inner self when the inner self has become too full. In order to prevent it from being torn, the I has to aim itself on objects outside the self; ". . . ultimately man must begin to love in order not to get ill." So that is what it is. Objects are of importance only in an extreme urgency. Human beings, too. The grief over their death is the sighing of a too-far distended covering, the groaning of an over-filled inner self.

Wordworth is a crisis-poet, Freud a crisis-analyst; the saving movement in each is backwards into lost time. But what is the movement of loss, in poet and in analyst? Van den Berg's suggestion is that Freud unnecessarily sacrificed the present moment, because he came at the end of a tradition of intellectual error that began with the extreme Cartesian dualism, and that progressively learned to devalue contact between the self and others, the self and the outer world, the self and the body. Wordsworth's prophecy, and Blake's, was overtly against dualism; they came, each said, to heal the division within man, and between man and the world, if never quite between man and man. But Wordsworth, the more influential because more apparently accessible of the two (I myself would argue that he is the more difficult because the more problematic poet), no more overcame a fundamental dualism than Freud did. Essentially this was Blake's complaint against him; it is certainly no basis for us to complain. Wordsworth made his kind of poetry out of an extreme urgency, and out of an overfilled inner self, a Blakean Prolific that nearly choked in an excess of its own delights. This is the Egotistical Sublime of which Keats complained, but Keats knew his debt to Wordsworth, as most poets since do not.

Wordsworth's Copernican revolution in poetry is marked by the evanescence of any subject but subjectivity, the loss of what a poem is "about." If, like the late Yvor Winters, one rejects a poetry that is not "about" something, one has little use for (or understanding of) Wordsworth. But, like Van den Berg on Freud, one can understand and love Wordsworth, and still ask of his radical subjectivity: was it necessary? Without hoping to find an answer, one can explore the question so as to come again to the central problem of Romantic (and post-Romantic) poetry: what, for men without belief and even without credulity, is the spiritual form of romance? How can a poet's (or any man's) life be one of continuous allegory (as Keats thought Shakespeare's must have been) in a reductive universe of death, a separated realm of atomized meanings, each discrete from the next? Though all men are questers, even the least, what is the relevance of quest in a gray world of continuities and homogenized enterprises? Or, in Wordsworth's own terms, which are valid for every major Romantic, what knowledge might yet be purchased except by the loss of power?

Frye, in his theory of myths, explores the analogue between quest-romance and the dream: "Translated into dream terms, the quest-romance is the search of the libido or desiring self for a fulfillment that will deliver it from the anxieties of reality but will still contain that reality." Internalized romance—and *The Prelude* and *Jerusalem* can be taken as the greatest examples of this kind—traces a Promethean and revolutionary quest, and cannot be translated into dream terms, for in it the libido turns inward into the self. Shelley's *Prometheus Unbound* is the most drastic High Romantic version of internalized quest, but there are more drastic versions still in our own age, though they present themselves as parodistic, as in the series of marvelous interior quests by Stevens, that go from *The Comedian As the Letter C* to the climactic *Notes Toward a Supreme Fiction.* The hero of internalized quest is the poet himself, the antagonists of quest are everything in the self that blocks imaginative work, and the fulfillment is never the poem itself, but the poem beyond that is made possible by the apocalypse of imagination. "A timely utterance gave that thought relief" is the Wordsworthian formula for the momentary redemption of the poet's sanity by the poem already written, and might stand as a motto for the history of the modern lyric from Wordsworth to Hart Crane.

The Romantics tended to take Milton's Satan as the archetype of the heroically defeated Promethean quester, a choice in which modern criticism has not followed them. But they had a genuine insight into the affinity between an element in their selves and an element in Milton that he would externalize only in a demonic form. What *is* heroic about Milton's Satan is a real Prometheanism and a thoroughly internalized one; he can steal only his own fire in the poem, since God can appear as fire, again in the poem, only when he directs it against Satan. In Romantic quest the Promethean hero stands finally, quite alone, upon a tower that is only himself, and his stance is all the fire there is. This realization leads neither to nihilism nor to solipsism, though Byron plays with the former and all fear the latter.

The dangers of idealizing the libido are of course constant in the life of the individual, and such idealizations are dreadful for whole societies, but the internalization of quest-romance had to accept these dangers. The creative process is the hero of Romantic poetry, and imaginative inhibitions, of every kind, necessarily must be the antagonists of the poetic quest. The special puzzle of Romanticism is the dialectical role that nature had to take in the revival of the mode of romance. Most simply, Romantic nature poetry, despite a long critical history of misrepresentation, was an anti-nature poetry, even in Wordsworth who sought a reciprocity or even a dialogue with nature, but found it only in flashes. Wordsworthian nature, thanks to Arnold and the critical tradition he fostered, has been misunderstood, though the insights of recent critics have begun to develop a better interpretative tradition, founded on A. C. Bradley's opposition to Arnold's view. Bradley stressed the strong side of Wordsworth's imagination, its Miltonic sublimity, which Arnold evidently never noticed, but which accounts for everything that is major in *The Prelude* and in the central crisis lyrics associated with it. Though Wordsworth came as a healer, and Shelley attacked him, in *Mont Blanc*, for attempting to reconcile man with nature, there is no such reconciliation in Wordsworth's poetry, and the healing function is performed only when the poetry shows the power of the mind over outward sense. The strength of renovation in Wordsworth resides only in the spirit's splendor, in what he beautifully calls "possible sublimity" or "something evermore about to be," the potential of an imagination too fierce to be contained by nature. This is the force that Coleridge sensed and feared in Wordsworth, and is remarkably akin to that strength in Milton that Marvell urbanely says he feared, in his introductory verses to *Paradise Lost*. As Milton curbed his own Prometheanism, partly by showing its dangers through Satan's version of the heroic quest, so Wordsworth learned to restrain his, partly through making his own quest-romance, in *The Prelude*, an account of learning both the enormous strength of nature, and nature's wise and benevolent reining-in of its own force. In the covenant between Wordsworth and nature, two powers that are totally separate from each other, and potentially destructive of the other, try to meet in a dialectic of love. "Meet" is too hopeful, and "blend" would express Wordsworth's ideal and not his achievement, but the try itself is definitive of Wordsworth's strangeness and continued relevance as a poet.

If Wordsworth, so frequently and absurdly called a pantheist, was not questing for unity with nature, still less were Blake, Shelley, and Keats, or their darker followers in later generations, from Beddoes, Darley, and Wade down to Yeats and Lawrence in our time. Coleridge and Byron, in their very different ways, were oddly closer both to orthodox Christian myth and to pantheism or some form of nature-worship, but even their major poems hardly approximate nature poetry. Romantic or internalized romance, especially in its purest version of the quest form, the poems of symbolic voyaging that move in a continuous tradition from Shelley's *Alastor* to Yeats's *The Wanderings of Oisin*, tends to see the context of nature as a trap for the mature imagination. This point requires much laboring, as the influence of older views of Romanticism is very hard to slough off. Even Northrop Frye, the leading romance theorist we have had at least since Ruskin, Pater, and Yeats, says that "in Romanticism the main direction of the quest of identity tends increasingly to be downward and inward, toward a hidden basis or ground of identity between man and nature." The directional part of this statement is true, but the stated goal I think is not. Frye still speaks of the Romantics as seeking a final unity between man and his nature, but Blake and Shelley do not accept such a unity as a goal, unless a total transformation of man and nature can precede unity, while Wordsworth's visions of "first and last and midst and without end" preserve the unyielding forms both of nature and of man. Keats's closest approach to an apocalyptic vision comes when he studies Moneta's face, at the climax of *The Fall of Hyperion*, but even that vision is essentially Wordsworthian, seeing as it does a perpetual change that cannot be ended by change, a human countenance made only more solitary in its growing alienation from nature, and a kind of naturalistic entropy that has gone beyond natural contraries, past "the lily and the snow."

Probably only Joyce and Stevens, in later Romantic tradition, can be termed unreconstructed naturalists, or naturalistic humanists. Later Romantics as various as Eliot, Proust, and Shaw all break through uneasy natural contexts, as though sexuality was antithetical to the imagination, while Yeats, the very last of the High Romantics, worked out an elaborate sub-myth of the poet as antithetical quester, very much in the mode of Shelley's poetry. If the goal of Romantic internalization of the quest was a wider consciousness that would be free of the excesses of self-consciousness, a consideration of the rigors of experiential psychology will show, quite rapidly, why nature could not provide an adequate context. The program of Romanticism, and not just in Blake, demands something more than a natural man to carry it through. Enlarged and more numerous senses are necessary, an enormous virtue of Romantic poetry clearly being that it not only demands such expansion but begins to make it possible, or at least attempts to do so.

The internalization of romance brought the concept of nature, and poetic consciousness itself, into a relationship they had never had before the advent of Romanticism in the later eighteenth century. Implicit in all the Romantics, and very explicit in Blake, is a difficult distinction between two modes of energy, organic and creative (Orc and Los in Blake, Prometheus bound and unbound in Shelley, Hyperion and Apollo in Keats, the Child and the Man, though with subtle misgivings, in Wordsworth). For convenience, the first mode can be called Prometheus and the second "the Real Man, the Imagination" (Blake's phrase, in a triumphant letter written when he expected death). Generally, Prometheus is the poet-as-hero in the first stage of his quest, marked by a deep involvement in political, social, and literary revolution, and a direct, even satirical attack on the institutional orthodoxies of European and English society, including historically oriented Christianity, and the neoclassic literary and intellectual tradition, particularly in its Enlightenment phase. The Real Man, the Imagination, emerges after terrible crises in the major stage of the Romantic quest, which is typified by a relative disengagement from revolutionary activism, and a standing aside from polemic and satire, so as to bring the search within the self and its ambiguities. In the Prometheus stage, the quest is allied to the libido's struggle against repressiveness, and nature is an ally, though always a wounded and sometimes a withdrawn one. In the Real Man, the Imagination stage, nature is the immediate though not the ultimate antagonist. The final enemy to be overcome is a recalcitrance in the self, what Blake calls the Spectre of Urthona, Shelley the unwilling dross that checks the spirit's flight, Wordsworth the sad perplexity or fear that kills or, best of all, the hope that is unwilling to be fed, and Keats, most simply and perhaps most powerfully, the Identity. Coleridge calls the antagonist by a bewildering variety of names since, of all these poets, he is the most hag-ridden by anxieties, and the most humanly vulnerable. Byron and Beddoes do not so much name the antagonist as mock it, so as to cast it out by continuous satire and demonic farce. The best single name for the antagonist is Keats's Identity, but the most traditional is the Selfhood, and so I shall use it here.

Only the Selfhood, for the Romantics as for such Christian visionaries as Eckhart before them, burns in Hell. The Selfhood is not the erotic principle, but precisely that part of the erotic that cannot be released in the dialectic of love, whether between man and man, or man and nature. Here the Romantics, all of them I think, even Keats, part company with Freud's dialectics of human nature. Freud's beautiful sentence on marriage is a formula against which the Romantic Eros can be tested: "A man shall leave father and mother—according to the Biblical precept—and cleave to his wife; then are tenderness and sensuality united." By the canons of internalized romance, that translates: a poet shall leave his Great Original (Milton, for the Romantics) and nature—according to the precept of Poetic Genius—and cleave to his Muse or Imagination; then are the generous and solitary halves united. But, so translated, the formula has ceased to be Freudian and has become High Romantic.

In Freud, part of the ego's own self-love is projected onto an outward object, but part always remains in the ego, and even the projected portion can find its way back again. Somewhere Freud has a splendid sentence that anyone unhappy in love can take to heart: "Object-libido was at first ego-libido and can be again transformed into ego-libido," which is to say that a certain degree of narcissistic mobility is rather a good thing. Somewhere else Freud remarks that all romance is really a form of what he calls "family-romance;" one could as justly say, in his terms, that all romance is necessarily a mode of ego-romance. This may be true, and in its humane gloom it echoes a great line of realists who culminate in Freud, but the popular notion that High Romanticism takes a very different view of love is a sounder insight into the Romantics than most scholarly critics ever achieve (or at least state).

All romance, literary and human, is founded upon enchantment; Freud and the Romantics differ principally in their judgment as to what it is in us that resists enchantment, and what the value of that resistance is. For Freud it is the reality principle, working through the great disenchanter, reason, the scientific attitude, and without it no civilized values are possible. For the Romantics, this is again a dialectical matter, as two principles intertwine in the resistance to enchantment—one "organic," an anxiety principle masquerading as a reality principle and identical to the ego's self-love that never ventures out to others, and the other "creative," which resists enchantment in the name of a higher mode than the sympathetic imagination.

This doubling is clearest in Blake's mythology, where there are two egos, the Spectre of Urthona and Los, who suffer the enchantments, real *and* deceptive, of nature and the female, and who resist, when and where they can, on these very different grounds. But, though less schematically, the same doubling of the ego into passive and active components is present in the other poets wherever they attempt their highest flights and so spurn the earth. The most intense effort of the Romantic quest is made when the Promethean stage of quest is renounced, and the purgatorial crisis that follows moves near to resolution. Romantic purgatory, by an extraordinary displacement of earlier mythology, is found just beyond the earthly paradise, rather than just before it, so that the imagination is tried by nature's best aspect. Instances of the interweaving of purgatory and paradise include nearly everything Blake says about the state of being he calls Beulah, and the whole development of Keats, from *Endymion*, with its den or cave of Quietude, on to the structure of *The Fall of Hyperion*, where the poet enjoys the fruit and drink of paradise just before he has his confrontation with Moneta, whose shrine must be reached by mounting purgatorial stairs.

Nothing in Romantic poetry is more difficult to comprehend, for me anyway, than the process that begins after each poet's renunciation of Prometheus; for the incarnation of the Real Man, the Imagination, is not like psychic maturation in poets before the Romantics. The love that transcends the Selfhood has its analogues in the renunciatory love of many traditions, including some within Christianity, but the creative Eros of the Romantics is not renunciatory though it is self-transcendent. It is, to use Shelley's phrasing, a total going-out from our own natures, total because the force moving out is not only the Promethean libido, but rather a fusion between the libido and the active or imaginative element in the ego; or, simply, desire wholly taken up into the imagination. "Shelley's love poetry," as a phrase, is almost a redundancy, Shelley having written little else, but his specifically erotic poems, a series of great lyrics and the dazzling *Epipsychidion*, have been undervalued because they are so very difficult, the difficulty being the Shelleyan and Romantic vision of love.

Blake distinguished between Beulah and Eden as states of being (Frye's essay, "The Keys to the Gates," included in this anthology, is definitive on this distinction), the first being the realm of family-romance and the second of apocalyptic romance, in which the objects of love altogether lose their object dimension. In family-romance or Beulah, loved ones are not confined to their objective aspect (that would make them denizens of Blake's state of Generation or mere Experience), but they retain it nevertheless. The movement to the reality of Eden is one of re-creation, or better, of knowledge not purchased by the loss of power, and so of power and freedom gained *through* a going-out of our nature, in which that last phrase takes on its full range of meanings. Though Romantic love, particularly in Wordsworth and Shelley, has been compared to what Charles Williams calls the Romantic Theology of Dante, the figure of Beatrice is not an accurate analogue to the various Romantic visions of the beloved, for sublimation is not an element in the movement from Prometheus to Man.

There is no useful analogue to Romantic or imaginative love, but there is a useful contrary in the melancholy wisdom of Freud on natural love, and the contrary has the helpful clarity one always finds in Freud. If Romantic love is the sublime, then Freudian love is the pathetic, and truer of course to the phenomenon insofar as it is merely natural. To Freud, love begins as ego-libido, and necessarily is ever after a history of sorrow, a picaresque chronicle in which the ever-vulnerable ego stumbles from delusion to frustration, to expire at last (if lucky) in the compromising arms of the ugliest of Muses, the reality principle. But the saving dialectic of this picaresque is that it is better thus, as there is no satisfaction in satisfaction anyway, since in the Freudian view all erotic partners are somewhat inadequate replacements for the initial sexual objects, parents. Romantic love, to Freud, is a particularly intense version of the longing for the mother, a love in which the imago is loved, rather than the replacement. And Romantic love, on this account, is anything but a dialectic of transformation, since it is as doomed to overvalue the surrogate as it compulsively overvalues the mother.

Our age begins to abound in late Romantic "completions" of Freud, but the Romantic critiques of him, by Jung and Lawrence in particular, have not touched the strength of his erotic pessimism. There is a subtly defiant attempt to make the imago do the work of the imagination by Stevens, particularly in the very Wordsworthian *The Auroras of Autumn*, and it is beautifully subversive of Freud, but of course it is highly indirect. Yet a direct Romantic counter-critique of Freud's critique of Romantic love emerges from any prolonged, central study of Romantic poetry. For Freud, there is an ironic loss of energy, perhaps even of spirit, with every outward movement of love away from the ego. Only pure self-love has a perfection to it, a stasis without loss, and one remembers again Van den Berg's mordant observation on Freud: "Ultimately the enigma of grief is the libido's inclination toward exterior things." All outward movement, in the Freudian psychodynamics, is a fall that results from "an overfilled inner self," which would sicken within if it did not fall outwards, and downwards, into the world of objects, and of other selves. One longs for Blake to come again and rewrite *The Book of Urizen* as a satire on this cosmogony of love. The poem would not require that much rewriting, for it can now be read as a prophetic satire on Freud, Urizen being a superego certainly over-filled with itself, and sickening into a false creation or creation-fall. If Romantic love can be castigated as "erotic illusion," Freudian love can be judged as "erotic reduction," and the prophets of the reality principle are in danger always of the Urizenic boast:

> I have sought for a joy without pain,
> For a solid without fluctuation
> Why will you die O Eternals?
> Why live in unquenchable burnings?

The answer is the Romantic dialectic of Eros and Imagination, unfair as it is to attribute to the Freudians a censorious repressive-ness. But to Blake and the Romantics, all available accounts of right reason, even those which had risen to liberate men, had the discon-certing tendency to turn into censorious moralities. Freud pain-fully walked a middle way, not unfriendly to the poetic imagination, and moderately friendly to Eros. If his myth of love is so sparse, rather less than a creative Word, it is still open both to analytic modification and to a full acceptance of everything that can come out of the psyche. Yet it is not quite what Philip Rieff claims for it, as it does not erase "the gap between therapeutic rationalism and self-assertive romanticism." That last is only the first stage of the Romantic quest, the one this discussion calls Prometheus. There remains a considerable gap between the subtle perfection to which Freud brought therapeutic rationalism, and the mature Romanti-cism which is self-transcendent in its major poets.

There is no better way to explore the Real Man, the Imagina-tion, than to study his monuments: *The Four Zoas, Milton,* and *Jerusalem; The Prelude* and the *Recluse* fragment; *The Ancient Mariner* and *Christabel; Prometheus Unbound, Adonais,* and *The Triumph of Life;* the two *Hyperions; Don Juan; Death's Jest-Book;* these are the definitive Romantic achievement, the words that were and will be, day and night. What follows is only an epitome, a rapid sketch of the major phase of this erotic quest. The sketch, like any which attempts to trace the visionary company of love, is likely to end in listening to the wind, hoping to hear an instant of a fleeting voice.

The internalization of quest-romance made of the poet-hero a seeker not after nature but after his own mature powers, and so the Romantic poet turned away, not from society to nature, but from nature to what was more integral than nature, within himself. The widened consciousness of the poet did not give him intimations of a former union with nature or the Divine, but rather of his former selfless self. One thinks of Yeats's Blakean declaration: "I'm looking for the face I had / Before the world was made." Different as the major Romantics were in their attitudes towards religion, they were united (except for Coleridge) in *not* striving for unity with anything but what might be called their Tharmas or id component, Tharmas being the Zoa or Giant Form in Blake's mythology who was the unfallen human potential for realizing instinctual desires, and so was the regent of Innocence. Tharmas is a shepherd-figure, his equivalent in Wordsworth being a number of visions of man against the sky, of actual shepherds Wordsworth had seen in his boyhood. This Romantic pastoral vision (its pictorial aspect can be studied in the woodcuts of Blake's Virgil series, and in the work done by Palmer, Calvert, and Richmond while under Blake's influence) is Biblical pastoralism, but not at all of a traditional kind. Blake's Tharmas is inchoate when fallen, as the id or appetite is inchoate, desperately starved and uneasily allied to the Spectre of Urthona, the passive ego he has projected outward to meet an object-world from which he has been severed so unwillingly. Wordsworth's Tharmas, besides being the shepherd image of human divinity, is present in the poet himself as a desperate desire for continuity in the self, a desperation that at its worst sacrifices the living moment, but at its best produces a saving urgency that protects the imagination from the strong enchantments of nature.

In Freud the ego mediates between id and superego, and Freud had no particular interest in further dividing the ego itself. In Romantic psychic mythology, Prometheus rises from the id, and can best be thought of as the force of libido, doomed to undergo a merely cyclic movement from appetite to repression, and then back again; any quest within nature is thus at last irrelevant to the mediating ego, though the quest goes back and forth through it. It is within the ego itself that the quest must turn, to engage the antagonist proper, and to clarify the imaginative component in the ego by its strife of contraries with its dark brother. Frye, writing on Keats, calls the imaginative ego *identity-with* and the selfhood ego *identity-as*, which clarifies Keats's ambiguous use of "identity" in this context. Hartman, writing on Wordsworth, points to the radical Protestant analogue to the Romantic quest: "The terror of discontinuity or separation enters, in fact, as soon as the imagination truly enters. In its restraint of vision, as well as its peculiar nakedness before the moment, this resembles an extreme Protestantism, and Wordsworth seems to quest for 'evidences' in the form of intimations of continuity."

Wordsworth's greatness was in his feeling the terror of discontinuity as acutely as any poet could, yet overcoming this terror nevertheless, by opening himself to vision. With Shelley, the analogue of the search for evidences drops out, and an Orphic strain takes its place, for no other English poet gives so continuous an impression of relying on almost literal inspiration. Where Keats knew the Selfhood as an attractive strength of distinct identity that had to be set aside, and Wordsworth as a continuity he longed for yet learned to resist, and Blake as a temptation to prophetic wrath and withdrawal that had to be withstood, Shelley frequently gives the impression of encountering no enchantment he does not embrace, since every enchantment is an authentic inspiration. Yet this is a false impression, though Yeats sometimes received it, as in his insistence that Shelley, great poet as he certainly was, lacked a Vision of Evil. The contrary view to Yeats is that of C. S. Lewis, who held that Shelley, more than any other "heathen" poet (the word is from Lewis), drove home the truth of Original Sin.

Both views are mistaken. For Shelley, the Selfhood's strong enchantment, stronger even than it is for the other Romantics, is one that would keep him from ever concluding the Prometheus phase of the quest. The Selfhood allies itself with Prometheus against the repressive force Shelley calls Jupiter, his version of Blake's Urizen or Freud's superego. This temptation calls the poet to perpetual revolution, and Shelley, though longing desperately to see the tyrannies of his time overturned, renounces it at the opening of *Prometheus Unbound*, in the Imagination's name. Through his renunciation, he moves to overturn the tyranny of time itself.

There are thus two main elements in the major phase of the Romantic quest, the first being the inward overcoming of the Selfhood's temptation, and the second the outward turning of the triumphant Imagination, free of further internalizations—though "outward" and "inward" become cloven fictions or false conceptual distinctions in this triumph, which must complete a dialectic of love by uniting the Imagination with its bride, who is a transformed ongoing creation of the Imagination rather than a redeemed nature. Blake and Wordsworth had long lives, and each completed his version of this dialectic. Coleridge gave up the quest, and became only an occasional poet, while Byron's quest, even had he lived into middle age, would have become increasingly ironic. Keats died at twenty-five, and Shelley at twenty-nine; despite their fecundity, they did not complete their development, but their death-fragments, *The Fall of Hyperion* and *The Triumph of Life*, prophesy the final phase of the quest in them. Each work breaks off with the Selfhood subdued, and there is profound despair in each, particularly in Shelley's; but there are still hints of what the Imagination's triumph would have been in Keats. In Shelley, the final despair may be total; but the man who had believed so fervently that the good time would come had already given a vision of imaginative completion in the closing Act of *Prometheus Unbound*, and we can go back to it and see what is deliberately lacking in *The Triumph of Life*. What follows is a rapid attempt to trace the major phase of quest in the four poets, taking as texts *Jerusalem* and *The Prelude*, and the *Fall* and *Triumph*, these two last with supplementary reference to crucial earlier erotic poems of Keats and Shelley.

Of Blake's long poems the first, *The Four Zoas*, is essentially a poem of Prometheus, devoting itself to the cyclic strife between the Promethean Orc and the moral censor, Urizen, in which the endless cycle between the two is fully exposed. The poem ends in an apocalypse, the explosive and Promethean *Night the Ninth, Being The Last Judgment*, which in itself is one of Blake's greatest works, yet from which he turned when he renounced the entire poem (by declining to engrave it). But this renunciation was completed not before he attempted to move the entire poem from the Prometheus stage to the Imagination, for Blake's own process of creative maturation came to its climax while he worked on *The Four Zoas*. The entrance into the mature stage of the quest is clearly shown by the two different versions of *Night the Seven*, for the later one introduces the doubling of the ego into Spectre of Urthona and Los, Selfhood or *Identity-As*, and Imagination or *Identity-With*. Though skillfully handled, it was not fully clarified by Blake, even to himself, and so he refused to regard the poem as a definitive vision.

Its place in his canon was filled, more or less, by the double-romance *Milton* and *Jerusalem*. The first is more palpably in a displaced romance mode, involving as it does symbolic journeys downwards to our world by Milton and his emanation or bride of creation, Ololon, who descend from an orthodox Eternity in a mutual search for one another, the characteristic irony being that they could never find one another in a traditional heaven. There is very little in the poem of the Prometheus phase, Blake having already devoted to that a series of prophetic poems, from *America* and *Europe* through *The Book of Urizen* and on to the magnificent if unsatisfactory (to him, not to us) *The Four Zoas*. The two major stages of the mature phase of quest dominate the structure of *Milton*. The struggle with the Selfhood moves from the quarrel between Palamabron (Blake) and Satan (Hayley) in the introductory "Bard's Song" on to Milton's heroic wrestling match with Urizen, and climaxes in the direct confrontation between Milton and Satan on the Felpham shore, in which Milton recognizes Satan as his own Selfhood. The recognition compels Satan to a full epiphany, and a subsequent defeat. Milton then confronts Ololon, the poem ending in an epiphany contrary to Satan's, in what Blake specifically terms a preparation for a going forth to the great harvest and vintage of the nations. But even this could not be Blake's final Word; the quest in *Milton* is primarily Milton's and not Blake's, and the quest's antagonist is still somewhat externalized.

In *Jerusalem, The Prelude*'s only rival as the finest long poem of the nineteenth century, Blake gives us the most comprehensive single version of the Romantic quest. Here there is an alternation between vision sweeping outwards into the nightmare world of the reality principle, and a wholly inward vision of conflict in Blake's ego between the Spectre and Los. The poet's antagonist is himself, the poem's first part being the most harrowing and tormented account of genius tempted to the madness of self-righteousness, frustrated anger, and solipsistic withdrawal even in the Romantic period. Blake-Los struggles on against this enchantment of despair, until the poem quietly, almost without warning, begins to move into the light of a Last Judgment, of a kind passed by every man upon himself. In the poem's final plates the reconciliation of Los and his emanative portion, Enitharmon, begins, and we approach the completion of quest.

Though Blake, particularly in *Jerusalem*, attempts a continuity based on thematic juxtaposition and simultaneity, rather than on consecutiveness, he is in such sure control of his own procedure that his work is less difficult to summarize than *The Prelude*, a contrast that tends to startle inexperienced readers of Blake and of Wordsworth. *The Prelude* follows a rough naturalistic chronology through Wordsworth's life down to the middle of the journey, where it, like any modern reader, leaves him in a state of preparation for a further greatness that never came. What is there already, besides the invention of the modern lyric, is a long poem so rich and strange it has defied almost all description.

The Prelude is an autobiographical romance that frequently seeks expression in the sublime mode, which is an invitation to aesthetic disaster. *The Excursion* is an aesthetic disaster, as Hazlitt, Byron, and many since happily have noted, yet there Wordsworth works within rational limits. *The Prelude* ought to be an outrageous poem, but its peculiar mixture of displaced genre and inappropriate style *works*, because its internalization of quest is the inevitable story for its age. Wordsworth did not have the Promethean temperament, yet he had absolute insight into it, as *The Borderers* already had shown.

In *The Prelude*, the initial quest phase of the poet-as-Prometheus is diffuse but omnipresent. It determines every movement in the growth of the child's consciousness, always seen as a violation of the established natural order, and it achieves great power in Book VI, when the onset of the French Revolution is associated with the poet's own hidden desires to surmount nature, desires that emerge in the great passages clustered around the Simplon Pass. The Promethean quest fails, in one way in the Alps when chastened by nature, and in another with the series of shocks to the poet's moral being when England wars against the Revolution, and the Revolution betrays itself. The more direct Promethean failure, the poet's actual abandonment of Annette Vallon, is presented only indirectly in the 1805 *Prelude*, and drops out completely from the revised, posthumously published *Prelude* of 1850, the version most readers encounter.

In his crisis, Wordsworth learns the supernatural and superhuman strength of his own imagination, and is able to begin a passage to the mature phase of his quest. But his anxiety for continuity is too strong for him, and he yields to its dark enchantment. The Imagination phase of his quest does not witness the surrender of his Selfhood and the subsequent inauguration of a new dialectic of love, purged of the natural heart, as it is in Blake. Yet he wins a provisional triumph over himself, in Book XII of *The Prelude*, and in the closing stanzas of *Resolution and Independence* and the Great Ode. And the final vision of *The Prelude* is not of a redeemed nature, but of a liberated creativity transforming its creation into the beloved:

> Prophets of Nature, we to them will speak
> A lasting inspiration, sanctified
> By reason, blest by faith: what we have loved
> Others will love, and we will teach them how;
> Instruct them how the mind of man becomes
> A thousand times more beautiful than the earth
> On which he dwells, above this frame of things . . .

Coleridge, addressed here as the other Prophet of Nature, renounced his own demonic version of the Romantic quest (clearest in the famous triad of *Kubla Khan, Christabel,* and *The Ancient Mariner*), his wavering Prometheanism early defeated not so much by his Selfhood as by his Urizenic fear of his own imaginative energy. It was a high price for the release he had achieved in his brief phase of exploring the romance of the marvelous, but the loss itself produced a few poems of unique value, the *Dejection* Ode in particular. The essay on the Greater Romantic Lyric, included in this book, is M. H. Abrams' pioneering and greatly illuminating explanation of how Coleridge preceded Wordsworth in the invention of a new kind of poetry that shows the mind in a dialogue with itself. The motto of this poetry might well be its descendant, Stevens' "The mind is the terriblest force in the world, father, / Because, in chief, it, only, can defend / Against itself. At its mercy, we depend / Upon it." Coleridge emphasizes the mercy,

Wordsworth the saving terror of the force. Keats and Shelley began with a passion closer to the Prometheus phase of Blake than of Wordsworth or Coleridge. The fullest development of the Romantic quest, after Blake's mythology and Wordsworth's exemplary refusal of mythology, is in Keats's *Endymion* and Shelley's *Prometheus Unbound*.

In this second generation of Romantic questers the same first phase of Prometheanism appears, as does the second phase of crisis, renounced quest, overcoming of Selfhood, and final movement towards imaginative love, but the relation of the quest to the world of the reality principle has changed. In Blake, the dream with its ambiguities centers in Beulah, the purgatorial lower paradise of sexuality and benevolent nature. In Wordsworth, the dream is rare, and betokens either a prolepsis of the imagination abolishing nature, or else a state the poet calls "visionary dreariness," in which the immediate power of the mind over outward sense is so great that the ordinary forms of nature seem to have withdrawn. But in Keats and Shelley, a polemical Romanticism matures, and the argument of the dream with reality becomes an equivocal one.

Romanticism guessed at a truth our doctors begin to measure; as infants we dream for half the time we are asleep, and as we age we dream less and less. The doctors have not yet told us that utterly dreamless sleep directly prophesies or equals death, but it is a familiar Romantic conceit, and may prove to be true. We are our imaginations, and die with them.

Dreams, to Shelley and Keats, are not wish fulfillments. It is not Keats but Moneta, the passionate and wrong-headed Muse in *The Fall of Hyperion*, who first confounds poets and dreamers as one tribe, and then insists they are totally distinct and even sheer opposites, antipodes. Freud is again a clear-headed guide; the manifest and latent content of the dream can be distinct, even opposite, but in the poem they come together. The younger Romantics do not seek to render life a dream, but to recover the dream for the health of life. What is called real is too often an exhausted phantasmagoria, and the reality principle can too easily be debased into a principle of surrender, an accommodation with death-in-life. We return to the observation of Van den Berg, cited earlier: Rousseau and the Romantics discovered not only the alienation between child and adult, but the second birth of psychic maturation or adolescence. Eliot thought that the poet of *Adonais* and *The Triumph of Life* had never "progressed" beyond the ideas and ideals of adolescence, or at least of what Eliot had believed in *his* own adolescence. Every reader can be left to his own judgment of the relative maturity of *Ash Wednesday* and *The Witch of Atlas*, or *The Cocktail Party* and *The Cenci*, and is free to formulate his own dialectics of progression.

The Promethean quest, in Shelley and in Keats, is from the start uneasy about its equivocal ally, nature, and places a deeper trust in the dream; for at least the dream itself is not reductive, however we reduce it in our dissections. Perhaps the most remarkable element in the preternatural rapidity of maturation in Keats and Shelley is their early renunciation of the Prometheus phase of the quest, or rather, their dialectical complexity in simultaneously presenting the necessity and the inherent limitation of this phase. In *Alastor*, the poem's entire thrust is at one with the Poet-hero's self-destruction; this is the cause of the poem's radical unity, which C. S. Lewis rightly observed as giving a marvelous sense of the poet's being at one with his subject. Yet the poem is also a daimonic shadow in motion; it shows us nature's revenge upon the imagination, and the excessive price of the quest in the poet's alienation from other selves.

On a cosmic scale, this is part of the burden of *Prometheus Unbound*, where the hero, who massively represents the bound prophetic power of all men, rises from his icy crucifixion by refusing to continue the cycles of revolution and repression that form an ironic continuity between himself and Jupiter. Demogorgon, the dialectic of history, rises from the abyss and stops history, thus completing in the macrocosmic shadow what Prometheus, by his renunciation, inaugurates in the microcosm of the individual imagination, or the liberating dream taken up into the self. Shelley's poetry after this does not maintain the celebratory strain of Act IV of his lyrical drama. The way again is down and out, to a purgatorial encounter with the Selfhood, but the Selfhood's temptations, for Shelley, are subtle and wavering, and mask themselves in the forms of the ideal. So fused do the ideal and these masks become that Shelley, in the last lines he wrote, is in despair of any victory, though it is Shelley's Rousseau and not Shelley himself who actually chants:

> . . . thus on the way
> Mask after mask fell from the countenance
> And form of all; and long before the day
>
> Was old, the joy which waked like heaven's glance
> The sleepers in the oblivious valley, died;
> And some grew weary of the ghastly dance,
>
> And fell, as I have fallen, by the wayside—

For Shelley, Rousseau was not a failed poet, but rather the poet whose influence had resulted in an imaginative revolution, and nearly ended time's bondage. So Rousseau speaks here not for himself alone, but for his tradition, and necessarily for Coleridge, Wordsworth, and the Promethean Shelley as well, indeed for poetry itself. Yet rightly or wrongly, the image Shelley leaves with us at his end is not this falling-away from the quest, but the image of the poet forever wakeful amidst the cone of night, illuminating it as the star Lucifer does, fading as the star, becoming more intense as it narrows into the light.

The mazes of romance in *Endymion* are so winding that they suggest the contrary to vision, a labyrinthine nature in which all quest must be forlorn. In this realm, nothing narrows to an intensity, and every passionate impulse widens out to a diffuseness, the fate of Endymion's own search for his goddess. In reaction, Keats chastens his own Prometheanism, and attempts the objective epic in *Hyperion*. Hyperion's self-identity is strong but waning fast, and the fragment of the poem's Book III introduces an Apollo whose self-identity is in the act of being born. The temptation to go on with the poem must have been very great after its magnificent beginnings, but Keats's letters are firm in renouncing it. Keats turns from the enchantments of identity to the romance-fragment, *The Fall of Hyperion*, and engages instead the demon of subjectivity, his own poetic ambitions, as Wordsworth had done before him. Confronted by Moneta, he meets the danger of her challenge not by asserting his own identity, but by finding his true form in the merged identity of the poethood, in the high function and responsibilities of a Wordsworthian humanism. Though the poem breaks off before it attempts the dialectic of love, it has achieved the quest, for the Muse herself has been transformed by the poet's persistence and integrity. We wish for more, necessarily, but only now begin to understand how much we have received, even in this broken monument.

I have scanted the dialectic of love in all of these poets. Romantic love, past its own Promethean adolescence, is not the possessive love of the natural heart, which is the quest of the Freudian Eros, moving always in a tragic rhythm out from and back to the isolated ego. That is the love Blake explicitly rejected:

> Let us agree to give up Love
> And root up the Infernal Grove
> Then shall we return and see
> The worlds of happy Eternity
>
> Throughout all Eternity
> I forgive you you forgive me . . .

The Infernal Grove grows thick with virtues, but these are the selfish virtues of the natural heart. Desire for what one lacks becomes a habit of possession, and the Selfhood's jealousy murders the Real Man, the imagination. All such love is an entropy, and as such Freud understood and accepted it. We become aware of others only as we learn our separation from them, and our ecstasy is a reduction. Is this the human condition, and love only its mitigation?

> To cast off the idiot Questioner who is always questioning,
> But never capable of answering . . .

Whatever else the love that the full Romantic quest aims at may be, it cannot be a therapy. It must make all things new, and then marry what it has made. Less urgently, it seeks to define itself through the analogue of each man's creative potential. But it learns, through its poets, that it cannot define what it is, but only what it will be. The man prophesied by the Romantics is a central man who is always in the process of becoming his own begetter, and though his major poems perhaps have been written, he has not as yet fleshed out his prophecy, nor proved the final form of his love.

SAMUEL H. MONK

The Sublime: Burke's *Enquiry* †

During the first half of the eighteenth century, as we have seen, theories of sublimity were all more or less derived from Longinus, although there was a general opinion that *Peri Hupsous* was inadequate in its methods of analysing the æsthetic experience. The preoccupation of critics and theorists such as Dennis, Jacob, and Lowth with the relation of the sublime to the pathetic bears witness to the continuation of the rhetorical tradition. They would, perhaps, never have studied the question had not the rhetoricians of antiquity and of their own age based much of the persuasive power of their art on the emotions which the great style evokes. Such a description as Quintilian gives of the effect of Cicero's defense of Cornelius is typical. He says that it was "the sublimity, splendour, the brilliance, and the weight of his eloquence that evoked such

† From *The Sublime: A Study of Critical Theories in XVIII-Century England* by Samuel H. Monk, Copyright © 1960 by the University of Michigan. Reprinted by permission of The University of Michigan Press.

clamorous enthusiasm." [1] Boileau had reinforced the conception of the sublime as primarily emotive in his much-paraphased *"en-lève, ravit, transporte,"* and the writers of manuals of oratory and rhetoric, both in France and in England, took over the word *sublime* and kept alive the conception that it represents a device for persuading through the emotions. Longinus lent himself as readily to this point of view as he did to that expressed in the nascent æsthetic of England.[2] It is against a background of rhetoric, then, that the sublime begins to emerge, and it is no matter for surprise that it should take on a certain coloring from its origins. It was only in the works which we have studied that the sublime began to free itself from rhetoric.

But Boileau had made it possible to consider the sublime apart from the high style, and it was this that the English began to do. The difference between the rhetorical sublime and the pathetic sublime of the early eighteenth-century theorists is largely that in the one emotions have a practical value, to persuade against the will and the reason of the audience, and in the other they are regarded as the source of æsthetic pleasure. In the latter case, the sublime can be sought in all the arts, and the question of why certain objects and certain subjects give pleasure can be approached. When the emotions that the sublime traditionally awakened could be regarded as an end in themselves, rather than as a means to an end, an æsthetic theory was possible.

The preoccupation with emotions on the part of theorists was in every way healthful. The latent danger of the neo-classical theory (almost always, in England, only latent) was a too great standardization of literature under the current theory of a universalized nature, and a tendency to overemphasize the value of reason in art. The sublime came as a justifiable category into which could be grouped the stronger emotions and the more irrational elements of art. The speed with which theorists assimilated under the Longinian sublime the emotions of terror, horror, and ecstasy, and the vast and more overwhelming aspects of the natural world bears witness to the need which was felt for a method of making respectable the more un-neo-classical elements of art.

Moreover, an interest in the emotional *effect* of objects definitely pointed to the individual response rather than to a code of externally

1. *Institutio Oratoria,* VIII, iii, Vol. III, 213.
2. It would be useless to quote from all of these works, for all of them say the same thing with damnable iteration. A few references, cited almost at random, can suffice. Le Clerc, *Parrhasiana,* Done into English by . . . (London, 1700), pp. 9, 16, 85; Gibert, *Réflexions sur la Rhetorique* (Paris, 1705), pp. 37, 38; Fénelon, *Dialogue Concerning Eloquence in General,* tr. Wm. Stevenson (London, 1722), p. 16; Rollin, *De la Manière d'Enseigner et d'Etudier les Belles Lettres,* Seconde Edition (Paris, 1728), pp. 103, 104; *Rhetoric* (London 1736), p. 41; *Traité de l'Eloquence* (Paris, 1752), pp. 54, 55.

applied rules as an æsthetic norm. The problem to be considered gradually came to be by what means objects in nature and art arouse pleasurable emotions, not to what degree a work of art follows the rules. Thus these early theories of the sublime consider the nature of sublime objects and the emotional responses that they awaken, and tend to stand midway between an objective and a subjective point of view. The lack of an adequate psychological method is apparent in all the men whose work we have considered, but Addison, Hume, and Baillie at least partially succeeded in creating an æsthetic of the sublime.

But though their method may be different from that of Longinus, almost all their ideas can be traced back to *Peri Hupsous*. The astonishment that the sublime awakens, the expansion and elevation of the soul when brought face to face with grandeur of thought or grandeur of scenery, the analogy between the effect of the vast in nature and of the sublime in art had all been suggested by Longinus. In working out their theories, these early writers cleared much ground, emphasized the important ideas in the Longinian discussion of sublimity, and in the case of Baillie clearly indicated the method of analysis that was to be followed in the more fruitful years after the middle of the century.

It was in an effort to correct the confusion and ambiguity of discussions of beauty and sublimity that young Burke undertook his investigation of the subject. The preface to the first edition [3] of the *Philosophical Enquiry into the Origin of our Ideas of the Sublime and Beautiful* called attention to the fact that "no exact theory of our passions, or a knowledge of their genuine sources" existed. Moreover, Burke had observed that the ideas of the sublime and the beautiful were frequently confounded, and that even Longinus had "comprehended things extremely repugnant to each other, under one common name of the *Sublime.*" The only escape from this "extremely inaccurate and inconclusive" reasoning seemed to him to be

3. I refer to the edition published by Dodsley in 1757. The question of the date of the *Enquiry* is puzzling. All of Burke's biographers name 1756 as the year in which it appeared. In *Notes and Queries*, CXLVIII (Jan. 31, 1925), 80, Mr. F. A. Pottle called attention to several facts which seem to indicate that the correct date is 1757. The most impressive of these facts are the failure of the contemporary periodicals to mention the book in the monthly "catalogue of new books" during 1756, and the appearance of all reviews of the *Enquiry* in 1757. On page 140 of the same volume of *N. and Q.* two answers to Mr. Pottle were printed. One gave reason for further doubt as to the existence of the edition of 1756; the second stated baldly: "I have myself seen and perused a copy of the 'Philosophical Enquiry into the Origin of our Ideas of the Sublime and Beautiful' dated 1756." Unfortunately, Mr. Theodore Prince, who makes this statement, did not see fit to be more specific. For further reasons for rejecting the earlier date see Helen E. Drew, "The Date of Burke's *Sublime and Beautiful*, *M.L.N.*, L (January, 1935), 29–31.

from a diligent examination of our passions in our own breasts; from a careful survey of the properties of things which we find by experience to influence those passions; and from a sober and attentive investigation of the laws of nature, by which these properties are capable of affecting the body, and thus of exciting our passions.[4]

This declaration indicates with sufficient clarity the point of view which Burke takes. He breaks with tradition in so far as he can, and sets out to make an original investigation of the nature of the beautiful and the sublime. But he carries over from the past several ideas. He holds (although we shall see that at times he almost escapes from the idea) that sublimity in some way depends on qualities residing in the object, but his analysis leaves ample room for a psychological and even a physiological investigation of the origin of the æsthetic experience. Moreover, he brings with him the idea of a relation between æsthetic and the pathetic, which largely predetermines his definitions. Finally the vagueness of past speculations impels him to that thorough and minute analysis which characterizes his work, and which leads him into statements that are often absurd. But despite absurdities that are patent, there are interesting passages in the *Enquiry*, and viewed historically it is certainly one of the most important æsthetic documents that eighteenth-century England produced.

The keystone of Burke's æsthetic is emotion, and the foundation of his theory of sublimity is the emotion of terror. We have observed how often in the first half of the century terror was related to sublimity, and have suggested that there is doubtless a connection between the taste for terror in the graveyard and descriptive poets and a desire to attain the sublime. It was Burke who converted the early taste for terror into an æsthetic system and who passed it on with great emphasis to the last decades of the century, during which it was used and enjoyed in literature, painting, and the appreciation of natural scenery. For this reason, even if the *Enquiry* had no importance as a treatise on æsthetic, even if it had not influenced Kant,[5] it would be of value as a study in taste.

There is reason to believe that Burke shared the fashionable

4. [Edmund Burke], *A Philosophical Enquiry into the Origin of Our Ideas of the Sublime and Beautiful* (London, 1757), pp. v–vii There is a well-authenticated tradition that the *Enquiry* was begun when Burke was a student at Trinity College, Dublin, and that, in its earliest form, it was read before the Club which he founded and sponsored. See A. P. I. Samuels, *The Early Life, Correspondence and Writings of Edmund Burke* (Cambridge, 1923), pp. 136, 137; 141. Burke states that it was completed four years before he published it (*Enquiry*, p. vii).

5. For a discussion of Burke's influence on Kant see George Candrea, *Der Begriff des Erhabenen bei Burke und Kant* (Strassburg, 1894); H. J. Hofmann, *Die Lehre vom Erhabenen bei Kant und seinen Vorgängern* (Halle, 1913).

tastes for ruins and melancholy and terror that found expression in the literature of his youth and early manhood, when the *Enquiry* was taking shape. His early love of the more horrid scenes of *Macbeth* [6] bears witness to such a taste. A letter to his friend, Shackleton, written on January 25, 1745/6, shows us how early this taste was formed, and points the way to the *Enquiry* in a vivid manner. He describes a flood in Dublin.

> It gives me pleasure to see nature in these great though terrible scenes. It fills the mind with grand ideas, and turns the soul in upon itself.[7]

In this one sentence we find an epitome of Burke's theory of the sublime—terror fills the mind with great ideas, and the soul delights in the experience. Like Wordsworth, Burke seems early to have sought "that beauty that hath terror in it."

The *Enquiry* was taking shape between the years 1747 and 1756. These and the immediately following years make up a period of transition and growth in English literature. They were years of changing values and new points of view, years in which the emotions and imagination began to destroy the perfect balance and harmony which neo-classic art had sought in theory, at any rate, between the different elements of the poetic act. Creative art led the way, and theory, ever a laggard, followed behind in the fifth and sixth decades of the century. The need of rationalizing the increasingly emotional art of the mid-century was met by such works as Hogarth's *Analysis of Beauty*, 1753, the first volume of Joseph Warton's *Essay on the Genius and Writings of Pope*, 1756, Young's *Conjectures on Original Composition* and Gerard's *Essay on Taste*, both of 1759, and Hurd's *Letters on Chivalry and Romance*, 1762. Burke's *Enquiry* is not the least important of these attempts to explain the age to itself.

Since Burke's sublime is based on terror, it may not be amiss at this point to take a brief glance at the part that the terrible was playing in poetry at about the time that he was writing the *Enquiry*. Such an account as can be given here must necessarily be no more than a reminder of the relation between Burke's theory and the general tendencies of the age. The presence of terror and horror in the poetry of the first half of the eighteenth century is familiar

6. Expressions of young Burke's admiration for the murder scene and the witch scenes from *Macbeth* can be found in Samuel's *Early Life*, pp. 100, 101; 168.

7. *Early Life*, p. 84. It is amusing to compare with this passage a similar "sublime" flood described by the terror-loving Anna Seward, in a letter to Miss Wingfield, May 21, 1795. *Letters* (Edinburgh, 1811), IV, 62.

to all students of that period, and needs not to be labored here.[8]
The poetry of the graveyard and of the ruined castle or abbey
comes readily to mind to illustrate the emotionalism of the third,
fourth, and fifth decades of the century. Whether the poet retires
to a graveyard or to a ruin, his aim is usually the melancholy one
of ruminating on the inconstancy of all sublunary things, a truism
which is emphasized and driven home by such horrid descriptions
as those of bodily decay or restless ghosts. With degree of emotion varying from the "white melancholy" of Gray to the black
despair and at times almost uncontrolled terror and horror of Blair,
the graveyard poetry sought to turn men's thoughts from health to
death, from the cheerful light of day to the horrors of the grave, and
in so doing it developed into an instrument for awakening the
strong emotion which the mid-century enjoyed. There is no need
to quote examples here.

But supernatural and charnel-house terrors were not the only
ones at the disposal of the poets. Thomson filled each successive
edition of *The Seasons* with increasingly long passages which
aimed at evoking terror before the vast and destructive forces of
nature. Such imitators of Thomson as Mallet and Savage went
considerably beyond their master in the use of volcanoes, storms,
plagues, and wild beasts; but a few quotations from *The Seasons*
will serve to illustrate how terror in nature was exploited. Summer
presents to the reader a picture of "the Savage Race," "the Tyger
darting fierce," "the lively-shining Leopard," "the keen Hyena, fel-
lest of the Fell."

> These, rushing from th' inhospitable Woods . . .
> Innumerous glare around their shaggy King,
> Majestic, stalking o'er the printed Sands.[9]

The terror-evoking description of the sharks [1] is too well known for
quotation, as are also perhaps the picture of the shepherd struck by
lightning,[2] and storm in the desert.[3] Among other horrors in
Summer, is the plague, which is described in great detail, and
which ends with the picture of the empty streets

> . . . with uncouth Verdure clad,
> And rang'd at open Noon, by Beasts of Prey,

---

8. Many discussions of this poetry exist. See Amy Louise Reed's *The Background of Gray's Elegy* (New York, 1924); Eino Railo's *Haunted Castle* (New York, 1927); Haferkorn's *Gotik und Ruine* (Leipzig, 1924); J. W. Draper's *The Funeral Elegy and the Rise of English Romanticism* (New York, 1929). For a discussion of the æsthetic of terror in the romantic period, see Mario Praz, *The Romantic Agony* (London, 1933); pp. 25–50.

9. James Thomson, *The Seasons*, ed. Otto Zippel (Berlin, 1908), Summer, D, 912–938.

1. Summer, D, 1013–1025.
2. *Ibid.*, D, 1103–1168.
3. *Ibid.*, D, 959–979.

> And birds of bloody Beak; while, all Night long,
> In spotted Troops, the recent Ghosts complain,
> Demanding but the covering Grave. . . .[4]

Perhaps the most terrible image in the *Seasons* is that of the starving wolves

> Cruel as Death, and hungry as the Grave!
> Burning for Blood, bony, and gaunt, and grim! . . .

They descend from the mountains,

> And pouring o'er the Country, bear along,
> Keen as the North-Wind sweeps the glossy Snow . . .
> Rapacious at the Mother's Throat they fly,
> And tear the screaming Infant from her Breast . . .
> But if, appriz'd of the severe Attack,
> The country be shut up, lur'd by the Scent,
> On Church-Yards drear (inhuman to relate!)
> The disappointed Prowlers fall, and dig
> The Shrouded Body from the Grave; o'er which
> Mix'd with foul Shades, and frighted Ghosts, they howl.[5]

Here the terrors of the destructive forces of nature mingle with the shudder of the graveyard mood.

There is no doubt that these are "sublime" passages, and that they are sublime because of the terror which they are intended to provoke. We recall how Dennis had introduced this particular emotion into the sublime, and how Jacob had given a long list of sublime objects, many of which became the stock-in-trade of the graveyard and descriptive poets. But we need not rely on conjecture, for we have Thomson's own ideas on the subject. Writing to Mallet in regard to *The Excursion*, he urges him to confound his confusion by the introduction of sublimities:

> Eruptions, earthquakes, the sea wrought into a horrible tempest, the abyss amidst whose amazing prospects, how pleasing must that be of a deep valley covered with all the tender profusions of Spring. Here if you could insert a sketch of the deluge, what more affecting and noble? Sublimity must be the character of your piece.[6]

And he tells Mallet that *The Excursion* displays "an inimitable mixture of animated simplicity and chastised sublimity," approving especially the line: "Shrieking witches in the desert—at the dead of night," and the passage

4. *Ibid.*, D, 1052–1092.
5. Winter, E, 389–413.
6. Peter Cunningham, "James Thomson and David Mallet," *Miscellanies of the Philobiblon Society* (London, 1857–58), IV, 30.

> . . . or to invert the year
> And bring wild Winter into summer's place,
> Or spread brown Night and tempest o'er the morn.

"This is Poetry," he exclaims; "this is arousing fancy—enthusiasm—rapturous terror." [7]

As a rule, in neither the graveyard nor the descriptive poetry did the emotion exist for its own sake. In the poetry of death, the purpose of terror was to prepare the mind for whatever moralizing the poet might choose to indulge in; in the descriptive poetry, terrible aspects of nature helped to show the greatness of the Creator and the inscrutability of His ways. Once this emotion was introduced into prose fiction, however, its moralistic purpose was soon lost, and it came to be the primary consideration. The gothic novel exists almost purely for the sake of evoking pleasant terror.

Before Burke published his *Enquiry*, fiction had begun to borrow mood and material from the contemporary poetry of terror. In 1753, Smollett introduced into *Ferdinand Count Fathom* a scene which, as has been frequently remarked, contains many of the elements of the gothic novel—a storm, a forest, banditti, a blood-stained corpse, the suggestions of a ghost, a hair-breadth escape.[8] In these chapters the sole desire of the author seems to be to stir strong emotion in the reader. Later in the book, when he recounts the visit of Renaldo to the supposed tomb of Monimia, Smollett borrows from the graveyard poets the mood and the properties of the scene. Darkness, silence, a lonely church, a clock striking midnight, an owl screeching from the ruined battlements, a glimmering taper, a tomb—all are crowded into one paragraph in order to pack it with emotive ideas.[9] In such scenes the emotion comes to be the important factor, to be enjoyed in and for itself.

It was this emotion—already widespread in theory and in art—that Burke came to strengthen and to place definitely and finally in the theory of art. The prevalence of terror perhaps accounts for some of the favor with which the *Enquiry* met, while certainly the *Enquiry* did much for the cause of the appreciation of terror in both art and nature. That Burke was not by nature incapacitated for sharing the tastes of his contemporaries is shown in a letter to Matthew Smith, written shortly after he came to London, in which he refers to *Il Penseroso* as "the finest poem in the English language" and imagines that it was composed "in the long resounding aisle of a mouldering cloister or ivy'd abbey." [1]

7. *Ibid.*, iv, 21; 24, 25.
8. [Tobias George Smollett], *The Adventures of Ferdinand Count Fathom* (London, 1753), i, 122–135.
9. *Ibid.*, ii, 236, 237.
1. *Early Life*, p. 221.

It is now time to turn to the *Enquiry* itself, and to analyse its chief ideas; this in spite of the fact that even today it is a not unfamiliar piece of writing.[2] The whole system is based on the antithesis of pain and pleasure, the one being the foundation of the sublime, the other of the beautiful. Hume, it will be recalled, had taken pain and pleasure as the effects of the ugly and the beautiful, and it may be said that in general this was the point of view of the first half of the century. Burke is interested in the fact that we can derive pleasure even from pain when we judge æsthetically, and in introducing pain as the basis of sublimity, he opens the way for the inclusion of ideas and images in art that had hitherto been considered as lying properly outside the sphere of æsthetic pleasure. The emotions of pleasure and pain Burke associates with the ideas of self-preservation and society (I, 6) and he makes them respectively the bases of the sublime and the beautiful. The relation between self-preservation, pain, and the sublime, he sums up in the following words:

> Whatever is fitted in any sort to excite the ideas of pain, and danger, that is to say, whatever is in any sort terrible, or is conversant about terrible objects, or operates in a manner analogous to terror, is a source of the *sublime*; that is, it is productive of the strongest emotion which the mind is capable of feeling. . . . When danger or pain press too nearly, they are incapable of giving any delight, and are simply terrible; but at certain distances, and with certain modifications, they may be, and they are delightful,[3] as we every day experience (I, 7).

Beauty, on the other hand, is social, and rests primarily on love and its attendant emotions (I, 8–17). No one had sought heretofore such a final and clear-cut distinction between the sublime and the beautiful, although, as we have seen, Addison and Akenside had contrasted them. Burke's æsthetic dualism has all the latent dangers of a too-exact pigeonholing. Neat as it is in theory, it is none the less an awkward splitting of the æsthetic experience; that it came to be considered unfortunate is shown by the invention, late in the century, of a third category, the picturesque, which had to come into existence in order to give those objects that are neither beautiful nor sublime (in Burke's sense of the words) a local habitation

---

2. The text from which I have quoted is that of the second (revised) edition, London, 1759. In order to avoid a superfluity of footnotes, it has seemed expedient to take advantage of Burke's rather minute division of his essay into sections, and to refer to them, rather than to pages. The reader will be able to refer conveniently to the context in any edition that happens to be at hand.

3. A note is needed on Burke's use of the word *delight*. He distinguishes between positive pleasure, which has an existence independent of pain, and that pleasure which arises from the removal of pain. It is this latter sensation that Burke terms "delight." Thus actual pain is kept out of the æsthetic experience.

and a name.[4] And the picturesque, by its very existence, bears witness to the influence of the *Enquiry* in æsthetic thought during the rest of the century.

In attempting to establish an æsthetic system on the "passions," and in relating it ultimately to bodily states, Burke takes a long step in the direction of realism. He is honestly interested in ascertaining how objects affect us, rather than in discussing, on the basis of pre-conceived ideas inherent in the neo-classic system, how they ought to affect us. He turns his back upon the work of artists and other critics, because he believes them to be too imitative, too traditional, too divorced from experience. Holding that "the true standard of the arts is in every man's power" (I, 19), he deliberately closes his mind to the dicta of the past, forgets Longinus, Boileau, *et al.*, and attempts the somewhat heroic task of building up a system on his own observations of his physical and mental being. For this reason, Burke is original as none of his predecessors had been, and the *Enquiry* marks a new departure in æsthetic thought.

In the second main part of his treatise, Burke is occupied wholly with a discussion of sublime objects and their effect. The great and sublime in nature cause the passion which Burke, in common with his age, called astonishment. In a definition that seems to be a para-phrase of Dr. Johnson's explanation of the word in his dictionary, Burke says that astonishment is "that state of the soul in which all its motions are suspended with some degree of horror." He goes on to point out that in such a state "the mind is so entirely filled with its object, that it cannot entertain any other, nor by conse-quence reason on that object which employs it." Thus the sublime, in its highest degree, "hurries us on by an irresistible force." The inferior effects of the sublime are admiration, reverence, and respect (II, 1).

Of all passions, fear has most power "to rob the mind of all its powers of acting and reasoning," and in this regard it resembles pain in all its action. Any object that threatens danger to man may produce the sublime, even small objects. Thus, unlike many theo-rists, Burke does not restrict the sublime to the grand; the emotion produced, not the object that produces it, is the important factor in Burke's aesthetic. For this reason, a wide expanse of plain is less sublime than an equally wide expanse of ocean, for we are accus-tomed to associate peril with the sea. "Indeed," he says, "terror is in all cases whatsoever, either more openly or latently, the ruling principle of the sublime" (II, 2). This recognition of the function of association in our æsthetic perceptions was familiar in speculation before Burke's day; Dennis, Hutcheson, Hume, and Baillie had all employed it, and Hartley had only recently erected a system of

4. See below, pp. 156 ff.

psychology on that idea alone. But Burke is careful in his use of association, and as we shall see, refuses to follow Hartley in adopting it as the sole explanation of our mental processes. He helps, however, to establish it definitely in speculation against the time when Alison exploits it fully. The idea that the sublime is completely irrational had been common since the ancients discussed the high style, but it should not be overlooked that in this, the most popular treatise of the century, irrationality is given what is at least a pseudo-scientific basis, and is passed on to the preromantic period, where it helps prepare the way for the overthrow of what Wordsworth calls "the meddling intellect" and Keats, "the dull brain."

There follows a classification of ideas that are sublime and an explanation of the sublimity of each. They are obscurity, where darkness and uncertainty arouse dread and terror (ii, 3); power, where the mind is impelled to fear because of superior force (ii, 5); privations, such as darkness, vacuity, and silence, which are great because they are terrible (ii, 6); vastness, whether in length, height, or depth, the last being the most powerful source of the sublime (ii, 7); infinity, or any object that because of its size seems infinite (ii, 8); difficulty—that is, any object that seems to owe its existence to a vast expenditure of labor and effort (ii, 12); and magnificence (ii, 13).

This is an interesting list. With the exception of power, none of these ideas would have been very much at home in neo-classic art. The age in which, as Austin Dobson puts it,

> . . . Phoebus touch'd the Poet's trembling Ear
> With one supreme Commandment, *Be thou Clear,*

was not an age to domicile the obscure in its art. It was a social art, and in its more characteristic moments preferred town and court to Burke's privations. It was, as we have seen, an art that sought proportion and that disliked the vast. It preferred the concrete and the bounded to the infinite, and it sought to give the impression of ease and urbanity, not of difficulty. This is not to attempt to convert Burke into a sort of philosophical Byron, but only to indicate that in the *Enquiry,* under the caption of the sublime, tastes that are not strictly compatible with neo-classic theory take up their position in a treatise that was extremely popular throughout the rest of the century, for the very reason that it chimed in so well with tastes that were to become dominant as the century drew to a close.

It is in relation to obscurity that Burke says: "A clear idea is therefore another name for a little idea" (ii, 4). This repudiation of clarity is especially important when we remember that Burke considered the sublime to be the highest domain of art, for it removes the greatest art from the atmosphere in which neo-classicism lived and moved and had its being. In his fifth *Méditation* Descartes had said: *"Toutes choses qui je connais clairement et distinctement sont vrais."* Hence French neo-classicism had preferred the *School of Athens* to the *Last Judgment;* hence deism, the typical religion of the neo-classical enlightenment, had stripped Christianity of its miracles; hence the truths which neo-classic art had sought to incarnate were clear and universal truths; and hence precision and proportion were regarded as valuable æsthetic qualities in all the arts. Burke's objection to clarity, his insistence on the essential pettiness of ideas that the reason can grasp, arises from his preoccupation with the non-rational element in art. "It is one thing to make an image clear, and another to make it affecting to the imagination," he avers (II, 4), and he sustains his opinion by pointing out that the greater emotive value of a verbal description as opposed to a drawing of the same scene, and the influence of music in arousing feeling without the aid of images. Such a position is clearly at variance with the standards of Augustan art, and it represents an advance toward that element in romantic art that manifests itself in half-lights, suggestions, and mystery. Much of that mood is expressed in the passage from Job that Burke quotes in this connection:

> In thoughts from the visions of the night, when deep sleep falleth upon man, fear came upon me and trembling, which made all my bones to shake. Then a spirit passed before my face. The hair of my flesh stood up. It stood still, *but I could not discover the form thereof;* an image was before mine eyes; there was silence; and I heard a voice: Shall mortal man be more just than God? (II, 4).

This evoking of awe through mystery is very much akin to the "sublimity" of Ossian and to many passages in the romantic poets.[5]

It is in discussing magnificence that Burke makes what Folkierski has claimed to be his chief contribution to æsthetic.[6] A profusion of splendid or valuable objects, he says, is magnificent. The "starry heavens" afford an example, and their number is the explanation of the fact that they always excite ideas of grandeur. "The apparent disorder augments the grandeur, for the appearance of care is highly contrary to our ideas of magnificence" (II, 13). The idea derives ultimately from Longinus's statement that a great genius, like a wealthy man, can afford to be careless, but its strict application to the practice of art would have been an innovation indeed. Once disorder is admitted into art, classic beauty, whose very essence is

---

5. Compare Coleridge's opinion: "Poetry gives most pleasure when only generally and not perfectly understood." *Anima Poetae,* ed. E. H. Coleridge

(London, 1895), p. 5.
6. *Entre le Classicisme et le Romantisme,* pp. 96, 97.

order, harmony, and proportion, is no more. Simplicity (which we found Boileau advancing as an appropriate dress for the sublime, and whose value Burke fully recognizes) was an essential element in neo-classical art, and cannot exist side by side with a magnificent disorder. It is true that Boileau had written of the ode:

> Son style impétueux souvent marche au hazard:
> Chez elle un beau désordre est un effet de l'art;[7]

but this disorder is merely a trick employed by a cunning craftsman who wishes to simulate the supposed disorder of the Pindaric ode. Burke's disorder produces "an appearance of infinity,"; else "you will have disorder only, without magnificence" (II, 13), so that there is evidently a distinction to be drawn between Boileau's "beau désordre" and Burke's "magnificent disorder." It is only fair to point out that the suggestion of the value of disorder is made very timidly, and is so qualified as to be almost revoked as soon as it is uttered, for Burke says that this kind of grandeur is "to be very cautiously admitted" because of its difficulty, and because "in many cases this splendid confusion would destroy all use, which should be attended to in most of the works of art with the greatest care" (II, 13). This statement is a sensible qualification of what must have seemed an anarchistic idea in æsthetic, but it does not obscure another instance of Burke's unorthodox tastes.

The remainder of Part II can be briefly summarized. Brilliant light, such as the direct light of the sun striking the eye, light moving with celerity (lightning), and quick transitions from light to darkness, or from darkness to light are sublime, but darkness is more productive of sublimity than is light, as quotations from Milton illustrate (II, 14); "sad and fuscous colours, as black and brown, or deep purple" belong to the same category, and bright colors are opposed to it because they militate against that "melancholy kind of greatness" which is the sublime (II, 16).[8] Excessively loud and regularly recurring sounds, low, tremulous, intermitting sounds, and inarticulate cries of pain or fear in beasts and in man evoke fear, and consequently operate on the soul as does the sublime (II, 17, 18, 19). Even the senses of smell and of taste play their part in producing these emotions; excessive bitters, or intolerable stenches(!), if they are not associated with mean ideas, create states of mind analogous to the sublime (II, 21). It is in this part of the *Enquiry* that one smiles to perceive how Burke's thesis is running away with him.

---

7. "L'Art Poétique," Canto II, *Œuvres Complètes*, II, 316.
8. Burke's taste in scenery is prophetic of the cult of wild nature that was to grow up in the next decade: "An immense mountain covered with a shining green turf is nothing, in this respect, to one dark and gloomy; the cloudy sky is more grand than the blue; and night more sublime and solemn than day" (II, 16).

In Part ɪᴠ Burke attempts to explain psychologically and physiologically, the effect of the ideas discussed in Parts ɪ and ɪɪ, so as to reach the "efficient cause" of the sublime, and it is at this point that he seems most original. Whatever one may think of his deductions, no one can deny that in seeking to observe the physiology of beauty and sublimity, in going beyond the passions to the body, and in bringing the whole organism into the æsthetic experience, Burke showed remarkable "modernity" of thought. Blake, the apostle of imagination and inspiration, was to feel "contempt and Abhorrence" for the *Enquiry*,[9] as he would have felt for most modern psychology, for in Burke's essay there is shadowed forth the materialistic implication of twentieth-century psychological investigation, the method that seeks a physical explanation even for art itself.[1] The empirical method of Burke's thought is seen in his statement: "When we go but one step beyond the immediate sensible qualities of things, we go out of our depth" (ɪᴠ, 1). He is therefore compelled to restrict his inquiry to sensation and its physical and emotional effect.

Burke uses association to explain the effect of objects, but the measure of his disagreement with the Hartleian psychology is shown in his refusal to explain all mental processes by that principle, preferring, as he does, to find when possible an explanation in the natural properties of the object and their physical effect upon a sense organ (ɪᴠ, 2).[2]

Arguing from the fact that pain and fear affect the body in much the same way—that is, they cause a violent contraction of the muscles and a tenseness of the nerves—Burke concludes that he is justified in treating the sensation and the emotion together, observing the distinction that pain operates on the mind through the body,

9. See the marginalia in the British Museum's copy of the second edition of the *Works* of Reynolds, ɪ, 282. In Blake's opinion the *Enquiry* mocks inspiration and vision, his "Element," and "Eternal Dwelling place."
1. See Francisco Mirabent's *La Estética Inglesa del Sigol XVIII* (Barcelona, 1927), pp. 118, 119.
2. It is not easy to trace Burke's indebtedness to the psychology of his time. The general method is, of course, that of Locke, whom Burke has constantly in mind, and with whom he differs on occasion (ɪ, 3 and ɪᴠ, 3). To Hume he may have been indebted, although here, too, specific borrowings are hard to find. The similarities which one can discover—such as their common opinion that there is no greater punishment that a man can suffer than perfect solitude—prove exactly nothing (see Hume's *Philosophical Works*, ɪɪ, 150). Burke's habit of regarding sensation as caused by the vibration of the nerves finds its parallel in Hume's writings, in which the mind is compared to a stringed instrument, whose vibrations gradually decay (*Philosophical Works*, ɪɪ, 140); and in Hartley's explanation of the continuation of the sense impression after direct stimulation has been removed as due to the vibrations of "Infinitesimal medullary Particles" (*Observations on Man*, ɪ, 9–11). Burke uses this bit of knowledge to show how a large, but uniform, building can create the impression of infinity on the senses. There are other minor, but equally unimpressive, parallels between Hartley and Burke who, in the main, disagree too much to have much in common. About all that one can say is that Burke seems to have studied the physiology and the psychology of his day.

and terror on the body through the mind (IV, 3). It follows that sublime objects must work their effect by causing such a tension and such a contraction in the subject, either through their natural properties or through association (IV, 5). But there remains the question as to why such an effect, which should be and which often is disagreeable, should in art and sometimes in reality prove capable of producing delight. The answer, which is suggested by Du Bos's statement that a state of rest and inactivity is disagreeable, is that as exercise is healthful for the body so it is good for the "finer organs" on which and by which the imagination acts.

> . . . if the pain and terror are so modified as not to be actually noxious; if the pain is not carried to violence, and the terror is not conversant about the present destruction of the person [that is, if it can be regarded theoretically], as these emotions clear the parts, whether fine or gross, of a dangerous and troublesome encumbrance, they are capable of producing delight; not pleasure, but a sort of delightful horror, a sort of tranquility tinged with terror; . . . Its object is the sublime. Its highest degree I call *astonishment*; the subordinate degrees are awe, reverence, and respect . . . (IV, 6, 7).

On this basis Burke explains why visual objects of great dimensions are sublime. Light from an object striking the retina causes tension and vibration, and when the object is large, this continued effect produces a state very like that which causes pain, and consequently produces an idea of the sublime. If the eye moves from one to another small and diversified object, it experiences an instant of relaxation, but if the object is both simple and vast, the eye (and therefore the mind) does not arrive readily at its bounds, and has no rest, since the image is everywhere the same. Hence the impression of an "artificial infinite" is created by a large and unified object which throws the retina into a state of tension and impresses itself so vividly on the mind that an idea of the sublime is suggested (IV, 9, 10, 13). The same reasoning is followed in regard to sounds (IV, 11, 12).

It is thus that Burke arrives at the conclusion that beauty and sublimity act directly on the nervous system through sense impressions. He removes the perception of the beautiful and the sublime from the realm of judgment, where the French neo-classicists had sought it, as well as from the realm of sentiment where some of his immediate predecessors had found it. Crousaz had referred aesthetic judgment to "sentiment," Du Bos had invented a "sixth sense," and Hutcheson had used the term "internal sense." These were vague ideas, but they all presupposed a separate faculty by which men perceive æsthetic values. Burke turned his back on these older theories, and had recourse to a sensationalism that has the advantage of being simpler and clearer. Moreover, although he cannot, by the very nature of his reasoning, refer beauty and sublimity to the perceiving mind alone, as Kant was to do and as Hume had already done, he does, perforce, concentrate most of his attention on the effect rather than on the qualities of objects. As we have seen, small objects may be regarded as sublime if they create terror, and even the ugly may be associated with sublimity if it is "united with such qualities as excite strong terror" (III, 21). This opinion represents a certain awareness of the supreme value of the individual impression, and is a step toward the abolition of purely objective formulæ in the labelling and consideration of æsthetic experiences.

The reviewers received the *Enquiry* kindly enough.[3] Burke's boast that his subject has led him "out of the common course of discourse" (I, 4) is well borne out by the dicta of the critics. The *London Chronicle* declares that the *Enquiry* gave "criticism a face that we never saw it wear before;" [4] Goldsmith, writing for the *Monthly Review*, dwells on the novelty of Burke's method, and points to the innovation therein when he says that the author "rejects all former systems, and founds his philosophy on his own particular feelings;" [5] the anonymous reviewer of the *Critical Review* mentions the same fact, and Arthur Murphy makes Burke's originality the point of a rather ill-humored attack.[6] But although in the main the essay was favorably received, the critics were unanimous in stating that Burke had attempted to restrict the sublime too closely when he excluded all emotions but terror from its sphere,[7] and Murphy demonstrates the hold that Longinus had on the thought of his time when he contrasts the *Enquiry* with *Peri Hupsous*, very much to the advantage of the Greek treatise.[8]

For nearly half a century the *Enquiry* continued in high favor with the public, no matter how often æstheticians might dissent from its views. Perhaps Burke's early biographer, Charles McCormick, does not much overestimate the popularity of the book when he declares that "the author was universally allowed to have surpassed LONGINUS in precision, and Addison in depth and comprehensiveness. . . ." [9] Certain it is that Burke had provided the

3. See Herbert A. Wicheln's "Burke's Essay on the Sublime and its Reviewers," *JEGP*, XXI (1922), 645–661. The article is a study of the relation between the reviews and the changes and additions that Burke made in the second edition.
4. *The London Chronicle, or Universal Evening Post*, II (1757), 52.
5. *Monthly Review*, XVI, 473.
6. *Critical Review*, III, 316; Johnson's *Works* (1787), X, 199, 200. Murphy's review was erroneously ascribed to Johnson by Sir John Hawkins, and was published by him in his edition of the complete works. For Boswell's denial of Johnson's authorship, and his ascription of the review to Murphy, see *Life*, I, 310.
7. See, for example, Goldsmith's views, *Monthly Review*, XVI, 475, note.
8. Johnson's *Works* (1787), X, 207.
9. Charles McCormick, *Memoirs of the Right Honourable Edmund Burke*, Second Edition (London, 1798), p. 29.

age with an idea of sublimity that suited nicely its increasingly sensational tastes, and that could easily be comprehended by those who were uninitiated into the deeper mysteries of philosophy. One of the most important phases of its influence will be pointed out in a later chapter.

Dr. Johnson considered it "an example of true criticism," [1] and in Reynolds' opinion it was an "admirable treatise." [2] But Burke was not dependent on praise from members of his own coterie. Blair, although he refused to limit sublimity to terror, did not hesitate to borrow from the *Enquiry*,[3] and in this respect he is typical of his fellow theorists, who seldom succeeded in ignoring Burke, even when they wrote from a totally different point of view. Quite late in the century, Richard Stack was to find the essay "in most respects perfectly just, in all its parts beautifully ingenious," [4] and Gregory, the translator of Lowth's lectures, was to speak of the author of the *Enquiry* as one "whose taste and imagination will be respected as long as the English language exists. . . ." [5] In 1792, the reviewer of Hickey's *History of Painting and Sculpture* could repeat the Burkean idea that terror is the "chief ingredient of the sublime," [6] and as we shall see, the *Enquiry* regained something of its early fame in the controversy over the picturesque that was in progress as the century came to its end. But certainly the prettiest compliment that Burke was paid is to be found in John Bennett's *Letters to a Young Lady on a Variety of Useful and Interesting Subjects*. The author describes one of those model young people who appear so often in the improving books of the eighteenth century. She retires to a garden, where "she indulges all the luxury of her taste," and then she reads the *Enquiry*, and thereby seems "more *beautiful* and more *sublime*, than the admired work of that well known and admired author." [7]

But none the less the treatise lost prestige as the century drew to a close. Something of this decline in fame is heralded by Plumer's fatuous attack in 1772,[8] but although the actual popularity of the book seems to decrease its influence continued, and the book is always to be reckoned with even during the early nineteenth century. Dugald Stewart recorded his opinion that Burke's was the best of the eighteenth-century essays on sublimity,[9] and Edward Mangin borrowed copiously from the *Enquiry* when he constructed

1. James Boswell, *Life of Johnson*, ed. G. B. Hill (Oxford, 1887), ii, 90.
2. Sir Joshua Reynolds, *Works*, ed. Edmond Malone (London, 1798), i, 282, note.
3. *Lectures*, i, 55.
4. *Transactions of the Royal Irish Academy*, i, 4.
5. *Lectures*, i, 302, 303, note.

6. *Analytical Review*, xiv (1792), 165.
7. John Bennett, *Letters to a Young Lady* (Warrington, 1789), ii, 59.
8. [F. Plumer], *A Letter from a Gentleman to his Nephew at Oxford* (London, 1772), *passim*.
9. Dugald Stewart, "On the Sublime," *Philosophical Essays* (Edinburgh, 1810), p. 344.

his theory of the sublime.[1]

But the work which had influenced so powerfully English æsthetic thought and taste during its formative years, and which had shaped some of Johnson's thoughts on poetry,[2] was ultimately to be regarded coldly, as when Coleridge dismissed it as "a poor thing." [3] But it had done its work by turning the attention of theorists to the sensations and the psychological influences that accompany and determine the æsthetic experience, and by helping to spread the cult of romantic terror throughout the literature of the era that just precedes the rise of romantic art.

OWEN BARFIELD

Symptoms of Iconoclasm †

We have seen that the theory of metaphor, as the means by which language originally acquired its 'inner' meanings, is incorrect. But it is important to remember how it arose. It arose because there *is* a close relation between language as it is used by a participating consciousness and language as it is used, at a later stage, metaphorically or symbolically. When we use language metaphorically, we bring it about of our own free will that an appearance means something other than itself, and, usually, that a manifest 'means' an unmanifest. We start with an idol, and we ourselves turn the idol into a representation. We use the phenomenon as a 'name' for what is not phenomenal. And this, it will be remembered, is just what is characteristic of participation. Symbolism, as we saw in Chapter XI, is made possible by the elimination of participation. But at the end

1. [Edward Mangin], *Essays on the Sources of the Pleasures Received from Literary Compositions* (London, 1809), pp. 51 ff.
2. Surely, when in *Rasselas*, Johnson says: "To the poet nothing can be useless. Whatever is beautiful; and whatever is dreadful, must be familiar to his imagination; he must be conversant with all that is awfully vast or elegantly little"; (*Works*, I, 221)— surely here he is thinking of the *Enquiry.*
3. *Table Talk and Omniana*, p. 54.
† From *Saving The Appearances: A Study in Idolatry* by Owen Barfield. Reprinted by permission of Harcourt, Brace & World, Inc. and the author.

of Chapter XVI it was observed that in certain circumstances this may give rise to a new kind of participation—one which could no longer be described as 'original'.

What then has occurred? If we rapidly review the whole historical development of 'the word', we must say that, as soon as unconscious or subconscious organic processes have been sufficiently polarized to give rise to phenomena on the one side and consciousness on the other, *memory* is made possible. As consciousness develops into self-consciousness, the remembered phenomena become detached or liberated from their originals and so, as images, are in some measure at man's disposal. The more thoroughly participation has been eliminated, the more they are at the disposal of his imagination to employ as it chooses. If it chooses to impart its own meaning, it is doing, *pro tanto*, with the remembered phenomena what their Creator once did with the phenomena themselves. Thus there *is* a real analogy between metaphorical usage and original participation; but it is one which can only be acknowledged at this high, or even prophetic, level. It can only be acknowledged if the crude conception of an evolution of idols, which has dominated the last two centuries, is finally abandoned, or at all events is enlightened by one more in line with the old teaching of the Logos. There is a valid analogy *if*, but only if, we admit that, in the course of the earth's history, something like a Divine Word has been gradually clothing itself with the humanity it first gradually created—so that what was first spoken by God may eventually be respoken by man.

This granted, we can see how language, in the course of its history, has indeed mediated the transformation of phenomena into idols. But we can also see how, by reason of this very fact, *within* man the phenomena have gradually ceased to operate as compulsive natural processes and have become, instead, mere memory-images available for his own creative 'speech'—using 'speech' now in the wide sense of Aquinas's 'word'.

We should expect, accordingly, that, with the progressive decrease of participation throughout the Graeco-Roman, or Aristotelian age, we should find a growing awareness—however faint— of this capacity of man for creative speech. And we should expect to find a marked increase in that awareness after the scientific revolution. It is what we do find. Let us take, for example, the Romantic theory of the 'creative imagination' and glance briefly at its previous history. Premonitory hints of an attribution of 'creative' power to man as artist or poet, appear as early as the first Christian century, with Dio Chrysostom. A century later Philostratus maintained of the works of Pheidias and Praxiteles, that:

Imagination made them, and she is a better artist than imitation; for where the one carves only what she has seen, the other carves what she has not seen.

By the third century Plotinus is maintaining that:

If anyone disparages the arts on the ground that they imitate nature, we must remind him that natural objects are themselves only imitations, and that the arts do not simply imitate what they see but reascend to those principles (λόγοι) from which Nature herself is derived.

For Scaliger in the sixteenth century (who was closely followed by Sidney in his *Apologie for Poesie*) the poet is one who 'maketh a new Nature and so maketh himself as it were a new God.' [1]

Coleridge's doctrine of the primary and secondary imagination, when it came, and the whole Romantic stress in England and Germany on the 'creative' function of art and poetry was, then, by no means a wholly new adventure in thought. It was rather that the whole attitude to nature, which it implied, had been rendered acceptable to a much wider circle by the rapidly increasing idolatry of the seventeenth and eighteenth centuries. Something very much like it had already been thought by a few. It became almost a popular movement in a world beginning at last to hunger for iconoclasm.

We have already had occasion to note the close relation between the apprehension of images and the making of them. As long as nature herself continued to be apprehended as image, it sufficed for the artist to imitate Nature. Inevitably, the life or spirit in the object lived on in his imitation, if it was a faithful one. For at the same time it could not help being more than an imitation, inasmuch as the artist himself participated in the being of the object. But the imitation of an *idol* is a purely technical process; which (as was quickly discovered) is better done by photography. To-day an artist cannot rely on the life inherent in the object he imitates, any more than a poet can rely on the life inherent in the words he uses. He has to draw the life forth from within himself.

It is for the same reason that an ever-increasing importance came to be attached to the *invented* image and men become more and more dissatisfied with imitations of nature both in the practice and in the theory of art. It is easy to see how it came to be held that 'the truest poetry is the most feigning'. For there is no doubt about where the life in an invented or fictitious image comes from. There

---

1. This important little piece of history will be found most effectively summarized at the beginning of Bk. III of Professor C. S. Lewis's *English Literature in the Sixteenth Century*. Clarendon Press. 1954.

can be no 'pathetic fallacy' there. What is peculiar to the Romantic Movement—as, indeed, its very name recalls—is the further reaction of this enthusiasm for fictitious and *fabulous* representations on the phenomena—on Nature herself. This is also what took the Romantic conception of art, properly understood, a step beyond the Neo-platonic theory referred to above. The Neo-platonic theory holds that man the artist is, in some measure, a creator. The Romantic conception agrees—but goes further and returns him, in this capacity, to Nature herself.

With what result? It is no longer simply that the arts 'reascend to those principles from which nature herself is derived'. The 'principles' themselves have changed their venue. For we are told by the Romantic theory that we must no longer look for the nature-spirits—for the Goddess Natura—on the farther side of the appearances; we must look for them *within ourselves*.

> *Unbewusst der Freuden, die sie schenket,*
> *Nie entzückt von ihrer Herrlichkeit,*
> *Nie gewahr des Geistes, der sie lenket,*
> *Sel'ge nur durch meine Seligkeit,*
>
> *Fühllos selbst für ihres Künstlers Ehre,*
> *Gleich dem toten Schlag der Pendeluhr,*
> *Dient sie knechtisch dem Gesetz der Schwere,*
> *Die entgötterte Natur.*[2]

Pan has shut up shop. But he has not retired from business; he has merely gone indoors. Or, in the well-known words of Coleridge:

> *We receive but what we give*
> *And in our life alone does Nature live.*[3]

It is again beyond the scope of this book to trace in detail the way in which the origin of the Romantic response to nature is exemplified in that association between Coleridge and Wordsworth which gave rise to the *Lyrical Ballads*. It was the dejected author of the *Ancient Mariner* who grasped the theory; but it was Wordsworth who actually *wrote* the nature-poetry.

If nature is indeed 'dis-godded', and yet we again begin to experience her, as Wordsworth did—and as millions have done since his time—no longer as dead but as alive; if there is no 'represented' on the far side of the appearances, and yet we begin to experience them once more *as* appearances, as representations—the question

2. From Schiller's *Die Götter Griech-enlands*: 'Unconscious of the joy she bestows, never transported by her own glory, never aware of the spirit that directs her, blest only through my blessedness, without feeling even for the honour of her artist—as with the dead stroke of a clock's pendulum she—disgodded Nature—slavishly obeys the law of gravity.'
3. *Ode to Dejection*.

arises, of *what* are they representations? It was no doubt the difficulty of answering this question which led Wordsworth to relapse occasionally into that nostalgic hankering after *original* participation, which is called pantheism—and from which Coleridge was rendered immune by his acquaintance with Kantian philosophy. We shall find somewhat the same contrast, in this respect, between Goethe and Schiller.

It is because of its failure to answer this question that the true, one might say the tremendous, impulse underlying the Romantic movement has never grown to maturity; and, after adolescence, the alternative to maturity is puerility. There is only one answer to the question. Henceforth, if nature is to be experienced as representation, she will be experienced as representation of—Man. But what is Man? Herein lies the direst possibility inherent in idolatry. It can empty of spirit—it has very nearly succeeded in doing so—not only nature, but also Man himself. For among all the other idols is his own body. And it is part of the creed of idolatry that, when we speak of Man, we mean only the body of this or that man, or at most his finite personality, which we are driven more and more to think an attribute of his body.

Thus it is, that the great change which the evolution of consciousness has brought about and the great lessons which men had begun to learn have all been wrenched awry. We had come at last to the point of realizing that art can no longer be content with imitating the collective representations, now that these are themselves turning into idols. But, instead of setting out to smash the idols, we have tamely concluded that nothing can now be art which in any way reminds us of nature—and even that practically anything may be art, which does not. We have learned that art can represent nothing but Man himself, and we have interpreted that as meaning that art exists for the purpose of enabling Mr. Smith to 'express his personality'. And all because we have not learnt—though our very physics shouts it at us—that nature herself is the representation of Man.

Hence the riot of private and personal symbolisms into which both art and poetry have degenerated. If I know that nature herself is the system of my representations, I cannot do otherwise than adopt a humbler and more responsible attitude to the representations of art and the metaphors of poetry. For in the case of nature there is no danger of my fancying that she exists to express my personality. I know in that case that what is meant, when I say she is my representation, is, that I stand, whether I like it or not, in—(I do not love the expression, but I can find no defter one in English) a 'directionally creator' relation to her. But I know also that what so stands is not my poor temporal personality, but the

Divine Name in the unfathomable depths behind it. And if I strive to produce a work of art, I cannot then do otherwise than strive humbly to create more nearly as *that* creates, and not as my idiosyncrasy wills.

After all, there is warrant for it. At the beginning of the first chapter I pointed to the phenomenon of the rainbow, because it is especially easy there to realize the extent of which it is 'our' creation. But we know equally well that it is not only the colours and curve of the rainbow which proceed from the eye; it is not only 'Iris' who has gone indoors; we know that light itself—*as light* (whatever we may think about the particles)—proceeds from the same source. Now for the Impressionist painters, this became a real experience. They really painted nature in the light of the eye, as no other painters had done before them. They were striving to realize in consciousness the n_____ __onscious activity of 'figuration' itself. They did not _____ __y expressed 'themselves'—inasmuch as they painted _____ __e representation of Man. They will serve as a remin___ ___ hey are not the only one—that the rejection of orig___ ___on may mean, not the destruction but the liberatio_____.

GEOFFREY H. HARTMAN

Romanticism and "Anti-Self-Consciousness" †

I

The dejection afflicting John Stuart Mill in his twentieth year was alleviated by two important events. He read Wordsworth, and he discovered for himself a view of life resembling the "anti-self-consciousness theory" of Carlyle. Mill describes this strangely named theory in his *Autobiography*:

Ask yourself whether you are happy, and you cease to be so. The only chance is to treat, not happiness, but some end external to

† Revised and expanded by the author from his essay in *Centennial Review*, Vol. VI, No. 4 (Autumn 1962). Copyright © 1962 by *Centennial Review* and

it as the purpose of life. Let your self-consciousness, your scrutiny, your self-interrogation exhaust themselves on that.[1]

It is not surprising that Wordsworth's poetry should also have served to protect Mill from the morbidity of his intellect. Like many Romantics, Wordsworth had passed through a depression clearly linked to the ravage of self-consciousness and the "strong disease" of self-analysis.[2] Book XI of the *Prelude*, chapter 5 of Mill's *Autobiography*, Carlyle's *Sartor Resartus*, and other great confessional works of the Romantic period, show how crucial these 'maladies' are for the adolescent mind. Endemic, perhaps, to every stage of life, they especially affect the transition from adolescence to maturity; and it is interesting to observe how man's attention has shifted from the fact of death and its *"rites de passage,"* to these trials in what Keats called "the Chamber of Maiden-Thought," and more recently still, to the perils of childhood. We can say, taking a metaphor from Donne, that "streights, and none but streights" are ways to whatever changes the mind must undergo; and that it is the Romantics who first explored the dangerous passageways of maturation.

Two trials or perils of the soul deserve special mention. We learn that every increase in consciousness is accompanied by an increase in self-consciousness, and that analysis can easily become a passion that "murders to dissect."[3] These difficulties of thought in

1. *Autobiography* (1873), chapter 5. Mill says that he had not heard, at the time, of Carlyle's theory. The first meeting between the writers took place in 1831; Mill's depression lasted, approximately, from autumn 1826 to autumn 1828. In a letter, Mill characterizes self-consciousness as "that demon of the men of genius of our time, from Wordsworth to Byron, from Goethe to Chateaubriand, and to which this age owes so much both of its cheerful and its mournful wisdom.'" See Wayne Shumaker, *English Autobiography* (Berkeley, 1954), p. 76.
2. Thought as a disease is an open as well as submerged metaphor among the Romantics. There are many hints in Novalis; Schelling pronounces naked reflection (analysis) to be a spiritual sickness of man (*Schellings Sämtliche Werke*, ed. K. F. Schelling, [Stuttgart, 1856–61], II, 13–14); the metaphor is explicit in Carlyle's *Characteristics* (1831), and commonplace by the time that E. S. Dallas in *The Gay Science* (1866) lays the 'modern disease" to ". . . excessive civilization and overstrained consciousness." The *mal du siècle* is not unrelated to the malady we are describing. Goethe's *Die Leiden des Jungen Werthers* (1774) may be

seen as its *terminus a quo,* and Kierkegaard's *Sickness unto Death* (1849) as its noonday point clarity.
3. Wordsworth, "The Tables Turned" (1798). For the first peril, see Kierkegaard's *Sickness unto Death,* and Blake, *e.g.* "The Negation is the Spectre, the Reasoning Power in Man;/ This is a false Body, an Incrustation over my Immortal/Spirit, a Selfhood which must be put off & annihilated alway" (*Milton,* Bk. II). This last quotation, like Wordsworth's "A reasoning, self-sufficient thing,/ An intellectual All-in-All" (A Poet's Epitaph") shows the closeness of the two perils. For the second, see also Coleridge, ". . . all the products of the mere reflective faculty [viz. the "understanding" contradistinguished from what Coleridge will call the "reason"] partook of DEATH" (*Biographia Literaria,* chapter 9); Benjamin Constant, defining one of the moral maladies of the age as ". . . the fatigue, the lack of strength, the perpetual analysis that saps the spontaneity of every feeling" (Draft Preface to *Adolphe*); and Hegel's preface to *The Phenomenology of Mind.* Hegel observes that ordinary analysis leads to a hardening of data, and he lays this

its strength question the ideal of absolute lucidity. The issue is raised of whether there exist what might be called *remedia intellectus:* remedies for the corrosive power of analysis and the fixated self-consciousness.

There is a remedy of great importance almost coterminous with art itself in the Romantic Period. This remedy differs from certain traditional proposals linked to the religious control of the intellect —the wild, living intellect of man, as Newman calls it in his *Apologia.*[4] As a remedy it is particularly Romantic and non-limiting with respect to the mind. It seeks to draw the antidote to self-consciousness from consciousness itself. A way is to be found not to escape from or limit knowledge but to convert it into an energy finer than intellectual. It is some such thought which makes Wordsworth in the preface to *Lyrical Ballads* describe poetry as the "breath and finer spirit of all knowledge," and as able to carry sensation into the midst of the most abstract or remotest objects of science. A more absolute figure for this cure, which is, strictly speaking, less a cure than a paradoxical faith, is given by Kleist. "Paradise is locked," says Kleist, ". . . yet to return to the state of innocence we must eat once more of the tree of knowledge." It is not by accident that Kleist is quoted by Adrian at a significant point in Mann's *Doktor Faustus,* which is *the* novel about self-consciousness and its relation to art.

This idea of a return, via knowledge, to naiveté—to a second naiveté—is a commonplace among the German Romantics. Yet its presence is perhaps more exciting, because suitably oblique, among the English and French Romantics. A. O. Lovejoy, of course, in his famous essay on the "Discrimination of Romanticisms," questions the possibility of unifying the various national movements. He rightly points out that the German Romantics insist on an art that rises from the plenitude of consciousness to absorb progressively the most sophisticated as well as naivest experience. But his claim that English Romanticism is marked by a more primitivistic "return to nature" is weakened by his use of second-rate poetry and isolated passages. One can show that the practice of the greater English Romantics is involved with a problematical self-consciousness similar to that of the Germans; and that, in the main, no primitivism or "sacrifice of intellect" is found. I do not mean to deny the obvious, that there are "primitivistic" passages in Cha-

to a persistence of the ego, whereas his *dialectic* is thought to reveal the true fluency of concepts., Carlyle most apodictically: "Had Adam remained in Paradise, there had been no Anatomy and no Metaphysics" (*Characteristics*). 4. *Apologia Pro Vita Sua* (1864), ch. 5. In the same chapter Newman calls reason "that universal solvent." Concerning Victorian remedies for "this disease/ My Self" (Marianne Moore), see also A. Dwight Culler, *The Imperial Intellect* (New Haven, 1955), pp. 234–37.

teaubriand and even Wordsworth; but the primary tendency should be distinguished from errors and epiphenomena.

The desire of the Romantics is perhaps for what Blake calls "organized innocence," but never for a mere return to the state of nature. The German Romantics, however, because of the contemporaneous philosophical tradition which centered on the relations between consciousness and consciousness of self (Fichte, Schelling, Hegel), gained in some respects a clearer though not more fruitful understanding of the problem. I cannot consider in detail the case of French Romanticism; but Shelley's visionary despair, Keats' understanding of the poetical character, and Blake's doctrine of the contraries, reveal that self-consciousness cannot be overcome; and the very desire to overcome it, which poetry and imagination encourage, is part of a vital, dialectical movement of "soul-making."

The link between consciousness and self-consciousness, or knowledge and guilt, is already expressed in the story of the expulsion from Eden. Having tasted knowledge, man realizes his nakedness, his sheer separateness of self. I have quoted Kleist's reflection; and Hegel, in his interpretation of the Fall, argues that the way back to Eden is via contraries: the naively sensuous mind must pass through separation and selfhood to become spiritually perfect. It is the destiny of consciousness, or as the English Romantics would have said, of Imagination, to separate from nature, so that it can finally transcend not only nature but also its own lesser forms. Hegel in his *Logic* puts it as follows:

> The first reflection of awakened consciousness in men told them they were naked. . . . The hour that man leaves the path of mere natural being marks the difference between him, a self-conscious agent, and the natural world. The spiritual is distinguished from the natural . . . in that it does not continue a mere stream of tendency, but sunders itself to self-realization. But this position of severed life has in its turn to be overcome, and the spirit must, by its own act, achieve concord once more. . . . The principle of restoration is found in thought, and thought only: the hand that inflicts the wound is also the hand that heals it.[5]

The last sentence states unequivocally where the remedy lies. Hegel, however, does not honor the fact that the meaning he derives from the Fall was originally in the form of myth. And the attempt to think mythically is itself part of a crucial defense against the self-conscious intellect. Bergson in *The Two Sources of Moral-*

5. *The Logic of Hegel*, tr. from the *Encyclopedia of the Sciences* by W. Wallace (2nd. ed., Oxford, 1904), pp. 54–57. The first two sentences given here come from passages in the original later than the remainder of the quotation.

ity and Religion sees both myth and religion as products of an *intellectual* instinct created by nature itself to oppose the analytic intellect, to preserve human spontaneities despite the hesitant and complicated mind.[6] Whether myth-making is still possible, and whether the mind can maintain something of the interacting unity of self and life, are central concerns of the Romantic poets.

Romantic art as myth-making has been discussed convincingly in recent years, and Friederich Schlegel's call in *"Rede über die Myth-ologie"* (1800) for a modern mythology is well-known. The renewal of myth is, nevertheless, a rather special response to the perplexities of reflective thought. "The poet," says Wallace Stevens in "Adagia," "represents the mind in the act of defending us against itself." Starting with the Romantics, this act is clearly focused, and poetry begins to be valued in contradistinction to directly analytic or purely conceptual modes of thought. The intelligence is seen as a perverse though necessary specialization of the whole soul of man, and art as a means to resist the intelligence intelligently.

It must be admitted, at the same time, that the Romantics themselves do not give (in their conceptual moments) an adequate definition of the function of art. Their criterion of pleasure or expressive emotion leads to some kind of art for art's sake formula, or to the sentimentalism which Mill still shared, and which marks the shift in sensibility from neoclassic to Romantic. That Mill wept over the memoirs of Marmontel, and felt his selfhood lightened by this evidence of his ability to feel, or that Lamartine saw the life of the poet as "tears and love," suggests that the *larmoyant* vein of the later eighteenth century persisted for some time; but also helped, when tears were translated into theory, or even when joy was so translated, to falsify the Romantic achievement and make Irving Babbitt's criticism possible.

The *art* of the Romantics, on the other hand, is often in advance of even their best thoughts. Neither a mere increase in sensibility nor a mere widening of self-knowledge constitutes its purpose. The Romantic poets do not exalt consciousness *per se*. They have recognized it as a kind of death-in-life, as the product of a division in the self. The mind which acknowledges the existence or past existence of immediate life knows that its present strength is based on a separation from that life. A creative mind desires not mere increase of knowledge, but "knowledge not purchased by the loss of power" (*Prelude* V). Life, says Ruskin, is the only wealth; yet childhood, or certain irrevocable moments, confront the poet

6. *Les Deux sources de la morale et da la religion* (1933), ch. 2. Both religion and "la function fabulatrice" are "une réaction défensive de la nature contre le pouvoir dissolvant de l'intelligence." (Cf. Newman calling the intellect "that universal solvent.") As Romanticism shades into Modernism, a third peril of over-consciousness comes strongly to the fore—that it leads to a (Hamlet-like) incapacity for action. Bergson, like Kierkegaard, tries to counter this aspect especially.

sharply, and give him the sense of having purchased with death the life of the mind. Constructing what Yeats calls an anti-self, or recovering deeply buried experience, the poet seeks a return to "Unity of Being." Consciousness is only a middle-term, the strait through which everything must pass; and the artist plots to have everything pass through whole, without sacrifice to abstraction.

One of the themes which best expresses this perilous nature of consciousness, and which has haunted literature since the Romantic period, is that of the Solitary, or Wandering Jew. He may appear as Cain, Ahasuerus, Ancient Mariner, and even Faust. He also resembles the later (and more static) figures of Tithonus, Gerontion, and the *poète maudit*. These solitaries are separated from life in the midst of life, yet cannot die. They are doomed to live a middle or purgatorial existence which is neither life nor death, and as their knowledge increases so does their solitude.[7] It is consciousness, ultimately, which alienates them from life and imposes the burden of a self which religion or death or a return to the state of nature might dissolve. Yet their heroism, or else their doom, is not to obtain a release from self. Rebels against God, like Cain, and men of God, like Vigny's Moses, are equally denied "le sommeil de la terre," and are shown to suffer the same despair, namely, "the self . . . whose worm dieth not, and whose fire is not quenched" (Kierkegaard). And in Coleridge's Mariner, as in Conrad's Marlow, the figure of the Wanderer approaches that of the Poet. Both are story-tellers who resubmit themselves to temporality and are compelled to repeat their experience in the purgatorial form of words. Yeats, deeply affected by the theme of the Wandering Jew, records a marvelous comment of Mme. Blavatsky's. "I write, write, write," said Mme. Blavatsky, "as the Wandering Jew walks, walks, walks."

The Solitary may also be said to create his own, peculiarly Romantic genre of poetry. In "Tintern Abbey," or "X Revisited," the poet looks back at a transcended stage and comes to grips with the fact of self-alienation. The retrospective movement may be visionary, as often in Hölderlin, or antiquarian, as in Scott, or deeply oblique, as in the lyrical ballad and monologue. In every case, however, there is some confrontation of person with shadow or self with self. The intense lyricism of the Romantics may well be related

---

7. "I lost the love of heaven above,/ I spurned the lust of earth below . . . ." John Clare, "A Vision." By this double exile, and their final madness, two poets as different as Clare and Hölderlin are joined. See Coleridge's intense realization of man's "between-ness," which increases rather than chastens the apocalyptic passion: "O Nature! I would rather not have been—let that which is to come so soon, come now—for what is all the intermediate space, but sense of utter worthlessness? . . . Man is truly and solely an immortal series of conscious mortalities and inherent Disappointments" (*Inquiring Spirit*, ed. K. Coburn [London, 1951], p. 142). But to ask death instead of life of nature is still to ask for finality, for some mental quietus: it is the bitter obverse, also met at the beginning of Goethe's *Faust*, of the quest for absolute truth.

to this confrontation. For the Romantic "I" emerges nostalgically when certainty and simplicity of self are lost. In a lyric poem it is clearly not the first person form that moves us (the poem need not be in the first person), but rather the "I" toward which that "I" reaches. The very confusion in modern literary theory concerning the fictive "I," whether it represents the writer as person or as persona, may reflect a dialectic inherent in poetry between the relatively self-conscious self, and that self within the self which resembles Blake's "emanation" and Shelley's "epipsyche."

It is true, of course, that this dialectic is found in every age. Mircea Eliade, following Nietzsche, has recently linked art to religion by interpreting the latter as originating in a periodic and ritually controlled abolition of the burden of self, or rather of this burden in the form of a nascent historical sense. It is not true, according to Eliade, that "primitive man" has no sense of history; on the contrary, his sense of it is too acute; he cannot tolerate the weight of responsibility accruing through memory and individuation; and only gradually does religious myth, and especially the Judaeo-Christian revelation, teach him to become a more conscious historical being. The question, therefore, is why the *Romantic* reaction to the problem of self-consciousness should be in the form of an aggrandizement of art, and why the entire issue should now achieve an urgency and explicitness previously lacking.

The answer requires a distinction between religion and art. This distinction can take a purely historical form. There clearly comes a time when art frees itself from its subordination to religion or religiously inspired myth, and continues or even replaces these. This time seems to coincide with what is generally called the Romantic period: the latter, at least, is a good *terminus a quo*. Though every age may find its own means to convert self-consciousness into the larger energy of "imagination," in the Romantic period it is primarily art on which this crucial function devolves. Thus, for Blake, all religion is a derivation of the Poetic Genius; and Matthew Arnold is already matter-of-fact rather than prophetic about a new age in which the religious passion is preserved chiefly by poetry. If Romantic poetry appears to the orthodox as misplaced religious feeling ("spilt religion"), to the Romantics themselves it *redeems* religion.[8]

8. I have omitted here the important role played by the French Revolution. The aggrandizement of art is due in no small measure to the fact that poets like Wordsworth and Blake cannot give up one hope raised by the Revolution—that a *terrestrial* paradise is possible—yet are eventually forced to give up a second hope—that it can be attained by direct political action. The shift from faith in the reformation of man through the prior reformation of society, to that in the prior reformation of man through vision and art, has often been noted. The "failure" of the French Revolution anchors the Romantic movement, or is the consolidating rather than primary cause. It closes, perhaps until the advent of Communism, the possibilty that politics rather than art should be invested with a passion previously subsumed by religion.

Yet as soon as poetry is separated from imposed religious or communal ends it becomes as problematic as the individual himself. The question, how is art possible, though post-Romantic in its explicitness, has its origin here, for the artist is caught up in a serious paradox. His art is linked to the autonomous and individual; yet that same art, in the absence of an actively received myth, must bear the entire weight of having to transcend or ritually limit these tendencies. No wonder that the problem of the subjective, the eccentric, the individual, grows particularly acute. Subjectivity— even solipsism—becomes the subject of poems which *qua* poetry seek to transmute it.

This paradox seems to inhere in all the seminal works of the Romantic period. "Thus my days are passed / In contradiction," Wordsworth writes sadly at the beginning of *The Prelude*. He cannot decide whether he is fit to be a poet on an epic scale. The great longing is there; the great (objective) theme eludes him. Wordsworth cannot find his theme because he already has it: himself. Yet he knows self-consciousness to be at once necessary *and* opposed to poetry. It will take him the whole of *The Prelude* to be satisfied *in actu* that he is a poet. His poem, beginning in the vortex of self-consciousness, is carried to epic length in the desire to prove that his former imaginative powers are not dead.

The *Ancient Mariner* is involved in the same problems. He depicts the soul's birth to the sense of separate (and segregated) being. In one of the really magical and hypnotic poems in the language, Coleridge evokes the travail of passing through self-consciousness to imagination. The slaying of an innocent creature, the horror of stasis, the weight of conscience or of the vertical eye (the sun), the appearance of the theme of deathlessness, and the terrible repetitive process of penitence, whereby the Wanderer becomes aware through the spirits above and the creatures below of his focal solitude between both—these point with archetypal force to the burden of selfhood, the straits of solitude, and the compensating plenary imagination that grows inwardly. The poem opens by evoking that *"rite de passage"* we call a wedding, and which leads to full human communion; but the Mariner's story interposes itself as a reminder of human separateness, and of the intellectual love (in Spinoza's sense) made possible by it.

To explore the transition from self-consciousness to imagination, and to achieve that transition while exploring it (and so to prove it still possible) is the Romantic purpose I find most crucial. The precariousness of that transition naturally evokes the idea of a journey; and in some later poets, like Rimbaud and Hart Crane, the motif of the journey has actually become a sustained metaphor for the experience of the artist during creation. This journey, of course, does not lead to what is generally called a *truth*: some final station for the mind. It remains as problematic a crossing as that from death to second life or from exile to redemption. These religious concepts, moreover, are often blended in, and remind us that Romantic art has a function analogous to that of religion. The traditional scheme of Eden, fall, and redemption merges with the new triad of nature, self-consciousness, imagination; while the last term in both involves a kind of return to the first.

Yet everything depends on whether it is the right and fruitful return. For the journey beyond self-consciousness is shadowed by cyclicity, by paralysis before the endlessness of introspection, and by the lure of false ultimates. Blake's "Mental Traveller," Browning's "Childe Roland to The Dark Tower Came," and Emily Dickinson's "Our journey had advanced" show these dangers in some of their forms. Nature in its childhood or sensuous radiance (Blake's "Beulah") exerts an especially deceptive lure. The desire to gain truth, finality, or revelation generates a thousand such enchantments. Mind has its blissful islands as well as its mountains, its deeps, and treacherous crossroads. Depicting these trials by horror and by enchantment Romanticism is genuinely a rebirth of Romance.

III

In the years following World War I it became customary to see Classicism and Romanticism as two radically different philosophies of life, and to place Modernism on the side of the anti-romantic. André Malraux defined the Classical element in modern art as a "lucid horror of seduction." Today it is clear that Romantic art shared that lucidity. Romanticism, at its profoundest, reveals the depth of the enchantments in which we live. We dream, we wake on the cold hillside, and our "sole self" pursues the dream once more. In the beginning was the dream; and the task of disenchantment never ends.

The nature-poetry of the Romantics is a case in point. Far from being an indulgence in dewy moments, it is the exploration of enchanted ground. The Romantic poets, like the Impressionist painters, refuse to "simplify the ghost" of nature. They begin to look steadfastly at all sensuous experience, penetrating its veils and facing its seductions. Shelley's "Mont Blanc" is not an enthusiastic nature-poem but a spirit-drama in which the poet's mind seeks to release itself from an overwhelming impression and to reaffirm its autonomy vis-à-vis nature. Keats also goes far in respecting illusions without being deluded. His starting-point is the dream of nature fostered by romance; he agrees to this as consciously as we lie down to sleep. But he intends such dreaming "beyond self" to unfold its own progressions, and to wake into truth. To this end he passes from a gentler to a severer dream-mode: from the romance of *Endymion* to the more austere *Hyperions.* Yet he is forced to give up the *Hyperions* because Saturn, Apollo, and others behave like quest-heroes instead of gods. Having stepped beyond romance into a sublimer mode, Keats finds the quest for self-identity elated rather than effaced. It has merely raised itself to a "divine" level. He cannot reconcile Miltonic sublimity with the utterly human pathos that keeps breaking through. The "egotistical sublime" remains.

It was Wordsworth, of course, whose poetry Keats had tried to escape by adhering to a less self-centered kind of sublimity: "Let us have the old Poets, and Robin Hood." Wordsworth had subdued poetry to the theme of nature's role in the growth of the individual mind. The dream of nature in Wordsworth does not lead to formal romance, but is an early, developmental step in converting the solipsistic into the sympathetic imagination: it entices the brooding soul out of itself, toward nature first, then toward humanity. Wordsworth knew the weight of self-consciousness:

> It seemed the very garments that I wore
> Preyed on my strength, and stopped the quiet stream
> Of self-forgetfulness.
>
> (1850 *Prelude*, V. 294 ff.)

The wound of self is healed, however, by "unconscious intercourse" with a nature "old as creation." Nature makes the "quiet stream" flow on. Wordsworth evokes a type of consciousness more integrated than ordinary consciousness, though deeply dependent on its early —and continuing—life in rural surroundings.[9]

The Romantic emphasis on "unconsciousness" and "organic form" is significant in this light. Unconsciousness remains an ambiguous term in the Romantic and Victorian periods, referring to a state distinctly other than consciousness or simply to un*self*consciousness. The characteristic of right performance, says Carlyle in *Characteristics* (1831), is an *unconsciousness*—" 'the healthy know not of their health, but only the sick.' " The term clearly approches here its alternate meaning of unselfconsciousness, and it is to such statements that Mill must be indebted when he mentions the "anti-

9. Mill, Hazlitt, and Arnold came to approximately the same estimate of Wordsworth's poetry. Comparing it to Byron's they found that the latter had too much fever of self in it to be remedial; they did not want their image cast back at them magnified. Carlyle prefers to compare Goethe and Byron ("Close your Byron, open your Goethe"), yet his point is the same: Goethe retains a strong simplicity in a tormented and divided age, while Byron seems to him a "spasmodically bellowing self-worshipper."

self-consciousness theory" of Carlyle. In America, Thoreau perpetuates the ambiguity. He also prescribes "unconsciousness" for his sophisticated age, and uses the word as an equivalent of vision: "the absence of the speaker from his speech." It does seem to me that the personal and expressive theory of poetry, ascribed to the Romantics, and the impersonal theory of poetry, claimed in reaction by the moderns, answer to the same problem and are quietly linked by the ambiguity in "unconsciousness." Both theories value art as thought recreated into feeling or self-consciousness into a more communal power of vision. Yet can the modern poet, whom Schiller called "sentimental" and whom we would describe as "alienated," achieve the directness of all great poetry, whatever its personal or historical source?

This is as crucial a matter today as when Wordsworth and Coleridge wrote *Lyrical Ballads* and Hölderlin pondered the fate of poetry in "Der Rhein." Is visionary poetry a thing of the past, or can it coexist with the modern temper? Is it an archaic revelation or a universal mode springing from every real contact with nature? "To interest or benefit us," says a Victorian writer, "Poetry must be reflective, sentimental, subjective; it must accord with the conscious, analytical spirit of present men." [1] The difficulties surrounding a modern poetry of vision vary with each national literature. In England the loss of "poesy" is laid by most Romantics to a historical though not irreversible fact—to the preceding century's infidelity to the line of Chaucer, Spenser, Shakespeare, and Milton. "Let us have the old Poets, and Robin Hood," as Keats said. Yet for the German and the French there was no easy return to a tradition deriving its strength from both learned and popular sources. "How much further along we would be," Herder remarks, "if we had used popular beliefs and myths like the British, if our poetry had built upon them as wholeheartedly as Chaucer, Spenser and Shakespeare did." [2] In the absence of this English kind of literary mediation, the gap between medieval romance and the modern spirit seemed too great. Goethe's *Faust* tried to bridge it, but, like *Wilhelm Meister*, anticipated a new type of literature which subsumed the philosophical character of the age and merged myth and irony into a "progressive" mode. The future belonged to the analytic spirit, to irony, to prose. The death of poetry had certainly occurred to the Romantics in idea, and Hegel's prediction of it was simply the overt expression of their own despair. Yet against this despair the greater Romantic poets staked their art, and often their sanity.

1. R. M. Milnes, *Palm Leaves* (1844), pp. XIV–XV.
2. *Von Ähnlichkeit der mittlern englischen und deutschen Dichtkunst* (1777). Cf. Louis Cazamian on French Romanticism: "Le romantisme n'a donc pas été pour la France, comme pour l'Angleterre, un retour facile et naturel à une tradition nationale, selon la pente du tempérament le plus profond. . . ." *Essais en deux langues* (Paris, 1938), p. 170.

J. H. VAN DEN BERG

The Subject and his Landscape †

The factualization of our understanding—the impoverishment of things to a uniform substantiality—and the disposal of everything that is not identical with this substantiality into the "inner self" are both parts of one occurrence. The inner self became necessary when contacts were devaluated.

When did this happen?

If a rather vague determination in time would do, it might be enough to point out the difference between St. Augustine's *Confessions* and Rousseau's. Gusdorf has called attention to this difference in his book, *La decouverte de soi*. Augustine, believing that the approach to himself is an aspect of his relation to God, wishes to speak of God and not of himself; Rousseau means to speak of the self of the individual, the "self" which is of significance because of itself. Augustine has no knowledge of this self, he does not know the self of this self-satisfied individualism; Rousseau points out, at the very beginning, that he will only concern himself with the description of the individual, himself, *"moi seul,"* Rousseau. "When the trumpet of the last judgment will sound, I shall come to present myself before the supreme judge with this book in my hand. I shall say in a loud voice: In this book is written what I have done, what I have thought, and what I have been. I have told the good things and the bad things with equal honesty. I have neither subtracted anything from the bad, nor added anything to the good." [1] These bold words would have been entirely alien to Augustine. But, in his turn, Rousseau had no idea of the boldness which later times would add to his. If he had lived today, Rousseau could not have left it at that. If he wished to appear before the supreme judge as an honest man, he would have had to add: "And in the folder in my other hand you will find, Oh, Lord, the result of an accurate psychological examination." Perhaps he might even

† From *The Changing Nature of Man* (*Metabletica*) by J. H. Van den Berg, M.D. Copyright © 1961 by W. W. Norton & Co., Inc. Reprinted by permission of the publisher.

1. "Que la trompette du jugement dernier sonne quand elle voudra, je viendrai, ce livre à la main, me présenter devant le souverain juge. Je dirai hautement: Voilà ce que j'ai fait, ce que j'ai pensé, ce que je fus. J'ai dit le bien et le mal avec la même franchise. Je n'ai rien tu de mauvais, rien ajouté de bon. . . ." J.-J. Rousseau, *Les Confessions*, I.

have added, with a humble inflection of his voice, "After me comes the psychiatrist who analyzed me; no doubt he will be able to fill in all the gaps in my thoughts and actions." There is no essential difference between Rousseau's words and these later additions.

LUTHER

Is it possible to determine the birth date of the inner self with greater accuracy? I will try. I shall discuss a few historical events which occurred between 400 and 1700 A.D. and put forward suggestions about connections between them. This reconnaissance will also be based on Dilthey's book, *Auffassung, und Analyse des Menschen im 15 und 16 Jahrundert*,[2] which emphasizes Luther's part in the personification of religion and its disappearance from public life.

In his essay "About the Freedom of a Christian" (1520), Luther made a distinction which became exceptionally significant. He distinguished the "inner" man from the outward and physical man. He needed this distinction, for he intended to dissent from a wrong conception of religion in order to assume a religious life which, to his mind, was more pure. Luther preferred the inner man, for the external and physical man is concerned with extraneous and physical things and is suspect for that reason. Luther had come to recognize extrinsic things as appearances and deceptions. "It is no help for the soul whether the body is wearing holy robes, as priests and clergymen do; neither does it help the soul whether it appears in churches or in holy places, nor whether it touches holy things." All this is of no importance; an evil man can do all these things just as well as a good man; any dissembler or hypocrite can. Consequently, it does not harm man to wear unholy clothes, to enter unholy places, and to touch unholy things; all this is of no importance. What is important is the inner man, the soul; for the soul has faith, the soul hears the word, and knows it must retain it. "The soul can do without anything except God's word, and without God's word it has no use for anything. But if it has God's word, it does not need anything else; in the word it has pleasure, food, gladness, peace, light, art, justice, truth, wisdom, freedom, and an abundance of other good things."[3] Man can do without all extraneous matters; the only objective thing he needs is God's word.

LESSING AND SCHLEIERMACHER

But this state of affairs did not last. Lessing, two hundred and fifty years later, doubted even this last extrinsic necessity. In his

2. *Archiv für Geschichte der Philosophie*, V, 1892, 337.
3. "Von der Freiheit eines Christenmenschen," *Martin Luthers reformatorische Schriften*, Deutsche Bibliothek, 94.

Axiomata he asks the question whether man can have faith without knowing God's word; he ultimately answers this in the affirmative.[4] The evidence of faith, which after all is faith itself, depends on an inner experience. This idea, cautiously put forward by Lessing, was developed fully by Schleiermacher, who, in his *Dialektik*, wrote that God is not given to us immediately, and that we have only understanding of God insofar as we are God ourselves, which means insofar as we have God within ourselves.[5]

Faith is not action had been said by Luther; action appeared to him to be contaminated with the objects involved in the action—the clothes, the candles, the relics. But Luther had clung to a faith that was knowledge, knowledge of something (there is no blind knowledge), knowledge of an extraneousness: the Word. Schleiermacher drops even this knowledge. "Faith is neither knowledge nor action; it is a trend of feeling, or a trend of the undividable self-consciousness," [6] is what he wrote in his *Theory of Faith*. The phrase, "a trend of the undividable self-consciousness" is especially significant; according to Schleiermacher, faith is a directly given quality, there is no need for an external intermediary. Faith is a matter of the inner self, an absolutely inner quality. And although these remarkable texts do not always agree with other texts of Schleiermacher's, these words do complete the transference of faith to the inner life. Anyway, the nineteenth century took the transference of faith to inner life more and more seriously; and the psychology of religion shows that by the beginning of this century, faith threatened to become a quality belonging entirely and only to the inner life.[7]

THE NECESSARY INNER LIFE

Luther was driven away from things because he had grown to suspect them. He knew how wrongly they could be used and how they were able to absorb a dangerous religiousness. The things he saw in Rome had filled him with amazement; that, apparently, was the meaning of the holy robes, the holy places, and the holy objects. His bewilderment is identical with ours when we see what the neurotic makes of things. And so is his reaction. We say: The world is a substratum, solid matter and nothing else; anything else that could be said about it is a human creation, projection. Luther said: The robes, candles, and relics are matter, nothing else; anything else that is said about it is a human creation, vanity. Luther did not know the word, projection.

---

4. "Axiomata, wenne es deren dergleichen Dingen gibt," *Lessing's Werke*, VII, 375.
5. *Dialektik*, 224.
6. *Der christliche Glaube*, 3.

7. It would carry us too far to go into this and to consider the striking similarities between the conclusions reached by psychologists of religion, psychologists, and belletrists.

Anything else that could be said about the world is projection because we will not and we cannot do without objects as means of understanding. Anxious to avoid a new Babel, we would rather reduce things to an extreme poverty. Was Luther moved toward just such a devaluation of extraneousnesses because he too feared a loss of understanding? Did Luther transfer things to a hastily constructed area called the "inner self," because his contemporaries were escaping from an all-embracing totality and were threatening to come adrift? One remembers how much against a rupture he was. "Do not leave each other," was what, after all, his aversion toward candles and robes meant. "Let the objects become poor—so long as we can stay together." But he had come too late.[8]

A SMILING INNER SELF

In the year Luther published his treatise on freedom, Da Vinci died. He left a canvas which portrays visibly the turn from outward to inward. Da Vinci's *Mona Lisa* and Luther's manuscript are essentially identical.

It is well-known how Da Vinci's contemporaries came, curious to see the smiling woman. The interest continues to our day. Why does she smile? What makes her smile so eloquent—and so secretive? What is it that she is confiding to us and keeping from us at the same time? No one who looks at this painting can escape these questions.

Her smile seals an inner self. Her contemporaries came to see her because they could behold a new way to live. They could see the face of later generations. What they saw was the inner self, although they did not know it—the secret inner self, the inner world in which everything the world has to offer is shut away. And a smile watches over this inner self. Mona Lisa holds that which is known, and she hides it. After this, that which is known will be that which is hidden, that which is unknown. And as time goes on everything will be within her, at once known and unknown. In Rilke's words, she is the first who "contains within herself all that is human."

At the same time she is the first (it is unavoidable) who is estranged from the landscape. The landscape behind her is justly famous; it is the first landscape painted as a landscape, just because

8. Luther was not the first. It is only logical that the urge to create and fill the inner man at the cost of exterior things was felt by all those who observed with anxiety the wrong use of exterior things. Savonarola was one of these. In his Psalm about the love of God, he spurns objects: they do not contain God, God is to be found in the soul. And also Thomas à Kempis:

Blessed are the eyes that are closed to exterior matters but attentive to inward things, *Imitation of Christ*, III, Chapter 1. Only one who is aware of the pulling power of the things, and who, perhaps, feels it personally, writes words like these. The Gospels rather suggest the opposite view. Nor is Luther's reasoning very evangelic.

it was a landscape. A pure landscape, not just a backdrop for human actions: nature, nature as the middle ages did not know it, an exterior nature closed within itself and self-sufficient, an exterior from which the human element has, in principle, been removed entirely. It is things-in-their-farewell, and therefore is as moving as a farewell of our dearest. It is the strangest landscape ever beheld by human eyes.

"This landscape," said Rilke, when he tried to put into words what is contained in the mountains, the trees, the water, and the bridges behind the smiling woman, when he wanted to express what all this lack of horizon implies, "This landscape is not the portrayal of an impression, it is not the judgment of a man on things at rest; it is nature coming into being, the world coming into existence, unknown to man as the jungle of an unknown island. It had been necessary to see the landscape in this way, far and strange, remote, without love, as something living a life within itself, if it ever had to be the means and the motive of an independent art; for it had to be far and completely unlike us—to be a redeeming likeliness of our fate. It had to be almost hostile in its exalted indifference, if, with its objects, it was to give a new meaning to our existence." [9]

A GROWING INNER SELF

Today the inner self has an impressive history. Rousseau was certainly wrong when he began his confessions with the words: "I am going to attempt something that has never been done before and will never be attempted again." [1] He was right as far as the first part of the statement was concerned; in the matter of form, the description of a solitary inner self, his confessions were a novelty. But as to the second part, history has certainly proved him wrong. In comparison to the inner self which came into existence after him, his was insignificant and poor. James Joyce [2] used as much space to describe the internal adventures of less than a day than Rousseau used to relate the story of half a life. The inner self, which in Rousseau's time was a simple, soberly filled, airy space, has become ever more crowded. Permanent residents have even been admitted; at first, only the parents, who could not stand being outside any longer, required shelter; finally it was the entire ancestry. As a result the space was divided, partitions were raised, and curtains appeared where in earlier days a free view was possible. The inner self grew

9. R. M. Rilke, *Von der Landschaft, Ausgewählte Werke*, 1938, II, 218.
1. "Je forme une enterprise qui n'eut jamais d'exemple, et dont l'exécution n'aura point d'imitateur. Je veux montrer à mes semblables un homme dans toute la vérité de la nature; et cet homme, ce sera moi." *Les Confessions*, Book I.
2. James Joyce, *Ulysses*, 1922.

into a complicated apartment building. The psychologists of our century, scouts of these inner rooms, could not finish describing all the things their astonished eyes saw. It did not take them long to surpass Joyce, and their work became endless in principle. The exploration of one apartment appeared to disturb another; and if the exploration moved to the next place, the first one again required attention. Something fell down or a threat was uttered; there was always something. The inner life was like a haunted house. But what else could it be? It contained everything. Everything extraneous had been put into it. The entire history of mankind had to be the history of the individual. Everything that had previously belonged to everybody, everything that had been collective property and had existed in the world in which everyone lived, had to be contained by the individual. It could not be expected that things would be quiet in the inner self.

THE LANDSCAPE

Almost unnoticed—for everybody was watching the inner self—the landscape changed. It became estranged, and consequently it became visible. In April, 1335, Petrarch climbs Mont Ventoux near Avignon, and was surprised and delighted at the view; he was seeing the landscape behind Mona Lisa, the "first landscape." But he apologized, afraid of having earned God's wrath; what he saw was Luther's robes, the jewels of Savonarola.

Four hundred years later Rousseau laid the foundation for the great change. The first observations on what since then has been called a "sense of nature" are contained in his *Confessions* of 1728.[3] That this is not coincidence is quite clear now. In the *Nouvelle Héloise* (1761), the emotion felt upon observing nature was completely described. Like an epidemic the new sensation spread through Europe. Everyone wished to see what Rousseau had seen, to experience the same ecstasy. Everybody visited Switzerland and climbed the Alps. This had not happened before Rousseau.[4] It was then that the Alps became a tourist attraction. Previously they had been an obstacle; a walk through the mountains had had few delights; the views were not in any way exceptional. Even in 1750, Hénault, a poet and a friend of Voltaire's, crossed the Jura and the Alps without the least enthusiasm, merely observing, "There is

3. *Confessions*, Book II, devoted to the experiences of 1728, the year Rousseau crossed the Alps.
4. "It was Rousseau who, with an extraordinary intensity and power of expression, created the emotion of the mountains. No doubt it existed before him, at least in elementary form; but it was he who molded these elements into a new shape and who forced the new emotion upon us as an exceptional timbre, composed of previously known sounds but determined by a new fundamental tone." E. de Bruyne, *Het aesthetisch beleven*, Antwerpen, 1942, 147.

always a creek at my side and rocks above my head, which seem about to fall in the creek or upon me." [5] These words would now-adays disqualify him as a poet—besides compromising his claim to be a human being.

Yet the estrangement of things, which brought Romanticism to ecstasy, belongs, for the most part, to the past. Many of the people who, on their traditional trip to the Alps, ecstatically gaze at the snow on the mountain tops and at the azure of the transparent distance, do so out of a sense of duty. They are only imitating Rousseau; they are simulating an emotion which they do not actually feel. It is simply not permissible to sigh at the vision of the great views and to wonder, for everyone to hear, whether it was really worth the trouble. And yet the question would be fully justified; all one has to do is see the sweating and sunburned crowd, after it has streamed out of the train or the bus, plunge with resignation into the recommended beauty of the landscape to know that for a great many the trouble is greater than the enjoyment. To a few the landscape is still delightful. But hardly anybody feels the delight is so great, so overpowering, that he is moved to tears.

For things have moved further away from us so that today they reveal the distance far more than the emotion that goes with it. Petrarch was delighted; his delight was caused by his seeing a reduction. (Otherwise he would have seen nothing.) Rousseau was deeply moved; his emotion was the sort felt by a mother when her child goes out alone for the first time. Rousseau and Petrarch made us believe that theirs was a discovery of something worthwhile, of a valuable matter which people for some inexplicable reason had never seen before. That their discovery was the discovery of a loss only became apparent in the twentieth century.

THE COMPLETE INNER SELF AND THE COMPLETELY ESTRANGED EXTERIOR

Modern psychology became possible because of an interiorization of all human realities. The interiorization founded a new domain: the inner self; psychology is its science. And of this science Freud is the undisputed master.

In 1915 (the date is significant), Freud expressed the following thoughts.

"We assume," he wrote, "that the human being has a certain amount of love, called libido, which, at the beginning, while remaining within the borders of its own self, is directed at its own

5. See D. Mornet, *Le sentiment de la Nature en France de J.-J. Rousseau à Bernadin de Saint Pierre*, Paris, 1907,

55. And R. Hening, *Die Entwicklung des Naturgefühls und das Wesen der Inspiration*, Leipzig, 1912.

self. Later on in the development, actually from a very early state on, this love detaches itself from the self, it aims itself on things outside, which are therefore, in a way, incorporated within us. If the things get lost or if they are destroyed, the love or libido which we had attached to those things, will become free again. This love can then aim itself on the things that took the place of the first things, but it can equally well return to the self. It appears that the latter is painful. Why it should be painful, why the detachment of things causes suffering, we do not understand; we are, as yet, unable to infer the painfulness from anything. What we see is that the libido clings to things, and that it does not want to give up things even if good substitutes are ready for it. This is the grief, the sadness, about the perishing of things and of people." [6]

These words could not be clearer. The *fons et origo* of the human existence is the libido; energy of the inner self. Nothing would seem more natural than that this energy remain close to its original source, within the I, within the subject. However, it does not happen this way. The energy partly detaches itself from the I and conveys itself to outside objects. The objects themselves are of secondary importance in the human existence; they remain foreign to it, and ultimately they are of no significance at all. If the objects get lost, the libido attached to them can be transported to other objects; or, if this is not feasible, it can return to the source from which it originated. If this is what happens, the libido will come home, and one is inclined to expect some satisfaction from it. Against all expectations, however, there is no satisfaction at all; on the contrary, there is suffering, mourning, and sadness. Why this suffering, mourning, and sadness? It is an enigma. "Suffering and sadness is a great mystification to the psychologist."

This is a painful remark. Sadness because of things lost—it cannot have been exceptional in the Vienna of 1915. Did the psychologist understand nothing of this grief?

Ultimately the enigma of grief is the libido's inclination toward exterior things. What prompts the libido to leave the inner self? In 1914 Freud asked himself this question—the essential question of his psychology, and the essential question of the psychology of

6. "Wir stellen uns vor, dass wir ein gewisses Mass von Liebesfähigkeit, genannt Libido, besitzen, welches sich in den Anfängen der Entwicklung dem eigenen Ich zugewendet hatte. Später, aber eigentlich von sehr frühe an, wendet es sich vom Ich ab und den Objecten zu, die wir solcherart gewissermassen in unser Ich hineinnehmen. Werden die Objekte zerstört oder gehen sie uns verloren, so wird unsere Liebesfähigkeit (Libido) weider frei. Sie kann sich andere Objekte zum Ersatz nehmen oder zeitweise zum Ich zurückkehren. Warum aber diese Ablösung der Libido von ihren Objekten ein so schmerzhafter Vorgang sein sollte, das verstehen wir nicht und können es derzeit aus keiner Annahme ableiten. Wir sehen nur, dass sich die Libido an ihre Objekte klammert und die verlorenen auch dann nicht aufgeben will wenn der Ersatz bereit liegt. Das also ist die Trauer." *Vergänglichkeit*, 1915, *Gesammelte Werke*, **X**, 360.

the twentieth century. His answer ended the process of interiorization. It is: the libido leaves the inner self when the inner self has become too full. In order to prevent it from being torn, the I has to aim itself on objects outside the self; ". . . ultimately man must begin to love in order not to get ill." [7] So that is what it is. Objects are of importance only in an extreme urgency. Human beings, too. The grief over their death is the sighing of a too-far distended covering, the groaning of an overfilled inner self.

PAUL DE MAN

Intentional Structure of the Romantic Image [†]

In the history of Western literature, the importance of the image as a dimension of poetic language does not remain constant. One could conceive of an organization of this history in terms of the relative prominence and the changing structure of metaphor. French poetry of the sixteenth century is obviously richer and more varied in images than that of the seventeenth, and medieval poetry of the fifteenth century has a different kind of imagery than that of the thirteenth. The most recent change remote enough to be part of history takes place towards the end of the eighteenth century and coincides with the advent of romanticism. In a statement of which equivalences can be found in all European literatures, Wordsworth reproaches Pope for having abandoned the imaginative use of figural diction in favor of a merely decorative allegorization. Meanwhile the term *imagination* steadily grows in importance and com-

7. The complete paragraph reads, "Von hier aus mag man es selbst wagen, an die Frage heranzutreten, woher denn überhaupt die Nötigung für das Seelenleben rührt, über die Grenzen des Narzissmus hinauszugehen und die Libido auf Objekte zu setzen. Die aus unserem Gedankengang abfolgende Antwort würde wiederum sagen, diese Nötigung trete ein, wenn die Ichbesetzung mit Libido ein gewisses Mass überschritten habe. Ein starker Egoismus schützt vor Erkrankung, aber endlich muss man beginnen zu lieben, um nicht krank zu werden, und muss, erkranken, wenn man infolge von Versagung nicht lieben kann." *Zur Einführung des Narzissmus,* 1914, *Gesammelte Werke,* **X,** 151–152.

† First printed, in a slightly different French version, under the title "Structure intentionelle de l'image romantique" in *Revue internationale de Philosophie,* 51, 1960. The translation is the author's. Copyright © 1968 by Paul de Man, and reprinted with his permission.

plexity, in the critical as well as in the poetic texts of the period. This evolution in poetic terminology—of which parallel instances could easily be found in France and in Germany—corresponds to a profound change in the texture of poetic diction. The change often takes the form of a return to a greater concreteness, a proliferation of natural objects that restores to the language the material substantiality which had been partially lost. At the same time, in accordance with a dialectic that is more paradoxical than may appear at first sight, the structure of the language becomes increasingly metaphorical and the image—be it under the name of symbol or even of myth—comes to be considered as the most prominent dimension of the style. This tendency is still prevalent today, among poets as well as among critics. We find it quite natural that theoretical studies such as, for example, those of Gaston Bachelard in France, of Northrop Frye in America, or of William Empson in England should take the metaphor as their starting point for an investigation of literature in general—an approach that would have been inconceivable for Boileau, for Pope, and even still for Diderot.

An abundant imagery coinciding with an equally abundant quantity of natural objects, the theme of imagination linked closely to the theme of nature, such is the fundamental ambiguity that characterizes the poetics of romanticism. The tension between the two polarities never ceases to be problematic. We shall try to illustrate the structure of this latent tension as it appears in some selected poetic passages.

In a famous poem, Hölderlin speaks of a time at which "the gods" will again be an actual presence to man:

> . . . nun aber nennt er sein Liebstes
> Nun, nun müssen dafür Worte, wie Blumen entstehn.
> ("Brot und Wein", stanza 5)

Taken by itself, this passage is not necessarily a statement about the image: Hölderlin merely speaks of words ("*Worte*"), not of images ("*Bilder*"). But the lines themselves contain the image of the flower in the simplest and most explicit of all metaphorical structures, as a straightforward simile introduced by the conjunction *wie*. That the words referred to are not those of ordinary speech is clear from the verb: to originate ("entstehn"). In everyday use words are exchanges and put to a variety of tasks, but they are not supposed to originate anew; on the contrary, one wants them to be as well known, as "common" as possible, to make certain that they will obtain for us what we want to obtain. They are used as established signs to confirm that something is recognized as being the same as before; and re-cognition excludes pure origination. But in poetic language words are not used as signs, not even as names, but in order *to name*: "Donner un sens plus pur aux mots de la tribu" (Mallarmé) or "erfand er für die Dinge eigene Nahmen" (Stefan George): poets know of the act of naming—"nun aber *nennt* er sein Liebstes"—as implying a return to the source, to the pure motion of experience at its beginning.

The word "entstehn" establishes another fundamental distinction. The two terms of the simile are not said to be identical with one another (the word = the flower), nor analogous in their general mode of being (the word is like the flower), but specifically in the way they originate (the word originates like the flower).[1] The similarity between the two terms does not reside in their essence (identity), or in their appearance (analogy), but in the manner in which both originate. And Hölderlin is not speaking of any poetic word taken at random, but of an authentic word that fulfills its highest function in naming being as a presence. We could infer, then, that the fundamental intent of the poetic word is to originate in the same manner as what Hölderlin here calls "flowers." The image is essentially a kinetic process: it does not dwell in a static state where the two terms could be separated and reunited by analysis; the first term of the simile (here, "words") has no independent existence, poetically speaking, prior to the metaphorical statement. It originates with the statement, in the manner suggested by the flower-image, and its way of being is determined by the manner in which it originates. The metaphor requires that we begin by forgetting all we have previously known about "words"—"donner un sens plus pur aux mots de la tribu"—and then informing the term with a dynamic existence similar to that which animates the "flowers." The metaphor is not a combination of two entities or experiences more or less deliberately linked together, but one single and particular experience: that of origination.

How do flowers originate? They rise out of the earth without the assistance of imitation or analogy. They do not follow a model other than themselves which they copy or from which they derive the pattern of their growth. By calling them *natural* objects, we mean that their origin is determined by nothing but their own being. Their becoming coincides at all times with the mode of their origination: it is as flowers that their history is what it is, totally defined by their identity. There is no wavering in the status of their existence: existence and essence coincide in them at all times. Un-

1. The line is ambiguous, depending on whether one gives the verb "entstehn" a single or a double subject. It can mean: words will originate that are like flowers ("Worte, die wie Blumen sind, müssen dafür entstehn"). But the meaning is much richer if one reads it: words will have to originate in the same way that flowers originate ("Worte müssen dafür entstehn wie Blumen entstehn"). Syntax and punctuation allow for both readings.

like words, which originate like something else ("like flowers"), flowers originate like themselves: they are literally what they are, definable without the assistance of metaphor. It would follow then, since the intent of the poetic word is to originate like the flower, that it strives to banish all metaphor, to become entirely literal.

We can understand origin only in terms of difference: the source springs up because of the need to be somewhere or something else than what is now here. The word "entstehn", with its distancing prefix, equates origin with negation and difference. But the natural object, safe in its immediate being, seems to have no beginning and no end. Its permanence is carried by the stability of its being, whereas a beginning implies a negation of permanence, the discontinuity of a death in which an entity relinquishes its specificity and leaves it behind, like an empty shell. Entities engendered by consciousness originate in this fashion, but for natural entities like the flower, the process is entirely different. They originate out of a being which does not differ from them in essence but contains the totality of their individual manifestations within itself. All particular flowers can at all times establish an immediate identity with an original Flower, of which they are as many particular emanations. The original entity, which has to contain an infinity of manifestations of a common essence, in an infinity of places and at an infinity of moments, is necessarily transcendental. Trying to conceive of the natural object in terms of origin leads to a transcendental concept of the Idea: the quest for the Idea that takes the natural object for its starting-point begins with the incarnated "minute particular" and works its way upwards to a transcendental essence. Beyond the Idea, it searches for Being as the category which contains essences in the same manner that the Idea contains particulars. Because they are natural objects, flowers originate as incarnations of a transcendental principle. "Wie Blumen entstehn" is to become present as a natural emanation of a transcendental principle, as an epiphany.

Strictly speaking, an epiphany cannot be a beginning, since it reveals and unveils what, by definition, could never have ceased to be there. Rather, it is the rediscovery of a permanent presence which has chosen to hide itself from us—unless it is we who have the power to hide from it:

> So ist der Mensch; wenn da ist das Gut und es sorget mitgaben
> Selber ein Gott für ihn, kennet und sieht er es nicht.
> ("Brot und Wein", stanza 5)

Since the presence of a transcendental principle, in fact conceived as omnipresence (parousia), can be hidden from man by man's own volition, the epiphany appears in the guise of a beginning rather than a discovery. Hölderlin's phrase: "Wie Blumen entstehn" is in fact a paradox, since origination is inconceivable on the ontological level; the ease with which we nevertheless accept it is indicative of our desire to forget. Our eagerness to accept the statement, the "beauty" of the line, stems from the fact that it combines the poetic seduction of beginnings contained in the word "entstehn" with the ontological stability of the natural object—but this combination is made possible only by a deliberate forgetting of the transcendental nature of the source.

That this forgetting, this ignorance, is also painful becomes apparent from the strategic choice of the word "flower," an object that seems intrinsically desirable. The effect of the line would have been thoroughly modified if Hölderlin had written, for instance, "Steinen" instead of "Blumen", although the relevance of the comparison would have remained intact as long as human language was being compared to a natural thing. The obviously desirable sensory aspects of the flower express the ambivalent aspiration towards a forgotten presence that gave rise to the image, for it is in experiencing the material presence of the particular flower that the desire arises to be reborn in the manner of a natural creation. The image is inspired by a nostalgia for the natural object, expanding to become nostalgia for the origin of this object. Such a nostalgia can only exist when the transcendental presence is forgotten, as in the "dürftiger Zeit" of Hölderlin's poem which we are all too eager to circumscribe as if it were a specific historical "time" and not Time in general. The existence of the poetic image is itself a sign of divine absence, and the conscious use of poetic imagery an admission of this absence.

It is clear that, in Hölderlin's own line, the words do *not* originate like flowers. They need to find the mode of their beginning in another entity; they originate out of nothing, in an attempt to be the first words that will arise as if they were natural objects, and, as such, they remain essentially distinct from natural entities. Hölderlin's statement is a perfect definition of what we call a natural image: the word that designates a desire for an epiphany but necessarily fails to be an epiphany, because it is pure origination. For it is in the essence of language to be capable of origination, but of never achieving the absolute identity with itself that exists in the natural object. Poetic language can do nothing but originate anew over and over again: it is always constitutive, able to posit regardless of presence but, by the same token, unable to give a foundation to what it posits except as an intent of consciousness. The word is always a free presence to the mind, the means by which the permanence of natural entities can be put into question and thus negated, time and again, in the endlessly widening spiral of the dialectic.

An image of this type is indeed the simplest and most fundamental we can conceive of, the metaphorical expression most apt to
gain our immediate acquiescence. During the long development that
takes place in the nineteenth century, the poetic image remains pre-
dominantly of the same kind that in the Hölderlin passage we took
for our starting-point—and which, be it said in passing, far from
exhausts Hölderlin's own conception of the poetic image. This type
of imagery is grounded in the intrinsic ontological primacy of the
natural object. Poetic language seems to originate in the desire to
draw closer and closer to the ontological status of the object, and its
growth and development are determined by this inclination. We
saw that this movement is essentially paradoxical and condemned in
advance to failure. There can be flowers that "are" and poetic
words that "originate," but no poetic words that "originate" as if
they "were."

Nineteenth century poetry reexperiences and represents the adventure of this failure in an infinite variety of forms and versions. It
selects, for example, a variety of archetypal myths to serve as the
dramatic pattern for the narration of this failure; a useful study
could be made of the romantic and post-romantic versions of Hel-
lenic myths such as the stories of Narcissus, of Prometheus, of the
War of the Titans, of Adonis, Eros and Psyche, Proserpine, and
many others; in each case, the tension and duality inherent in the
mythological situation would be found to reflect the inherent tension that resides in the metaphorical language itself. At times, romantic thought and romantic poetry seem to come so close to
giving in completely to the nostalgia for the object that it becomes
difficult to distinguish between object and image, between imagination and perception, between an expressive or constitutive and a
mimetic or literal language. This may well be the case in some passages of Wordsworth and Goethe, of Baudelaire and Rimbaud,
where the vision almost seems to become a real landscape. Poetics of
"unmediated vision," such as those implicit in Bergson and explicit
in Bachelard, fuse matter and imagination by amalgamating perception and reverie, sacrificing, in fact, the demands of consciousness
to the realities of the object. Critics who speak of a "happy relationship" between matter and consciousness fail to realize that the
very fact that the relationship has to be established within the
medium of language indicates that it does not exist in actuality.

At other times, the poet's loyalty towards his language appears
so strongly that the object nearly vanishes under the impact of
his words, in what Mallarmé called "sa presque disparition vibra-
toire." But even in as extreme a case as Mallarmé's, it would be a
mistake to assume that the ontological priority of the object is being
challenged. Mallarmé may well be the nineteenth century poet

who went further than any other in sacrificing the stability of the object to the demands of a lucid poetic awareness. Even some of his own disciples felt they had to react against him by reasserting the positivity of live and material substances against the annihilating power of his thought. Believing themselves to be in a situation where they had to begin their work at the point where Mallarmé had finished his, they took, like Claudel, the precise counterpart of his attitudes or, like Valéry, reversed systematically the meaning of some of his key-images. Yet Mallarmé himself had always remained convinced of the essential priority of the natural object. The final image of his work, in *Un Coup de Dés*, is that of the poet drowned in the ubiquitous "sea" of natural substances against which his mind can only wage a meaningless battle, "tenter une chance oiseuse." It is true that, in Mallarmé's thought, the value-emphasis of this priority has been reversed and the triumph of nature is being presented as the downfall of poetic defiance. But this does not alter the fundamental situation. The alternating feeling of attraction and repulsion that the romantic poet experiences towards nature becomes in Mallarmé the conscious dialectic of a reflective poetic consciousness. This dialectic, far from challenging the supremacy of the order of nature, in fact reasserts it at all times. "Nous savons, victimes d'une formule absolue, que certes n'est que ce qui est," writes Mallarmé, and this absolute identity is rooted, for him, in la premiere en date, la nature. Idée tangible pour intimer quelque réalité aux sens frustes. . . ."

Mallarmé's conception and use of imagery is entirely in agreement with this principle. His key-symbols—sea, winged bird, night, the sun, constellations, and many others—are not primarily literary emblems but are taken, as he says, "au répertoire de la nature"; they receive their meaning and function from the fact that they belong initially to the natural world. In the poetry, they may seem disincarnate to the point of abstraction, generalized to the point of becoming pure ideas, yet they never entirely lose contact with the concrete reality from which they spring. The sea, the bird, and the constellation act and seduce in Mallarmé's poetry, like any earthly sea, bird, or star in nature; even the Platonic "oiseau qu'on n'ouit jamais" still has about it some of the warmth of the nest in which it was born. Mallarmé does not linger over the concrete and material details of his images, but he never ceases to interrogate, by means of a conscious poetic language, the natural world of which they are originally a part—while knowing that he could never reduce any part of this world to his own, conscious mode of being. If this is true of Mallarmé, the most self-conscious and anti-natural poet of the nineteenth century, it seems safe to assert that the priority of the natural object remains unchallenged among the inheritors of romanticism. The detailed study of Mallarmé bears this out; the same is true, with various nuances and reservations, of most Victorian and post-Victorian poets. For most of them, as for Mallarmé, the priority of nature is experienced as a feeling of failure and sterility, but nevertheless asserted. A similar feeling of threatening paralysis prevails among our own contemporaries and seems to grow with the depth of their poetic commitment. It may be that this threat could only be overcome when the status of poetic language or, more restrictively, of the poetic image, is again brought into question.

The direction that such a reconsideration might take can better be anticipated by a reading of the precursors of romanticism than by the study of its inheritors. Assumptions that are irrevocably taken for granted in the course of the nineteenth century still appear, at an earlier date, as one among several alternative roads. This is why an effort to understand the present predicament of the poetic imagination takes us back to writers that belong to the earlier phases of romanticism such as, for example, Rousseau. The affinity of later poets with Rousseau—which can well be considered to be a valid definition of romanticism as a whole—can, in turn, be best understood in terms of their use and underlying conception of imagery. The juxtaposition of three famous passages can serve as an illustration of this point and suggest further developments.

The three passages we have selected each represent a moment of spiritual revelation; the use of semi-religious, "sacred," or outspokenly sublime language in all three makes this unquestionably clear. Rousseau is probably the only one to have some awareness of the literary tradition that stands behind the topos: his reference to Petrarch (*La Nouvelle Héloise*, Part I, XXIII) suggests the all-important link with the Augustinian lesson contained in Petrarch's letter narrating his ascent of Mont Ventoux. A similar experience, in a more Northern Alpine setting, is related in the three passages. The Rousseau text is taken from the letter in *La Nouvelle Héloise* in which Saint-Preux reports on his sojourn in the Valais:

> Ce n'était pas seulement le travail des hommes qui rendait ces pays étranges si bizarrement contrastés; la nature semblait encore prendre plaisir à s'y mettre en opposition avec elle-même, tant on la trouvait différente en un même lieu sous divers aspects. Au levant les fleurs du printemps, au midi les fruits de l'automne, au nord les glaces de l'hiver: elle réunissait toutes les saisons dans le même instant, tous les climats dans le même lieu, des terrains contraires sur le même sol, et formait l'accord inconnu partout ailleurs des productions des plaines et de celles des Alpes. . . . J'arrivai ce jour là sur des montagnes les moins élevées, et, parcourant ensuite leurs inégalités, sur celles des plus hautes qui étaient à ma portée. Après m'être promené dans les nuages,

j'atteignis un séjour plus serein, d'ou l'on voit dans la saison le tonerre et l'orage se former au-dessous de soi; image trop vaine de l'âme du sage, dont l'exemple n'exista jamais, ou n'existe qu'aux mêmes lieux d'où l'on en a tiré l'emblême.

Ce fut là que je démêlai sensiblement dans la pureté de l'air où je me trouvais la véritable cause du changement de mon humeur, et du retour de cette paix intérieure que j'avais perdue depuis si longtemps. En effet, c'est une impression générale qu'éprouvent tous les hommes, quoiqu'ils ne l'observent pas tous, que sur les hautes montagnes, où l'air est pur et subtil, on se sent plus de facilité dans la respiration, plus de légèreté dans le corps, plus de sérénité dans l'esprit; les plaisirs y sont moins ardents, les passions plus modérées. Les méditations y prennent je ne sais quel caractère grand et sublime, proportionné aux objets qui nous frappent, je ne sais quelle volupté tranquille qui n'a rien d'âcre et de sensuel. Il semble qu'en s'élévant au-dessus du séjour des hommes on y laisse des sentiments bas et terrestres, et qu'à mesure qu'on approche des régions éthérées, l'âme contracte quelque-chose de leur inaltérable pureté. On y est grave sans mélancolie, paisible sans indolence, content d'être et de penser. . . . Imaginez la variété, la grandeur, la beauté de mille étonnants spectacles; le plaisir de ne voir autour de soi que des objets tout nouveaux, des oiseaux étranges, des plantes bizarres et inconnues, d'observer en quelque sorte une autre nature, et de se trouver dans un nouveau monde. Tout cela fait aux yeux un mélange inexprimable, dont le charme augmente encore par la subtilité de l'air qui rend les couleurs plus vives, les traits plus marqués, rapproche tous les points de vue; les distances paraissent moindres que dans les plaines, où l'épaisseur de l'air couvre la terre d'un voile, l'horizon présente aux yeux plus d'objets qu'il semble n'en pouvoir con-tenir: enfin le spectacle a je ne sais quoi de magique, de sur-naturel, qui ravit l'esprit et les sens; on oublie tout, on s'oublie soi-même, on ne sait plus où l'on est . . .

Wordsworth's text is taken from Book VI of *The Prelude* and describes the poet's impressions in crossing the Alps, after having taken part in one of the celebrations that mark the triumph of the French Revolution. Wordsworth begins by praying for the safe-guard of the Convent of the Grande Chartreuse, threatened with destruction at the hands of the insurrection; his prayer is first aimed at God, then "for humbler claim" at nature:

> . . . and for humbler claim
> Of that imaginative impulse sent
> From these majestic floods, yon shining cliffs,
> The untransmuted shapes of many worlds,
> Cerulian ether's pure inhabitants,
> These forests unapproachable by death,
> That shall endure as long as man endures,
> To think, to hope, to worship, and to feel,

> To struggle, to be lost within himself
> In trepidation, from the blank abyss
> To look with bodily eyes, and be consoled.
>
> (The Prelude, VI, 11, 477–487)

Somewhat later in the same section, Wordsworth describes the descent of the Simplon pass:

> . . . The immeasurable height
> Of woods decaying, never to be decayed,
> The stationary blasts of waterfalls,
> And in the narrow rent at every turn
> Winds thwarting winds, bewildered and forlorn,
> The torrents shooting from the clear blue sky,
> The rocks that muttered close upon our ears,
> Black drizzling crags that spake by the way-side
> As if a voice were in them, the sick sight
> And giddy prospect of the raving stream,
> The unfettered clouds and region of the Heavens,
> Tumult and peace, the darkness and the light—
> Were all like workings of one mind, the features
> Of the same face, blossoms upon one tree;
> Characters of the great Apocalypse,
> The types and symbols of Eternity,
> Of first, and last, and midst, and without end.
>
> (*The Prelude*, VI, 624–640)

Hölderlin's poem "Heimkunft" begins by the description of a sunrise in the mountains, observed by the poet on his return from Switzerland to his native Swabia:

> Drin in den Alpen ists noch helle Nacht und die Wolke,
> Freudiges dichtend, sie deckt drinnen das gähnende Tal.
> Dahin, dorthin toset und stürzt die scherzende Bergluft,
> Schroff durch Tannen herab glänzet und schwindet ein Strahl.
> Langsam eilt und kämpft das freudigschauernde Chaos,
> Jung an Gestalt, doch stark, feiert es liebenden Streit
> Unter den Felsen, es gärt und wankt in den ewigen Schranken,
> Denn bacchantischer zieht drinnen der Morgen herauf.
> Denn es wächst unendlicher dort das Jahr und die heilgen
> Stunden, die Tage, sie sind kühner geordenet, gemischt.
> Dennoch merket die Zeit der Gewittervogel und zwischen
> Bergen, hoch in der Luft weilt er und rufet den Tag.
>
> . . . .
> Ruhig glänzen indes die silbernen Höhen draüber,
> Voll mit Rosen ist schon droben der leuchtende Schnee.
> Und noch höher hinauf wohnt über dem Lichte der reine
> Selige Gott vom Speil heiliger Strahlen erfreut.
> Stille wohnt er allein, und hell`erscheinet sein Antlitz,
> Der ätherische scheint Leben zu geben geneigt. . . .
>
> ("Heimkunft", st. I and II)

Each of these texts describes the passage from a certain type of nature, earthly and material, to another nature which could be called mental and celestial, although the "Heaven" referred to is devoid of specific theological connotations. The common characteristic that concerns us most becomes apparent in the mixed, transitional type of landscape from which the three poets start out. The setting of each scene is located somewhere between the inaccessible mountain peaks and the humanized world of the plains; it is a deeply divided and paradoxical nature that, in Rousseau's terms, "seems to take pleasure in self-opposition." Radical contradictions abound in each of the passages. Rousseau deliberately mixes and blurs the order of the seasons and the laws of geography. The more condensed, less narrative diction of Wordsworth transposes similar contradictions into the complexity of a language that unites irreconcilable opposites; he creates a disorder so far-reaching that the respective position of heaven and earth are reversed: ". . . woods decaying, never to be decayed . . . ," ". . . torrents shooting from the sky . . . ," ". . . the stationary blast of waterfalls. . . ." Hölderlin's text also is particularly rich in oxymorons; every word-combination, every motion expresses a contradiction: "helle Nacht," "langsam eilt," "liebenden Streit," "toset und stürzt," "geordnet, gemischt," "freudigschauernde," etc. One feels everywhere the pressure of an inner tension at the core of all earthly objects, powerful enough to bring them to explosion.

The violence of this turmoil is finally appeased by the ascending movement recorded in each of the texts, the movement by means of which the poetic imagination tears itself away, as it were, from a terrestrial nature and moves towards this "other nature" mentioned by Rousseau, associated with the diaphanous, limpid and immaterial quality of a light that dwells nearer to the skies. Gaston Bachelard has described similar images of levitation very well, but he may not have stressed sufficiently that these rêveries of flight not only express a desire to escape from earth-bound matter, to be relieved for a moment from the weight of gravity, but that they uncover a fundamentally new kind of relationship between nature and consciousness; it is significant, in this respect, that Bachelard classifies images of repose with earth and not with air, contrary to what happens in the three selected texts. The transparency of air represents the perfect fluidity of a mode of being that has moved beyond the power of earthly things and now dwells, like the God in Hölderlin's "Heimkunft," higher even than light ("über dem Lichte"). Like the clouds described by Wordsworth, the poets become "Cerulian ether's pure inhabitants." Unlike Mallarmé's "azur" or even the constellation at the end of *Un Coup de Dés* which are always seen from the point of view of the earth by a man about to sink away, their language has itself become a celestial entity, an inhabitant of the sky. Instead of being, like the "flower" in Hölderlin's "Brot und Wein," the fruit of the earth, the poetic word has become an offspring of the sky. The ontological priority, housed at first in the earthly and pastoral "flower," has been transposed into an entity that could still, if one wishes, be called "nature," but could no longer be equated with matter, objects, earth, stones, or flowers. The nostalgia for the object has become a nostalgia for an entity that could never, by its very nature, become a particularized presence.

The passages describe the ascent of a consciousness trapped within the contradictions of a half-earthly, half-heavenly nature "qui semblait prendre plaisir à (se) mettre en opposition avec elle-même," towards another level of consciousness, that has recovered "cette paix intérieure . . . perdue depuis si lontemps." (It goes without saying that the sequel of the three works from which the passages have been taken indicates that this tranquillity is far from having been definitively reconquered. Yet the existence of this moment of peace in *La Nouvelle Héloise*, in *The Prelude*, and in the poem "Heimkunft"—"*Ruhig* glänzen indes die silbernen Höhen darüber . . ."—determines the fate of the respective authors and marks it as being an essentially poetic destiny.) In the course of this movement, in a passage that comes between the two descriptions we have cited, Wordsworth praises the faculty that gives him access to this new insight, and he calls this faculty "Imagination":

> Imagination! lifting up itself
> Before the eye and progress of my Song
> Like an unfather'd vapour; . . .
>   . . . in such strength
> Of usurpation, in such visitings
> Of awful promise, when the light of sense
> Goes out in flashes that have shewn to us
> The invisible world, doth Greatness make abode,
>
> The mind beneath such banners militant
> Thinks not of spoils or trophies, nor of aught
> That may attest its prowess, blest in thoughts
> That are their own perfection and reward,
> Strong in itself, and in the access of joy
> Which hides it like the overflowing Nile.
>   (*The Prelude*, VI, 591–614)

But this "imagination" has little in common with the faculty that produces natural images born "as flowers originate." It marks instead a possibility for consciousness to exist entirely by and for itself, independently of all relationship with the outside world, without being moved by an intent aimed at a part of this world. Rousseau stressed that there was nothing sensuous ("rien d'âcre et de sensuel") in Saint-Preux's moment of illumination; Wordsworth, who goes so far as to designate the earth by the astonishing periphrase of "blank abyss," insists that the imagination can only come into full play when "the light of sense goes out" and when thought reaches a point at which it is "its own perfection and reward"—as when Rousseau, in the Fifth *Rêverie*, declares himself "content d'être" and "ne jouissant de rien d'extérieur à soi, de rien sinon de soi-même et de sa propre existence."

We know very little about the kind of images that such an imagination would produce, except that they would have little in common with what we have come to expect from familiar metaphorical figures. The works of the early romantics give us no actual examples, for they are, at most, *underway* towards renewed insights and inhabit the mixed and self-contradictory regions that we encountered in the three passages. Nor has their attempt been rightly interpreted by those who came after them, for literary history has generally labeled "primitivist," "naturalistic," or even pantheistic the first modern writers to have put into question, in the language of poetry, the ontological priority of the sensory object. We are only beginning to understand how this oscillation in the status of the image is linked to the crisis that leaves the poetry of today under a steady threat of extinction, although, on the other hand, it remains the depositary of hopes that no other activity of the mind seems able to offer.

WILLIAM K. WIMSATT, JR.

The Structure of Romantic Nature Imagery [†]

Students of romantic nature poetry have had a great deal to tell us about the philosophic components of this poetry: the specific blend of deistic theology, Newtonian physics, and pantheistic naturalism which pervades the Wordsworthian landscape in the period

[†] From *The Verbal Icon* by W. K. Wimsatt, Jr. Copyright © 1954 by the University of Kentucky Press. Reprinted by permission of the publisher.

of "Tintern Abbey," the theism which sounds in the "Eolian Harp" of Coleridge, the conflict between French atheism and Platonic idealism which even in "Prometheus Unbound" Shelley was not able to resolve. We have been instructed in some of the more purely scientific coloring of the poetry—the images derived from geology, astronomy, and magnetism, and the coruscant green mystery which the electricians contributed to such phenomena as Shelley's Spirit of Earth. We have considered also the "sensibility" of romantic readers, distinct, according to one persuasive interpretation, from that of neoclassic readers. What was exciting to the age of Pope, "Puffs, Powders, Patches, Bibles, Billet-doux" (even about these the age might be loath to admit its excitement), was not, we are told, what was so manifestly exciting to the age of Wordsworth. "High mountains are a feeling, but the hum of cities torture." Lastly, recent critical history has reinvited attention to the romantic theory of imagination, and especially to the version of that theory which Coleridge derived from the German metaphysicians, the view of poetic imagination as the *esemplastic* power which reshapes our primary awareness of the world into symbolic avenues to the theological.[1]

We have, in short, a *subject*—simply considered, the nature of birds and trees and streams—a *metaphysics* of an animating principle, a special *sensibility*, and a *theory* of poetic imagination—the value of the last a matter of debate. Romantic poetry itself has recently suffered some disfavor among advanced critics. One interesting question, however, seems still to want discussion; that is, whether romantic poetry (or more specifically romantic nature poetry) exhibits any imaginative *structure* which may be considered a special counterpart of the subject, the philosophy, the sensibility, and the theory—and hence perhaps an explanation of the last. Something like an answer to such a question is what I would sketch.

For the purpose of providing an antithetic point of departure, I quote here a part of one of the best known and most toughly reasonable of all metaphysical images:

> If they be two, they are two so
> As stiff twin compasses are two,
> Thy soul the fixed foot, makes no show
> To move, but doth, if th' other do.

1. This paragraph alludes especially to Joseph Warren Beach, *The Concept of Nature in Nineteenth-Century English Poetry* (New York, 1936), chaps. II–VIII; Newton P. Stallknecht, *Strange Seas of Thought* (Durham, 1945), chaps. II–IIIV Carl H. Grabo, *A Newton among Poets* (Chapel Hill, 1930), chaps. VI–VII, and *Prometheus Unbound: An Interpretation* (Chapel Hill, 1935), 142–43, 151; Frederick A. Pottle, *The Idiom of Poetry* (Ithaca, 1941), chap. I. For a survey of recent writing on the English romantic theory of imagination, see Thomas M. Raysor (ed.), *The English Romantic Poets, A Review of Research* (New York, 1950).

It will be relevant if we remark that this similitude, rather far-fetched as some might think, is yet unmistakable to interpretation because quite overtly stated, but again is not, by being stated, precisely defined or limited in its poetic value. The kind of similarity and the kind of disparity that ordinarily obtain between a drawing compass and a pair of parting lovers are things to be attentively considered in reading this image. And the disparity between living lovers and stiff metal is not least important to the tone of precision, restraint, and conviction which it is the triumph of the poem to convey. Though the similitude is cast in the form of statement, its mood is actually a kind of subimperative. In the next age the tension of such a severe disparity was relaxed, yet the overtness and crispness of statement remained, and a wit of its own sort.

> 'Tis with our judgments as our watches, none
> Go just alike, yet each believes his own.

We may take this as typical, I believe, of the metaphoric structure in which Pope achieves perfection and which survives a few years later in the couplets of Samuel Johnson or the more agile Churchill. The difference between our judgments and our watches, if noted at all, may be a pleasant epistemological joke for a person who questions the existence of a judgment which is taken out like a watch and consulted by another judgment.

But the "sensibility," as we know, had begun to shift even in the age of Pope. Examples of a new sensibility, and of a different structure, having something to do with Miltonic verse and a "physico-theological nomenclature," are to be found in Thomson's *Seasons*. Both a new sensibility and a new structure appear in the "hamlets brown and dim-discovered spires" of Collins' early example of the full romantic dream. In several poets of the mid century, in the Wartons, in Grainger, or in Cunningham, one may feel, or rather see stated, a new sensibility, but at the same time one may lament an absence of poetic quality—that is, of a poetic structure adequate to embody or objectify the new feeling. It is as if these harbingers of another era had felt but had not felt strongly enough to work upon the objects of their feelings a pattern of meaning which would speak for itself—and which would hence endure as a poetic monument.

As a central exhibit I shall take two sonnets, that of William Lisle Bowles "To the River Itchin" (1789) [2] and for contrast that of Coleridge "To the River Otter" (1796)—written in confessed imitation of Bowles.[3] Coleridge owed his first poetic inspiration to

2. The sonnet "To the River Lodon" (1777) by Bowles' Oxford senior, Thomas Warton, shows sensibility with even less structural support.

3. Coleridge's sonnet first appears in its entirety and as a separate poem in the pamphlet collection which he published privately in 1796; the sonnet reappears in the 1797 *Poems* of Coleridge under the half-title "Sonnets attempted in the manner of the Rev. W. L. Bowles."

Bowles (the "father" of English romantic poetry) and continued to express unlimited admiration for him as late as 1798. That is, they shared the same sensibility—as for that matter did Wordsworth and Southey, who too were deeply impressed by the sonnets of Bowles. As a schoolboy Coleridge read eagerly in Bowles' second edition of 1789 [4] (among other sonnets not much superior):

> Itchin, when I behold thy banks again,
> Thy crumbling margin, and thy silver breast,
> On which the self-same tints still seem to rest,
> Why feels my heart the shiv'ring sense of pain?
> Is it—that many a summer's day has past
> Since, in life's morn, I carol'd on thy side?
> Is it—that oft, since then, my heart has sigh'd,
> As Youth, and Hope's delusive gleams, flew fast?
> Is it—that those, who circled on thy shore,
> Companions of my youth, now meet no more?
> Whate'er the cause, upon thy banks I bend
> Sorrowing, yet feel such solace at my heart,
> As at the meeting of some long-lost friend,
> From whom, in happier hours, we wept to part.

Here is an emotive expression which once appealed to the sensibility of its author and of his more cultivated contemporaries, but which has with the lapse of time gone flat. The speaker was happy as a boy by the banks of the river. Age has brought disillusion and the dispersal of his friends. So a return to the river, in reminding him of the past, brings both sorrow and consolation. The facts are stated in four rhetorical questions and a concluding declaration. There is also something about how the river looks and how its looks might contribute to his feelings—in the metaphoric suggestion of the "crumbling" margin and in the almost illusory tints on the surface of the stream which surprisingly have outlasted the "delusive gleams" of his own hopes. Yet the total impression is one of simple association (by contiguity in time) simply asserted—what might be described in the theory of Hume or Hartley or what Hazlitt talks about in his essay "On the Love of the Country." "It is because natural objects have been associated with the sports of our child-hood, . . . with our feelings in solitude . . . that we love them as we do ourselves."

Coleridge himself in his "Lines Written at Elbingerode in 1799" was to speak of a "spot with which the heart associates Holy remembrances of child or friend." His enthusiasm for Hartley in this period is well known. But later, in the *Biographia Literaria* and in the third of his essays on "Genial Criticism," he was to repudiate

---

4. "I made, within less than a year and a half, more than forty transcrip-tions, as the best presents I could offer." *Biographia Literaria*, chap. I.

explicitly the Hartleyan and mechanistic way of shifting back burdens of meaning. And already, in 1796, Coleridge as poet was concerned with the more complex ontological grounds of association (the various levels of sameness, of correspondence and analogy), where mental activity transcends mere "associative response"— where it is in fact the unifying activity known both to later eighteenth century associationists and to romantic poets as "imagination." The "sweet and indissoluble union between the intellectual and the material world" of which Coleridge speaks in the introduction to his pamphlet anthology of sonnets in 1796 must be applied by us in one sense to the sonnets of Bowles, but in another to the best romantic poetry and even to Coleridge's imitation of Bowles. There is an important difference between the kinds of unity. In a letter to Sotheby of 1802 Coleridge was to say more emphatically: "The poet's heart and intellect should be *combined*, intimately combined and unified with the great appearances of nature, and not merely held in solution and loose mixture with them." [5] In the same paragraph he says of Bowles' later poetry: "Bowles has indeed the *sensibility* of a poet, but he has not the passion of a great poet . . . he has no native passion because he is not a thinker."

The sententious melancholy of Bowles' sonnets and the asserted connection between this mood and the appearances of nature are enough to explain the hold of the sonnets upon Coleridge. Doubtless the metaphoric coloring, faint but nonetheless real, which we have remarked in Bowles' descriptive details had also something to do with it. What is of great importance to note is that Coleridge's own sonnet "To the River Otter" (while not a completely successful poem) shows a remarkable intensification of such color.

> Dear native Brook! wild Streamlet of the West!
> How many various-fated years have past,
> What happy and what mournful hours, since last
> I skimmed the smooth thin stone along thy breast,
> Numbering its light leaps! yet so deep imprest
> Sink the sweet scenes of childhood, that mine eyes
> I never shut amid the sunny ray,
> But straight with all their tints thy waters rise,
> Thy crossing plank, thy marge with willows grey,
> And bedded sand that veined with various dyes
> Gleamed through thy bright transparence! On my way,
> Visions of Childhood! oft have ye beguiled

5. Coleridge has in mind such loose resemblances as need to be stated "in the shape of formal similes." *Letters* (Boston, 1895), I, 404. Cp. Bowles, *Sonnets* (2d ed., Bath, 1789), Sonnet V, "To the River Wenbeck," "I listen to the wind, And think I hear meek sorrow's plaint"; Sonnet VI, "To the River Tweed," "The murmurs by thy wand'ring wave below Seem to his ear the pity of a friend."

Lone manhood's cares, yet waking fondest sighs:
Ah! that once more I were a careless Child!

Almost the same statement as that of Bowles' sonnet—the sweet scenes of childhood by the river have only to be remembered to bring both beguilement and melancholy. One notices immediately, however, that the speaker has kept his eye more closely on the object. There are more details. The picture is more vivid, a fact which according to one school of poetics would in itself make the sonnet superior. But a more analytic theory will find it worth remarking also that certain ideas, latent or involved in the description, have much to do with its vividness. As a child, careless and free, wild like the streamlet, the speaker amused himself with one of the most carefree motions of youth—skimming smooth thin stones which leapt lightly on the breast of the water. One might have thought such experiences would sink no deeper in the child's breast than the stones in the water—"yet so deep imprest"—the very antithesis (though it refers overtly only to the many hours which have intervened) defines imaginatively the depth of the impressions. When he closes his eyes, they *rise* again (the word *rise* may be taken as a trope which hints the whole unstated similitude); they rise like the tinted waters of the stream; they gleam up through the depths of memory —the "various-fated years"—like the "various dyes" which vein the sand of the river bed. In short, there is a rich ground of meaning in Coleridge's sonnet beyond what is overtly stated. The descriptive details of his sonnet gleam brightly because (consciously or unconsciously—it would be fruitless to inquire how deliberately he wrote these meanings into his lines) he has invested them with significance. Here is a special perception, "invention" if one prefers, "imagination," or even "wit." It can be explored and tested by the wit of the reader. In this way it differs from the mere flat announcement of a Hartleian association, which is not open to challenge and hence not susceptible of confirmation. If this romantic wit differs from that of the metaphysicals, it differs for one thing in making less use of the central overt statement of similitude which is so important in all rhetoric stemming from Aristotle and the Renaissance. The metaphor in fact is scarcely noticed by the main statement of the poem.[6] Both tenor and vehicle, furthermore, are wrought in a parallel process out of the same material. The river landscape is both the occasion of reminiscence and the source of the metaphors by which reminiscence is described.[7] A poem of this structure is a

6. See the more overt connections in the poem "Recollection" (*Watchman,* no. V, April 2, 1796) from which lines 2–11 of this sonnet were taken. "Where blameless Pleasures dimpled Quiet's cheek, As water-lilies *ripple* thy slow stream!" "Ah! fair tho' faint those forms of memory seem, Like Heaven's bright bow on thy smooth evening stream."

7. "It is among the chief excellencies of Bowles that his imagery appears almost always prompted by surrounding scenery." Coleridge to Southey, December 17, 1794 (*Letters,* I, 115).

signal instance of that kind of fallacy (or strategy) by which death in poetry occurs so often in winter or at night, and sweethearts meet in the spring countryside. The tenor of such a similitude is likely to be subjective—reminiscence or sorrow or beguilement—not an object distinct from the vehicle, as lovers or their souls are distinct from twin compasses. Hence the emphasis of Bowles, Coleridge, and all other romantics on spontaneous feelings and sincerity. Hence the recurrent themes of One Being and Eolian Influence and Wordsworth's "ennobling interchange of action from within and from without." In such a structure again the element of tension in disparity is not so important as for metaphysical wit. The interest derives not from our being aware of disparity where likeness is firmly insisted on, but in an opposite activity of discerning the design which is latent in the multiform sensuous picture.

Let us notice for a moment the "crossing plank" of Coleridge's sonnet, a minor symbol in the poem, a sign of shadowy presences, the lads who had once been there. The technique of this symbol is the same as that which Keats was to employ in a far more brilliant romantic instance, the second stanza of his "Ode to Autumn," where the very seasonal spirit is conjured into reality out of such haunted spots—in which a gesture lingers—the half-reaped furrow, the oozing cider press, the brook where the gleaners have crossed with laden heads.[8] To return to our metaphysics—of an animate, plastic Nature, not transcending but immanent in and breathing through all things—and to discount for the moment such differences as may relate to Wordsworth's naturalism, Coleridge's theology, Shelley's Platonism, or Blake's visions: we may observe that the common feat of the romantic nature poets was to read meanings into the landscape. The meaning might be such as we have seen in Coleridge's sonnet, but it might more characteristically be more profound, concerning the spirit or soul of things—"the one life within us and abroad." And that meaning especially was summoned out of the very surface of nature itself. It was embodied imaginatively and without the explicit religious or philosophic statements which one will find in classical or Christian instances—for example in Pope's "Essay on Man":

> Here then we rest: "The Universal Cause
> Acts to one end, but acts by various laws,"

or in the theological divines, More, Cudworth, Bentley, and others of the seventeenth and eighteenth centuries, or in Paley during the same era as the romantics. The romantic poets want to have it and not have it too—a spirit which the poet himself as superidealist creates by his own higher reason or esemplastic imagination. Here one may recall Ruskin's chapter of *Modern Painters* on the differ-

8. Compare the "wooden bridge" in Arnold's Keatsian "Scholar Gipsy."

ence between the Greek gods of rivers and trees and the vaguer suffusions of the romantic vista—"the curious web of hesitating sentiment, pathetic fallacy, and wandering fancy, which form a great part of our modern view of nature." Wordsworth's "Prelude," from the cliff that "upreared its head" in the night above Ullswater to the "blue chasm" that was the "soul" of the moonlit cloudscape beneath his feet on Snowdon, is the archpoet's testament, both theory and demonstration of this way of reading nature. His "Tintern Abbey" is another classic instance, a whole pantheistic poem woven of the landscape, where God is not once mentioned. After the "soft inland murmur," the "one green hue," the "wreaths of smoke . . . as , . . Of vagrant dwellers in the houseless woods" (always something just out of sight or beyond definition), it is an easy leap to the "still, sad music of humanity," and

> a sense sublime
> Of something far more deeply interfused,
> Whose dwelling is the light of setting suns.

This poem, written as Wordsworth revisited the banks of a familiar stream, the "Sylvan Wye," is the full realization of a poem for which Coleridge and Bowles had drawn slight sketches. In Shelley's "Hymn to Intellectual Beauty" the "awful shadow" of the "unseen Power" is substantiated of "moonbeam" showers of light behind the "piny mountain," of "mist o'er mountains driven." On the Lake of Geneva in the summer of 1816 Byron, with Shelley the evangelist of Wordsworth at his side, spoke of "a living fragrance from the shore," a "floating whisper on the hill." We remark in each of these examples a dramatization of the spiritual through the use of the faint, the shifting, the least tangible and most mysterious parts of nature—a poetic counterpart of the several theories of spirit as subtile matter current in the eighteenth century, Newton's "electric and elastic" active principle, Hartley's "infinitesimal elementary body." The application of this philosophy to poetry by way of direct statement had been made as early as 1735 in Henry Brooke's "Universal Beauty," where an "elastick Flue of fluctuating Air" pervades the universe as "animating Soul." In the high romantic period the most scientific version to appear in poetry was the now well recognized imagery which Shelley drew from the electricians.

In such a view of spirituality the landscape itself is kept in focus as a literal object of attention. Without it Wordsworth and Byron in the examples just cited would not get a start. And one effect of such a use of natural imagery—an effect implicit in the very philosophy of a World Spirit—is a tendency in the landscape imagery to a curious split. If we have not only the landscape but the spirit which either informs or visits it, and if both of these must be rendered for

the sensible imagination, a certain parceling of the landscape may
be the result. The most curious illustrations which I know are in
two of Blake's early quartet of poems to the seasons. Thus, "To
Spring":

> O THOU with dewy locks, who lookest down
> Thro' the clear windows of the morning, turn
> Thine angel eyes upon our western isle,
> Which in full choir hails thy approach, O Spring!
>
> The hills tell each other, and the list'ning
> Vallies hear; all our longing eyes are turned
> Up to thy bright pavillions; issue forth,
> And let thy holy feet visit our clime.
>
> Come o'er the eastern hills, and let our winds
> Kiss thy perfumed garments; let us taste
> Thy morn and evening breath; scatter thy pearls
> Upon our love-sick land that mourns for thee.

And "To Summer":

> O THOU, who passest thro' our vallies in
> Thy strength, curb thy fierce steeds, allay the heat
> That flames from their large nostrils! thou, O Summer,
> Oft pitched'st here thy golden tent, and oft
> Beneath our oaks hast slept, while we beheld
> With joy thy ruddy limbs and flourishing hair.
> Beneath our thickest shades we oft have heard
> Thy voice, when noon upon his fervid car
> Rode o'er the deep of heaven; beside our springs
> Sit down, and in our mossy vallies, on
> Some bank beside a river clear, throw thy
> Silk draperies off, and rush into the stream.

Blake's starting point, it is true, is the opposite of Wordsworth's or
Byron's, not the landscape but a spirit personified or allegorized.
Nevertheless, this spirit as it approaches the "western isle" takes on
certain distinctly terrestrial hues. Spring, an oriental bridegroom,
lives behind the "clear windows of the morning" and is invited to
issue from "bright pavillions," doubtless the sky at dawn. He has
"perfumed garments" which when kissed by the winds will smell
much like the flowers and leaves of the season. At the same time,
his *own* morn and evening breaths are most convincing in their
likeness to morning and evening breezes. The pearls scattered by
the hand of Spring are, we must suppose, no other than the flowers
and buds which literally appear in the landscape at this season.
They function as landscape details and simultaneously as properties
of the bridegroom and—we note here a further complication—as

properties of the land taken as lovesick maiden. We have in fact a double personification conjured from one nature, one landscape, in a wedding which approximates fusion. Even more curious is the case of King Summer, a divided tyrant and victim, who first appears as the source and spirit of heat, his steeds with flaming nostrils, his limbs ruddy, his tent golden, but who arrives in our valleys only to sleep in the shade of the oaks and be invited to rush into the river for a swim. These early romantic poems are examples of the Biblical, classical, and Renaissance tradition of allegory as it approaches the romantic condition of landscape naturalism—as Spring and Summer descend into the landscape and are fused with it. Shelley's Alastor is a spirit of this kind, making the "wild his home," a spectral "Spirit of wind," expiring "Like some frail exhalation; which the dawn Robes in its golden beams." Byron's Childe Harold desired that he himself might become a "portion" of that around him, of the tempest and the night. "Be thou, Spirit fierce," said Shelley to the West Wind, "My spirit! Be thou me."

An English student of the arts in the Jacobean era, Henry Peacham, wrote a book on painting in which he gave allegorical prescriptions for representing the months, quoted under the names of months by Dr. Johnson in his *Dictionary*:

April is represented by a young man in green, with a garland of myrtle and hawthorn buds; in one hand primroses and violets, in the other the sign Taurus.

July I would have drawn in a jacket of light yellow, eating cherries, with his face and bosom sunburnt.[9]

But that would have been the end of it. April would not have been painted into a puzzle picture where hawthorn buds and primroses were arranged to shadow forth the form of a person.[1] There were probably deep enough reasons why the latter nineteenth century went so far in the development of so trivial a thing as the actual landscape puzzle picture.

In his Preface of 1815 Wordsworth spoke of the *abstracting* and "*modifying* powers of the imagination." He gave as example a passage from his own poem, "Resolution and Independence," where an old leech gatherer is likened to a stone which in turn is likened to a sea beast crawled forth to sun itself. The poems which we have just considered, those of Coleridge, Wordsworth, and Blake especially, with their blurring of literal and figurative, might also be

---

9. With these prescriptions compare the allegorical panels of seasons and months in Spenser's *Cantos of Mutabilitie*, VII, xxvii ff.

1. Perhaps too sweeping. See, for instance, Alfred H. Barr, Jr. (ed.), *Fantastic Art, Dada, Surrealism* (New York, 1947), 83, "Head–Landscape" in the tradition of Arcimboldo.

taken, I believe, as excellent examples. In another of his best poems Wordsworth produced an image which shows so strange yet artistic a warping, or modification, of vehicle by tenor that, though not strictly a nature image, it may be quoted here with close relevance. In the ode "Intimations of Immortality":

> Hence, in a season of calm weather,
> Though inland far we be,
> Our souls have sight of that immortal sea
> Which brought us hither;
> Can in a moment travel thither—
> And see the children sport upon the shore,
> And hear the mighty waters rolling evermore.

Or, as one might drably paraphrase, our souls in a calm mood look back to the infinity from which they came, as persons inland on clear days can look back to the sea by which they have voyaged to the land. The tenor concerns souls and age and time. The vehicle concerns travelers and space. The question for the analyst of structure is: Why are the children found on the seashore? In what way do they add to the solemnity or mystery of the sea? Or do they at all? The answer is that they are not strictly parts of the traveler-space vehicle, but the soul-age-time tenor, attracted over, from tenor to vehicle. The travelers looking back in both space and time see themselves as children on the shore, as if just born like Venus from the foam. This is a sleight of words, an imposition of image upon image, by the *modifying* power of imagination.

Poetic structure is always a fusion of ideas with material, a statement in which the solidity of symbol and the sensory verbal qualities are somehow not washed out by the abstraction. For this effect the iconic or directly imitative powers of language are important —and of these the well known onomatopoeia or imitation of sound is only one, and one of the simplest. The "stiff twin compasses" of Donne have a kind of iconicity in the very stiffness and odd emphasis of the metrical situation. Neoclassic iconicity is on the whole of a highly ordered, formal, or intellectual sort, that of the "figures of speech" such as antithesis, isocolon, homoeoteleuton, or chiasmus. But romantic nature poetry tends to achieve iconicity by a more direct sensory imitation of something headlong and impassioned, less ordered, nearer perhaps to the subrational. Thus: in Shelley's "Ode to the West Wind" the shifts in imagery of the second stanza, the pell-mell raggedness and confusion of loose clouds, decaying leaves, angels and Maenads with hair uplifted, the dirge, the dome, the vapors, and the enjambment from tercet to tercet combine to give an impression beyond statement of the very wildness, the breath and power which is the vehicle of the poem's radical metaphor. If we think of a scale of structures having at one end logic, the completely reasoned and abstracted, and at the other some form of madness or surrealism, matter or impression unformed and undisciplined (the imitation of disorder by the idiom of disorder), we may see metaphysical and neoclassical poetry as near the extreme of logic (though by no means reduced to that status) and romantic poetry as a step toward the directness of sensory presentation (though by no means sunk into subrationality). As a structure which favors implication rather than overt statement, the romantic is far closer than the metaphysical to symbolist poetry and the varieties of postsymbolist most in vogue today. Both types of structure, the metaphysical and the romantic, are valid. Each has gorgeously enriched the history of English poetry.

PART TWO

Nature and Revolution

Romantic poetry rose, in England, out of English reactions to the French Revolution and the revolution's "failure," and in a sense out of the English failure to follow the French in revolution. The effect of the revolution upon the English Protestant temperament is, in depth, the subject of M. H. Abrams' essay on "The Spirit of the Age," the most advanced discussion to date on the relation between the apocalyptic yearnings of the period and the poets' emergent "natural supernaturalism." The fullest study of a single Romantic poet in his political context is David V. Erdman's *Blake: Prophet Against Empire*, a work difficult to excerpt. Northrop Frye's "The Road of Excess" is printed in this section, though it is concerned largely with Blake, and as readily would suit the "Nature and Literary Form" section, since it presents central insights into Blake's deliberate use of discontinuity. But it is also a seminal essay on the revolutionary element in Romanticism, and prefigures Frye's later writings on the theme of the "growing feeling that the origin of human civilization was human too." Uneasily allied to this feeling was a contrary impulse in Romanticism, fostered by Burke and taken up by the Lake Poets. Burke taught Wordsworth and Coleridge to think of "individuals in society," rather than of the natural man in relation to the state, and so encouraged them in a kind of romance politics or mystique of nationality. This is the subject of the historian Alfred Cobban, with his enviable understanding of the political vision of Romanticism.

M. H. ABRAMS

English Romanticism: The Spirit of the Age †

My title echoes that of William Hazlitt's remarkable book of 1825, which set out to represent what we now call the climate of opinion among the leading men of his time. In his abrupt way Hazlitt did not stay to theorize, plunging into the middle of things with a sketch of Jeremy Bentham. But from these essays emerges plainly his view that the crucial occurrence for his generation had been the French Revolution. In that event and its repercussions, political, intellectual, and imaginative, and in the resulting waves of hope and gloom, revolutionary loyalty and recreancy, he saw both the promise and the failures of his violent and contradictory era.

The span covered by the active life of Hazlitt's subjects—approximately the early 1790s to 1825—coincides with what literary historians now call the Romantic period; and it is Hazlitt's contention that the characteristic poetry of the age took its shape from the form and pressure of revolution and reaction. The whole "Lake school of poetry," he had said seven years earlier, "had its origin in the French revolution, or rather in those sentiments and opinions which produced that revolution." [1] Hazlitt's main exhibit is Wordsworth (the "head" of the school), whose "genius," he declares, "is a pure emanation of the Spirit of the Age." The poetry of Wordsworth in the period of *Lyrical Ballads* was "one of the innovations of the time."

> It partakes of, and is carried along with, the revolutionary movement of our age: the political changes of the day were the model on which he formed and conducted his poetical experiments. His Muse (it cannot be denied, and without this we cannot explain its character at all) is a levelling one.[2]

Neither the concept that the age had an identifying "spirit," nor that this spirit was one of revolutionary change, was unique with Hazlitt. Just after the revolution of July, 1830, John Stuart Mill

† From *Romanticism Reconsidered*, ed. Northrop Frye. Copyright © 1963 by Columbia University Press. Reprinted by permission of the publisher.
1. *Lectures on the English Poets* (1818), in *The Complete Works of William Hazlitt*, ed. P. P. Howe (21 vols.; London, 1930–34), V, 161.
2. *The Spirit of the Age, ibid.*, XI, 86–87.

wrote a series of essays on *The Spirit of the Age* in which he said that the phrase, denoting "the dominant idea" of the times, went back only some fifty years, and resulted from the all but universal conviction "that the times are pregnant with change"—a condition "of which the first overt manifestation was the breaking out of the French Revolution." [3] Shelley, in A *Philosophical View of Reform* (1819), after reviewing the European outbreaks of liberty against tyranny which culminated in the American and French revolutions, asserted that the related crisis of change in England had been accompanied by a literary renascence, in which the poets displayed "a comprehensive and all-penetrating spirit" that was "less their own spirit than the spirit of their age." [4] Conservative critics, like the radical Shelley, recognized the fact of a great new poetry and associated its genesis with political events. "The revolution in our literature," Francis Jeffrey claimed in 1816, had as one of its primary causes "the agitations of the French revolution, and the discussions as well as the hopes and terrors to which it gave occasion." [5] And De Quincey said (1839) that the almost "miraculous" effect of the "great moral tempest" of the Revolution was evident "in all lands . . . and at the same time." "In Germany or England alike, the poetry was so entirely regenerated, thrown into moulds of thought and of feeling so new, that the poets everywhere felt themselves . . . entering upon the dignity and the sincere thinking of mature manhood." [6]

It seems to me that Hazlitt and his contemporary viewers of the literary scene were, in their general claim, manifestly right: the Romantic period was eminently an age obsessed with the fact of violent and inclusive change, and Romantic poetry cannot be understood, historically, without awareness of the degree to which this preoccupation affected its substance and form. The phenomenon is too obvious to have escaped notice, in monographs devoted to the French Revolution and the English poets, singly and collectively. But when critics and historians turn to the general task of defining the distinctive qualities of "Romanticism," or of the English Ro-

3. John Stuart Mill, *The Spirit of the Age*, ed. Frederick A. von Hayek (Chicago, 1942), pp. 1–2, 67. In 1812 Thomas Belsham spoke of "the spirit of the times," the "mania of the French Revolution," which "pervaded all ranks of society" (*Memoirs of the Late Reverend Theophilus Lindsey* [2d ed.; London, 1820], p. 216). See also "Letter on the Spirit of the Age," *Blackwood's Magazine*, XXVIII (Dec., 1830), 900–920.
4. *Shelley's Prose*, ed. David Lee Clark (Albuquerque, 1954), pp. 239–40; the passage was later used, almost verbatim, as the conclusion of *A De-*fence *of Poetry*. See also the Preface to *Prometheus Unbound*, *ibid.*, pp. 327–28, and the letter to C. and J. Ollier, Oct. 15, 1819. Shelley called the French Revolution "the master theme of the epoch in which we live" (*Lord Byron's Correspondence*, ed. John Murray [2 vols.; London, 1922], II, 15).
5. Review of Walter Scott's edition of *The Works of Jonathan Swift*, in *Contributions to the Edinburgh Review* (4 vols.; London, 1844), I, 158–67.
6. "William Wordsworth," in *The Collected Writings of Thomas De Quincey*, ed. David Masson (14 vols.; Edinburgh, 1889–90), II, 273–74.

mantic movement, they usually ignore its relations to the revolutionary climate of the time. For example, in an anthology of "the 'classic' statements" on Romanticism, especially in England, which came out in 1962, the few essays which give more than passing mention to the French Revolution do so to reduce the particularity of Romantic poems mainly to a distant reflection of an underlying economic reality, and to an unconscious rationalization of the bourgeois illusion of "freedom." [7]

It may be useful, then, to have a new look at the obvious as it appeared, not to post-Marxist historians, but to intelligent observers at the time. I shall try to indicate briefly some of the ways in which the political, intellectual, and emotional circumstances of a period of revolutionary upheaval affected the scope, subject-matter, themes, values, and even language of a number of Romantic poems. I hope to avoid easy and empty generalizations about the *Zeitgeist*, and I do not propose the electrifying proposition that "le romantisme, c'est la révolution." Romanticism is no one thing. It is many very individual poets, who wrote poems manifesting a greater diversity of qualities, it seems to me, than those of any preceding age. But some prominent qualities a number of these poems share, and certain of these shared qualities form a distinctive complex which may, with a high degree of probability, be related to the events and ideas of the cataclysmic coming-into-being of the world to which we are by now becoming fairly accustomed.

I. THE SPIRIT OF THE 1790S

By force of chronological habit we think of English Romanticism as a nineteenth-century phenomenon, overlooking how many of its distinctive features had been established by the end of the century before. The last decade of the eighteenth century included the complete cycle of the Revolution in France, from what De Quincey called its "gorgeous festival era" [8] to the *coup d'état* of November 10, 1799, when to all but a few stubborn sympathizers it seemed betrayed from without and within, and the portent of Napoleon loomed over Europe. That same decade was the period in which the poets of the first Romantic generation reached their literary maturity and had either completed, or laid out and begun, the greater number of what we now account their major achievements. By the end of the decade Blake was well along with *The Four Zoas;* only *Milton* and *Jerusalem* belong to the nineteenth century. By the end of the year 1800 Wordsworth had already announced the

7. *Romanticism: Points of View*, ed. Robert F. Gleckner and Gerald E. Enscoe (Englewood Cliffs, N.J., 1962).

8. "William Wordsworth," *Collected Writings*, II, 274.

over-all design and begun writing the two great undertakings of his poetic career; that is, he had finished most of the the first two books and a number of scattered later passages of *The Prelude*, and of *The Recluse* he had written "Home at Grasmere" (which included the extraordinary section he later reprinted as the "Prospectus of the design and scope of the whole poem") as well as the first book of *The Excursion*. Coleridge wrote in the 1790s seven-tenths of all the nondramatic material in his collected poems.

"Few persons but those who have lived in it," Southey reminisced in his Tory middle age, "can conceive or comprehend what the memory of the French Revolution was, nor what a visionary world seemed to open upon those who were just entering it. Old things seemed passing away, and nothing was dreamt of but the regeneration of the human race." [9] The early years of the Revolution, a modern commentator has remarked, were "perhaps the happiest in the memory of civilized man," [1] and his estimate is justified by the ecstasy described by Wordsworth in *The Prelude*—"bliss was it in that dawn to be alive"—and expressed by many observers of France in its glad dawn. Samuel Romilly exclaimed in May, 1792: "It is the most glorious event, and the happiest for mankind, that has ever taken place since human affairs have been recorded." Charles James Fox was less restrained in his evaluation: "How much the best!" [2] A generation earlier Dr. Johnson had written a concluding passage for Goldsmith's *The Traveller* which summed up prevailing opinion:

> How small, of all that human hearts endure,
> That part which laws or kings can cause or cure!
> Still to ourselves in every place consigned,
> Our own felicity we make or find.

But now it seemed to many social philosophers that the revolution against the king and the old laws would cure everything and establish felicity for everyone, everywhere. In 1791 Volney took time out from his revolutionary activities to publish *Les ruines, ou méditations sur les révolutions des empires*, in which a supervisory Genius unveils to him the vision of the past, the present, and then the "New Age," which had in fact already begun in the American Revolution and was approaching its realization in France. "Now," cries the author, "may I live! for after this there is nothing which

9. *The Correspondence of Robert Southey with Caroline Bowles*, ed. Edward Dowden (Dublin, 1881), p. 52.
1. M. Ray Adams, *Studies in the Literary Backgrounds of English Radicalism* (Lancaster, Pa., 1947), p. 7.
2. Romilly in Alfred Cobban, ed., *The Debate on the French Revolution, 1789–1800* (London, 1950), p. 354;

Fox as cited by Edward Dowden, *The French Revolution and English Literature* (New York, 1897), p. 9. "Era of happiness in the history of the world!" John Thelwall described the Revolution; "Dawn of a real golden age" (Charles Cestre, *John Thelwall* [London, 1906], p. 171).

I am not daring enough to hope." [3] Condorcet wrote his *Outline of the Progress of the Human Spirit* as a doomed man hiding from the police of the Reign of Terror, to vindicate his unshaken faith that the Revolution was a breakthrough in man's progress; he ends with the vision of mankind's imminent perfection both in his social condition and in his intellectual and moral powers.[4] The equivalent book in England was Godwin's *Political Justice*, written under impetus of the Revolution in 1791–93, which has its similar anticipation of mankind morally transformed, living in a state of total economic and political equality.[5]

The intoxicating sense that now everything was possible was not confined to systematic philosophers. In 1793, Hazlitt said, schemes for a new society "of virtue and happiness" had been published "in plays, poems, songs, and romances—made their way to the bar, crept into the church . . . got into the hearts of poets and the brains of metaphysicians . . . and turned the heads of almost the whole kingdom." [6] Anyone who has looked into the poems, the sermons, the novels, and the plays of the early 1790s will know that this is not a gross exaggeration. Man regenerate in a world made new; this was the theme of a multitude of writers notable, forgotten, or anonymous. In the Prologue to his highly successful play, *The Road to Ruin* (1792), Thomas Holcroft took the occasion to predict that the Revolution in France had set the torrent of freedom spreading,

> To ease, happiness, art, science, wit, and genius to give birth;
> Ay, to fertilize a world, and renovate old earth! [7]

"Renovate old earth," "the regeneration of the human race"— the phrases reflect their origin, and indicate a characteristic difference between French and English radicalism. Most French philosophers of perfectibility (and Godwin, their representative in England) were anticlerical skeptics or downright atheists, who claimed that they based their predictions on an inductive science of history and a Lockian science of man. The chief strength and momentum of English radicalism, on the other hand, came from the religious Nonconformists who, as true heirs of their embattled ancestors in the English Civil War, looked upon contemporary politics through the perspective of biblical prophecy. In a sermon on the

3. C. F. C. de Volney, *The Ruins* (5th ed.; London, 1807), pp. 92, 98–113.
4. Marquis de Condorcet, *Outlines of an Historical View of the Progress of the Human Mind* (London, 1795), pp. 261–62, 370–72.
5. William Godwin, *Enquiry Concerning Political Justice*, ed. F. E. L. Priestley (3 vols.; Toronto, 1946); see, e.g., II, 463–64, 528–29; III, 180–81.

6. *Complete Works*, VII, 99. Some of this minor revolutionary literature is reviewed in M. Ray Adams, *Literary Backgrounds of English Radicalism*, and Allene Gregory, *The French Revolution and the English Novel* (New York, 1915).
7. *The Road to Ruin* (1st ed.; London, 1792).

French Revolution preached in 1791 the Reverend Mark Wilks proclaimed: "Jesus Christ was a Revolutionist; and the Revolution he came to effect was foretold in these words, 'He hath sent me to proclaim liberty to the captives.' " [8] The Unitarians—influential beyond their numbers because they included so large a proportion of scientists, literary men, and powerful pulpit orators—were especially given to projecting on the empirical science of human progress the pattern and detail of biblical prophecies, Messianic, millennial, and apocalyptic. "Hey for the New Jerusalem! The millennium!" Thomas Holcroft cried out, in the intoxication of first reading Paine's The Rights of Man (1791); [9] what this notorious atheist uttered lightly was the fervent but considered opinion of a number of his pious contemporaries. Richard Price, in 1785, had viewed the American Revolution as the most important step, next to the introduction of Christianity itself, in the fulfillment of the "old prophecies" of an empire of reason, virtue, and peace, when the wolf will "dwell with the lamb and the leopard with the kid." "May we not see there the dawning of brighter days on earth, and a new creation rising?" In the sermon of 1789 which evoked the hurricane of Burke's Reflections on the French Revolution, he sees that event capped by one even greater and more immediately promising: "I am thankful that I have lived to [see] it: and I could almost say, Lord, now lettest thou thy servant depart in peace, for mine eyes have seen thy salvation." [1] By 1793 the increasingly violent course of the Revolution inspired the prophets to turn from Isaiah's relatively mild prelude to the peaceable kingdom and "the new heavens and the new earth" to the classic text of apocalyptic violence, the Book of Revelation. In February of that year Elhanan Winchester's The Three Woe Trumpets interpreted the Revolution in France as the precise fulfillment of those prophecies, with the seventh trumpet just about to sound (Rev. 11) to bring on the final cataclysm and announce the Second Advent of Christ, in a Kingdom which should be "the greatest blessing to mankind that

8. The Origin and Stability of the French Revolution: A Sermon Preached at St. Paul's Chapel, Norwich, July 14, 1791, p. 5; quoted by Mark Schorer, William Blake: The Politics of Vision (New York, 1946), p. 205. For apocalyptic thinking among the Illuminists in France, see A. Viatte, Les sources occultes du Romantisme (2 vols.; Paris, 1928), chap. vi.
9. C. Kegan Paul, William Godwin: His Friends and Contemporaries (2 vols.; London, 1876), I, 69.
1. Richard Price, Observations on the Importance of the American Revolution (London, 1785), pp. 6–7, 21; A Discourse on the Love of Our Country

(Nov. 4, 1789), in S. MacCoby, ed., The English Radical Tradition, 1763–1914 (London, 1952), p. 54. The dissenter Nash wrote in reply to Burke's Reflections: "As I am a believer in Revelation, I, of course, live in the hope of better things; a millennium . . . a new heaven and a new earth in which dwelleth righteousness . . . a state of equal liberty and equal justice for all men." (A Letter to the Right Hon. Edmund Burke from a Dissenting Country Attorney [Birmingham, 1790]. Quoted by Anthony Lincoln, Some Political and Social Ideas of English Dissent, 1763–1800 [Cambridge, 1938], p. 3.)

ever they enjoyed, or even found an idea of." [2] In 1791 Joseph Priestley, scientist, radical philosopher, and a founder of the Unitarian Society, had written his *Letters* in reply to Burke's *Reflections*, in which he pronounced the American and French revolutions to be the inauguration of the state of universal happiness and peace "distinctly and repeatedly foretold in many prophecies, delivered more than two thousand years ago." Three years later he expanded his views in *The Present State of Europe Compared with Antient Prophecies*. Combining philosophical empiricism with biblical fundamentalism, he related the convulsions of the time to the Messianic prophecies in Isaiah and Daniel, the apocalyptic passages in various books of the New Testament, and especially to the Book of Revelation, as a ground for confronting "the great scene, that seems now to be opening upon us . . . with tranquillity, and even with satisfaction," in the persuasion that its "termination will be glorious and happy," in the advent of "the millennium, or the future peaceable and happy state of the world." [3] Wordsworth's Solitary, in *The Excursion*, no doubt reflects an aspect of Wordsworth's own temperament, but the chief model for his earlier career was Joseph Fawcett, famous Unitarian preacher at the Old Jewry, and a poet as well. In Wordsworth's rendering, we find him, in both song and sermon, projecting a dazzling vision of the French Revolution which fuses classical myth with Christian prophecy:

> I beheld
> Glory—beyond all glory ever seen,
> Confusion infinite of heaven and earth,
> Dazzling the soul. Meanwhile, prophetic harps
> In every grove were ringing, "War shall cease."
>   . . . I sang Saturnian rule
> Returned,—a progeny of golden years
> Permitted to descend and bless mankind.
> —With promises the Hebrew Scriptures teem.
>   . . . the glowing phrase
> Of ancient inspiration serving me,
> I promised also,—with undaunted trust
> Foretold, and added prayer to prophecy. [4]

2. Elhanan Winchester, *The Three Woe Trumpets* (1st American ed.; Boston, 1794), pp. 37–38, 71. Winchester also published in 1793 *The Process and Empire of Christ: An Heroic Poem* in blank verse, in which Books VIII to XII deal with the Second Advent, the Millennium, and the apocalyptic "New Creation; or, The Renovation of the Heavens and Earth after the Conflagration."
3. *Letters to the Right Honourable Edmund Burke* (2d ed.; Birmingham, 1791), pp. 143–50; *The Present State of Europe Compared with Antient Prophecies* (4th ed.; London, 1794), pp. 18 ff., 30–32. See also Priestley's *Sermon Preached in Hackney, Apr. 19, 1793*, and *Observations on the Increase of Infidelity* (1796).
4. *The Excursion*, III, 716–65; also II, 210–23. On the relation of the Solitary to Joseph Fawcett see M. Ray Adams, *Literary Backgrounds of English Radicalism*, Chap. VII.

The formative age of Romantic poetry was clearly one of apocalyptic expectations, or at least apocalyptic imaginings, which endowed the promise of France with the form and impetus of one of the deepest rooted and most compelling myths in the culture of Christian Europe.

II. THE VOICE OF THE BARD

In a verse-letter of 1800 Blake identified the crucial influences in his spiritual history as a series beginning with Milton and the Old Testament prophets and ending with the American War and the French Revolution.[5] Since Blake is the only major Romantic old enough to have published poems before the Revolution, his writings provide a convenient indication of the effects of that event and of the intellectual and emotional atmosphere that it generated.

As Northrop Frye has said in his fine book on Blake, his *Poetical Sketches* of 1783 associate him with Collins, Gray, the Wartons, and other writers of what Frye later called "The Age of Sensibility." [6] As early as the 1740s this school had mounted a literary revolution against the acknowledged tradition of Waller-Denham-Pope—a tradition of civilized and urbane verse, controlled by "good sense and judgment," addressed to a closely integrated upper class, in which the triumphs, as Joseph Warton pointed out, were mainly in "the didactic, moral, and satiric kind." [7] Against this tradition, the new poets raised the claim of a more daring, "sublime," and "primitive" poetry, represented in England by Spenser, Shakespeare, Milton, who exhibit the supreme virtues of spontaneity, invention, and an "enthusiastic" and "creative" imagination—by which was signified a poetry of inspired vision, related to divinity, and populated by allegorical and supernatural characters such as do not exist "in nature." [8]

Prominent in this literature of revolt, however, was a timidity, a sense of frustration very different from the assurance of power and of an accomplished and continuing literary renascence expressed by a number of their Romantic successors: Coleridge's unhesitating judgment that Wordsworth's genius measured up to Milton's, and Wordsworth's solemn concurrence in this judgment; Leigh Hunt's opinion that, for all his errors, Wordsworth is "at the head of a new and great age of poetry"; Keats's conviction that "Great spirits now

5. *The Complete Writings of William Blake*, ed. Geoffrey Keynes (London, 1957), p. 799.
6. *Fearful Symmetry* (Princeton, 1947), pp. 167 ff.; "Towards Defining an Age of Sensibility," in *Eighteenth-Century English Literature: Modern*

Essays in Criticism, ed. James L. Clifford (New York, 1959), pp. 311–18.
7. *An Essay on the Genius and Writings of Pope*, II (London, 1782), 477.
8. See M. H. Abrams, *The Mirror and the Lamp* (New York, 1953), pp. 274–76 and notes.

on earth are sojourning"; Shelley's confidence that "the literature of England . . . has arisen, as it were, from a new birth." [9] The poets of sensibility, on the contrary, had felt that they and all future writers were fated to be epigones of a tradition of unrecapturable magnificence. So Collins said in his "Ode on the Poetical Character" as, retreating from "Waller's myrtle shades," he tremblingly pursued Milton's "guiding steps"; "In Vain—

> Heaven and Fancy, kindred powers,
> Have now o'erturned the inspiring bowers,
> Or curtained close such scene from every future view.

And Gray:

> But not to one in this benighted age
> Is that diviner inspiration given,
> That burns in Shakespeare's or in Milton's page,
> The pomp and prodigality of Heaven.

So, in 1783, Blake complained to the Muses:

> How have you left the antient love
> That bards of old enjoy'd in you!

Besides *Poetical Sketches*, Blake's main achievements before the French Revolution were *Songs of Innocence* and *The Book of Thel*, which represent dwellers in an Eden trembling on the verge of experience. Suddenly in 1790 came *The Marriage of Heaven and Hell*, boisterously promulgating "Energy" in opposition to all inherited limits on human possibilities; to point the contemporary relevance, Blake appended a "Song of Liberty," which represents Energy as a revolutionary "son of fire," moving from America to France and crying the advent of an Isaian millennium:

EMPIRE IS NO MORE! AND NOW THE LION AND WOLF SHALL CEASE.

In 1791 appeared Blake's *The French Revolution*, in the form of a Miltonic epic. Of the seven books announced, only the first is extant, but this is enough to demonstrate that Blake, like Priestley and other religious radicals of the day, envisioned the Revolution as the portent of apocalypse. After five thousand years "the ancient dawn calls us/To awake," the Abbé de Sieyès pleads for a peace, freedom, and equality which will effect a regained Eden—"the happy earth sing in its course,/ The mild peaceable nations be opened to heav'n, and men walk with their fathers in bliss"; when his plea is ignored, there are rumblings of a gathering Armageddon, and the book ends with the portent of a first resurrection: "And

9. Leigh Hunt, *The Feast of the Poets* (London, 1814), p. 90; Keats, sonnet, "Great Spirits Now on Earth"; *Shelley's Prose*, pp. 239–40.

the bottoms of the world were open'd, and the graves of arch-angels unseal'd."

The "Introduction" to *Songs of Experience* (1794) calls on us to attend the voice which will sing all Blake's poems from now on: "Hear the voice of the Bard!/ Who Present, Past, & Future, sees," who calls to the lapsèd Soul and enjoins the earth to cease her cycle and turn to the eternal day. This voice is that of the poet-prophets of the Old and New Testaments, now descending on Blake from its specifically British embodiment in that "bard of old," John Milton. In his "minor prophecies," ending in 1795, Blake develops, out of the heroic-scaled but still historical agents of his *French Revolution*, the Giant Forms of his later mythical system. The Bard becomes Los, the "Eternal Prophet" and father of "red Orc," who is the spirit of Energy bursting out in total spiritual, physical, and political revolution; the argument of the song sung by Los, however, remains that announced in *The French Revolution*. As David Erdman has said, *Europe: A Prophecy* (1794) was written at about the time Blake was illustrating Milton's "On the Morning of Christ's Nativity," and reinterprets that poem for his own times.[1] Orc, here identified with Christ the revolutionary, comes with the blare of the apocalyptic trumpet to vex nature out of her sleep of 1,800 years, in a cataclysmic Second Coming in "the vineyards of Red France" which, however, heralds the day when both the earth and its inhabitants will be resurrected in a joyous burst of un-bounded and lustful energy.[2]

By the year 1797 Blake launched out into the "strong heroic Verse" of *Vala, or The Four Zoas*, the first of his three full-scale epics, which recounts the total history of "The Universal Man" from the beginning, through "His fall into Division," to a future that explodes into the most spectacular and sustained apocalyptic set-piece since the Book of Revelation; in this holocaust "the evil is all consum'd" and "all things are chang'd, even as in ancient times." [3]

III. ROMANTIC ORACLES

No amount of historical explanation can make Blake out to be other than a phoenix among poets; but if we put his work into its historical and intellectual context, and alongside that of his poetic contemporaries of the 1790s, we find at least that he is not a freak without historical causes but that he responded to the common circumstances in ways markedly similar, sometimes even to odd

1. *Blake, Prophet Against Empire* (Princeton, 1954), pp. 264 ff.; and see Frye, *Fearful Symmetry*, p. 262.
2. *Europe: A Prophecy*, Plates 9, 12–15. See also *America: A Prophecy* (1793), Plates 6, 8, 16; *The Song of Los* (1795), Plates 3, 7.
3. *Vala, or The Four Zoas*, I, 5, 21; IX, 827, 845.

details. But while fellow-poets soon left off their tentative efforts to evolve a system of "machinery" by which to come to terms with the epic events of their revolutionary era, Blake carried undauntedly on.

What, then, were the attributes shared by the chief poets of the 1790s, Blake, Wordsworth, Southey, Coleridge?—to whom I shall add, Shelley. Byron and Keats also had elements in common with their older contemporaries, but these lie outside the immediate scope of my paper. Shelley, however, though he matured in the cynical era of Napoleon and the English Regency, reiterated remarkably the pattern of his predecessors. By temperament he was more inclusively and extremely radical than anyone but Blake, and his early "principles," as he himself said, had "their origin from the discoveries which preceded and occasioned the revolutions of America and France." That is, he had formed his mind on those writers, from Rousseau through Condorcet, Volney, Paine, and Godwin, whose ideas made up the climate of the 1790s—and also, it should be emphasized, on the King James Bible and *Paradise Lost*.[4]

1. First, these were all centrally political and social poets. It is by a peculiar injustice that Romanticism is often described as a mode of escapism, an evasion of the shocking changes, violence, and ugliness attending the emergence of the modern industrial and political world. The fact is that to a degree without parallel, even among major Victorian poets, these writers were obsessed with the realities of their era. Blake's wife mildly complained that her husband was always in Paradise; but from this vantage point he managed to keep so thoroughly in touch with mundane reality that, as David Erdman has demonstrated, his epics are hardly less steeped in the scenes and events of the day than is that latter-day epic, the *Ulysses* of James Joyce. Wordsworth said that he "had given twelve hours thought to the conditions and prospects of society, for one to poetry";[5] Coleridge, Southey, and Shelley could have made a claim similarly extravagant; all these poets delivered themselves of po-

4. *Proposals for an Association of Philanthropists* (1812), in *Shelley's Prose*, p. 67. Concerning the early formative influences on Shelley's thought, see K. N. Cameron, *The Young Shelley* (London, 1951). Mary Shelley testified that "in English, the Bible was [Shelley's] constant study," that the sublime poetry of the Old Testament "filled him with delight," and that over an extended period in 1816 and 1817, Shelley read both the *Bible and Paradise Lost* aloud to her (*The Complete Poetical Works of P. B. Shelley*, ed. Thomas Hutchinson [London, 1948], pp. 156, 536, 551). See Bennett Weaver, *Toward the Understanding of Shelley* (Ann Arbor, 1932).

5. F. M. Todd, *Politics and the Poet: A Study of Wordsworth* (London, 1957), p. 11. Both of Wordsworth's long poems turn on an extended treatment of the French Revolution—in *The Prelude* as the crisis of his own life as exemplary poet, and in *The Excursion* as the crisis of his generation. See also Carl R. Woodring, *Politics in the Poetry of Coleridge* (Madison, 1961), William Haller, *The Early Life of Robert Southey* (New York, 1917), and K. N. Cameron, *The Young Shelley*.

litical and social commentary in the form of prose-pamphlets, essays, speeches, editorials, or sermons; and all exhibit an explicit or submerged concern with the contemporary historical and intellectual situation in the greater part of their verses, narrative, dramatic, and lyric, long and short.

2. What obscures this concern is that in many poems the Romantics do not write direct political and moral commentary but (in Schorer's apt phrase for Blake) "the politics of vision," uttered in the persona of the inspired prophet-priest. Neoclassic poets had invoked the muse as a formality of the poetic ritual, and the school of sensibility had expressed nostalgia for the "diviner inspiration" of Spenser, Shakespeare, and Milton. But when the Romantic poet asserts inspiration and revelation by a power beyond himself—as Blake did repeatedly, or Shelley in his claim that the great poets of his age are "the priests of an unapprehended inspiration, the mirrors of gigantic shadows which futurity casts upon the present" [6] —he means it. And when Wordsworth called himself "A youthful Druid taught . . . Primeval mysteries, a Bard elect . . . a chosen Son," and Coleridge characterized *The Prelude* as "More than historic, that prophetic Lay," "An Orphic song" uttered by a "great Bard," [7] in an important sense they meant it too, and we must believe that they meant it if we are to read them aright.

The Romantics, then, often spoke confidently as elected members of what Harold Bloom calls "The Visionary Company," the inspired line of singers from the prophets of the Old and New Testaments through Dante, Spenser, and above all Milton. For Milton had an exemplary role in this tradition as the native British (or Druidic) Bard who was a thorough political, social, and religious revolutionary, who claimed inspiration both from a Heavenly Muse and from the Holy Spirit that had supervised the Creation and inspired the biblical prophets, and who, after the failure of his millennial expectations from the English Revolution,[8] had kept his singing voice and salvaged his hope for mankind in an epic poem.

3. Following the Miltonic example, the Romantic poet of the 1790s tried to incorporate what he regarded as the stupendous events of the age in the suitably great poetic forms. He wrote, or planned to write an epic, or (like Milton in *Samson Agonistes*) emulated Aeschylean tragedy, or uttered visions combining the

6. For example, Blake's letter to Thomas Butts, April 25, 1803; Shelley, "A Philosophical View of Reform," *Shelley's Prose*, p. 240.
7. MS A, III, 82–93, in *William Wordsworth, The Prelude*, ed. Ernest De Selincourt and Helen Darbishire (2d ed.; Oxford, 1959), p. 75; Coleridge "To William Wordsworth," ll. 3, 45, 48.
8. On Milton's millennialism see H. J. C. Grierson, *Milton and Wordsworth* (Cambridge, 1937), pp. 32–36.

mode of biblical prophecy with the loose Pindaric, "the sublime" or "greater Ode," which by his eighteenth-century predecessors had been accorded a status next to epic, as peculiarly adapted to an enthusiastic and visionary imagination. Whatever the form, the Romantic Bard is one "who present, past, and future sees"; so that in dealing with current affairs his procedure is often panoramic, his stage cosmic, his agents quasi-mythological, and his logic of events apocalyptic. Typically this mode of Romantic vision fuses history, politics, philosophy, and religion into one grand design, by asserting Providence—or some form of natural teleology—to operate in the seeming chaos of human history so as to effect from present evil a greater good; and through the mid-1790s the French Revolution functions as the symptom or early stage of the abrupt culmination of this design, from which will emerge a new man on a new earth which is a restored Paradise.

To support these large generalizations I need to present a few particulars.

Robert Southey, the most matter-of-fact and worldly of these poets, said that his early adoration of Leonidas, hero of Thermopylae, his early study of Epictetus, "and the French Revolution at its height when I was just eighteen—by these my mind was moulded." [9] The first literary result came a year later, in 1793, when during six weeks of his long vacation from Oxford he wrote *Joan of Arc: An Epic Poem* [1]—with Blake's *French Revolution*, the first English epic worth historical notice since Glover's *Leonidas*, published in 1737. Southey's Joan has been called a Tom Paine in petticoats; she is also given to trances in which "strange events yet in the womb of Time" are to her "made manifest." In the first published version of 1796, Book IX consists of a sustained vision of the realms of hell and purgatory, populated by the standard villains of the radicals' view of history. To Joan is revealed the Edenic past in the "blest aera of the infant world," and man's fall, through lust for gold and power, to this "theatre of woe"; yet "for the best/ Hath he ordained all things, the ALL-WISE!" because man, "Samson-like" shall "burst his fetters" in a violent spasm not quite named the French Revolution,

> and Earth shall once again
> Be Paradise, whilst WISDOM shall secure
> The state of bliss with IGNORANCE betrayed.
> "Oh age of happiness!" the Maid exclaim'd,

9. Quoted by Edward Dowden, *Southey* (New York, 1880), p. 189.
1. Southey's Preface to *Joan of Arc* (1837), *The Poetical Works of Robert Southey* (10 vols.; Boston, 1860), I,

11-12 The next year (1794) with even greater revolutionary élan, Southey dashed off in three mornings the Jacobin *Wat Tyler: A Drama* (*ibid.*, II, 28).

> "Roll fast thy current, Time, till that blest age
> Arrive!" [2]

To the second book of *Joan* Coleridge (then, like Southey, a Unitarian, and like both Southey and Wordsworth, considering entering the clergy) contributed what he called an "Epic Slice," which he soon patched up into an independent poem, *The Destiny of Nations: A Vision*. The vision, beamed "on the Prophet's purgèd eye," reviews history, echoes the Book of Revelation, and ends in the symbolic appearance of a bright cloud (the American Revolution) and a brighter cloud (the French Revolution) from which emerges "A dazzling form," obviously female, yet identified in Coleridge's note as an Apollo-figure, portending that "Soon shall the Morning struggle into Day." [3] With the epomania of the age, Coleridge considered writing an epic of his own, laid out plans which would take twenty years to realize, and let it go at that.[4] His ambition to be the Milton of his day was, in practice, limited to various oracular odes, of which the most interesting for our purpose is *Religious Musings*, his first long poem in blank verse; on this, Coleridge said, "I build all my poetic pretensions." [5] The poem as published bore the title "Religious Musings on Christmas Eve. In the year of Our Lord, 1794," and Coleridge had earlier called it "The Nativity." [6] The year is precisely that of Blake's *Europe: A Prophecy*, and like that poem, *Religious Musings* is clearly a revision for the time being of Milton's "On the Morning of Christ's Nativity," which had taken the occasion of memorializing Christ's birth to anticipate "the wakefull trump of doom" and the universal earthquake which will announce His Second Coming:

> And then at last our bliss
> Full and perfect is.

There is never any risk of mistaking Coleridge's voice for that of Blake, yet a reading of Coleridge's poem with Blake's in mind reveals how remarkably parallel were the effects of the same his-

---

2. *Joan of Arc: An Epic Poem* (Bristol, 1796), Book I, ll. 497–99; Book IX, ll. 825–27, 837–72. In the MS version of 1793, the references to the French Revolution are explicit; see Book XI, ll. 633–749, in Benjamin W. Early, "Southey's *Joan of Arc:* The Unpublished Manuscript, the First Edition, and a Study of the Later Revisions" (MS doctoral thesis, Duke University Library, 1951). Southey wrote in 1830 that "forty years ago I could partake the hopes of those who expected that political revolutions were to bring about a political millennium" (*Correspondence with Caroline Bowles*, p. 200). By 1797, however, he seems to have been prepared to give back to Christ the task of realizing the dreams of Plato and Milton for total "happiness on earth": "Blessed hopes! awhile/ From man withheld, even to the latter days,/ When CHRIST shall come and all things be fulfill'd." ("Inscription IV. For the Apartment in Chepstow Castle," *Poems*, 1797.)

3. "The Destiny of Nations," 11, 464, 326–38, 421–58. See Woodring, *Politics in the Poetry of Coleridge*, pp. 169–73.

4. To Joseph Cottle, April, 1797, in *Collected Letters*, ed. E. L. Griggs (Oxford, 1956–), I, 320–21.

5. *Collected Letters*, I, 197, 205.

6. *Ibid.*, I, 147, 162 and footnote.

torical and literary situation, operating simultaneously on the imagination of the two poets.

Coleridge's opening, "This is the time," echoes "This is the Month" with which Milton begins his Prologue, as Blake's "The deep of winter came" reflects "It was the Winter wild" with which Milton begins the Hymn proper. (Blake's free verse is also at times reminiscent of the movement of Milton's marvelous stanza.) Musing on the significance of the First Advent, Coleridge says, "Behold a VISION gathers in my soul," which provides him, among other things, a survey of human history since "the primeval age" in the form of a brief theodicy, "all the sore ills" of "our mortal life" becoming "the immediate source/ Of mightier good." The future must bring "the fated day" of violent revolution by the oppressed masses, but happily "Philosophers and Bards" exist to mold the wild chaos "with plastic might" into the "perfect forms" of their own inspired visions. Coleridge then presents an interpretation of contemporary affairs which, following his Unitarian mentor, Joseph Priestley, he neatly summarizes in his prose "Argument" as: "The French Revolution. Millennium. Universal Redemption. Conclusion." His procedure is to establish a parallel (developed in elaborate footnotes) between current revolutionary events and the violent prophecies of the Book of Revelation. The machinery of apocalypse is allegorical, with the "Giant Frenzy" given the function of Blake's Orc in "Uprooting empires with his whirlwind arm." In due course the "blest future rushes on my view!" in the form of humankind as a "vast family of Love" living in a communist economy. "The mighty Dead" awaken, and

> To Milton's trump
> The high groves of the renovated Earth
> Unbosom their glad echoes,

in the adoring presence of three English interpreters of millennial prophecy, Newton, Hartley, and Priestley, "patriot, and saint, and sage." [7] (In Blake's *Europe*, not Milton but Newton had "siez'd the trump & blow'd the enormous blast"; as in Coleridge's poem, however, he seemingly appears not in his capacity as scientist but as author of a commentary on the Book of Revelation.)

Wordsworth thought the concluding section of *Religious Musings* on "the renovated Earth" to be the best in Coleridge's *Poems*

7. *Complete Poetical Works*, ed. E. H. Coleridge (2 vols.; Oxford, 1912), I, 108–23, and notes. David Hartley had included his interpretation of millennial prophecy in his *Observations on Man*, Part II, Sections IV and V. In ll. 126–58 of *Religious Musings* Coleridge, like Blake in his later prophecies, interpreted the fall of man as a splintering of social fraternity into anarchic individuality, and his redemption at the Second Coming as a rejunction of separate selves into a single "Self, that no alien knows!" Cf. the opening of Blake's *The Four Zoas*, I, 9–23.

of 1796. On this subject Wordsworth was an expert, for a year prior to the writing of the poem, in 1793, he had concluded his own *Descriptive Sketches* with the prophecy (precisely matching the prophecy he attributed to the Wanderer in his *Excursion*) that the wars consequent on the French Revolution would fulfill the predictions both of the Book of Revelation and of Virgil's Fourth Eclogue:

> —Tho' Liberty shall soon, indignant, raise
> Red on his hills his beacon's comet blaze . . .
> Yet, yet rejoice, tho' Pride's perverted ire
> Rouze Hell's own aid, and wrap thy hills in fire.
> Lo! from th' innocuous flames, a lovely birth!
> With its own Virtues springs another earth:
> Nature, as in her prime, her virgin reign
> Begins, and Love and Truth compose her train . . .
> No more . . .
> On his pale horse shall fell Consumption go.

"How is it," Blake was to ask in his conclusion of *The Four Zoas*, "we have walk'd thro' fires & yet are not consum'd?/ How is it that all things are chang'd, even as in ancient times?"[8]

Some two decades later Shelley recapitulated and expanded these poetic manifestations of the earlier 1790s. At the age of nineteen he began his first long poem, *Queen Mab*, in the mode of a vision of the woeful past, the ghastly present, and the blissful future, and although the concepts are those of the French and English *philosophes*, and the Spirit of Necessity replaces Providence as the agent of redemption, much of the imagery is imported from biblical millennialism. The prophecy is that "A garden shall arise, in loveliness/ Surpassing fabled Eden"; when it eventuates, "All things are recreated," the lion sports "in the sun/ Beside the dreadless kid," and man's intellectual and moral nature participates in "The gradual renovation" until he stands "with taintless body and mind" in a "happy earth! reality of Heaven!" the "consummation of all mortal hope!"[9]

If I may just glance over the fence of my assigned topic: in Germany, as in England, a coincidence of historical, religious, and literary circumstances produced a comparable imaginative result. In the early 1790s the young Hölderlin was caught up in the

8. *Descriptive Sketches* (1793 version), ll. 774–91. Blake, *The Four Zoas*, IX, 844–45; see also *America*, VIII, 15. For Wordsworth's opinion of the apocalyptic passage in Coleridge's *Religious Musings* see Coleridge's *Collected Letters*, I, 215–16. As late as 1808 the Spanish insurrection against Napoleon revived Wordsworth's millennial hopes: "We must trust that Regeneration is at hand: these are works of recovered innocence and wisdom . . . *redeunt Saturnia regna*" (Wordsworth, *The Convention of Cintra*, ed. A. V. Dicey [London, 1915], p. 122; also pp. 10–11). 9. *Queen Mab*, IV, 88–89; VIII, 107 ff.; IX, 1–4.

intoxication of the revolutionary promise; he was at the time a student of theology at Tübingen, and immersed in the literary tradition of *Sturm und Drang* libertarianism, Schiller's early poems, and Klopstock's *Messias* and allegoric odes. A number of Hölderlin's odes of that decade (the two "Hymnen an die Freiheit," the "Hymne an die Menschheit," "Der Zeitgeist") are notably parallel to the English form I have been describing; that is, they are visionary, oracular, panoramic, and see history on the verge of a blessed culmination in which the French Revolution is the crucial event, the Book of Revelation the chief model, and the agencies a combination of Greek divinities, biblical symbols, and abstract personifications of his own devising. In the "Hymne an die Freiheit" of 1792, for example, the rapt poet chants a revelation of man's first pastoral innocence, love, and happiness; this "Paradise" is destroyed by a "curse"; but then in response to a call by the Goddess Liberty, Love "reconciles the long discord" and inaugurates "the new hour of creation" of a free, fraternal, abundantly vital, and radiant century in which "the ancient infamy is cancelled" and "der Erndte grosser Tag beginnt"—"there begins the great day of the harvest." [1]

IV. THE APOCALYPSE OF IMAGINATION

The visionary poems of the earlier 1790s and Shelley's earlier prophecies show imaginative audacity and invention, but they are not, it must be confessed, very good poems. The great Romantic poems were written not in the mood of revolutionary exaltation but in the later mood of revolutionary disillusionment or despair. Many of the great poems, however, do not break with the formative past, but continue to exhibit, in a transformed but recognizable fashion, the scope, the poetic voice, the design, the ideas, and the imagery developed in the earlier period. This continuity of tradition converts what would otherwise be a literary curiosity into a matter of considerable historical interest, and helps us to identify and interpret some of the strange but characteristic elements in later Romantic enterprises.

Here is one out of many available instances. It will have become apparent even from these brief summaries that certain terms, images, and quasi-mythical agents tend to recur and to assume a specialized reference to revolutionary events and expectations: the earthquake and the volcano, the purging fire, the emerging sun, the dawn of glad day, the awakening earth in springtime, the Dionysian

---

1. Hölderlin, *Sämtliche Werke*, ed Friedrich Beissner (Stuttgart, 1946–), Vol. I, Part I, pp. 139–42. See Geneviève Bianquis, "Hölderlin et la révolution française," *Études Germaniques*, VII (1952), 105–16, and Maurice Delorme, *Hölderlin et la révolution française* (Monaco, 1959). The relevance of Hölderlin was pointed out to me by my colleague, Paul de Man.

figure of revolutionary destruction and the Apollonian figure of the
promise of a bright new order. Prominent among these is a term
which functions as one of the principal leitmotifs of Romantic
literature. To Europe at the end of the eighteenth century the
French Revolution brought what St. Augustine said Christianity
had brought to the ancient world: hope. As Coleridge wrote, on
first hearing Wordsworth's *Prelude* read aloud, the poet sang of his
experience "Amid the tremor of a realm aglow,"

> When from the general heart of human kind
> Hope sprang forth like a full-born Deity!

and afterward, "Of that dear Hope afflicted and struck down.
. . ."[2] This is no ordinary hope, but a universal, absolute, and
novel hope which sprang forth from the Revolutionary events sudden and complete, like Minerva. Pervasively in both the verse and
prose of the period, "hope," with its associated term, "joy," and its
opposites, "dejection," "despondency," and "despair," are used in
a special application, as shorthand for the limitless faith in human
and social possibility aroused by the Revolution, and its reflex, the
nadir of feeling caused by its seeming failure—as Wordsworth had
put it, the "utter loss of hope itself/ And things to hope for."
(*The Prelude*, 1805, XI, 6–7.)

It is not irrelevant, I believe, that many seemingly apolitical
poems of the later Romantic period turn on the theme of hope and
joy and the temptation to abandon all hope and fall into dejection
and despair; the recurrent emotional pattern is that of the key
books of *The Excursion*, labeled "Despondency" and "Despondency Corrected," which apply specifically to the failure of millennial hope in the Revolution. But I want to apply this observation
to one of those passages in *The Prelude* where Wordsworth
suddenly breaks through to a prophetic vision of the hidden
significance of the literal narrative. In the sixth book Wordsworth
describes his first tour of France with Robert Jones in the summer
of 1790, the brightest period of the Revolution. The mighty forms
of Nature, "seizing a youthful fancy," had already "given a charter
to irregular hopes," but now all Europe

> was thrilled with joy,
> France standing on the top of golden hours,
> And human nature seeming born again.

2. "To William Wordsworth," ll. 34–
38. Cf., e.g., *The Prelude* (1805), II,
448–66, X, 355–81, 690–728; *The Excursion*, II, 210–23; *The Convention
of Cintra*, pp. 10–11, 157–58, 187–88;
Shelley, Preface to *The Revolt of Islam*,
Poetical Works, pp. 33–34; Hazlitt,
Complete Works, IV, 119–20, XVII,
196–98, 316, and his *Life of Thomas
Holcroft*, ed. Elbridge Colby (2 vols.;
London, 1925), II, 92–93.

Sharing the universal intoxication, "when joy of one" was "joy for tens of millions," they join in feasting and dance with a "blithe host/ Of Travellers" returning from the Federation Festival at Paris, "the great spousals newly solemnised/ At their chief city, in the sight of Heaven." In his revisions of the 1805 version of *The Prelude*, Wordsworth inserted at this point a passage in which he sees, with anguished foreboding, the desecration by French troops of the Convent of the Chartreuse (an event which did not take place until two years later, in 1792). The travelers' way then brings them to the Simplon Pass.

Wordsworth's earlier account of this tour in the *Descriptive Sketches*, written mainly in 1791–92, had ended with the prophecy of a new earth emerging from apocalyptic fires, and a return to the golden age. Now, however, he describes a strange access of sadness, a "melancholy slackening." On the Simplon road they had left their guide and climbed ever upward, until a peasant told them that they had missed their way and that the course now lay downwards.

> Loth to believe what we so grieved to hear,
> For still we had hopes that pointed to the clouds,
> We questioned him again, and yet again;

but every reply "Ended in this,—*that we had crossed the Alps*."

> Imagination . . .
> That awful Power rose from the mind's abyss
> Like an unfathered vapour that enwraps,
> At once, some lonely traveller; I was lost;
> Halted without an effort to break through;
> But to my conscious soul I now can say—
> "I recognise thy glory". . . .

Only now, in retrospect, does he recognize that his imagination had penetrated to the emblematic quality of the literal climb, in a revelation proleptic of the experience he was to recount in all the remainder of *The Prelude*. Man's infinite hopes can never be matched by the world as it is and man as he is, for these exhibit a discrepancy no less than that between his "hopes that pointed to the clouds" and the finite height of the Alpine pass. But in the magnitude of the disappointment lies its consolation; for the flash of vision also reveals that infinite longings are inherent in the human spirit, and that the gap between the inordinacy of his hope and the limits of possibility is the measure of man's dignity and greatness:

> Our destiny, our being's heart and home,
> Is with infinitude, and only there;

> With hope it is, hope that can never die,
> Effort, and expectation, and desire,
> And something evermore about to be.

In short, Wordsworth evokes from the unbounded and hence impossible hopes in the French Revolution a central Romantic doctrine; one which reverses the cardinal neoclassic ideal of setting only accessible goals, by converting what had been man's tragic error—the inordinacy of his "pride" that persists in setting infinite aims for finite man—into his specific glory and his triumph. Wordsworth shares the recognition of his fellow-Romantics, German and English, of the greatness of man's infinite *Sehnsucht*, his saving insatiability, "Blake's "I want! I want!" [3] Shelley's "the desire of the moth for the star"; but with a characteristic and unique difference, as he goes on at once to reveal:

> Under such banners militant, the soul
> Seeks for no trophies, struggles for no spoils
> That may attest her prowess, blest in thoughts
> That are their own perfection and reward. . . .

The militancy of overt political action has been transformed into the paradox of spiritual quietism: under such militant banners is no march, but a wise passiveness. This truth having been revealed to him, Wordsworth at once goes on to his apocalypse of nature in the Simplon Pass, where the *coincidentia oppositorum* of its physical attributes become the symbols of the biblical Book of Revelation:

> Characters of the great Apocalypse,
> The types and symbols of Eternity,
> Of first, and last, and midst, and without end. [4]

This and its companion passages in *The Prelude* enlighten the orphic darkness of Wordsworth's "Prospectus" for *The Recluse*, drafted as early as 1800, when *The Prelude* had not yet been

---

3. It is an interesting coincidence that Blake's "I want! I want!" (which is illustrated by a man climbing a ladder reaching to the moon) was his retort to a political cartoon by Gillray caricaturing the inordinacy of revolutionary hope, by depicting a short ladder pointing futilely toward the moon. See Erdman, *Blake, Prophet Against Empire*, pp. 186–88. The parable, in its political application, was a familiar one; thus Edmund Burke had said (1780): "If we cry, like children, for the moon, like children we must cry on" (*The Works of the Right Honorable Edmund Burke* [12 vols., London, 1899], II, 357).

4. *The Prelude* (1850), VI, 322–640. On the glory of infinite promise aroused by the Revolution see also *ibid.*, XI, 105–23. Wordsworth's later revision of the passage of apocalyptic hope in the *Descriptive Sketches* of 1793 parallels the emblematic significance of the Alpine crossing:
Lo, from the flames, a great and
     glorious birth;
As if a new-made heaven were hailing
     a new earth!
—All cannot be: the promise is too fair
For creatures doomed to breathe
     terrestrial air. . . .
(*Poetical Works*, I, 89)

differentiated from the larger poem. Woodsworth's aim, he there reveals, is still that of the earlier period of millennial hope in revolution, still expressed in a fusion of biblical and classical imagery. Evil is to be redeemed by a regained Paradise, or Elysium: "Paradise," he says, "and groves/ Elysian, Fortunate Fields . . . why should they be/ A history only of departed things?" And the restoration of Paradise, as in the Book of Revelation, is still symbolized by a sacred marriage. But the hope has been shifted from the history of mankind to the mind of the single individual, from militant external action to an imaginative act; and the marriage between the Lamb and the New Jerusalem has been converted into a marriage between subject and object, mind and nature, which creates a new world out of the old world of sense:

> For the discerning intellect of Man,
> When wedded to this goodly universe
> In love and holy passion, shall find these
> A simple produce of the common day.
> —I, long before the blissful hour arrives,
> Would chant, in lonely peace, the spousal verse
> Of this great consummation . . .
> And the creation (by no lower name
> Can it be called) which they with blended might
> Accomplish:—this is our high argument.[5]

In the other Romantic visionaries, as in Wordsworth, naive millennialism produced mainly declamation, but the shattered trust in premature political revolution and the need to reconstitute the grounds of hope lay behind the major achievements. And something close to Wordsworth's evolution—the shift to a spiritual and moral revolution which will transform our experience of the old world—is also the argument of a number of the later writings of Blake, Coleridge, Shelley, and, with all his differences, Hölderlin. An example from Shelley must suffice. Most of Shelley's large enterprises after *Queen Mab*—*The Revolt of Islam, Prometheus Unbound, Hellas*—were inspired by a later recrudescence of the European revolutionary movement. Shelley's view of human motives and possibilities became more and more tragic, and, like Blake after his *French Revolution*, he moved from the bald literalism of *Queen Mab* to an imaginative form increasingly biblical, symbolic, and mythic; but the theme continues to be the ultimate promise of a renovation in human nature and circumstances. In *Prometheus Unbound* this event is symbolized by the reunion of Prometheus and Asia in a joyous ceremony in which all the cosmos participates. But this new world is one which reveals itself to the purged

5. *Poetical Works*, ed. De Selincourt, V, 3–5.

imagination of Man when he has reformed his moral nature at its deep and twisted roots; and the last words of Demogorgon, the inscrutable agent of this apocalypse, describe a revolution of spirit whose sole agencies are the cardinal virtues of endurance, forgiveness, love, and, above all, hope—though a hope that is now hard to distinguish from despair:

> To suffer woes which Hope thinks infinite . . .
> To love, and bear; to hope till Hope creates
> From its own wreck the thing it contemplates . . .
> This is alone Life, Joy, Empire, and Victory!

v. WORDSWORTH'S OTHER VOICE

"Two voices are there. . . . And, Wordsworth, both are thine." I have as yet said nothing about Wordsworth's *Lyrical Ballads* and related poems, although Hazlitt regarded these as the inauguration of a new poetic era and the close poetic equivalent to the revolutionary politics of the age. Yet the *Ballads* seem in every way antithetical to the poetry I have just described: instead of displaying a panoramic vision of present, past, and future in an elevated oracular voice, these poems undertake to represent realistic "incidents and situations from common life" in ordinary language and to employ "humble and rustic life" as the main source of the simple characters and the model for the plain speech.

Here are some of the reasons Hazlitt gives for his claim that "the political changes of the day were the model on which [Wordsworth] formed and conducted his poetical experiments":

> His Muse (it cannot be denied, and without this we cannot explain its character at all) is a levelling one. It proceeds on a principle of equality, and strives to reduce all things to the same standard. . . .
> His popular, inartificial style gets rid (at a blow) of all the trappings of verse, of all the high places of poetry. . . . We begin *de novo*, on a tabula rasa of poetry. . . . The distinctions of rank, birth, wealth, power . . . are not to be found here. . . . The harp of Homer, the trump of Pindar and of Alcaeus, are still.[6]

Making due allowance for his love of extravagance, I think that Hazlitt makes out a very plausible case. He shrewdly recognizes

6. *The Spirit of the Age, Complete Works*, XI, 87. Cf. "On the Living Poets," *ibid.*, V. 161–64. Christopher Wordsworth, though his loyalties were the polar opposites of Hazlitt's, also accounted for the theory of *Lyrical Ballads* in political terms: "The clue to his *poetical* theory, in some of its questionable details, may be found in his *political* principles; these had been democratical, and still, though in some degree modified, they were of a republican character." (*Memoirs of William Wordsworth* [2 vols., Boston, 1851], I, 127.)

that Wordsworth's criteria are as much social as literary, and that by their egalitarianism they subvert the foundations of a view of poetry inherited from the Renaissance. This view assumed and incorporated a hierarchical structure of social classes. In its strict form, it conceived poetry as an order of well-defined genres, controlled by a theory of decorum whereby the higher poetic kinds represent primarily kings and the aristocracy, the humbler classes (in other than a subsidiary function) are relegated to the lowlier forms, and each poem is expressed in a level of style—high, middle, or low—appropriate, among other things, to the social status of its characters and the dignity of its genre. In England after the sixteenth century, this system had rarely been held with continental rigor, and eighteenth-century critics and poets had carried far the work of breaking down the social distinctions built into a poetic developed for an aristocratic audience. But Wordsworth's practice, buttressed by a strong critical manifesto, carried an existing tendency to an extreme which Hazlitt regarded as a genuine innovation, an achieved revolution against the *ancien régime* in literature. He is, Hazlitt said, "the most original poet now living, and the one whose writings could least be spared: for they have no substitute elsewhere." And Wordsworth has not only leveled, he has transvalued Renaissance and neoclassic aesthetics, by deliberately seeking out the ignominious, the delinquent, and the social outcast as subjects for serious or tragic consideration—not only, Hazlitt noted, "peasants, pedlars, and village-barbers," but also "convicts, female vagrants, gipsies . . . ideot boys and mad mothers." [7] Hence the indignation of Lord Byron, who combined political liberalism with a due regard for aristocratic privilege and traditional poetic decorum:

> "Peddlers," and "Boats," and "Wagons"! Oh! ye shades
> Of Pope and Dryden, are we come to this?

In his Preface to *Lyrical Ballads* Wordsworth justified his undertaking mainly by the ultimate critical sanctions then available, of elemental and permanent "nature" as against the corruptions and necessarily short-lived fashions of "art." But Wordsworth also dealt with the genesis and rationale of *Lyrical Ballads* in several other writings, and in terms broader than purely critical, and these passage clearly relate his poems of humble lives in the plain style to his concept and practice of poetry in the grand oracular style.

In the crucial thirteenth book of *The Prelude* Wordsworth describes how, trained "to meekness" and exalted by "humble faith," he turned from disillusionment with the "sublime/ In

---

7. *Complete Works*, **XI**, 89, V, 162– 63. On the novelty of Wordsworth's   poems see also V, 156, and **XVII**, 117.

what the Historian's pen so much delights/ To blazon," to "fraternal love" for "the unassuming things that hold/ A silent station in this beauteous world," and so to a surrogate for his lost revolutionary hopes:

> The promise of the present time retired
> Into its true proportion; sanguine schemes,
> Ambitious projects, pleased me less; I sought
> For present good in life's familiar face,
> And built thereon my hopes of good to come.

He turned, that is, away from Man as he exists only in the hopes of naive millennialists or the abstractions of the philosophers of perfectibility to "the man whom we behold/ With our own eyes"; and especially to the humble and obscure men of the lower and rural classes, "who live/ By bodily toil," free from the "artificial lights" of urban upper-class society, and utter the spontaneous overflow of powerful feelings ("Expressing liveliest thoughts in lively words/ As native passion dictates"). "Of these, said I, shall be my song." But, he insists, in this new subject he continues to speak "things oracular," for though he is "the humblest," he stands in the great line of the "Poets, even as Prophets, each with each/ Connected in a mighty scheme of truth," each of whom possesses "his own peculiar faculty,/ Heaven's gift, a sense that fits him to perceive/ Objects unseen before." And chief among the prophetic insights granted to Wordsworth is the discovery that Nature has the power to "consecrate" and "to breathe/ Grandeur upon the very humblest face/ Of human life," as well as upon the works of man, even when these are "mean, have nothing lofty of their own." [8]

We come here to a central paradox among the various ones that lurk in the oracular passages of Wordsworth's major period: the oxymoron of the humble-grand, the lofty-mean, the trivial-sublime —as Hazlitt recognized when he said that Wordsworth's Muse "is distinguished by a proud humility," and that he "elevates the mean" and endeavors "(not in vain) to aggrandise the trivial." [9] The ultimate source of this concept is, I think, obvious, and Wordsworth several times plainly points it out for us. Thus in *The Ruined Cottage* (1797–98) the Pedlar (whose youthful experiences parallel Wordsworth's, as the poet showed by later transferring a number of passages to *The Prelude*) had first studied the Scriptures, and only afterward had come to "*feel* his faith" by discovering the corresponding symbol-system, "the writing," in the great book of nature, where "the least of things/ Seemed infinite," so that (as a "chosen son") his own "being thus became/ Sublime and compre-

8. *The Prelude* (1850), XIII, 11–312.   9. *Complete Works*, XI, 87–89.

hensive. . . . Yet was his heart/ Lowly"; he also learned to recognize in the simple people of rural life what Wordsworth in a note called "the aristocracy of nature." [1] The ultimate source of Wordsworth's discovery, that is, was the Bible, and especially the New Testament, which is grounded on the radical paradox that "the last shall be first," and dramatizes that fact in the central mystery of God incarnate as a lowly carpenter's son who takes fishermen for his disciples, consorts with beggars, publicans, and fallen women, and dies ignominiously, crucified with thieves. This interfusion of highest and lowest, the divine and the base, as Erich Auerbach has shown, had from the beginning been a stumbling-block to readers habituated to the classical separation of levels of subject-matter and style, and Robert Lowth in the mid-eighteenth century still found it necessary to insist, as had Augustine and other theologians almost a millennium and a half earlier, that the style of the Bible had its special propriety and was genuinely sublime, and not, as it seemed to a cultivated taste, indecorous, vulgar, barbarous, grotesque.[2] Wordsworth, it should be recalled, had had a pious mother, attended a church school at Hawkeshead, and was intended for the clergy. In this aspect his poetic reflects a movement in eighteenth-century pietism and evangelicalism which had emphasized, in the theological term, God's "condescension" or "accommodation" in revealing his immense divinity to the limited human mind through the often trivial events of Scripture, as well as in sending his son to be born as the lowliest among men. The archetypal figure, among Wordsworth's many numinous solitaries, is the humble shepherd magnified in the mist, "glorified" by the setting sun, and "descried in distant sky,"

> A solitary object and sublime,
> Above all height! like an aerial cross
> Stationed alone upon a spiry rock
> Of the Chartreuse, for worship. Thus was man
> Ennobled outwardly before my sight—

apotheosized, rather, as *figura Christi*, the Good Shepherd himself; for by such means Wordsworth learned, he says, to see Man

1. "The Ruined Cottage," in *Poetical Works*, V, 379 ff., ll. 53–59, 145–66, 264–75; and p. 411, note to l. 341 of the revised version in *The Excursion*, Book I.

2. Robert Lowth, *Lectures on the Sacred Poetry of the Hebrews* (1753) (London, 1874), pp. 79–84 and *passim*. On earlier theological discussions of the Christian paradox of *humilitas-sublimitas*, see Erich Auerbach, *Mimesis* (Princeton, 1953), pp. 72–73, 151–55, "Sermo Humilis," *Romanische Forschungen*, LXIV (1952), 304–64, and "St. Francis of Assisi in Dante's *Commedia*," in *Scenes from the Drama of European Literature* (New York, 1959), pp. 79–98; also Joseph Mazzeo, "St. Augustine's Rhetoric of Silence," *Journal of the History of Ideas*, XXIII (1962), 183 ff.

"As, more than anything we know, instinct/ With godhead," while yet "acknowledging dependency sublime." [3]

An important document connecting the religious, political, and aesthetic elements in his poetic theory is Wordsworth's neglected "Essay, Supplementary to the Preface" of 1815, in which he undertakes to explain at length why his *Lyrical Ballads* had been met with almost "unremitting hostility" ever since they appeared. The argument is extraordinarily contorted, even for Wordsworth's prose; but this, I believe, is the gist of it. "The higher poetry," especially when it "breathes the spirit of religion," unites "grandeur" and "simplicity," and in consequence is apt to evoke dislike, contempt, suspicion from the reader.

> For when Christianity, the religion of humility, is founded upon the proudest faculty of our nature [imagination], what can be expected but contradictions? . . .
>
> The commerce between Man and His Maker cannot be carried on but by a process where much is represented in little, and the Infinite Being accommodates himself to a finite capacity. In all this may be perceived the affinity between religion and poetry.

(In the sentence before the last, Wordsworth defines exactly the theological concept of "accommodation" or "condescension.") Wordsworth then puts himself at the end of a long list of great poets who had been neglected or misunderstood; necessarily so, for original genius consists in doing well "what was never done before," and so introducing "a new element into the intellectual universe"; hence such an author has "the task of *creating* the taste by which he is to be enjoyed." Wordsworth's originality, he says (Hazlitt made essentially the same claim), lies in producing a revolutionary mode of sublimity in poetry. Can it, then,

> be wondered that there is little existing preparation for a poet charged with a new mission to extend its kingdom [i.e., of sublimity] and to augment and spread its enjoyments?

The "instinctive wisdom" and "heroic" (that is, epic) "passions" of the ancients have united in his heart "with the meditative wisdom of later ages" (that is, of the Christian era) to produce the imaginative mode of "sublimated humanity," and "*there*, the poet must reconcile himself for a season to few and scattered hearers." For he must create the taste by which his innovation is to be enjoyed by stripping from the reader's literary responses their

3. *The Prelude* (1850), VIII, 256–76, 492–94. Cf. Philippians 2:7–9: Christ took on "the form of a servant" and humbled himself" even unto "the death of the cross. Wherefore God also hath highly exalted him. . . ." See also, e.g., Matthew 23:11–12 and I Cor-inthians 1:27–28. On the history of the theological concept of "condescensio," with special reference to the eighteenth century, see Karlfried Gründer, *Figur und Geschichte* (Freiburg/Munich, 1958).

ingrained class-consciousness and social snobbery—what Wordsworth calls "the prejudices of false refinement," "pride," and
"vanity"—so as to establish "that dominion over the spirits of
readers by which they are to be humbled and humanised, in order
that they may be purified and exalted." [4] Having given up the hope
of revolutionizing the social and political structure, Wordsworth
has discovered that his new calling, his divine "mission," con-
demning him to a period of inevitable neglect and scorn, is to effect
through his poetry an egalitarian revolution of the spirit (what he
elsewhere calls "an entire regeneration" of his upper-class readers) [5]
so that they may share his revelation of the equivalence of souls, the
heroic dimensions of common life, and the grandeur of the ordinary
and the trivial in Nature.

In his account of this same discovery in *The Prelude*, Book XIII,
Wordsworth says that in his exercise of a special power, unprece-
dented in literature, "Upon the vulgar forms of present things,/
The actual world of our familiar days,"

> I remember well
> That in life's every-day appearances
> I seemed about this time to gain clear sight
> Of a new world,

capable of being made visible "to other eyes," which is the product
of "A balance, an ennobling interchange," between "the object
seen, and eye that sees." [6] This carries us back to the "Prospectus"
to *The Recluse*, for it is clear that this "new world" is an aspect of
the re-created universe there represented as "A simple produce of
the common day," if only we learn to marry our mind to nature
"In love and holy passion." And if we put the "Prospectus" back
into its original context in the concluding section of *Home at
Grasmere*, we find that this document, written precisely at the turn
of the century, gathers together the various themes with which we
have been dealing: the sense of divine mission and illumination,
the conversion of his aspiration for millennial achievements beyond
possibility into its spiritual equivalent in a militant quietism, and
the replacement of his epic schemes by a new poetic enterprise, to
communicate his transforming vision of the common man and the
ordinary universe.

In the seclusion of Grasmere vale, Wordsworth has dismissed

---

4. "Essay, Supplementary to the Preface" of 1815, in *Poetical Works*, II,
411–29. Cf. the letter to J. K. Miller,
Dec. 17, 1831. De Quincey agreed with
Wordsworth (and Hazlitt) that the
Lyrical Ballads were without literary
precedent: "I found in these poems . . .
an absolute revelation of untrodden
worlds . . ." (*Collected Writings*, II,
139).
5. In a letter to Lady Beaumont, May
21, 1807, on the same subject as the
"Essay Supplementary," in *Wordsworth's Literary Criticism*, ed. Nowell
C. Smith (London, 1905), p. 54.
6. *The Prelude* (1850), XIII, 352–78.

"all Arcadian dreams,/ All golden fancies of the golden Age" that is "to be/ Ere time expire," yet finds remaining a "sufficient hope." He proclaims that "yet to me I feel/ That an internal brightness is vouchsafed," something that "is shared by none," which impels him, "divinely taught," to speak "Of what in man is human or divine." The voice of Reason sanctions the lesson which Nature has stealthily taught him:

> Be mild and cleave to gentle things,
> Thy glory and thy happiness be there.
> Nor fear, though thou confide in me, a want
> Of aspirations that *have* been, of foes
> To wrestle with, and victory to complete,
> Bounds to be leapt, darkness to be explored . . .
> All shall survive—though changed their office. . . .

Therefore he bids "farewell to the Warrior's schemes," as well as to "that other hope, long mine, the hope to fill/ The heroic trumpet with the Muse's breath!" But having given up his ambition for a Miltonic epic, he at once finds that his new argument exceeds in its scope the height of Milton's "heaven of heavens" and the depths of Milton's hell, and that it presents its imaginative equivalent of a restored Paradise. Hence he will need, he claims— in that union of arrogance with humility which characterizes all poet-prophets who know they are inspired, but by a power for which they are not responsible—a Muse that will outsoar Milton's, just as Milton had claimed that his Muse would outsoar "th' Aonian Mount" of the pagan Homer. "Urania," Wordsworth says,

> I shall need
> Thy guidance, or a greater Muse, if such
> Descend to earth or dwell in highest heaven! [7]

Wordsworth, then, in the period beginning about 1797, came to see his destiny to lie in spiritual rather than in overt action and adventure, and to conceive his radical poetic vocation to consist in communicating his unique and paradoxical, hence inevitably misunderstood, revelation of the more-than-heroic grandeur of the humble, the contemned, the ordinary, and the trivial, whether in the plain style of direct ballad-like representation, or in the elevated voice in which he presents himself in his office as recipient of this gift of vision. In either case, the mode in which Wordsworth conceived his mission evolved out of the ambition to participate in the renovation of the world and of man which he had shared with his fellow-poets during the period of revolutionary enthusiasm. Both the oracular and the plain poetry, in the last

7. *Home at Grasmere* (1800), in   664–750; "Prospectus," ll. 25–71.
Poetical Works, V, 334 ff., ll. 625–34,

analysis, go back beyond Milton, to that inexhaustible source of radical thought, the Bible—the oracular poetry to the Old Testament prophets and their descendant, the author of the Book of Revelation, and the plain poetry to the story of Christ and to His pronouncements on the exaltation of the lowly and the meek. For the Jesus of the New Testament, as the Reverend Mark Wilks had said in 1791, was indeed "a revolutionary," though not a political one; and Wordsworth, in his long career as apologist for the Anglican Establishment, never again came so close to the spirit of primitive Christianity as in the latter 1790s when, according to Coleridge, he had been still "a Republican & at least a *Semi*-atheist." [8]

NORTHROP FRYE

The Road of Excess [†]

It will be easiest for me to begin with a personal reference. My first sustained effort in scholarship was an attempt to work out a unified commentary on the prophetic books of Blake. These poems are mythical in shape: I had to learn something about myth to write about them, and so I discovered, after the book was published, that I was a member of a school of "myth criticism" of which I had not previously heard. My second effort, completed ten years later, was an attempt to work out a unified commentary on the theory of literary criticism, in which again myth had a prominent place. To me, the progress from one interest to the other was inevitable, and it was obvious to anyone who read both books that my critical ideas had been derived from Blake. How completely the second book was contained in embryo in the first, however, was something I did not realize myself until I recently read through *Fearful Symmetry*, for the first time in fifteen years, in order to write a preface to a new paperback edition. It seems perhaps worth while to examine what has been so far a mere assumption, the actual connecting links between my study of Blake and my study of the

8. To John Thelwall, May 13, 1796, *Collected Letters*, I, 216.
† From *Myth and Symbol*, ed. Bernice Slote. Copyright © 1963 by the University of Nebraska Press. Reprinted by permission of the publisher.

theory of criticism. At least the question is interesting to me, and so provides the only genuine motive yet discovered for undertaking any research.

Blake is one of the poets who believe that, as Wallace Stevens says, the only subject of poetry is poetry itself, and that the writing of a poem is itself a theory of poetry. He interests a critic because he removes the barriers between poetry and criticism. He defines the greatest poetry as "allegory addressed to the intellectual powers," and defends the practice of not being too explicit on the ground that it "rouzes the faculties to act." His language in his later prophecies is almost deliberately colloquial and "unpoetic," as though he intended his poetry to be also a work of criticism, just as he expected the critic's response to be also a creative one. He understood, in his own way, the principle later stated by Arnold that poetry is a criticism of life, and it was an uncompromising way. For him, the artist demonstrates a certain way of life: his aim is not to be appreciated or admired, but to transfer to others the imaginative habit and energy of his mind. The main work of criticism is teaching, and teaching for Blake cannot be separated from creation.

Blake's statements about art are extreme enough to make it clear that he is demanding some kind of mental adjustment to take them in. One of the Laocoon Aphorisms reads: "A Poet, a Painter, a Musician, an Architect: the Man Or Woman who is not one of them is not a Christian." If we respond to this in terms of what we ordinarily associate with the words used, the aphorism will sound, as Blake intended it to sound, like someone in the last stages of paranoia. Blake has an unusual faculty for putting his central beliefs in this mock-paranoid form, and in consequence has deliberately misled all readers who would rather believe that he was mad than that their own use of language could be inadequate. Thus when a Devil says in *The Marriage of Heaven and Hell:* "those who envy or calumniate great men hate God; for there is no other God," our habitual understanding of the phrase "great men" turns the remark into something that makes Carlyle at his worst sound by comparison like a wise and prudent thinker. When we read in the *Descriptive Catalogue,* however, that Chaucer's Parson is "according to Christ's definition, the greatest of his age," we begin to wonder if this paradoxical Devil has really so sulphurous a smell. Similarly, Blake's equating of the arts with Christianity implies, first, that his conception of art includes much more than we usually associate with it, and, second, that it excludes most of what we do associate with it. Blake is calling a work of art what a more conventional terminology would call a charitable act, while at the same time the painting of, say, Reynolds is for him not bad painting but antipainting. Whether we agree or sympathize with Blake's attitude, what he says does involve a whole theory of criticism, and this theory we should examine.

One feature of Blake's prophecies which strikes every reader is the gradual elimination, especially in the two later poems *Milton* and *Jerusalem* that form the climax of this part of his work, of anything resembling narrative movement. The following passage occurs in Plate 71 of *Jerusalem:*

> What is Above is Within, for every-thing in Eternity is
> translucent:
> The Circumference is Within, Without is formed the
> Selfish Center,
> And the Circumference still expands going forward to
> Eternity,
> And the Center has Eternal States; these States we now
> explore.

I still have the copy of Blake that I used as an undergraduate, and I see that in the margin beside this passage I have written the words "Something moves, anyhow." But even that was more of an expression of hope than of considered critical judgement. This plotless type of writing has been discussed a good deal by other critics, notably Hugh Kenner and Marshall McLuhan, who call it "mental landscape," and ascribe its invention to the French *symbolistes*. But in Blake we not only have the technique already complete, but an even more thoroughgoing way of presenting it.

If we read *Milton* and *Jerusalem* as Blake intended them to be read, we are not reading them in any conventional sense at all: we are staring at a sequence of plates, most of them with designs. We can see, of course, that a sequence of illustrated plates would be an intolerably cumbersome and inappropriate method of presenting a long poem in which narrative was the main interest. The long poems of other poets that Blake illustrated, such as Young's *Night Thoughts* and Blair's *Grave*, are meditative poems where, even without Blake's assistance, the reader's attention is expected to drop out of the text every so often and soar, or plunge, whichever metaphor is appropriate, although perhaps wander is even more accurate. No doubt the development of Blake's engraving technique had much to do with the plotlessness of the engraved poems. We notice that the three poems of Blake in which the sense of narrative movement is strongest—*Tiriel, The French Revolution, The Four Zoas*—were never engraved. We notice too that the illustration on a plate often does not illustrate the text on the same plate, and that in one copy of *Jerusalem* the sequence of plates in Part Two is slightly different. The elimination of narrative movement is clearly central to the structure of these poems, and the device of a sequence of plates is consistent with the whole scheme, not a mere accident.

The theme of *Milton* is an instant of illumination in the mind of the poet, an instant which, like the moments of recognition in Proust, links him with a series of previous moments stretching back to the creation of the world. Proust was led to see men as giants in time, but for Blake there is only one giant, Albion, whose dream is time. For Blake in *Milton*, as for Eliot in *Little Gidding*, history is a pattern of timeless moments. What is said, so to speak, in the text of *Milton* is designed to present the context of the illuminated moment as a single simultaneous pattern of apprehension. Hence it does not form a narrative, but recedes spatially, as it were, from that moment. *Jerusalem* is conceived like a painting of the Last Judgement, stretching from heaven to hell and crowded with figures and allusions. Again, everything said in the text is intended to fit somewhere into this simultaneous conceptual pattern, not to form a linear narrative. If I ever get a big enough office, I shall have the hundred plates of my *Jerusalem* reproduction framed and hung around the walls, so that the frontispiece will have the second plate on one side and the last plate on the other. This will be *Jerusalem* presented as Blake thought of it, symbolizing the state of mind in which the poet himself could say: "I see the Past, Present & Future existing all at once Before me." In the still later Job engravings the technique of placing the words within a pictorial unit is of course much more obvious.

Many forms of literature, including the drama, fiction, and epic and narrative poetry, depend on narrative movement in a specific way. That is, they depend for their appeal on the participation of the reader or listener in the narrative as it moves along in time. It is continuity that keeps us turning the pages of a novel, or sitting in a theatre. But there is always something of a summoned-up illusion about such continuity. We may keep reading a novel or attending to a play "to see how it turns out." But once we know how it turns out, and the spell ceases to bind us, we tend to forget the continuity, the very element in the play or novel that enabled us to participate in it. Remembering the plot of anything seems to be unusually difficult. Every member of this audience is familiar with many literary narratives, could even lecture on them with very little notice, and yet could not give a consecutive account of what happened in them, just as all the evangelical zeal of the hero of *The Way of All Flesh* was not equal to remembering the story of the resurrection of Christ in the Gospel of John. Nor does this seem particularly regrettable. Just as the pun is the lowest form of wit, so it is generally agreed, among knowledgeable people like ourselves, that summarizing a plot is the lowest form of criticism.

I have dealt with this question elsewhere, and can only give the main point here. Narrative in literature may also be seen as theme, and theme *is* narrative, but narrative seen as a simultaneous unity. At a certain point in the narrative, the point which Aristotle calls *anagnorisis* or recognition, the sense of linear continuity or participation in the action changes perspective, and what we now see is a total design or unifying structure in the narrative. In detective stories, when we find out who done it, or in certain types of comedy or romance that depend on what are now called "gimmicks," such as Jonson's *Epicoene*, the point of *anagnorisis* is the revelation of something which has previously been a mystery. In such works Aristotle's word *anagnorisis* is best translated "discovery." But in most serious works of literature, and more particularly in epics and tragedies, the better translation is "recognition." The reader already knows what is going to happen, but wishes to see, or rather to participate in, the completion of the design.

Thus the end of reading or listening is the beginning of critical understanding, and nothing that we call criticism can begin until the whole of what it is striving to comprehend has been presented to it. Participation in the continuity of narrative leads to the discovery or recognition of the theme, which *is* the narrative seen as total design. This theme is what, as we say, the story has been all about, the point of telling it. What we reach at the end of participation becomes the center of our critical attention. The elements in the narrative thereupon regroup themselves in a new way. Certain unusually vivid bits of characterization or scenes of exceptional intensity move up near the center of our memory. This reconstructing and regrouping of elements in our critical response to a narrative goes on more or less unconsciously, but the fact that it goes on is what makes remembering plot so difficult.

Thus there are two kinds of response to a work of literature, especially one that tells a story. The first kind is a participating response in time, moving in measure like a dancer with the rhythm of continuity. It is typically an uncritical, or more accurately a precritical response. We cannot begin criticism, strictly speaking, until we have heard the author out, unless he is a bore, when the critical response starts prematurely and, as we say, we can't get into the book. The second kind of response is thematic, detached, fully conscious, and one which sees and is capable of examining the work as a simultaneous whole. It may be an act of understanding, or it may be a value-judgement, or it may be both. Naturally these two types of response overlap more in practice than I suggest here, but the distinction between them is clear enough, and fundamental in the theory of criticism. Some critics, including Professors Wimsatt and Beardsley in *The Verbal Icon*, stress the deficiencies of "holism" as a critical theory; but we should distinguish between "holism" as a critical theory and as a heuristic principle.

There are of course great differences of emphasis within literature itself, according to which kind of response the author is more interested in. At one pole of fiction we have the pure storyteller, whose sole interest is in suspense and the pacing of narrative, and who could not care less what the larger meaning of his story was, or what a critic would find in it afterwards. The attitude of such a storyteller is expressed in the well-known preface to *Huckleberry Finn*: "Persons attempting to find a motive in this narrative will be prosecuted; persons attempting to find a plot in it will be shot." Motive and moral and plot certainly are in *Huckleberry Finn*, but the author, or so he says, doesn't want to hear about them. All the storyteller wants to do is to keep the attention of his audience to the end: once the end is reached, he has no further interest in his audience. He may even be hostile to criticism or anti-intellectual in his attitude to literature, afraid that criticism will spoil the simple entertainment that he designed. The lyrical poet concerned with expressing certain feelings or emotions in the lyrical conventions of his day often takes a similar attitude, because it is natural for him to identify his conventional literary emotions with his "real" personal emotions. He therefore feels that if the critic finds any meaning or significance in his work beyond the intensity of those emotions, it must be only what the critic wants to say instead. Anti-critical statements are usually designed only to keep the critic in his place, but the attitude they represent, when genuine, is objective, thrown outward into the designing of the continuity. It is the attitude that Schiller, in his essay on *Naive and Sentimental Poetry*, means by naive, and which includes what we mean in English by naive. Naive writers' *obiter dicta* are often repeated, for consolation, by the kind of critic who is beginning to suspect that literary criticism is a more difficult discipline than he realized when he entered into it. But it is not possible for any reader today to respond to a work of literature with complete or genuine naivete. Response is what Schiller calls sentimental by its very nature, and is hence to some degree involved with criticism.

If we compare, let us say, Malory with Spenser, we can see that Malory's chief interest is in telling the stories in the "French book" he is using. He seems to know that some of them, especially the Grail stories, have overtones in them that the reader will linger with long after he has finished reading. But Malory makes no explicit reference to this, nor does one feel that Malory himself, preoccupied as he was with a nervous habit of robbing churches, would have been much interested in a purely critical reaction to his book. But for Spenser it is clear that the romance form, the quest of the knight journeying into a dark forest in search of some sinister villain who can be forced to release some suppliant female, is merely a projection of what Spenser really wants to say. When he says at the end of Book II of *The Faerie Queene*:

> Now gins this goodly frame of Temperance
> Fayrely to rise

it is clear that his interest is thematic, in the emergence of a fully articulated view of the virtue of Temperance which the reader can contemplate, as it were, like a statue, seeing all of its parts at once. This simultaneous vision extends over the entire poem, for Temperance is only one of the virtues surrounding the ideal Prince, and the emergence of the total form of that Prince is the thematic mould into which the enormous narrative is finally poured. The stanza in Spenser, especially the final alexandrine, has a role rather similar to the engraved design in Blake: it deliberately arrests the narrative and forces the reader to concentrate on something else.

In our day the prevailing attitude to fiction is overwhelmingly thematic. Even as early as Dickens we often feel that the plot, when it is a matter of unplausible mysteries unconvincingly revealed, is something superimposed on the real narrative, which is more like a procession of characters. In our day the born storyteller is even rather peripheral to fiction, at best a border-line case like Somerset Maugham, and the serious novelist is as a rule the novelist who writes not because he has a story to tell but because he has a theme to illustrate. One reason for this present preference of the thematic is that the ironic tone is central to modern literature. It is the function of irony, typically in Greek tragedy, to give the audience a clearer view of the total design than the actors themselves are aware of. Irony thus sets up a thematic detachment as soon as possible in the work, and provides an additional clue to the total meaning.

There may be, then, and there usually is, a kind of empathic communion set up in the reader or audience of a work of literature, which follows the work continuously to the end. The sense of empathy may be established by a story, where we read on to see what happens. Or by a pulsating rhythm, such as the dactylic hexameter in Homer, which has a surge and sweep that can carry us through even the longueurs referred to by Horace. We notice the effectiveness of rhythm in continuity more clearly in music, and most clearly in fast movements. I recall a cartoon of a tired man at a concert consulting his program and saying: "Well, the next movement is *prestissimo molto ed appassionato*, thank God." Or by the fluctuating intensity of a mood or emotion, again most clearly in music and in lyrical poetry. Or by a continuous sense of lifelikeness in realistic fiction, a sense which can extend itself even to realistic painting, as the eye darts from one detail to another. All these empathic responses are "naive," or essentially pre-critical.

Certain forms of art are also designed to give us the strongest possible emphasis on the continuous process of creation. The sketch, for example, is often more prized than the finished painting because of the greater sense of process in it. *Tachisme* and action-painting, spontaneous improvisation in swing, jazz, or more recently electronic music, and the kind of action-poetry, often read to jazz, which evokes the ghosts of those primeval jam-sessions postulated by early critics of the ballad, are more complete examples. All forms of art which lay great stress on continuous spontaneity seem to have a good deal of resistance to criticism, even to the education which is the natural context of criticism. We are told in Professor Lord's *Singer of Tales* that the most continuous form of poetry ever devised, the formulaic epic, demands illiteracy for success on the part of the poet, and there seems to be an inevitable affinity between the continuous and the unreflecting.

It is this continuity which is particularly Aristotle's imitation of an action. One's attention is completely absorbed in it: no other work of art is demanding attention at the same time, hence one has the sense of a unique and novel experience, at least as an ideal (for of course one may be rereading a book or seeing a familiar play). But, as in the world of action itself, one cannot participate and be a spectator at the same time. At best one is what Wyndham Lewis calls a "dithyrambic spectator." Lewis's disapproval of the dithyrambic spectator indicates an opposed emphasis on the detached contemplation of the entire work of art, and one so extreme that it talks of eliminating the sense of linear participating movement in the arts altogether. It would not clarify our argument to examine Lewis's very muddled polemics at this point, but they have some interest as documents in a tradition which strongly emphasized a visual and contemplative approach to art. Blake's plotless prophecies are, somewhat unexpectedly, in a similar (though by no means identical) tradition.

Just as the sense of participation in the movement of literature is absorbed, unique and novel, isolated from everything else, so the contemplative sense of its simultaneous wholeness tends to put the work of literature in some kind of framework or context. There are several such contexts, some of them indicated already. One of them is the allegorical context, where the total meaning or significance of the literary work is seen in relation to other forms of significance, such as moral ideas or historical events. A few works of literature, such as *The Pilgrim's Progress*, are technically allegories, which means that this explicit relation to external meaning is also a part of its continuity. Most literary works are not allegorical in this technical sense, but they bear a relation to historical events and moral ideas which is brought out in the kind of criticism usually called commentary. As I have explained elsewhere, commentary allegorizes the works it comments on.

We notice that Blake is somewhat ambiguous in his use of the term "allegory." He says in a letter to Butts, "Allegory addressed to the Intellectual powers . . . is My Definition of the Most Sublime Poetry." But in commenting on one of his paintings of the Last Judgement, he says: "The Last Judgment is not Fable or Allegory, but Vision. Fable or Allegory are a totally distinct & inferior kind of Poetry." The first use of the term recognizes the fact that "the most sublime poetry," including his own prophecies, will demand commentary. The second use indicates that his own poems and pictures are not allegorical in the Spenserian or continuous sense, nor are they allegorical in a much more obvious and central way. They do not subordinate their literary qualities to the ideas they convey, on the assumption that the latter are more important. In the second passage quoted above Blake goes on to say with great precision: "Fable is allegory, but what Critics call The Fable, is Vision itself." Fable is here taken in its eighteenth-century critical sense of fiction or literary structure. Aristotle's word for intellectual content, *dianoia*, "thought," can be understood in two ways, as a moral attached to a fable, or as the structure of the fable itself. The latter, according to Blake, contains its own moral significances by implication, and it destroys its imaginative quality to assume that some external moral attached to it can be a definitive translation of its "thought."

We touch here on a central dilemma of literature. If literature is didactic, it tends to injure its own integrity; if it ceases wholly to be didactic, it tends to injure its own seriousness. "Didactic poetry is my abhorrence," said Shelley, but it is clear that if the main body of Shelley's work had not been directly concerned with social, moral, religious, philosophical, political issues he would have lost most of his self-respect as a poet. Nobody wants to be an ineffectual angel, and Bernard Shaw, one of Shelley's most direct descendants in English literature, insisted that art should never be anything but didactic. This dilemma is partly solved by giving an ironic resolution to a work of fiction. The ironic resolution is the negative pole of the allegorical one. Irony presents a human conflict which, unlike a comedy, a romance, or even a tragedy, is unsatisfactory and incomplete unless we see in it a significance beyond itself, something typical of the human situation as a whole. What that significance is, irony does not say: it leaves that question up to the reader or audience. Irony preserves the seriousness of literature by demanding an expanded perspective on the action it presents, but it preserves the integrity of literature by not limiting or prescribing for that perspective.

Blake is clearly not an ironic writer, however, any more than he is an allegorist, and we must look for some other element in his thematic emphasis. A third context to which the theme of a literary work may be attached is its context in literature itself, or what we may call its archetypal framework. Just as continuous empathy is naive and absorbed in a unique and novel experience, so the contemplation of a unified work is self-conscious, educated, and one which tends to classify its object. We cannot in practice study a literary work without remembering that we have encountered many similar ones previously. Hence after following a narrative through to the end, our critical response includes the establishing of its categories, which are chiefly its convention and its genre. In this perspective the particular story is seen as a *projection* of the theme, as one of an infinite number of possible ways of getting to the theme. What we have just experienced we now see to be a comedy, a tragedy, a courtly love lyrical complaint, or one of innumerable treatments of the Tristan or Endymion or Faust story.

Further, just as some works of literature are explicitly or continuously allegorical, so some works are continuously, or at least explicitly, allusive, calling the reader's attention to their relation to previous works. If we try to consider *Lycidas* in isolation from the tradition of the pastoral elegy established by Theocritus and Virgil, or *Ash Wednesday* in isolation from its relation to Dante's *Purgatorio,* we are simply reading these works out of context, which is as bad a critical procedure as quoting a passage out of context. If we read an Elizabethan sonnet sequence without taking account of the conventional nature of every feature in it, including the poet's protests that he is not following convention and is really in love with a real person, we shall merely substitute the wrong context for the right one. That is, the sonnet sequence will become a biographical allegory, as the sonnets of Shakespeare do when, with Oscar Wilde, we reach the conclusion that the profoundest understanding of these sonnets, the deepest appreciation of all their eloquence and passion and power, comes when we identify the "man in hue" of Sonnet 20 with an unknown Elizabethan pansy named Willie Hughes.

Blake's prophecies are intensely allusive, though nine-tenths of the allusions are to the Bible. "The Old & New Testaments are the Great Code of Art," Blake says, and he thinks of the framework of the Bible, stretching from Creation to Last Judgement and surveying the whole of human history in between, as indicating the framework of the whole of literary experience, and establishing the ultimate context for all works of literature whatever. If the Bible did not exist, at least as a form, it would be necessary for literary critics to invent the same kind of total and definitive verbal structure out of the fragmentary myths and legends and folk tales we have outside it. Such a structure is the first and most indispensable of critical conceptions, the embodiment of the whole of literature as an order of words, as a potentially unified imaginative experience. But although its relation to the Bible takes us well on toward a solution of the thematic emphasis in Blake's illuminated poetry, it does not in itself fully explain that emphasis. If it did, the prophecies would simply be, in the last analysis, Biblical commentaries, and this they are far from being.

Blake's uniqueness as a poet has much to do with his ability to sense the historical significance of his own time. Up to that time, literature and the arts had much the same educational and cultural value that they have now, but they competed with religion, philosophy, and law on what were at best equal and more usually subordinate terms. Consequently when, for example, Renaissance critics spoke of the profundity of poetry, they tended to locate that profundity in its allegorical meaning, the relations that could be established between poetry and ideas, more particularly moral and religious ideas. In the Romantic period, on the other hand, many poets and critics were ready to claim an authority and importance for poetry and the imaginative arts prior to that of other disciplines. When Shelley quotes Tasso on the similarity of the creative work of the poet to the creative work of God, he carries the idea a great deal further than Tasso did. The fact of this change in the Romantic period is familiar, but the trends that made it possible are still not identified with assurance.

My own guess is that the change had something to do with a growing feeling that the origin of human civilization was human too. In traditional Christianity it was not: God planted the garden of Eden and suggested the models for the law, rituals, even the architecture of human civilization. Hence a rational understanding of "nature," which included the understanding of the divine as well as the physical origin of human nature, took precedence over the poetic imagination and supplied a criterion for it. The essential moral ideas fitted into a divine scheme for the redemption of man; we understand the revelation of this scheme rationally; literature forms a series of more indirect parables or emblems of it. Thus poetry could be the companion of camps, as Sidney says: it could kindle an enthusiasm for virtue by providing examples for precepts. The sense of excitement in participating in the action of the heroic narrative of, say, the Iliad was heightened by thinking of the theme or total meaning of the Iliad as an allegory of heroism. Thus, paradoxically, the Renaissance insistence on the allegorical nature of major poetry preserved the naivete of the participating response. We see this principle at work wherever poet and audience are completely in agreement about the moral implications of a poetic theme, as they are, at least theoretically, in a hiss-the-villain melodrama.

Blake was the first and the most radical of the Romantics who identified the creative imagination of the poet with the creative power of God. For Blake God was not a superhuman lawgiver or the mathematical architect of the stars; God was the inspired suffering humanity of Jesus. Everything we call "nature," the physical world around us, is sub-moral, subhuman, sub-imaginative; every act worth performing has as its object the redeeming of this nature into something with a genuinely human, and therefore divine, shape. Hence Blake's poetry is not allegorical but mythopoeic, not obliquely related to a rational understanding of the human situation, the resolution of which is out of human hands, but a product of the creative energy that alone can redeem that situation. Blake forces the reader to concentrate on the meaning of his work, but not didactically in the ordinary sense, because his meaning is his theme, the total simultaneous shape of his poem. The context into which the theme or meaning of the individual poem fits is not the received ideas of our cultural tradition, of which it is or should be an allegory. It is not, or not only, the entire structure of literature as an order of words, as represented by the Bible. It is rather the expanded vision that he calls apocalypse or Last Judgement: the vision of the end and goal of human civilization as the entire universe in the form that human desire wants to see it, as a heaven eternally separated from a hell. What Blake did was closely related to the Romantic movement, and Shelley and Keats at least are mythopoeic poets for reasons not far removed from Blake's.

Since the Romantic movement, there has been a more conservative tendency to deprecate the central place it gave to the creative imagination and to return, or attempt to return, to the older hierarchy. T. S. Eliot is both a familiar and a coherent exponent of this tendency, and he has been followed by Auden, with his Kierkegaardian reinforcements. According to Eliot, it is the function of art, by imposing an order on life, to give us the sense of an order in life, and so to lead us into a state of serenity and reconciliation preparatory to another and superior kind of experience, where "that guide" can lead us no further. The implication is that there is a spiritually existential world above that of art, a world of action and behavior, of which the most direct imitation in this world is not art but the sacramental act. This latter is a form of uncritical or pre-critical religious participation that leads to a genuinely religious contemplation, which for Eliot is a state of heightened consciousness with strong affinities to mysticism. Mysticism is a word which has been applied both to Blake and to St. John of the Cross: in other words it has been rather loosely applied, because these two poets have little in common. It is clear that Eliot's mystical affinities are of the St. John of the Cross type. The function of art, for Eliot, is again of the subordinated or allegorical kind. Its order represents a higher existential order, hence its greatest ambition should be to get beyond itself, pointing to its superior reality with such urgency and clarity that it disappears in that reality. This, however, only happens either in the greatest or the most explicitly religious art: nine-tenths of our literary experience is on the subordinate plane where we are seeing an order in life without worrying too much about the significance of that order. On this plane the naive pre-critical direct experience of participation can still be maintained, as it is in Renaissance critical theory. The Romantics, according to this view, spoil both the form and the fun of poetry by insisting so much on the profundity of the imaginative experience as to make it a kind of portentous *ersatz* religion.

This leads us back to the aphorism of Blake with which we began, where the artist is identified with the Christian. Elsewhere he speaks of "Religion, or Civilized Life such as it is in the Christian Church," and says that poetry, painting and music are "the three Powers in Man of conversing with Paradise, which the flood did not Sweep away." For Blake art is not a substitute for religion, though a great deal of religion as ordinarily conceived is a substitute for art, in that it abuses the mythopoeic faculty by creating fantasies about another world or rationalizing the evils of this one instead of working toward genuine human life. If we describe Blake's conception of art independently of the traditional myth of fall and apocalypse that embodies it, we may say that the poetic activity is fundamentally one of identifying the human with the nonhuman world. This identity is what the poetic metaphor expresses, and the end of the poetic vision is the humanization of reality, "All Human Forms identified," as Blake says at the end of *Jerusalem*. Here we have the basis for a critical theory which puts such central conceptions as myth and metaphor into their proper central place. So far from usurping the function of religion, it keeps literature in the context of human civilization, yet without limiting the infinite variety and range of the poetic imagination. The criteria it suggests are not moral ones, nor are they collections of imposing abstractions like Unity, but the interests, in the widest sense, of mankind itself, or himself, as Blake would prefer to say.

In this conception of art the productive or creative effort is inseparable from the awareness of what it is doing. It is this unity of energy and consciousness that Blake attempts to express by the word "vision." In Blake there is no either-or dialectic where one must be either a detached spectator or a preoccupied actor. Hence there is no division, though there may be a distinction, between the creative power of shaping the form and the critical power of seeing the world it belongs to. Any division instantly makes art barbaric and the knowledge of it pedantic—a bound Orc and a bewildered Urizen, to use Blake's symbols. The vision inspires the act, and the act realizes the vision. This is the most thoroughgoing view of the partnership of creation and criticism in literature I know, but for me, though other views may seem more reasonable and more plausible for a time, it is in the long run the only one that will hold.

ALFRED COBBAN

The Revolt Against the Eighteenth Century †

The religious revival was evidently not the decisive fact in the revolt against the eighteenth century. As one by one the different religious movements lost their initial ardour, it was seen that they belonged to a constantly recurring and essentially evanescent type of phenomenon. They revived old religious institutions and created new ones, but they introduced nothing into Western civilization that was not already in existence, and they presented no permanent obstacle to the advance of eighteenth-century ideas. The eighteenth century, insurgent in the Revolution, did but stay its course for a brief space; its principles swept over into the next century with accumulated force, on the crest of a wave mounting higher and higher as it rushed on, as it rushes on to-day—towards we know not yet what goal.

But though there was nothing that could answer eighteenth-century criticism satisfactorily in the Wesleyan and Evangelical move-

† From *Edmund Burke and the Revolt Against the Eighteenth Century* by Alfred Cobban. Second Edition © George Allen & Unwin Ltd. 1960. Reprinted by permission of George Allen & Unwin Ltd. and Barnes & Noble, Inc.

ments, in the Catholic revival and in Tractarianism, this is not to say that there were not religious thinkers whose views, if given a hearing, were capable of modifying profoundly and perhaps even entirely upsetting the eighteenth-century world-view. The Revolution, we must agree, was but the culmination of the previous century. But among the eddying and swirling waters of the revolutionary period are signs of another and very different current, come thither from unknown seas, surging upward from unfathomed depths. Almost contemporaneously, in England, France and Germany, appear three thinkers—Burke, Rousseau and Kant—whose influence, acting through various forms, was to undermine much that the eighteenth century had believed in profoundly. The influence of Burke was primarily political, that of Kant philosophic and that of Rousseau literary and religious.

An ill-assorted company they seem, the Anglo-Irish party orator, the old philosopher of Königsberg, and the wild, fleeting, inspired Genevese. What could they have in common—save that each was in revolt against the eighteenth century? Now to be in revolt against that century was essentially to be in revolt against a theory of the mind—that superficial psychology of sensations described above. It is in their revolt against the psychological school founded by Locke that Burke, Rousseau and Kant find a principle of union, and it would not be untrue to say that they were all three inspired less by the scientific weakness of this theory than by its inability to satisfy the eternal demand of the human spirit for a sense of reality. For Lockian psychology seemed to admit the reality only of things of immediate perception. Hence for Burke it excluded from politics the whole field of tradition, the whole work of the genius of the race; for Rousseau it prohibited that penumbra of the conscious mind on which he relied to supply him with artistic and religious inspiration; and, for Kant, by making the scepticism of Hume unavoidable, it denied the possibility of philosophic truth.

Like the religious revival, however, the break away from Lockian psychology proved inadequate in itself to overthrow the ideas of the *philosophes*. If it had not been so the eighteenth-century system would have collapsed before it had well begun, because the sensational psychology showed signs of developing inconsistently from the very beginning. Let us trace this process. As befitted an intensely didactic age, one of the principal problems of Locke's school was the problem of ethics. The old religious sanctions had vanished and were to be replaced by utilitarianism, as we saw in the first chapter. Utilitarianism, moreover, was interpreted in a very narrow rationalistic sense, and being combined with a strict individualism it presented the problem of the reconciliation of the interests of the individual with those of the rest of the community in an acute form.

A section of opinion represented by Mandeville's *Fable of the Bees* solved the problem by apotheosizing selfishness and calling it universal harmony; the philosophical radicals and some of the economists accepted this solution. Another, and for a time a more influential school of thought, in effect abandoned the severe individualism of the stricter utilitarians. They incorporated social virtue into the conception of man's nature in the form of a "moral sense." Universal harmony, says Shaftesbury, the leader of this school, is represented in man by an innate principle of morality. To accept this was to admit a considerable breach in the fabric of Locke's system; it was fatal to strict rationalism.

The reaction is carried a stage further by Hume, who adopts Shaftesbury's moral sense as an alternative to Locke's deductive ethics. For Hume, however, this is only part of a general campaign against intellectualist theories of the mind. By the mechanism of association he is able to explain the working of the mind without the intervention of a rational faculty. He holds that "when the mind passes from the idea or impression of one object to the idea or belief of another, it is not determined by reason, but by certain principles, which associate together the ideas of these objects, and unite them in the imagination." [1] By means of this theory he is enabled to purge thought and knowledge of their rational element and to reduce opinion and belief to simple feeling, "more properly an act of the sensitive, than of the cogitative part of our natures." [2] Nor does it derogate from their significance and validity for him that moral and political opinions are only sentiments. Rejecting intellectualism and the deductive ethics of Locke, he does not fall back on the moral scepticism of Hobbes. Inexorable custom and the unfailing passions of man provide him with a point of rest less elusive than the arguments of the abstract reason. For the reason is a vain thing, he says, which by its very nature is incapable of motivating the will; only the passions can do that.[3] Hence, as moral philosophy is a practical science aiming at practical results, it cannot be derived from the reason.[4] Thus, declining to derive morality from either supernatural ordinance or from a rationalistic calculation of consequences, he is left with the necessity of deriving it from sentiment or feeling.[5]

This same tendency, which in Hume took philosophic shape, was represented for his contemporaries by a literary phenomenon. We need not look further than to the arid utilitarianism and the gross materialism which formed the popular interpretation of the ideas of the school of Locke for an explanation of the wave of sentimen-

1. Hume: Treatise on Human Nature, I. iii. 6.
2. Id. I. iv. 1.
3. Id. II. iii. 3.
4. Hume: Treatise on Human Nature, III. i. 1.
5. Id. III. i. 2.

tality in the latter half of the century. The sentimentalists are of little importance in the history of thought, nevertheless this phase marks the first line of revolt against intellectualism and the beginning of the reassertion of the actual individual. Moreover, the greatest of the sentimentalists—such as Diderot and Rousseau in France —represent something more than mere sentiment. They mark a further stage in the movement back to reality. Sentiment is the first step, an effort towards simplification the second; and both of these are absorbed in the broader movement, that "return to nature" with which romanticism is inaugurated.

With Rousseau, the petty bourgeois, started the cult of the wild, unregulated, primitive passions, of barbaric nature and of innocent, uncivilized natural man. Nothing that Rousseau wrote subsequently ever effaced the memory of his first essay. This was only fair, for the note which he struck in the *Discours sur les Arts et les Sciences* is heard again and again, in the *Émile*, the *Nouvelle Héloïse*, and at the end of his life in the *Mèditations d'un promeneur solitaire*. Nature, in all the various meanings of that much-abused word, was the goddess of Rousseau's adoration. Naturalism, of course, had been the result for the whole Enlightenment of the abandonment of the religious attitude; but the austere Nature deity of Voltaire appeared transformed by Dionysiac traits at the hands of the author of the *Confessions*. The importance of this transformation must not be exaggerated, however: it was not this side of Rousseau's teachings which counted politically. The influence of the sentimentalists is to be found rather in literature, in religion, and in social movements—in the floods of sentiment that deluged the revolutionary assemblies and that poured from the printing presses of France, Germany and England, in the religious history of a Chateaubriand, in the increasing simplicity of dress, and in the lachrymose sensuality that saw a child of nature in every errant Marquise.

Still, Rousseau did have at times a true if theatrical vision of nature, and could see a mountain or a forest as it had not been seen before; and after him, along the same path came a whole school of writers, for whom, moreover, nature had a new meaning. For Wordsworth nature was not merely the uncivilized, the primitive, the world as yet untouched by man, but man himself was part of nature. Wordsworth and his contemporaries loved Nature as perhaps no generation before or since, for they saw in her not only infinite beauty, but behind the ceaseless mutations of changing colour and transient scene they knew her at heart, the mysterious mother of humanity, brooding in omnipresence. The Renaissance had discovered Man; it was left for Romanticism to make the real discovery of Nature, and wondering to guess "with a wild surmise" at who knows what arcana hidden therein from unpoetic gaze. In

Wordsworth, more than in any other poet of nature, was the feeling greater than simple appreciation of natural beauty; it was more even than man; it was a knowledge of oneness with all the animate and inanimate world, a refusal to put nature on one side and man on the other and leave them thus eternally divided; it was a faith reaching in many a glowing invocation almost to pantheism.

> Dust as we are, the immortal spirit grows
> Like harmony in music; there is a dark
> Inscrutable workmanship that reconciles
> Discordant elements, makes them cling together
> In one society.[6]

From a literary point of view we are now in the midst of the revolt against the eighteenth century, but as regards politics it is altogether a different matter. "Nature" is a term which may mean much or little—or sometimes nothing at all. Politically, "back to nature" was captured by the Revolution; thus illustrating the manner in which the fundamental tendencies of an age persist through apparent changes in terminology and remould themselves to suit a new spirit. The Nature of most of the romanticists is simply an emotionalized version of the Reason of the *philosophes*, its political effect being to place their views of society in a democratic setting. Thus it was that the leaders of the second generation of romanticism in England—to give only two names, Shelley and Byron—were descendants of the eighteenth-century system of thought, inspired by a sentimentalized version of the ideas of the *philosophes*, rather than by those of Wordsworth, Coleridge and Burke. The sentimental and naturalistic movements, beginning in a revolt against the intellectualist theory of the mind, ended by declining into a mere superficial ornamentation to a view of man and society, and their place in nature, which was in fact based on that intellectualist psychology itself. This revolt against the eighteenth century had thus failed, and failed badly, and that precisely because it took the first and easiest line of attack. The Ideas of the Enlightenment were of no great philosophic profundity, but they were not to be overcome in favour of such a baseless fabric as the romanticism of the sentimental and "back to nature" school.

Herein lay the essential weakness of Rousseau, and the explanation of the ineffectiveness of his ideas in the realm of practical politics. Burke himself had never had any truck with these tendencies, but the youthful fancy of the Lake Poets had been captivated at once. Yet though sentimentalism and naturalism left a lasting mark on their contribution to English literature, the influence on their ideas in general was very transitory and passed away with the

6. Prelude, I. 340–4.

waning of their revolutionary enthusiasm. If we are to find a clue to their political or social philosophy it is certainly not to be found in this.

II. THE INFLUENCE OF THE HISTORIC IDEA

The religious revival, sentimentalism, and "back to nature," though they all have some connections with the political thought of Burke and the Lake Poets, obviously fail to provide us with a satisfactory clue to the inmost nature of their revolt against the prevailing system of ideas. If we turn back to our chapters on Burke, we will remember that very closely connected with his religious views was his idea of the nation as a community held together by long tradition, in other words by history. The belief that political values are to be judged in their relation with the historical community seemed to us the final teaching of Burke's political theory, and the lesson which the Lake Poets learned from him. Perhaps in this historic idea is to be found the ultimate explanation of what was original in the theory of Burke's followers as well as in his own theory: perhaps a historical sense is the creative force in their revolt against the eighteenth century. As Renan writes, *"L'histoire est la vraie philosophie du XIXe siècle"*: it certainly was not of the eighteenth.

On the whole it is true to say that the sense of historical background, implicit in the philosophy which the Middle Ages had derived from the *Civitas Dei*, had been obscured since the decline of mediaeval theology. There lingered, however, even in the ideology occasioned by a Protestant environment, a belief in Providence and in the value of the traditional and customary. The eighteenth century changed all this. Confident in the power of reason, it challenged all existing creeds and institutions with the test of reasonableness and utility, ignoring completely the play of historic forces which had gone to their shaping, and looking for nothing but conscious and self-interested motives from the actors in the great drama of history.

It is true that quite early in the century there appeared a thinker for whom the history of man was more than a mere set of chronologically related but fortuitous phenomena. Vico definitely describes his *Scienza Nuova* as a "history of the ideas, customs and actions of the human race." [7] But Vico, whether because Italy was out of the main stream of European thought, or because his views were too novel and too far in advance of his time, failed to gain a hearing. Montesquieu incorporated some of his principles in the *Esprit des Lois*, but the glimpses of historical method in this work are far

7. Vico: Scienza Nuova, II. i. 3.

more rudimentary. The French writer lays great stress on the universal rule of law, an idea he derives from Vico, and he recognizes also the need to allow for the influence of physical environment in studying the varying customs of different peoples, but that is as far as he goes. The relativity of institutions in time does not enter his mind; no attempt is made to conceive history as more than a useful storehouse of precedents. Bolingbroke, despite his pompous "philosophy teaching by examples" phrase, is equally unenlightened. Similarly, Hume, although he turned to historical writing in his later years, revealed only a chronicler's conception of events. Leslie Stephen has attributed the defects of Hume and of most contemporary historians to their narrow view of their own functions as discoverers of causal relations among the phenomena they had to describe. Now as Hume's philosophy contained a destructive criticism of the very idea of causation, this was only to be expected in his case. His *Essays*, on the other hand, show some disposition to generalize from historical evidence. There was great progress in the writing of history at this time, but it was principally in technique, in the searching out and more critical examination of evidence. History remained an external account with the usual intellectualist bias.

In the midst of so much historical research, men were bound to begin to look for something more from their material. But this they were not likely to get so long as they remained subject to the intellectualist psychology and extreme individualism of the school of Locke. History was bound to be a curiously distorted study so long as its characters were assumed to act always rationally and on motives of self-interest. It was bound to be an aimless phantasmagoria unless some relation besides that of a chronological succession of events was found in it, which meant unless it dealt with some entities more permanent than fleeting unrelated individuals. The intellectualist psychology had been undermined early, and so the more serious problem for historians was to find some corrective or supplement for the individualist theory of society. The first attempted solution was Voltaire's "history of civilization," a *genre* of historiography in which the subject became not men but Man. Two favourite principles of the eighteenth century—empiricism and universality—were united in the idea of humanity which perhaps formed Voltaire's greatest contribution to the development of modern thought. His idea is to be distinguished from mere cosmopolitanism; it was the rebirth of the ecumenical idea, forgotten since the decline of Stoicism in the ancient world and the shattering of the Roman Empire—for the mediaeval outlook was parochial, if at the same time eternal. Mediaeval man was a citizen of the City of God and a member of the Church of Christ on earth; he was a subject of a local lord, but he was not a citizen of the world. Voltaire's philosophy as well as his pose made him essentially such, and under his teaching the Enlightenment learned to despise local and national prejudices. His success was only negative, for he found few followers to develop the positive aspects of his idea, and the religion of humanity as the revolutionaries tried to develop it proved a sorry farce. Individualism captured the idea of humanity and turned it into an invertebrate cosmopolitanism, which soon collapsed under the stress of the national and racial jealousies of the following century.

The next attempt to give substance to the historic idea came not from a professed historian but from the English statesman, Burke, and he, unconscious that he was sharing in an epoch-making discovery, ignorant of the world-shattering events that were to follow when the people of Europe came for themselves to the same realization, applied it to the national community, and so doing gained for himself a place among the prime founders of nationalism.

When, however, we speak of the thought of Burke and his successors as historical, it can only be with certain qualifications. Their merit was to have introduced general conceptions into the view of history. But it was not without reason that Wordsworth was described by his biographer as a thinker with "small value for anything but contemporary history." [8] Although this statement is not strictly true, certainly his historical feeling was manifested in a very different way from that of Savigny and his generation. To Burke, Wordsworth and Southey, history was primarily a religious process; to Coleridge, as a disciple of the Idealists, it was partly also a philosophic unrolling of ideas; and both the providential views of Burke's followers and the dialectical evolution of the Idealists were in rivalry rather than in alliance with the true historical movement. Yet, as Leslie Stephen has pointed out, history found its disciples in the ranks of the intuitionists, while the empirical school, which professed to base itself on experience, totally neglected historical evidence. It was not until the empiricism of the one school and the evolutionary ideas of the other had become linked that the historical movement proper was possible. Meanwhile, the conservatism of Burke and the early Romantic poets could be described as religious or philosophic rather than historical. Though there is a certain relationship, no logically inevitable connection exists between the historical movement proper of the nineteenth century and that historic conception of society which played so large a part in early Romantic political theory in England, and which was perhaps even the nucleus of romanticism.

Let us leave for a moment the broad principles and consider in more detail to what in fact the historical spirit of the Lake Poets

8. C. Wordsworth: Memoirs of Wordsworth, II. 445.

amounted. Southey alone was a professed historian, and apart from the biographies of Nelson and Wesley the work that won him his reputation is almost completely forgotten. Those huge tomes on South American history rest undisturbed on their shelves; Anglicanism does not now go for support to the *Book of the Church*. But Southey's labours must not be dismissed as altogether fruitless. He helped to elevate both the standard and the reputation of his own class of writers. Contemporaries were more appreciative of his historical talents than posterity has proved, and he himself perhaps gained more than any from his studies. They moderated a mind naturally prone to take extreme views and deepened a naturally superficial understanding. "A man," he wrote, "ought well to have studied history before he is fit for any direct share in national policy," [9] and such signs of political and social enlightenment above the ordinary as we discover in him are to be attributed in large measure to his own historical studies.

The revival of history had involved the discovery of the Middle Ages, of which Southey had been a close student. The main effect on him, as on his generation, was to substitute an idealized mediaevalism for the equally idealized and even more misconceived classicism of the eighteenth century. How the Romantic movement discovered the Middle Ages, and how the Middle Ages reacted on the romanticists by revealing to them a set of ideas which, wholly alien from the ideas of the eighteenth century and almost forgotten, were yet the original basis of the customs and institutions of pre-revolutionary society, we need not linger to explain. The result was on the one hand to assist in propping up the tottering fabric of society and on the other to rehabilitate mediaeval ideas on social relationships. To this influence can be attributed the combination, most marked in Southey, but noticeable in many others, of pronounced Toryism with an outlook on social problems which put them far in advance of their more enlightened contemporaries. They did not become any the less Tories. The initial affiliations of the mediaeval revival may have been Whig, since the Parliamentarians of the seventeenth century had looked back beyond Tudor despotism to Lancastrian constitutionalism, but with Burke its true tendency becomes apparent. Conservatives, it has been said, put their golden age in the past; while those of progressive views look to a Utopia of the future. If we agree with this we shall understand why the influence of Rousseau with his state of nature proved in the long run conservative, and why the cult of mediaevalism also, in spite of its reforming aspect, is rightly classed among the forces of reaction.

Reaction, that is, more particularly against the eighteenth cen-

9. Essays, Moral and Political, I. 14.

tury. We have remarked above how, wearied by the intellectualism of the *philosophes,* men had thrown themselves back on authority, and how transcendentalism had offered them the categorical imperative, and Catholicism the Church. But the former had provided little satisfaction except to a few philosophers, and the latter was not a solution for Protestants with no infallible Church to fall back on. Their only resource was to take refuge from the demands of the future in the authority of the past. Now this could not be the immediate past, for historical development since the Renaissance and Reformation had led only too obviously up to the Enlightenment. Nor was classical antiquity much more acceptable. Not only was it non-Christian, it was also notoriously the idol of the eighteenth century, the pseudo-classical absurdities of which the Romantic movement did well not to attempt to emulate. On the other hand the Enlightenment had been supremely contemptuous of the Middle Ages. What appeal more suitable, then, than from an age of unbelief to the Ages of Faith, from an age of rebellion and self-assertion to the age of subordination and caste, from an age of the breaking of all bonds and loosening of all ties—social, moral and religious—to the age of fixed feudal hierarchy and unalterable law? Where else, too, should the reborn spirit of romance find inspiration and sympathy? These modern novelists, your Fielding and your Smollet, were all very well in their plain, prosaic way, but the new generation wanted heroic deeds, mystery, colour, and all the war-paint of romanticism. And the age found the first and greatest of Romantic novelists ready to supply its want.

Scott's novels no doubt intensified the mediaeval trend, but they did not call it into being in the first place. Thus it did not require the enchantments of the Wizard of the North to bring Southey under the spell of the Middle Ages. As early as 1803 he writes to Rickman, "Coleridge says there has never been a single line of common sense written about the dark ages. He was speaking of the knowledge and philosophy of that period; and I believe his assertion is true in a more extensive sense." [1] Southey, as soon as his conversion had been effected, took up feudalism with as much ardour as he had taken up Godwinism. He came to look on the disharmony in Europe as primarily a struggle "between the feudal system of society as variously modified throughout Europe, and the levelling principle of democracy"; in which struggle, he feared, the spirit of trade was gradually superseding the "rude but kindlier principle" of the feudal system. "Bad as the feudal times were, they were far less injurious than these commercial ones to the kindly and generous feelings of human nature, and far, far more favourable to the principles of honour and integrity." "While gain is the great object

1. Sel. Lett., I. 228, 1803.

of pursuit, selfishness must ever be the uppermost feeling. I cannot dissemble from myself that it is the principle of our social system, and that is awfully opposed to the spirit of Christianity." [2] The connection in Southey's mind between the revived cult of feudalism and a religious conception of society is obvious. Similarly, Words worth asks, "Why should not great landowners look for a substitute for what is lost of feudal paternity in the higher principles of christianized humanity and humble-minded brotherhood?" [3] Feudalism was not necessarily religious, nor Christianity feudal, but they both implied the same thing—that spirit of community life which Wordsworth and Southey assumed to have been lost in the anarchy of eighteenth-century individualism and the economic revolution and which it was their desire to see restored.

To what extent the Romantic writers were ignorant of the darker side of mediaeval life is difficult to say. Scott, at any rate, does not hesitate on occasion to deck his characters in sombre panoply and to hang his scenes with the trappings of sorrow and guilt. We need to be careful of exaggerating the prevalence of mediaeval barbarism: but though some very fine things can exist alongside the grossest brutality and superstition there can be no doubt that the Romantic school on the whole painted the Middle Ages in unjustifiably roseate hues.

However this may be, one of the best clues to the ideals of an age is the fiction it reads, because people do on the whole prefer to read not of what they are but of what they would like to be, not of their environment as it is, but of the environment in which they would like to be placed. Scott was the first to discover, or at least the first to exploit on a large scale, the mediaeval sentiment. It is consequently all the more significant that we can see in Scott, the high priest of mediaevalism himself, that the taste for the Middle Ages was more than a taste merely for a picturesque period of history. It was for certain things which could be found more particularly in the Middle Ages, it is true, but which could be found also in other fields. Was not feudal society supremely distinguished from modern by its recognition both in theory and practice of the value and significance of communal life, of the natural interdependence of individuals and of classes, and of the beauty of self-devotion to a corporate ideal? Not only in mediaeval Europe, but wherever he find qualities such as these Sir Walter is at home. Does not his voice take on a new ring of spiritual exaltation when he comes to his Highland clans? The love of comradeship which had to be satisfied with drilling in the Volunteers, and the loyalty which could be bestowed on no worthier object than the Prince Regent, found in

---

2. Colloquies, I. 79; II. 414, 246–7, 250.   3. C. Wordsworth: Memoirs, II. 409.

the devotion of clansmen to their clan and its chief a more stirring social relationship, even as he had found the same in mediaeval ties of allegiance and the code of chivalry.

Thus, to sum up, we see that the historic revival at this time amounted very largely to a revival of interest in the Middle Ages, and from Scott as well as from Coleridge and Southey we can see what it was that the Middle Ages gave them. We can see that they pass from the historic process of development to the implied subject of that process, to something in which are reconciled the principles of permanence and development, to something that is —over centuries and generations—what the individual man is for some threescore years and ten—a body in which the elements are always changing without the body losing its identity, and which is the family, the clan, the city, the community, the nation. Behind religion, behind the historic idea itself, behind nationalism and the cry for social reform, the rediscovery of this is the root of all that is really new in the development of political theory at the end of the eighteenth and in the first decades of the nineteenth century, and *that* is the significance of the political thinking of Burke and Coleridge, Wordsworth, Southey, with Scott, Cobbett and a few lesser writers of their time.

III. CONCLUSION

We have arrived at what—it seems to us—is the ultimate significance in political thinking of the revolt against the eighteenth century, for we have discovered its definition of the State, in which, in a sense, all the rest is implied. It is one of the real definitions in which a science culminates, not one of the formal definitions in which it begins, and for Burke and the Lake Poets it is to be found in their idea of the national community. To attempt further to build up into a complete system the ideas we have analysed in this book would be to pass from the field of history to that of theory. In this matter the ideas of Burke and his followers must be left to speak for themselves without being artificially arranged into some system which their authors never had in mind when they evolved them. At the same time it will be worth our while in conclusion to emphasize what is the peculiar feature which distinguishes their political theory from other theories.

There have been, roughly speaking, two leading tendencies in political thinking—towards individualism and towards absolutism. Let us pass these rapidly under review. In the Middle Ages political theory proper did not exist. It came to birth in the form of absolutism with the development of the sovereign prince of the Renaissance and Reformation. The divine right of the mediaeval ruler persisted for a while in its new form, but the process which began with the attack on the authority of the Catholic Church of necessity could not end there. Divine right monarchs exhibited too few of the characteristics of divinity for their power to last once it had occurred to men to challenge it. As a final political result of the Protestant Reformation the sovereign prince was replaced by the sovereign individual, on whose behalf a theory of natural rights was elaborated by Locke. This culminated in the French Revolution and in economic individualism, and showed no further capacity for development, utilitarianism as a political doctrine being simply Lockian individualism with the assumptions of the pleasure-pain calculus put in place of the assumptions of natural law.

Before the Revolution, however, the absolutist theory had revived, although now with the sovereign State in place of the sovereign prince. The transition is to be observed in the political writings of Rousseau, who, beginning always with the abstract individual of the state of nature, ends with the General Will. Idealist philosophy took up the heritage of Rousseau, but whereas Rousseau certainly tried, if with doubtful success, to distinguish between the rules of political technology, the historical evolution, and the philosophical theory of the State, Idealism was too often content merely to identify them. With even more disastrous results, the philosophical desire for a closed system was allowed to result in an air of finality being given to the dialectical evolution traced out by Hegel, and so to the actual State as it was in his day. Unfortunately this meant the Kingdom of Prussia. Thus, under cover of the philosophical Absolute, all the evils of State absolutism—a very different matter—were sanctioned in an accentuated form.

These theories of the absolute State and of the absolute individual provided the twin bases of nineteenth-century politics, which are to a large extent vitiated by the fact that they spring in the ultimate resort from two extreme, untenable, and mutually incompatible principles. The attempt to work these theories out in practice has proved calamitous. The assertion of individual rights as such leads to anarchy, the attribution of all rights to the political State to tyranny, a practical inconvenience which is, of course, but a reflection of the theoretical weakness. The trouble with political theories based on the natural rights of the individual or on the absolute State, or on any combination of these two extremes, was that they were basing themselves on abstractions. The eighteenth-century "individual" was an invention of Locke. No one has ever isolated a natural man, and it would be of little use if anyone ever did: what the political theorist has to deal with is the individual in society. No government has, in fact, worked on the assumptions of natural man, and none ever could. More apparent practical success has been attained by the idea of the absolute State, but the results wherever men have attempted to put it into effect have been equally calamitous. No State has ever been able in fact to depend for its strength and cohesion merely on the exercise of sovereignty. Natural man and the sovereign State—the two conceptions from which most modern political thinking has sprung—are equally unreal and mischievous, because they arise not from observation and meditation on the facts of political society, but from the need to find theories which would justify claims to power.

It may be asked whether a less partial view of politics can be expected from Burke, who "to party gave up what was meant for mankind." The great advantage of Burke, however, was that he was not a professed political theorist; he was under no obligation to erect a theory at all, and he was therefore free from the artificial world of the system-makers. His position was more akin to that of the scientific observer, and as a practical politician he had unusual opportunities for studying the behaviour of man as a political animal. Similarly, the Lake Poets were merely students of the political life of their day, not professional dealers in theories. No previous political thinker, with the possible exception of Machiavelli, had been equally willing to start from the actual facts of human experience instead of from abstract ideas such as "sovereignty," "laws of nature," "natural man," "the felicific calculus," and the like.

Starting in this way from actual experience, they naturally found that the ultimate fact with which they had to deal, the basic material of politics, was neither the natural man nor the sovereign State, but simply individuals in society. The implication of this is that for political theory individuals must always be taken as they exist in society, on the one hand, and on the other, that political society is simply a feeling of relationship in the minds of individuals. This is the primary fact for the political theorist, who thus starts by assuming neither the rights of individuals nor the rights of the State. The recognition that neither of these are absolute rights lies at the base of all sound political thinking. So long as either the State or the individual was regarded as having absolute natural rights, no *modus vivendi* could be arranged between them, political speculation was doomed to oscillate vainly between anarchy and tyranny, and political practice could hope to see any abuse justified in the name of natural right. In declining to trace back all political right either to the State or to the individual, in acknowledging the priority of neither, Burke liberated political theory from the task of attempting to solve an insoluble problem.

How Burke's theory of the nature of the political relationship worked out in practice has been told at length in previous chapters. It was in essence a theory of nationality, because it founded itself on the historic unit called the nation, and neither on the State nor the individual, and it was destined to be followed by a widespread assertion of the claims of nationality in practice. The time has not yet come to pass judgment on a movement the possibilities of which for good and for evil have still to be exhausted. This we can say, that the theorists of the nation-state have been justified by the practical logic of events; for it has proved itself one of the strongest and most stable institutions in the world. Nations have been partitioned, suppressed for centuries, and out of the long historical memories of middle Europe have been born again. The whole fabric of society has been subverted and the nation has remained. Only, in speaking of Burke and his followers as theorists of the nation-state, we must be careful to point out that it is of the nation-state *minus* the idea of sovereignty. To pass on to those who first recognized the fact of nationality any of the blame for the numerous excesses committed in its name would be patently unfair. The aggressive nationalism of a later day has taken over unchanged the heritage of the eighteenth-century despotisms—*corruptio optimi pessima*—but the aberrations of modern politics must not cause us to ignore the true fact of nationality.

The nature of the nation as a political body was first taught by Burke. Wordsworth re-echoes and deepens the call to the national spirit. Southey applies what is fundamentally the same idea to social problems. In Coleridge the attack on the eighteenth-century State finds its most unequivocal and philosophic exponent. He goes a long way towards building up a complete alternative system—and is perpetually frustrated by his own weakness and the spirit of the age. There was no doubt on which side this was. Burke's political theory has not even been given a distinguishing name. He founded no school, except in so far as the Lake Poets can be said to form one. Among Continental thinkers, despite occasional borrowings, the influence of his thought as a whole was negligible. And so the leaders of the first generation of romanticism died one by one, beaten and broken men, perishing among the spears of triumphant Victorianism.

PART THREE

Nature and Literary Form

It is assumed, in this anthology, that the central spiritual problem of Romanticism is the difficult relation between nature and consciousness, and its prime historical problem the relation between changing concepts of nature and the French Revolution. The leading formal problem results directly from these spiritual and historical stimuli, and is a problem of innovations in literary form: in questions of aesthetic theory, verbal mode, verse forms and metrics, and the new genres or modifications of genre that appeared. The essays in this section concern these matters, in sequence. W. J. Bate correctively emphasizes the empiricism and eclecticism of Romantic aesthetic theory, which restrained the English critics and poets of the period from too profound a plunge into the deep well of "emotionalism and subjectivism," and kept their modifications of traditional forms within the compass of rational imagination. Josephine Miles eloquently defines the Romantic style, finding its vital idea "of the spirit's narrative, the individual's lyrical story, half articulated and half heard, but powerful in its force of implication." John Hollander inaugurates a new kind of study of Romantic prosody, one which traces in the minute articulations of the verse the larger patterns of Prometheanism and the internalized quest. The introductory essay in this volume, by the editor, attempts to study the new genre of internalized romance as the characteristic form of the Romantic long poem. The concluding essay of this section is M. H. Abrams' pioneering definition of the most prevalent of the new Romantic genres, the Greater Romantic Lyric of Coleridge, Wordsworth, and their followers.

WALTER JACKSON BATE

The English Romantic Compromise †

In the former part of the last century [wrote an admirer of rural life in 1803], it was usual with writers on moral subjects to insist much on the reason and fitness of things, their several natures and mutual relations . . . and to have deserted these grounds for the sake of a theory which leaves everyone to resolve his duty by his *feelings,* would have been thought at best extremely unphilosophical. How different are the times in which we live! [1]

The two preceding chapters attempted to point out that, as the eighteenth century progressed, the inevitable mechanistic and emotional reactions to neo-classic rationalism, as well as to what remained of classical and Renaissance humanism, received effective and consistent support from British empirical psychology. The closing years of the century were accordingly characterized by a general conviction decidedly different from that which it had inherited: a conviction that the essential nature of man was not reason—whether it be the ethical insight into the ideal or even the sheer mathematicism of the Cartesians—but that it consisted, in effect, either of a conglomeration of instincts, habits, and feelings, or else, as German subjectivism was beginning to illustrate, of an ego which creates and projects its own world, and which has little real hope of knowing anything else. There are frequent indications of a restless and at times startled awareness of the newly-discovered inadequacy of man's mind and knowledge—an awareness which somewhat stimulated and also received temporary balm from man's increasing scientific conquest of external nature. A more widespread temptation was to glorify at least one aspect of the discovery: to find the sole attainable validity and worth either in one form or another of sentiment or else in some other essentially non-rational capacity.

This glorification, however diverse in its aspects, is one of the most distinguishing characteristics of the romanticism which the later eighteenth century formulated and bequeathed to Western

† From *From Classic to Romantic* by Walter Jackson Bate (Cambridge, Mass.: Harvard University Press). Copyright © 1946 by the President and Fellows of Harvard College. Reprinted by permission of the publisher.

1. Ely Bates, *Rural Philosophy: or Reflections on Knowledge, Virtue, and Happiness* (1803), pref. p. vii.

Europe. Examples are both numerous and extremely familiar. We may recall the widespread wave of primitivism which took rise at this time, and which Johnson continually combated: the confidence—so familiarly exemplified by Rousseau—that the "natural" man is good, and that, once his fetters are removed, he will inevitably fulfill himself and reattain the Golden Age. This confidence in the "natural" man was many-sided in its effects and manifestations. It was partly humanitarian and political, and its influence on the French Revolution, of course, is a byword. It also encouraged the common romantic emphasis on the virtues of simple and rural life, and, in its extremer form, as Mr. Fairchild has shown, found outlet in continuing the cult of the "noble savage" who is unspoiled by contact with civilization. It lent a kind of sanction to the vogue of the untutored and "original genius"; and the frequent dilation on the "natural" innocence and goodness of childhood is an equally common expression of it.

A trust in natural sentiment and inclination was not only primitivistic: it also gave a heartening impetus to the conception of progress which retained so marked a prominence throughout the whole nineteenth century. Few books have ever achieved so quick if temporary a vogue as William Godwin's *Political Justice* (1793), where the basic equality of all men's innate goodness is urged in conjunction with the theory of "perfectibility." In 1800, said Hazlitt twenty-five years later, Godwin "was in the very zenith of a sultry and unwholesome popularity . . . no one was more talked of, more sought after, and wherever liberty, truth, and justice was the theme, his name was not far off. . . . Tom Paine was for the time considered as Tom Fool to him, Paley an old woman, and Edmund Burke a flashy sophist." "Throw away your books of Chemistry," said the younger Wordsworth to a student, "and read Godwin"; and Shelley and others were not slow in taking heed. It is significant that, although Godwin at first considered himself a "rationalist," he was really very much in the English benevolist tradition; that he adopted Hume's principle of sympathy; and that he planned ultimately to rewrite his *Political Justice*, and found his system upon "feeling." This combination of the belief in natural goodness and in progress was to some extent drawn upon by British utilitarianism—with its creed of "the greatest happiness of the greatest number"—and may be illustrated in its popular form by such works as Mary Hays' novel, *Emma Courtney* (1796), where the heroine makes it her goal to facilitate progress and to work "towards the great end of life—*general utility*." In France, where so many English tendencies have been carried to their logical extremes, the fruition of one aspect of romantic utilitarianism was soon typified by the positivist sociolatry of Auguste Comte. Since "nothing is absolute, but all is relative"—a statement he never tired of repeating—Comte, like the French mechanist, Du Marsais, concluded that "Society is the only Divinity," and preached a "religion of humanity." This religion he later elaborated under the "angelic influence" of Mme Clotilde de Vaux, without which, as he modestly said, he would have been merely another Aristotle. The uncharitable may find a warning, as did M. Gilson, in the list of books which Comte made out for the "Positivist Library": such men as Plato, Spinoza, and Leibniz are omitted, whereas some of the British empiricists are present side by side with Mme de Lambert's *Counsels of a Mother.* "Hume," said Comte, "is my principal predecessor in philosophy." We may remember that, when Hume considered the possible consequences of his philosophy, he was "affrighted and confounded."

Though it attempted to combat both empiricism and emotional relativism, contemporary German thought stemmed from the same source and revealed some of the same general characteristics which attended upon other aspects of subjectivism. Having proved that reality is forever unknowable to the intellect, Kant was forced to find a non-rational means for feeling or manifesting, if not actually knowing, the good; and this he discovered in the "will." Kant was keenly aware of possible misinterpretations, and continually qualified himself. It was left for his truant pupil, Fichte, to conclude that nature itself is only the creation of the ego—or the will —which is in turn the product and manifestation of the "Eternal and Infinite Will": "Thou and I," said Fichte to the "Infinite Will," "are not divided! Thy voice sounds within me; mine resounds in Thee!" And after the close of the eighteenth century, Hegel, attempting to find a unity and direction which would transcend individual subjectivism, preached that truth is the "realization or actualization of the Whole," and that in any form of "individuality" there is a "negation" involved. But being a relativist— at least in the classical sense—he could find no real "whole," for all moral intents and purposes, beyond that of the state; and with the progressive welfare of the state thus constituting "the onward march of God," it is perhaps inevitable that he should have added that "the military class is the class of universality." "Had there been no Rousseau," and Napoleon, "there would have been no Revolution; had there been no Revolution, *I* should have been impossible."

The recollection of such broad tendencies as the few which have been mentioned here is perhaps necessary in any general consideration of romanticism. They may serve to remind us of the extent, the pervasiveness, and the variety of the anti-rationalistic movement of which romanticism reflects or comprises the first stage. They may also remind us of the problems that begin to confront any system of values, whether ethical or aesthetic, which abandons a rational conception of the objective good as the distinctive characteristic of man. If something in man, such as emotion or the will, is postulated as independent of reason or as transcending it in attaining the good, the question then arises what the good is and how it is possibly to be known. And the answer is too often one which either begs the question or else cites a purely empirical or utilitarian end. Even Friedrich Schlegel noted that, since Hume, "nothing more has been attempted than merely to erect all sorts of barriers against the *practical* influence of this destructive tendency"; and this attempt to divert or glorify certain effects of relativism rather than to strike at its source has resulted, he adds, either in making social and "national welfare the ruling principle of thought"—a principle "quite unfitted to be the center and oracle of *all* knowledge and science"—or else in relying upon "moral feeling and on sympathy," which, since individual predilection diverges boundlessly, "are too frail and uncertain for a rule of moral action." The continued application of either result necessitates a sanguine belief in a progress inherent in man's natural and even subjective self or else in the general empirical scheme of things. The gradual evaporation of this belief was mirrored in art, as the nineteenth century wore to a close, by a decay and growing aimlessness in romanticism and by a subsequent transition to a barer, more searching, and occasionally a more naturalistic relativism.

Owing to an array of extraordinary individual talent, the early nineteenth century, especially in music and literature, takes rank among the greatest periods of western art; and few generalizations consistently apply to the outstanding exponents of romanticism. Yet because it did not exist in an aesthetic vacuum but was so closely interrelated with a general relativistic subjectivism, romantic art has been frequently censured during the twentieth century, and perhaps with some justice. It may certainly be admitted that if art is to emancipate and give voice to the subjective associations and feelings of the individual, it is difficult to draw the line between what is valid and what is not. The ultimate temptation is to abandon a line of demarcation. Criticism, in that case, assumes an "expressionist" point of view, like that of Croce: it merely inquires what the artist's intention was and how well he succeeded; and it neglects a third question, upon which Goethe was careful to insist: what is the worth of the artist's intention? Moreover, "a subjective nature," as he remarked, "has soon talked out his little internal material, and is at last ruined by mannerism. . . . I call the classic *healthy*, and the romantic *sickly*." Wordsworth himself was aware that his "associations must have sometimes been particular instead of general, and that consequently, giving to things a false importance, I may sometimes have written on unworthy subjects." We may also admit that self-expression too often results, as Irving Babbitt pointed out, in a corruption of the Aristotelean *katharsis* —a degeneration into the *katharisis* which a recent critic exalts as the same "grateful feeling . . . a hen achieves every time she lays an egg": "I am aware," said Rousseau, "that the reader need not know these details, but I need to tell him." The accompanying self-absorption which is sometimes found in extreme romanticism had various ramifications. As distinct from that of more recent art, it was often marked by the sort of sensibility of which Hazlitt complained in Rousseau: "His alternate pleasures and pains are the bead-roll that he tells over and piously worships." Furthermore, the common romantic conception of the spontaneous "unconsciousness" of genius—as it was urged, that is, by its more extreme spokesmen—admittedly bears affinities with the hasty and primitivistic opposition between the "natural" and the "artificial." On the continent, its interrelation with the general extolling of mere expansiveness was extremely pronounced—as Babbitt, again, has amusingly if at times unfairly shown—in the French Rousseauists and in the German *Sturm und Drang;* and we may remember Fichte's praise of the Germans as an *Urfolk* in whom the natural and the unconscious spontaneously wells up. Similarly, at least some of the "communion" with nature—though not that of Wordsworth, yet that of many lesser figures—was undeniably a mere communion with one's own mood. An awareness of this was perhaps one of the sources of romantic melancholy. Though they might at times believe that "Nature never did betray The heart that loved her," some romanticists realized only too well that they "pined for what is not." But the matter can easily be pushed too far. It was admittedly in an *Ode on Dejection,* for example, that Coleridge wrote "in *our* life alone doth Nature live"; but the "shaping spirit of imagination" which, for Coleridge, illuminates the "inanimate cold world" could be confused with "mood" or an outrush of sentiment only by the most determined anti-romantic.

II

Indeed, recent censuring of the subjective element in romanticism, both by critics who have merely substituted another and less effusive form of individualism and by writers who have condemned all forms of modern relativistic subjectivism, has suffered from the quick generalization which tempts any judgment by one age of another immediately preceding it. Much adverse criticism is particularly vulnerable to the charge of indiscrimination in its view of the strictly aesthetic aims and qualities of early

nineteenth-century romanticism. There has especially been an occasional but blatant failure to distinguish between, on the one hand,
the spontaneity and emotional intensity which are prized—and
attained—in romantic criticism and art, and, on the other hand, the
expansive egocentricity and aimless sentimentality of which it is only
too easy to find indications throughout the later eighteenth and
entire nineteenth centuries.

The romantic use of suggestion, to take but one instance, may be
condemned as capable of becoming indeterminate and limp: of
evoking merely such random recollections and images as are already
near the surface; of inducing a revery or a kind of Paterian "stirring
of the senses," which may "set the spirit free for a moment" but
which admittedly leaves it undisciplined, unsettled, and without
purpose. That this has encouraged an occasional cultivation of nostalgia for its own sake is a familiar and indeed valid charge. But it
is a charge which has been hastily and indiscriminately flung about,
especially by the followers of Irving Babbitt, who felt that even a
little yearning was a dangerous thing. For, except during the later
seventeenth and early eighteenth centuries, a use of suggestion far
transcending that in classical antiquity had been intrinsic and traditional in much European art and literature, particularly in the
individualization of emotions which flowered in one aspect of the
baroque and in the early seventeenth-century interest in the dramatic. Instances had abounded, not least of all in Shakespeare,
Milton, and Rembrandt, of its indispensability in prompting
imaginative reach and a vitality of inference; and these instances
may be especially paralleled by recourse to much of the English
poetry of the romantic movement. Similarly, the more felicitous
attempts of romantic poetry to reveal analogies and significances
which exist to subjective reaction alone rarely transgressed the
limits which English criticism had marked out during the second
half of the eighteenth century; and as such they should be sharply
distinguished from the marked subjectivity of less happy and later
efforts of romanticism. Even in the much-ridiculed interest in "syn-
aesthesia," there is a difference between the moderate and legitimate speculations of the eighteenth-century associationists, of
Hazlitt, or of Coleridge, and the more extreme and self-indulging
notions of Rousseau and Diderot; between Keats's masterly use
of several senses in strengthening an image and the sort of thing
later exemplified by Rimbaud's comparison of the five vowels to
various colors, by the aesthete of the nineties who wished to "say
mad scarlet things and awaken the night with silver silences," or
by the hero of Huysmans's novel, *A Rebours*, who devotes himself
to composing concerts of perfumes and liqueurs, and who at length
collapses in the arms of a nerve-specialist.

Critics who rather too arbitrarily oppose the classic and the romantic as diametrical opposites often take pause to caution us not to judge the various ramifications of classicism by what they degenerated into; yet the same critics, in upbraiding European romanticism, have cited as illustration and tended to think in terms of the several extremes into which romanticism was capable of degenerating. To say, for example, that the stylistic premises and values of such writers as Wordsworth, Hazlitt, or Keats were admissions inevitably leading to the diffuse "dampness" which often characterizes poorer romantic art and criticism, and which seems to repel many critics of the present day, is almost as weak a generalization as to say that in Aristotle are the inevitable seeds of Thomas Rymer; and if one judges by potential degeneration in both instances, the question seems to subside into whether one is more averse to a marsh than a desert.

In common with much other nineteenth and twentieth-century art, many of even the most successful examples of romanticism admittedly lack a certain moral centrality which is familiar in so much classical, Renaissance, and even neo-classic art. But the various styles of the most successful romantic art were at least guided by purposes which transcend the mere exploitation of emotional mood or technical interest. It should be noted, indeed, that a romanticization of subject matter long precedes the deliberate romanticization of the aesthetic medium. The poems of Goldsmith are characteristic in this respect; and even through the *Lyrical Ballads* (1798) of Wordsworth and Coleridge, and the narrative poems of Scott, Byron, and Keats, an almost orthodox interest in action and event is still retained, and the romantic themes tend to dictate the imagery, the vocabulary, and even the versification. In the *Lyrical Ballads*, said Wordsworth, "each of these poems has a purpose . . . the feeling therein developed gives importance to the action and situation, and not the action and situation to the feeling"; and, although the statement—as Hazlitt pointed out—is not strictly true, its intention, at least, is significant. A contrast is thus offered to the later poetry of the nineteenth century, where, as notoriously in Swinburne's poems on classical themes, subjects are assumed of any sort, and are then employed as a mere backdrop to the conscious romanticization of style *per se*. In Victorian poetry, the past, for example, is frequently reverted to not because it offers romantic subjects but because of what it can offer associationally to the diction and the imagery: because the very nostalgia evoked by it furnishes an easy and immediate emotional response which would permit a stylistic manipulation and development of mood. The poetic aestheticism of this period gave additional opportunity to the development of the novel as one of the few remaining *genres* which could still have pertinence to life.

A parallel is to be observed in the evolution of nineteenth-century painting. Whereas Michelangelo had sought to idealize the human being, and Rembrandt to portray him as he is, early nineteenth-century painting romanticized its subject matter. But the delineation of object, action, or scene was still a basic concern. It remained for the latter half of the century to busy itself primarily with problems of light and shade, of color, and of form as ends in themselves; and the parallel with the music of that period and with its interest in tonal coloring is even more pronounced. Many twentieth-century reactions to this tendency were reactions against languor, insipidity, or exhausted conventions, but constituted no break in fundamental direction; and the subjectivistic concern with the aesthetic medium itself, either for its emotional and associational potentialities or for a somewhat more formalistic conception of technique, not only remained but became almost scientific.

The moderation in the general stylistic character of romantic art at its best is also to be attributed to its ability to profit from tradition without becoming eclectic and reminiscent. The comparative restraint of English romanticism, in particular, was partly due to an acute if occasionally confined awareness of English poetic tradition. And, more than any other European people, the English possessed a large body of creative literature which had been written before neo-classic rationalism became extensively reflected in European art; and this literature, in addition to its other attributes, had been characterized by an imaginative strength and an emotional spontaneity which were at once congenial to romanticism and which at the same time had been channeled to either a religious, formal, or objectively dramatic end.

The subjectivistic assumptions of romantic criticism itself, however, have perhaps been more vulnerable. Throughout the eighteenth century, British empirical and psychological criticism had increasingly created a temptation to regard the beautiful as a by-product of the mind's subjective working rather than as the selective "imitation" of an idealized nature. It therefore sought to analyze the character of the reactions which make up both taste and aesthetic creation before it pronounced upon art. It is somewhat in this vein that Coleridge insisted that the poet's aim is less to "copy nature" than to "create forms according to the severe laws of the intellect"; and he consequently attempted, as he said, "to ground my opinions in the component faculties of the human mind itself, and their comparative dignity and importance. According to the faculty or source, from which the pleasure given by any poem or passage was derived, I estimated the merit of such poem or passage." The crystallization of this tendency is preeminently exemplified on the continent, of course, by Kant: any estimate of the beautiful, said Kant, must be based upon the analysis of the aesthetic sense or taste; and the determinations of taste "can be no other than subjective." The conception of art as a kind of excrescence of mind rather than as an imitation of significant objective reality was, like other legacies of eighteenth-century British empiricism, extremely profitable to particularized aesthetic criticism; but as a basic conception it was in some respects a potential Trojan Horse, and one, it may be noted, which was hardly the sort that the Greeks would have bestowed. Less happy possibilities accrued in proportion as the mind was seen to be increasingly restricted in its communication with the external world; for the assumption that the reactions of the subjective mind are the only certain phenomena is one which may lead to almost any eventuality. The methods of meeting this problem were multifarious; they became more so as the nineteenth century progressed, and have varied from an almost complete relativism to attempted ramifications of Schiller's and Schelling's "objective idealism" and of the Kantian doctrine of "the universal subjective validity of taste."

Yet many of the generalizations which may be made about the basic character of romantic aesthetic theory are as little applicable to the more sober criticism of this period as they would be to that of any other. For major romantic critics were far from prepared to accept all the extreme consequences of the problem of subjective taste. As in the notable examples of Goethe and Hazlitt, they occasionally turned back to classical antiquity and especially the Renaissance; they turned directly, that is, to art itself, as it flourished in its greatest epochs, and sought to derive their standards from it; nor should it be forgotten that, among the severest judges of this period, were men who themselves dwelt in it. The general stream of lesser romantic criticism also refused at last to follow the exclusive lead of psychological speculation, but with less success; and by the middle of the nineteenth century, aesthetics and criticism became effectively divorced and traveled in substantially the same direction but by very different roads. The English in particular, having virtually created the modern science of aesthetics, or having at least established the subjective basis from which aesthetics was to proceed, in general refused to become professional aestheticians, and abandoned the subject to the academic dialectic and later the pragmatic experimentation of the German universities. They themselves turned either to the favorite and often suggestively fruitful English pastime of appreciative description or else to the historical study of their own literature and of the classics;

and a Victorian or Edwardian critic of philosophical inclination became almost as rare as an aesthetician who possessed an extensive knowledge of art or any genuine susceptibility to it.

III

Despite its strong empirical bent, English criticism especially tended to avoid excessive subjectivism during the early nineteenth century. Subjectivism in one form or another is perhaps an inevitable companion of extreme empiricism. But the British confidence in the teaching of experience at least prevented an acceptance, by the more sober, either of "natural" feeling and inclination as a guide or of the elaborate subjectivistic systems which were being worked out in Germany; indeed, Hazlitt's reaction to the first of these two tendencies—and Hazlitt, in his fundamental premises, is perhaps the most representative English critic of the period—was one of strong and often clear-sighted antagonism.

It has been one of the purposes of the two preceding chapters to show that, as these terms were evolved in later eighteenth-century British criticism, "imagination" is hardly to be confused with revery or rank illusion, and that "feeling" is seldom to be regarded as equivalent to "impulse." Such terms—like any others—were admittedly capable of the loosest connotation, and, in popular moral and semi-critical writing, sometimes bore a marked Rousseauistic coloring. But most early-nineteenth-century critics of any significance continued to use them as means of implying a broader and more intense awareness and employment of experience than can be achieved by analytical enumeration or by the artificial postulation of separate categories and concepts. In its unification, for example, of all varieties of mental exercise and response, eighteenth-century associationism had occasionally tended to designate them all, in a loose way, as "feelings": thus sensations, as Hartley said, are those "internal feelings of the mind which are produced by sense-impressions," whereas "all of our other internal feelings may be called ideas." Indeed, as Hugh Blair had said, though with a different implication, the divergence

> between the authors who found the standard of taste upon the common feelings of human nature ascertained by general approbation, and those who found it upon established principles which can be ascertained by reason, is more an apparent than a real difference. Like many other controversies, it turns chiefly upon modes of expression.[2]

The use of the word "feeling" in this sense survived well into the nineteenth century, and may be characteristically exemplified

2. Hugh Blair, *Lectures on Rhetoric and Belles-Lettres* (1783), I, 32n.

by the Scottish intuitionist, Thomas Brown, whose works comprise one of the most detailed and descriptive syntheses of the joint associationist-intuitionist tendency. To Brown, all intellection is distinguished by "feelings of relation" and also by a central "desire" —by a purpose, interest, or concern, that is. This dominant and controlling "desire,"

> like every other vivid feeling, . . . [according to] its permanence, tends to keep the accompanying conception of the subject, which is the object of the desire, also permanent before us; and while it is thus permanent, the usual spontaneous suggestions [i.e., associations] take place; conception following conception, in rapid but relative series. . . .[3]

It is this "desire" or interest, "co-existing with successive *feelings of relation* as they arise . . . to which we commonly give the name of reasoning." In addition to innate capacity, therefore, experience is obviously necessary: it broadens and even creates desire or interest, and it feeds and disciplines the associations by which "feelings of relation" arise. "Taste" is simply the application of this combinatory function of mind to the aesthetic realm: it presupposes, first, an "emotion" which is directed to an end, and which reacts in proportion to the significance of that end, whether it be an ideal, a design of action, a disclosure of character, or the self-sufficient form of a simple object; but it also includes a sensitive "feeling of the relations of fitness" towards that end—a feeling schooled by an extensive acquaintance not only with the specific medium of art but with all facets of life which can come within the province of art.

Similarly, Wordsworth tended to apply the term "feeling" to a state of comparatively vivid awareness, and "thought" to a later and vestigial "representative" of that awareness. It is necessary that the feeling be intense if the subsequent thought is to have pertinence and substance; "deep thinking," said Coleridge, "is attainable only by a man of deep feeling." It is with this implication of the word that, in terms and outlines which were later echoed and modified by Keats, Wordsworth took such pains to describe the evolution of the thinking mind. Thus, "boyhood" is a period of "glad animal movement" and of thoughtless and chaotic sensation; "youth," if sufficient native endowment is present, is characterized by intense feeling of various sorts which is not necessarily translated into thought; and, with the attainment of "maturity," the immediate delight in sensation disappears, while feeling continues but culminates in thought—"feelings," said Coleridge, "die by flowing into the mould of the intellect, becoming ideas." It should be noted

3. Thomas Brown, *Lectures on the Philosophy of the Human Mind* (Edinburgh: 1820), II, 398.

parenthetically that an absorption in external nature was far from Wordsworth's intention. It was only in his youth that he "had a world about me . . . I made it, for it only lived to me"; and this was a period of mere "fancy," when "Imagination slept." In maturity, he said in the *Intimations of Immortality,*

> What though the radiance which was once so bright
> Be now forever taken from my sight,
> Though nothing can bring back the hour
> Of splendor in the grass, of glory in the flower;
> We will grieve not, rather find
> Strength in what remains behind;
>   .   .   .
> In years that bring the philosophic mind.

The genuine philosophic mind, then, presupposes and necessitates feeling, particularly in youth. Art of any excellence, said Wordsworth, is produced only "by a man who, being possessed of more than usual organic sensibility, had also thought long and deeply. For our continued influxes of feeling are modified and directed by our thoughts, which are indeed the representatives of all our past feelings." [4]

"Without passion," as Hume had said, "no idea has any force." Similarly, taste—although it includes "a judgment that cannot be duped into admiration by aught that is unworthy for it"—must rest, added Wordsworth, upon "a natural sensibility that has been tutored into correctness without losing any of its quickness"; and those critics alone are to be heeded "who, never having suffered their youthful love of poetry to remit much of its force, have applied to the consideration of the laws of this art the best power of their understandings." The control of learning and experience by such a sensibility may hardly be regarded as the mere following of impulse, and, as Dugald Stewart said, actually prevents an aimless subservience or inclination to the temporary:

> A sensibility, deep and permanent, to those objects of affection, admiration, and reverence, which interested the youthful heart . . . gives rise to the habits of attentive observation by which such a Taste alone can be formed; and it is this also that, binding and perpetuating the associations which such a Taste supposes, fortifies the mind against the fleeting caprices which the votaries of fashion watch and obey.[5]

Since thought is a kind of conceptualization or abstraction from more immediate and vital experiences, "feeling" may thus be pos-

4. William Wordsworth, Preface to the *Lyrical Ballads, Prose Works* (ed. Grosart, 1876), II, 82.

5. Dugald Stewart, "On Taste," *Philosophical Essays* (Edinburgh: 1810), pp. 470–471.

tulated as the groundwork of taste. But it also characterizes taste in an even more inclusive sense. For coalesced "aggregates of simple ideas by association" in time tend themselves, as Hartley said, to form an "emotion." Ideas, evolved from primary or primitive feelings, may in turn pass into conceptions which, though broadened and rendered more valid after this intermediary process of abstraction, may be sufficiently unified and vivid in their appearance to deserve the designation of "feelings." It is in this respect that Wordsworth defined poetry as "the spontaneous overflow of powerful feelings"—of feelings which have been previously screened, as it were, by the process of thought; and poetry thus

> take its origin from emotion recollected in tranquillity: the emotion is contemplated till, by a species of re-action, the tranquillity gradually disappears, and an emotion, kindred to that which was before the subject of contemplation, is gradually produced, and does itself actually exist in the mind.[6]

IV

Wordsworth's definition of the poetic process manifests a loose but very British assumption, and one which is rather prevalent in English romantic criticism, that "ideas" in general, when held with any intensity, can coalesce into almost emotional convictions. Thus sympathy, as Hume had stated, "is nothing but the conversion of an idea into an impression by the force of the imagination"; and this impression, when felt with sufficient vivacity, is in turn fused and transformed into the emotion which was originally observed in another human being. According to such a process, perceptions and ideas are capable of becoming melted, so to speak, into this crucible of imaginative and emotional response. Hazlitt's *Principles of Human Action* (1805), which probably had a strong influence on Keats, especially exemplifies this assumption. The theme of the book, which is an argument against the Hobbist doctrine of innate self-love as the dominant principle of human action, is the formative adaptability of man's emotional character, and the complete dependence of the will upon whatever may be said to constitute mind. These principles are of course far from unclassical; they are among the primary suppositions of classicism. The mind inclines to that of which it possesses the most vivid idea; self-love is an effect rather than a cause, and arises when the individual has a clearer and more vivid idea, through direct experience, of his own "identity" than of the identities of others. But if the imagination is sufficiently wide and intense in its working, he may attain an equally clear and vigorous idea of the "identity" of another—an idea which, accord-

6. Wordsworth, *Prose Works*, II, 96.

ing as it is supported by intelligent and attentive observation, becomes transmuted into a sympathetic feeling of proportionate justness, and results in a consequent moral concern as strong as self-love, if not stronger.

This assumption that ideas can be resolved, converted, or as it were energized into persuasions and responses which are instantaneous in their working, and which thus deserve to be called "feelings," manifests—like the prevalent conception of the imagination in the English criticism of the period—a common conviction of British associationism and intuitionalism generally: the conviction, which was discussed in a previous chapter, that instinct of whatever sort feeds upon experience, and digests into its own automatic working the accumulated results of past impressions, reactions, thoughts, and judgments, however subtle or minute they may be when considered separately. Conceptions "may exist together," said Thomas Brown, "forming one complex feeling": each of the several parts of this feeling may branch out with endless associational tentacles, as it were; but, by means of a guiding emotional centrality, still be united in "one harmonizing whole"; and an appropriate use of "suggestion" in art will elicit these connected and relevant associations, not in piecemeal succession, but, under the control of a central feeling, in such a way that they "multiply and mingle as they arise."

In this awareness, the most fluid and elusive interrelations will be sensed; and, in the aesthetic realm especially, a truth and significance will be observed through all "the innumerable compositions and decompositions"—as Keats wrote—"which take place between the intellect and its thousand materials before it arrives at that trembling, delicate and snail-horn perception of beauty." And such an insight, with its grasp of the unique and organic totality of a phenomenon, will stand opposed to that artificial and abstracting faculty by which, as Wordsworth said in the *Prelude*, we

> pore, and dwindle as we pore,
> Viewing all objects unremittingly
> In disconnection dead and spiritless.

It is because of the spontaneity of its function, said Dugald Stewart, that taste is sometimes mistakenly assumed to be a simple sentiment; for "the transition from a Taste for the beautiful to that more comprehensive Taste," which extends its scope to all the several aspects of an art, is easy and gradual, and is characterized by an "insensible swelling in dimension." A familiar ramification of this attitude in Victorian criticism, though more restrictedly stylistic in its object, is found in Matthew Arnold's insistence that, in order to discern poetic excellence, one should have assimilated "lines and expressions of the great masters," and employ them as a kind of "touchstone" to other poetry:

> Of course we are not to require this other poetry to resemble them; it may be very dissimilar. But if we have any tact we shall find them, when we have lodged them well in our minds, an infallible touchstone for detecting the presence or absence of high poetic quality, and also the degree of this quality. . . .[7]

Such an extended and trained fusion of feelings, then, is far from being confused by English romantic criticism with mere native "impulse"; and it is characteristic that Hazlitt, who profoundly distrusted "natural" inclination of the primitivistic sort, regarded taste as inevitably vitiated in proportion as it became public. Although Keats, again, was "certain of nothing but the holiness of the Heart's affections and the truth of the Imagination," he had little patience with Godwin's belief in "perfectibility"—"the nature of the world will not admit of it"; and the "Heart's affections" of which he speaks are as far removed from the temperamental "benevolism" of a John Gilbert Cooper as is the "reason" of Erasmus or Johnson from that of Charles Gildon. "I know nothing, I have read nothing," said the youthful Keats: ". . . there is but one way for me—the road lies through application, study, and thought." For

> The difference of high Sensations with and without knowledge appears to me this—in the latter case we are falling continually ten thousand fathoms deep and being blown up again without wings and with all the horror of a bare shouldered creature—in the former case, our shoulders are fledge, and we go thro' the same air and space without fear.[8]

And following Reynolds—whose *Discourses* he greatly admired—Wordsworth dismissed any argument for taste which presupposes the validity of untutored sentiment: taste, he said, "can only be produced by severe thought and a long-continued intercourse with the best models of composition"; and the fundamental principles and intentions of such poets as Chaucer, Shakespeare, and Milton must be imbibed by any English poet or critic and woven into the texture of his mind. The poet, said Coleridge, must regulate himself "by principles, the ignorance or neglect of which would convict him of being no *poet*, but a silly or presumptuous usurper of the name"—

> In a word by such knowledge of the facts, material and spiritual, that most appertain to his art, as, if it have been governed and

7. Matthew Arnold, "Study of Poetry," *Essays in Criticism, Second Series* (1896), pp. 16–17.

8. Keats to J. H. Reynolds, May 3, 1818, *Letters* (ed. M. B. Forman, 1935), p. 140.

applied by *good sense*, and rendered instinctive by habit, becomes the representative and reward of our past conscious reasonings, insights, and conclusions, and acquires the name of TASTE.[9]

Indeed, "genius" is almost determined by the extent to which knowledge and experience are rendered intuitively and spontaneously applicable by strong conception and feeling. Shakespeare, said Hazlitt, possessed a knowledge "of the connecting links of the passions" which "anticipated and outdid all the efforts of the most refined art, not inspired and rendered instinctive by genius." "Talent," he added, "is a voluntary power, while genius is involuntary." And the emphasis by British romantic critics on the "spontaneity" and "unconsciousness" of genius is by no means to be confused, as it occasionally has been, with an infinite capacity for not taking pains, and with the admittedly rather general desire in the nineteenth century to emancipate individual temperament. Shakespeare, said Coleridge, was "no mere child of nature": rather, he "studied patiently, meditated deeply, understood minutely, till knowledge, become habitual and intuitive, wedded itself to his habitual feelings, and at length gave birth to that stupendous power, by which he stands alone, with no equal or second in his class." [1] August von Schlegel contended that the Greeks were able to assume "a unison and proportion between all the faculties," whereas modern art and thought are aware of an "internal discord," and attempt to reconcile it by "hallowing the impressions of the senses, as it were, through a mysterious connection with higher feelings; while the soul, on the other hand, embodies its forebodings, or indescribable intuitions of infinity, in types and symbols borrowed from the visible world." [2] This "internal discord," and the struggle to reconcile it, were somewhat less pronounced in England. For "intuition" and the "impressions of the senses" had never been effectively separated there; and, as a consequence, it was not felt that sense-impressions particularly needed to be "hallowed" nor that intuitions, on the other hand, were completely "indescribable."

The intuitional assimilation of experience, and the capacity of feeling to capture interrelations, qualities, and significances, however elusive, and then to modify and render them organically and instantaneously pertinent, form the background of almost all the various conceptions of taste, genius, and imagination advanced in early-nineteenth-century English criticism and aesthetics; and had Hazlitt written his contemplated history of British philosophy, he would perhaps have sketched the rise and ramifications of this

9. Coleridge, *Biographia Literaria* (1817; ed. Shawcross, 1907), II, 64.
1. *Ibid.*, II, 19–20.

2. Schlegel, *Lectures on Dramatic Art and Literature* (1809–1811), Lect. I.

background with a revealing and certainly sympathetic insight. This conception of mind, which is very British both in looseness and in its joint empiricism and intuitionalism, was capable of many modifications which varied from a mildly skeptical relativism to a potential coöperation—such as Reynolds had earlier achieved— with many of the tenets of humanistic classicism. The extent of its flexibility and of its unusual capacity for eclecticism is peculiarly exemplified by Coleridge, who, as Mr. Wellek has well shown, was far from being the Kantian he is usually supposed to have been. A French writer has said that Mme Clotilde de Vaux, whom Comte regarded as his "inspiration," "never inspired Comte except with his own ideas"; and—certainly without implying any similarity in mental stature between Clotilde and Kant—we may say that Kant rarely inspired Coleridge except with his own ideas or with those which he had imbibed, as a youth, from the Christian Platonists.

v

By its loose and compromising empiricism, therefore, English romantic thought avoided both excessive relativism and mere emotionalism. Its major departure from classical precept and practice was in being somewhat naturalistic in its direction rather than frankly subjectivistic; for the intuitional empiricism upon which it relied was tempted to concentrate on the particular, and upon the revelation of its essential nature *as* a particular. This concentration had occasionally an almost scientific direction, as in Sir Charles Bell's *Lectures on the Anatomy and Philosophy of Expression* (1806), which took as their concern the natural expression of character in the face and figure of the human being, and the cause and control of this expression by the focusing of the various natural forces and relations which propel and animate the empirical universe. *King Lear*, said Hazlitt in a passage which evoked admiration from Keats, continually presents

> the highest examples not only of the force of individual passion, but of its dramatic vicissitudes and striking effects arising from the different circumstances and characters of the persons speaking. We see the ebb and flow of the feeling, its pauses and feverish starts, its impatience of opposition, its accumulating force when it has time to recollect itself, the manner in which it avails itself of every passing word or gesture . . .[3]

The expression and character of the particular itself might thus become an objective goal for imaginative grasping; and beauty, accordingly, would be viewed as a sort of by-product which attends

3. Hazlitt, *Character of Shakespeare's Plays* (1817), in *Works* (ed. Howe. 1931–1934), IV, 259.

the fulfillment by a creature, object, or even an empirically rendered aesthetic form of its distinctive and individual function, significance, and nature. "Nothing seemed to escape him," said Joseph Severn, recalling his walks with Keats:

> the motions of the wind—just how it took certain tall flowers . . . even the features and gestures of the passing tramps, the colour of one woman's hair, the smile on one child's face, the furtive animalism below the deceptive humanity in many of the vagrants, even the hats, clothes, shoes, wherever these conveyed the remotest hint as to the real self of the wearer.[4]

It was the naturally "instinctive" and elusive character and meaning of the particular in which, for Keats, the poetical resided:

> I go among the Fields and catch a glimpse of a Stoat or a fieldmouse peeping out of the withered grass—the creature hath a purpose and its eyes are bright with it. I go amongst the buildings of a city and I see a Man hurrying along—to what? the Creature has a purpose and his eyes are bright with it.

The "reasonings" of the human being are themselves a pursuit of "the same instinctive course as the veriest human animal you can think of," and possess a higher but fundamentally similar "grace":

> May there not be superior beings amused with any graceful, though instinctive attitude my mind may fall into, as I am entertained with the alertness of a Stoat or the anxiety of a Deer? Though a quarrel in the Streets is a thing to be hated, the energies displayed in it are fine; the commonest Man shows a grace in his quarrel—By a superior being our reasonings may take the same tone—though erroneous they may be fine—This is the very thing in which consists poetry.[5]

Yet we may recall the striking evolution which took place in Keats two years before his premature death; and there is reason to believe that, had he lived even another twenty-five years longer, the course of both the poetry and the criticism of nineteenth-century England would have been somewhat different. "Some think," he later wrote, "I have lost that poetic ardor and fire 'tis said I once had." It gave him no regret; for "I hope," he continued, "I shall substitute a more thoughtful and quiet power." And even when he stated that the poetical is to be found in the distinctive function and "identity" of the particular alone, he was not really certain; for he added, "If so, [poetry] is not so fine a thing as philosophy—For the same reason that an eagle is not so fine a thing as a truth."

Indeed, it must not be forgotten that at least some awareness of

---

4. William Sharp, *Life and Letters of Joseph Severn* (1892), p. 20.
5. To George and Georgiana Keats, Feb. 14 to May 3, 1819, *Letters*, pp. 316–317.

the necessity of the universal is implied throughout most English romantic criticism. The object of poetry, said Wordsworth, "is truth, not individual and local, but general, and operative." Yet if English romantic criticism was cognizant of the universal, it tended to regard the universal as attainable only through the particular; it would have agreed, for example, with Sir Joshua Reynolds that Michelangelo's use of particularization was indispensable as a means of enlivening and enforcing the presentation of the ideal. "Nothing becomes real," said Keats, "till it is experienced"; "axioms in philosophy are not axioms until they are proved upon our pulses." And Hazlitt, who considered drama "the closest imitation of nature" because of its capacity to exhibit both the individual and the representative, felt that the concrete must serve as the starting point; if we know little of humanity, for example, "but its abstract and common properties, . . . we shall care just as little. . . . If we understand the texture and vital feeling, we can then fill up the outline, but we cannot supply the former from having the latter given." There seems also to have been an occasional hope, inferable if unformulated, of disclosing the naturalistic and almost independent "truth" or character of the particular and at the same time of revealing its participation or reflection of the ideal; and it is indicative of the compromising spirit of the English criticism of this period that it should have thus essayed to preserve this precarious and at bottom loosely empirical balance between the ideal and the concrete.

Perhaps the most successful attempt, certainly the most familiar, was that of Coleridge. Through a brilliant eclecticism, he tried to establish at least a theoretical mutual dependence between particular and universal by maintaining the vital ferment of potentiality inherent in the former and its organic transmutation into the latter. The particular, indeed, is not a separate and fixed totality at all: what appears as a finite and self-sufficient entity is only "a framework which the human imagination forms by its own limits, as the foot measures itself on the snow." Shakespeare, accordingly, did not merely abstract generalizations from his knowledge of specific individuals: rather, in addition, to this secondary and merely assisting process, he grasped the living force, the law and active thread of connection, which binds the specific with the general; and it is characteristic that "in the Shakespearian drama there is a vitality which grows and evolves itself from within." It was the prerogative of Shakespeare

> to have the *universal*, which is potential in each *particular*, opened out to him . . . not as an abstraction from observation of a variety of men, but as the substance capable of endless modifications, of which his own personal existence was but one, and to

use *this one* as the eye that beheld the other, and as the tongue that could convey the discovery.[6]

Beaumont and Fletcher, for example, portray only "what could be put together and represented to the eye." Their piecemeal synthesis, that is, was a mere "abstraction" from the observation of various particulars, and lacks the germinating potentiality, the organic unfolding of process, which Shakespeare continually discloses. Their achievement is comparable to that of a man who

> might put together a quarter of an orange, a quarter of an apple, and the like of a lemon and a pomegranate, and make it look like one round diverse coloured fruit. But nature, who works from within by evolution and assimilation according to a law, cannot do it. Nor could Shakespeare, for he too worked in the spirit of nature, by evolving the germ within by the imaginative power according to an idea.[7]

A power which can unite the relatively passive and empirical conception of the particular with the comprehension of the universal is necessarily an active one. "Taste," said Coleridge, therefore, must be "an intermediate faculty which connects the active with the passive powers of our nature, the intellect with the senses; and its appointed function is to elevate the *images* of the latter, while it realizes the *ideas* of the former." Coleridge's later assignment of this function to the imagination itself is characteristic of English romantic terminology. The later eighteenth century, in establishing and analyzing what constitutes taste, had so emphasized the active properties of the mind that the imagination gradually usurped the place which taste had been given. For "taste," as Wordsworth said, too often bears a popular connotation of a "passive" faculty or combination of faculties, whereas aesthetic insight is really impossible "without the exertion of a coöperating power in the mind of the Reader." Romantic criticism believed that it had found an appropriate term in "imagination"; for it wished to postulate a faculty which is at all times acutely aware, as "consequitive reasoning" is not, of the empirically concrete, and which is at the same time cognizant of all that reason, in its widest sense, can attain: a capacity, in other words, which, by drawing upon all facets of mind and feeling, conceives the particular as "adequate to an idea of reason," and effects an indissoluble "reconcilement," as Coleridge said, of "the general with the concrete; the idea with the image." Such an achievement is characterized by a "union of all that is essential in all the functions of our spirit,"

---

6. Coleridge, Lecture vii (1818), *Miscellaneous Criticism* (ed. Raysor, 1936), p. 44.

7. *Ibid.*, pp. 42–43.

and by "an emotion tranquil from its very intensity"; and the imagination, since it connotes this comprehensive and energizing capacity, "is but another name," as Wordsworth stated, for "Reason in her most exalted mood."

VI

As it was resurrected during the eighteenth century, the conception of art as a unique and independent function or aspect of life was inevitably distinguished by a growing self-consciousness. Yet many of the figures of that century, including some who themselves advanced or indirectly aided this conception, seem to have felt that this self-consciousness, with its accompanying interest in aesthetic theory, was a symptom that Western art was moving into a more sophisticated and a less vital and gifted stage. Certainly, the general relativistic movement in Western European art is not without historical parallels which would possibly suggest as much. It is especially to be compared—as indeed it often has been—with the general tenor of classical art after the age of Pericles. The growing concern with the particularized character, which gathered impetus in sculpture and painting under the Alexandrian realists; the emphasis on "originality," which seems to have stemmed from the time of Alexander the Great and then to have augmented with the opening of the Christian era; the ultimate rejection of the mimetic theory of art by such theorists as Philostratus and the evoking of the creative imagination, "a wiser and subtler artist"—as Philostratus said—"than imitation":—such tendencies, of course, were merely surface indications of a growing self-consciousness in art, and of an increasing emphasis upon art as an independent exercise of the mind.

It has been well said that "The Greek knew not that he was an artist till his arts were well past their prime": his dominant conscious concern had been "Gods, heroes, and men" rather than art as such. The Greek use of art as a formative means to a further end is not to be confused, of course, with didacticism in the ordinary sense of the word. The assumption that art has little excuse for existence unless it discloses and inculcates the fundamental verities of life was therefore no more peculiar to Plato than it was unusually Philistine for Aristotle to state that "Children are to be instructed in painting . . . primarily because it makes them judges of the beauties of the human form." Mr. F. P. Chambers has justly contended that "If morality is an obstruction to the free creative impulses of Fine Art,—as modern aesthetics believe—under such obstruction did Fine Art in Greece begin her course; nor was she freed when she ran most strongly." And when Greece at length

emancipated art: when it turned, that is, to the deliberate cultivation and study of art for itself, and to aesthetic theorizing, it
discovered that its highest attainment in art was already in the
past. Without pushing the parallel too far, or by any means col-
lapsing into the ever-waiting arms of Spengler, we may admit that,
like the pervasive philosophical shift which it mirrored, the great
relativistic emancipation of art in the later eighteenth century at
least brought with it a few of the problems which ancient art, as
it acquired self-consciousness, had finally been forced to confront.
The main problem with which European art was now faced was to
find a centrality of purpose and direction. It may be questioned
whether this centrality has really been found. Nor can criticism,
from the onset of this epoch until the present day, be said to have
furnished much lasting aid in the attempt to descry it, despite the
isolated insights of its major spokesmen and the later addition of
unparalleled technical means.

The manner in which leading English critics of the early nineteenth century avoided the excesses of both emotionalism and subjectivism is mainly attributable to a more than usually active
presence in this period of qualities which are distinctively British:
to the empirical but compromising good-sense which traditionally
characterizes British thought at its happiest, and to a stubborn
refusal to accept for long any systematization. Ways of thinking
which have been customarily thought of as British have almost invariably shown a certain moderation as long as they have been confined to their homeland; and it is one of the interesting paradoxes
of European history that, from the time of Duns Scotus, intellectual, as well as social, economic, and aesthetic tendencies, which
have taken rise in Britain, have been carried to their logical conclusions elsewhere. We may agree, for example, with Engels, who,
in praising England with faint damns, stated that "materialism is
the natural-born son of Great Britain." Yet materialism in England, like so many other tendencies there, has largely preserved an
amateur status; it remained for the later French Cartesians to
systematize mechanism, and to conclude, by applying the rationalism of Descartes to the empiricism of Locke, that man is really a
"machine." "In the eighteenth century," said Friedrich Schlegel at
its close, "the English were the first people of Europe, in literature,
as in everything else. The whole of modern French philosophy was
produced by that of Bacon, Locke, and other Englishmen. . . . Yet
what a different appearance it assumed in France, from that which
it had always had in England!" The paradox of English thought
may be likened "to a man who bears every external mark of health
and vigor, but who is by nature prone to a dangerous distemper";
the distemper never became extreme enough to "break out openly,"

and was therefore never "cured." Schlegel seems almost to have surmised that the "materialistic disease" has been mildly inherent in the English for so long that they themselves have become relatively immune to the epidemics with which they periodically infect the continent. Utilitarianism, again, is unquestionably the offspring of Britain. Yet few gifted English thinkers were consistent in their utilitarianism; and the disparity between the effeminate sociolatry of Comte and the liberal individualism of John Stuart Mill may serve as an exaggerated but pertinent indication.

French critics often remind us, moreover, that the English are traditionally "romantic." Some substantiation may perhaps be found in the prevalent tenor of English literature as a whole. It is also certainly true that many general tendencies which are thought of as congenial to romanticism have been traditional with the English. One may note, for example, that Gothic architecture, long after it had expired on the continent, survived in England well into the seventeenth century. It even lingered on afterwards in the provincial counties; and its eighteenth-century "revival" was hardly so great a break with tradition as has occasionally been believed. British thought, moreover, which tends to prize immediacy and timeliness rather than abstraction and finality, has in all periods exhorted "instincts" and "intuitions" which have a rather emotional tinge. Yet it would be difficult to find a major British figure who was comparable to Rousseau. The romantic "regeneration of literature in the eighteenth century," said Friedrich Schlegel, "received its first impetus and its principal ruling direction from the poetry and the criticism of the English"; but he felt that German poetry and the earnest professionalism of German thought were required to develop its full romantic potentialities.

An enviable capacity to reconcile apparently inconsistent elements has been a familiar example of this moderation. We may recall the genuinely humanistic temper of many of Locke's sentiments. "The most singular phenomenon in the whole history of philosophy," said the puzzled Schlegel, "is perhaps the existence of such a man as Berkeley, who carried the attitudes of Locke so far as utterly to disbelieve the existence of the material world, and yet continued all the while a devout Christian bishop." Similarly, Hume, the prince of those that would live in the subjective, could retain and justify his neo-classic tastes, and associationism, under the Reverend John Gay, took rise within the tolerant confines of the Anglican church. This very moderation, with its resulting plasticity of mind, has permitted England to be the soil from which modern empirical relativism has stemmed and at the same time to remain a persistent seat of a broad, flexible, and unsystematized classical tradition. It may be questioned whether the strain of platonism which sometimes emerges in English thought is not more genuine, because more pliable and less methodized, than that on the continent; and there is also reason to believe that the spirit if not the letter of Christian humanism was perhaps more closely approached by a few Englishmen in the Renaissance than by its more ardent but less plastic exponents elsewhere. It is equally characteristic that the more representative figures of eighteenth-century England could reflect an almost Horatian sanity and good sense without degenerating into the bodiless and self-conscious urbanity typified by Voltaire; nor should one overlook the anomaly at this time of so authentic a Christian humanist as Dr. Johnson.

For British thought is especially the product of individuals rather than the collective architectural achievement of a movement or an age. "In speculation as in other things," Mr. Santayana has stated, "the Englishman trusts his inner man; his impulse is to soliloquize even in science." It is certainly true that although he may adopt from others—and occasionally with unparalleled sympathy and timeliness—elements which he deems "sensible" or which may seem to him to help explain his intuitions, the English thinker, from his suspicion of systems, has continually reverted to his own convictions as an individual, and reworked his philosophy afresh. The individual variety of British thought, which often transcends or disregards the general outlines of a movement or a period, is a consequence. But it also chances that, from the time of William of Occam, his convictions have usually been empirical; he is confident that experience both exists and teaches; and his watchword ultimately becomes the sensible remark of Edmund Burke—that "though no man can draw a stroke between the confines of day and night, yet darkness and light are upon the whole tolerably distinguishable." Hence the repetitive character of British thought— which also transcends the proclivities of an age—and its capacity to evoke despair in French logicians and bewilderment in German historians of philosophy. Indeed, English history as a whole, said Goethe, "repeats itself over and over again," and because it possesses so intrinsic a character, is "genuine, healthy, and therefore universal." Whether for better or worse, the history of British thought—like the British Constitution—almost deserves Johnson's description of Dryden's prose: it is "always another and the same."

The eighteenth-century transition in conceptions of art and taste is admittedly far-reaching in its implications. For if art is the interpreter of human values, aesthetic criticism, which must estimate the worth of this interpretation, is ultimately interwoven with man's entire thinking: it is interwoven with his ability to respond emotionally to rational ends, with his ethical premises and ideals, his religious aspirations, his various cosmologies, and the scientific abstractions he may choose to employ. Yet if this transition marks the general subsiding and interchange of certain very basic conceptions and values, it also witnessed the perseverance and readaptation of others. For, in varying degree, major figures of any age break through the shell of whatever concepts or premises of thinking that age may construct or generally accept. Moreover, through its traditional moderation, eclecticism, and repetitive self-scrutiny, the prevalent English thought of this transition retained a certain continuity both of procedure and, in some respects, of aim. It reworked and modified the empiricism and intuitionalism which it had inherited, and which had produced such troubled reverberations elsewhere. In doing so, it gradually evolved a loose but persistent body of aesthetic, moral, and psychological conceptions which underlay and even guided a notable flowering of literature. The pervasiveness of this body of assumptions renders it one of the few really effective means of linking together the English romantic poets and critics, while its elasticity is illustrated by the individuality, and even marked dissimilarity, which it permitted to these writers. But the unque fusion of its qualities gives it a broader and even perennial significance. For it is characteristically English, both in the varied adaptability which its looseness and lack of system permit and in its simultaneous continuity with British thought as a whole.

JOSEPHINE MILES

The Romantic Mode †

Whom shall we call the romantics? Was there actually a sufficient number of poets in agreement at the turn of the century to make what one would call a style or mode? Certain traits of attitude, or of material, or of structure, could take us back as far as Addison with his sense of a new world, or Thomson, to whom Wordsworth went for images, or the stanzaic experiments of Collins, or any poet any time for a certain cut of jib. I think we should not answer theoretically, but look to see if there was indeed in England any whole

† From *Eras & Modes in English Poetry* by Josephine Miles. Copyright, 1957, © 1964, by the Regents of the University of California. Reprinted by permission of University of California Press.

group of poets who agreed together, if only tacitly, in abandoning the full complex of the earlier mode, its epic and panoramic pentameters, for a new complex of attitude, terminology, and construction. Did any new meter take over the poetry of 1800, any new vocabulary, any whole new sort of statement?

We know that throughout the eighteenth century there had been a strong consolidation of poetic techniques which endured even through the work of Wordsworth and Keats and included much free play of virtuosity without strain on the bonds of agreement. We know that this solid agreement had made for a thematic sense of moral universality, a full and regular pentameter line, a descriptive adjectival richness, in the sublime terms of Longinus. We recognize the primary vocabulary—that is, the nouns, adjectives, and verbs used most often, over and over, by a majority of the poets —to have been especially general and emotional, in terms of *art, beauty, fate, friend, joy, life, love, land, head, heart, mind, muse, nature, power, thought, virtue,* modified by such approving epithets as *divine, fair, gay, happy, proud, soft, sweet,* a vocabulary in all well suited to generalization about natural human forces, brought home to the heart by direct image and simile.

Poems in this mode were as various as Thomson's *Seasons,* Dyer's *Ruins,* and Cowper's *Task.* In the later years of the century the tone and vocabulary grew more gloomy, more *woe* and *weeping, cold* and *sad* came into the pattern, and more details of analysis, but the pattern was easily adaptable to such modifications, and held its own as if to last forever.

The beginning of Cowper's *Task* is a good sample of the type; the epically descriptive flights have taken in humbler and humbler objects more and more seriously:

> I sing the Sofa. I, who lately sang
> Truth, Hope, and Charity, and touch'd with awe
> The solemn chords, and, with a trembling hand,
> Escap'd with pain from that advent'rous flight,
> Now seek repose upon an humbler theme;
> The theme, though humble, yet august, and proud
> Th' occasion—for the fair commands the song.

And, in the details of description:

> Nor rural sights alone, but rural sounds,
> Exhilarate the spirit, and restore
> The tone of languid Nature. Mighty winds,
> That sweep the skirt of some far-spreading wood
> Of ancient growth, make music not unlike
> The dash of Ocean on his winding shore,
> And lull the spirit while they fill the mind;

Unnumber'd branches waving in the blast,
And all their leaves fast flutt'ring, all at once.
Nor less composure waits upon the roar
Of distant floods, or on the softer voice
Of neighb'ring fountain, or of rills that slip
Through the cleft rock, and, chiming as they fall
Upon loose pebbles, loose themselves at length
In matted grass, that with a livelier green
Betrays the secret of their silent course.
Nature inanimate employs sweet sounds,
But animated nature sweeter still,
To soothe and satisfy the human ear.

This is all deft progressive analysis, and it can go on and on, through many long volumes of the nineteenth century, in a structure which needs three nouns and adjectives to every verb, so discriminated are the details of quality within the universal whole, so substantially and thoroughly received are the sensations and concepts.

We have said we should look for a new mode where a new complex of idea, material, and structure clearly began. But the pentameter epical description was too strong in itself to admit any new complexes. And by 1800, when we should be growing restless, most of the poetry written was still of this sort, still even-coupleted and satirical in its popular reaches, still wistfully voluminous and substantival at its most lofty. Were, then, could a new mode get a hold?

Well, on various fine mornings close to 1800, various poets had begun writing verses like these:

> "And wear thou this"—she solemn said,
> And bound the holly round my head;
> The polish'd leaves, and berries red,
>   Did rustling play;
> And, like a passing thought, she fled
>   In light away.
> > (Burns's "The Vision")

> My mother groan'd! my father wept.
> Into the dangerous world I leapt:
> Helpless, naked, piping loud;
> Like a fiend hid in a cloud.
> > (Blake's "Infant Sorrow")

> No more to chiefs and ladies bright
>   The harp of Tara swells;
> The chord alone, that breaks at night,
>   Its tale of ruin tells.
> Thus Freedom now so seldom wakes,
>   The only throb she gives

> Is when some heart indignant breaks,
>   To show that still she lives.
>   (Moore's "Harp")

Now in all ways, as the quickest ear or eye will tell you, this is a
new and a different mode of poetry all of a sudden. It comes of
course from "Sir Patrick Spence" and "Lord Randall" and "Chevy
Chase," but it comes not gradually, but freely, with full intent to
transform its sources. Remember how "Chevy Chase" began?—the
very first of Bishop Percy's *Reliques*—

> The Persé owt of Northombarlande,
>   And a vowe to God mayd he,
> That he wolde hunte in the mountayns
>   Off Chyviat within dayes thre,
> In the mauger of doughtè Dogles,
>   And all that ever with him be.

> The fattiste hartes in all Cheviat
>   He sayd he wold kill, and cary them away:
> Be my feth, sayd the doughtei Doglas agayn,
>   I wyll let that hontyng yf that I may.

This is the measure and structure of Blake in some of the *Songs*,
Coleridge and Wordsworth in the *Lyrical Ballads*, Thomas Moore,
and Byron. Vary it as they will to their own purposes, this is the
basic pattern of what will be a major nineteenth-century mode: the
lyrical narrative of dramatic confrontation.

One may ask whether, since Addison praised "Chevy Chase" so
early in the century, there was not an early beginning of ballad
poetry in the mid-eighteenth century, as one of the strands of preromanticism. We should look for such an early version of the mode
in Chatterton, for example, or Smart. But poets like these, we find,
were too deeply involved in their own conventions to put new forms
to use. Except in his "Battle of Bristowe," Chatterton was writing
the poetry of a Spenserian antiquarianism, full of rich raiments,
sceneries, sorrows, and *bedights*, not the book of the ballad. Even
Percy's *Reliques*, so strong was the time, presented a sort of Shen-
stonian structure in 1765, an array of Spenserian Elizabethans, and
some pure ballads, but some so rewritten, like "Barbara Allen" and
"Child Maurice," that they contain the whole vocabulary of eighteenth-century emotionalism and descriptive weight: enameled
fields and deadly sorrows, rages, despairs, sighs, and repentances.

It remained for the poets of the century's end to find in Percy the
actual power of a new mode, and to use it for their own new pur-

poses. Technically, the results may be described as follows: a sentence structure of dramatic confrontation, which employs more verbs than adjectives, more subordinate than serial constructions, more actions and arguments than descriptions and invocations. That is, the structure presents people in situations, with much suggestion and implication of surroundings, rather than surroundings with a suggestion of situation as the eighteenth century did. The focus has shifted to foreground figures. At the same time, the meter breaks, to allow for the effects of silence as well as sound in the verse line. In dramatic colloquy, lack of answer may be as vivid as answer itself, and the various modifications of ballad measure allow for this, as Coleridge pointed out indirectly in his discussion of "Christabel." Coleridge sought, as his contemporaries sought, a varied and broken line pattern, the constant remission of four stresses to three, with the consequent effects of easy repetition or implication, the lightness of assonance as the shade of rhyme, feminine as the shade of masculine endings, shadings of echo and progression from stanza to stanza, and indeed in every new form of modification in sound, the quality of shadow, echo, or answer, rather than the massed and cumulative quality of the old pentameters.

It was Coleridge too who brought the full effect of a new vocabulary to play in this complex of sound and structure. The vocabulary of the ballads themselves bore four main emphases: first, the great human terms of most English poetry, *man, love, heart,* and the verbs of action; second, the terms of a concrete reality, specific colors and objects, the *red blood* and the *burnished sword*; third, the terms of family relationship, *father, mother, daughter, son, brother*; fourth, the terms of station, *king, knight, lady, lord,* and so on. What Scott and the straight ballad imitators did was to preserve and reëmphasize these special terms, adding more of the same, more colors, more brothers, barons, harps, halls, steeds, and general trappings. For them an old mode was renovated, but did not become really new. Coleridge, on the other hand, with the aid of his contemporaries Byron, Moore, and Landor, following Rogers, Campbell, Burns, and Southey, made the mode realize its new language.

This new language was hard-won from the eighteenth century; it had to break away from the antiquarian trappings of the knights and ladies on the one hand and from the whole sublime gross of descriptions and emotions on the other. What it could save from the old ballads was the family relation and the qualities of immediacy; what it could save from the eighteenth century was that century's own new sort of immediacy, the sensory world of sun, sky, sea, star, and tree. Like stars coming out one by one in the sky, these terms had appeared as primary for a few poets: *sun, wind,* and *cloud* in Thomson, *deep, little, wild,* and *sad,* in Dyer, Gray, and Collins, and colors in the Wartons, in the very poets for whom Wordsworth has given us the clue of liking; and now, at century's end, the terms moved into constellation. Over and over in the narrative verses of the romantics and their colleagues, the major terms of nature take part in the action. The king has gone from Dumferling town, and in his meter and story the sea has taken over. Or even the first person "I" may have become the actor, with moon and cloud as other dramatis personae. And the child has become a protagonist, descended from the son of the ballads, now younger in age, and taking the stage from the father.

In the main, then, we may say that with the generation of 1800 to 1840 there grew up a mode which by sheer contemporality and by its integration of special characteristics we may call new and whole and romantic. The vocabulary of this poetry is in part the basic human terms which prevail through all English poetry, and in part the terms of the surrounding century, and in at least one-half the terms which serve to characterize and identify it, the sensory epithets of *bright, deep, sad, wild,* the active natural forces of *flower, light, moon, mountain, sea, star, sun,* the human concepts of *hope, spirit, father, tear,* and *woe,* and the sensitive receptive verbs of *feeling, falling, lying, looking, praying, seeming.* These materials, with their total characterizing quality of a mysterious, fearful, yet hopeful nighttime in which men meet and pray, are given shape in the implicative and dramatic structures of ballad form with results familiar to us over and over in Hebrew Melodies, West Winds, Mariners.

> I pass, like night, from land to land;
> I have strange power of speech;
> The moment that his face I see,
> I know the man that must hear me:
> To him my tale I teach.

> What loud uproar bursts from that door!
> The wedding-guests are there:
> But in the garden-bower the bride
> And bride-maids singing are:
> And hark the little vesper bell,
> Which biddeth me to prayer!

Of Coleridge's inheritance from the ballads, Professor Lowes has said that it was mechanically literary, not so vigorous as his use of travel books. But Lowes referred mainly to the archaic diction. Actually, I think we may see, it was the oblique narrative progression of ballad sound and structure, as he uses it here to his own moral ends, that allowed Coleridge to find moral pertinence in the books of nature and travel which would otherwise have been too strange and oblique for his purpose.

Or Byron, without the harp of the ballad, would not have broken the pentameter line into such famous melodies as

> And there lay the steed with his nostril all wide,
> But through it there roll'd not the breath of his pride;
> And the foam of his gasping lay white on the turf,
> And cold as the spray of the rock-beating surf.
>
> And there lay the rider distorted and pale,
> With the dew on his brow, and the rust on his mail;
> And the tents were all silent—the banners alone—
> The lances unlifted—the trumpet unblown.

Such lilt of measure and pure romantic vocabulary Byron continues even into his most so-called classical satires. While Shelley in steadier and more sober measure manages to blur the edges of all his images in the romantic fashion of implication and in layers of metaphor:

> Methought that of these visionary flowers
>   I made a nosegay, bound in such a way
> That the same hues, which in their natural bowers
>   Were mingled or opposed, the like array
> Kept these imprisoned children of the Hours
>   Within my hand,—and then, elate and gay,
> I hastened to the spot whence I had come,
> That I might there present it!—oh! to whom?

When we come to the very center of the romantic mode in these poems of Byron and Shelley, Coleridge and Wordsworth and Keats, we may see that there is technical justification for thinking of the five together, sheer descriptive criteria, apart from greatness and goodness. What can be said about the mode in general can be said most particularly about them. Their agreements were interwoven, with no great splits between them. Their structural sense was vividly stanzaic, their sense of narrative not epic but lyric and episodic, their ear for sound tuned to undertone, their eye for concrete detail bright but seeing always blurred edges of emotional significance, as Professor Fogle has shown us; their metaphors glancing and complex, their verbs stronger and more structurally determining than their adjectives; their own especially abundant vocabulary shared in the characteristic terms of *bright, deep, cloud, light, spirit, star, sun,* and *wind,* in lightness and darkness, sound and silence.

This is not to say that the new mode, once it had come for these five poets, came immediately to stay. The five themselves kept to the mode with varying fidelity. Wordsworth, as we know, turned back from the flexible improvisations of ballads and the poems of 1806 to the more explicit earlier modes in which *The Excursion* and *The River Duddon* are written. Keats, always half faithful to the richness of Miltonic preromanticism, wrote in the *Odes* and *Hyperion* the finest sort of culmination of eighteenth-century poetry, though he worried about the very mode as he wrote. At the same time, minor figures like Hunt, Kirke White, Campbell, and Bryant in America, carried on for a while what the earlier century had so firmly established. But there is no reason to expect that the presence of a new style should immediately silence an old one. And, on the other hand, the new style spread and grew, not only in the later work of Byron, but in the minor poetry, as of Moore and Beddoes.

What makes the extent and strength of the new mode most explicit is the pattern of simple facts like these: by about 1820 most of the leading poets' work was stanzaic in structure, while a half century before it had been mostly linear; the measures were freely trisyllabic where they had been disyllabic; by about 1820 half the major terms, the nouns, adjectives, and verbs most used by the majority, were new terms, characteristically sensory, concrete, and thus often symbolic, while oblique metaphors had taken the place of explicit similes; by about 1820 the sentence structures were more narrative than descriptive, more complex than coördinate, using more verbs and sometimes only half as many adjectives as in the century before. By about 1820, in other words, the substance and structure of poetry had physically altered in determinable degree, to carry a new attitude by a new mode of statement.

The idea which gave life to this romantic mode was the idea of the spirit's narrative, the individual's lyrical story, half articulated and half heard, but powerful in its force of implication. It is one triumphant solution to the long Augustan search for a great heroic poem or a cosmical epic, which should reconcile the inheritances of classical culture and of contemporary science, in a descriptive panorama of heroic proportions, stressing scenes and sublimities and subordinating Sir Patrick Spence to Virgil, Spenser, and Milton. When the heroic story finally came to be told, it was of the individual self, of the Mariner, the adventurer Childe, even the infant of the *Songs* and *The Prelude*, the self who was the son of Sir Patrick Spence, who said little, and felt much, and implied more, and died deeply. For such a narration, the form could be better lyrical than epical, the structure better repetitive than cumulative, the terms better active than descriptive, as the individual poet is both hero and minstrel, both tree-harp and the wind in it, both the story and the storyteller, in the romantic mode.

JOHN HOLLANDER

Romantic Verse Form and the Metrical Contract †

The fascination of Romantic literary thought with the interplay of nature and convention has at least one infrequently studied aspect in some questions of metrical theory. This lies close to the problems about the framing of poetic utterance that so occupied, from time to time, the utterance itself, and, in fact, comes as near to the heart of the poem as some of the more specific studies of the actual poetic rhythms of particular poets and texts. It would be absurd to suggest that all Romantic poetry falls along one line of prosodic tradition, or even along one line of approach: while the first generation of poets was more concerned with freeing poetry from the institution of eighteenth-century literature, the second was seeking new affirmations in re-engagements, stylistically speaking, with older voices. Keats, Shelley, and Byron contribute virtually nothing to any continuing discussion of formal theory. Leigh Hunt, aided by the most sophisticated knowledge of music of all the English Romantics, has left a few trenchant observations of the subject of what, following Coleridge, he calls "variety in uniformity" as being the basis of verse, but his concern is primarily with "metrical excitement" or actual rhythmic effects. Had he been able to expand adequately upon his opening remark to a discussion of versification, "Poetry stands between nature and convention, keeping alive among us the enjoyment of the external and the physical world," [1] he might have led straight to the heart of the problem I should like to raise.

For this problem has some interesting repercussions for the

† From *From Sensibility to Romanticism: Essays Presented to Frederick A. Pottle*, ed. Frederick H. Hilles and Harold Bloom. Copyright © 1965 by Oxford University Press, Inc. Revised and expanded from "Blake and the Metrical Contract" by the author. Copyright © 1968 by John Hollander. Reprinted by permission of the publisher and author.

1. Leigh Hunt, "An Answer to the Question What is Poetry Including Remarks on Versification," in *Imagination and Fancy* (London, 1891), 1. The discussion of "variety in uniformity" occurs on pp. 31 ff. and 43 ff. The relevant passage from Coleridge is one from *Anima Poetae* quoted by Shawcross in his edition of *Biographia Literaria* (Oxford, 1967), II, 278, although Hunt's application of it to meter is his own. Cf. also Wordsworth's "preception of similitude and dissimilitude".

whole idea of what a literary program is. That even Romantic poetry is doomed to become literature, as antinomian heroes become locked into the laws of their eventual worship, seems inevitable. But the poets who knew this all too well wished to exercise their control over the ways in which this would happen, and in the following remarks I should like to try to set out some of the formal mechanisms of this control. But first, a few words about the whole matter of metrical theory and practice.

In recent years, the most illuminating studies of prosody in general have been devoted to showing the relation of patterned sound and semantic sense in particular poems. This concern with the music of poetry, with the expressive function of rhythm, has centered primarily on the analysis of how the poem's sound structure, formed within the limits of a particular metrical scheme, amplifies from moment to moment what is being said. This is an important matter, of course, and for lyric poetry in particular; since the fundamental separation between the lyric poem and the actual text for music early in the seventeenth century, the expressive rhythms of language have come to permit the lyric poem to sing its own song.

But by and large, prosodists since Saintsbury have been less concerned with another dimension along which the problems of poetic meter may be viewed. This dimension I should call purely conventional, or formal, rather than expressive, and its function is rather like a definitive or axiomatic one for the whole literary work. It involves the elements of convention which link a metrical style or type to a whole poetic genre and, hence, a poet's choice of meter to a larger intention. In an age of canonical metrical styles like the Augustan period, the relation between meter and intention is very clear. In the nineteenth century it is less so, and in our own day the *sine qua non* of originality has led to an almost obsessive concern, in American poetry in particular, with metrical format.

As Northrop Frye has suggested, [2] the Age of Sensibility represents an interesting period of transition in the history of English meter as well as in the history of the literary imagination. In very different ways and for very different reasons, Smart, Ossian, Chatterton and, finally, Blake, all seem to threaten the very basis of English literary meter—the accentual-syllabic system that is normal from Chaucer through Tennyson—in outbursts of self-made song. This threat may be brought about as the result of the influence of the English Bible, as in the case of Ossian; or it may result from the completely graphic reality of Chatterton's fake dialect, a speech that his heart may have heard but his ears, never. In any event, the major

2. Northrop Frye, "Toward Defining an Age of Sensibility," in *Fables of   Identity* (New York, 1963), pp. 132–4.

Romantic poets' extremely sophisticated sense of literary history and of their own various relationships to the past gave them to understand that iambic verse, official though it may have been, was by no means necessarily the strained, cruel voice of an enemy. But this *rapprochement* had to be accomplished, I think, only after an expense of some awkwardness, and I think that the whole problem of metrical choice may be usefully reconsidered for a moment.

The stylistic choices (which I am calling *metrical*, rather than *rhythmic*) [3] occur at a different level of decision-making from those of mysterious choices which must occur in actual composition. (This remains true, I think, even though the poet himself could not or would not differentiate between the types of choice.) The metrical choice provides a basic schematic fabric of contingencies governing the range of expressive effect. But it also establishes a kind of frame around the work as a whole. Like a title, it indicates how it is to be taken, what sort of thing the poem is supposed to be, and, perhaps, taken in historical context, what the poet thought he was doing by calling his curious bit of language a poem at all.

But there are some cases in English literary history where a poet does seem to acknowledge the importance of metrical choice. One with which we are probably all familiar is that of the prose apology prefaced to *Paradise Lost*. In it, Milton defends his choice of blank verse as a measure for the poem, and seems to allow his choice of meter to stand emblematically for the entire mode of language of his epic. He never touches upon his Latinate syntax, reinterpretation of the use and structure of epic simile and so forth, and only in the poem itself does he deal with his choice of subject or his myth of the poem's origins. The metrical mode is there, we are told, both a fabric and a frame for what will be worked within it.

Now we know that Milton, even more than most learned writers of the seventeenth century, was acutely aware of the classical notion of musical modality. Although unable to understand its empirical bases, Renaissance and later neoclassicism often took as a model notion of style this canonical correspondence in Greek music between each type of musical scale and its particular *ethos* or persuasive quality. One knew from Plato alone, who admitted to or excluded from his Just City certain scales because of their necessary effects upon a listener, that the Dorian scale was considered vigorous and manly, the Lydian, relaxing, the Phrygian, wild, etc.

The relation of a mode or scale to its particular *ethos* was held to be as fixed as that of a word to its meaning. Thinkers since the Renaissance have looked in vain for some necessary, unwavering connection between melodic contours and feelings generated by

---

3. I have discussed this at greater length in "The Metrical Emblem," *Kenyon Review* XXI (1959), pp. 279–96.

their perception; the association between musical mode and human mood remained one that was maintained by convention alone. The words of the poetic text to which the melody was sung, we must remember, gave to the melody's succession of intervals its duration and accent: the meter gave to the pitches half of what we would call its melodic quality. The meaning of the text, its form and poetic occasion seem to have been the decisive factors in maintaining the convention of *ethos.* [4]

There are good grounds for suspecting that Greek thinkers themselves believed that modality had its affective consequences for human behavior because of connections established by nature rather than by convention. In any event, successive ages would conclude, from their experience of classical theoretic and mythological writings only, that music and poetry in Antiquity had been mysteriously wed, and that subsequent literary history was a record of their divorce. Moreover, it was easy to move from the close connection of mode and mood in music to an analogical correspondence, longingly pursued by the Renaissance, of meter, diction, image, subject, presentation or performance style, and occasion. Certainly Alexandrian literature contained the modern notion of the literary occasion *per se* (rather than the public ones of theatre, ritual ceremony, games, formal inscription, etc.). And in any event, what had been for classical Greek poets canonical metrical uses became for Roman ones a matter of choice, a choice personal and in its own way expressive.

The very idea of literature is in some senses based upon an extension of this notion of modality. Even in Latin poetry, where we see the beginning of the dislocation of stylistic genre from its original context in Greek life, there emerges the phenomenon of metrical forms beginning to take on a life of their own, and something very like a kind of *ethos* developing for them. As early as Longinus, we see hexameters being praised as the proper meter for epic because of their stirring manly qualities, rather than the other way around.[5] A Roman poet will imitate a Greek metrical form, sometimes for an analogous type of poem and sometimes not; but in any case the form constitutes a kind of badge of literary authenticity. We are faced, quite early in the history of Western literature, with the problem of metrical genre and its relation to individual intention and the history of style in general.

Of the genres of Greek poetry, all clearly differentiated by form, occasion, musical accompaniment, and presentation style, as well as by context, only comedy, tragedy, epic, and lyric have in any way been transmitted to successive cultural epochs. Distinctions among

---

4. Also see my *The Untuning of the Sky* (Princeton, 1961), pp. 206–20.

5. (Pseudo-) Longinus, *On the Sublime,* XXXIX, 4.

various types of solo and choral lyric, dithyrambic, iambic and elegiac poetry became blurred even in Latin poetry, and traditional forms began to be used for different purposes. The modern theories of genre propounded by literary historians tend, as René Wellek has observed, to treat literary types as something very like political or social institutions, preserving either form or content, but not both, throughout changing historical contexts.[6] Studies of genre may concentrate upon form or underlying strand of content; their classification may be modeled either on taxonomy or on embryology, or, as we might say, on either a synchronic or diachronic linguistic approach. Hobbes's famous tripartite distinction in his letter to Davenant divided the world of human affairs into three realms, court, city, and country, and suggested that to each of these there corresponded tragedy and epic (courtly), comedy and satire (urban), and pastoral (rural);[7] this association is full of historical mistakes (about pastoral, for example) if taken as a genetic approach. But it seems to anticipate certain strains in modern criticism both by taking very seriously the concept of literary occasion and by establishing a kind of central mythic pattern within which genres may be said to have a kind of analogically general significance (as in the critical theory of Northrop Frye).

Meter has always remained a curiously strong indication or emblem of genre. Whether or not a seventeenth-century writer like Milton might choose to use the names of the Greek musical modes metaphorically to describe a general shift of poetic style (or even use the word "monody" in such an extended sense in the subtitle of "Lycidas"), he would certainly tend to think of the meter of a particular poem in a frame of previous ancient and modern use. And although the stylistic connotations of certain metrical schemes from the early sixteenth through the late eighteenth centuries in England may be seen, from a historical point of view, to have been rather grotesquely acquired, it nevertheless remains true that during that period, English poetry is written in a framework of canonical metrical style; innovation and individual invention tend usually to consist of a unique rhythmic style, using and interpreting the underlying formal fabric of the meter.

Milton's defense of his blank verse, against the expectation, for example, that he might, like Sylvester in his translation of Du Bartas, use couplets, is addressed then to those who might feel he was inventing the *use of* a meter, a subject and genre and occasion for a particular formal pattern so wrenched away from previous traditions of use that it might be said to be actually a new meter.

6. See René Wellek and Austin Warren, *Theory of Literature* (New York, 1949), pp. 235–47.

7. In *Critical Essays of the XVIIth Century*, ed. J. E. Spingarn (New York, 1908), I, 54–5.

But let us look for a moment at some particularly perceptive remarks on meter, also produced in the course of stylistic polemic,
nearly 150 years after Milton. They represent at the same time an
unusually clear understanding about just this question of genre
being entailed by meter, and an eventual refusal to consider meter
as being too important in itself.

"It is supposed that by the act of writing in verse an author
makes a formal engagement that he will gratify certain known
habits of association; that he not only thus apprises the reader that
certain classes of ideas and expressions will be found in his book,
but that others will be carefully excluded. This exponent or symbol held forth by metrical language must in different eras of literature have excited very different expectations: for example in the
age of Catullus, Terence and Lucretius, and that of Statius or
Claudian; and in our own country, in the Age of Shakespeare and
Beaumont and Fletcher, and that of Donne and Cowley, or Dryden,
or Pope. I will not take upon me to determine the exact import of
the promise which, by the act of writing in verse, an author in the
present day makes to his reader; but it will undoubtedly appear to
many persons that I have not fulfilled the terms of an engagement
thus voluntarily contracted."

This is Wordsworth, writing in the 1800 preface to *Lyrical Ballads*.[8] In the 1802 appendix to the preface, he again says of the
"unusual" language of poetry: "In process of time metre became a
symbol or promise of this unusual language." Wordsworth's concern here, of course, is not with type or style of meter, just as he
gives no indication of even a trivial neoclassical interest in poetic
genre. His problem was to defend an attitude about poetic diction,
and his discussion of poetic language comes down to that matter
almost immediately. Still, the sense that a meter as distinguished
from a prose format does represent a kind of contract, involving
"certain known habits of association," is a keen and sure one. It is
interesting to find a poet dealing with the question of meter from
the point of view of a choice conditioned by variables of expectation
on the part of an audience—a modern literary-historical concept, in
short, of convention.

Coleridge, in his revision of Wordsworth's remarks in *Biographia
Literaria*, goes on to assert the contractual basis of metrical choice
quite unequivocally, albeit in connection with some additional
concerns of his own. Discussing "the interpenetration of passion
and will, of *spontaneous* impulse and *voluntary* purpose" (in which,
incidentally, our two domains of the metrical and the rhythmic
might be said to operate), he remarks of the union of the two: "It

8. Text from *Wordsworth's Literary Criticism*, ed. Nowell C. Smith (London,
1905), pp. 12–13.

not only dictates, but of itself tends to produce, a more frequent employment of picturesque and vivifying language, than would be natural in any other case, in which there did not exist, as there does in the present, a previous and well-understood, though tacit, *compact* between the poet and his reader, that the latter is entitled to expect, and the former bound to supply, this species and degree of pleasurable excitement." [9]

Insofar as the early Romantics considered the question of the effect of rhythm at all, it was a matter eliciting feeling or giving pleasure; here is Wordsworth again, from the 1800 preface: "Now the music of harmonious metrical language, the sense of difficulty overcome, and the blind association of pleasure which has been previously received from works of rhyme or meter of the same or similar construction, an indistinct perception perpetually renewed of language closely resembling that of real life, and yet, in the circumstance of meter, differing from it so widely—all these imperceptibles make up a complex feeling of delight, which is of the most important use in tempering the painful feeling always found intermingled with powerful descriptions of the deeper passions." "The sense of difficulty overcome," of course, is more that of the poet than of the reader, who in a sense shares the poet's feeling through sympathy if he has it at all. This is a theme which becomes more and more important in the informal metrical remarks of twentieth-century poets; we can see it in Frost's casual "Free verse is like playing tennis without a net," or in Valéry's famous prescription: "The exigencies of a strict prosody constitute the artifice which bestows upon natural speech the qualities of an unyielding material, foreign to our spirit, and almost deaf to our desires. If they were not a bit mad, and if they did not encourage our rebellion, they would be basically absurd." [1] Again, we can see a touch of this notion in Coleridge's remark on the origin of meter (although "origin" is used in an extremely peculiar sense): "This I would trace to the balance in the mind effected by that spontaneous effort which strives to hold in check the workings of passion. It might be easily explained likewise in what manner this salutary antagonism is assisted by the very state, which it counteracts; and how this balance of antagonists became organized into *metre* (in the usual acceptation of that term) by a supervening act of the will and judgement, consciously and for the foreseen purpose of pleasure." [2] But Coleridge, like Wordsworth, goes on to talk about poetic diction, which is far more important to his concerns at the moment.

9. *B.L.*, ed. Shawcross, II, 50.
1. Paul Valéry, "Au Sujet d'Adonis," in *Variété* (Paris, 1924), p. 70 (my translation).
2. *B.L.*, ed. cit., II, 50.

Here, then, is the notion of the metrical contract. For Wordsworth it covers only the commitment engendered by writing verse rather than prose; but what I have been pointing out as the framing or defining function of a particular metrical choice extends the idea of the contract to cover the choice among various metrical possibilities. Wordsworth and Coleridge would dismiss meter as a criterion for the poetic character of an utterance. But unless we are judging or being polemical, I think we must take the fact of verse form as an indication that the writer feels he has written a poem—whatever he may mean by that—and expects it to be recognized as such.

In a sense, they are both struggling against "the tendency of metre to divest language, in a certain degree, of its reality," as Wordsworth put it in the Preface; [3] for both of them, there is a disposition to regard metrical structure as an element *added to* potentially poetic language. Thus Wordsworth, in discussing the process of "selection" from among human utterances in order to distinguish poetic language from mere speech, adds that "if metre be superadded thereto," the distinction will have been made complete. For Coleridge, chemical images presented themselves, whether of "yeast, worthless or disagreeable by itself, but giving vivacity and spirit to the liquor with which it is traditionally combined," or of something more like the modern notion of catalysis for which perhaps he was groping: "Metre therefore having been connected with *poetry* most often and by a peculiar fitness, whatever else is combined with *metre* must, though it be not itself *essentially* poetic, have nevertheless some property in common with poetry, as an intermedium of affinity, a sort (if I may dare borrow a well-known phrase from technical chemistry) of *mordaunt* between it and the super-added metre." [4]

This aspect of the metrical contract, the choice of a particular style, did not interest the Romantics very much. They attended to it at the pragmatic level, and their actual choices and inventions had far-reaching effects. Even so, Wordsworth, in the first of his remarks quoted, realizes that different historical epochs embody various accepted styles of meter, with various modal significances which serve as the unstated terms against which the contract is drawn. (I am ignoring for the moment Blake's marginalia on Wordsworth's remarks: "I do not know who wrote these Prefaces, they are very mischievous & direct contrary to Wordsworth's own practise.") The real difficulty here comes from the fact that every canonical style has evolved from some earlier one, and that the metrical forms take on new modal significances with each new use,

3. *Wordsworth's Literary Criticism*, p. 31.   4. *B.L.*, II, 55.

and with different sorts of awareness of past ones. Perhaps the test of the canonical status of a metrical mode is the inability of anyone working within its range and age of power to see that it rules not by divine right but, as Milton's Satan said of God, by convention.

Metrical traditions in English have evolved, however. Aside from the metrical crises—Whitman, Hopkins, twentieth-century free verse—that underline dramatically the drawing up of a new contract, there remains the long history of the so-called iambic tradition itself. As opposed to these crises, the milder variations of metrical evolution occur within the boundaries of a particular system. Even the briefest sketch of the normative pattern of accentual-syllabic verse in English shows that, time and again, certain formal patterns within the system have become displaced from previous sorts of usage and adapted to new ones. In the centuries before Chaucer, English had replaced the pure accentualism of Germanic verse with the fairly regular tendency, in octosyllabic lines borrowed from the French romance, to alternate stressed and unstressed syllables; it was Chaucer's stroke of invention to see this system as capable of embracing an adaptation of the Italian *ende-casillabo*, which, because of the invariable placement of a final /e/ at the end of the line, regularized itself into the pentameter line of English verse. Chaucer's adaptation, it must be remembered, was made not to preserve a form for its own, or for some symbolic sake, but in order to write in a genre that had previously existed only in other languages—Italian and French. The *Canterbury Tales* contain examples of many genres and types of medieval storytelling; most of them usually appeared in English in completely different metrical clothing from Chaucer's pentameter couplets (octosyllabics, for the most part). But his triumph of accomplishment depends in some part on his having seized upon one style for his overall voice in the poem: such a choice is always basic to the conception of literary, or, as C. S. Lewis calls it, *secondary* epic.

In the century after Chaucer, however, we begin to see instances of metrical evolution through utter formal dislocation, occasioned by an interest in practicing a particular form without regard to any of its significance as an emblem of literary type. The extremely complicated stanza-forms of the medieval drama in England, of the Wakefield cycle in particular, are derived from lyric poetry, where we expect in the later middle ages to see more complication and flexibility in stanza form than in narrative verse. Through the early Tudor morality play we see this use of a lyrical verse form for dramatic poetry continuing, and it is only odd when humanist drama, written with the eye glued to the Senecan and Plautine model, begins to enmesh actual popular theatrical conventions that the modern use of a unilinear form for poetic drama develops.

Perhaps the modern sense of the peculiar rightness of such an association of unilinear forms with narrative and dramatic verse is the
result of unavowed latent neoclassicism: it was only Greek lyric
poetry, it will be remembered, which was strophic, while narrative
and iambic dramatic verses were always arranged *kata kôlon,* or
unilinearly.

There are many other examples of metrical evolution or transfer
in the sixteenth through the eighteenth centuries in England.
They vary in the degree to which the new or adapted use of the
metrical pattern wishes to engage prior associations—and which
associations in particular—generated by other uses. The history of
blank verse in English is obviously a case in point: it moves from
the early dramatists, through the later ones, to Milton, through the
eighteenth-century speculative poem consciously connected with
Milton's spirit, through *The Prelude* and eventually toward the
later Romantic lyric. The crisis here occurs with Milton; and yet
it is during the eighteenth century that all poetry save for the sung
lyric begins to have to confront the growth of prose as an authentic
vehicle of imaginative expression. For Milton, blank verse had the
virtues of a canonical poetic cadence, but by the middle of the eighteenth century, it was important that it be more like prose in some
ways than rhymed verse could ever be.

Then again, there is the case of the preservation of lyric stanza
forms over the categorical change in genre from the Elizabethan to
the Metaphysical lyric. The Elizabethan lyric poem is a song text
per se; it may merely extend a popular or courtly convention, or it
may, like the songs in Shakespeare's plays, play itself off against
those conventions in order to perform the far more intense and
exacting work of a kind of summarizing symbolist lyric, catching up
and embodying the themes and movements of the whole play. But
the Metaphysical lyric, starting with Donne, is not in any essential
way modeled on the song, but rather on the written text for study.
Emblem verses, patristic writings, and other theological disputation,
natural philosophy, all lie behind Donne's *Songs and Sonnets,* with
the additional complication that each poem generates its own immediate dramatic context. There is always a particular erotic situation behind the rhetorical one of every poem, and the relation
behind the lyric ego and the "you" is quite complex. It is as if
the stylized Petrarchan lover, the "I" of the sonnet tradition, had
suddenly acquired real knowledge instead of lore, and real feelings
in place of gesture. But Donne and his followers invariably employ
the variety of line and strophe forms used by the Elizabethan lyric,
wherein a density of formal texture is compensated for by an atten-
uation of semantic and iconographic complexity—they can be comprehended upon hearing, or rapid reading, for the most part. The

Metaphysical lyric is to be read and studied and considered, and the overall formal shape of the poem is often at ironic odds with the cognitive density of the thought and language. But the effect of the maintenance of the song forms, of the name "song" for poem, is the literary justification for the new departure, and the justification is based, as it is so often, upon the authority supplied by continuity itself.

The Romantic reinterpretation of sonnet form is another case in point. More revealing for literary history than the eighteenth-century restorations of the sonnet by Warton, Thomas Russell, or even by Bowles, is Wordsworth's reconstitution of the form, as a total lyric mode, in the essentiality of its Miltonic type. Wordsworth's sense of the implications of the form as resulting from its being short, binding, and historically complex is well-known through the "sonnets on the sonnet"; the heart of the question, however, lies in the form as representing a fit instrument for the "soul-animating strains" of Milton's strong, self-contained bursts of utterance, an eloquence too complete to display its structure. In a letter to Dyce in 1833, he puts quite clearly the central, pregnant formal difference between the Elizabethan and the Miltonic types: "Instead of looking at this composition as a piece of architecture, making a whole out of three parts, I have been much in the habit of preferring the image of an orbicular body—a sphere—or a dew drop." [5] It is, in fact, by virtue of its providing a rounded period, not unlike a blank verse paragraph in that the rhymes do not force logical and rhetorical units, that it serves Wordsworth so well. And it is finally, the rhetorical model of Milton's invocations, prophecies, and confessions, rather than that of the more meditative or painterly sonnets in the eighteenth century, that helped him to shape his own. It is almost safe to say that despite his archaeological interests in Shakespeare's sonnets, it was Milton alone whom Wordsworth's sonnet writing was, in a peculair formal sense, about.

The concept of "elegy" in English, insofar as it involves purely metrical matters, is an interesting one too. The genre is metrically defined by neoclassical poetry, and entails a longish poem in couplets, often indistinguishable from the sort of poem called a "satire" in the seventeenth century, as well as from the verse epistle imitated also from the Latin poets. It is only toward the end of the eighteenth century, when Gray's tranquilly recollected quatrains, or Cowper's hippity-hop anapests in "The Poplar-Field" define for romanticism and ever after the elegiac tone as a mood, rather than as a formal mode:

5. See *Poetical Works*, ed. E. de Sélincourt (Oxford, 1946), III, 417, for a letter, also, to Landor, on 20 April, 1822. Also for some valuable reminiscences on the sonnet, Christopher Wordsworth, *Memoir of William Wordsworth* (London, 1841), p. 277.

> Twelve years have elaps'd since I first took a view
> Of my favorite field and the bank where they grew;
> And now in the grass behold they are laid,
> And the tree is my seat that once lent me a shade.

would have served, in the seventeenth century, as the proper meter
in which to frame a coyly erotic lyric; in the earlier eighteenth
century, they would have violated the voice of seriousness. But for
Cowper, the form of these lines stands for the emotional authenticity of the personal. It is the meter alone which is significant
here, by the way, for the parallelism of syntactic and rhetorical structure is firmly in the eighteenth-century tradition.

Cowper's "elegiac" use of the anapestic tetrameter, incidentally,
has interesting consequences for Romantic prosodic practice. It
echoes more than faintly through Blake's distortion of it in the
dimeters of "The Echoing Green." Wordsworth employs it, most
successfully in "The Reverie of Poor Susan," but also in the overly
willed attentiveness to the city fiddler in "The Power of Music";
"The Two Thieves," "A Character," "The Childless Father," and
"The Farmer of Tillsbury Vale," all early, and the later "At Vallam-
brosa" all use the anapestic elegiac as well, whether in pairs of
couplets or *abab* quatrains. "Repentance, A Pastoral Ballad" is
more immediately suggestive of Cowper. The contractual effects of
Cowper's version of the meter seem to have been not unconnected,
for Wordsworth, with a sense of smoothness and evenness of flow,
rather than with an equally justifiable sense of the meter's jumpi-
ness and abruptness, which suited it not only to drinking songs and
bawdy in earlier times, but to an alternative convention in Romantic
verse. Coleridge, as well, seems to have acknowledged this smoothness: in a letter to Wordsworth in which he discusses the meter of
The White Doe of Rylstone, he makes the distinction between
meters that are "in general, rather dramatic than lyric, i.e. not such
an arrangement of syllables, not such a metre, as acts a priori and
with complete self-subsistence (as the simple anapestic in its
smoothest form) . . ." [6]

The subsequent course of the anapestic elegiac mode is easy to
trace. The Cowper-Wordsworth tradition is clearly marked in such
uses of the form as John Clare's (in Grigson's edition alone, for
sixteen poems); William Barnes' (in seven poems in standard English and nine in dialect); the young Shelley's (five times in the
Esdaile Notebook); Darley's; and in countless song texts. These last
may be as overtly minor-Wordsworthian as the "How dear to my
heart are the scenes of my childhood/When fond recollection
presents them to view" of the grossly familiar "The Old Oaken

6. See E. K. Chambers, *Samuel Taylor Coleridge, a Biographical Study* (Oxford, 1938), p. 35.

Bucket." On the other hand, the 6/8 rhythms of the transcribed salon-versions of many Scotch and Irish melodies seemed frequently to call for texts in this meter, such as Burns' words to "Afton Water." The irrepressible Thomas Moore also presents a case in point, with no less than fifty-four elegiac anapestic poems throughout his works, from the *Irish Melodies* to pieces set into *Lalla Rookh*. On the other hand, Moore, who could not be accused of much direct Wordsworthian influence, uses the same anapestic tetrameter almost twice as often in the alternative modality. Ninety-seven of his satiric and comical poems are written in it; *The Fudge Family*, and comic poems by Hunt and Landor, undoubtedly contribute to the use of the form in subsequent society verse (James Russell Lowell comes immediately to mind here). The two different modalities of the anapestic four-stressed line, in fact, tend to make us forget that the words of "The Star-Spangled Banner," on the one hand (on the model of its originally bibulous eighteen-century melody), and the blank verses parodying Persian poetry in the standard English translation of *Vathek* (unrhymed so as to give the effect of Oriental translationese verse, perhaps) on the other, share the same verse form.

The specifically discontinuous quality of the rhythm is used by Byron in a lyric like "The Destruction of Sennacherib" for its expressive force; his rhythmic interest in the form points neither toward the elegiac nor the satiric-comic metrical modes, and this sense of expressive vigor is refined even more sharply by the selective ear of Browning for the suggestion of hoofbeats in "How They Carried the Good News from Ghent to Aix." But in general, the smooth flow and the hippity-hop, attainable rhythms in the same metrical schema, provide the bases for reflective lyric and satirical verse respectively.

All of these instances, however, represent what I have called metrical evolution within the limits of a metrical system. The emblematic character of particular forms is employed to cover the shifts in literary milieu, in a kind of eternal struggle to maintain the condition of a poem as a Platonic entity: as if a poem were a poem always, by virtue of some quintessential character which different ages may merely call by different names. Metrical form (and we have, of course, been considering the larger variations in form, line lengths, stanza forms, rhyme patterns, etc.), then, acts to define a type of poem, even a poem itself, as well as to set up formal contingencies within which some linguistic event will become a poetic one, and something literary may be said to have happened.

What, then, of the metrical crisis, where the very conditions of the metrical system seem to be questioned? What looks to be a pathological form emerges, and it appears that the contract of meter has been broken. For example, there is an interesting aspect of Christopher Smart's *Jubilate Agno*: it ought properly never to have been an eighteenth-century poem at all. Written while its author, in his late thirties, was confined in a madhouse with the degenerative psychosis from which he never fully recovered, the poem consists of 32 foolscap sheets covered with 1735 long, unmeasured lines. Lost in Smart's lifetime, it seems to have ceased to exist in its own age and come to life only in the literary Bedlam of the twentieth century when the MS. was discovered and first edited in 1939. *Jubilate Agno* could really only be considered a poem in our time, for its methodical madness, prophetic bursts of energy, obsessive learning, and almost symbolist associative coherence could only be read as a realized poem by an audience with the Romantics, Whitman, and Pound's *Cantos* behind it.

Smart's meter in the poem is aggressively Hebraic. Not only is it conditioned by the language of the English Bible, but by the cadences of the actual Hebrew which Smart knew. The verses are all self-contained and end-stopped, and the most recent edition [7] suggests that many of them may have been written antiphonally, in pairs. They all exhibit intralinear or line-to-line parallelism. The actual rhythm of these lines is exceedingly complicated and various, and to describe it would entail an involved analysis of syntax, classical and biblical references, interlingual puns and the like, as well as some consideration of the rhythmic effects of lists and catalogues, acrostic sections, balancing of symbolic allusion and autobiographical detail and other rhetorical devices. Representing a complete break with accentual-syllabism in English, Smart's meter had no immediate results. Had the poem been made public in its time, it would have been dismissed as lunatic ravings; by the time it was discovered, it could begin to be read with recognition.

Jubilate Agno, historically speaking, is an encapsulated event. For the modern notion of a personal meter that flows, like rhetoric, like personality, from the source of the self, we must turn to the specialized consequences of Romanticism in Whitman and Hopkins. In both cases, a new type of metrical contract is being drawn, in which the commitment is made not to convention, but to the poetic self. For both poets, the terms of the metrical contract become the bases of a whole aesthetic, but in radically different ways. Hopkins's constant allegorization of metrical terms like "stress" and his very clear historical commitment to what he feels are "inner" or underlying prosodic traditions—Old English, Celtic—are in one sense a far cry from the myth of organic form in Whitman. When Whitman says: "I and mine do not convince by arguments,

7. *Jubilate Agno*, ed. W. H. Bond (London, 1954).

similes, rhymes,/We convince by our presence," he is insisting that readers recognize his attempt to finesse all the framing, formal implications of meter which I have been discussing. In a prose passage,[8] he is even more explicit about his verse: "Its analogy is *the Ocean* . . . the liquid, billowy waves, ever rising and falling, perhaps wild with storm, always moving, always alike in their nature as rolling waves, but hardly any two exactly alike in size or measure, never having the sense of something finished and fixed, always suggesting something beyond." In our terms, it might be said that Whitman is claiming to have made a metrical principle out of the unique shapes of rhythm. The actual constituents of his metrical style are syntactic; his invariably end-stopped lines are connected by parallelisms, expansions of sentence matrices, types of catalogue and so forth, and the interactions of recognizable stress-pattern with these syntactic formulae are frequently reminiscent of the prophetic and lyric sections of the English Bible. But his claim nevertheless remains that expression takes on natural form from the self that releases it.

The study of metrical choice in the eclectic twentieth century must start from these two crucial breaks with tradition. But much of their avowed intention to allow an idiosyncratic meter almost to stand for an aesthetic manifesto is foreshadowed earlier, not by Smart's aesthetically unavowed poem, not by Milton's thundering choice of what had been a dramatic meter for his epic one, but by the very problematic metrical invention of William Blake.

Blake's metrical contract has deceived some of his most sympathetic readers.[9] Swinburne, for example, spoke of "an exquisite and lyrical excellence of form, when the subject is well in keeping with the poet's tone of spirit" as characterizing the verse of both Blake and Whitman, and he is constantly treating Blake's long lines as if they were the undulant outpourings of the other poet. In short, he was able to take the meter of, for example, *Jerusalem* and consider it as an example of what I have been calling a crisis. But it surely represents within Blake's own development a carefully and even systematically evolved style. Even the barest outlines of this development reveal an astonishingly consistent attempt to evolve a whole metrical system to serve as an alternative to the normal one, emblematic of the profoundly systematic undertaking of the en-

8. See Horace Traubel, *With Walt Whitman in Camden* (Boston, 1906), I, 414.

9. I am grateful to Professor L. C. Knights for calling my attention to Jack Lindsay's sensitive and powerful "The Metric of William Blake," prefaced to the Scholartis Press edition of *Poetical Sketches* (London, 1927). He is sensitive to the essence of Blake's struggle with the Miltonic epic line, but keeps reading undue invention and improvisation into the long line of the so-called prophetic books. Alicia Ostriker's *Vision and Verse in William Blake* (Madison, Wis., 1965) also largely ignores the metrical dimension as opposed to the rhythmic one.

graved canon of Blake's works.

In the *Poetical Sketches,* the move toward freer accentualism than one would find in, say, Collins, is perhaps even less significant than the atmosphere of real experimentation that prevails. There seems to be a conscious formal perversity to the Spenserian imitation, for example, in which every stanza is "defective" if taken from one point of view, or "adapted" if from another. There are startling enjambments that quite exceed some of Donne's in his *Satyrs.* In the closing strophe of "To Summer," he writes blank verse as perfectly end-stopped as that of the Elizabethan "drab" style, and in the conclusion of "To Winter," he will appear to employ not merely a different mode, but a different system. In any event, the two poems represent considerably different versions of what iambic pentameter is to be. What emerges from this experimentation is, of course, a commitment to a traditional-sounding accentualism. There are overtones of balladry in the freely accentual stanzas of the short poems from the manuscripts and from the *Songs of Innocence and of Experience,* but this is inevitable in such cases. Just as "free verse" in English so often turns out to be a version of the English Bible (or, in the twentieth century, to be modeled on line-for-line prose translations of the classics), loosely handled rhymed quatrains will smack of popular poetry, particularly when there is a dactyllic flavor to them.

The pure fourteeners of "Holy Thursday" are rhymed and are among the most syllabically regular of all the verses in *Songs of Innocence.* These are probably Blake's first production [1] in a meter which is to become profoundly important for him later on. The unrhymed fourteeners of *The Book of Thel* and *Tiriel,* still quite regular in their alternations of stressed and unstressed syllables, present no problems to the prosodist or to the critic. It is only what Blake was to make of his inherited line that became problematic.

The fourteener in English verse had been the meter of Chapman, Phaer, Golding, and Warner's *Albion's England.* Moreover, fourteeners in couplets are merely an alternate way of notating ballad-stanzas, and their use in broadsides, Leveller verses, and other popular and even sub-literary verse continued through Blake's own day. For Blake to use the strict, unrhymed fourteener as the basis for further expansion and modulation of a metrical style is more than merely an unfettering of poetry by enlarging its cell to the size of a long line. It seems to result from a positive attempt to create an anti-meter, as opposed to the norm of blank verse. Just as the iambic pentameter had crowded out the late Elizabethan experiments in seven-stressed lines, consigning them to the sub-literary

---

1. It predates the version in *Songs of Innocence,* appearing first in *An Island in the Moon.*

dungeon of doggerel, so Blake may have thought to resurrect them and some of what they stood for. His attempts to undermine metrical conventions are present everywhere in his shorter poems. The last two lines of *The Garden of Love,* for example, break the expected conclusion of what begins like a sentimental song in quatrains, and thunder out in a little sub-quatrain of their own, with the epigrammatic tension of the kind of inscription or motto Blake uses elsewhere. "The Question Answered" is an anti-epigram:

> What is it men in women do require?
> The lineaments of gratified desire.
> What is it women do in men require?
> The lineaments of gratified desire.

The whole Augustan tradition of the two-couplet epigram is undermined by the unyielding hammered insistence of the repeated line and the ironic absence of wit. The reader is implicitly rebuked for expecting a logical movement toward the discovery of a conclusion —as if all epigrams were merely circular, just as logical proofs produce only new tautologies—and the form plunges us into the identity without remorse. It is not surprising, then, to find one of Blake's most explicit anti-epigrams couched in a couplet of fourteeners: "Her whole Life is an Epigram, smart smooth & neatly pen'd,/Platted quite neat to catch applause with a sliding noose at the end." Epigrammatic tautology, for Blake, seems to be a kind of death.

Blake's subversion of English meter proceeds through his modulation of the strict fourteener in the later long poems. In the puzzling, longer, still early lines of "The French Revolution," an accentual seven-stressed core remains, the number of syllables varying from fifteen to more than twenty-one or twenty-two within a group of five or six lines. After this rather peculiar poem, Blake evidently decided that his modulation of the septenarius lay not in the direction of free-accentual expansion, and in the subsequent longer poems we see him adapting the basic line in forms analagous to those of normative meter. His stanza-forms in *Europe*, in *Nights* 2 and 5 of *Vala*, and various staves of three, four, and five lines in other poems, even the enigmatic short lines in *Ahania, Los,* and *Urizen* (where it has been suggested that the engraving called for longer, thinner columns) [2] involve combinations and units of four and three stresses—the relation of Blake's meters to traditional iambic lines of varying length are like that of a duodecimal modulo number system to a decimal one.

The rhythmic possibilities established by the fourteener are in-

2. By George Saintsbury in *A History Of English Prosody* (London, 1910), III, 26.

teresting, for the tendency of the familiar ballad-rhythm to intrude on the ears of the reader allows for frequent syntactic juncture after the fourth stress. Blake's rhythmic derivations from Ossian and from the English Bible, which have been so frequently commented upon, often involve structural parallelism hung across such a juncture—again, an underground substitute for the balance and antithesis of Augustan verse. But Blake never completely surrenders to the Whitmanesque program of claiming that rhythm is its own meter. At first glance, the metrical apology prefaced to *Jerusalem* suggests this, in terms clearly implying an alternative to the apology to *Paradise Lost*:

> Of the measure in which
> the following poem is written.
> . . . When this Verse was first dictated to me, I consider'd a Monotonous Cadence, like that used by Milton & Shakespeare & all writers of English Blank Verse, derived from the modern bondage of Rhyming, to be a necessary and indispensible part of Verse. But I soon found that in the mouth of a true Orator such monotony was not only awakward, but as much a bondage as rhyme itself. I therefore have produced a variety in every line, both of cadences & of number of syllables. Every word and every letter is studied and put into its fit place; the terriffic numbers are reserved for the terrific parts, the mild & gentle for the mild & gentle parts, and the prosaic for inferior parts; all are necessary to each other. Poetry Fetter'd Fetters the Human Race. Nations are Destroy'd or Flourish in proportion as Their Poetry, Painting and Music are Destroy'd or Flourish! The Primeval State of Man was Wisdom, Art and Science.

Blake is suggesting here a kind of traditional modality of meter, albeit in the guise of a declaration of rhythmic independence. It would be the expressive rhythms that would be fettered for him in a "Monotonous Cadence." What he in fact does in *Jerusalem* is to extend the loosening of the fourteener in several directions, from regular to loose, from syllabic fourteeners with only five or six major stresses to cluttered ones of eight. He frequently enjambs lines in ways that he had only done previously in the blank verse of the *Poetical Sketches,* allowing a mono- or disyllabic word at the line-break to count for a strong stress, even though the principle of his free accentualism throughout his work has been to let speech stress, in its syntactic and rhetorical context, govern the metrical role of syllables.

As for his rhythmic modes of mild, terrific, and prosaic, it is obvious from the text that the key is provided not by the measure of syllable or stress, nor by some referential rhythmic pattern alone, but by the diction. In some ways, Blake's sense of meter here is closer to the concerns of Wordsworth than one might think. But throughout the poem, the fourteener is never far away, and the poem's meter is most like a transformed equivalent of the freest kind of blank verse. Were the norm to have been five stresses rather than seven, there would never have been as much puzzling about Blake's meter as there has been.

Among all the Romantics, then, Blake's meter is perhaps the most programmatic, and perhaps the most paradigmatically contractual. His evolved metrical style results not from a nihilistic smashing of metrical conventions in order to free an oppressed rhythm (he is not Whitman), but rather to use metrical choices in the way in which certain twentieth-century poets, historically self-conscious, have used them: to engage certain prior conventions, and, rejecting others, to form a new tradition, discontinuous in some ways as it might be. His contract was, in a way, with the Devil's party which, he felt, Milton finally betrayed, "though sublime/In Number, Weight and Measure," as Marvell had put it. But echoing the same text in his *Proverbs of Hell*, Blake was engaging the literal sense of poetic "numbers" as well as conceptual ones: "Bring out number, weight & measure in a year of dearth," he half-snarls, and we can perhaps too easily leap from what we think Blake's intentions might be to the unfetterings of a Whitman, or even beyond, to some kind of transcendence of the very ways in which intense language controls its own shape. But in that realm there is never plenitude. For art, the task is always "What to make of a diminished thing." Blake could no more have abandoned numbers entirely than he could have dispensed with, say, the containing power of line over color in his graphics.

Blake's metrical practice typifies Romantic critical thought generally in its ability to resist the actual linguistic analysis of metrical schemata and rhythmic processes which so plagued eighteenth-century prosodic theorists.[3] At one point, Coleridge accuses Wordsworth of evading this same issue, and yet he is himself only able to come up with one example, and that a crude and obvious one,

3. Southey, for one, ventures deeper into these waters than one might have supposed. He is naturally concerned to defend the English adaptation of the German stressed hexameter which he used so skillfully in the otherwise ill-fated *A Vision of Judgment*. Although as confused in his terminology (in such concepts as "accent" and "emphasis") as any eighteenth-century prosodist, he nevertheless shows some sophistication in grasping the notion of phrase-stress. See *Poetical Works* (London, 1838), X, 198 f. Southey is perceptive in other ways as well; in discussing the complicated stanza-form of *Thalaba*, he correctly observes, *op. cit.* p. 199, that his variations of line length are bound to commit him to monosyllables in English unlike German and Latin (a phenomenon the present author observed in the development of the double-dactyl). He observes that "the English greatly exceeds the ancient one in literal length," so that, given typographical conventions, it gets too long for the page. He sees this, perhaps rightly, as causing the break-up of the fourteener couplet into the ballad stanza, claiming that "that fine measure of the Elizabethan age" thereby suffered "diminution of its powers."

of the more elementary operations of rhythmic modality: "The discussion on the powers of metre in the preface," he says, "is highly ingenious and touches at all points on truth. But I cannot find any statement of its powers considered absolutely and separately. On the contrary, Mr. Wordsworth seems always to estimate metre by the powers, which it exerts during (and, as I think, in *consequence of*) its combination with other elements of poetry. Thus the previous difficulty is left unanswered, *what* the elements are, with which it must be combined in order to produce its own effects to any pleasurable purpose. Double and tri-syllable rhymes, indeed, form a lower species of wit, and attended to exclusively for their own sake, may become a source of moderate amusement. . . ." Coleridge is no doubt right about the "*in consequence of,*" as the most sophisticated modern linguistic studies of poetic language are showing. In his own thoughts on metrical matters, Coleridge is most concerned with such questions as getting the German versions of Greek meters into English, and so forth, the kind of thing that occupied Southey and Landor as well. A tantalizing fragment from an earlyish notebook [4] seems to indicate an awareness on Coleridge's part of the problems that result from thinking of a meter as something "super-added": "Metre distinct and artificial—till at length poetry forgot its existence in those forms which were only hieroglyphics of it." Yes; but whether he really means this to be true of phylogeny or ontogeny, of poetic process in literary history or internalized creation, we cannot be sure.

Romantic metrical theory, as informal a body of thought as it is, finally avows the emblematic, framing, defining role of metrical format as consistently as does that of Whitman, Hopkins, or some of the poets of our own day. Even more clearly, perhaps, the stylistic revolutions of English Romantic poetry which look forward to the intent, if not the methods, of some of the manifestoes of its devouring offspring, Modernism, can only be fully understood in the light of the programs of meter, the wisely-schooled heart of poetry, as well as the profuse strains of actual rhythmic instances.

4. *Notebooks*, ed. K. Coburn (New York, 1957), Vol. I, note no. 786.

M. H. ABRAMS

Structure and Style in the Greater Romantic Lyric †

There is no accepted name for the kind of poem I want to talk about, even though it was a distinctive and widely practiced variety of the longer Romantic lyric and includes some of the greatest Romantic achievements in any form. Coleridge's "Eolian Harp," "Frost at Midnight," "Fears in Solitude," and "Dejection: An Ode" exemplify the type, as does Wordsworth's "Tintern Abbey," his "Ode: Intimations of Immortality," and (with a change in initial reference from scene to painting) his "Elegiac Stanzas Suggested by a Picture of Peele Castle in a Storm." Shelley's "Stanzas Written in Dejection" follows the formula exactly, and his "Ode to the West Wind" is a variant on it. Of Keats's odes, that to a Nightingale is the one which approximates the pattern most closely. Only Byron, among the major poets, did not write in this mode at all.

These instances yield a paradigm for the type. Some of the poems are called odes, while the others approach the ode in having lyric magnitude and a serious subject, feelingfully meditated. They present a determinate speaker in a particularized, and usually a localized, outdoor setting, whom we overhear as he carries on, in a fluent vernacular which rises easily to a more formal speech, a sustained colloquy, sometimes with himself or with the outer scene, but more frequently with a silent human auditor, present or absent. The speaker begins with a description of the landscape; an aspect or change of aspect in the landscape evokes a varied but integral process of memory, thought, anticipation, and feeling which remains closely intervolved with the outer scene. In the course of this meditation the lyric speaker achieves an insight, faces up to a tragic loss, comes to a moral decision, or resolves an emotional problem. Often the poem rounds upon itself to end where it began, at the outer scene, but with an altered mood and deepened understanding which is the result of the intervening meditation.

What shall we call this Romantic genre? To label these poems

† From *From Sensibility to Romanticism: Essays Presented to Frederick A. Pottle*, edited by Frederick W. Hilles and Harold Bloom. Copyright © 1965 by Oxford University Press, Inc. Reprinted by permission of the publisher.

simply nature lyrics is not only inadequate, but radically misleading. We have not yet entirely recovered from the earlier critical
stress on Wordsworth's statement that "I have at all times endeavored to look steadily at my subject," to the neglect of his repeated warnings that accurate natural description, though a
necessary, is an inadequate condition for poetry. Like Blake and
Coleridge, Wordsworth manifested wariness, almost terror, at the
threat of the corporeal eye and material object to tyrannize over
the mind and imagination, in opposition to that normative experience in which

> The mind is lord and master—outward sense
> The obedient servant of her will.[1]

In the extended lyrics we are considering, the visual report is invariably the occasion for a meditation which turns out to constitute
the *raison d'être* of the poem. Romantic writers, though nature
poets, were humanists above all, for they dealt with the non-human
only insofar as it is the occasion for the activity which defines man:
thought, the process of intellection.

"The descriptive-meditative poem" is a possible, but a clumsy
term. *Faute de mieux*, I shall call this poetic type "the greater Romantic lyric," intending to suggest, not that it is a higher achievement than other Romantic lyrics, but that it displaced what
neoclassical critics had called "the greater ode"—the elevated
Pindaric, in distinction to "the lesser ode" modeled chiefly on
Horace—as the favored form for the long lyric poem.

The repeated out-in-out process, in which mind confronts nature
and their interplay constitutes the poem, is a remarkable phenomenon in literary history. If we don't find it strange, it is because our
responses have been dulled by long familiarity with such a procedure not only in the Romantic poets, but in their many successors
who played variations on the mode, from Matthew Arnold and Walt
Whitman—both "Dover Beach" and "Crossing Brooklyn Ferry,"
for example, closely follow the pattern of the greater Romantic
lyric—to Wallace Stevens and W. H. Auden. But at the beginning
of the nineteenth century this procedure in the lyric was part of a
new and exciting poetic strategy, no less epidemic than Donne's in
his day, or T. S. Eliot's in the period after the first World War. For
several decades poets did not often talk about the great issues of
life, death, love, joy, dejection, or God without talking at the same

1. *The Prelude* (1850), XII, 222–3.
Even Keats, though he sometimes
longed for a life of sensations rather
than of thought, objected to the poems
of John Clare that too often "the
Description overlaid and stifled that
which ought to be the prevailing Idea."
(Letter to John Clare from John
Taylor, 27 September 1820, quoted by
Edmund Blunden, *Keats' Publisher*
[London, 1936], p. 80).

time about the landscape. Wordsworth's narrative of Michael emerges from a description of the scene around "the tumultuous brook of Green-head Ghyll," to which in the end it returns:

> and the remains
> Of the unfinished Sheep-fold may be seen
> Beside the boisterous brook of Green-head Ghyll.

Coleridge's great, neglected love-poem, "Recollections of Love," opens with a Quantock scene revisited after eight years have passed, and adverts suddenly to the River Greta at the close:

> But when those meek eyes first did seem
> To tell me, Love within you wrought—
> O Greta, dear domestic stream!
>
> Has not, since then, Love's prompture deep,
> Has not Love's whisper evermore
> Been ceaseless, as thy gentle roar?
> Sole voice, when other voices sleep,
> Dear under-song in clamor's hour.

Keats's first long poem of consequence, though it is his introduction to an *ars poetica*, represents what he saw, then what he thought, while he "stood tiptoe upon a little hill." Shelley treats the theme of permanence in change by describing the mutations of a cloud, defines the pure Idea of joy in a meditation on the flight and song of a skylark, and presents his ultimate concept of the secret and impersonal power behind all process in a description of Mont Blanc and the Vale of Chamouni. Wordsworth's *Prelude* can be viewed as an epic expansion of the mode of "Tintern Abbey," both in overall design and local tactics. It begins with the description of a landscape visited in maturity, evokes the entire life of the poet as a protracted meditation on things past, and presents the growth of the poet's mind as an interaction with the natural milieu by which it is fostered, from which it is tragically alienated, and to which in the resolution it is restored, with a difference attributable to the intervening experiences; the poem ends at the time of its beginning.

What I have called "the greater lyric," then, is only a special instance of a very widespread manner of proceeding in Romantic poetry; but it is of great interest because it was the earliest Romantic formal invention, which at once demonstrated the stability of organization and the capacity to engender successors which define a distinct lyric species. New lyric forms are not as plenty as blackberries, and when one turns up, it is worth critical attention. Suppose, therefore, that we ask some questions about this one: about its genesis, its nearest literary antecedents, and the reasons why this way of proceeding, out of the alternatives in common lyric practice, should have appealed so powerfully to the Romantic sensibility. Inquiry into some probable causes of the structure and style of the greater lyric will take us not only to the evolution of certain descriptive genres in the seventeenth and eighteenth centuries, but also to contemporary developments in philosophy and in theology, and to the spiritual posture in which many poets, as well as philosophers, found themselves at the end of the Enlightenment.

I. COLERIDGE AND WORDSWORTH

In this investigation Coleridge must be our central reference, not only because he had the most to say about these matters in prose but because it was he, not Wordsworth, who inaugurated the greater Romantic lyric, firmly established its pattern, and wrote the largest number of instances. Wordsworth's first trial in the extended lyric was "Tintern Abbey," which he composed in July 1798. Up to that time his only efforts in the long descriptive and reflective mode were the schoolboy effort, "The Vale of Esthwaite," and the two tour-poems of 1793, "An Evening Walk" and "Descriptive Sketches." The first of these was written in octosyllabic and the latter two in heroic couplets, and all differ in little but merit and the detail of single passages from hundreds of eighteenth-century predecessors.[2] Coleridge, however, as early as 20 August 1795, composed a short first version of "The Eolian Harp," and in 1796—two years before "Tintern Abbey"—expanded it to fifty-six lines which established, in epitome, the ordonnance, materials, and style of the greater lyric.[3] It is in the dramatic mode of intimate talk to an unanswering auditor in easy blank-verse paragraphs. It begins with a description of the peaceful outer scene; this, in parallel with the vagrant sounds evoked from a wind-harp, calls forth a recollection in tranquillity of earlier experiences in the same setting and leads to a sequence of reflections which are suggested by, and also incorporate, perceptual qualities of the scene. The poem closes with a summary reprise of the opening description of "PEACE, and this COT, and THEE, heart-honour'd Maid!"

Between the autumn of 1796 and the spring of 1798 Coleridge

2. *Descriptive Sketches* (1793) drew from a contemporary reviewer the cry: "More descriptive poetry! Have we not yet enough? . . . Yes; more, and yet more: so it is decreed." *The Monthly Review,* 2d series, XII (1793), 216–17; cited by Robert A. Aubin, *Topographical Poetry in XVIII-Century England* (New York, 1936), p. 255; see also pp. 217–19.

3. Perhaps that is the reason for Coleridge's later judgment that "The Eolian Harp" was "the most perfect poem I ever wrote." (Quoted by J. D. Campbell, ed., *The Poetical Works of S. T. Coleridge,* London, 1893, p. 578). The first version of the poem and a manuscript version of 1797 (Coleridge then entitled it "Effusion") are reproduced in *The Complete Poetical Works,* ed. E. H. Coleridge (2 vols.; Oxford, 1912), II, 1021–3. For an account of the revisions of the poem, see H. J. W. Milley, "Some Notes on Coleridge's 'Eolian Harp,'" *Modern Philology,* XXXVI (1938–39), 359–75.

composed a number of variations on this lyric type, including "Reflections on Having Left a Place of Retirement," "This Lime-tree Bower," "Fears in Solitude," and "The Nightingale." To these writings Professor G. M. Harper applied the term which Coleridge himself used for "The Nightingale," "conversation poems"; very aptly, because they are written (though some of them only intermittently) in a blank verse which at its best captures remarkably the qualities of the intimate speaking voice, yet remains capable of adapting without strain to the varying levels of the subject matter and feeling. And within this period, in February of 1798, Coleridge produced one of the masterpieces of the greater lyric, perfectly modulated and proportioned, but so successful in the quiet way that it hides its art that it has only recently attracted its meed of critical admiration. The poem is "Frost at Midnight," and it follows, but greatly enlarges and subtilizes the pattern of "The Eolian Harp." What seems at first impression to be the free association of its central meditation turns out to have been called forth, qualified, and controlled by the opening description, which evokes the strangeness in the familiar surroundings of the solitary and wakeful speaker: the "secret ministry" of the frost, the "strange and extreme silentness" of "sea, and hill, and wood," the life of the sleeping village "inaudible as dreams," and the film that flutters on the grate "the sole unquiet thing." In consonance with these elements, and directed especially by the rhythm of the seemingly unnoticed breathing of a sleeping infant, the meditative mind disengages itself from the physical locale, moves back in time to the speaker's childhood, still farther back, to his own infancy, then forward to express, in the intonation of a blessing, the hope that his son shall have the life in nature that his father lacked; until, in anticipating the future, it incorporates both the present scene and the results of the remembered past in the enchanting close—

> Whether the eave-drops fall
> Heard only in the trances of the blast,
> Or if the secret ministry of frost
> Shall hang them up in silent icicles,
> Quietly shining to the quiet Moon.

In the original version this concluding sentence trailed off in six more verse-lines, which Coleridge, in order to emphasize the lyric rondure, later excised. Plainly, Coleridge worked out the lyric device of the return-upon-itself—which he used in "Reflections on Having Left a Place of Retirement" and "Fears in Solitude," as well as in "The Eolian Harp" and "Frost at Midnight"—in a deliberate endeavor to transform a segment of experience broken out of time into a sufficient aesthetic whole. "The common end of all *narrative*, nay, of *all*, Poems," he wrote to Joseph Cottle in 1815, "is to convert a *series* into a *Whole*: to make those events, which in real or imagined History move on in a *strait* Line, assume to our Understandings a *circular* motion—the snake with it's Tail in its Mouth." [4] From the time of the early Greek philosophers, the circle had been the shape of perfection; and in occult philosophy the *ouroboros*, the tail-eating snake, had become the symbol for eternity and for the divine process of creation, since it is complete, self-sufficient, and endless. For Coleridge the perfect shape for the descriptive-meditative-descriptive poem was precisely the one described and exemplified in T. S. Eliot's "East Coker," which begins: "In my beginning is my end," and ends: "In my end is my beginning;" another modern writer who knew esoteric lore designed *Finnegans Wake* so that the headless sentence which begins the book completes the tailless sentence with which it ends.

Five months after the composition of "Frost at Midnight," Wordsworth set out on a walking tour with his sister. Reposing on a high bank of the River Wye, he remembered this among others of Coleridge's conversation poems—the dramatic mode of address to an unanswering listener in flexible blank verse; the opening description which evolves into a sustained meditation assimilating perceptual, personal, and philosophical elements; the free movement of thought from the present scene to recollection in tranquillity, to prayer-like prediction, and back to the scene; even some of Coleridge's specific concepts and phrases—and in the next four or five days' walk, worked out "Lines Composed a Few Miles above Tintern Abbey" and appended it forthwith to *Lyrical Ballads*, which was already in press.

To claim that it was Coleridge who deflected Wordsworth's poetry into a channel so entirely congenial to him is in no way to derogate Wordsworth's achievement, nor his powers of invention. "Tintern Abbey" has greater dimension and intricacy and a more various verbal orchestration than "Frost at Midnight." In its conclusion Wordsworth managed Coleridge's specialty, the return-upon-itself, with a mastery of involuted reference without match in the poems of its begetter. "Tintern Abbey" also inaugurated the wonderfully functional device Wordsworth later called the "two consciousnesses": a scene is revisited, and the remembered landscape ("the picture of the mind") is superimposed on the picture before the eye; the two landscapes fail to match, and so set a problem ("a sad perplexity") which compels the meditation. Wordsworth played variations on this stratagem in all his later trials in the greater lyric, and in *The Prelude* he expanded it into a persisting double awareness of things as they are and as they were, and so

4. *Collected Letters*, ed. Earl Leslie Griggs (Oxford, 1956), IV, 545.

anticipated the structural principle of the most influential masterpiece of our own century, Proust's À *la recherche du temps perdu*.

II. THE LOCAL POEM

What was the closest poetic antecedent of this controlled and
shapely lyric genre? It was not the ancient lyric formula, going back
to the spring-songs of the troubadors, which set forth an ideal
spring scene (the *Natureingang*) and then presented a human
experience in harmony or contrast—a formula which survived in
Burns's

> Ye flowery banks o' bonie Doon,
> How can ye blume sae fair?
> How can ye chant, ye little birds,
> And I sae fu' o' care?

Nor was it Thomson's *Seasons*, that omnibus of unlocalized description, episodic narration, and general reflection, in which the
pious observer moves from Nature to Nature's God with the help
of Isaac Newton's *Principia*. And certainly it was not the formal
descriptive poem such as Collins's "Ode to Evening," which
adapted Pindar's ceremonial panegyric to landscape mainly by the
device of transforming descriptive and meditative propositions into
a sequence of tableaux and brief allegories—a mode which Keats
revitalized in his "Ode to Autumn." [5] The clue to the provenance
of the greater Romantic lyric is to be found in the attributes of the
opening description. This landscape is not only particularized; it is
in most cases precisely localized, in place, and sometimes in time
as well. Critics have often remarked on Wordsworth's scrupulosity
about specifying the circumstances for his poems, but his fellow-
poets were often no less meticulous in giving their greater lyrics
an exact locality. We have "The Eolian Harp, Composed at Cleve-
don, Somersetshire" (the first versions also appended to the title a
date, 20 August 1795); "This Lime-Tree Bower My Prison," sub-
titled: "In the June of 1797 . . . the author's cottage. . . . Composed . . . in the garden-bower"; "Fears in Solitude written April,
1798. . . . The Scene, the Hills near Stowey"; [6] "Lines Written a

5. Keats used a different figure for the
poetic return. In a letter of Dec. 1818–
Jan. 1819, he transcribed "Ever let
the Fancy roam" and "Bards of Passion and of Mirth," in which the last
lines are variants of the opening lines,
and said: "These are specimens of a
sort of rondeau which I think I shall
become partial to" (*The Letters*, ed.
H. E. Rollins, 2 vols., Cambridge,
Mass., 1958, II, 21–6). In the next
few months he exemplified the rondeau
form in "The Eve of St. Agnes" and
"La Belle Dame sans Merci," as well
as in the descriptive-meditative lyric,
"Ode to a Nightingale."

6. So titled in the Dowden MS. in
the Morgan Library; see Carl R.
Woodring, *Politics in the Poetry of
Coleridge* (Madison, Wisconsin, 1961),
p. 255, note 16.

Few Miles above Tintern Abbey . . . July 13; 1798"; "Stanzas Written in Dejection, Near Naples." Even when its setting is not named in the title, the poem usually has an indentifiable local habitation, such as the milieu of Coleridge's cottage at Nether Stowey for "Frost at Midnight," or the view from Coleridge's study at Keswick in "Dejection: An Ode." To his "Ode to the West Wind," Shelley was careful to add the note: "Written in a wood that skirts the Arno, near Florence. . . ."

There existed in the eighteenth century a well-defined and immensely popular poetic type, in which the title named a geographical location, and which combined a description of that scene with the thoughts that the scene suggested. This was known as the "local" or "loco-descriptive" poem; Robert A. Aubin, in his compendious and amusing survey of *Topographical Poetry in XVIII-Century England*, lists almost two thousand instances of the form. "Local poetry," as Dr. Johnson concisely defined it in his life of John Denham, was

> a species of composition . . . of which the fundamental subject is some particular landscape, to be poetically described, with the addition of such embellishments as may be supplied by historical retrospection or incidental meditation.[7]

The evidence, I think, makes it clear that the most characteristic Romantic lyric developed directly out of one of the most stable and widely employed of all the neoclassic kinds.

By general consent Sir John Denham, as Dr. Johnson said, was the "author" of the genre, in that excellent poem, "Cooper's Hill," of which the first version was written in 1642. In it the poet inventories the prospect of the Thames valley visible from the hilltop, with distant London on one side and Windsor Castle on the other. As Earl Wasserman has shown, the poem is a complex construction, in which the topographical elements are selected and managed so as to yield concepts which support a Royalist viewpoint on the eve of the Civil Wars.[8] But if, like Dr. Johnson, we abstract and classify Denham's incidental meditations, we find that some are historical and political, but that others are broadly sententious, and are achieved by the device of adducing to a natural object a correspondent moral idea. Thus the "aery Mountain" (lines 217–22), forced to endure the onslaught of winds and storms, instances "The common fate of all that's high or great," while the Thames (lines 163–4) hastens "to pay his tribute to the Sea,/Like mortal life to meet Eternity."

This latter procedure is worth dwelling on for a moment, because for many of Denham's successors it displaced history and

---

7. *The Works of Samuel Johnson*, ed. Arthur Murphy (12 vols.; London, 1824), IX, 77.   8. *The Subtler Language* (Baltimore, 1959), Chap. III.

politics to become the sole meditative component in local poems, and it later evolved into the extended meditation of the Romantic lyric. The *paysage moralisè* was not invented as a rhetorical device by poets, but was grounded on two collateral and pervasive concepts in medieval and Renaissance philosophy. One of these was the doctrine that God has supplemented the Holy Scriptures with the *liber creaturarum*, so that objects of nature, as Sir Thomas Browne said, carry "in Stenography and short Characters, something of Divinity" [9] and show forth the attributes and providence of their Author. The second concept, of independent philosophic origin but often fused with the first, is that the divine Architect has designed the universe analogically, relating the physical, moral, and spiritual realms by an elaborate system of correspondences. A landscape, accordingly, consists of *verba visibilia* which enable pious interpreters such as Shakespeare's Duke in *As You Like It* to find "books in the running brooks,/Sermons in stones, and good in everything."

The metaphysic of a symbolic and analogical universe underlay the figurative tactics of the seventeenth-century metaphysical poets who were John Denham's predecessors and contemporaries. The secular and amatory poems exploited unexpected correspondences mainly as display rhetoric, positing the analogue in order to show the author's wit in supporting an argument and to evoke in the reader the shock of delightful discovery. In their devotional poems, however, the poets put forward their figures as grounded in the divine plan underlying the universe. Thus Henry Vaughan, musing over a waterfall, was enabled by the guidance of its Creator to discover its built-in correspondences with the life and destiny of man:

> What sublime truths and wholesome themes,
> Lodge in thy mystical deep streams!
> Such as dull man can never find
> Unless that spirit lead his mind
> Which first upon thy face did move,
> And hatched all with his quick'ning love.

In 1655, the year in which Vaughan published "The Waterfall," Denham added to his enlarged edition of "Cooper's Hill" the famous pair of couplets on the Thames which link description to concepts by a sustained parallel between the flow of the stream and the ideal conduct of life and art:

> O could I flow like thee, and make thy stream
> My great example, as it is my theme!
> Though deep, yet clear, though gentle, yet not dull,
> Strong without rage, without o'erflowing, full.

9. *Works*, ed. Geoffrey Keynes (6 vols.; London, 1928), I, 17.

The metaphysical device and ingenuity are still apparent, but we can see why this became the best-known and most influential passage in the poetry of neoclassicism—a model not only for its versification, but also for some of its most characteristic ideas and rhetorical devices. In these lines the metaphysical wit has been tamed and ordered into the "true wit" which became the eighteenth-century ideal; Denham's "strength" (which Dr. Johnson defined as "much meaning in few words"), so universally admired, has replaced the "strong lines" (the compressed and hyperbolic ingeniousness) of John Donne; while the startling revelation of *discordia concors* between object and idea has been smoothed to a neoclassic decency, moulded to the deft play of antitheses around the caesura, and adapted to the presentation of the cardinal neoclassic norm of a mean between extremes.[1]

In the enormous number of eighteenth-century local poems the organization of "Cooper's Hill" around a controlling political motif was soon reduced mainly to the procedure of setting up parallels between landscape and moral commonplaces. The subtitle of Richard Jago's long "Edge Hill" (1767) neatly defines the double-function: "The Rural Prospect Delineated and Moralized"; while the title of an anonymous poem of 1790 reveals how monstrous this development could be: "An Evening's Reflection on the Universe, in a Walk on the Seashore." The literal belief in a universe of divine types and correspondences, which had originally supported this structural trope, faded,[2] and the coupling of sensuous phe-

---

1. The opening eight lines of "Cooper's Hill," despite some approximation to neoclassic neatness and dispatch, are much closer to Donne's couplets, in the cramped syntax of their run-on lines, which deploy a tortuous analogical argument to demonstrate a paradox that inverts and explodes a mythological cliché:

> Sure there are Poets which did not dream
> Upon *Parnassus*, nor did taste the stream
> Of *Helicon*, we therefore may suppose
> Those made no Poets, but the Poets those.
> And as Courts make not Kings, but Kings the Court,
> So where the Muses and their train resort,
> *Parnassus* stands; if I can be to thee
> A Poet, thou Parnassus are to me.

Compare the opening of Andrew Marvell's "Upon the Hill and Grove at Billborow" (probably written in the early 1650's for the jolting movement, the doughty hyperbole, and witty shock-tactics of the thoroughly metaphysical management of a local hill-poem.

2. See Earl R. Wasserman, "Nature Moralized: The Divine Analogy in the Eighteenth Century," *ELH*, XX (1953), 39–76. For commentators on the local poem, the chief structural problem was how to establish easy, just, yet varied connections between its two components, the *visibilia* and the *moralia*. Joseph Warton's observation is typical, that "it is one of the greatest and most pleasing arts of descriptive poetry, to introduce moral sentences and instructions in an oblique and indirect manner." *An Essay on the Genius and Writings of Pope*, 1756 (London, 1806), I, 29.

nomena with moral statements came to be regarded as a rhetorical
device particularly apt to the descriptive poet's double aim of combining instruction with delight. John Dyer's "Grongar's Hill"
(1726) was justly esteemed as one of the most deft and agreeable
of prospect poems. Mounting the hill, the poet describes the
widening prospect with a particularity beyond the call of the
moralist's duty. Yet the details of the scene are duly equated with
sententiae; and when he comes to moralize the river (always, after
Denham's passage on the Thames, the favorite item in the topog-
raphic inventory), Dyer echoes the great theological concept of a
typological universe lightly, as a pleasant conceit:

> And see the rivers how they run . . .
> Wave succeeding wave, they go
> A various journey to the deep,
> Like human life to endless sleep!
> Thus is nature's vesture wrought,
> To instruct our wand'ring thought;
> Thus she dresses green and gay,
> To disperse our cares away.

Thomas Gray's "Ode on a Distant Prospect of Eton College"
(1747) provides significant evidence that the local poem evolved
into the greater Romantic lyric. It is a hill-poem, and its setting
—Windsor heights and the Thames valley—is part of the very
prospect which Denham had described. The topographical form,
however, has been adapted to the Horatian ode, so that the focus
of interest is no longer in the analogical inventory of scenic detail,
but in the mental and emotional experience of a specific lyric
speaker. The meditation becomes a coherent and dramatic sequence of thought, triggered by what was to become Wordsworth's
favorite device of *dèja vu:* the scene is a scene revisited, and it
evokes in memory the lost self of the speaker's youth.

> I feel the gales that from ye blow
> A momentary bliss bestow,
> As, waving fresh their gladsome wing,
> My weary soul they seem to soothe,
> And, redolent of joy and youth
> To breathe a second spring.

As he watches the heedless schoolboys at their games, the speaker's
first impulse is to warn them of the ambuscades which the "minis-
ters of human fate" are even now laying for them: "Ah, tell them
they are men!" But a new thought leads to a reversal of intention,
for he suddenly realizes that since life's horrors are inescapable,
forewarning is a useless cruelty.

We are a long way, however, from the free flow of consciousness,
the interweaving of thought, feeling, and perceptual detail, and

the easy naturalness of the speaking voice which characterize the Romantic lyric. Gray deliberately rendered both his observations and reflections in the hieratic style of a formal odic *oratio*. The poet's recollection of times past, for example, is managed through an invocation to Father Thames to tell him "Who foremost now delight to cleave/With pliant arm thy glassy wave," and the language throughout is heightened and stylized by the apostrophe, exclamation, rhetorical question, and studied periphrasis which Wordsworth decried in Gray—"more than any other man curiously elaborate in the structure of his . . . poetic diction." [3] Both reminiscence and reflection are depersonalized, and occur mainly as general propositions which are sometimes expressed as *sententiae* ("where ignorance is bliss/'Tis folly to be wise"), and at other times as proposition which, in the standard artifice of the contemporary ode, are converted into the tableau-and-allegory form that Coleridge derogated as Gray's "translations of prose thoughts into poetic language." [4] Gray's poem is structurally inventive, and excellent in its kind, but it remains distinctly a mid-century period piece. We need to look elsewhere for the immediate occasion of Coleridge's invention of the greater Romantic lyric.

III. COLERIDGE AND BOWLES

I have quoted Coleridge's derogation of Gray from the first chapter of the *Biographia Literaria*, in which Coleridge reviewed his own early development as a poet. To Gray's style he opposed that of three poems, the only contemporary models he mentioned with approval; and all three, it is important to note, were of a type which combines local description with associated meditation. One was William Crowe's conventional prospect poem, *Lewesdon Hill* (1788) and another was Cowper's *The Task*, which incorporated a number of episodic meditations evoked by the environs of the river Ouse. Both these poems, however, he read later—*The Task*, he says, "many years" later—than a publication which at once seized irresistibly upon his sensibility, William Lisle Bowles's *Sonnets* of 1789. By these poems he was "year after year . . . enthusiastically delighted and inspired," and he worked zealously to win "proselytes" to his poetic divinity by buttonholing strangers and friends alike, and by sending out as gifts more than forty copies of Bowles's volume, which he had himself transcribed.[5]

Coleridge mentioned also Bowles's "Monody Written at Matlock" (1791), which is a long prospect-poem written in blank

3. Preface to *Lyrical Ballads, The Poetical Works of William Wordsworth*, ed. E. de Selincourt (5 vols.; Oxford, 1949), II, 391.

4. *Biographia Literaria*, ed. J. Shawcross (2 vols.; Oxford, 1907), I, 13.
5. *Ibid*, pp. 8–16.

verse. But most of Bowles's poems of 1789 were obvious adapta-
tions of this local-meditative formula to the sonnet form. As in both
the local poems and the Romantic lyric, a number of Bowles's
titles specify the place, and even the time: "To the River Wens-
beck"; "To the River Itchin Near Winton"; "On Dover Cliffs. July
20, 1787"; "Written at Ostend. July 22, 1787." The whole was
"Written," as the title of 1789 points out, "Chiefly on Picturesque
Spots, during a Tour," and constitutes a sonnet-sequence uttered
by a latter-day wandering *penseroso* who, as the light fades from the
literal day, images his life as a metaphoric tour from its bright
morning through deepening shadow to enduring night. Within this
over-arching equation, the typical single poem begins with a rapid
sketch of the external scene—frequently, as in so many of Denham's progeny, a river scene—then moves on to reminiscence and
moral reflection. The transition is often managed by a connecting
phrase which signalizes the shift from objects to concepts and
indicates the nature of the relation between them: "So fares it with
the children of the earth"; "ev'n thus on sorrow's breath/A kindred
stillness steals"; "Bidding me many a tender thought recall/Of
summer days"; "I meditate/On this world's passing pageant."

Bowles wrote in a Preface of 1805, when his poems had already
achieved a ninth edition, that his sonnets "describe his personal
feelings" during excursions taken to relieve "depression of spirits."
They exhibit "occasional reflections which naturally rose in his
mind" and were

> in general suggested by the scenes before them; and wherever such
> scenes appeared to harmonise with his disposition at the moment,
> the sentiments were involuntarily prompted.[6]

The local poem has been lyricized. That is, Bowles's sonnets present a determinate speaker, whom we are invited to identify with
the author himself, whose responses to the local scene are a spontaneous overflow of feeling and displace the landscape as the center
of poetic interest; hence the "occasional reflections" and "sentiments," instead of being a series of impersonal *sententiae* linked to
details of the setting by analogy, are mediated by the particular
temperament and circumstances of the perceiving mind, and tend
to compose a single curve of feelingful meditation. "To the River
Itchin, Near Winton"—which so impressed Coleridge that he
emulated it in his sonnet "To the River Otter"—will represent
Bowles's procedure, including his use of the recollection of an
earlier visit to stimulate the meditation:

---

6. *The Poetical Works of William Lisle Bowles*, ed. George Gilfillan (2 vols;
Edinburgh, 1855), I, 1.

Itchin, when I behold thy banks again,
    Thy crumbling margin, and thy silver breast,
    On which the self-same tints still seem to rest,
Why feels my heart the shiv'ring sense of pain?
    Is it—that many a summer's day has past
Since, in life's morn, I carol'd on thy side?
Is it—that oft, since then, my heart has sigh'd,
    As Youth, and Hope's delusive gleams, flew fast?
Is it—that those, who circled on thy shore,
Companions of my youth, now meet no more?
    Whate'er the cause, upon thy banks I bend
Sorrowing, yet feel such solace at my heart,
    As at the meeting of some long-lost friend,
    From whom, in happier hours, we wept to part.

Why Coleridge should have been moved to idolatry by so slender, if genuine, a talent as that of Bowles has been an enigma of literary history. It is significant, however, that Bowles's *Sonnets* of 1789 had an impact both on Southey and Wordsworth which was also immediate and powerful. As Wordsworth later told Samuel Rogers:

> I bought them in a walk through London with my dear brother. . . . I read them as we went along; and to the great annoyance of my brother, I stopped in a niche of London Bridge to finish the pamphlet.[7]

And if we take into account Coleridge's intellectual preoccupations between the ages of seventeen and twenty-five, as well as his growing discontent with current modes of poetry, including his own, we find a sufficiency of reasons to explain the power of Bowles over his sensibility and his practice as a poet. Some of these are literary reasons, pertaining to Bowles's characteristic subjects and style, while others concern the philosophy of mind and its place in nature which, Coleridge believed, was implicit in Bowles's habitual manner of proceeding.

Bowles's sonnets represent the lonely mind in meditation, and their *fin de siècle* mood of weary and self-pitying isolation—what Coleridge called their "lonely feeling"[8]—proved irresistible to a

7. *Recollections of the Table-Talk of Samuel Rogers* (New York, 1856), p. 258, note. For Bowles's effect on Southey see William Haller, *The Early Life of Robert Southey* (New York, 1917), pp. 73–6. As late as 1806–20, in *The River Duddon*, Wordsworth adopted Bowles's design of a tour represented in a sequence of local-meditative sonnets.
8. Coleridge, Introduction to his

"Sheet of Sonnets" of 1796, *The Complete Poetical Works, II*, 1139. As early as November of 1797, however, Coleridge as "Nehemiah Higginbottom" parodied "the spirit of *doleful egotism*" in the sonnet. See *Biographia Literaria*, I, 17, and David Erdman, "Coleridge as Nehemiah Higginbottom," *Modern Language Notes*, LXXIII (1958), 569–80.

vigorous young newcomer to poetry. Of much greater and more enduring importance, however, as Coleridge emphasized in his *Biographia*, was the revelation to him of the possibility of a style "so tender and yet so manly, so natural and real, and yet so dignified and harmonious, as the sonnets etc. of Mr. Bowles!" [9] Even while he was absorbedly reading and tentatively imitating Bowles, Coleridge himself in his major efforts was primarily the poet "To turgid ode and tumid stanza dear," of Byron's unadmiring comment. In his poetic volume of 1796, as enlarged in 1797, the most ambitious undertakings were the "Religious Musings" and "Ode on the Departing Year." Of this publication Coleridge said in the *Biographia* that though, even then, he clearly saw "the superiority of an austerer and more natural style" than his own obscure and turgid language, he failed to realize his ideal, partly out of "diffidence of my own comparative talent," and "partly owing to a wrong choice of subjects, and the desire of giving a poetic colouring to abstract and metaphysical truths, in which a new world then seemed to open upon me." [1] In the turbulence and crises of the early period of the French Revolution, he had been obsessed with the need to give public voice to his political, religious, and philosophical beliefs, and he had tried to poetize such materials in the fashion current in the 1790's. [2] That is to say, he had adopted a visionary and oracular persona—in accordance, as he said in the Dedication to his "Ode on the Departing Year," with the practice of the ancients, when "the Bard and the Prophet were one and the same character" [3]—and had compounded Biblical prophecy, the hieratic stance of Milton, and the formal rhetoric, allegorical tactics, and calculated disorder of what he called "the sublimer Ode" of Gray and Collins, in the effort to endow his subjects with the requisite elevation, passion, drama, and impact. As Coleridge wrote to Southey in December of 1794, while Bowles's poems were his "morning Companions," helping him, "a thought-bewilder'd Man," to discover his own defects: "I am so habituated to philosophizing, that I cannot divest myself of it even when my own Wretchedness is the subject."

> And I cannot write without a *body* of *thought*—hence my *Poetry* is crowded and sweats beneath a heavy burthen of Ideas and Imagery! It has seldom Ease. [4]

9. *Biographia Literaria*, I, 10.
1. Ibid. pp. 2–3, and pp. 203–4, note. Coleridge's claim that he had recognized the defects of the "swell and glitter" of his elevated style, even as he employed it, is borne out by his Preface to the Poems of 1797, *Complete Poetical Works*, II, 1145.

2. See M. H. Abrams, "English Romanticism: The Spirit of the Age," in *Romanticism Reconsidered*, ed. Northrop Frye (New York, 1963), pp. 37–72.
3. *Complete Poetical Works*, II, 1113–14; see also p. 1145.
4. 11 December 1794, *Collected Letters*, I, 133–7.

This "Ease" Coleridge had early discovered in Bowles. And as he said in the *Biographia*, the example of Bowles—together with Cowper the first of the living poets who, in the style "more sustained and elevated" than in Percy's collection of popular ballads, "combined natural thoughts with natural diction; the first who reconciled the heart with the head"—rescued him from the unnatural division between intellect and feeling, and consonantly, from his use of "a laborious and florid diction"; but only, as he adds, "gradually." [5] The reason for the delay in making, as he put it, his "practice" conform to his "better judgment" is, I think, plain. Coleridge succeeded in emulating Bowles's ease only after he learned to adopt and commit himself to the lyric persona which demands such a style. That is, in place of philosophical, moral, historical pronouncements translated into allegoric action by Pindaric artifice and amplified for public delivery in a ceremonious bardic voice, Bowles's sonnets opened out to Coleridge the possibilities in the quite ordinary circumstances of a private person in a specific time and place whose meditation, credibly stimulated by the setting, is grounded in his particular character, follows the various and seemingly random flow of the living consciousness, and is conducted in the intimate yet adaptive voice of the interior monologue. (Bowles's style, as Coleridge said, unites the possibilities both of colloquialism and elevation—it is "natural and real, and yet . . . dignified and harmonious.") It was in "the compositions of my twenty-fourth and twenty-fifth years," Coleridge goes on to say, including "the shorter blank verse poems"—that is, the poems of 1796–97, beginning with "The Eolian Harp," which established the persona, idiom, materials, and ordonnance of the greater Romantic lyric—that he achieved his "present ideal in respect of the general tissue of the style." [6] No doubt the scholars are right who claim some influence on these poems of the relaxed and conversational blank verse of Cowper's *The Task*,[7] in the recurrent passages, within its mock-Miltonic manner, of serious description or meditation. I see no reason, however, to doubt Coleridge's repeated assertion that Bowles's sonnets and blank-verse poems were for him the prior and by far the pre-eminent models.

So much for the speaker and voice of Bowles's sonnets. Now

---

5. *Biographia Literaria*, I, 10, 15–16.
6. Ibid. p. 16.
7. See, for example, Humphry House, *Coleridge* (London, 1953), Chap. III; George Whalley, "Coleridge's Debt to Charles Lamb," *Essays and Studies* (1958), pp. 68–85; and Max F. Schulz, *The Poetic Voices of Coleridge* (Detroit, 1963), Chap. 5. A comment of Lamb to Coleridge in December 1796 substantiates Coleridge's own statements about the relative importance for him of Bowles and Cowper: "Burns was the god of my idolatry, as Bowles of yours. I am jealous of your fraternising with Bowles, when I think you relish him more than Burns or my old favourite, Cowper." *The Works of Charles and Mary Lamb*, ed. E. V. Lucas (7 vols.; London, 1903–5), VI, 73.

what of their central structural trope, by which, as Coleridge described it in 1796, "moral Sentiments, Affections, or Feelings, are deduced from, and associated with, the scenery of Nature"? Even so early in his career Coleridge was an integral thinker for whom questions of poetic structure were inseparable from general philosophic issues, and he at once went on to interpret this device as the correlate of a mode of perception which unites the mind to its physical environment. Such compositions, he said,

> create a sweet and indissoluble union between the intellectual and the material world. . . . Hence the Sonnets of BOWLES derive their marked superiority over all other Sonnets; hence they domesticate with the heart, and become, as it were, a part of our identity.[8]

This philosophical and psychological interpretation of Bowles's lyric procedure was not only, as Coleridge indicates, a cardinal reason for his early fascination with Bowles, but also the chief clue to his later disenchantment, and it merits attention.

IV. THE COALESCENCE OF SUBJECT AND OBJECT

In the opening chapter of his *Literary Life*, Coleridge introduces Bowles's sonnets not on their own account, but as representing a stage in his total intellectual development—"as introductory to the statement of my principles in Politics, Religion, and Philosophy, and an application of the rules, deduced from philosophical principles, to poetry and criticism." [9] Hence he moves from his account of the shaping influence of Bowyer, Bowles, and Wordsworth into a summary review of the history of philosophy, as preliminary to establishing his own metaphysical and critical premises, of which the culmination was to be the crucial distinction between fancy and imagination.

In the course of his survey of the dominant philosophy of the preceding age, it becomes clear that Coleridge found intolerable two of its main features, common both to philosophers in the school of Descartes and in the school of Locke. The first was its dualism, the absolute separation between mind and the material universe, which replaced a providential, vital, and companionable world by a world of particles in purposeless movement. The second was the method of reasoning underlying this dualism, that pervasive elementarism which takes as its starting point the irreducible element or part and conceives all wholes to be a combination of discrete parts, whether material atoms or mental "ideas."

8. Introduction to the "Sheet of Sonnets" of 1796, *Complete Poetical Works*, II, 1139. 9. *Biographia Literaria*, I, 1.

Even in 1797, while Coleridge was still a Hartleian associationist in philosophy, he had expressed his recoil from elementarist thinking. The fault of "the Experimentalists," who rely only on the "testimony of their senses," is that "they contemplate nothing but *arts*—and all *parts* are necessarily little—and the Universe to them is but mass of *little things*." "I can contemplate nothing but parts, & parts are all *little*—!—My mind feels as if it ached to behold & know something *great*—something *one & indivisible*. . . . [1] And he wrote later in *The Friend* about that particular separation between part and part which divides mind from nature:

> The ground-work, therefore, of all true philosophy is the full apprehension of the difference between . . . that intuition of things which arises when we possess ourselves, as one with the whole . . . and that which presents itself when . . . we think of ourselves as separated beings, and place nature in antithesis to the mind, as object to subject, thing to thought, death to life.[2]

As to Coleridge, so to Wordsworth in 1797–98, "solitary objects . . . beheld/In disconnection" are "dead and spiritless," and division, breaking down "all grandeur" into successive "littleness," is opposed to man's proper spiritual condition, in which "All things shall live in us and we shall live/In all things that surround us." [3] Absolute separation, in other words, is death-dealing—in Coleridge's words, it is "the philosophy of Death, and only of a dead nature can it hold good" [4]—so that the separation of mind from nature leads inevitably to the conception of a dead world in which the estranged mind is doomed to lead a life-in-death.

To the Romantic sensibility such a universe could not be endured, and the central enterprise common to many post-Kantian German philosophers and poets, as well as to Coleridge and Wordsworth, was to join together the "subject" and "object" that modern intellection had put asunder, and thus to revivify a dead nature, restore its concreteness, significance, and human values, and re-domiciliate man in a world which had become alien to him. The pervasive sense of estrangement, of a lost and isolated existence in an alien world, is not peculiar to our own age of anxiety, but was a commonplace of Romantic philosophy. According to Friedrich Schelling, the most representative philosopher of that age, division from unity was the fall of man consequent upon his eating the fruit of the tree of knowledge in the Enlightenment. The guilt of modern men must be

---

1. *Collected Letters*, I, 354, 349. See also ibid. IV, 574–5, and *The Notebooks of Samuel Taylor Coleridge* (New York, 1957), II, note 2151.
2. *The Friend* (3 vols.; London, 1818), III, 261–2.
3. *The Ruined Cottage*, addendum to MS. B (1797–98), *The Poetical Works*, V, 402.
4. *Theory of Life*, ed. Seth B. Watson (London, 1848), p. 63.

ascribed to their own will, which deviated from unity. . . . [This is] a truly Platonic fall of man, the condition in which man believes that the dead, the absolutely manifold and separated world which he conceives, is in fact the true and actual world.[5]

Long before he read Schelling, and while at the height of his enthusiasm for Bowles, Coleridge had included in his visionary "Religious Musings" (1794) an outline of human history in which mankind's highest good had been "to know ourselves/Parts and proportions of one wondrous whole"; the present evil was defined as a fall into an anarchic separation in which each man, "disherited of soul," feels "himself, his own low self the whole"; and man's redemption at the Second Coming was anticipated as a reintegration into his lost unity by a "sacred sympathy" which makes "The whole one Self! Self, that no alien knows! . . . all of all possessing!"[6] And in 1815 Coleridge recalled that the plan of Wordsworth's projected masterpiece, *The Recluse*, as he had understood it, had also been to affirm "a Fall in some sense, as a fact," to be redeemed by a

> Reconciliation from this Enmity with Nature . . . by the substitution of Life, and Intelligence . . . for the Philosophy of mechanism which in every thing that is most worthy of the human Intellect strikes *Death*.[7]

In the *Biographia Literaria*, when Coleridge came to lay down his own metaphysical system, he based it on a premise designed to overcome both the elementarism in method and the dualism in theory of knowledge of his eighteenth-century predecessors, by converting their absolute division between subject and object into a logical "antithesis," in order to make it eligible for resolution by the Romantic dialectic of thesis-antithesis-synthesis. The "primary ground" of his theory of knowledge, he says, is "the coincidence of an object with a subject" or "of the thought with the thing," in a synthesis, or "coalescence," in which the elements lose their separate identities. "In the reconciling, and recurrence of this contradiction exists the process and mystery of production and life."[8] And the process of vital artistic creation reflects the process of this vital creative perception. Unlike the fancy, which can only rearrange the "fixities and definites" of sense-perception without altering their identity, the "synthetic and magical power" of the secondary imagination repeats the primal act of knowing by dissolving the elements of perception "in order to recreate" them, and "reveals

5. Schelling, *Sämmtliche Werke* (Stuttgart and Augsburg, 1857), Pt. I, Vol. VII, 81–2.
6. "Religious Musings," ll. 126–58, *Complete Poetical Works*, I, 113–15.

7. To Wordsworth, 30 May 1815, *Collected Letters*, IV, 574–5.
8. *Biographia Literaria*, I, 174–85.

itself in the balance or reconciliation of opposite or discordant qualities"—including the reconciliation of intellect with emotion, and of thought with object: "the idea, with the image." [9]

In short, the reintegration of the divided self (of "head and heart") and the simultaneous healing of the breach between the ego and the alien other (of "subject and object") was for Coleridge a profound emotional need which he translated into the grounds both of his theory of knowledge and his theory of art. How pivotal the concept of human-nonhuman reconciliation came to be for Coleridge's aesthetics is apparent in his essay "On Poesy or Art," in which he specifically defined art as "the reconciler of nature and man . . . the power of humanizing nature, of infusing the thoughts and passions of man into every thing which is the object of his contemplation." It is "the union and reconciliation of that which is nature with that which is exclusively human." [1]

Perhaps now, to return at last to the sonnets of Bowles, we can understand better why those seemingly inconsequential poems made so powerful an impact on Coleridge, in their materials as well as their structure and style. Bowles's primary device by which sentiments and feelings "are deduced from, and associated with, the scenery of Nature" had seemed to Coleridge evidence of a poetry which not only "reconciled the heart with the head," but also united the mind with nature; in the terms available to him in 1796, it created "a sweet and indissoluble union between the intellectual and the material world." Through the next half-decade, however, Coleridge carried on his own experiments in the descriptive and meditative lyric, came to know the early poetry of Wordsworth, had his introduction to German metaphysics, and, in intense and almost fevered speculation, groped his way out of the mechanism and associationism of David Hartley and other English empiricists. Increasingly in the process he became dissatisfied with the constitution of Bowles's poems, and the reasons came sharply into focus in 1802, at about the time he was recasting his verse "Letter to [Asra]" into his highest achievement in the greater Romantic lyric, "Dejection: An Ode." On 10 September he wrote a letter to William Sotheby which shows that his working his way through and beyond Bowles was an integral part of his working his way toward a new poetry, a new criticism, and a new world view. The letter is a preliminary sketch for the *Biographia Literaria*, for like that work it moves from a critique of Bowles through a view of

9. Ibid. I, 202, 12. See *The Friend*, III, 263–4, on the "one principle which alone reconciles the man with himself, with other [men] and with the world."

1. In *Biographia Literaria*, II, 253–5. Though "On Poesy or Art" takes its departure from Schelling's "On the Relation of the Plastic Arts to Nature," the quoted statements are Coleridge's own.

the relation of mind to nature in perception to a theory of poetic production, and culminates in Coleridge's first explicit distinction between the elementaristic fancy and the synthetic imagination.

Bowles had just published a new edition of his sonnets, supplemented by several long poems in blank verse which reverted to a process of scenic inventory and incidental meditation very close to the eighteenth-century local poem. Bowles's second volume, Coleridge begins, "is woefully inferior to it's Predecessor."

> There reigns thro' all the blank verse poems such a perpetual trick of *moralizing* every thing—which is very well, occasionally— but never to see or describe any interesting appearance in nature, without connecting it by dim analogies with the moral world, proves faintness of Impression. Nature has her proper interest; & he will know what it is, who believes & feels, that every Thing has a Life of it's own, & that we are all *one Life*. A Poet's *Heart & Intellect* should be *combined, intimately* combined & *unified*, with the great appearances in Nature—& not merely held in solution & loose mixture with them, in the shape of formal Similes. . . . The truth is—Bowles has indeed the *sensibility* of a poet; but he has not the *Passion* of a great Poet. . . . He has no native Passion, because he is not a Thinker.[2]

Bowles's exaggeration in his later poems of his earlier devices has opened out to Coleridge his inherent failings. Bowles is able to reconcile the heart with the head, but only because of an equality of weakness in the antagonist powers of intellect and passion. And what Coleridge had earlier described as an "indissoluble union between the intellectual and material world" now turns out to be no better than "a loose mixture," in which the separate parts, instead of being "*intimately* combined & *unified*," are merely held together by the rhetorical expedient of "formal Similes." In other words, what to Coleridge, the Hartleian associationist, had in 1796 appeared to be an adequate integration of mind and its milieu reveals itself—when he had learned to think of all higher mental processes in terms of a synthesis of contraries—to be what he later called the "conjunction-disjunctive" of neoclassic unity by a decorum of the parts.

In the letter to Sotheby, Coleridge goes on to draw a parallel distinction between the treatment of nature in Greek mythology and in the Hebrew poets, and ends by assigning the former type to the collocative process of the lower productive faculty, or Fancy. To the Greek poets

> all natural Objects were *dead*—mere hollow Statues—but there was a Godkin or Goddessling *included* in each. . . . At best it is

but Fancy, or the aggregating Faculty of the mind—not *Imagination*, or the *modifying*, and co-adunating Faculty. . . . In the Hebrew Poets each Thing has a Life of it's own, & yet they are all one Life.

Bowles's poems, it becomes apparent, remain in the mode of the Fancy because they fail to overcome the division between living mind and a dead nature by that act of the coadunating Imagination which fuses the two into "one Life"; for when Bowles joins the parts *a* and *b* they form an aggregate *ab*, instead of "interpenetrating" (in terms of Coleridge's critique of elementarist thinking) to "generate a higher third, including both the former," the product *c*.[3] For the "mystery of genius in the Fine Arts," as Coleridge said in "On Poesy or Art," is

> so to place these images [of nature] . . . as to elicit from, and to superinduce upon, the forms themselves the moral reflexions to which they approximate, to make the external internal, the internal external, to make nature thought, and thought nature.[4]

The shift in Coleridge's theory of descriptive poetry corresponded with a change in his practice of the form; and in the sequence of sonnets and conversation poems that he wrote under Bowles's influence we can observe him in the process of converting the conjunction of parts, in which nature stays on one side and thought on the other, into the Romantic interfusion of subject and object. W. K. Wimsatt has acutely remarked that Coleridge's sonnet "To the River Otter"—though written in express imitation of Bowles's "To the River Itchin," perhaps so early as 1793—has begun to diverge from Bowles's "simple association . . . simply asserted" by involving the thought in the descriptive details so that the design "is latent in the multiform sensuous picture." [5] "The Eolian Harp" (1795–96) set the expanded pattern of the greater lyric, but in it the meditative flight is a short one, while the thought is still at times expressed in the mode of *sententiae* which are joined to the details of the scene by formal similes. We sit

> beside our Cot, our Cot o'ergrown
> With white-flower'd Jasmin, and the broad-leav'd Myrtle,
> (Meet emblems they of Innocence and Love!)
> And watch the Clouds, that late were rich with light,
> Slow-sadd'ning round, and mark the Star of eve
> Serenely brilliant (such should WISDOM be!)
> Shine opposite.

3. *Theory of Life*, p. 63.
4. *In Biographia Literaria*, II, 258.
5. "The Structure of Romantic Nature Imagery," in *The Verbal Icon* (New York, 1958), pp. 106–10.

In "Frost at Midnight," however, written two years later, the images in the initial description are already suffused with an unstated significance which, in Coleridge's terms, is merely "elicited" and expanded by the subsequent reflection, which in turn "superinduces" a richer meaning upon the scene to which it reverts. "Fears in Solitude," a few months after that, exemplifies the sustained dialogue between mind and landscape which Coleridge describes in lines 215–20 of the poem: the prospect of sea and fields

> seems like society—
> Conversing with the mind, and giving it
> A livelier impulse and a dance of thought!

And "Dejection: An Ode," on which Coleridge was working in 1802 just as he got Bowles's poems into critical perspective, is a triumph of the "coadunating" imagination, in the very poem which laments the severance of his community with nature and the suspension of his shaping spirit of imagination. In unspoken consonance with the change of the outer scene and of the responsive wind-harp from ominous quiet to violent storm to momentary calm, the poet's mind, momentarily revitalized by a correspondent inner breeze, moves from torpor through violence to calm, by a process in which the properties earlier specified of the landscape— the spring rebirth, the radiated light of moon and stars, the clouds and rain, the voice of the harp—reappear as the metaphors of the evolving meditation on the relation of mind to nature; these culminate in the figure of the one life as an eddy between antitheses:

> To her may all things live, from pole to pole,
> Their life the eddying of her living soul!

On Coleridge's philosophical premises, in this poem nature is made thought and thought nature, both by their sustained interaction and by their seamless metaphoric continuity.

The best Romantic meditations on a landscape, following Coleridge's examples, all manifest a transaction between subject and object in which the thought incorporates and makes explicit what was already implicit in the outer scene. And all the poets testify independently to a fact of consciousness which underlay these poems, and was the experiential source and warrant for the philosophy of cognition as an interfusion of mind and nature. When the Romantic poet confronted a landscape, the distinction between self and not-self tended to dissolve. Coleridge asserted that from childhood he had been accustomed to "unrealize . . . and then by a sort of transfusion and transmission of my consciousness to identify myself with the Object"; also that in looking at objects of Nature while I am thinking . . . I seem rather to be seeking, as it were *asking*, a symbolical language for something within me that already and forever exists, than observing anything new.

So with Wordsworth: "I was often unable to think of external things as having external existence, and I communed with all that I saw as something not apart from, but inherent in, my own immaterial nature." Shelley witnessed to "the state called reverie," when men "feel as if their nature were dissolved into the surrounding universe, or as if the surrounding universe were absorbed into their being. They are conscious of no distinction." Even Byron's Childe Harold claimed that "I live not in myself," but that mountains, waves, and skies become "a part/Of me, and of my soul, as I of them." Keats's experience differs, but only in the conditions that, instead of assimilating the other to the self, the self goes out into the other, and that the boundary of self is "annihilated" when he contemplates, not a broad prospect, but a solid particular endowed with outline, mass, and posture or motion. That type of poet of which "I am a Member . . . has no self" but "is continually [informing] and filling some other Body"—a moving billiard ball, a breaking wave, a human form in arrested motion, a sparrow, an urn, or a nightingale.[6]

V. THE ROMANTIC MEDITATION

The greater Romantic lyric, then, as established by Coleridge, evolved from the descriptive-meditative structure of the eighteenth-century local poem, primarily through the intermediate stage of Bowles's sequence of sonnets. There remains, however, a wide disparity between the Romantic lyric and its predecessors, a disparity in the organization and nature of the meditation proper. In local poetry the order of the thoughts is the sequence in which the natural objects are observed; the poet surveys a prospect, or climbs a hill, or undertakes a tour, or follows the course of a stream, and he introduces memories and ideas intermittently, as the descriptive occasion offers. In Bowles's sonnets, the meditation, while more continuous, is severely limited by the straitness of the form, and consists mainly of the pensive commonplaces of the typical late-century man of feeling. In the fully developed Romantic lyric, on the other hand, the description is structurally subordinate to the meditation, and the meditation is sustained, continuous, and highly serious. Even when the initial impression is of the casual

6. Coleridge, *Collected Letters*, IV, 974–5, and *The Notebooks*, II, 2456; Wordsworth, *Poetical Works*, IV, 463; *Shelley's Prose*, ed. David Lee Clark (Albuquerque, 1954), p. 174; Byron, *Childe Harold*, III, lxxii, lxxv; Keats, *The Letters*, I, 387.

movement of a relaxed mind, retrospect reveals the whole to have been firmly organized around an emotional issue pressing for resolution. And in a number of the greatest lyrics—including Coleridge's "Dejection," Wordsworth's "Intimations," Shelley's "Stanzas Written in Dejection" and "West Wind," Keats's "Nightingale"—the issue is one of a recurrent state often called by the specialized term "dejection." This is not the pleasing melancholy of the eighteenth-century poet of sensibility, nor Bowles's muted self-pity, but a profound sadness, sometimes bordering on the anguish of terror or despair, at the sense of loss, dereliction, isolation, or inner death, which is presented as inherent in the conditions of the speaker's existence.

In the English literary tradition these Romantic meditations had their closest analogue in the devotional poems of the seventeenth century. In his study *The Poetry of Meditation* Professor Louis Martz has emphasized the importance, for the religious poets we usually class as "metaphysical," of the numerous and immensely popular devotional handbooks which undertook to discipline the casual flow of ordinary consciousness by setting down a detailed regimen for evoking, sustaining, and ordering a process of meditation toward resolution. A standard sub-department was the "meditation on the creatures" (that is, on the created world) in order, as the title of Robert Bellarmine's influential treatise of 1615 put it, to achieve *The Ascent of the Mind to God by a Ladder of Things Created.* The recommended procedure, as this became stabilized at the turn of the century, tended to fall into three major divisions. The first involved what Loyola called the "composition of place, seeing the spot"; that is, envisioning in vivid detail the person, object, or scene which initiates the meditation. The second, the meditation proper, was the analysis of the relevance to our salvation of this scene, interpreted analogically; it often included a turn inward to a close examination of conscience. The last specified the results of this meditation for our affections and will, and either included, or concluded with, a "colloquy"—usually a prayer, or discourse with God, although as St. Francis de Sales advises, "while we are forming our affections and resolutions," we do well to address our colloquy also "to ourselves, to our own hearts . . . and even to insensible creatures." [7]

Few seventeenth-century meditative poems accord exactly with the formulas of the Catholic or Anglican devotional manuals, but many of them unmistakably profited from that disciplining of fluid thought into an organized pattern which was a central enterprise in the spiritual life of the age. And those poetic meditations on the

7. *Introduction to the Devout Life,* translated by John K. Ryan (Garden City, N. Y., 1955), p. 88.

creatures which envision a natural scene or object, go on, in sorrow, anguish, or dejection, to explore the significance for the speaker of the spiritual signs built into the object by God, and close in reconciliation and the hope of rebirth, are closer to the best Romantic lyrics in meditative content, mood, and ordonnance than any poem by Bowles or his eighteenth-century predecessors. Good instances of the type are Vaughan's "The Waterfall," "Regeneration," "Vanity of Spirit," and "I walkt the other day (to spend my hour,)/Into a field"—an hour being a standard time set aside for formal meditation. "Regeneration," for example, begins with a walk through a spring landscape which stands in sharp contrast to the sterile winter of the poet's spirit, finds its resolution in a sudden storm of wind which, as *spiritus*, is the material equivalent both of the breath of God and the spirit of man, and ends in a short colloquy which is a prayer for a spiritual dying-into-life:

> Here musing long, I heard
>   A rushing wind
> Which still increas'd, but whence it stirr'd
> No where I could not find. . . .
> Lord, then said I, on me one breath,
> And let me die before my death!

The two key figures of the outer and inner seasons and of the correspondent, regenerative wind later served as the radical metaphors in a number of Romantic poems, including Coleridge's "Dejection" and Shelley's "Ode to the West Wind." [8]

Or consider the meditation on a creature which—at least in his later life—was Coleridge's favorite poem by one of his favorite lyrists, George Herbert's "The Flower." [9] Reflecting upon the annual death and rebirth of the plant, the poet draws a complex analogy with his own soul in its cycles of depression and joy, spiritual drought and rain, death and springlike revival, alienation from God and reconcilement; in the concluding colloquy he also (as Coleridge and Shelley were to do) incorporates into the analogy the sterility and revival of his poetic powers:

> And now in age I bud again,
> After so many deaths I live and write;
> I once more smell the dew and rain,
> And relish versing. Oh, my only light,
>   It cannot be

8. See M. H. Abrams, "The Correspondent Breeze: A Romantic Metaphor," in *English Romantic Poets: Modern Essays in Criticism* (New York, 1960), pp. 37–54.

9. Coleridge's comments on Herbert are gathered in *Coleridge on the Seventeenth Century*, ed. Roberta Florence Brinkley (Duke University Press, 1955), pp. 533–40.

> That I am he
> On whom thy tempests fell all night.[1]

Herbert is describing the state of inner torpor through alienation from God known in theology as accidie, dejection, spiritual dryness, interior desolation; this condition was often analogized to circumstances of the seasons and weather, and was a matter of frequent consideration in the devotional manuals. As St. Francis de Sales wrote, in his section "Of Spiritual Dryness and Sterility":

> Sometimes you will find yourself so deprived and destitute of all devout feelings of devotion that your soul will seem to be a fruitless, barren desert, in which there is no . . . water of grace to refresh her, on account of the dryness that seems to threaten her with a total and absolute desolation. . . . At the same time, to cast her into despair, the enemy mocks her by a thousand suggestions of despondency and says: "Ah! poor wretch, where is thy God? . . . Who can ever restore to thee the joy of His holy grace?" [2]

Coleridge, during the several years just preceding "Dejection: An Ode," described in his letters a recurrent state of apathy and of the paralysis of imagination in terms which seem to echo such discussions of spiritual dryness: "My Imagination is tired, down, flat and powerless. . . . As if the *organs* of Life had been dried up; as if only simple BEING remained, blind and stagnant!" "I have been . . . undergoing a process of intellectual *exsiccation*. . . . The Poet is dead in me." [3]

The Romantic meditations, then, though secular meditations, often turn on crises—alienation, dejection, the loss of a "celestial light" or "glory" in experiencing the created world—which are closely akin to the spiritual crises of the earlier religious poets. And at times the Romantic lyric becomes overtly theological in expression. Some of them include not only colloquies with a human auditor, real or imagined, and with what De Sales called "insensible creatures," but also with God or with a Spirit of Nature, in the mode of a formal prayer ("Reflections on Having Left a Place of Retirement," "Ode to the West Wind"), or else of a terminal benediction. Thus Coleridge's "Frost at Midnight" falls into the ritual language of a blessing ("Therefore all seasons shall be sweet to thee")—a tactic which Wordsworth at once picked up in "Tintern Abbey" ("and this prayer I make. . . . Therefore let the

---

1. Coleridge wrote his later poem of aridity in a spring landscape, "Work Without Hope" (1825), expressly "in the manner of G. HERBERT." See *Complete Poetical Works*, II, 1110–11.
2. *Introduction to the Devout Life*, pp. 256–7; on "spiritual desolation," see also Loyola's *Spiritual Exercise*, ed. Orby Shipley (London, 1870), pp. 139–40.
3. *Collected Letters*, I, 470; II, 713–14; also I, 643.

moon/Shine on thee in thy solitary walk") and which Coleridge himself repeated in *Dejection* ("Visit her, gentle Sleep! with wings of healing. . . . To her may all things live, from pole to pole").

We must not drive the parallel too hard. There is little external evidence of the direct influence of the metaphysical poem upon the greater Romantic lyric; the similarity between them may well be the result of a common tradition of meditations on the creatures—a tradition which continued in the eighteenth century in so prodigiously popular a work as James Hervey's *Meditations and Contemplations* (1746–47).[4] And there is a very conspicuous and significant difference between the Romantic lyric and the seventeenth-century meditation on created nature—a difference in the description which initiates and directs the process of mind. The "composition of place" was not a specific locality, nor did it need to be present to the eyes of the speaker, but was a typical scene or object, usually called up, as St. Ignatius and other preceptors said, before "the eyes of the imagination," [5] in order to set off and guide the thought by means of correspondences whose interpretation was firmly controlled by an inherited typology. The landscape set forth in Vaughan's "Regeneration," for example, is not a particular geographical location, nor even a literal setting, but the allegorical landscape common to the genre of spiritual pilgrimages, from the *Divine Comedy* to *Pilgrim's Progress*. And Herbert's flower is not a specified plant, described by the poet with his eye on the object, but a generic one; it is simply the class of all perennials, in which God has inscribed the invariable signatures of his providential plan. In the Romantic poem, on the other hand, the speaker merely happens upon a natural scene which is present, particular, and almost always precisely located; and though Coleridge occasionally alludes to it still as "that eternal language, which thy God utters," [6] the primary meanings educed from the scene are not governed by a public symbolism, but have been brought to it by the private mind which perceives it. But we know already that these attributes also had a seventeenth-century origin, in a poet who inherited the metaphysical tradition yet went on, as Dryden and many of his successors

4. In the *Meditations and Contemplations* (7th ed., 2 vols.; London, 1750), II, xv–xvii, Hervey describes his aim to "exhibit a Prospect of still *Life*, and grand *Operation*" in order "to *open* the *Door* of Meditation," and show how we may "*gather up* the unstable, fluctuating *Train* of Fancy: and collect her fickle Powers into a consistent regular, and useful Habit of Thinking."
5. See Louis L. Martz, *The Poetry of Meditation* (New Haven, 1954), pp. 27–8.

6. "Frost at Midnight," ll 58–62; cf. "This Lime-Tree Bower," ll. 39–43, and "Fears in Solitude," ll. 22–4. In Coleridge's "Hymn before Sunrise" (1802), unlike his greater lyrics, the meditation moves from the creatures to the Creator by a hereditary symbolism as old as Psalm 19: "The heavens declare the glory of God; and the firmament sheweth his handywork."

commented,[7] to alter it in such a way as to establish the typical meter, rhetoric, and formal devices of neoclassic poetry. The crucial event in the development of the most distinctive of the Romantic lyric forms occurred when John Denham climbed Cooper's Hill and undertook to describe, in balanced couplets, the landscape before his eyes, and to embellish the description with incidental reminiscence and meditation.

7. Dr. Johnson listed Denham among the metaphysical poets, then added, in the great commonplace of neoclassical literary history, that he "and Waller sought another way to fame, by improving the harmony of our numbers." (*The Life of Cowley, Works,* IX, 23.)

PART FOUR

The Major Poets

The criticism devoted to the major English Romantic poets has been, with honorable exceptions, inadequate to the complexity and power of their achievement. The bibliography at the end of this volume represents the editor's judgment as to what is most valuable in the available criticism. In this section, a group of representative essays or excerpts are gathered together, as a critical introduction to the six major poets. Since Blake and Wordsworth are the most difficult, and most eminent of modern poets, two essays are given for each, representing contrasting critical approaches.

Useful criticism of Blake began with Swinburne, was set back by Yeats, and moved forward again with S. Foster Damon, the first scholar to follow Blake's own systematic approach to poetic mythology. The essay by Northrop Frye here is the apex of Damon's tradition, and introduces Blake as he wished to be introduced. Martin Price's study is more historically oriented, and seeks to explore the affinities, as well as the conscious differences, between Blake and the Augustans, particularly as intellectual satirists. It is, I think, the best criticism of Blake done outside the Damon-Frye tradition.

Wordsworth criticism has two rival traditions, the "poet of Nature" line descending from Arnold, and the "poet of the Sublime" grouping that stems from Bradley's rebuttal of Arnold. Frederick A. Pottle's lucid essay explains "what Wordsworth meant by looking steadily at his subject," and can be considered the finest mediating effort between the two traditions. The excerpts from Geoffrey H. Hartman, laced together by the editor from two separate studies by that critic, revitalize Bradley and illuminate the problematic dialectic of nature and imagination by Wordsworth.

The essay on Coleridge, by Humphry House, comprehensively discusses Coleridge's most important poems beyond those investigated by M. H. Abrams in his essay on the greater Romantic lyric. The exception is *The Ancient Mariner*, on which the best criticism available is also by House. W. J. Bate's definitive investigation of Negative Capability is at the center of his lifetime of work on Keats's conceptions of imagination. The study of *Don Juan*, by Alvin B. Kernan, is uniquely valuable for exposing the almost universal structure of satire in Byron's major poem. Lastly, the essay on Shelley is both a general introduction to his poetry, and an "appreciation," to use an unfortunately outmoded term, of a poet who in proportion to his actual merits remains probably the most underrated in the language.

NORTHROP FRYE

The Keys to the Gates †

The criticism of Blake, especially of Blake's prophecies, has developed in direct proportion to the theory of criticism itself. The complaints that Blake was "mad" are no longer of any importance, not because anybody has proved him sane, but because critical theory has realized that madness, like obscenity, is a word with no critical meaning. There are critical standards of coherence and incoherence, but if a poem is coherent in itself the sanity of its author is a matter of interest only to the more naïve type of biographer. Those who have assumed that the prophecies are incoherent because they have found them difficult often use the phrase "private symbolism." This is also now a matter of no importance, because in critical theory there is no such thing as private symbolism. There may be allegorical allusions to a poet's private life that can only be interpreted by biographical research, but no set of such allusions can ever form a poetic structure. They can only be isolated signposts, like the allusions to the prototypes of the beautiful youth, dark lady, and rival poet which historians and other speculative critics are persuaded that they see in the Shakespeare sonnets. When I first embarked on any intensive study of Blake's prophecies, I assumed that my task was to follow the trail blazed by Foster Damon's great book, and take further steps to demonstrate the coherence of those poems. My primary interests, like Damon's, were literary, not occult or philosophical or religious. Many other writers had asserted that while the prophecies were doubtless coherent enough intellectually, they would turn out to depend for their coherence on some extra-poetic system of ideas. A student interested in Blake's prophecies as poems would have to begin by rejecting this hypothesis, which contradicts all Blake's views about the primacy of art and the cultural disaster of substituting abstractions for art. But as I went on, I was puzzled and annoyed by a schematic quality in these prophecies that refused to dissolve into

† From *Some British Romantics: A Collection of Essays*, ed. James V. Logan, John E. Jordan, and Northrop Frye. Copyright © 1966 by Ohio State University Press. Reprinted by permission of the publishers. All Rights Reserved.

what I then regarded as properly literary forms. There were even diagrams in Blake's own designs which suggested that he himself attached a good deal of value to schematism, and such statements as "I must create a system." Perhaps, then, these critics I had begun by rejecting were right after all: perhaps Blake was not opposed to abstraction but only to other people's abstractions, and was really interested merely in expounding some conceptual system or other in an oblique and allegorical way. In any event, the schematic, diagramatic quality of Blake's thought was there, and would not go away or turn into anything else. Yeats had recognized it; Damon had recognized it; I had to recognize it. Like Shelley, Blake expressed an abhorrence of didactic poetry but continued to write it.

This problem began to solve itself as soon as I realized that poetic thought is inherently and necessarily schematic. Blake soon led me, in my search for poetic analogues, to Dante and Milton, and it was clear that the schematic cosmologies of Dante and Milton, however they got into Dante and Milton, were, once they got there, poetic constructs, examples of the way poets think, and not foreign bodies of knowledge. If the prophecies are normal poems, or at least a normal expression of poetic genius, and if Blake nevertheless meant to teach some system by them, that system could only be something connected with the principles of poetic thought. Blake's "message," then, is not simply *his* message, nor is it an extra-literary message. What he is trying to say is what he thinks poetry is trying to say: the imaginative content implied by the existence of an imaginative form of language. I finished my book in the full conviction that learning to read Blake was a step, and for me a necessary step, in learning to read poetry, and to write criticism must be so too. I began to notice that as soon as a critic confined himself to talking seriously about literature, his criticism tightened up and took on a systematic, even a schematic, form.

The nature of poetic "truth" was discussed by Aristotle in connection with action. As compared with the historian, the poet makes no specific or particular statements: he gives the typical, recurring, or universal event, and is not to be judged by the standards of truth that we apply to specific statements. Poetry, then, does not state historical truth, but contains it: it sets forth what we may call the *myth* of history, the kind of thing that happens. History itself is designed to record events, or, as we may say, to provide a primary verbal imitation of events. But it also, unconsciously perhaps, illustrates and provides examples for the poetic vision. Hence we feel that *Lear* or *Macbeth* or *Oedipus Rex*, although they deal almost entirely with legend rather than actual history, contain infinite reserves of historical wisdom and insight. Thus poetry is "something more philosophical" than history.

This last observation of Aristotle's has been of little use to critics except as a means of annoying historians, and it is difficult to see in what sense Anacreon is more philosophical than Thucydides. The statement is best interpreted, as it was by Renaissance critics, schematically, following a diagram in which poetry is intermediate between history and philosophy, pure example and pure precept. It follows that poetry must have a relation to thought paralleling its relation to action. The poet does not think in the sense of producing concepts, ideas or propositions, which are specific predications to be judged by their truth or falsehood. As he produces the mythical structures of history, so he produces the mythical structures of thought, the conceptual frameworks that enter into and inform the philosophies contemporary with him. And just as we feel that the great tragedy, if not historical, yet contains an infinity of the kind of meaning that actual history illustrates, so we feel that great "philosophical" poetry, if not actually philosophical, contains an infinity of the kind of meaning that discursive writing illustrates. This sense of the infinite treasures of thought latent in poetry is eloquently expressed by several Elizabethan critics, and there is perhaps no modern poet who suggests the same kind of intellectual richness so immediately as Blake does.

Blake, in fact, gives us so good an introduction to the nature and structure of poetic thought that, if one has any interest in the subject at all, one can hardly avoid exploiting him. There are at least three reasons why he is uniquely useful for this purpose. One is that his prophecies are works of philosophical poetry which give us practically nothing at all unless we are willing to grapple with the kind of poetic thought that they express. Another is that Blake also wrote such haunting and lucid lyrics, of which we can at first say little except that they seem to belong in the center of our literary experience. We may not know why they are in the center, and some readers would rather not know; but for the saving remnant who do want to know, there are the prophecies to help us understand. The third reason is Blake's quality as an illustrator of other poets. If a person of considerable literary experience is reading a poem he is familiar with, it is easy for him to fall—in fact it is very difficult for him not to fall—into a passive habit of not really reading the poem, but merely of spotting the critical clichés he is accustomed to associate with it. Thus, if he is reading Gray's "Ode on the Death of a Favorite Cat," and sees the goldfish described as "angel forms," "genii of the stream," and with "scaly armour," his stock response will start murmuring: "Gray means fish, of course, but he is saying so in terms of eighteenth-century personification, Augustan artificiality, his own peculiar demure humour," and the like.

Such a reading entirely obliterates Gray's actual processes of poetic thought and substitutes something in its place that, whatever it is, is certainly not poetry or philosophy, any more than it is history. But if he is reading the poem in the context of Blake's illustrations, Blake will compel him to see the angel forms, the genii of the stream, and the warriors in scaly armour, as well as the fish, in such a way as to make the unvisualized clichés of professional reading impossible, and to bring the metaphorical structure of the poem clearly into view.

I am suggesting that no one can read Blake seriously and sympathetically without feeling that the keys to poetic thought are in him, and what follows attempts to explain how a documentation of such a feeling would proceed. I make no claim that I am saying anything here that I have not said before, though I may be saying it in less compass.

EASTERN GATE: TWOFOLD VISION

The structure of metaphors and imagery that informed poetry, through the Middle Ages and the Renaissance, arranged reality on four levels. On top was heaven, the place of the presence of God: below it was the proper level of human nature, represented by the stories of the Garden of Eden and the Golden Age; below that was the physical world, theologically fallen, which man is in but not of: and at the bottom was the world of sin, death and corruption. This was a deeply conservative view of reality in which man, in fallen nature, was confronted with a moral dialectic that either lowered him into sin or raised him to his proper level. The raising media included education, virtue, and obedience to law. In the Middle Ages, this construct was closely linked with similar constructs in theology and science. These links weakened after the sixteenth century and eventually disappeared, leaving the construct to survive only in poetry, and, even there, increasingly by inertia. It is still present in Pope's *Essay on Man*, but accompanied with a growing emphasis on the limitation of poetic objectives. This limitation means, among other things, that mythopoeic literature, which demands a clear and explicit framework of imagery, is in the age of Pope and Swift largely confined to parody.

As the eighteenth century proceeded, the imaginative climate began to change, and we can see poets trying to move toward a less conservative structure of imagery. This became a crucial problem when the French Revolution confronted the Romantic poets. No major poet in the past had been really challenged by a revolutionary situation except Milton, and even Milton had reverted to the traditional structure for *Paradise Lost*. Blake was not only older than

Wordsworth and Coleridge, but more consistently revolutionary in his attitude: again, unlike most English writers of the period, he saw the American Revolution as an event of the same kind as its French successor. He was, therefore, the first English poet to work out the revolutionary structure of imagery that continues through Romantic poetry and thought to our own time.

At the center of Blake's thought are the two conceptions of innocence and experience, "the two contrary states of the human soul." Innocence is characteristic of the child, experience of the adult. In innocence, there are two factors. One is an assumption that the world was made for the benefit of human beings, has a human shape and a human meaning, and is a world in which providence, protection, communication with other beings, including animals, and, in general, "mercy, pity, peace and love," have a genuine function. The other is ignorance of the fact that the world is not like this. As the child grows up, his conscious mind accepts "experience," or reality without any human shape or meaning, and his childhood innocent vision, having nowhere else to go, is driven underground into what we should call the subconscious, where it takes an essentially sexual form. The original innocent vision becomes a melancholy dream of how man once possessed a happy garden, but lost it forever, though he may regain it after he dies. The following diagram illustrates the process as well as the interconnection of *Songs of Innocence and Experience*, *The Marriage of Heaven and Hell*, and the early political prophecies *The French Revolution* and *America* in Blake's thought:

child's
innocence $>$ adult
experience $=$ Urizen $=$ "heaven" of status quo

$\longrightarrow$ frustrated
desire $=$ Orc $=$ "hell" of rebelliousness

In place of the old construct, therefore, in which man regains his happy garden home by doing his duty and obeying the law, we have an uneasy revolutionary conception of conscious values and standards of reality sitting on top of a volcano of thwarted and mainly sexual energy. This construct has two aspects, individual or psychological, and social or political. Politically, it represents an ascendant class threatened by the growing body of those excluded from social benefits, until the latter are strong enough to overturn society. Psychologically, it represents a conscious ego threatened by a sexually-rooted desire. Thus the mythical structure that informs both the psychology of Freud and the political doctrines of Marx is present in *The Marriage of Heaven and Hell*, which gives us both aspects of the Romantic movement: the reaction to political revolu-

tion and the manifesto of feeling and desire as opposed to the
domination of reason.

In the associations that Blake makes with Urizen and Orc, Urizen
is an old man and Orc a youth: Urizen has the counterrevolutionary
color white and Orc is a revolutionary red. Urizen is therefore associated with sterile winter, bleaching bones, and clouds; Orc with
summer, blood, and the sun. The colors white and red suggest the
bread and wine of a final harvest and vintage, prophesied in the
fourteenth chapter of Revelation. Orc is "underneath" Urizen,
and underneath the white cliffs of Albion on the map are the "vineyards of red France" in the throes of revolution. In a map of
Palestine, the kingdom of Israel, whose other name, Jacob, means
usurper, sits on top of Edom, the kingdom of the red and hairy
Esau, the rightful heir. Isaiah's vision of a Messiah appearing in
Edom with his body soaked in blood from "treading the winepress"
of war, haunts nearly all Blake's prophecies. There are many other
associations; perhaps we may derive the most important from the
following passage in *America:*

> The terror answerd: I am Orc, wreath'd round the accursed
>   tree:
> The times are ended: shadows pass the morning gins to
>   break
> The fiery joy, that Urizen perverted to ten commands,
> What night he led the starry hosts thro' the wide wilder-
>   ness:
> That stony law I stamp to dust: and scatter religion abroad
> To the four winds as a torn book, & none shall gather the
>   leaves:
> But they shall rot on desart sands, & consume in bottomless
>   deeps:
> To make the desarts blossom, & the deeps shrink to their
>   fountains,
> And to renew the fiery joy, and burst the stony roof.
> That pale religious letchery, seeking Virginity,
> May find it in a harlot, and in coarse-clad honesty
> The undefil'd tho' ravish'd in her cradle night and morn:
> For every thing that lives is holy, life delights in life:
> Because the soul of sweet delight can never be defil'd.
> Fires inwrap the earthly globe, yet man is not consumd:
> Amidst the lustful fires he walks: his feet become like
>   brass,
> His knees and thighs like silver, & his breast and head like
>   gold.[1]

At various times in history, there has been a political revolution
symbolized by the birth or rebirth of Orc, the "terrible boy": each
one, however, has eventually subsided into the same Urizenic form

---

1. Blake's punctuation is retained.

as its predecessor. Orc is the human protest of energy and desire, the impulse to freedom and to sexual love. Urizen is the "reality principle," the belief that knowledge of what is real comes from outside the human body. If we believe that reality is what we bring into existence through an act of creation, then we are free to build up our own civilization and abolish the anomalies and injustices that hamper its growth; but if we believe that reality is primarily what is "out there," then we are condemned, in Marx's phrase, to study the world and never to change it. And the world that we study in this way we are compelled to see in the distorted perspective of the human body with its five cramped senses, not our powers of perception as they are developed and expanded by the arts. Man in his present state is so constructed that all he can see outside him is the world under the law. He may believe that gods or angels or devils or fairies or ghosts are also "out there," but he cannot see these things: he can see only the human and the subhuman, moving in established and predictable patterns. The basis of this vision of reality is the world of the heavenly bodies, circling around automatically and out of reach.

One early Orc rebellion was the Exodus from Egypt, where Orc is represented by a pillar of fire (the "fiery joy") and Urizen by a pillar of cloud, or what *Finnegans Wake* calls "Delude of Isreal." Orc was a human society of twelve (actually thirteen) tribes; Urizen, a legal mechanism symbolized by the twelvefold Zodiac with its captive sun, which is why Urizen is said to have "led the starry hosts" through the wilderness. The eventual victory of Urizen was marked by the establishing of Aaron's priesthood (the twelve stones in his breastplate symbolized the Zodiac as well as the tribes, according to Josephus), and by the negative moral law of the Decalogue, the moral law being the human imitation of the automatism of natural law. The final triumph of Urizen was symbolized by the hanging of the brazen serpent (Orc) on the pole, a form of the "accursed tree," and recalling the earlier association of tree and serpent with the exile of Adam into a wilderness, as well as anticipating the Crucifixion.

Jesus was another Orc figure, gathering twelve followers and starting a new civilization. Christian civilization, like its predecessors, assumed the Urizenic form that it presented so clearly in Blake's own time. This historical perversion of Christianity is studied in *Europe*, where Enitharmon, the Queen of Heaven, summons up twelve starry children, along with Orc as the captive sun, to reimpose the cult of external reality, or what Blake calls natural religion, on Christendom. With the Resurrection, traditionally symbolized by a red cross on a white ground, Jesus made a definitive step into reality: the revolutionary apocalypse Blake hopes for in his day is a second coming or mass resurrection, which is why resurrection imagery is prominently displayed in *America*. Now, at the end of European civilization, comes another rebellion of Orc in America, bearing on its various banners a tree, a serpent, and thirteen red and white stripes. The spread of this rebellion to Europe itself is a sign that bigger things are on the way.

The Israelites ended their revolt in the desert of the moral law: now it is time to reverse the movement, to enter the Promised Land, the original Eden, which is to Israel what Atlantis is to Britain and America. The Promised Land is not a different place from the desert, but the desert itself transformed (Blake's imagery comes partly from Isaiah 35, a chapter he alludes to in *The Marriage of Heaven and Hell*). The "deeps shrink to their fountains" be cause in the apocalypse there is no more sea: dead water is transformed to living water (as in Ezekiel's vision, Ezek. 47:8). The spiritual body of risen man is sexually free, an aspect symbolized by the "lustful fires" in which he walks. Man under the law is sexually in a prison of heat without light, a volcano: in the resurrection he is unhurt by flames, like the three Hebrews in Nebuchadnezzar's furnace who were seen walking with the son of God. According to *The Marriage of Heaven and Hell*, Jesus became Jehovah after his death, and Jehovah, not Satan, is the one who dwells in flaming fire. The risen man, then, is the genuine form of the metallic statue of Nebuchadnezzar's dream, without the feet of clay that made that statue an image of tyranny and the cycle of history.

The Resurrection rolled the stone away covering the tomb ("burst the stony roof"). The stone that covers the tomb of man under the law is the vast arch of the sky, which we see as a concave "vault of paved heaven" (a phrase in the early "Mad Song") because we are looking at it from under the "stony roof" of the skull. The risen body would be more like the shape of one of Blake's Last Judgment paintings, with an "opened centre" or radiance of light on top, in the place which is the true location of heaven. Finally, the entire Bible or revelation of the divine in and to man can be read either as the charter of human freedom or as a code of restrictive and negative moral commands. Orc proposes to use Urizen's version of the holy book as fertilizer to help make the desert blossom: what he would do, in other words, is to internalize the law, transform it from arbitrary commands to the inner discipline of the free spirit.

NORTHERN GATE: SINGLE VISION

The optimistic revolutionary construct set up in Blake's early prophecies is found again in Shelley, whose Prometheus and Jupiter correspond to Orc and Urizen. But in later Romanticism, it quickly turns pessimistic and once more conservative, notably in Schopenhauer, where the world as idea, the world of genuine humanity, sits on top of a dark, threatening, and immensely powerful world as will. A similar construct is in Darwin and Huxley, where the ethical creation of human society maintains itself precariously against the evolutionary force below it. In Freud, civilization is essentially an anxiety structure, where the "reality principle," Blake's Urizen, must maintain its ascendancy somehow over the nihilistic upthrusts of desire. It may permit a certain amount of expression to the "pleasure principle," but not to the extent of being taken over by it. And in Blake, if every revolt of Orc in history has been "perverted to ten commands," the inference seems to be that history exhibits only a gloomy series of cycles, beginning in hope and inevitably ending in renewed tyranny. In Blake's later prophecies, we do find this Spenglerian view of history, with a good many of Spengler's symbols attached to it.

The cyclical movement of history is summarized by Blake in four stages. The first stage is the revolutionary birth of Orc; the second, the transfer of power from Orc to Urizen at the height of Orc's powers, accompanied by the binding or imprisoning of Orc; the third, the consolidating of "natural religion" or the sense of reality as out there, symbolized by Urizen exploring his dens; the fourth, a collapse and chaos symbolized by the crucifixion of Orc, the hanging of the serpent on the dead tree. This fourth stage is the one that Blake sees his own age entering, after the triumph of natural religion or "Deism" in the decades following Newton and Locke. It is an age characterized by mass wars (Isaiah's treading of the winepress), by technology and complex machinery, by tyranny and "empire" (imperialism being the demonic enemy of culture), and by unimaginative art, especially in architecture. The central symbol of this final phase is the labyrinthine desert in which the Mosaic exodus ended. Jesus spent forty days in the desert, according to Mark, "with the wild beasts": the passage from empire to ruin, from the phase of the tyrant to the phase of the wild beast, is symbolized in the story of Nebuchadnezzar, whose metamorphosis is illustrated at the end of *The Marriage of Heaven and Hell*. The figure of Ijim in *Tiriel* has a parallel significance.

As Blake's symbolism becomes more concentrated, he tends to generalize the whole cycle in the conception of "Druidism." The Druids, according to Blake's authorities, worshipped the tree and the serpent, the Druid temple of Avebury, illustrated on the last plate of *Jerusalem*, being serpent-shaped; and they went in for orgies of human sacrifice which illustrate, even more clearly than warfare, the fact that the suppression or perversion of the sexual impulse ends in a death wish (I am not reading modern conceptions into Blake here, but following Blake's own symbolism). This "Druid" imagery is illustrated in the following passage from *Europe*, describing the reaction of the tyrannical "King" or guardian angel of the reactionary Albion and his councillors to the American revolution and kindred portents of apocalyptic disaffection:

> In thoughts perturb'd they rose from the bright
>   ruins silent following
> The fiery King, who sought his ancient temple
>   serpent-form'd
> That stretches out its shady length along the
>   Island white.
> Round him roll'd his clouds of war; silent the
>   Angel went,
> Along the infinite shores of Thames to golden
>   Verulam.
>
> There stand the venerable porches that high-
>   towering rear
> Their oak-surrounded pillars, form'd of massy
>   stones, uncut
> With tool: stones precious: such eternal in
>   the heavens,
> Of colours twelve, few known on earth, give
>   light in the opake,
> Plac'd in the order of the stars, when the five
>   senses whelm'd
> In deluge o'er the earth-born man: then turn'd
>   the fluxile eyes
> Into two stationary orbs, concentrating all
>   things.
> The ever-varying spiral ascents to the heavens
>   of heavens
> Were bended downward, and the nostrils golden
>   gates shut,
> Turn'd outward barr'd and petrify'd against the
>   infinite . . .
>
> Now arriv'd the ancient Guardian at the southern
>   porch.
> That planted thick with trees of blackest leaf,
>   & in a vale
> Obscure, inclos'd the Stone of Night; oblique
>   it stood, o'erhung
> With purple flowers and berries red: image of
>   that sweet south
> Once open to the heavens and elevated on the
>   human neck,

Now overgrown with hair and cover'd with a
stony roof:

Downward 'tis sunk beneath th' attractive north,
that round the feet
A raging whirlpool draws the dizzy enquirer to
his grave.

It is an intricate passage, but it all makes sense. The serpent
temple of Avebury is identified with the white-cliffed Albion in its
Druid phase. It is centered at Verulam, which, as the site of a Roman camp, a "Gothic" cathedral, and the baronial title of Bacon,
takes in the whole cycle of British civilization. As we approach the
temple, it appears to be a Stonehenge-like circle of twelve precious
stones, "plac'd in the order of the stars," or symbolizing the Zodiac. The imagery recalls the similar decadence of Israel in the
desert: the twelve Zodiacal gems of Aaron's breastplate have been
mentioned, and the Israelites also built megalithic monuments on
which they were forbidden to use iron (Jos. 8:31), hence "uncut
with tool," iron being in Blake the symbol of Los the blacksmith,
the builder of the true city of gems (Isa. 54:16).

The central form of Druid architecture is the trilithic cromlech
or dolmen, the arch of three stones. According to Blake, the two
uprights of this arch symbolize the two aspects of creative power,
strength and beauty, or sublimity and pathos, as he calls them in
the *Descriptive Catalogue*, the horizontal stone being the dominant
Urizenic reason. Human society presents this arch in the form of
an "Elect" class tyrannizing over the "Reprobate," the unfashion-
able artists and prophets who embody human sublimity, and the
"Redeemed," the gentler souls who are in the company of the beautiful and pathetic. This trilithic structure reappears in such later
militaristic monuments as the Arch of Titus: in its "Druid"
form, it is illustrated with great power in *Milton*, Plate 6, and
Jerusalem, Plate 70. In the former, the balancing rock in front may
represent the "Stone of Night" in the above passage. To pass under
this arch is to be subjugated, in a fairly literal sense, to what is,
according to the *Descriptive Catalogue*, both the human reason
and the "incapability of intellect," as intellect in Blake is always
associated with the creative and imaginative. Another form of tyrannical architecture characteristic of a degenerate civilization is the
pyramid, representing the volcano or imprisoning mountain under
which Orc lies. Blake connects the pyramids with the servitude of
the Israelites among the brickkilns and the epithet "furnace of
iron" (I Kings 8:51) applied to Egypt in the Bible. The association
of pyramids and fire is as old as Plato's pun on the word πύρ.

The temple of Verulam is a monument to the fall of man, in

Blake the same event as the deluge and the creation of the world in its present "out there" form. This form is that of the law, the basis of which is revolution in its mechanical sense of revolving wheels, the symbol of which is the *ouroboros*, the serpent with its tail in its mouth (indicated in a passage omitted above). We see the world from individual "opake" centers, instead of being identified with a universal Man who is also God, who created what we see as alien to us, and who would consequently see his world from the circumference instead of the center, the perspective reinstated in man by the arts. Such a God-Man would be "full of eyes," like the creatures of Ezekiel's vision, and by an unexpected but quite logical extension of the symbolism, Blake makes him full of noses too. Burning meat to gods on altars, after all, does assume that gods have circumferential noses.

The "Stone of Night," the opposite of the "lively stones" (I Peter 2:5) of the genuine temple, is an image of the human head, the phrase "stony roof" being repeated from the passage in *America* quoted above. It is in the south because the south is the zenith, the place of the sun in full strength in Blake's symbolism. Now it is covered with purple flowers and red berries, probably of the nightshade: the colors are those of the dying god, which is what Orc (usually Luvah in this context) comes to be in Blake's later poems. The Stone of Night has fallen like a meteor through the bottom or nadir of existence, represented by the north, and now has the same relation to its original that a gravestone has to a living body. We may compare the "grave-plot" that Thel reached when she passed under the "northern bar," and the black coffin which is the body of the chimney sweep (and the enslaved Negro, who also belongs in the "southern clime"). Blake's imagery of the north combines the magnetic needle and the legend of the northern maelstrom, the latter supplying a demonic parody of the ascending spiral image on the altar.

From the perspective of single vision, then, our original diagram of buried innocence trying to push its way into experience has to be completed by the death in which all life, individual or historical, ends. Death in Blake's symbolism is Satan, the "limit of Opacity," reduction to inorganic matter, who operates in the living man as a death wish or "accuser" of sin. His source in the outer world is the sky, Satan being the starry dragon of Revelation 12:4. Blake identifies this dragon with the Covering Cherub of Ezekiel 28, and the Covering Cherub again with the angel trying to keep us out of the Garden of Eden. Thus the sky is, first, the outward illusion of reality that keeps us out of our proper home; second, the macrocosmic Stone of Night, the rock on top of man's tomb designed to prevent his resurrection; and third, the circumference of what Blake calls the "Mundane Shell," the world as it appears to the embryonic and unborn imagination. Thus:

child's innocence > adult experience > death = Satan or Covering Cherub

life under moral law = Urizen

frustrated -desire = Orc or Luvah

Ordinary human life, symbolized in Blake first by "Adam" and later by "Reuben," oscillates between the two submerged states.

The conception of Druidism in Blake, then, is a conception of human energy and desire continuously martyred by the tyranny of human reason, or superstitition. The phrase "dying god" that we have used for Luvah suggests Frazer, and Blake's Druid symbolism has some remarkable anticipations of Frazer's *Golden Bough* complex, including the mistletoe and the oak. The anticipations even extend to Frazer's own unconscious symbolism: the colors of the three states above are, reading up, red, white, and black; and Frazer's book ends with the remark that the web of human thought has been woven of these three colors, though the status of the white or scientific one in Blake is very different. The following passage from *Jerusalem* 66 illustrates Blake's handling of sacrificial symbolism:

> The Daughters of Albion clothed in garments
> of needle work
> Strip them off from their shoulders and bosoms,
> they lay aside
> Their garments, they sit naked upon the
> Stone of trial.
> The knife of flint passes over the howling
> Victim: his blood
> Gushes & stains the fair side of the fair
> Daughters of Albion.
> They put aside his curls: they divide his
> seven locks upon
> His forehead: they bind his forehead with
> thorns of iron,
> They put into hand a reed, they mock,
> Saying: Behold
> The King of Canaan, whose are seven hundred
> chariots of iron!
> They take off his vesture whole with their
> Knives of flint:
> But they cut asunder his inner garments:
> searching with

Their cruel fingers for his heart, & there
   they enter in pomp,
In many tears: & there they erect a temple
   & an altar:
They pour cold water on his brain in front,
   to cause
Lids to grow over his eyes in veils of tears:
   and caverns
To freeze over his nostrils, while they feed
   his tongue from cups
And dishes of painted clay.

The imagery combines the mockery and passion of Jesus with features from Aztec sacrifices, as Blake realizes that the two widely separated rituals mean essentially the same thing. In the Mexican rites, the "vesture whole" is the skin, not the garment, and the heart is extracted from the body, not merely pierced by a spear as in the Passion. As the passage goes on, the victim expands from an individual body into a country: that is, he is beginning to embody not merely the dying god, but the original universal Man, Albion, whose present dead body is England. The veils and caverns are religious images derived from analogies between the human body and the landscape. Serpent worship is for Blake a perennial feature of this kind of superstition, and the victim is fed from dishes of clay partly because, as Blake says in *The Everlasting Gospel*, "dust & Clay is the Serpent's meat." An early Biblical dying-god figure is that of Sisera, the King of Canaan, whose murder at the hands of Jael suggests the nailing down of Jesus and Prometheus; and the reference to "needle work" in the first line also comes from Deborah's war song. The role given to the Daughters of Albion shows how clearly Blake associates the ritual of sacrifice, many features of which are repeated in judicial executions, with a perversion of the erotic instinct; and in fact Blake is clearer than Frazer about the role of the "white goddess" in the dying god cult, the Cybele who decrees the death of Attis.

SOUTHERN GATE: THREEFOLD VISION

The conception of a cycle common to individual and to historical life is the basis of the symbolism of several modern poets, including Yeats, Joyce in *Finnegans Wake*, and Graves in *The White Goddess*. In its modern forms, it usually revolves around a female figure. *The Marriage of Heaven and Hell* prophesies that eventually the bound Orc will be set free and will destroy the present world in a "consummation," which means both burning up and the climax of a marriage. When the marriage is accomplished "by an improvement of sensual enjoyment," the world of form and reason will be possessed by energy and desire, and will be their "outward bound or circumference" instead of a separate and therefore tyrannizing principle. One would think then that a female figure would be more appropriate for the symbolism of the world of form than the aged and male Urizen.

In traditional Christian symbolism, God the Creator is symbolically male, and all human souls, whether of men or of women, are creatures, and therefore symbolically female. In Blake, the real man is creating man; hence all human beings, men or women, are symbolically male. The symbolic female in Blake is what we call nature, and has four relations to humanity, depending on the quality of the vision. In the world of death, or Satan, which Blake calls Ulro, the human body is completely absorbed in the body of nature —a "dark Hermaphrodite," as Blake says in *The Gates of Paradise*. In the ordinary world of experience, which Blake calls Generation, the relation of humanity to nature is that of subject to object. In the usually frustrated and suppressed world of sexual desire, which Blake calls Beulah, the relation is that of lover to beloved, and in the purely imaginative or creative state, called Eden, the relation is that of creator to creature. In the first two worlds, nature is a remote and tantalizing "female will"; in the last two she is an "emanation." Human women are associated with this female nature only when in their behavior they dramatize its characteristics. The relations between man and nature in the individual and historical cycle are different, and are summarized in *The Mental Traveller*, a poem as closely related to the cyclical symbolism of twentieth-century poetry as Keats's *La Belle Dame Sans Merci* is to pre-Raphaelite poetry.

The Mental Traveller traces the life of a "Boy" from infancy through manhood to death and rebirth. This Boy represents humanity, and consequently the cycle he goes through can be read either individually and psychologically, or socially and historically. The latter reading is easier, and closer to the center of gravity of what Blake is talking about. The poem traces a cycle, but the cycle differs from that of the single vision in that the emphasis is thrown on rebirth and return instead of on death. A female principle, nature, cycles in contrary motion against the Boy, growing young as he grows old and vice versa, and producing four phases that we may call son and mother, husband and wife, father and daughter, ghost (Blake's "spectre") and ghostly bride (Blake's "emanation"). Having set them down, we next observe that not one of these relations is genuine: the mother is not really a mother, nor the daughter really a daughter, and similarly with the other states. The "Woman Old," the nurse who takes charge of the Boy, is Mother Nature, whom

Blake calls Tirzah, and who ensures that everyone enters this world in the mutilated and imprisoned form of the physical body. The sacrifice of the dying god repeats this symbolism, which is why the birth of the Boy also contains the symbols of the Passion (we should compare this part of *The Mental Traveller* with the end of *Jerusalem* 67).

As the Boy grows up, he subdues a part of nature to his will, which thereupon becomes his mistress: a stage represented elsewhere in the Preludium to *America*. As the cycle completes what Yeats would call its first gyre, we reach the opposite pole of a "Female Babe" whom, like the newborn Boy, no one dares touch. This female represents the "emanation" or accumulated form of what the Boy has created in his life. If she were a real daughter and not a changeling, she would be the Boy's own permanent creation, as Jerusalem is the daughter of Albion, "a City, yet a Woman"; and with the appearance of such a permanent creation, the cycle of nature would come to an end. But in this world all creative achievements are inherited by someone else and are lost to their creator. This failure to take possession of one's own deepest experience is the theme of *The Crystal Cabinet* (by comparing the imagery of this latter poem with *Jerusalem* 70 we discover that the Female Babe's name, in this context, is Rahab). The Boy, now an old man at the point of death, acquires, like the aged king David, another "maiden" to keep his body warm on his deathbed. He is now in the desert or wilderness, which symbolizes the end of a cycle, and his maiden is Lilith, the bride of the desert, whom Blake elsewhere calls the Shadowy Female. The Boy as an old man is in an "alastor" relation to her: he ought to be still making the kind of creative effort that produced the Female Babe, but instead he keeps seeking his "emanation" or created form outside himself, until eventually the desert is partially renewed by his efforts, he comes again into the place of seed, and the cycle starts once more.

A greatly abbreviated account of the same cycle, in a more purely historical context, is in the "Argument" of *The Marriage of Heaven and Hell*. Here we start with Rintrah, the prophet in the desert, the Moses or Elijah or John the Baptist, who announces a new era of history; then we follow the historical cycle as it makes the desert blossom and produces the honey of the Promised Land. We notice how, as in the time of Moses, water springs up in the desert and how Orc's "red clay" puts life on the white bones of Urizen. Eventually the new society becomes decadent and tyrannical, forcing the prophet out into the desert once more to begin another cycle.

The poem called *The Gates of Paradise*, based on a series of illustrations reproduced in the standard edition of Blake, describes the same cycle in slightly different and more individualized terms.

Here conception in the womb, the mutilation of birth which produces the "mother's grief," is symbolized by the caterpillar and by the mandrake. The mandrake is traditionally an aphrodisiac, a plant with male and female forms, an opiate, the seed of hanged men, a "man-dragon" that shrieks when uprooted (i.e., born), and recalls the frustrated sunflower of the *Songs of Experience*. The association of the mandrake with the mother in Genesis 30:14 is the main reason why Blake uses "Reuben" instead of "Adam" as the symbol of ordinary man in *Jerusalem*. The embryo then takes on the substance of the four elements and the four humors that traditionally correspond to them, of which "Earth's Melancholy" is the dominant one. Then the infant is born and grows into an aggressive adolescent, like the Boy in *The Mental Traveller* binding nature down for his delight. This attitude divides nature into a part that is possessed and a part that eludes, and the separation indicates that the boy in this poem also is bound to the cyclical movement. The youth then collides with Urizen, the spear in the revolutionary left hand being opposed to the sword of established order in the right. The caption of this emblem, "My Son! My Son!", refers to Absalom's revolt against David. Orc is not the son of Urizen, but Absalom, hung on a tree (traditionally by his golden hair, like the mistletoe: cf. *The Book of Ahania*, II, 9) is another dying god or Druid victim.

The other plates are not difficult to interpret: they represent the frustration of desire, the reaction into despair, and the growing of the youthful and rebellious Orc into a wing-clipping Urizen again. Finally the hero, like the early Tiriel and like the Boy of *The Mental Traveller* in his old age, becomes a wandering pilgrim making his way, like the old man in the Pardoner's Tale, toward his own death. He enters "Death's Door," the lower half of a design from Blair's *Grave* omitting the resurrection theme in the upper half, and is once more identified with Mother Nature, with a caption quoted from Job 17:14. The Prologue asks us why we worship this dreary womb-to-tomb treadmill as God—that is, why we think of God as a sky-god of automatic order, when this sky-god is really Satan, the corpse of God. The Epilogue returns to the same attack, and concludes by calling Satan "The lost traveller's Dream under the Hill." Apart from the general theme of the dreaming traveller which is common to this poem and to *The Mental Traveller* (where the "mental" travelling is done by the poet and reader, not the hero), there is a more specific allusion to the passage in *The Pilgrim's Progress* where Christian, after falling asleep under Hill Difficulty and losing his roll, is forced to retrace his steps like the Israelites in the desert, to whom Bunyan explictly refers.

The passage from death to rebirth is represented in Blake's symbolism by Tharmas, the power of renewing life. The ability of the individual to renew his life is resurrection, and the resurrection is a break with the cycle, but in ordinary life such a renewal takes place only in the group or species, and within the cycle. Tharmas is symbolized by the sea, the end and the beginning of life. As the original fall of man was also the deluge, we are in this world symbolically under water, our true home being Atlantis, or the Red Sea, which the Israelites found to be dry land. Tharmas and Orc are the strength and beauty, the sublime and the pathetic, the uprights of the Druid trilithon already mentioned, with Urizen, the antiintellectual "reason," connecting them. Thus:

$$
\begin{array}{l}
\text{childhood} \\
\text{and youth}
\end{array}
>
\begin{array}{l}
\text{maturity} \\
\text{and old age}
\end{array}
>
\begin{array}{l}
\text{death and return} \\
\text{to place of seed}
\end{array}
= \text{Tharmas} =
\begin{array}{l}
\text{fallen} \\
\text{power}
\end{array}
$$

$$
\longrightarrow \text{life under law} \quad = \text{Urizen} = \begin{array}{l}\text{fallen}\\\text{wisdom}\end{array}
$$

$$
\longrightarrow \text{frustrated desire} \quad = \text{Orc} \quad = \begin{array}{l}\text{fallen}\\\text{love}\end{array}
$$

WESTERN GATE: FOURFOLD VISION

In *The Marriage of Heaven and Hell*, Blake presents the revolutionary vision of man as a self-centered anxious ego sitting on top of a rebellious desire, and he associates the emancipating of desire with the end of the world as we know it. The Proverbs of Hell say: "He who desires but acts not, breeds pestilence." Putting desire into action does not lead to anarchy, for the fires of Orc are "thought-creating": what it does lead to is an apocalypse in which "the whole creation will be consumed and appear infinite and holy, whereas it now appears finite & corrupt." But when we read other works of Blake, we begin to wonder if this "Voice of the Devil" tells the whole story. Blake certainly means what he says in *The Marriage of Heaven and Hell*, but that work is a satire, deriving its norms from other conceptions. As we read further in Blake, it becomes clear that the emancipating of desire, for him, is not the cause but the effect of the purging of reality. There was some political disillusionment as Blake proceeded—the perversion of the French Revolution into Napoleonic imperialism, the strength of the reactionary power in Britain, the continued ascendancy of the slave-owners in America, and a growing feeling that Voltaire and Rousseau were reactionaries and not revolutionaries were the main elements in it—but although this leads to some changes in emphasis in later poems, there is no evidence that he was ever really confused about the difference between the apocalyptic and the historical versions of reality.

Blake dislikes any terminology which implies that there are two perceivers in man, such as a soul and a body, which perceive different worlds. There is only one world, but there are two kinds of things to be done with it. There is, first, what Blake calls the natural vision, which assumes that the objective world is essentially independent of man. This vision becomes increasingly hypnotized by the automatic order and tantalizing remoteness of nature, creates gods in the image of its mindless mechanism, and rationalizes all evils and injustices of existence under some such formula as "Whatever is, is right." In extreme forms, this alienating vision becomes the reflection of the death wish in the soul, and develops annihilation wars like those of Blake's own time. Then there is the human vision, which takes the objective world to be the "starry floor," the bottom of reality, its permanence being important only as a stable basis for human creation. The goal of the human vision is "Religion, or Civilized Life such as it is in the Christian Church." This is a life of pure creation, such as is ascribed in Christianity to God, and which for Blake would participate in the infinite and eternal perspective of God. We note that Blake, like Kierkegaard, leads us toward an "either/or" dilemma, but that his terms are the reverse of Kierkegaard's. It is the aesthetic element for Blake which moves in the sphere of existential freedom; it is the ethical element which is the spectator, under the bondage of the law and the knowledge of good and evil.

We begin, then, with the view of an orthodox or moral "good," founded on an acceptance of the world out there, contrasted with the submerged "evil" desires of man to live in a world that makes more human sense. This vision of life turns out to be, when examined, a cyclical vision, completed by the more elaborate cycles just examined. But in addition to the cyclical vision there is also a dialectic, a separating-out of the two opposing human and natural visions. The categories of these visions are not moral good and evil, but life and death, one producing the real heaven of creation and the other the real hell of torture and tyranny. We have met one pole of this dialectic already in the conception of Satan, or death, as the only possible goal of all human effort from one point of view. The other pole is the impulse to transform the world into a human and imaginative form, the impulse that creates all art, all genuine religion, all culture and civilization. This impulse is personified by Blake as Los, the spirit of prophecy and creativity, and it is Los, not Orc, who is the hero of Blake's prophecies. Los derives, not from the suppressed desires of the individual child, but from a deeper creative impulse alluded to in Biblical myths about the unfallen state. These myths tell us that man's original state was not primitive, or derived from nature at all, but civilized, in the environment of a garden and a city. This unfallen state is, so to speak, the previous tree of which contemporary man is the seed, and the form he is attempting to recreate. Thus:

unfallen state	>	child's innocence	>	adult experience	= Urizen	= England	= Israel
				frustrated desire	= Orc	= France and America	= Edom
				creative power	= Los	= Atlantis	= Eden

It seems curious that, especially in the earlier prophecies, Los appears to play a more reactionary and sinister role than Urizen himself. We discover that it is Los, not Urizen, who is the father of Orc; Los, not Urizen, who actively restrains Orc, tying him down under Mount Atlas with the "Chain of Jealousy"; and Los who is the object of Orc's bitter Oedipal resentments. In the Preludium to *America*, he is referred to by his alternative name of Urthona, and there it is he and not Urizen who rivets Orc's "tenfold chains." These chains evidently include an incest taboo, for Orc is copulating with his sister in this Preludium. Evidently, as Blake conceives it, there is a deeply conservative element in the creative spirit that seems to help perpetuate the reign of Urizen. In fact certain functions given to Urizen in earlier prophecies are transferred to Los in later ones. According to William Morris, the joy that the medieval craftsman took in his work was so complete that he was able to accept the tyranny of medieval society: similarly, Blake is able to live in the age of Pitt and Nelson and yet be absorbed in building his palace of art on the "Great Atlantic Mountains," which will be here after the "Sea of Time and Space" above it is no more.

This principle that effective social action is to be found in the creation of art and not in revolution is, of course, common to many Romantics in Blake's period. It should not, however—certainly not in Blake—be regarded as a mere neurotic or wish-fulfilment substitute for the failure of revolution. Apart from the fact that the creation of art is a highly social act, Blake's conception of art is very different from the dictionary's. It is based on what we call the arts, because of his doctrine that human reality is created and not observed. But it includes much that we do not think of as art, and excludes much that we do, such as the paintings of Reynolds.

We notice that in *The Gates of Paradise* cycle there is one point at which there is a break from the cycle, the plate captioned "Fear & Hope are—Vision," and described in the commentary as a glimpse of "The Immortal Man that cannot Die." The corresponding point in *The Mental Traveller* comes in describing the form ("emanation") of the life that the Boy has been constructing, just before it takes shape as the elusive "Female Babe":

> And these are the gems of the Human Soul,
> The rubies & pearls of a lovesick eye,
> The countless gold of the akeing heart,
> The martyr's groan & the lover's sigh.

The curiously wooden allegory is not characteristic of Blake, but it recurs in *Jerusalem* 12, where the same theme is under discussion. Evidently, Blake means by "art" a creative life rooted in the arts, but including what more traditional language calls charity. Every act man performs is either creative or destructive. Both kinds seem to disappear in time, but in fact it is only the destructive act, the act of war or slavery or parasitism or hatred, that is really lost.

Los is not simply creative power, but the spirit of time: more accurately, he is the power that constructs in time the palace of art (Golgonooza), which is timeless. As Blake says in a grammatically violent aphorism, the ruins of time build mansions in eternity. The products of self-sacrifice and martyrdom and endurance of injustice still exist, in an invisible but permanent world created out of time by the imagination. This world is the genuine Atlantis or Eden that we actually live in. As soon as we realize that we do live in it, we enter into what Blake means by the Last Judgement. Most people do not make this act of realization, and those who do make it have the responsibility of being evangelists for it. According to Blake, most of what the enlightened can do for the unenlightened is negative: their task is to sharpen the dialectic of the human and natural visions by showing that there are only the alternatives of apocalypse and annihilation.

Blake obviously hopes for a very considerable social response to vision in or soon after his lifetime. But even if everybody responded completely and at once, the City of God would not become immediately visible: if it did, it would simply be one more objective environment. The real "heaven" is not a glittering city, but the power of bringing such cities into existence. In the poem "My Spectre around me," Blake depicts a figure like the Boy of *The Mental Traveller* in old age, searching vainly for his "emanation," the total body of what he can love and create, outside himself instead of inside. The natural tendency of desire (Orc) in itself is to find its object. Hence the effect of the creative impulse on desire is bound to be restrictive until the release of desire becomes the inevitable by-product of creation.

The real world, being the source of a human vision, is human and not natural (which means indefinite) in shape. It does not stretch away forever into the stars, but has the form of a single giant man's body, the parts of which are arranged thus:

       Urizen   = head = city
       Tharmas = body = garden
       Orc   = loins = soil or bed of love
       Urthona = legs = underworld of dream and repose
       (Los)

Except that it is unfallen, the four levels of this world correspond very closely to the four traditional levels that we find in medieval and Renaissance poetry. The present physical world, by the "improvement of sensual enjoyment," would become an integral part of nature, and so Comus' attempt to seduce the Lady by an appeal to "nature" would no longer be a seduction or a specious argument. But the really important distinction is that for earlier poets the two upper levels, the city and the garden, were divine and not human in origin, whereas for Blake they are both divine and human, and their recovery depends on the creative power in man as well as in God.

The difference between the traditional and the Blakean versions of reality corresponds to the difference between the first and the last plates of the Job illustrations. In the first plate, Job and his family are in the state of innocence (Beulah), in a peaceful pastoral repose like that of the twenty-third Psalm. They preserve this state in the traditional way, by obeying a divine Providence that has arranged it, and hence are imaginatively children. There is nothing in the picture that suggests anything inadequate except that, in a recall of a very different Psalm (137), there are musical instruments hung on the tree above. In the last plate, things are much as they were before, but Job's family have taken the instruments down from the tree and are playing them. In Blake, we recover our original state, not by returning to it, but by recreating it. The act of creation, in its turn, is not producing something out of nothing, but the act of setting free what we already possess.

MARTIN PRICE

The Standard of Energy †

In *The Book of Urizen* (1794) we find the beginnings of the myth that was to occupy Blake in his later poetry. This is the account of a fall. Like Milton, Blake sees all human existence as shot through with moments of fall and moments of redemption, and one fall provides an archetype for all others. This is the story of the emergence of "the primeval Priest's assum'd power," and Urizen (whose name seems to derive, as does our word "horizon," from the Greek form of "to limit") is the archetypal State of false Priesthood. We first see Urizen separating off from the rest of existence, creating a void, a "soul-shudd'ring vacuum" that keeps out the spirit and secedes, as it were, from Eternity: it is pictured as a landscape of turbulence—vast forests, mountains of ice, thunderous voices —which embodies the "tormenting passions" of a "self-contemplating shadow."

Urizen explains his divorce from life as the desire for fixity:

> I have sought for a joy without pain,
> For a solid without fluctuation.
> Why will you die, O Eternals?
> Why live in unquenchable burnings? (II, 4:10–13.)

Urizen cannot tolerate the openness of eternal movement, that is, the vital energy of imagination. He fights its irregular and unpredictable freedom until he produces a "wide world of solid obstruction." He has wrested from the moral conflict with the "Seven deadly Sins of the soul" (his way of conceiving the freedom of energy) a book of "eternal brass," and he has reduced all seeming disorder to law and to simple regularity:

> One command, one joy, one desire,
> One curse, one weight, one measure,
> One King, one God, one Law (II, 4:38–40).

The effrontery of Urizen's speech is much like that of the Dunces or of Dulness' addresses. Urizen is less a character than a State revealing itself in its fullness.

† From *To the Palace of Wisdom* by Martin Price. Copyright © 1964 by Martin Price. Reprinted by permission of Doubleday & Co., Inc.

The Eternals seem, at least to Urizen, to rage furiously about him after this speech, separating themselves from him, although he has, of course, broken away from them. And now, in fear, he seeks a hiding-place, piling up mountains until he builds a "roof vast, petrific around / On all sides . . . like a womb" (III, 5:28–29). The Eternals send Los to watch over Urizen, and we encounter one of those poetic condensations that run through all of Blake's later poetry. Blake breaks down conventional narrative continuities by embodying relationships in constantly shifting images. As characters enter into new States, or as States enter into new relationships, the characters' natures alter, and they undergo the transformations that we recognize in the "condensation" of dream-processes. Here Los is sent to watch over Urizen, but Urizen is described as being rent from Los's side. If we take Los as the redeeming power of imagination, we can see Blake's desire to dramatize once more the separation of Urizen from all those other powers in man with which he should be in harmony. Urizen, wrenched apart from Los, is even more clearly a figure of pure rationality, a version of lifeless order. Tellingly, Urizen cannot generate a meaningful order even at the level he has reached. His "one law" needs some form of embodiment, and creates the senses through which he can receive awareness; for example, his eyes—"two little orbs . . . fixed in two little caves." As he takes on bodily form, Urizen's "eternal life" is "obliterated," and Los himself is dazed and paralyzed by this act. What horrifies Los is not the turbulence of life but the vacuity of "Space, undivided by existence" that now surrounds them.

When Los feels pity for Urizen's world, Pity itself grows into Enitharmon, the "first female now separate." As Urizen has fallen into a life bounded by the senses, so Los, out of more generous motives, falls into a State where he may be overcome by passivity. Enitharmon becomes a separate dominating will. The Eternals cover over the world with a great curtain they call Science; this may in turn be taken as Los's remoter view of eternal life now that he accepts a separate female partner. Los's marriage (which is, of course, like Adam's need for the Eve who will later seduce him) is an archetype of man's acceptance of a natural world about him as real as his own mind; a resignation of imaginative power. Enitharmon's first action is "perverse and cruel" coyness as she flees from his embrace. When she bears a male child, who issues howling with fierce flames, the Eternals close the tenting curtain: "No more Los beheld Eternity" (VI, 20:2). The descent has gone further: the prophet-poet is now committed to the world of his fallen self. He is absorbed into that world as a jealous father, and he becomes like Urizen.

Two actions follow, each the counterpart of the other. Los and

Enitharmon chain to a rock their son, Orc, who embodies the rebellious' principle of renewed and independent life. Los keeps
Enitharmon protected and enclosed while she bears "an enormous
race." At the same time Urizen awakes from sleep, "Stung with
the odours of Nature," and explores his world. To his horror he
finds his order is unworkable:

> he curs'd
> Both sons & daughters; too he saw
> That no flesh nor spirit could keep
> His iron laws one moment
> For he saw that life liv'd upon death (VIII, 23:23–26).

Urizen wanders, pitying his creations; and his tears become a
web, the Net of Religion. At this point we have Blake's savage parody of the creation of man in Genesis, as Urizen's creatures contract
into earthbound humans:

> 3.   Six days they shrunk up from existence,
> And on the seventh day they rested,
> And they bless'd the seventh day, in sick hope,
> And forgot their eternal life.
>
> 4.   And their thirty cities divided
> In form of a human heart.
> No more could they rise at will
> In the infinite void, but bound down
> To earth by their narrowing perceptions
> They lived a period of years;
> Then left a noisom body
> To the jaws of devouring darkness.
>
> 5.   And their children wept, & built
> Tombs in the desolate places,
> And form'd laws of prudence, and call'd them
> The eternal laws of God
>   (IX, 27:39–28:7).

At the close, Urizen's oldest son—a counterpart of the bound Orc
—calls together the children of Urizen and leads them from "the
pendulous earth": "They called it Egypt, & left it." We are at the
point of an exodus of the spirit from the domination of the merely
natural. The consolidation of error has brought the spirit to the
point of rebellion.

The irony of Blake's poem is strongest when he describes the fall
in the language of the Biblical creation. But this parody is simply
the most transparent instance of the inverted order that the poem
discloses. Blake's great satiric theme is the displacement of a true
order by a grotesque mock order:

Such is that false
And Generating Love, a pretence of love to destroy love
(*Jerusalem* I, 17:25–36).
A pretence of Art to destroy Art; a pretence of Liberty
To destroy Liberty; a pretence of Religion to destroy Religion
(*Jerusalem* II, 43:35–36).

This verbal pattern is Blake's most compressed statement of the inversion that insensibly creeps over man and his world, offering itself in the guise of what it seeks to usurp. Only the prophetic awareness of Los discerns what is taking place; others may sustain this
awareness for a time and feel the wearying eclipse—as Dulness'
sons lapse into sleep—but soon all is night. Like Pope, Blake presents the grandeur and terror of the usurpation:

Loud Satan thunder'd . . .
Coming in a Cloud with Trumpets & with Fiery Flame,
An awful Form eastward from midst a bright Paved-work
Of precious stones by Cherubim surrounded, so permitted
(Lest he should fall apart in his Eternal Death) to imitate
The Eternal Great Humanity Divine surrounded by
His Cherubim & Seraphim in every happy Eternity
(*Milton* II, 39:22–28).

In the same way, Blake's Urizen absorbs much of the traditional
image of God the Father, making clearer the kind of God man must
worship once he has resigned the energies that demand free movement and has contracted into the security of a closed system.

Blake's interweaving of mental states and outward structures, of
political programs and philosophic doctrines, gives any moment
in the later poems a formidable complexity. Characters voice the
world view that underlies the moral and social errors they embody.
Their frankness, like the shamelessness of Pope's dunces, shows how
completely they are enclosed in their limited order; they are com-
placently untroubled by the claims of a rival order, or at most
blusteringly defiant. When the Saviour appeals to Albion, the
primal man who is now fallen mankind, he offers the vision of
charity: "Lo! we are one, forgiving all Evil." But Albion's denial
opens out into an opposed vision of reality:

But the perturbed Man away turns down the valleys dark:
Saying we are not One, we are Many, thou most simulative
Phantom of the over heated brain! shadow of immortality!
Seeking to keep my soul a victim to thy Love! which binds
Man, the enemy of man, into deceitful friendship . . .
By demonstration man alone can live, and not by faith.
My mountains are my own, and I will keep them to myself:
The Malvern and the Cheviot, the Wold, Plinlimmon & Snowden

Are mine: here will I build my Laws of Moral Virtue.
Humanity shall be no more, but war & princedom & victory!

(*Jerusalem* I, 1:22–32.)

The fullness with which Albion reveals his error moves the passage toward ironic satire. Like the great speeches by Aristarchus or Silenus in the fourth book of *The Dunciad* it exposes itself in every assertion. The denial of Jesus becomes rabid empiricism ("most simulative Phantom"), Hobbesian politics ("Man, the enemy of man"), dogmatic rationalism ("By demonstration . . . alone"), and acquisitive materialism ("My mountains are my own"). Pascal's disjunction of orders was never more complete than this.

It is in such passages that we can best see Blake's resemblance to the Augustans. Like them he is acutely aware of how deeply all attitudes are rooted in systems of belief. A madman inhabits a mad world, where values are turned inside out, and each sane pattern of order has its reverse image. This takes us back to the problem of orders, to the view that each discrete order of experience tends to become self-subsistent in a world of its own making. The most insistent irony in Blake is the irony of the "mind-forg'd manacles," the enclosure and stultification of man's vision and the loss of the power even to discern the change.

Blake's constant effort is to give unmistakable form to error and thus rob it of vague and mysterious authority. To do this, he must become a master of satiric symbols and ironic confrontations. "Every honest man is a Prophet; he utters his opinion both of private & public matters. Thus: If you go on So, the result is So. He never says, such a thing shall happen let you do what you will. A Prophet is a Seer, not an Arbitrary Dictator. It is man's fault if God is not able to do him good, for he gives to the just & to the unjust, but the unjust reject his gift" (392). This is precisely the satirist's task: to appeal to men's responsibility by projecting the consequences of their action into the actions themselves, as Swift dramatizes our failure of charity in the cannibalism of *A Modest Proposal*. Such satiric prophecy is uncomfortable; it is designed to disturb. "What do these Knaves mean by Virtue? Do they mean War & its horrors & its Heroic Villains?" (400.)

It is important to make certain distinctions. Blake hates the "Accusers of Sin," the moralists who make impossible demands, rob the self of spontaneity and confidence, then punish its inevitable transgressions with a righteous show of pity. Everything that lives is holy; each man lives in the imagination. Each individual is unique, a law to itself so long as it remains truly alive and does not harden into the negation of life, the hindering of energy in itself and others. Judgments of good and evil deny this uniqueness and demand characterless passivity. For Blake, therefore, the prophet does not defend a moral code; he keeps the divine vision, and he seeks to restore life where men have chosen death. As a satirist he attacks not individuals but States. "Man Passes on, but States remain for Ever; he passes thro' them like a traveller who may as well suppose that the places he has pass'd thro' Exist no more. Every thing is Eternal" (606). States must be identified, so that man may recognize them and pass beyond those that are conditions of death. Man must be made to see:

> . . . What seems to Be, Is, To those to whom
> It seems to Be, & is productive of the most dreadful
> Consequences to those to whom it seems to Be, even of
> Torments, Despair, Eternal Death
> *(Jerusalem* II, 36:51–54).

The satirist exposes the nature and thereby dissolves the solidity of those structures men build as resting places from thought. The most splendid structures may be the denial of life, either through externalization or through simple inversion of values.

> The Walls of Babylon are Souls of Men, her Gates the Groans
> Of Nations, her Towers are the Miseries of once happy Families,
> Her Streets are paved with Destruction, her Houses built with Death,
> Her Palaces with Hell & the Grave, her Synagogues with Torments
> Of ever-hardening Despair, squar'd & polish'd with cruel skill
> *(Jerusalem* I, 24:31–35).

Blake insists upon the world man inhabits as a world of his making. Everything is an imaginative act, and every demon is born of terror. Satan springs into monstrous proliferation,

> Producing many Heads, three or seven or ten, & hands & feet
> Innumerable at will of the unfortunate contemplator
> Who becomes his food: such is the way of the Devouring Power
> *(Jerusalem* II, 33:22–24).

In such a situation, the prophet must become a liberator who destroys the Babylons men build around themselves and dispels the Satan they feed with their doubt or despair. To the extent that man accepts error through a failure of insight, through dishonesty or willful rejection of what he knows to be true, he may be treated with that therapeutic scorn we have seen in Pope. Blake's prophet-poet Los exclaims:

> "I care not whether a Man is Good or Evil; all that I care
> Is whether he is a Wise Man or a Fool. Go, put off Holiness
> And put on Intellect, or my thund'rous Hammer shall drive thee
> To wrath which thou condemnest, till thou obey my voice"
> *(Jerusalem* IV, 91:55–8).

The prophet, like the satirist, must reject the saving lie, and he must commit himself with "triumphant honest pride" to the vision that strips away illusion. The power to penetrate the wishful blindness and the plausible pretext is the prophetic gift that leads to the satiric image. The prophet in his vision shares the detachment of the God he interprets, sees earthly power in its imminent frailty: "Though they dig into hell, thence shall mine hand take them; though they climb up to heaven, thence will I bring them down." It is this detachment, both in range of vision and in elevation of spirit above the fears of worldly power, that Blake portrayed in his version of Gray's Bard: "King Edward and his Queen Elenor are prostrated, with their horses, at the foot of the rock on which the Bard stands; prostrated by the terrors of his harp on the margin of the river Conway. . . ." As Blake says (576–77), "Weaving the winding sheet of Edward's race by means of sounds of spiritual music and its accompanying expressions of articulate speech is a bold, and daring, and masterly conception. . . ." If the Bard's spiritual music is bitter denunciation, we can turn to Chaucer, who "was very devout, and paid respect to true enthusiastic superstition. He has laughed at his knaves and fools. . . . But he has respected his True Pilgrims . . ." (575). The spiritual music of the Bard, the laughter of Chaucer, the "triumphant honest pride" of Jesus (750) —these go to compose the satirist's scorn and outrage at the pretensions of the corrupt.

What primarily distinguishes Blake as satirist from the Augustans is the shift from moral judgment to a standard of energy. It is not the evil man so much as the soulless and dead man that Blake disdains. In fact, of course, any standard of vitality tends to transform itself into one of morality, as death-in-life becomes a state of bondage to false gods. But the prophetic stance fits well, in its sense of inspiration and commanding power, with the scorn for the materialized, the rigid, the timorous and self-protective. The exposed grandeur of Gray's Bard, as well as his sacrifice of himself to the cause of liberty, becomes a dramatization of titanic energies confronting legal tyrants. So long as these titanic forces remain tied to a system or dogma, they seem oppressive. When they shake off all commitment to the limited and regular, they become symbols of infinity. They overleap doctrines and stand for the spirit that gives life and demands life of others. The pride of such a force is essential to its nature; itself infinite and divine, it can only mock any limited conceptions of its will or any simulation of its energy. And out of such pride scorn must naturally follow: the infinite can only shatter with its breath those mechanical representations of life that men devoutly compose. The spiritual music is nothing less than the whirlwind, the destruction of worldly order in the name of energy that cannot be ordered unless it orders itself.

The myths of Blake's later poetry are designed to show life under the aspect of energy. They show the primal unity of man sundered into the warring elements of the Four Zoas. Reason has been divided from feeling, Urizen from Luvah; the instinctual unity of the body from its imaginative direction, Tharmas from Urthona. Each of the Zoas is at war with the others, except for momentary conspiracies, and the conflict drives each to the impoverished extreme of its nature.

Again, Blake creates the cyclic myth of the four realms of man, which are also four conditions of spirit. Eden is a place of mastery, of active engagement in intellectual warfare and hunting, or what Shaw calls the creation of new mind. The condition of Eden is a limit of life as we customarily know it; it fixes in myth those moments of heightened intensity, confident achievement, and harmonious self-realization that confer a sense of transcendence. The principle of active mastery is crucial, for the pleasant state of repose that Blake calls Beulah carries the threat of inducing passivity. To move from Eden to Beulah is to descend from the battlefield or hunt to the domestic ease of simple accord, from vital conflict of contraries to unresisting acceptance by a benign world, like the arms of the delighted bride or the cradle of the mother's embrace. Like every descent from difficulty to shelter, it can become a movement toward dependence.

The next phase of passivity is the most important, for in the descent from Beulah to Ulro, man forgets that his imagination creates his world and accepts as solid reality what he has unconsciously imposed upon himself. Once he submits to this reality, he sets out giving it form and making it a self-subsistent order. He is under the domination of Urizen, and in *The Book of Urizen* we see the primal pattern of this self-enclosure. Just as Urizen fails to impose his law upon all of existence, so man remains aware of more than he can rationalize. The affective life he fails to acknowledge erupts into institutional warfare and sacrificial religion, the perversions of the feelings that have been repressed. (We may recall the emperor in Swift's *A Tale of a Tub*, whose blocked semen shoots up into his brain and fosters dreams of conquest.) The life man creates for himself in Ulro becomes unendurable; he is, like Pope's fallen men in the *Essay on Man*, forced into virtue. For Blake the pattern of recovery is the painful struggle of rebellion that marks the condition of Generation, the condition of the *Songs of Experience* or the *Visions of the Daughters of Albion*.

Finally, a third myth Blake uses is that of Spectre and Emanation. The Emanation that embodies man's aspirations and his vision of self-realization is driven away by doubt and jealous suspicion.

The Emanation may be replaced, as Jerusalem is, by the temptress, at first in the benign image of pastoral nature, later as the whore of mystery and abominations. This is another way of seeing the descent into Ulro and the tyranny of a partial vision. The Spectre is Selfhood that encrusts man's spirit with opacity, diverts him from transcendent vision to rationalism. "Thou art my Pride & Self righteousness," Los declares to his Spectre. Opposed to the Spectre is the vision of selflessness and forgiveness:

> And if God dieth not for Man & giveth not himself
> Eternally for Man, Man could not exist; for Man is Love
> As God is Love
> (*Jerusalem* IV, 96:25–27).

The complex interaction of these myths and others creates the pattern of Blake's later poetry. At any moment the forward narrative movement may give way to the sense of depth, or the opening out of levels of meanings that have been compressed into massive symbols. Blake encourages this process by stressing the simultaneity of actions on various levels and by moving abruptly from one level to another. The myths, as we see, can easily merge into each other and produce dreamlike fluidity of epic movement. One is reminded of Spenser's world in *The Faerie Queene*, where the extravagances of chivalric romance are only the outward surface of a spiritual movement within the heroes. Spenser's scene is a landscape of soul, embodied in sinister palaces or castles, deserts of despair, fountains of renewal; his dragons and witches are the temptations that live within the soul. Blake carries this further. The myths he superimposes upon history in the earlier works, such as *America* or *The French Revolution*, are at last wholly internalized, and the cosmic drama is played out within the mind and soul of fallen man, the sleeping Albion. Instead of characters as distinct as Milton's angels or Spenser's Archimago or Orgoglio, Blake creates States through which man passes, and the movement from one State to another may be apparent transformation of identity. There is always the need to identify in Blake's poems. Oothoon recognizes Urizen in Bromion's voice; Los and Enitharmon (in *Milton* 10:1) see "that Satan is Urizen."

This process of naming and identifying is a process of satiric reduction. The Augustan satirists dramatize the plausible power of error in elaborate ironic structures: the systems of belief in Swift's *Tale of a Tub*, the worship of Dulness in *The Dunciad*, the queenly hauteur of Dryden's Panther. Perhaps the finest brief instance is Pope's vision, in the *Epilogue to the Satires*, I, of the triumphal procession of Vice. But all of this ironic appreciation that seems to give in to pretension and to admire appearance prepares for the act of naming, as the satirist reveals the order within which this grandeur is contained. Swift's Peter and Jack prove to be two aspects of the same selfhood; Pope's Dulness is a phantom by which man enslaves himself; and Dryden's Panther, the more dangerous for a deceptively mild manner. Significantly, all of the great Augustan satires are works whose narrative structure seems to bend or halt under their weight of symbolic meaning. Narrative gives way to dialectic.

Blake's Urizen—reason grown to a deity and despot—is a counterpart to Pope's Dulness, the usurping deity who has undone true order and blinded her adherents to their former existence. Urizen is the impoverishing tyranny of reason, Dulness the paralyzing tyranny of pure matter; but these different tyrants achieve their power in similar ways. The uncreating word of Dulness grows in the human brain as surely as Urizen's tree of mystery. Pope's skill is to make of his ridiculous pedants, poetasters, grubs, and charlatans a formidable army of the Enemy. So in Blake, the tyranny or malice of each man creates the more formidable and frightful system, the world view in which man imprisons himself. Like Dulness, Urizen is a part of the human soul usurping the rule of other parts. Dulness represents the atavistic unconscious of self-gratification and self-absorption that may include overt pride, less obvious laziness, more fundamental selfhood. Blake's Urizen is selfhood in another guise: the selfhood of prostration before one's guilt and anxiety, of assertion through vindictive law and frustration before repressive fear, a cycle—in familiar modern terms—of frustration and aggression, the aggression turned against oneself as well as others and projected into an institution that gives it impersonal authority. Dulness surrounds her sons and herself with fogs, Urizen encloses man's mind in a mundane shell.

In a larger sense, one might compare Pope's conception of Dulness with Freud's conception of the Unconscious, as Philip Rieff presents it:

The unconscious is fertile "nature," the womb of darkness, the identity in which every distinction fades and all things reunite. . . . Freud's notion of the unconscious stresses the lack of differentiation in feeling: all unconscious desires are impersonal, as all persons are creatures of a vaguely instinctual demiurge. . . .
Freud thought of the unconscious as somewhat like a hidden god—indifferent, impersonal, unconcerned about the life of its creation. It is inferred always in negative terms. . . . Consciousness is discriminating and selective. The unconscious never says No. . . . Consciousness is alterable. Unconscious forces are "indestructible." Instincts fill the unconscious with energy, "but it has no organization, no unified will . . . the laws of logic—

above all the laws of contradiction" do not apply to it; it knows "no values, no good and evil, no morality" (*Freud, The Mind of the Moralist*, New York, 1961, pp. 36–37).

One may, as Rieff points out, see form and order as prior to the "fundamental substrate" that it shapes, or one may see the substrate as the source from which order is derived. Mandeville takes the second position, as does Freud; but Pope takes the first. Dulness seeks "to blot out Order, and extinguish Light"; their primacy is essential to Pope's conception. He recognizes the energies of self-love and the ruling passion (in the *Essay on Man*), or of wit (in the *Essay on Criticism*). But in each case there is a forming power to which the energy must be wedded, and its presence is what distinguishes creativity from destructiveness or art from madness. Pope can treat the emergence of society from chaotic selfishness, but the emergence is, for him, a restoration of primal order.

Therefore Pope suggests that the failure of mind is the failure of an energy different from, but no less important than, that of Dulness' unconscious and instinctive force. Much of the treatment of Dulness dramatizes the loss of this energy of mind. She is the mistress of the great yawn, the creator of moral inanition, the dissolver of critical effort and vigilance, the coddler of a boozy son. She may be busy and bold, but she is also heavy and blind. Her characteristic motion is the self-enclosing vortex, her characteristic form is sluggish and formless viscosity. Her followers are a "vast involuntary throng," led along by the mechanics of magnetism like steel filings or ball bearings, by "strong impulsive gravity of head." Here again heaviness represents a dehumanized lethargy of mind.

Blake, in his conception of Urizen, stresses the ongoing process of energy, which Urizen tries to block and freeze with rational structures. Yet Blake recognizes that Urizen's tyranny is not true reason. Like Wordsworth, Blake prizes "reason in her most exalted mood," when reason acts in unity with imagination and feeling. Urizen exemplifies A. O. Lovejoy's point that "rationality, when conceived as complete, as excluding all arbitrariness, becomes itself a kind of irrationality" (*The Great Chain of Being*, p. 331). As the promulgator of laws that can never be fully obeyed and the creator of excessive self-demands that can yield only neurasthenic paralysis, Urizen inevitably collapses into superstition and mystery. His rationalism produces a world more and more abstract and inhuman, ruled by a God that is a mere phantom lawgiver. What has been denied returns in a corrupt form. Urizen's temples are the scene of an erotic mystery cult, like that of the Magna Mater to whom Pope likens Dulness, and his religion is allied with war, that is, with "energy enslav'd." Just as Dulness' own energy is matched with mental languor, so Urizen's rationalism is matched with the debased emotions that Blake embodies in Rahab, the whore of Babylon: "Religion hid in War, a Dragon red & hidden Harlot" (*Jerusalem* III, 75:20).

Pope and Blake deal with the failure of both order and energy. Pope, whose concern is for order, shows Dulness foisting a mock order with the irresistible power that is freed by the mind's abdication. Blake, whose concern is for the energy that makes its own constantly renewed forms of order, shows Urizen checking all movement and renewal or forcing energy into perverse and wasteful forms. Pope shows Dulness ruling the world by corrupting institutions and inverting their original nature. Blake shows Urizen's power in the false authority of all institutions, which by their nature seek to preserve and extend the power surrendered to them. Both poets work, by means of dialectical encounters, toward the ultimate exposure and consolidation of error so that it may be thrown off. Once the orders are distinguished, the self-enclosure of each has been broken, and a choice can be made. Pope dramatizes the choice in the satires as a moral intensity that leads man beyond selfhood and makes his will one with God's. Blake, who regards moral judgment, based as it is upon universal law, as the worst form of institutional tyranny, sees Urizen finally absorbed into the restored unity of all the Zoas, as the primal man, Albion, at last accepts Jesus and His doctrine of forgiveness.

> They walked
> To & fro in Eternity as One Man, reflecting each in each & clearly seen
> And seeing, according to fitness & order (*Jerusalem* IV, 98:38–40).

Blake can use the mathematical symbolism of Revelation, once it is purged of the taint of Pythagorean rationalism. Elsewhere he fuses the artifice of order with the vitality of organic life, and, like Milton, he does this through the metaphor of the dance:

> Thou seest the gorgeous clothed Flies that dance & sport in summer
> Upon the sunny brooks & meadows: every one the dance
> Knows in its intricate mazes of delight artful to weave:
> Each one to sound his instruments of music in the dance,
> To touch each other & recede, to cross & change & return
> (*Milton* I, 26:2–6).
> every Flower,
> The Pink, the Jessamine, the Wall-flower, the Carnation,
> The Jonquil, the mild Lilly, opes her heavens; every Tree
> And Flower & Herb soon fill the air with an innumerable Dance,
> Yet all in order Sweet & lovely (*Milton* II, 31:58–62).

Blake regards the authority of the imagination as absolute, and his critical remarks are a fierce attack upon any doctrine that seems in any way to undermine that authority. In this respect, he differs greatly from writers of more skeptical temper or tentative attitudes. Perhaps the greatest threat to the visionary is the sense of self-division and doubt. Where so much depends upon the strong assertion of a vision, any flickering of its brightness or blurring of its clarity may become utterly destructive, and any attempt to see the emergence of the vision from the natural man may seem betrayal or blasphemy. Among the fragments of Blake's *The Everlasting Gospel* (c. 1818) we have one "Spoke by My Spectre to Voltaire, Bacon, &c.":

> Did Jesus teach doubt? or did he
> Give any lessons of Philosophy,
> Charge Visionaries with deceiving,
> Or call Men wise for not Believing? (756).

Doubt, as Blake puts it, "is Self-Contradiction" (753), the self divided into the visionary and the questioner. He writes to Thomas Butts (25 April 1803) of his planned departure from Hayley's patronage at Felpham. In London, Blake hopes, he

> may converse with my friends in Eternity, See Visions, Dream Dreams & prophecy and speak Parables unobserv'd & at liberty from the Doubts of other Mortals; perhaps Doubts proceeding from Kindness, but Doubts are always pernicious, Especially when we Doubt our Friends.

Blake, far more than the earlier enthusiastic poets of the sublime, is aware of the internal struggle that is necessary to achieve and to maintain visionary power. The threat from within is as great as that from without, and one's doubts of one's friends or one's friends' doubts have the power of internalizing what might otherwise be more easily fought without oneself. Blake makes the division of self, between Los and his Spectre, as well as between Albion and his Emanation, Jerusalem, the central theme of his last major work. One passage will make this clear. In this speech Los recognizes the "consolidation of error" as the point where redemption can begin. To recognize error is to be free of it. "It is Burnt up the Moment Men cease to behold it" (617):

Deny a Conscience in Man & the Communion of Saints & Angels, Contemning the Divine Vision & Fruition, Worshiping the Deus Of the Heathen, The God of This World, & the Goddess Nature, Mystery, Babylon the Great, The Druid Dragon & hidden Harlot, Is it not that Signal of the Morning which was told us in the Beginning? (*Jerusalem* IV, 93:21–26.)

Here apparent disorder begins to reveal its inherent order. The function of error has become clear, and the total design of man's redemption is made manifest. The Spectre, as Los says, "is become One with me." This pattern of reintegration is essential to Blake's dialectical conception of contraries, and it is also at work in his own struggles within himself. In his most famous letter, he writes to William Hayley (23 October 1804):

> For now! O Glory! and O Delight! I have entirely reduced that spectrous Fiend to his station, whose annoyance has been the ruin of my labours for the last passed twenty years of my life. . . . he is become my servant who domineered over me, he is even as a brother who was my enemy. . . . thank God that I courageously pursued my course through darkness.

And we have a fragment of another letter to Hayley (4 December 1804) in a similar vein:

> I have indeed fought thro' a Hell of terrors and horrors . . . in a divided existence; now no longer divided nor at war with myself, I shall travel on in the strength of the Lord God, as Poor Pilgrim says.

The horror of doubt underlies much of Blake's writing on art. It does not, of course, affect the validity of Blake's arguments, but it helps to explain the violence and indiscriminate arrogance he shows toward such painters as Titian, Rubens, and Rembrandt. Blake rejects any attempt to derive the imagination from man's natural impulses. The purpose of the seventh of Reynolds' *Discourses on Art*, he writes on his copy, "is to Prove that Taste and Genius are not of Heavenly Origin" (437). As we have seen, Blake insists upon the innate or connatural, upon the descent of the divine rather than emergence from below. But, apart from this question of the grounds of imaginative vision, there remains the problem of its form. Here Blake insists, against the mockery and doubts of others, that vision is not mere phantasy; it is more determinate than the imitation of empirical reality. "He who does not imagine in stronger and better light than his perishing and mortal eye can see, does not image at all" (576).

The assertion of the determinate is, for Blake, the defense of the linear against the colorist method. "The more distinct, sharp, and wirey the bounding line, the more perfect the work of art" (585). The "want of this determinate and bounding form" is evidence of slackness and plagiarism. Each individual is marked off by its distinctive form. "How do we distinguish the oak from the beech, the horse from the ox, but by the bounding outline?" The bounding line becomes the test of authentic vision and, even more, of moral sincerity. "What is it that distinguishes honesty from knavery, but the hard and wiry line of rectitude and certainty in the actions and intentions? Leave out this line, and you leave out life itself; all is chaos again, and the line of the almighty must be drawn out upon it before man or beast can exist" (585). The visionary holds to the "certainty" of line even though he be "molested continually by blotting or blurring demons" (581). The certainty of line is given only to those who are Copiers of Imagination. Those who are Copiers of Nature prove only "that Nature becomes to its Victim nothing but Blots & Blurs" (595).

The colorists are Copiers of Nature, passive before empirical appearances, which they try to unify by imposing a harmony of color at the expense of sharp outlines. Blake favors clear fresco or water colors "unmuddied by oil, and firm and determinate lineaments unbroken by shadows" (504). The colorists "put the original Artist in fear and doubt of his original conception." The spirit of Titian "was particularly active in raising doubts concerning the possibility of executing without a model, and when once he had raised the doubt, it became easy for him to snatch away the vision time after time" (582). Mere memory of nature comes to possess the mind of the painter whose power of imagination is weakened. This is a surrender of the artist's individual character, a state of possession by "Venetian and Flemish demons." True painting, for Blake, is "drawing on Canvas" (594), just as true art is firm and confident invention, not imitation. The vision is "organized and minutely articulated beyond all that the mortal and perishing nature can produce" (576).

Related to Blake's defense of invention is his rejection of the charges that his own invention was far more impressive than his execution, or as Blake quotes them, "he can conceive but he cannot execute" (602). Blake acknowledges that his execution "is not like Any Body Else." But he does not intend that it should be; and he refuses to separate invention from execution. "The Man's Execution is as his Conception & No Better" (461)—the two must, in fact, be "Just Equal" (602) because they are the indivisible parts of the same act. "Ideas cannot be Given but in their minutely Appropriate Words, nor Can a Design be made without its minutely Appropriate Execution" (596). This becomes an eloquent attack upon the slavery of the official artist to the preconceived form. Blake defends the uniqueness of the individual vision against the tyranny of "one law." What he cannot conceive is that the heroic couplet is the proper and necessary vehicle of Dryden and Pope or that the colorist method of Rubens and Rembrandt has its own authenticity as execution.

The confrontation of Blake and Reynolds is perhaps the clearest indication of Blake's difference from the prevailing attitudes of his age. We do not, unfortunately, have his annotations on the later *Discourses*, where the dialectic of Reynolds' doctrines moves out most boldly to absorb the sublime and the picturesque. But even in those discourses, Reynolds hesitates to accept with Blake's tenacity and whole-heartedness the gospel of imagination. At the close of the great thirteenth discourse, Reynolds defends the dominion of Art over History. In language reminiscent of Sidney and Bacon, Reynolds describes the "object and intention of all the Arts" as

> to supply the natural imperfection of things, and often to gratify the mind by realizing and embodying what never existed but in the imagination. . . . Because these Arts, in their highest province, are not addressed to the gross senses, but to the desires of the mind, to that spark of divinity which we have within, impatient of being circumscribed by the world which is about us.

But Reynolds goes on, with a qualification that Blake would have abhorred: "Just so much as our Art has of this, just so much of dignity, *I had almost said of divinity*, it exhibits" (italics added). So again, when Reynolds speaks in the following discourse of Gainsborough, he insists upon "the slow progress of advancement" which is "in general imperceptible to the man himself who makes it; it is the consequence of the accumulation of various ideas which his mind received, he does not perhaps know how or when." Sometimes, an artist may recognize the hint that stirs him, when "he has received, as it were, some new and guiding light, *something like inspiration*, by which his mind has been expanded" (italics added). We can assume that Blake would object to the "almost" and the "something like" with the same ferocity he showed toward the earlier *Discourses*; he would have condemned Reynolds' stress upon slow growth, unconscious assimilation, and the determination of a man's art by "accidental circumstance." This, to Blake, would be the old Epicureanism that undermined the validity of imagination.

Reynolds opposes to the imitation of external nature the appeal to the disposition of the internal fabric of mind or imagination. But, in his constant reference to artistic illusion, he makes clear that this fabric of mind has at most a limited authority as truth. He distinguishes between the imitation that is narrowly conceived as deception and the ideal imitation (of a "higher order of beings") that depends upon legitimate artistic illusion. His most striking instance of this is the appeal to our "reverence for antiquity" of Gothic archiecture and its "Towers and battlements . . . Bosom'd high in tufted trees." And he points out that the Gothic, "though not so ancient as the Grecian, is more so to our imagination, with which the Artist is more concerned than with absolute truth." (So, too, Shaftesbury wrote "historically true, poetically false";) Blake does not make such distinctions; if art is conceived as invention or vision, its use of deception or illusion does not even enter into consideration.

Reynolds also shows a nice appreciation of the picturesque. Interestingly, when Blake had earlier used Reynolds in his own defense (22 November 1802), he had quoted the letter to Gilpin in which Reynolds likened the picturesque to colorist painting as "excellence of an inferior order." In the thirteenth discourse, however, Reynolds praises the architect's "use of accidents; to follow when they lead, and to improve them rather than always to trust to a regular plan." Buildings to which additions have been made for convenience often "acquire something of scenery by this accident." And the streets of London or other old towns are more pleasant in their "forms and turnings . . . produced by accident" than Wren's regular design for the rebuilt City might have been. Reynolds, like Uvedale Price, appeals from a more formal or limited art (here architecture; in Price landscape design) to the principles of painting. Vanbrugh, "who was a poet as well as an Architect understood light and shadow, and had great skill in composition." In Discourse XIV Reynolds recounts Gainsborough's frequent use of accident and arbitrary hints" ("broken stones, dried herbs, and pieces of looking glass, which he magnified into rocks, trees, and water"). Reynolds mentions the danger of mere trifling, but he pays tribute to Gainsborough's desire to "keep his faculties in exercise."

Finally, in his fifteenth discourse, Reynolds moves back to the grand style, but with an emphasis now more upon its expressiveness than its ideal imitation: Michelangelo carried painting to its "highest point of possible perfection" by "the divine energy of his own mind," and in doing so he "discovered to the world the hidden powers" that painting possessed. But Reynolds also emphasizes Michelangelo's labors, and cites Michelangelo's statement about Raphael, "that he did not possess his art from nature, but by long study." And when Reynolds acknowledges the individualism of students, he is cautious: "something must be conceded to great and irresistible impulses: perhaps every Student must not be strictly bound to general methods, if they strongly thwart the peculiar turn of his own mind."

This brings us to the best known of Blake's marginal comments: "To Generalize is to be an Idiot. To Particularize is the Alone distinction of Merit. General Knowledges are those Knowledges that Idiots possess" (451). These observations are a response to Edmund Burke's praise of Reynolds' intellectual powers of abstraction as a critic, rather than to Reynolds' remarks on painting; but we find their counterpart later when Blake is annotating the *Discourses* themselves. In the earlier discourses Reynolds defends the grandeur of generality against that art, whether Gothic or Dutch, which "attends to the minute accidental discriminations of particular and individual objects." And Blake's immediate response is, "Minute Discrimination is Not Accidental. All Sublimity is founded on Minute Discrimination" (453).

What Blake is doing in this passage (as in many others) is to equate generality with abstraction, vagueness, or indeterminacy. He defends the "characteristic." Yet, as we have seen, the characteristic may signify the qualities of a class of objects as well as an individual. "We see the same character," Blake writes, "repeated again and again, in animals, vegetables, minerals, and in men" (567). When he writes on Chaucer's pilgrims, Blake insists upon their generality or universality; and elsewhere it is clear that he wants to preserve this generality of high art through those archetypes that are both concrete and universal—the representations of "states" in figures that embody them with memorable clarity. Like Reynolds (and Shaftesbury) Blake rejects the mean particularity of those who "represent Christ uniformly like a Drayman" (596). But, unlike Reynolds, he does not seek his archetypes in the classical figures that are common to all modern European culture and therefore a shared imagery, concrete in itself but free of the fashionable and limiting particulars of a given place or time. He rejects Reynolds' "invariable" standard of beauty, and he rejects Reynolds' description of the attainment of generality as the stripping away of limiting particulars. But it is clear enough that Reynolds did not forsake concreteness and that Blake did not reject generality so much as indeterminacy.

Blake's attack upon generality gains its edge by a transference of terms, through analogy, from a moral to an artistic realm. We can see this happening in a passage of *Jerusalem* (91:19–22, 30–31):

He who would see the Divinity must see him in his Children,
One first, in friendship & love, then a Divine Family, & in the midst
Jesus will appear; so he who wishes to see a Vision, a perfect Whole,
Must see it in its Minute Particulars, Organized. . . .
. . . General Forms have their vitality in Particulars, & every
Particular is a Man, a Divine Member of the Divine Jesus.

The product of such analogical use of terms is a coherent system that excludes accidents. Blake refuses to contemplate the natural history of mind, and he derives all acts from the imagination. Just as he cuts through the dualism of mind and body, so he does with the dualism of God and man. God is nothing if He is not human.

"No man hath seen God at any time. If we love one another, God dwelleth in us, and his love is perfected in us" (I John 4:12). Blake can hardly be identified as theist or humanist; the distinction becomes meaningless for him. God can only exist within man, but man must be raised to a perception of the infinite. Blake rejects both transcendental deity and natural man: "God becomes as we are, that we may be as he is" (98).

The mind, in Blake's system, absorbs into itself all those limiting forces that might—in a writer like Sterne—exist outside its power. All resistances become dialectical, all necessity internal. "There is no Such Thing as a Second Cause nor as a Natural Cause for any Thing in any Way" (403). Blake gives us a world conceived as the manifestation of imaginative energy, hardened into opacity as energy fails, raised through intense and confident assertion to the image of One Man, containing all powers within himself and exercising them in the creation of works of art.

FREDERICK A. POTTLE

The Eye and the Object in the Poetry of Wordsworth †

A centenary year invites the publication of a great many essays with some such title as "Wordsworth Today." The purpose of these essays would be to judge Wordsworth as though he were a contemporary poet, to decide what portion of his works is really available to present-day sensibility. My purpose in the remarks that follow is descriptive rather than judicial: I shall try to isolate qualities of Wordsworth's poetry that look as though they were going to be apparent to all historical varieties of sensibility, though the values assigned to them by different sensibilities may differ. And I think I can best get to what I want to say by the method of texts: by inviting you to consider two prose statements made by Wordsworth himself about poetry in general and about his own poetry in particular. They are both from the famous Preface:

† From *The Yale Review*, Vol. XL (Autumn 1950). Copyright © 1950 by Yale University Press. Reprinted by permission of *The Yale Review*.

"Poetry takes its origin from emotion recollected in tranquillity" and "I have at all times endeavoured to look steadily at my subject." It is my notion that the latter of these texts usually gets, if not a false, at least an impoverished, interpretation; and that the two, taken together and rightly understood, go a long way toward placing Wordsworth in literary history.

At first sight it looks as though they were what Bacon calls "cross clauses": that is, they appear to be hopelessly contradictory. The natural image that rises in one's mind as one reads the statement "I have at all times endeavoured to look steadily at my subject" is that of an artist painting from a model or an actual landscape; and since Wordsworth's poetry contains a good deal of landscape, the obvious meaning of his words would appear to be that he composed poetry while looking earnestly and steadily at the natural objects that he introduces into his poems. But if poetry takes its rise from "emotion recollected in tranquillity," it is hard to see how this can happen. In fact, the only way in which we can leave any place for the actual model, in poetry that starts from recollection, is to suppose that after poetry *has* taken its rise, the poet goes back to natural objects and pores over them as he composes. And we know that Wordsworth did not do that. His normal practice, like that of other poets, was to paint without the model. He very seldom made a present joy the matter of his song, but rather turned habitually for the matter of poems to joys that sprang from hiding-places ten years deep.

More than that, a good many of his poems, including several of his finest, either have no basis in personal experience at all, or show autobiography so manipulated that the "subject" corresponds to nothing Wordsworth ever saw with the bodily eye. His extensive critical writings deride the matter-of-fact and speak over and over again of the power of the imagination to modify and create. Yet there is a widespread belief that Wordsworth was Nature's Boswell, in the old erroneous sense which defined Boswell as a man who followed Johnson about with a notebook, taking down his utterances on the spot. Actually, like Boswell, Wordsworth relied on memory, and says so quite explicitly. But then he says other things in which he appears to be vindicating the rightness of his poetry, not on the ground that it is well-imagined, but on the ground that the things described in the poem really did happen in that fashion and in no other. I do not mean merely the notes which he dictated in old age to Miss Fenwick. There is his impassioned defense of *The Leech Gatherer* against the mild and sisterly strictures of Sara Hutchinson, a defense made before the poem was published: "A young Poet in the midst of the happiness of Nature is described as overwhelmed by the thought of the miserable reverses which have befallen the happiest of all men, viz Poets—I think of this till I am so deeply impressed by it, that I consider the manner in which I was rescued from my dejection and despair almost as an interposition of Providence. . . . 'A lonely place, a Pond' 'by which an old man *was*, far from all house or home'—not stood, not sat, but '*was*'—the figure presented in the most naked simplicity possible. . . . I cannot conceive a figure more impressive than that of an old Man like this, the survivor of a Wife and ten children, travelling alone among the mountains and all lonely places, carrying with him his own fortitude, and the necessities which an unjust state of society has entailed upon him. . . . Good God! Such a figure, in such a place, a pious self-respecting, miserably infirm . . . Old Man telling such a tale!" [1]

Who would believe from reading this that in real life Wordsworth met the old man, not on the lonely moor, but in the highway; that the old man in real life was not demonstrating resolution and independence by gathering leeches under great difficulties, but was begging? In short, that the narrative is from first to last an imaginative construction—the account of an imagined meeting between Wordsworth and the beggar as Wordsworth imagined him to have been before he was finally reduced to beggary? [2]

What, then, are we to make of Wordsworth's boast that he endeavored at all times to look steadily at his subject? I shall try to answer the question by tracing the steps that he followed in writing one of his most famous poems, *I wandered lonely as a cloud*, commonly (though with no authority from Wordsworth) called *Daffodils*. The starting point is the entry in Dorothy Wordsworth's *Journal* for April 15, 1802. That entry is fairly long, but it is all good reading; and I have my reasons for not eliminating any of it:

"It was a threatening, misty morning, but mild. We set off after dinner from Eusemere. Mrs. Clarkson went a short way with us, but turned back. The wind was furious, and we thought we must have returned. We first rested in the large boat-house, then under a furze bush opposite Mr. Clarkson's. Saw the plough going in the field. The wind seized our breath. The Lake was rough. There was a boat by itself floating in the middle of the bay below Water Millock. We rested again in the Water Millock Lane. The hawthorns are black and green, the birches here and there greenish, but there is yet more of purple to be seen on the twigs. We got over into a field to avoid some cows—people working. A few primroses by the roadside—woodsorrel flower, the anemone, scentless violets, straw-

1. Letter of June 14, 1802. *The Early Letters of William and Dorothy Wordsworth: (1787–1805)*, ed. by E. de Selincourt, Oxford, 1935, 305–6.

2. Dorothy Wordsworth's *Journal*, Friday, October 3, 1800. *Journals of Dorothy Wordsworth*, ed. by E. de Selincourt, 2 vols., New York, 1941, I, 63.

berries, and that starry, yellow flower which Mrs. C. calls pile wort. When we were in the woods beyond Gowbarrow Park we saw a few daffodils close to the water-side. We fancied that the lake had floated the seeds ashore, and that the little colony had so sprung up. But as we went along there were more and yet more; and at last, under the boughs of the trees, we saw that there was a long belt of them along the shore, about the breadth of a country turnpike road. I never saw daffodils so beautiful. They grew among the mossy stones about and about them; some rested their heads upon these stones as on a pillow for weariness; and the rest tossed and reeled and danced, and seemed as if they verily laughed with the wind, that blew upon them over the lake; they looked so gay, ever glancing, ever changing. This wind blew directly over the lake to them. There was here and there a little knot, and a few stragglers a few yards higher up; but they were so few as not to disturb the simplicity, unity, and life of that one busy highway. We rested again and again. The bays were stormy, and we heard the waves at different distances, and in the middle of the water, like the sea. Rain came on—we were wet when we reached Luff's, but we called in. Luckily all was chearless and gloomy, so we faced the storm—we *must* have been wet if we had waited—put on dry clothes at Dobson's. I was very kindly treated by a young woman, the landlady looked sour, but it is her way. She gave us a goodish supper, excellent ham and potatoes. We paid 7/- when we came away. William was sitting by a bright fire when I came downstairs. He soon made his way to the library, piled up in a corner of the window. He brought out a volume of Enfield's *Speaker*, another miscellany, and an odd volume of Congreve's plays. We had a glass of warm rum and water. We enjoyed ourselves, and wished for Mary. It rained and blew, when we went to bed. N.B. Deer in Gowbarrow Park like skeletons." [3]

I said this was the starting point, for it is as near the raw matter of the poem as we can get. The true raw matter consisted of certain perceptions, visual, auditory, tactile, which Wordsworth and his sister had on that windy April morning—and those we have no way of recovering. In Dorothy's entry this raw matter has already been grasped and shaped by a powerful imagination, and it has been verbalized. The entry is not a poem, because it contains a good deal of true but inconsequential statement (the rum and water, the volume of Congreve), but much of it is prefabricated material for a poem. And the fact is (though this is doctrine little heard of among men) that Wordsworth made grateful use of prefabricated material whenever he could get it of the right sort. As Professor Lane

---

3. *Journals of Dorothy Wordsworth,* I, 131–2.

Cooper showed us long ago,[4] he went regularly to books of travel for material of the right sort, but his best source was his sister's journal.

The function of the imagination, as Wordsworth and Coleridge insisted, is, at the first level, to make sense out of the undifferentiated manifold of sensation by organizing it into individual objects or things; at the second, and specifically poetic, level, to reshape this world of common perception in the direction of a unity that shall be even more satisfactory and meaningful. Dorothy has made extensive use of the secondary or poetic imagination. Notice the devices by which she has unified and made sense of the experience of the daffodils. First, and most important, she has endowed them with human qualities. They are a social group engaged in busy concerted activity. The notion of the social group, the crowd (she does not actually use the word) is reinforced by her further figure of stragglers. Secondly, besides being active, the crowd of daffodils is happy: they look gay, they toss and reel and dance (their very activity is sport) and seem verily to laugh. And thirdly, some of the crowd have danced so hard that they are tired: they rest their heads upon the stones as on pillows.

Wordsworth recollected the scene in tranquillity and wrote his poem a full two years afterwards. He fixes on Dorothy's fine central perception of "the simplicity, unity, and life of that one busy highway," and condenses it into the one word "crowd," which, as we have seen, she did not use. He takes over, too, her impression that the daffodils were "dancing," that they were "gay," that they were even "laughing." Ever since 1807, when Wordsworth published this poem, daffodils have danced and laughed, but there is nothing inevitable about it. The Greek myth of Narcissus is not exactly hilarious; and even Herrick, when he looked at a daffodil, saw something far from jocund:

> When a Daffadill I see,
> Hanging down his head t'wards me;
> Guesse I may, what I must be:
> First, I shall decline my head;
> Secondly, I shall be dead;
> Lastly, safely buryed.

The literal, positivistic, "scientific" fact was that Wordsworth and his sister saw a large bed of wild daffodils beside a lake, agitated by a strong, cold spring wind. The rest is all the work of the imagination.

---

4. A Glance at Wordsworth's Reading," *Modern Language Notes*, Vol. XXII, Nos. 3 and 4 (March and April 1907), 83–9, 110–17; reprinted with altera- tions in *Methods and Aims in the Study of Literature*, ed. by Lane Cooper, Boston, 1915.

The mark of the poetic imagination is to simplify: to make the manifold of sensation more meaningful by reducing it to a number of objects that can actually be contemplated. Wordsworth continues Dorothy's process of simplification: he eliminates the bitterness of the wind, which is so prominent in her account; reduces the wind, in fact, to a breeze. It may appear here that he has simplified more than was necessary or wise. Shakespeare, in the most famous lines ever written about daffodils, kept the wind:

> daffodils
> That come before the swallow dares, and take
> The winds of March with beauty.

Admittedly, it is a higher mode. Wordsworth, on some occasions, would have kept the wind, too; but to have kept it here would have made a more complex—if you will, a more tragic—poem than he felt like writing. He felt this poem as something very simple and very pure; when he came to publish it, he put it in a group called "Moods of My Own Mind." But he is impartial: as he throws out matter on the one hand because it is too serious, he throws out matter on the other because it is too playful. The prettiest thing in Dorothy's realization—her image of the daffodils pillowing their heads on the stones—drops out. He dispenses too with Dorothy's stragglers. He fastens on her central image of the dancing, laughing crowd, and lets everything else go.

But now the idea of the crowd calls for a modification, and a modification of a fundamental sort. The social glee of the crowd can be made more significant if it is set over against solitary joy; and so in the poem he makes himself solitary, which in literal fact he was not. He now has what for him is a promising situation. The solitariness of the poet and the sociability of the daffodils are set up as poles between which the poem discharges itself. I have said that the situation is for him a promising one. Everyone knows of Wordsworth's love of solitude, his conviction that the highest experiences came to him when he was alone. What we need constantly to remind ourselves of is that his theory assigned an only slightly lower value to the love of men in societies. (The subtitle of Book VIII of *The Prelude* is "Love of Nature Leading to Love of Man.") The trouble was that, though he had the best of intentions, he could never handle close-packed, present, human crowds in the mode of imagination. If he were to grasp the life of a great city imaginatively, it had to be at night or early in the morning, while the streets were deserted; or at least in bad weather, when few people were abroad.[5] The Seventh Book of *The Prelude* ("Residence in London") is one of the most delightful things Wordsworth ever

5. *The Prelude* (1850), vii, 654–68; *Earth has not anything to show more fair.*

wrote, but as he himself tells us, it is almost all in the mode of fancy—almost all poetry that groups with *The Kitten and the Falling Leaves*.[6] But in the figure of a bed of daffodils endowed with human characteristics, he can handle with feelings of approval and exhilaration the concept of a crowd, of ten thousand individuals packed close together. He begins and ends solitary: at the beginning, we may assume, filled with joy, but a joy somewhat solemn, somewhat cold and remote, as the symbol of the cloud indicates. He is surprised by the sensation of mere unmixed human gaiety and lightheartedness, yields to it, and finds it good; so good that ever after he can derive refreshment from the memory of the experience.

I ought perhaps to be no more specific, but my purposes demand a somewhat closer analysis of Wordsworth's formal devices. The extension in space which he secures by linking the daffodils to other objects in nature—stars and waves—is characteristic of his poems of the imagination, but I shall defer discussion of this. The second stanza is ostensibly introduced merely to reinforce the idea of number ("continuous" echoing "crowd" and "host"), but of course there are other meaningful parallels. "Stars" looks back to "golden," and "twinkle" echoes "fluttering."[7] So, too, the third stanza professes only to reinforce the idea of dancing, but actually reinforces also the idea of number (waves are always numberless); and "sparkling" looks back to "twinkle," and back of that to "fluttering." The progress toward explicit identification of the symbol is gradual. First we have "fluttering" (literal: the flowers are self-moved); then "tossing their heads in sprightly dance." (The flowers are self-moved and are having a wonderful time. "Dance" is the key word: you will have noticed that it occurs in either the last or the first line of each of the four stanzas.) Finally—but not until the third stanza is reached—we get the quite explicit series "glee," "gay," "jocund," "pleasure." Wordsworth is always (or almost always) explicit in this fashion: he tells you just how you are expected to take his figures. Of course it is the figures that convey the emotion. No one can make us joyful merely by using the word "joy" or any of its synonyms. But there is impressive agreement among readers of all periods that by giving us a simple figure, reinforcing it by certain devices of varied iteration, and explicitly interpreting it, Wordsworth does evoke the emotion of joy.

We can now see what Wordsworth meant by looking steadily at his subject. So far as his subject is expressed in imagery drawn from nature (and that means in all his best poetry), there is implied a lifelong habit of close, detailed, and accurate observation of the

6. *The Prelude* (1850), VII, 436–41.
7. The second stanza was added in 1815. To accommodate it, some very skillful changes were made in the first stanza. Line 4 read originally "A host of dancing daffodils" and line 6, "Ten thousand dancing in the breeze."

objects composing the external universe. By "accurate" I mean something the same thing as "naturalistic," but not entirely so. Wordsworth scorned the merely analytic vision of the naturalist ("One that would peep and botanize Upon his mother's grave") because in his opinion that kind of apprehension empties the object of life and meaning by detaching it from its ground. "His theme is nature *in solido*, that is to say, he dwells on that mysterious presence of surrounding things, which imposes itself on any separate element that we set up as an individual for its own sake. He always grasps the whole of nature as involved in the tonality of the particular instance." [8] But, except for those portions of the scientist's vision which require (let us say) dissection and magnification, there is little in the scientist's vision that Wordsworth misses. A *merely* matter-of-fact, an *exclusively* positivistic view of nature fills him with anger, but his own apprehension includes the matter-of-fact view without denying any of it. Dr. Leavis has perhaps put this more intelligibly when he remarks, as the chief virtue of Wordsworth's poetry, a "firm hold upon the world of common perception," [9] though I myself should like to phrase it, "in the mode of perception which has been common in Western civilization since some time in the late eighteenth century." In a literal, physiological sense, Wordsworth did look steadily at the natural objects that appear in his poetry.

But the subject he is talking about in the sentence in the Preface is not an object in external nature; and the eye that looks steadily is not the physical eye. The subject is a mental image, and the eye is that inward eye which is the bliss of solitude. The mental image accompanies or is the source of the emotion recollected in tranquillity; it recurs in memory, not once but many times; and on each occasion he looks at it steadily to see what it *means*. Wordsworth in his best poetry does not start with an abstraction or a generalization, a divine commonplace which he wishes to illustrate. He starts with the mental image of a concrete natural object. He feels this object to be very urgent, but at first he does not know why. As he looks steadily at it, he simplifies it, and as he simplifies it, he sees what it means. He usually continues to simplify and interpret until the object becomes the correlative of a single emotion. It is a great mistake to consider Wordsworth a descriptive poet. When he is writing in the mode of the imagination, he never gives catalogues, in fact never provides a profusion of imagery.[1] He

8. *Science and the Modern World*, by Alfred North Whitehead, New York, 1925, 121.
9. *Revaluation*, London, 1936, 175.
1. E.g., in a poem of the imagination he could have done nothing with Dorothy's pleasant sentence, "A few primroses by the roadside—woodsorrel flower, the anemone, scentless violets, strawberries, and that starry, yellow flower which Mrs. C. calls pile wort." That would have suited Shelley's mode: see *The Question*.

employs few images. His images are firm and precise ("literal"), but, as one of my undergraduate students acutely said, they are very spare.[2] Of the daffodils we are given nothing but their habit of growing in clumps, their color, and their characteristic movement when stirred by the wind. Wordsworth's method (I am trying to be just as hard-headed and precise as I know how) is not the method of beautification (Tennyson), nor the method of distortion (Carlyle); it is the method of transfiguration. The primrose by the river's brim remains a simple primrose but it is also something more: it is a symbol (to use Hartley's quaint terminology) of sympathy, theopathy, or the moral sense.[3]

We can also see now the main cause of Wordsworth's dissatisfaction with the poetry of Pope: "It is remarkable that, excepting the nocturnal Reverie of Lady Winchilsea, and a passage or two in the Windsor Forest of Pope, the poetry of the period intervening between the publication of the Paradise Lost and the Seasons does not contain a single new image of external nature; and scarcely presents a familiar one from which it can be inferred that the eye of the Poet had been steadily fixed upon his object, much less that his feelings had urged him to work upon it in the spirit of genuine imagination. To what a low state knowledge of the most obvious and important phenomena had sunk, is evident from the style in which Dryden has executed a description of Night in one of his Tragedies, and Pope his translation of the celebrated moonlight scene in the Iliad. A blind man, in the habit of attending accurately to descriptions casually dropped from the lips of those around him, might easily depict these appearances with more truth." [4] For Pope's usual method is the exact contrary of that which I have been describing. Pope starts with an abstraction or a generalization concerning human nature and then looks for a correlative in the world of nature apart from man. His habit of observation of external nature is not detailed and precise; indeed, he thinks it unimportant whether the "facts" of nature which he alleges in his illustrations are really facts or superstitions. The natural history of Pliny and the old bestiaries are as much grist to his mill as the latest papers of the Royal Society. He appears also to me to have at times no clear, detailed, and consistent mental picture of his own figures. To illustrate: in the couplet near the beginning of the *Essay on Man,*

> The latent tracts, the giddy heights explore
> Of all who blindly creep or sightless soar,

2. He perhaps picked up the adjective from John Crowe Ransom's *The World's Body,* New York, 1938, 141, though it is there used of the Metaphysicals, not of Wordsworth.

3. Loving awareness of men ("the still,

sad music of humanity"), loving awareness of God ("something far more deely interfused"), morality ("all my moral being").

4. Essay, Supplementary to the Preface, 1815.

he means, I suppose, moles and birds of some sort. If so, in order to enforce his doctrine that "the proper study of mankind is man," he appears to be making use of the ancient and medieval notion that all birds except the eagle blind themselves by looking at the sun. Surely, by Pope's time it was generally known that the high-flying birds are not "sightless"; that on the contrary they have telescopic vision.

When in the same poem he says that man

Touches some wheel, or verges to some goal,[5]

I cannot convince myself that he could draw a diagram of the machine he has in mind. Or consider a famous passage from the Second Dialogue of the *Epilogue to the Satires* (he is referring to satire itself):

> O sacred Weapon! left for truth's defense,
> Sole Dread of Folly, Vice, and Insolence!
> To all but Heav'n-directed hands deny'd,
> The Muse may give thee, but the Gods must guide.
> Rev'rent I touch thee! but with honest zeal;
> To rowze the Watchmen of the Publick Weal,
> To Virtue's Work provoke the tardy Hall,[6]
> And goad the Prelate slumb'ring in his Stall.
> Ye tinsel Insects! whom a Court maintains,
> That counts your Beauties only by your Stains,
> Spin all your Cobwebs o'er the Eye of Day!
> The Muse's wing shall brush you all away.[7]

"Tinsel" to me means "shining or glittering like cheap metal foil," [8] and my natural image of a "tinsel insect" would be some kind of beetle ("this Bug with gilded wings"). But the word can mean no more than "pretentiously showy" and so may not have been intended to identify the kind of insect Pope has in mind. "Stains," however, can hardly mean anything else than moths or butterflies ("Innumerable of stains and splendid dyes, As are the tiger-moth's deep-damask'd wings"). But the trouble with that is that Pope's insects spin cobwebs, which no butterfly or moth can do. I think we shall do Pope no injustice if we conclude that his insects have the combined characteristics of beetles, moths, and spiders, and hence do not belong to any order known to naturalists.[9]

---

5. I, 58–9.
6. Westminster Hall, the hall of justice.
7. Lines 212–23.
8. My sense of the word is probably affected by unconscious false etymology: *tinsel* from *tin*. The word is actually derived from French *étincelle*.
9. "Tinsel," "stains," and "cobwebs" would all be appropriate for certain varieties of spiders, but only arachnologists "count the beauties" of spiders. It would undoubtedly be a quibble to point out that spiders are not insects!

May I remind the reader again that this essay is descriptive, not judicial? Wordsworth is right in maintaining that many of Pope's images are "false"

Looking steadily at a subject, then, for Wordsworth means grasping objects firmly and accurately in the mode of common perception and then looking at them imaginatively. And we have not said all that needs to be said about the second half of the process. I have made a great deal of *I wandered lonely*, and must add now that Wordsworth had doubts about putting that poem in the central group of his short pieces called "Poems of the Imagination." In the collected edition of 1815, where the grouping first appeared, he added the following note to *I wandered lonely:* "The subject of these Stanzas is rather an elementary feeling and simple impression (approaching to the nature of an ocular spectrum) upon the imaginative faculty, than an *exertion* of it."

It is hard for us nowadays to understand why Blake, Wordsworth, Coleridge, and Shelley made such a fuss about the imagination, and why Wordsworth and Coleridge labored so to distinguish the imagination from the fancy. Make no mistake about it: it was for them a matter of vital importance, nothing less than a vindication of their right to exist as poets. In the reigning psychology of Locke extended by Hartley, imagination and fancy—pretty much interchangeable terms—were handled as modes of memory. That in itself was proper enough, but there was a strong tendency to make a total and exclusive philosophy out of this mechanistic naturalism. Wordsworth and Coleridge were convinced that imagination and fancy were creative; and they wished to make imagination not merely creative but a power for apprehending truth. It is a pity that neither of them was ever very clear on the subject. Perhaps the problem is too profound to allow of perfectly clear statement, but it is possible to be a lot clearer than either of them ever was.[1] In particular, I should advise the reader to note carefully what Wordsworth says about fancy in the Preface of 1815, but not to bother with what is said there about the imagination, for he will only find it confusing. Here is the passage about fancy:

"The law under which the processes of Fancy are carried on is as capricious as the accidents of things, and the effects are surprising, playful, ludicrous, amusing, tender, or pathetic, as the objects happen to be appositely produced or fortunately combined. Fancy depends upon the rapidity and profusion with which she scatters her thoughts and images; trusting that their number, and the felicity with which they are linked together, will make amends for the want of individual value: or she prides herself upon the curious subtilty

from the naturalistic point of view, but I should be willing to argue that they are appropriate for the kind of poetry Pope was writing. In the metaphor just discussed, a general idea of insect-ness is what Pope wants, and he can produce it better by eclecticism than by sharp individuation.

1. The clearest and most useful treatment of the matter is by D. G. James, in *Scepticism and Poetry*, London, 1937, a book to which I am deeply indebted.

and the successful elaboration with which she can detect their lurking affinities. If she can win you over to her purpose, and impart to you her feelings, she cares not how unstable or transitory may be her influence, knowing that it will not be out of her power to resume it upon an apt occasion. But the Imagination is conscious of an indestructible dominion;—the Soul may fall away from it, not being able to sustain its grandeur; but, if once felt and acknowledged, by no act of any other faculty of the mind can it be relaxed, impaired, or diminished.—Fancy is given to quicken and to beguile the temporal part of our nature, Imagination to incite and to support the eternal."

Fancy deals with images that are fixed, detailed, and sharply defined; its effects are "surprising, playful, ludicrous, amusing, tender, or pathetic." Furthermore (and most important), these effects are transitory because the deep relationships of things will not permit a serious, steady contemplation of them in that mode. Dorothy's charming image of the tired daffodils resting their heads on the stones was for Wordsworth an image of fancy; her image of the daffodils as a busy crowd expressing social glee, an image of the imagination. He did not disparage poetry of the fancy, but he considered it inferior to poetry of the imagination. He thought that an unfortunately large portion of metaphysical poetry was fanciful rather than imaginative, because of the definiteness and fixity of its images; and he would probably have passed the same judgment on modern poetry. Imagination, in his opinion, gets at relationships that are true at the deepest level of experience. He was, in short, a religious poet; and nothing for him was deeply imaginative unless it attained (I fall back on Hartley's terminology again) to theopathy and the moral sense. And since Wordsworth was a mystic, subject to occasional mystic rapture, he felt that the deepest truth was not attained until the light of sense went out. He always connected deeply imaginative effects with the sense of infinity. So long as you can see sharply, clearly, with the kind and degree of detail that accompanies common perception, he might say, you should suspect that you are either engaged in merely practical activity or are resting in the mode of fancy. You will know that you are dealing with imagination when the edges of things begin to waver and fade out. In two brief texts he sums up the whole business far more satisfactorily than in the entire Preface devoted to the subject. The first is in the Sixth Book of *The Prelude* (he is speaking specifically of the imagination):

> in such strength
> Of usurpation, when the light of sense
> Goes out, but with a flash that has revealed

> The invisible world, doth greatness make abode,
> There harbours; whether we be young or old,
> Our destiny, our being's heart and home,
> Is with infinitude, and only there;
> With hope it is, hope that can never die,
> Effort, and expectation, and desire,
> And something evermore about to be.[2]

The second occurs in a letter to Walter Savage Landor, January 21, 1824. Landor has said that he is disgusted with all books that treat of religion. Wordsworth replies that it is perhaps a bad sign in himself, but he has little relish for any other kind. "Even in poetry it is the imaginative only *viz.*, that which is conversant [with], or turns upon infinity, that powerfully affects me—perhaps I ought to explain: I mean to say that, unless in those passages where things are lost in each other, and limits vanish, and aspirations are raised, I read with something too much like indifference." [3]

It is not difficult by Wordsworth's own standards to establish the right of *I wandered lonely* to be considered an imaginative poem. The impression that the daffodils are joyous is not for him what Ruskin called pathetic fallacy. Under steady, prolonged, and serious contemplation daffodils can remain for him a symbol of joy because it is his faith (literally—no figure of speech) that every flower enjoys the air it breathes.[4] Again, *I wandered lonely* is imaginative because the impression of joy deepens into *social* joy: since the daffodils stand for men in society, the poem attains to sympathy on Hartley's ladder. But Wordsworth was not willing to rank the poem as an example of the higher exercise of the imagination, because it lacks the fade-out. In it things only just begin to be lost in each other, and limits to vanish, and aspirations to be raised. He was quite aware of the fact that *I wandered lonely* is a very simple poem.

The Solitary Reaper has the degree of complexity necessary for full illustration of Wordsworth's theory.[5] The Highland Lass is *single*, is *solitary*, is *alone*, and her song is *melancholy*. I said that the situation of *I wandered lonely* was promising, but here is what

2. Text of 1850, VI, 599–608.
3. *The Letters of William and Dorothy Wordsworth: The Later Years*, ed. by E. de Selincourt, 3 vols., Oxford, 1939, I, v34–5.
4. *Lines Written in Early Spring*.
5. Like *I wandered lonely*, the lines had a verbalized source, the then unpublished *Tour in Scotland* by Wordsworth's agriculturist friend Thomas Wilkinson. Dorothy's *Recollections of a Tour Made in Scotland* seems to say that though she and William saw companies of reapers, they knew of the solitary reaper only from Wilkinson's account. *Journals of Dorothy Wordsworth*, I, 380. After appearing among "Poems of the Imagination" in the editions of 1815 and 1820, the poem was put back into "Memorials of a Tour in Scotland, 1803," the classification which it had in the first place (1807). It was written in November 1805, just about two years after the actual tour.

is for Wordswoth the optimum situation: solitude, in the single human figure against the landscape with more than a hint of visionary dreariness in it; society, its affections and passions presented not directly but felt in the distanced, muted, managed form of song. Actual men in crowds are to him an unmanageable sight,[6] a crowd of daffodils can stand for humanity if no more is called for than a gush of social joy; but this symbol of the singing reaper will express the whole solemn mystery of human existence. The limits begin to vanish in the first stanza with the figure of the sound overflowing the rim of the vale.

The mystery of human existence: that is the first meaning of the bird metaphors of the second stanza. The song can stand for mystery because it is itself mysterious. Like the song of the nightingale and the song of the cuckoo, it is in a foreign tongue. It is one of those Gaelic occupational chants that go on and on like the drone of a bagpipe ("the Maiden sang As if her song could have no ending"):[7] the poet feels it to be melancholy from its tone and rhythm, though he cannot understand the words. But he is also at work in other ways to make limits vanish: he pushes his boundaries out in space from Arabia to St. Kilda. And the third stanza, besides reinforcing "melancholy" by the more explicit "old, unhappy, far-off things, And battles long ago," extends the boundaries in time: from "long ago" to "to-day," a plane of extension cutting across the plane of space. Again, we have the extension in human experience: from the unnatural sorrows of battles to the natural pain of everyday life.[8] It is by devices such as these that Wordsworth transfigures the matter of common perception.

It would be perverse to attempt to identify the basic ideas of Wordsworth and Blake on the imagination. Blake by his "double vision" no doubt meant much the same thing as Wordsworth with his two ways of looking steadily at objects. Wordsworth might well have joined Blake's prayer to be kept from single vision and Newton's sleep.[9] But Wordsworth believed that poetry must hold firm to the vision of the outward eye, and Blake, I think, wanted to relinquish the control of common perception altogether. "I assert for My Self that I do not behold the outward Creation & that to me it is hindrance & not Action; it is as the dirt upon my feet, No part of Me. . . . I question not my Corporeal or Vegetative Eye any more than I would Question a Window concerning a Sight. I

6. *The Prelude* (1850), vii, 732.
7. The literal precision of these lines was pointed out to me by Professor David Daiches.
8. This borrows a good deal from W. K. Wimsatt, "The Structure of the 'Concrete Universal' in Literature,"

PMLA, Vol. lxii, No. 1 (March 1947), 274–5.
9. Letter to Thomas Butts, November 22, 1802. *Poetry and Prose of William Blake* (Nonesuch one-volume), ed. by Geoffrey Keynes, third edition, London, 1932, 1066–8.

look thro' it & not with it." [1] Still, detached from Blake's private interpretations, his lines state very well what Wordsworth proposed:

> To see a World in a Grain of Sand
> And a Heaven in a Wild Flower,
> Hold Infinity in the palm of your hand
> And Eternity in an hour.

GEOFFREY H. HARTMAN

The Romance of Nature and the Negative Way [†]

I

We know from "Tintern Abbey" that in certain "'blessed" moods, the eye is quieted. Book XII of *The Prelude* relates that the tyranny of sight was, as well as "almost inherent in the creature," especially oppressive at a particular point in Wordsworth's life. This time coincided with an excessive sitting in judgment and may safely be identified with the period when the poet, disillusioned by the French Revolution and with Godwin, sought formal proof in everything till "yielding up moral questions in despair":

> I speak in recollection of a time
> When the bodily eye, in every stage of life
> The most despotic of our senses, gained
> Such strength in *me* as often held my mind
> In absolute dominion. (XII, 127 ff.)

1. *Ibid.*, 844 (end of "A vision of the Last Judgment"). See Blake's note written in Wordsworth's *Poems*, 1815: "Natural Objects always did & now do weaken, deaden & obliterate Imagination in Me. Wordsworth must know that what he Writes Valuable is Not to be found in Nature" (*Ibid.*, 1024–5); see also Crabb Robinson's record of Blake's remark, "Everything is Atheism" which assumes the reality of the Natural & Unspiritual world," and of Blake's repeated charge that Wordsworth was an atheist because he loved Nature. *Blake, Coleridge, Wordsworth,*

Lamb, etc., being Selections from the Remains of Henry Crabb Robinson, ed. by Edith J. Morley, London, 1922, 6, 10, 11, 15, 23.

† Section I is pp. 129–132, with modifications, from *The Unmediated Vision* by Geoffrey H. Hartman. Copyright © 1954 by Yale University. Sections II and III are pp. 42–48 and pp. 328–338, with modifications, from *Wordsworth's Poetry 1787–1814* by Geoffrey H. Hartman. Copyright © 1964 by Yale University. Reprinted by permission of the Yale University Press.

He refuses to enter upon abstruse argument to show how Nature thwarted such despotism by summoning all the senses to counteract each other; but his reflections lead him somewhat later in the same book to think of those "spots of time" which preserved and renovated him. One of them is the famous episode of the young boy, separated from his companion on a ride in the hills, dismounting out of fear and stumbling onto a murderer's gibbet, mouldered down, and of which nothing remained except the murderer's name carved nearby and kept clean because of local superstitution:

> The grass is cleared away, and to this hour
> The characters are fresh and visible:
> A casual glance had shown them, and I fled,
> Faltering and faint, and ignorant of the road:
> Then, reascending the bare common, saw
> A naked pool that lay beneath the hills,
> The beacon on the summit, and, more near,
> A girl, who bore a pitcher on her head,
> And seemed with difficult steps to force her way
> Against the blowing wind. It was, in truth,
> An ordinary sight. . . .   (XII, 244 ff.)

The nudity of such scenes has often been remarked and various hypotheses invented, for example that Wordsworth lacked sexual sensibility, saw in Nature a father substitute, etc. But a correct detailing of the characteristics of this moment would have to note first the cause of the faltering and fleeing, which is not so much the mouldered gibbet as the fresh and visible characters engraved by an unknown hand. The name evidently doesn't matter, only the characters as characters, and the effect on the boy is swift and out of proportion to the simple sight, a casual glance sufficing. Suggested first is the indestructibility of human consciousness, exemplified by the new characters, and after that the indestructibility of a consciousness in Nature, figured in the skeletal characters of a scene denuded of all color, sketched in a permanent black and white, yet capable of immense physical impact. The mystical chord is touched, and the eye overpowered by an intuition of characters affecting no single sense but compelling a comparison between the indestructibility of human consciousness and a physical indestructibility. The same effect will be found suggested in the second of the spots of time:

> I sate half-sheltered by a naked wall;
> Upon my right hand couched a single sheep,
> Upon my left a blasted hawthorn stood;   (XII, 299 ff.)

and the description of the characters of the great Apocalpyse likewise starts with an intuition of indestructibility:

> the immeasurable height
> Of woods decaying, never to be decayed (VI, 623 ff.)

This, moreover, is coupled with a hint of the Last Judgment in the trumpeting of waterfalls that to the eye seem to possess the rigidity of rock,

> The stationary blasts of waterfalls.

But before reaching a conclusion we should consider one more event, the most significant perhaps that enters through, yet overpowers, the eye. Wandering among London crowds the poet is smitten

> Abruptly, with the view (a sight not rare)
> Of a blind Beggar, who, with upright face,
> Stood, propped against a wall, upon his chest
> Wearing a written paper, to explain
> His story, whence he came, and who he was.
> Caught by the spectacle my mind turned round
> As with the might of waters; and apt type
> This label seemed of the utmost we can know,
> Both of ourselves and of the universe;
> And, on the shape of that unmoving man,
> His steadfast face and sightless eyes, I gazed,
> As if admonished from another world.   (VII, 638 ff.)

As in the gibbet scene, the poet emphasizes that the sight was ordinary and sudden, that is, having no intrinsic claim on the mind, nor worked up by meditation. But a greater similarity obtains between the two, though it is by no means complete. Both events focus on a label written by an impersonal hand. But whereas the characters in the one case seem indestructible, here the label is a sign of human impotence. Yet the superficial label clearly points to a set of deeper and indestructible characters, for the suggestion is that the lost eyes of the beggar were only like a piece of paper, a visual surface, and that, being removed, they leave the man more steadfast, fixed, eternal. We rediscover Wordsworth's constant concern with denudation, stemming from both a fear of visual reality and a desire for physical indestructibility. And the fine image of the mind turned by the spectacle as if with the might of waters, refers to that vast identity established throughout the poems of Wordsworth, an identity against sight, its fever and triviality, and making all things tend to the sound of universal waters; subduing the eyes by a power of harmony, and the reason by the suggestion of a Final Judgment which is God's alone. The intuition of indestructibility in the midst of decay, and the identity of the power in light with the power of sound ("by form or image unprofaned") are the two modes of a vision in which the mind knows itself almost without exterior cause or else as no less real, here, no less indestructible than the object of its perceptions.

II

Nature, for Wordsworth, is not an "object" but a presence and a power; a motion and a spirit; not something to be worshiped and consumed, but always a guide leading beyond itself. This guidance starts in earliest childhood. The boy of *Prelude* I is fostered alike by beauty and by fear. Through beauty, nature often makes the boy feel at home, for, as in the Great Ode, his soul is alien to this world. But through fear, nature reminds the boy from where he came, and prepares him, having lost heaven, also to lose nature. The boy of *Prelude* I, who does not yet know he must suffer this loss as well, is warned by nature itself of the solitude to come.

I have suggested elsewhere how the fine skating scene of the first book (425–63), though painted for its own sake, to capture the animal spirits of children spurred by a clear and frosty night, moves from vivid images of immediate life to an absolute calm which foreshadows a deeper and more hidden life.[1] The Negative Way is a gradual one, and the child is weaned by a premonitory game of hide-and-seek in which nature changes its shape from familiar to unfamiliar, or even fails the child. There is a great fear, either in Wordsworth or in nature, of traumatic breaks: *Natura non facit saltus.*

If the child is led by nature to a more deeply meditated understanding of nature, the mature singer who composes *The Prelude* begins with that understanding or even beyond it—with the spontaneously creative spirit. Wordsworth plunges into *medias res,* where the *res* is Poetry, or Nature only insofar as it has guided him to a height whence he must find his own way. But Book VI, with which we are immediately concerned, records what is chronologically an intermediate period, in which the first term is neither Nature nor Poetry. It is Imagination in embryo: the mind muted yet also strengthened by the external world's opacities. Though imagination is with Wordsworth on the journey of 1790, nature seems particularly elusive. He goes out to a nature which seems to hide as in the crossing of the Alps.

The first part of this episode is told to illustrate a curious melancholy related to the "presence" of imagination and the "absence" of nature. Like the young Apollo in Keats' *Hyperion*, Wordsworth is strangely dissatisfied with the riches before him, and compelled to seek some other region:

1. *The Unmediated Vision* (New Haven, 1954), pp. 17–20.

> Where is power?
> Whose hand, whose essence, what divinity
> Makes this alarum in the elements,
> While I here idle listen on the shores
> In fearless yet in aching ignorance? [2]

To this soft or "luxurious" sadness, a more masculine kind is added, which results from a "stern mood" or "underthirst of vigor"; and it is in order to throw light on this further melancholy that Wordsworth tells the incident of his crossing the Alps.

The stern mood to which Wordsworth refers can only be his premonition of spiritual autonomy, of an independence from sense-experience foreshadowed by nature since earliest childhood. It is the 'underground' form of imagination, and *Prelude* II.315 ff. describes it as "an obscure sense / Of possible sublimity," for which the soul, remembering *how* it felt in exalted moments, but no longer *what* it felt, continually strives to find a new content. The element of obscurity, related to nature's self-concealment, is necessary to the soul's capacity for growth, for it vexes the latter toward self-dependence. Childhood pastures become viewless; the soul cannot easily find the source from which it used to drink the visionary power; and while dim memories of a passionate commerce with external things drive it more than ever to the world, this world makes itself more than ever inscrutable.[3] The travelers' separation from their guides, then that of the road from the stream (VI.568), and finally their trouble with the peasant's words that have to be "translated," express subtly the soul's desire for a *beyond*. Yet only when poet, brook, and road are once again "fellow-travellers" (VI.622), and Wordsworth holds to Nature, does that reveal—a Proteus in the grasp of the hero—its prophecy.

This prophecy was originally the second part of the adventure, the delayed vision which compensates for his disappointment (the "Characters of the great Apocalypse," VI.617–40). In its original sequence, therefore, the episode has only two parts: the first term or moment of natural immediacy is omitted, and we go straight to the second term, the inscrutability of an external image, which leads via the gloomy strait to its renewal. Yet, as if this pattern demanded a substitute third term, Wordsworth's tribute to "Imagination" severs the original temporal sequence, and forestalls nature's renewal of the bodily eye with ecstatic praise of the inner eye.

The apocalypse of the gloomy strait loses by this the character of a *terminal* experience. Nature is again surpassed, for the poet's imagination is called forth, at the time of writing, by the barely scrutable, not by the splendid emotion; by the disappointment, not

2. *Hyperion* III.103–07.
3. Cf. the Intimations Ode; also *Prelude* I.597 ff.

the fulfillment. This (momentary) displacement of emphasis is the more effective in that the style of VI.617 ff., and the very characters of the apocalypse, suggest that the hiding places of power cannot be localized in nature.[4] Though the apostrophe to Imagination—the special insight that comes to Wordsworth in 1804—is a real peripety, reversing a meaning already established, it is not unprepared. But it takes the poet many years to realize that nature's "end" is to lead to something "without end," to teach the travelers to transcend nature.

The three parts of this episode, therefore, can help us understand the mind's growth toward independence of immediate external stimuli. The measure of that independence is Imagination, and carries with it a precarious self-consciousness. We see that the mind must pass through a stage where it experiences Imagination as a power separate from Nature, that the poet must come to think and feel as if by his own choice, or from the structure of his mind.[5]

VI-a (557–91) shows the young poet still dependent on the immediacy of the external world. Imagination frustrates that dependence secretly, yet its blindness toward nature is accompanied by a blindness toward itself. It is only a "mute Influence of the soul, / An Element of nature's inner self" (1805, VIII.512–13).

VI-b (592–616) gives an example of thought or feeling that came from the poet's mind without immediate external excitement. There remains, of course, the memory of VI-a (the disappointment), but this is an internal feeling, not an external image. The poet recognizes at last that the power he has looked for in the outside world is really within and frustrating his search. A shock of recognition then feeds the very blindness toward the external world which helped to produce that shock.

In VI-c (617–40) the landscape is again an immediate external object of experience. The mind cannot separate in it what it desires to know and what it actually knows. It is a moment of revelation, in which the poet sees not as in a glass, darkly, but face to face.

4. Of the four sentences which comprise lines 617–40, the first three alternate the themes of eager and of restrained movement ("melancholy slackening . . . Downwards we hurried fast . . . at a slow pace"); and the fourth sentence, without explicit transition, commencing in mid-verse (line 624), rises very gradually and firmly into a development of sixteen lines. These depend on a single verb, an unemphatic "were," held back till the beginning of line 636; the verb thus acts as a pivot that introduces, without shock or simply as the other side of the coin, the falling and interpretative movement. This structure, combined with a skillful interchange throughout of asyndetic and conjunctive phrases, always avoids the sentiment of abrupt illumination for that of a majestic swell fed by innumerable sustaining events, and thereby strengthens our feeling that the vision, though climactic, is neither terminal nor discontinuous.

5. Cf. Preface (1802) to *Lyrical Ballads:* "[The poet] has acquired a greater readiness and power in expressing . . . especially those thoughts and feelings which, by his own choice, or from the structure of his own mind, arise in him without immediate external excitement."

VI-c clarifies, therefore, certain details of VI-a and *seems* to actualize figurative details of VI-b.[6] The matter-of-fact interplay of quick and lingering movement, of up-and-down perplexities in the ascent (VI.567 ff.), reappears in larger letters; while the interchanges of light and darkness, of cloud and cloudlessness, of rising like a vapor from the abyss and pouring like a flood from heaven have entered the landscape bodily. The gloomy strait also participates in this actualization. It is revealed as the secret middle term which leads from the barely scrutable presence of nature to its resurrected image. The travelers who move freely with or against the terrain, hurrying upward, pacing downward, perplexed at crossings, are now led narrowly by the pass as if it were their rediscovered guide.

The Prelude, as history of a poet's mind, foresees the time when the "Characters of the great Apocalypse" will be intuited without the medium of nature. The time approaches even as the poet writes, and occasionally cuts across his narrative, the imagination rising up, as in Book VI, "Before the eye and progress of my Song" (version of 1805). This phrase, at once conventional and exact, suggests that imagination waylaid the poet on his mental journey. The "eye" of his song, trained on a temporal sequence with the vision in the strait as its final term, is suddenly obscured. He is momentarily forced to deny nature that magnificence it had shown in the gloomy strait, and to attribute the glory to imagination, whose interposition in the very moment of writing proves it to be a power more independent than nature of time and place, and so a better type "Of first, and last, and midst, and without end" (VI. 640).

We know that VI-b records something that happened during composition, and which enters the poem as a new biographical event. Wordsworth has just described his disappointment (VI-a) and turns in anticipation to nature's compensatory finale (VI-c). He is about to respect the original temporal sequence, "the eye and progress" of his song. But as he looks forward, in the moment of composition, from blankness toward revelation, a new insight cuts him off from the latter. The original disappointment is seen not as a test, or as a prelude to magnificence, but as a revelation in itself. It suddenly reveals a power—imagination—that could not be satisfied by anything in nature, however sublime. The song's progress comes to a halt because the poet is led beyond nature. Unless he can respect the natural (which includes the temporal) order, his song, at least as narrative, must cease. Here Imagination, not Nature (as in I.96 ff.), defeats Poetry.

This conclusion may be verified by comparing the versions of

---

6. VI-c was composed before VI-b, so that while the transference of images goes structurally from VI-b to VI-c, *chronologically* the order is reversed.

1805 and 1850. The latter replaces "Before the eye and progress of my Song" with a more direct metaphorical transposition. Imagination is said to rise from the mind's abyss "Like an unfathered vapour that enwraps, / At once, some lonely traveller." The (literal) traveler of 1790 becomes the (mental) traveler at the moment of composition. And though one Shakespearean doublet has disappeared,[7] another implicitly takes its place: does not imagination rise from "the dark backward and abysm of time" (*The Tempest*, I.2.50)? The result, in any case, is a disorientation of time added to that of way; an apocalyptic moment in which past and future overtake the present; and the poet, cut off from nature by imagination, is, in an absolute sense, lonely.

The last stage in the poet's "progress" has been reached. The travelers of VI-a had already left behind their native land, the public rejoicing of France, rivers, hills, and spires; they have separated from their guides, and finally from the unbridged mountain stream. Now, in 1804, imagination separates the poet from all else: human companionship, the immediate scene, the remembered scene. The end of the via negativa is near. There is no more "eye and progress"; the invisible progress of VI-a (Wordsworth crossing the Alps unknowingly) has revealed itself as a progress independent of visible ends,[8] or engendered by the desire for an "invisible world" —the substance of things hoped for, the evidence of things not seen. Wordsworth descants on the Pauline definition of faith:

> in such strength
> Of usurpation, when the light of sense
> Goes out, but with a flash that has revealed
> The invisible world, doth greatness make abode,
> There harbours; whether we be young or old,
> Our destiny, our being's heart and home,
> Is with infinitude, and only there;
> With hope it is, hope that can never die,
> Effort, and expectation, and desire,
> And something evermore about to be. (VI.599–608)

Any further possibility of progress for the poet would be that of song itself, of poetry no longer subordinate to the mimetic function, the experience faithfully traced to this height. The poet is a traveler insofar as he must respect nature's past guidance and retrace his route. He did come, after all, to an important instance of bodily vision. The way is the song. But the song often strives to become the way. And when this happens, when the song seems to

---

7. De Selincourt, *William Wordsworth, The Prelude* (1959), p. 559, calls "Before the eye and progress of my Song" a Shakespearean doublet, which is right except that the text he refers to should be *Much Ado about Nothing*, IV.1.238, rather than *King John*, II.1.224.

8. Cf. *The Unmediated Vision*, pp. 129–32.

capture the initiative, in such supreme moments of poetry as VI-b or even VI-c, the way is lost. Nature in VI-c shows "Winds thwarting winds, bewildered and forlorn," as if they too had lost their way. The apocalypse in the gloomy strait depicts a self-thwarting march and counter-march of elements, a divine mockery of the concept of the Single Way.

But in VI-c, nature still stands over and against the poet; he is still the observer, the eighteenth-century gentleman admiring a new manifestation of the sublime, even if the lo! or mark! is suppressed. He moves haltingly but he moves; and the style of the passage emphasizes continuities. Yet with the imagination athwart there is no movement, no looking before and after. The song itself must be the way, though that of a blinded man, who admits, "I was lost." Imagination, as it shrouds the poet's eye, also shrouds the eye of his song, whose tenor is nature guiding and fostering the power of song.

It is not, therefore, till 1804 that Wordsworth discovers the identity of his hidden guide. VI-c was probably composed in 1799, and it implies that Wordsworth, at that time, still thought nature his guide. But now he sees that it was imagination moving him by means of nature, just as Beatrice guided Dante by means of Virgil. It is not nature as such but nature indistinguishably blended with imagination that compels the poet along his Negative Way. Yet, if VI-b prophesies against the world of sense-experience, Wordsworth's affection and point of view remain unchanged. Though his discovery shakes the foundation of his poem, he returns after a cloudburst of verses to the pedestrian attitude of 1790, when the external world and not imagination seemed to be his guide ("Our journey we renewed, / Led by the stream," etc.).[9] Moreover, with the exception of VI-b, imagination does not move the poet directly, but always through the agency of nature. The childhood "Visitings of imaginative power" depicted in Books I and XII also appeared in the guise or disguise of nature. Wordsworth's journey as a poet can only continue with eyes, but the imagination experienced as a power distinct from nature opens his eyes by putting them out. Wordsworth, therefore, does not adhere to nature because of natural fact, but despite it and because of human and poetic fact. Imagination is indeed an *awe-full* power.

III

Wordsworth's attempt to revive the Romance mode for a consciously Protestant imagination had no issue in his own poetry,

---

9. The "return to nature" is anticipated by the last lines of VI-b (lines 613–16).

or even in English poetry as a whole, which will follow the freer romances of Keats, Shelley, and Scott. But in America, where Puritanism still questioned the sacred and also secular rights of imagination, a similar development is found. The possibility of a consciously Protestant romance is what inspires or self-justifies Hawthorne, Melville, and Henry James. If the Christian poets of the Renaissance wondered how they could use Pagan forms and themes, the neo-Puritan writers wonder how they can use the Christian superstitions. Not only do we find the often directly presented schism between an old-world and a new-world imagination, in which the old world is, sometimes nobly, under the spell of "superstitious fancies strong," but the action centers on the manner in which a strange central apparition, a romance phenomenon, is imaginatively valued. In the European society in which she moves, James' Daisy Miller is a white doe, and there are those who do the gentle creature wrong, who kill her, in fact, by knowing her wrongly. I have chosen, of course, a very simple case; but there is no need to ascend the scale of Jamesian or Melvillean fiction to the final white mystery. Wordsworth's scruples concerning the imagination are Puritan scruples even though they are gradually associated with Anglican thought.

That Wordsworth was seeking to develop a new kind of romance, one that would chasten our imaginations, is already suggested by the stanzas dedicating *The White Doe* to his wife. A moving personal document, they trace the history of his relation to romantic fiction. He describes his and Mary's love of Spenser, their innocent enjoyment of "each specious miracle." But then a "lamentable change"—the death of Wordsworth's brother—pierces their hearts:

> For us the stream of fiction ceased to flow,
> For us the voice of melody was mute.

Romance and realism are suddenly opposed. The truth is too harsh, and fiction is even blamed for deceiving the mind, for veiling reality with "the light that never was." [1] Spenser, however, is so soothing, that he beguiles them once more, and the story of the Nortons, with its own "mild Una in her sober cheer," is composed.

But the death of Wordsworth's brother leaves its mark. Though Wordsworth returns to Spenser, the stream of fiction is troubled, it will never again flow lightly "in the bent of Nature." The poet seems to have interpreted his brother's death, like his father's, as a "chastisement" following an over-extension of imaginative hopes

---

1. "Elegiac Stanzas Suggested by a Picture of Peele Castle." Cf. Wordsworth's dedicatory sts. with T. Warton's ode "Sent to Mr. Upton on His edition of the Faerie Queene."

(cf. *Prelude* XII.309–16). The dream of happiness built on John's return was something *hyper moron*, secretly apocalyptic, or beyond the measure nature could fulfill. This is not to say that John's loss was the decisive cause for Wordsworth's decline as a poet—I have abjured speculation on this matter. Some speculations, however, are simply a way of describing the later poetry, and it is quite true that whether or not the decisive shock came in 1805, Wordsworth's mind is now much less inclined to "wanton" in "the exercise of its own powers . . . loving its own creation." [2] If we compare his dedicatory stanzas to Mary with those Shelley wrote to *his* Mary and which preface "The Witch of Atlas," the distance between one poet's light-hearted espousal of "visionary rhyme" and the other's weight of scruples becomes fully apparent. It is as if Shelley and Wordsworth had polarized Spenserian romance, the former taking its *dulce*, the latter, its *utile*.[3]

It might not seem possible that the later poetry could be beset by even more scruples, but this is what happens. Wordsworth's attitude toward his mind's "exercise of its powers" suffers a further restraint. He begins to watch on *two* fronts: to be deluded that "the mighty Deep / Was even the gentlest of all gentle things" [4] is as dangerous as to gaze into the bottomless abyss. He is now as careful about an idealizing impulse as about the apocalyptic intimation. The presence of a Sympathetic Nature, which is the one superstition for which he had kept his respect, for it is vital not only to poetry but also to human development, being a necessary illusion in the growth of the mind, this too is falling away. Yet the story of the white doe is his attempt to save the notion once more in some purer form. He knows that to give it up entirely is to return to a holy, but stern and melancholy, imagination.

Under the pressure of these many restraints, Wordsworth's mind has little chance to fall in love with or explore its own impressions. Self-discovery, which informs the meditative lyrics (the act of recall there is never a passive thing but verges on new and often disturbing intuitions) almost disappears. And, by a curious irony, the unpublished *Prelude*, which is his greatest testimony to the living mind, now discourages further self-exploration. Such later sentiments as:

2. Letter to Lady Beaumont, May 21, 1807, concerning the sonnet "With ships the sea . . ." (*Middle Years, 1,* 128–29).
3. There may be a direct polemical relationship between Shelley's dedication and Wordsworth's, but the younger poet's explicit comments on Wordsworth indicate rather his displeasure with *Peter Bell* and *its* prologue. At the beginning of 1808, when completing *The White Doe,* Wordsworth wrote to Sir George Beaumont that "Every great Poet is a Teacher: I wish either to be considered as a Teacher, or as nothing" (*Middle Years, 1,* 170).
4. "Elegiac Stanzas."

Earth prompts—Heaven urges; let us seek the light,
Studious of that pure intercourse begun
When first our infant brows their lustre won,[5]

do not rely, in their weakness, on the external authority of the church,[6] but on the internal authority of his own greatest poem, which is kept private, and as scripture to himself abets the flat re-iteration of his ideas in a slew of minor poems. J. M. Murry is right in feeling that the later Wordsworth represents the process of self-discovery as much more orthodox from the beginning than it was; and Coleridge, severely disappointed by *The Excursion*, of-fers a similar diagnosis: Wordsworth's opinions, he said, were based on "self-established convictions" and did not have for readers in general the special force they had for the poet.[7]

There are, nevertheless, strange happenings in the later poetry, which has a precarious quality of its own. Though Wordsworth no longer dallies with surmise, he cannot entirely forego apocalyptic fancies, or the opposite (if more generous) error which attributes to nature a vital and continuous role in the maturing of the mind. The old imaginative freedoms continue to rise up, like Proteus or Triton, against the narrow-minded materialism of his time—a living Pagan is better than a dead Christian spirit. He is not beyond being surprised by his imagination. It continues to defy his censorship, even if he queries every fancy, every moment of "quickened subjec-tivity." I shall conclude by considering certain incidents from the later poetry that show in what relation to his own mind Wordsworth stands.

In 1820, thirty years after his journey through the Alps, he takes Mary and Dorothy to the Continent. Dorothy keeps her usual jour-nal, to which he probably turned in composing the "memorials" of that tour.[8] While in the valley of Chamonix (a place sacred to the poet) the travelers hear voices rising from the mountain's base and glimpse below them a procession making its way to the church. Dorothy describes the scene for us:

[we saw] a lengthening Procession—the Priest in his robes—the host, and banners uplifted; and men following two and two;— and, last of all, a great number of females, in like order; the head and body of each covered with a white garment. The stream con-tinued to flow on for a long time, till all had paced slowly round the church. . . . The procession was grave and simple, agreeing

5. *Ecclesiastical Sonnets* (1822), Pt. III 46.
6. See the suggestion of Charles Wil-liams in *The English Poetic Mind* (Ox-ford, 1932), pp. 166–67.
7. J. M. Murry, *Keats* (4th ed. New York, 1955), p. 281; Coleridge, letter to Lady Beaumont, April 3, 1815 (Harper, *Wordsworth*, p. 528).
8. *Memorials of a Tour on the Con-tinent. 1820*.

with the simple decorations of a village church; the banners made no glittering shew; the Females composed a moving girdle round the Church; their figures, from head to foot, covered with one piece of white cloth, resembled the small pyramids of the Glacier, which were before our eyes; and it was impossible to look at one and the other without fancifully connecting them together. Imagine the *moving* Figures, like a stream of pyramids,—the white Church, the half-concealed Village, and the Glacier close behind, among pine-trees,—a pure sun shining over all! and remember that these objects were seen at the base of those enormous mountains, and you may have some faint notion of the effect produced upon us by that beautiful spectacle.[9]

Wordsworth is inspired by this to a 'progress poem' entitled "Processions. Suggested on a Sabbath Morning in the Vale of Chamouny" which traces the spirit of religious ceremonies from ancient times to the present. The Alps, archaic strongholds, allow him to recognize in Pagan ritual the impure basis of Christian pageantry. Shrill canticles have yielded to sober litanies; silver bells and pompous decorations to "hooded vestments fair"; and noisy feasts to an assembly breathing "a Spirit more subdued and soft." Moreover, as he looks on, another archaic vestige suggests itself, which is hinted at in Dorothy's account: that the procession is born of the mountain, like the white pillars above it. Indeed, the glacier columns, juxtaposed with the moving column of white figures, bring to mind the theory of Creation by Metamorphosis. The mountain, in this Blakean insight, is "men seen afar."

Wordsworth is strangely frightened at this—not at the mere thought of metamorphosis but at a reflexive knowledge connected with it. He realizes he has viewed more than a transformed archaic ritual, or ancient truth: he has seen the *source* of that truth in his mind's excited and spontaneous joining of the living stream of people to the frozen of nature. As in his greatest poetry, the mind is moved by itself after being moved by something external. He writes a stanza similar in tenor and directness to the apostrophe to Imagination in the sixth book of *The Prelude,* similar at least in its magnificent opening:

> Trembling, I look upon the secret springs
> Of that licentious craving in the mind
> To act the God among external things,
> To bind, on apt suggestion, or unbind;
> And marvel not that antique Faith inclined
> To crowd the world with metamorphosis,
> Vouchsafed in pity or in wrath assigned;
> Such insolent temptations wouldst thou miss,
> Avoid these sights; nor brood o'er Fable's dark abyss!

9. Journal for September 16, 1820: *PW*, 3, 484–85.

Wordsworth's reaction, visceral first, pontific later, differs from the usual religious decision to relinquish a profane subject or style. He does not say, in Herbert's sweet manner, farewell dark fables, or censor their use in Christian poetry. But he turns in the moment, and explicitly, from a power of his own mind without which poetry is not conceivable. It is not fabling merely, but "Fable's dark abyss"—the mind of man itself—he now fears to look on. He is afraid of fables because of their reaction on a mind that might brood too pregnantly on what they reveal of its power. Yet at the time of *The White Doe* he had still tried to 'convert' a fable by purifying its superstition and cleansing its mystery: the doe is not a metamorphosed spirit and her powers of sympathy are due to natural not supernatural causes. What a difference, also, between this sacred tremor and his earlier, almost cavalier attitude toward all mythologies! In 1798, and again in 1814, he professes to be unalarmed at their conceptions because of the greater "fear and awe" that fall on him when he regards "the Mind of Man— / My haunt, and the main region of my song." He did not fear his fear then as he does now, trembling before his own creative will.

Wordsworth's diffidence is no sudden thing; we found it at the beginning of his career, and related it to an extraordinary, apocalyptic consciousness of self. At that time religion seemed to him too much a product of that same apocalyptic consciousness. Nature had to be defended against a supernatural religion as well as against the barren eye of Science. Was it ever meant, he asks,

> That this majestic imagery, the clouds
> The ocean and the firmament of heaven
> Should lie a barren picture on the mind? [1]

In the later poetry, however, religion has changed its role. It now protects rather than threatens nature. He begins to identify with the Anglo-Catholic concept of the *via media* his ideal of Nature, of England, even of Poetry. The poet, he had said in 1802, is "the rock of defence for human nature; an upholder and preserver, carrying everywhere with him relationship and love." He now sees the church as part of that rock: an *ecclesia* mediating by a divine principle of mercy the sterner demands of God, State, and Imagination, demands which have often threatened human nature, and led to individual or collective fanaticisms. Religion and imagination are intervolved (Wordsworth and Blake are in perfect accord on *this*), and whereas Catholicism incites an apocalyptic response:

1. From an addendum to "The Ruined Cottage," *PW*, 5, 402. Cf. Barfield's remarks on "the liberation of images" in *Saving the Appearances*, p. 132 and passim.

> Mine ear has rung, my spirit sunk subdued,
> Sharing the strong emotion of the crowd,
> When each pale brow to dread hosannas bowed
> While clouds of incense mounting veiled the rood,
> That glimmered like a pine-tree dimly viewed
> Through Alpine vapours . . .

the Anglican Church, which is the *religio loci* corresponding to the *genius loci* of England, rejects such appalling rites in the hope that nature, man, and God constitute ultimately "one society":

> the Sun with his first smile
> Shall greet that symbol crowning the low Pile:
> And the fresh air of incense-breathing morn
> Shall wooingly embrace it; and green moss
> Creep round its arms through centuries unborn.

Covenant has replaced, as completely as possible, apocalypse: his emblem marries nature, time, and the spirit.

The *Ecclesiastical Sonnets,* from which the above extracts are taken,[2] show Wordsworth is suspicious of everything that could rouse the apocalyptic passions. This is also an important clue to his later politics, which seem illiberal, apostate even; a failure of nerve like his poetry. The evidence against him is indeed black. "That such a man," cries Shelley, "should be such a poet!" Shelley did not know Wordsworth personally, but even the faithful Crabb Robinson, who made all the possible allowances, is compelled to address Dorothy in 1827: "I assure you it gives me a real pain when I think that some further commentator may possibly here-after write: 'This great poet survived to the fifth decennary of the nineteenth century, but he appears to have died in the year 1814, as far as life consisted in an active sympathy with the temporary [viz. temporal] welfare of his fellow-creatures.' "[3] Only in matters of Church doctrine, as distinguished from Church or national politics, does something of Wordsworth's liberalism remain. His views, says H. N. Fairchild, praising where he thinks to blame, are "wholly consistent with modern Christian liberalism . . . very loose and vague, however, for a nineteenth-century High Church-man."[4]

Wordsworth, it is clear, has passed from the idea that change (let alone revolutionary change) intends a repossession of the earth to the idea that it might cause a greater dispossession than ever. Harper has documented his panic fear of change. It is a deeply emotional and imaginative thing, and has almost no relation to his own very small prosperity. The Reform Bill of 1832, for instance, seems

2. Pt. III, 49: *PW, 3,* 403–04.
3. The quotations from Shelley and Crabb Robinson are found in two hard-hitting chapters (23–24) of Harper's *Wordsworth.*
4. *Religious Thought, 3,* 260.

to him to herald a revolt of the masses. He prophesies ruin and destruction to England and thinks of having to leave it. His jeremiads indicate a soul which knows itself too well, and is still afraid in others of those "blasts of music" and "daring sympathies with power" to which he had given ear at the time of the French Revolution.[5]

Dark thoughts—"blind thoughts" as he calls them in "Resolution and Independence"—certainly continue to impinge on him. Yet how deep they lie, almost too deep for notice. They come to the surface only in matters of politics, and in exceptionally self-conscious verses, like those in memory of Chamonix. The most famous of the River Duddon sonnets, the "After-thought" of the series, runs truer to course. The whole series, less conventional than it seems, participates in the poet's desire to bind together the powers of his mind and of nature; and to know this illumines the character of his final sonnet.

The "After-thought" begins very simply:

> I thought of Thee, my partner and my guide,
> As being passed away.

It makes us wonder, this quiet human directness, whom the poet is addressing, but then Willard Sperry's observation that "his brief for nature's morality was based upon her openness to our address" [6] comes to mind. The more remarkable aspect of the verses is what Wordsworth can have meant by the river "passing away."

He must have recalled the prophecy of streams shrinking in the final fire, of "Old Ocean, in his bed left singed and bare." [7] This must have come to him and threatened the entire basis of his sonnets, which is the partnership of mind and nature. Or is it his own death which he foresaw, as in "Tintern Abbey"? But why, in that case, would he talk of Duddon's death rather than of his own?

I suspect, in any case, that the personal fact of his dying seemed to him a small matter compared to the river's loss and the foreboded severing of the loves of man and nature.[8] Duddon is mortal in that it may die in man or to him as he grows older, but especially in that it may die to the human imagination, generally, on Wordsworth's death. For if his special mission among poets is to marry nature to the mind, his death takes on a cosmic meaning. The rest of the poem, of course, dispels his strange fear concerning Duddon:

5. *Prelude* X.437–63.
6. *Wordsworth's Anti-Climax* (Cambridge, Mass., 1935), p. 184.
7. *Prelude* V.33; cf. II Peter 3:10 and "Lycidas," lines 132–33. In the last of the *Ecclesiastical Sonnets*, the scriptural "there shall be no more sea" (Revelation) is quietly displaced by a reference to the "living waters."
8. Cf. Intimations Ode, st. xi.

> —Vain sympathies!
> For, backward, Duddon! as I cast my eyes,
> I see what was, and is, and will abide;
> Still glides the Stream, and shall for ever glide;
> The Form remains, the Function never dies;
> While we, the brave, the mighty, and the wise,
> We Men, who in our morn of youth defied
> The elements, must vanish;—be 'it so!
> Enough, if something from our hands have power
> To live, and act, and serve the future hour;
> And if, as toward the silent tomb we go,
> Through love, through hope, and faith's transcendent dower,
> We feel that we are greater than we know.

This is pure consolation and too easy. His sympathies (for the stream!) are "vain" because nature outlives man and will continue to inspire him; and because man, too, has the promise, through religion, of an immortality that hopefully does not exclude the tie of nature.

Yet the distance between "Tintern Abbey" and the River Duddon "After-thought" is not great. The primary experience is one of nature, of the Wye or the Duddon or other great presences. In the earlier poems we are told directly of how the cataracts haunted the boy or how the objects of nature "lay upon his mind like substances" and "perplexed the bodily sense." The same kind of perplexity is produced by the appearance of the white doe. The mystery in nature is that of our relation to it, which is darkly sympathetic, so that Goethe calls it "das offenbare Geheimniss," an incumbent natural mystery. But this experience of relationship, open to all, is followed by the further mystery of its diminution, also shared by all. The poet who returns to Tintern Abbey knows his loss; he sees it in the glass of the landscape, darkly; and a prophetic fear, despite nature's continuing importance, leads him to envisage severance and even death. The conclusion that his death may mean the passing away of nature from the human mind is not yet drawn, for he prays that his sister may continue a relationship to which he is dying. But in the "after-thought" his fear touches that furthest point. It does so fleetingly, yet still bespeaks either a delusion of grandeur or a remarkable conviction that man and nature are growing irremediably apart, and that the gap between them, whether a historical error or a providential test, already verges on apocalypse. "The sun strengthens us no more, neither does the moon." [9]

The burden of this secret consciousness in Wordsworth should not be underestimated. It is he who stands between us and the

9. D. H. Lawrence, *Apocalypse* (London, 1932).

death of nature; and this is also the truest justification for the
"egotistical sublime" in his poetry. He values his own lightest feeling for the sufficiencies of mother earth—

> The night that calms, the day that cheers;
> The common growth of mother-earth
> Suffices me—her tears, her mirth
> Her humblest mirth and tears [1]

—because her call to him, unregarded, augurs a loss in our capacity
to respond to nature, and hence the virtual opposite of that "great
consummation" of which he sings in the verses that preface the 1814
Excursion. He feels that he must personally fasten or newcreate
the links between nature and the human mind. The "Adonais"
Shelley laments is strangely like his own conception of himself.

I may seem to exaggerate Wordsworth's sense of mission; but no
one has yet explained the heart-sickness and melancholia of the aging poet. These are prompted, of course, by political fears (which
are really imaginative fears) and by personal grief, yet do they differ,
except in persistence, from earlier dejections? Is his "fixed despondency, uncorrected" [2] human weakness merely, and the effect
of old age, or may it not accord with his own younger picture of
himself as a "meditative, oft a suffering man"? [3] What his meditations were, and why linked intimately to a certain kind of suffering,
may now be clear. The selfhood Wordsworth knew, and which is
always related to a fear of the death of nature, is at first alleviated
by his sense of special mission, then cruelly confirmed by what he
takes to be his growing isolation. [4] At the time of "Michael," he is
still thinking "Of youthful Poets, who among these hills / Will be
my second self when I am gone"; it is in hope of these that he spins
his homely ballads. But he never recognizes Shelley or Keats or any
of the following generation as his second self. He is a stubborn,

---

1. *Peter Bell,* Prologue.
2. Edward Quillinan to Crabb Robinson, letter of October 14, 1849 (quoted
in Harper, *Wordsworth,* p. 609): "You
will find your old and faithful friend,
the poet, pretty much as he was on
your last visit. The same social cheerfulness — company cheerfulness — the
same fixed despondency, uncorrected
[an illusion to Bk. IV of *The Excursion,* 'Despondency Corrected']. I
esteem him for both; I love him best
for the latter."
3. *Prelude* (1805) XIII. 126.
4. This isolation is more the result
of a spiritual judgment brought by
Wordsworth against his age than an
apparent fact. It is true that the
Poems of 1807 received a more
overtly hostile reception than *Lyrical
Ballads;* the former, indeed, were com-

paratively well received (cf. Oswald
Doughty, "The Reception of Wordsworth by His Contemporaries," *English Miscellany,* ed. M. Praz, *13,*
Rome, 1962, 81–97). But his reputation grows into national fame, even
if we discount the acknowledgments he
receives from close friends like Coleridge and Lamb, and from the Leigh
Hunt circle. Leigh Hunt writes in his
Feast of the Poets (1814) that Wordsworth is "capable of being at the head
of a new and great age of poetry; and
in point of fact, I do not deny he is so
already, as the greatest poet of the
present." Wordsworth's notorious judgment of Keats's Hymn to Pan
(*Endymion*) as "a pretty piece of
paganism" shows either provincial
bigotry or an acute and intransigent
awareness of his own difference.

old, opinionated man—perhaps; the fact remains that Shelley and
Keats, though concerned with the humanizing of imagination, have
greater affinities with the Renaissance poets and that these have
greater affinities with one another than Wordsworth has with any of
them. Milton, whose sense of mission is as strong as his, could turn
to Spenser and even to Virgil; Blake, though almost unknown in
his time, thought of himself as continuing or correcting Milton
and the Bible; but Wordsworth, despite his love for the older
writers, and especially for Milton, can turn to no one in his desire
to save nature for the human imagination. He is the most isolated
figure among the great English poets.

HUMPHRY HOUSE

Kubla Khan, Christabel and *Dejection* †

If Coleridge had never published his Preface, who would have
thought of "Kubla Khan" as a fragment? Who would have guessed
at a dream? Who, without the confession, would have supposed that
"in consequence of a slight indisposition, an anodyne had been pre-
scribed"? Who would have thought it nothing but a "psychological
curiosity"? Who, later, would have dared to talk of its "patchwork
brilliance"? [1] Coleridge played, out of modesty, straight into the
hands of critics.

Were it not for Livingston Lowes, it would hardly still be necessary to point out the poem's essential unity and the relation between
its two parts. But Lowes's book has such deserved prestige for other
reasons that his view may still have underserved currency. He treats
the relation between the parts as "inconsequential".

> With utter inconsequence, as the caves of ice glance and are
> gone, the Abyssinian damsel with a dulcimer is there, a tantalising
> phantom of a dream-remembered dream, unlocalized, without the
> slightest sense of unreality, in space; while the Tartar youth with
> flashing eyes is projected against the background of that twice
> phantasmal dome in air, dream-built within the dream. It is a

† From *Coleridge: The Clark Lectures
1951–52* by Humphry House (London:
Rupert Hart-Davis, 1953). Reprinted
by permission of the publisher.
1. P. H. B. Lyon, *The Discovery of
Poetry,* p. 101.

bafflingly complex involution—dreams within dreams, like a nest of Oriental ivories, "sphere in sphere".[2]

He also talks of the "vivid incoherence" of the second part.[3] This shows, more clearly than anything could, the prejudice under which readers labour from having been told beforehand that the poem was a dream, or the result of a dream. For it is exactly on the relationship between these two parts that the poem's character and the whole interpretation of it depend.

The "flashing eyes and floating hair" could only have been attributed to a "Tartar youth" by somebody who had momentarily forgotten the *Phaedrus*, say, and *A Midsummer Night's Dream*. For this is poetic frenzy, and the "symphony and song" are the emblemised conditions of poetic creation. The unity of the poem focuses on just that transition from the first part to the second, and the pivot of all interpretation is in the lines:

> Could I revive within me
> Her symphony and song,
> To such a deep delight 'twould win me,
> That with music loud and long,
> I would build that dome in air. . . .[4]

For "Kubla Khan" is a poem about the act of poetic creation, about the "ecstasy in imaginative fulfilment".[5] Interpretations have diverged to opposite poles of major meaning on the treatment of the emphasis and rhythm of that single line—"Could I revive within me". If a strong emphasis (and therefore necessarily also a strong metrical stress) is put upon "could", the word can be taken to imply "If only I could, but I can't", and the whole poem can be made to appear to be about the failure and frustration of the creative power. But if the emphasis on "could" is slight, then the condition is an "open" condition, like "Could you make it Wednesday instead of Thursday, it would be easier for me"; and the matter is the very possibility of creative achievement. The word "once" in the line "In a vision once I saw" then also becomes a light syllable, not implying "Once, only once and, I fear, never again", but rather indicating delight, surprise and the sense of unique privilege.

In this choice I have no hesitation in taking the second alternative; not only is it biographically relevant to point out that in 1797-8 Coleridge, so far from bemoaning the loss of creative power, was only just discovering its strength; but also the whole rhythmic character of the paragraph requires this view. The metre is light and

2. Lowes, p. 409.
3. *ibid.*, p. 363, where it is called an attribute of dreams.
4. *PW* I.298.
5. Maud Bodkin, *Archetypal Patterns in Poetry*, p. 95.

fast; the paragraph moves from delight and surprise, through enthu-siasm to 'ecstasy; no sensitive reader can read it otherwise. The verse is asserting, not denying, the ecstasy. If this were a poem of frustra-tion and failure, the movement would be slow and the stresses heavy. Another verbal detail points the same way—"I would build *that* dome in air". What dome? Of course, the dome that has been described in the first part. And if it had not there been fully described, the music of the singing and the dulcimer would not have any substantial and evident power. It is just because the first part presents the dome and the river with all its setting so com-pletely, beautifully and finally, that we accept the authenticity of the creative impulse in the second part, and find in the last word "Paradise" a fact, not a forlorn hope. "Kubla Khan" is a triumphant positive statement of the potentialities of poetry. How great those potentialities are is revealed partly in the description of its *effects* at the ending of the second part and partly in the very substance and content of the first.

The precision and clarity of the opening part are the first things to mark—even in the order of the landscape. In the centre is the pleasure-dome with its gardens on the river bank: to one side is the river's source in the chasm, to the other are the "caverns measureless to man" and the "sunless sea" into which the river falls: Kubla in the centre can hear the "*mingled* measure" of the fountain of the source from one side, and of the dark caves from the other. The river winds across the whole landscape. Nobody need keep this mere geographical consistency of the description prominently in mind as he reads (though once established it remains clear and constant); but I suggest that if this factual-visual consistency had been absent, and there had been a mere random sequence or col-location of items, such as a dream might well have provided—items which needed a symbol-system to establish relations at all—then the absence *would* be observed: the poem would have been quite different, and a new kind of effort would have been needed to apprehend what unity it might have had. Within this main land-scape, too, there is a pervasive order. The fertility of the plain is only made possible by the mysterious energy of the source. The dome has come into being by Kubla's decree: the dome is stately; the gardens are girdled round with walls and towers.

It is so often said that "Kubla Khan" achieves its effect mainly by "far-reaching suggestiveness", or by incantation or by much con-notation, with little denotation, that it is worth emphasising this element of plain clear statement at the outset, statement which does particularise a series of details inter-related to each other, and deriving their relevance from their interrelation and their order. Furthermore, the use of highly emotive and suggestive proper names is proportionately no large source of the poem's effect; it is only necessary to watch the incidence of them. Xanadu, Kubla Khan and Alph occur once in that form within the poem's opening two-and-a-half lines: and none of them occurs again except for the single repetition of Kubla in line 29. Abyssinian and Mount Abora occur once each, in the three lines 39–41. There are no other proper names in the poem at all, unless we should count the final word Paradise.

Next, the mode of appraisal which relies on suggestiveness is likely to underestimate the strength and firmness of the descriptions. In particular, lines 17–24, describing the source of the river, do not in method employ "suggestiveness" at all.

> And from this chasm, with ceaseless turmoil seething,
> As if this earth in fast thick pants were breathing,
> A mighty fountain momently was forced:
> Amid whose swift half-intermitted burst
> Huge fragments vaulted like rebounding hail,
> Or chaffy grain beneath the thresher's flail:
> And 'mid these dancing rocks at once and ever
> It flung up momently the sacred river.

We may well believe that this is based on a combination of William Bartram's description of the "chrystal fountain" with his description of the "Alligator Hole",[6] but he did not provide the organisation of the words to convey so fully the sense of inexhaustible energy, now falling now rising, but persisting through its own pulse. We have here in verse the counterpart to such later prose descriptions as that of the starlings or the "white rose of eddyfoam". The whole passage is full of life because the verse has both the needed energy and the needed control. The combination of energy and control in the rhythm and sound is so great, as in

> at once and ever
> It flung up momently the sacred river

that we are even in danger of missing the force of the imagery, as in "rebounding hail" and "dancing rocks". If we miss it, it is our fault not Coleridge's; and it sometimes appears as if readers are blaming or underestimating him because they have improperly allowed themselves, under the influence of the rhythm, to be blind to the "huge fragments" and "dancing rocks" which lay another kind of weight upon it, and to be blind to the construction of the thought, which holds together the continuity and the intermission.

A different kind of clarity and precision in the first part leads us nearer to the poem's central meaning—the consistency with which the main facts of this landscape are treated, the dome and

6. Lowes, pp. 367–9; *PW*, I, 297.

the river. The dome (apart from the biographists' concern about
its oriental connection with opium—all the more important to
them because Purchas did not mention it and archaeologists have
found no trace) is an agreed emblem of fulfilment and satisfaction,
it is breast-like, full to touch and eye, rounded and complete. In
the first part it is mentioned three times, as "a stately pleasure-
dome" in line 2, as "the dome of pleasure" in line 31, and as "A
sunny pleasure-dome" in line 36. Each time the word "pleasure"
occurs with it. So too, the word *river* is used three times in the first
part, and each time, without fail, it is "the *sacred* river": this is its
constant, invariable epithet. The centre of the landscape of this part
is, as we have seen, the point at which the dome and the river
join:

> The shadow of the dome of pleasure
> Floated midway on the waves.

Here, without possibility of doubt, the poem presents the conjunction of pleasure and sacredness: that is the core of Part One. And
in Part Two the poet who has been able to realise this fusion of
pleasure and sacredness is himself regarded as a holy or sacred person, a seer acquainted with the undivided life: and this part is
clinched by the emphatic and final word Paradise. The conditional
form of Part Two does not annul the presentation of Paradise in
Part One, though it may hold out the hope of a future fuller vision.

What is this Paradise? Those who are intent on making "Kubla
Khan" either a poem about imaginative failure or a document for
the study of opium dreams, remind us that many of the sources
for Coleridge's details were descriptions of false paradises; there
was Aloadine's trick Mohammedan Paradise to which young men
were lured and entertained with music and girls, so that they might
be willing to die in battle in the hope of winning such joys for ever.
There were, still more notably, the pseudo-Paradises of Milton,

> that faire field
> Of *Enna*,[7]

and the place

> where *Abassin* Kings thir issue Guard,
> Mount *Amara*, though this by som suppos'd
> True Paradise under the *Ethiop* Line
> By *Nilus* head.[8]

Of course we have in "Kubla Khan" a fruit of Coleridge's Miltonis-
ing, but because the Abassin kings and Mount Amara belong with
one false paradise it does not follow that the Abyssinian maid and

7. *Paradise Lost*, IV, 268–9.   8. *ibid.*, 280–3.

Mount Abora belong with another.

There is only one answer to those who want to make this a false Paradise—that is, an appeal to the poem as a whole, its rhythmical development, its total effect as a poem of fulfilment, and to say "If you still want to make that experience a spurious experience, do so: 'Thy way thou canst not miss, me mine requires'." Acceptance of the Paradise, in sympathy, is the normal response, from childhood and unsophistication to criticism: to most people rejection would mean a ruinous and purposeless wrench. But what is being accepted?

Positively, it causes a distortion of the poem if we try to approximate this Paradise either to the earthly Paradise of Eden before the Fall or to the Heavenly Paradise which is the ultimate abode of the blest. It may take its imagery from Eden, but it is not Eden because Kubla Khan is not Adam. Kubla Khan himself is literally an oriental prince with his name adapted from Purchas. We may, if we persist in hankering after formal equations, incline to say he *is* the Representative Man, or Mankind in general: but what matters is not his supposed fixed and antecedent symbolic character, so much as his activity. Within the landscape treated as literal he must be of princely scope, in order to decree the dome and gardens: and it is this decree that matters, for it images the power of man over his environment and the fact that man makes his Paradise for himself. Just as the whole poem is about poetic creation at the imaginative level, so, within the work of the imagination, occurs the creativeness of man at the ethical and practical levels. This is what the poet, of all men, is capable of realising.

I have already noticed that the name Kubla is repeated only once after the first line; and the place of its repetition is significant:

> And 'mid this tumult Kubla heard from far
> Ancestral voices prophesying war!

This is essential to the full unity of the conception: the Paradise contains knowledge of the threat of its own possible destruction. It is not held as a permanent gift; the ideal life is always open to forces of evil; it must be not only created by man for himself, but also defended by him. It is not of the essence of this Paradise that it must be lost; but there is a risk that it may be lost.

About the river, again, we need not aim to be too precise and make equations. Its function in the poem is clear. The bounding energy of its source makes the fertility of the plain possible: it is the sacred given condition of human life. By using it rightly, by building on its bank, by diverting its water into his sinuous rills, Kubla achieves his perfect state of balanced living. It is an image of these non-human, holy, given conditions. It is not an allegorical river which would still flow across that plain if Kubla was not there. It is an imaginative statement of the abundant life in the universe, which begins and ends in a mystery touched with dread, but it is a statement of this life as the ground of ideal human activity.

The "caves of ice" need special attention. Some discussions of the poem seem to imply that they belong with the "caverns measureless to man"; but there surely can be no doubt that in the poem they belong closely and necessarily with the dome.

> It was a miracle of rare device,
> A sunny pleasure-dome, with caves of ice!

The very line shows the closeness by the antithesis, the convex against the concave, the warm against the cold. It is not necessary to invoke Coleridge's own statement of the theory of the reconciliation of opposites in art [9] ("the heat in ice" is even one of his examples) to see that it is the holding together of these two different elements in which the miracle consists. They are repeated together, also within the single line, 47, in Part Two. Lowes shows clearly how in Coleridge's memory the caves of ice came to be associated with the sacred river [1]; and in his sources the ice does not indicate terror or torment or death (as Miss Bodkin [2] seems to think Coleridge's ice does here), but rather the marvellous, and the delight which accompanies the marvellous; the ice is linked specifically to the fountains sacred to the moon. This marvellousness is present also in "Kubla Khan", but there is more: ice is shining, clear, crystalline, hard: and here it adds greater strength and austerity to what would be otherwise the lush, soft, even sentimental, core of the poem. As it is, the miracle of rare device consists in the combination of these softer and harder elements. And when this is seen in relation to the act of poetic creation, in the light of which all Part One must be understood, its function is still plainer: such creation has this element of austerity in it.

For this is a vision of the ideal human life *as the poetic imagination can create it*. Part One only exists in the light of Part Two. There may be other Paradises, other false Paradises too: but this is the creation of the poet in his frenzy. And it is because he can create it that he deserves the ritual dread.

II

The critique of "Christabel" is an entirely different matter: for not only is it inescapably a fragment, but the two parts differ so much from each other, that they scarcely seem to belong to the

9. "On Poesy or Art", printed in *BL*, II, 255–6; *cf. BL*, II, 12.
1. Lowes, pp. 379–80.
2. *Archetypal Patterns in Poetry*, p. 135.

same poem. The unlikeness here would have been altogether apparent even if Coleridge had not himself, as usual, used a Preface to explain that the two parts were written in different years, with the visit to Germany between them, and even if all his letters and other comments on the business were unknown.

One of the most obvious differences between the two parts is caused by his physical move from Somerset to the Lake District. In Part I there is the castle in the woodland, with oak and moss and mistletoe, a landscape which has its function only in relation to the persons and the atmosphere. There are no proper names but those of the three main persons. In Part II we plunge straight into the detailed geography of the region; Wyndermere, Langdale Pike, Dungeon-ghyll, Borodale and the rest, organise the reader's attention as if this were matter of history rather than of imagery.

It is generally agreed that the experience of reading the First Part of "Christabel" is more an acquaintance with an atmosphere than the apprehension of a poetic unity. This atmosphere is achieved partly through the description of the setting, partly by the mystery surrounding Geraldine.

One of the familiar examples of description will illustrate also a point mentioned in passing in Chapter II, the relationship between Coleridge's descriptions and Dorothy Wordsworth's.

Dorothy, 25 January 1798:

> The sky spread over with one continuous cloud, whitened by the light of the moon . . .[3]

Dorothy, 31 January:

> When we left home the moon immensely large, the sky scattered over with clouds. These soon closed in, contracting the dimensions of the moon without concealing her.[4]

Coleridge, Gutch Memorandum Book:

> Behind the thin
> Grey cloud that covered but not hid the sky
> The round full moon looked small.[5]

Coleridge, "Christabel", Part I, lines 14–19:

> Is the night chilly and dark?
> The night is chilly, but not dark.
> The thin gray cloud is spread on high,
> It covers but not hides the sky.
> The moon is behind, and at the full;
> And yet she looks both small and dull.

3. *Journals of Dorothy Wordsworth*, ed.   4. *ibid.*, I, 5.
E. de Selincourt, I, 4.   5. Quoted in *C*, p. 3.

We do not know whose original observation this may have been, but one thing is clear—that Coleridge did more than merely take over an existing observation of Dorothy's or his own, and transfer it straight into "Christabel"; because he has very much modified his own first verse draft in the Gutch book. Especially by adding the moon's dullness—perhaps he even did pronounce the word "dull" to rhyme with "full"—he has increased the mysteriousness and vagueness of the midnight light, and has reached an effect which is altogether absent from Wordsworth's lines in "A Night-Piece". which also belong with the same entry in Dorothy's Journal. Wordsworth wrote:

> The sky is overcast
> With a continuous cloud of texture close,
> Heavy and wan, all whitened by the Moon,
> Which through that veil is indistinctly seen,
> A dull, contracted circle, yielding light
> So feebly spread that not a shadow falls,
> Chequering the ground.[6]

The difference of atmosphere from "Christabel" is very marked. The whole Wordsworth poem is an attempt to expand, rather in the manner of Cowper, according to a method in which rhythm has little part; to win assent to the delight by mere accumulation of circumstance and detail. But in the result there is no particularity of mood. The Coleridge lines, by contrast, suggest, both by vocabulary and rhythm that cloud and moon are behaving oddly and ominously, just out of the way of ordinary behaviour, as if proportion is thrown out and normal vision perplexed. At point after point in "Christabel" descriptions are used to heighten the mystery by such suggestions of slight distortion in behaviour, or of contrast, or surprise—

> And wildly glittered here and there
> The gems entangled in her hair.

> in moonshine cold

> The brands were flat, the brands were dying,
> Amid their own white ashes lying;
> But when the lady passed, there came
> A tongue of light, a fit of flame;
> And Christabel saw the lady's eye

> The silver lamp burns dead and dim.

But it is all fragmentary and finally unsatisfying because it leads up to a mystery which is both incomplete and clueless. The enigmatic

6. *Poetical Works*, ed. E. de Selincourt, II, 208.

Geraldine entirely swamps Part I. I do not propose to go into the questions of how far she was a vampire or a Lamia or whether she was a victim of metempsychosis.[7] But Ernest Hartley Coleridge was surely right when he said that there are a number of indications that in Part I Geraldine is "at the mercy of some malign influence not herself".[8] She is in "sore distress" and asks for pity (l. 73); "in wretched plight" (l. 188); she first (apparently without irony) wishes Christabel's mother were there, and even after the malignant wish for the mother to be off, she will still try to requite Christabel well; she must even pray: "for I Must pray, ere yet in bed I lie" (ll. 233–4). The critical act of revealing her bosom is approached with extreme reluctance. She acts "drawing in her breath aloud Like one that shuddered". Then comes the main passage on which Ernest Hartley Coleridge comments:

> Ah! what a stricken look was hers!
> Deep from within she seems half-way
> To lift some weight with sick assay,
> And eyes the maid and seeks delay;
> Then suddenly, as one defied,
> Collects herself in scorn and pride,
> And lay down by the Maiden's side! [9]

These lines did not occur in the original version of 1816; they were not published till 1828; and that edition is the basis of the *textus receptus*. They occur in none of the main manuscripts. Their insertion seems rather to underline what was already implied, than to declare a later change of purpose; and they were, further, a protection against the misrepresentation of critics.

The whole of this scene has unquestionably a genuine horror in it: the mitigating explanatory lines were absent from the version reviewed so malignantly in *The Examiner* (very probably by Hazlitt) on 2 June 1816:

> There is something disgusting at the bottom of his subject, which is but ill glossed over by a veil of Della Cruscan sentiment and fine writing—like moon-beams playing on a charnelhouse, or flowers strewed on a dead body.

An anonymous pamphlet later "pronounced poor Christabel 'the most obscene Poem in the English Language' "—which prompted Coleridge's comment: "I saw an old book at Coleorton in which the Paradise Lost was described as an 'obscene Poem', so I am in

7. For an exhausting exploration of these questions, see Nethercot, Bk. II.
8. *C*, p. 76 n. 2. But Gillman (p. 284) calls her "an evil being, not of this world".

9. ll. 256–62; the earlier versions read, simply, for these lines:
  She took two paces and a stride,
  And lay down by the maiden's side.

good company." [1]

There are three extant accounts of how "Christabel" was to have been finished that are near enough to Coleridge himself to have serious claim to be considered authentic. Two come from Gillman, in whose house at Highgate Coleridge lived from 1816 till his death; the other from Coleridge's son Derwent. The shorter Gillman account is this:

> The story of Christabel is partly founded on the notion, that the virtuous of this world save the wicked. The pious and good Christabel suffers and prays for
> "The weal of her lover that is far away,"
> exposed to various temptations in a foreign land; and she thus defeats the power of evil represented in the person of Geraldine. This is one main object of the tale.[2]

The Derwent Coleridge account is also short and general:

> The sufferings of Christabel were to have been represented as vicarious, endured for her "lover far away"; and Geraldine, no witch or goblin, or malignant being of any kind, but a spirit, executing her appointed task with the best good will, as she herself says.—
>
> > All they, who live in the upper sky,
> > Do love you, holy Christabel, &c. (ll. 227–32).
>
> In form this is, of course, accommodated to "a fond superstition", in keeping with the general tenour of the piece; but that the holy and the innocent do often suffer for the faults of those they love, and are thus made the instruments to bring them back to the ways of peace, is a matter of fact, and in Coleridge's hands might have been worked up into a tale of deep and delicate pathos.[3]

The longer Gillman account of the projected third and fourth parts is this:

> Over the mountains, the Bard, as directed by Sir Leoline, "hastes" with his disciple; but in consequence of one of those inundations supposed to be common to this country, the spot only where the castle once stood is discovered,—the edifice itself being washed away. He determines to return. Geraldine being acquainted with all that is passing, like the Weird Sisters in Macbeth, vanishes. Re-appearing, however, she waits the return of the Bard, exciting in the mean time, by her wily arts, all the anger

1. *UL,* II, 247; *To* Southey, February 1819. The letter also says: "It seems that Hazlitt from pure malignity has spread about the report that Geraldine was a Man in disguise."
2. Gillman, p. 283.
3. *C,* p. 52, *n.* 1: from *The Poems of*

Samuel Taylor Coleridge, ed. Derwent and Sara Coleridge, [?] 1870. This undated issue first contained an introductory essay by Derwent Coleridge. I have not seen a copy of it, and *C* is my only authority for the quotation.

she could rouse in the Baron's breast, as well as that jealousy of which he is described to have been susceptible. The old Bard and the youth at length arrive, and therefore she can no longer personate the character of Geraldine, the daughter of Lord Roland de Vaux, but changes her appearance to that of the accepted though absent lover of Christabel. Next ensues a courtship most distressing to Christabel, who feels—she knows not why—great disgust for her once favoured knight. This coldness is very painful to the Baron, who has no more conception than herself of the supernatural transformation. She at last yields to her father's entreaties, and consents to approach the altar with his hated suitor. The real lover returning, enters at this moment, and produces the ring which she had once given him in sign of her betrothment. Thus defeated, the supernatural being Geraldine disappears. As predicted, the castle bell tolls, the mother's voice is heard, and to the exceeding great joy of the parties, the rightful marriage takes place, after which follows a reconciliation and explanation between the father and daughter.[4]

James Dykes Campbell said in his edition of the poems (1893) that he suspected and hoped Coleridge was merely quizzing Gillman with the shorter account of the ending.[5] Dante Gabriel Rossetti took the longer Gillman ending seriously.[6] In two modern American articles it has been accepted as highly probable.[7] But the chief objection against the long Gillman ending is plain—that, as it is presented, it makes the story seem like a vulgar, trivial Gothic Romance; and Donald R. Tuttle has virtually accepted the idea that it is simply as a Gothic Romance that the poem is to be read. The shorter Gillman account of the ending, and the account given by Derwent Coleridge, both agree in making Christabel the centre of the main interest; and agree moreover on the view that the primary subject of the poem was Christabel's vicarious suffering for her lover.

This leads to the one other interesting recorded remark made by Coleridge himself about the poem—that Crashaw's verses on St. Theresa beginning

> Since 'tis not to be had at home,
> She'l travel to a martyrdome

were ever present to my mind whilst writing the second part of Christabel; if, indeed by some subtle process of the mind they did not suggest the first thought of the whole poem.[8]

4. Gillman, pp. 301–2.
5. p. 604.
6. Hall Caine, *Recollections of Dante Gabriel Rossetti* (1882), p. 154.
7. *Studies in Philology*, XXXIII, July 1936, B. R. McElderry Jr., "Coleridge's Plan for Completing *Christabel*". *P.M.L.A.* LIII, June 1938, Donald R. Tuttle, "*Christabel* Sources in Percy's *Reliques* and the Gothic Romance".
8. *Letters Conversations and Recollections of S. T. Coleridge*, edited by Thomas Allsop, 3rd edn. (1864), pp. 104–5.

Now since the central theme of the Crashaw poem is the desire for martyrdom, and since the traditional view of martyrdom, and of the virtue in the blood of martyrs, includes the idea of the value to others of vicarious suffering, this one remark of Coleridge's tends strongly to reinforce the evidence of Derwent Coleridge and the shorter account given by Gillman.

A. H. Nethercot, whose book *The Road to Tryermaine* contains the fullest and fairest modern attempt to interpret the poem, found himself forced in his conclusion to the belief that its theme was relatively "simple and straightforward". He argues that "Christabel" was to exemplify the "preternatural", just as "The Ancient Mariner" was to exemplify the "supernatural". Coleridge used the word "preternatural" at the beginning of his critique of *The Monk*: in 1801 he was planning to publish "Christabel" with two essays prefixed, one on the Preternatural and one on Metre.[9] Nethercot links this to the lines on Joan of Arc in "The Destiny of Nations", which speak of "Beings of higher class than Man", who take on human form for their own purposes, and make

> Of transient Evil ever-during Good
> Themselves probationary, and denied
> Confess'd to view by preternatural deed
> To o'erwhelm the will, save on some fated day.[1]

Geraldine, Nethercot argues, is such a being as this, in Derwent Coleridge's words, "a spirit, executing her appointed task with the best good will". She is the agency through whom Christabel (whose name has "Christ's name in 't'") is to be brought to "an abbreviated but concentrated form"[2] of martyrdom at her father's castle. By this means Christabel would make atonement for the wrongs committed by her absent lover.

This is neat, and consistent with various evidence; but, as Nethercot fully admits, it is hard to reconcile with Coleridge's overwhelming difficulties in completing the poem, his references to his "vision" of it, all the suggestions that the theme was subtle and complicated. The underlying fact is that none of Coleridge's poems at this period can be covered by a short, neat statement of their theme, any more than "The Ancient Mariner" is explained by quoting the epigrammatic moral at its end. In view of Coleridge's statement about the importance to him, in a "subtle" way, of Crashaw's poem on St. Theresa, there seems a strong likelihood that he was hampered by problems which belong to the psychological borderland where matters of religion overlap with matters of sex:

9. *L*, I. 349; To Thomas Poole, 16 Mar 1801. See Nethercot, pp. 200–1.
1. *PW*, I, 136 *n*. The text is that included in Southey's *Joan of Arc*, 1796. See Nethercot, pp. 201–5.
2. Nethercot, p. 210.

> Shee never undertooke to know,
> What death with love should have to doe
> Nor has shee ere yet understood
> Why to show love shee should shed blood.

In the seventeenth century such double references could be carried together in the mind without any intellectual unease, and without any moral shame or awkwardness. In 1800 that was not so. Yet Coleridge, of all Englishmen then living, was the one most likely to have had some understanding of this borderland, and to have known intimately the difficulties of using that, perhaps dim, understanding at the centre of a narrative poem. He was not writing an elementary story of Gothic horror, but was trying to explore more deeply the serious psychological areas which such stories just touched in their own trivial way.

III

I do not mean to discuss the metre of "Christabel" or the controversies which have arisen from Coleridge's note upon it. But it is worth pausing to call attention, in an interlude, to the part which metrical experiment played in Coleridge's life. Many of his experiments were published by his grandson, and the Note-Books contain a number of discussions of metrical forms and theories which have not yet been printed.

Along with many others from Harvey and Spenser to Clough and Robert Bridges, he was interested in the experimental adaptation of classical Greek and Latin metres to English verse. He did this partly as Clough did, for a joke:

> Read with a nod of the head in a humoring recitativo

made a good hexameter. But these lines about his hexameters themselves carry the effectiveness a good deal further:

> All my hexameters fly, like stags pursued by the stag-hounds,
> Breathless and panting, and ready to drop, yet flying still
> onwards,
> I would full fain pull in my hard-mouthed runaway hunter.[3]

And altogether beyond this they sometimes reveal poetic achievement of a special kind. This comes about, I think, because the mere exercise of trying to produce English verses in classical metres gave him a sort of mental distraction from the *duty* of poeticising his thoughts, which was so often his greatest handicap; he was too intellectually clever. But to write hexameters or hendecasyllables acted on him like the use of a rosary on the ideal Catholic, providing

3. *PW, I,* 304–5.

a focus for distractions so that the heart-felt stream of prayer might flow. For Coleridge the attention to the metrical ingenuity acted just like that; it kept his mind off the conscious poeticising of his thoughts and left them free to run, in much the same way as for different reasons in "Kubla Khan" they ran. There is one passage which seems to me most of all to bear this out: and to be very relevant to other matters we have already discussed. It is from the hexameters in the letter to William and Dorothy Wordsworth which I have already been quoting, written from Ratzeburg in the winter of 1798-9 to them at Goslar. He had been suffering from a pain in his eyes; he had written to his wife: "a stye, or something of that kind, has come upon and enormously swelled my eyelids, so that it is painful or improper for me to read or write". Then in the hexameter verses to the Wordsworths he wrote:

> Five long hours have I tossed, rheumatic heats, dry and
> flushing,
> Gnawing behind in my head, and wandering and throbbing
> about me,
> Busy and tiresome, my friends, as the beat of the boding night-
> spider.

So much alone is impressive as a description of the state of pain. But after saying in the letter "I forget the beginning of the line", he continues, with a wonderfully expressive diagnosis of the relation of blindness to sight:

> . . . my eyes are a burthen,
> Now unwillingly closed, now open and aching with darkness.
> O! what a life is the eye! what a strange and inscrutable
> essence!
> Him that is utterly blind, nor glimpses the fire that warms
> him;
> Him that never beheld the swelling breast of his mother;
> Him that smiled in his gladness as a babe that smiles in its
> slumber;
> Even for him it exists, it moves and stirs in its prison;
> Lives with a separate life, and "Is it a Spirit?" he murmurs:
> "Sure it has thoughts of its own, and to see is only a language."

"And to see is only a language." What a brilliant insight this is into experience! It is not philosophy, but it is the expression of the concrete experience which is the ground of philosophy. It links to that Note-Book entry about looking over the Barnard Castle bridge:

> What would it be if I had the eyes of a fly!—What if the
> blunt eye of a Brobdignag!—[4]

4. See above, pp. 56 and 75-6.

What if I had no working eyes at all? To see is only a language. This comes as the finish of a sequence of thought, where it could hardly be bettered. The relativity of visual experience is a familiar theme, one which Coleridge often explored; but here he slips out in unpremeditated verse a far deeper critique of the senses; and it was premeditated just because he was playing a metrical game; and it had its immediate origin in illness.

IV

For nearly sixteen years now the original full text of "Dejection: an Ode" has been known.[5] But the current editions and selections of Coleridge's poems still necessarily print the *textus receptus*, and consequently the relation between the various versions is not widely known and its import not generally understood. The *textus receptus* is called an Ode; it is divided into eight stanzas, which altogether amount to 139 lines. But the original version was written as a verse letter to Sara Hutchinson on 4 April 1802, in 340 lines.

The whole matter of these original "verses" and of the resulting Ode belongs so closely with that long prose entry in a Note-Book which I quoted in the first chapter that I would like just to refer to what I then said: the passage is a long meditation on personal unhappiness, with this at its centre:

> O Sara wherefore am I not happy! Why for years have I not enjoyed one pure & sincere pleasure! one full joy!—one genuine Delight, that rings sharp to the Beat of the Finger!—all cracked, & dull with base Alloy!—

I said that there, in the rough, is the kind of personal experience from which there grew his insistence on the distinction between the primary and the secondary imagination: and that the secondary imagination appears not in its achievement—for the "recreation" is here "rendered impossible"—but in its "essentially vital" activity, as it "*struggles* to idealise and unify". In such prose passages we are watching a half-act of artistic creation.

In the various stages of "Dejection: an Ode" we can, I think, see these "struggles" working on very similar material, carried into further stages towards artistic creation, towards unity. I think it is the opinion of many readers of the Ode, that brilliantly successful as most of it is, as *parts*, yet it fails to achieve complete artistic unity. By comparison with "Frost at Midnight" or "The Ancient Mariner" or "Kubla Khan" it is not a whole poem.

In the received text, the opening of Stanza VII especially, and its

5. Ernest de Selincourt, "Coleridge's Dejection: an Ode", *Essay & Studies*, XXII, 1937; and also de Selincourt, *Wordsworthian and other Studies*, pp. 57–76.

placing and relevance, are serious obstacles to accepting the poem
as a whole. The stanza opens with a sudden twist of thought, in
very awkward language:

> Hence, viper thoughts, that coil around my mind,
>> Reality's dark dream!
> I turn from you, and listen to the wind,
>> Which long has raved unnoticed.[6]

And the "viper thoughts" against which this revulsion occurs are
the famous meditative stanza about the loss of his "shaping spirit
of Imagination", ending with the lines:

> Till that which suits a part infects the whole,
> And now is almost grown the habit of my soul.

The phrase "reality's dark dream" then applies to the firm, sad
honesty of self-analysis which make the greatness of that stanza.
This result has come about by taking over the word "dream" from
the original version (l. 185), where the "dark distressful Dream",
from which he turns, is the thought of his misery if Sara were ill in
body or in mind and he, necessarily absent, were unable to comfort her. The "dream" was not the honest self-analysis at all. And in
the original version the passage about the loss of "the shaping spirit
of imagination", though substantially the same in wording, follows, instead of preceding, the vital change in the weather: it
follows the groans, and smarting wounds and the screams of the
lost child. The "tender lay" is not Otway's, but William's. The
course of the weather is very important to the argument, and they
move parallel.

Another major change is this: in the published Ode the praise
and description of "joy" is divided between Stanza v and the end of
Stanza viii, at the end of the poem. In the original verses these two
parts are undivided, and form one long strain, at the end of the
poem, a strain of forty-four lines, beginning

> O Sara! we receive but what we give,

including the images of the wedding garment, the shroud, the
luminous cloud, the light, the glory, the fair luminous mist; and
these images focus not on Coleridge and his loss of joy, but on Sara
and her possession of it. It is thus a paean to her happiness, not a
wail over his misery. Moreover, this long strain contains one important and beautifully developed image which was dropped altogether in the published version:

> Thou being innocent and full of love,
> And nested with the Darlings of thy Love,

6. ll. 94–7; *PW*, I, 367.

> And feeling in thy Soul, Heart, Lips, and Arms
> Even what the conjugal and mother Dove,
> That borrows genial Warmth from those, she warms,
> Feels in the thrill'd wings, blessedly outspread—⁷

The loss of this from inside the praise of joy is perhaps the worst the poem has suffered. "Thy Soul, Heart, Lips, and Arms" and "the thrill'd wings" make the union of the physical and emotional in the mood of joy more concrete than anything retained in the public poem. In its original place the "conjugal and mother Dove" stood as a contrast to a long explicit passage about Coleridge's unhappiness in his own marriage,

> those habitual Ills
> That wear out Life, when two unequal Minds
> Meet in one House and two discordant Wills; ⁸

about the fact

> that my coarse domestic Life has known
> No Habits of heart-nursing Sympathy.

In the light of these passages the line "Ours is her Wedding Garment, our's her Shroud" acquires its force: the two garments may be the same.

The main theme of the unpublished passages of the verses was the contrast between Sara Hutchinson's "joyous" membership of the Wordsworth group, with its permanency of gladness and affection, and Coleridge's own separation from it, and lack of an equivalent—

> To *visit* those, I love, as I love thee,
> Mary, and William, and dear Dorothy,
> It is but a temptation to repine—
> The transientness is Poison in the Wine,
> Eats out the pith of Joy, makes all Joy hollow,
> All Pleasure a dim Dream of Pain to follow! ⁹

All this personal detail had to be cut out before publication, and in the cutting the sequence of the poem was altered as well as its direction and tone.

As the poem originally stood, the relation of the change in weather to the sequence of mood was quite different. The crescent moon and the "Green Light that lingers in the West" were the

---

7. App. I, ll. 325–30; *cf.* for both theme and imagery these lines from "To Two Sisters" (1807), ll. 1–5; *PW*, I, 410.
To know, to esteem, to love,—and then to part—
Makes up life's tale to many a feeling heart;

Alas for some abiding-place of love,
O'er which my spirit like the mother dove,
Might brood with warming wings!
8. App. I, ll. 243–5.
9. *ibid.*, ll. 157–62.

setting of the "stifling, drowsy, unimpassion'd Grief"; of "I see, not feel, how beautiful they are"; of

> I may not hope from outward Forms to win
> The Passion and the Life, whose Fountains are within!

just as they are in the received text; the first, more quiet, mood of self-analysis. This passes on to the pain that he has caused Sara, to the happiness of the Wordsworth group, and to the dream of his absence from Sara in illness, which I have mentioned. The change in the wind has been happening "unnoticed" during these thoughts. The fierce, active variable wind then breaks in, and governs all the rest of the poem. The wind that is the "Mad Lutanist", the "Actor, perfect in all tragic Sounds"; the "mighty Poet, even to frenzy bold", is the wind which leads into the lines about the suspense of imagination, the "abstruse research", and into the final forty-four lines about the power of joy inside the soul itself, the "strong music in the Soul",

> This Light, this Glory, this fair luminous Mist,
> This beautiful and beauty-making Power!

This wind has several different aspects: as tragic actor, and bold mighty poet it may express the wounds and groans of a host in rout together with a "Tale of less Affright, And tempered with Delight": but it is also the destructive wind from which regeneration may follow, at once destroyer and creator. The line

> And be this Tempest but a Mountain Birth

which now, slightly altered, comes in Stanza VIII, originally preceded the "Imagination" lines: the imagination has not come into the matter before that point.[1]

A case cannot be made out for the full coherence of the original version; but this major difference is important. For it is under the stimulus of this strong creative wind that the deepest self-analysis occurs, and also the fullest realisation of the power of joy, as it is actually achieved in Sara herself.

In the longer version, too, the Eolian harp is less prominent; the lines given to it are in length and substance virtually the same as in the shorter poem; and its function is rather to declare the character of the wind than to poise the doubtful question of the passivity or activity of the mind. I. A. Richards's long discussion of the harp image in *Coleridge on Imagination* [2] was written before the longer text was available; but he has since expressed (more or less) his adherence to what he then said.[3]

1. See Appendix II, p. 166.
2. Esp. pp. 150, ff.

3. *The Portable Coleridge*, ed. I. A. Richards (Viking Press, New York, 1950), pp. 15–16, 41–2.

Now I would suggest that the emphasis on it and on Coleridge's modes of imagining the relation between the mind and external nature, the treatment of his poems too much as embryo philosophy, has tended to obscure the place of the affections and feelings in them. "Dejection: an Ode" is not primarily a poem about modes of perception. It is a poem about unhappiness and about love and about joy. Of the later autobiographical poems there is least of self-pity in it, the self-analysis being all the clearer and more mature therefore, because the sense of love and of joy is so strong. This idea of joy was a guiding principle of Coleridge's life.

The "joy" of "Dejection" must be understood as involving the "deep delight" which "Kubla Khan" shows at the centre of creative happiness. To give some further indication of what "joy" meant to Coleridge I shall quote two entries in one of his Note-Books: the first comes before the writing of "Dejection" and describes a particular kind of joy in his son Hartley with splendid distinction:

> Sunday, November 1. 1801. Hartley breeched—dancing to the jingling of the money—but eager & solemn Joy, not his usual whirl-about gladness—but solemn to & fro eager looks, as befitted the importance of the æra.[4]

That belongs partly with the "Conclusion to Part II" of "Christabel", and partly looks forward to "Dejection" in the following year. The other note was written after "Dejection", probably in October 1803, and applies to himself:

> I write melancholy, always melancholy: you will suspect that it is the fault of my natural Temper. Alas! no.—This is the great Cross in that my Nature is made for Joy—impelling me to Joyance—& I never—never can yield to it.—I am a genuine *Tantalus*—[5]

That is one of the most aweful things he ever wrote.

I said in Chapter I that there are passages in the later autobiographical poems where one can put one's finger on a word, phrase or rhythm which declares, in its poetic weakness, an emotional weakness which suddenly obtrudes, as if it came there through a lack of alert attention. And I suggested also that this weakness is often due to self-pity. It is the Tantalus who cannot reach his Joy.

Self-pity is exceedingly hard to sympathise with, to understand, to assess; it is easy to sweep it all away as undignified whining, lacking control and decorum, as evidence of a deep and distasteful psychological malaise. There are many parts of Coleridge's published writings, especially in his letters, which it is tempting to

4. MS Note-Book No. 21. Add. MSS 47518, ff. 34v–35. 5. MS Note-Book No. 21. Add. MSS 47518, ff. 70v–71.

treat in this way. And he does suffer by comparison with others. There are many parallels, for instance, between his circumstances and those of Hopkins: both suffered from ill-health, the sense of isolation, and from a thwarting of the creative impulse; both planned or began many works which were never finished; both were faced, though in rather different ways, with the problem of bringing their creative poetical powers into relation with their scholarship and their technical interest in philosophy. Coleridge might well have taken as the motto or the basis of a poem that passage from the twelfth chapter of Jeremiah which opens Hopkins's sonnet:

> Thou art indeed just, Lord, if I contend
> With thee; but, sir, so what I plead is just.
> Why do sinners' ways prosper? and why must
> Disappointment all I endeavour end? [6]

In fact, this very idea is expressed in the ending of Coleridge's "Pains of Sleep", of 1803—

> Such punishments, I said, were due
> To natures deepliest stained with sin,—
> For aye entempesting anew
> The unfathomable hell within,
> The horror of their deeds to view,
> To know and loathe, yet wish and do!
> Such griefs with such men well agree,
> But wherefore, wherefore fall on me? [7]

And his sonnet "Work without Hope" exactly parallels Hopkins's contrast of the fertility and life of nature with his own eunuch-like unproductiveness; "birds build, but not I build", wrote Hopkins: and Coleridge—

> All Nature seems at work. Slugs leave their lair—
> The bees are stirring—birds are on the wing—
> And Winter slumbering in the open air,
> Wears on his smiling face a dream of Spring!
> And I the while, the sole unbusy thing,
> Nor honey make, nor pair, nor build, nor sing.[8]

The parallels in the circumstances, the ideas, even the images are striking. But the comparison is in Hopkins's favour, because he avoids just that kind of weakness. In that stanza from "The Pains of Sleep", it is only in the last line that they appear. Where Hopkins twice boldly uses the strong interrogative "Why"

> Why do sinners' ways prosper? and why must

6. *Poems,* 3rd edn., ed. W. H. Gardner p. 113.
7. ll. 43–50; *PW,* I, 390–1.
8. Dated in first draft 21 Feb 1825;
PW, I, 447 and II, 1110–1; Hopkins may well have known this sonnet, and also "The Pains of Sleep".

Coleridge twice side-by-side uses the weak interrogative "where-fore"; it occurred in the verses to Sara, it occurred in the prose meditation of October 1803; and here it comes twice at the critical point in a stanza otherwise strong and terrible:

> wherefore, wherefore fall on me?

It is a tone which his admirers have to face.

But the ending of the verses to Sara as a paean of joy was not an isolated break from a lasting mood of self-pity. She was for several years his focus-point and stay, and I should like to end this chapter by quoting without comment the sonnet he wrote to her in 1801:

> Are there two things, of all which men possess,
> That are so like each other and so near,
> As mutual Love seems like to Happiness?
> Dear Asra, woman beyond utterance dear!
> This Love which ever welling at my heart,
> Now in its living fount doth heave and fall,
> Now overflowing pours thro' every part
> Of all my frame, and fills and changes all,
> Like vernal waters springing up through snow,
> This Love that seeming great beyond the power
> Of growth, yet seemeth ever more to grow,
> Could I transmute the whole to one rich Dower
> Of Happy Life, and give it all to Thee,
> Thy lot, methinks, were Heaven, thy age, Eternity! [9]

WALTER JACKSON BATE

Negative Capability [†]

The "Negative Capability" letter is best understood as another phrasing of these thoughts, with at least three further extensions. First, the problem of form or style in art enters more specifically.

9. *PW*, I, 361–2. First published 1893. This sonnet was prefixed to the MS of "Christabel" which Coleridge presented to Sara Hutchinson.
† From *John Keats* by Walter Jackson Bate (Cambridge, Mass.: The Belknap Press of Harvard University Press). Copyright © 1963 by the President and Fellows of Harvard College. Reprinted by permission of the publisher. Deletions have been made by the author.

Second, the ideal toward which he is groping is contrasted more strongly with the egoistic assertion of one's own identity. Third, the door is further opened to the perception—which he was to develop within the next few months—of the sympathetic potentialities of the imagination.

He begins by telling his brothers that he has gone to see Edmund Kean, has written his review, and is enclosing it for them. Then on Saturday, December 20, he went to see an exhibition of the American painter, Benjamin West, particularly his picture, "Death on the Pale Horse." Keats was altogether receptive to any effort to attain the "sublime," and West's painting had been praised for succeeding. Yet it struck Keats as flat—"there is nothing to be intense upon; no women one feels mad to kiss; no face swelling into reality." Then the first crucial statement appears:

> The excellence of every Art is its intensity, capable of making all disagreeables evaporate, from their being in close relationship with Beauty & Truth—Examine King Lear & you will find this exemplified throughout; but in this picture we have unpleasantness without any momentous depth of speculation excited, in which to bury its repulsiveness.

In the active cooperation or full "greeting" of the experiencing imagination and its object, the nature or "identity" of the object is grasped so vividly that only those associations and qualities that are strictly relevant to the central conception remain. The irrelevant and discordant (the "disagreeables") "evaporate" from this fusion of object and mind. Hence "Truth" and "Beauty" spring simultaneously into being, and also begin to approximate each other. For, on the one hand, the external reality—otherwise overlooked, or at most only sleepily acknowledged, or dissected so that a particular aspect of it may be abstracted for special purposes of argument or thought—has now, as it were, awakened into "Truth": it has been met by that human recognition, fulfilled and extended by that human agreement with reality, which we call "truth." And at the same time, with the irrelevant "evaporated," this dawning into unity is felt as "Beauty." Nor is it a unity solely of the object itself, emerging untrammeled and in its full significance, but a unity also of the human spirit, both within itself and with what was at first outside it. For in this "intensity"—the "excellence," he now feels, "of every Art"—we attain, if only for a while, a harmony of the inner life with truth. It is in this harmony that "Beauty" and "Truth" come together. The "pleasant," in the ordinary sense of the word, has nothing to do with the point being discussed; and to introduce it is only to trivialize the conception of "Beauty." Hence Keats's reference to *Lear*. The reality disclosed may be distressing and even cruel to human nature. But the harmony with truth will remain, and even deepen, to the extent that the emerging reality is being constantly matched at every stage by the "depth of speculation excited"—by the corresponding release and extension, in other words, of human insight. "Examine King Lear and you will find this exemplified throughout."

Hazlitt's short essay "On Gusto" had aroused his thinking about style when he read it at Oxford in the *Round Table*; and what he is saying now is partly the result of what he has assimilated from Hazlitt.[1] By "gusto," Hazlitt means an excitement of the imagination in which the perceptive identification with the object is almost complete, and the living character of the object is caught and shared in its full diversity and given vital expression in art. It is "power or passion defining any object." But the result need not be subjective. By grasping sympathetically the overall significance of the object, the "power or passion" is able to cooperate, so to speak, with that significance—to go the full distance with its potentialities, omitting the irrelevant (which Keats calls the "disagreeables"), and conceiving the object with its various qualities coalescing into the vital unity that is the object itself. One result is that the attributes or qualities that we glean through our different senses of sight, hearing, touch, and the rest are not presented separately or piecemeal, but "the impression made on one sense excites by affinity those of another." Thus Claude Lorrain's landscapes, through "perfect abstractions of the visible images of things," lack "gusto": "They do not interpret one sense by another. . . . That is, his eye wanted imagination; it did not strongly sympathise with his other faculties. He saw the atmosphere, but he did not feel it." Chaucer's descriptions of natural scenery have gusto: they give "the very feeling of the air, the coolness or moisture of the ground." "There is gusto in the colouring of Titian. Not only do his heads seem to think—his bodies seem to feel."

II

This interplay and coalescence of impressions was to become a conscious aim in Keats's own poetry within the next six months, and, by the following autumn, to be fulfilled as richly as by any English poet of the last three centuries. Meanwhile, only a few days before he wrote the "Negative Capability" letter to his brothers, he had followed Hazlitt's use of the word "gusto" in his own review "On Edmund Kean as a Shakesperian Actor" (though

---

1. Keats had also read Hazlitt's own essay on Benjamin West in the December issue of the *Edinburgh Review* (*Works*, XVIII [1933], 135–140), where West is censored for lack of "gusto."

he later returns to the word "intensity"—"gusto" perhaps suggesting a briskness or bounce of spirit he does not have in mind). He had been trying in this review to describe how "a melodious passage in poetry" may attain a fusion of "both sensual and spiritual," where each extends and declares itself by means of the other:

> The spiritual is felt when the very letters and points of charactered language show like the hieroglyphics of beauty;—the mysterious signs of an immortal free-masonry! . . . To one learned in Shakespearian hieroglyphics,—learned in the spiritual portion of those lines to which Kean adds a sensual grandeur: his tongue must seem to have robbed "the Hybla bees, and left them honeyless."

Hence "there is an indescribable gusto in his voice, by which we feel that the utterer is thinking of the past and future, while speaking of the present." [2]

Keats is here extending the notion of "gusto" in a way that applies prophetically to his own maturer style—to an imaginative "intensity" of conception, that is, in which process, though slowed to an insistent present, is carried in active solution. So with the lines he had quoted a month before to Reynolds as an example of Shakespeare's "intensity of working out conceits":

> When lofty trees I see barren of leaves
> Which erst from heat did canopy the herd,
> And Summer's green all girded up in sheaves,
> Borne on the bier with white and bristly beard.

Previous functions, and the mere fact of loss itself, are a part of the truth of a thing as it now is. The nature of the "lofty trees" in this season, now "barren of leaves," includes the fact that they formerly "from heat did canopy the herd"; nor is it only the dry, completed gain of the autumn that is "girded up in sheaves," but the "Summer's green" that it once was. This entire way of thinking about style is proving congenial to Keats in the highest degree; for though it has independent developments, it has also touched and is giving content to the ideal briefly suggested a year before in *Sleep and Poetry*—even before he saw the Elgin Marbles for the first time: an ideal of poetry as "might half slumb'ring on its own right arm." The delight in energy caught in momentary repose goes back to the idea he had "when a Schoolboy . . . of an heroic painting": "I saw it somewhat sideways," he tells Haydon, "large prominent round and colour'd with magnificence—somewhat like the feel I have of Anthony and Cleopatra. Or of Alcibiades, leaning on his Crimson Couch in his Galley, his broad shoulders imperceptibly heaving with the Sea." So with the line in *Henry VI*, "See how the surly Warwick mans the Wall." One of the comments he wrote in his copy of Milton during the next year gives another illustration:

> Milton in every instance pursues his imagination to the utmost —he is "sagacious of his Quarry," he sees Beauty on the wing, pounces upon it and gorges it to the producing his essential verse. . . . But in no instance is this sort of perseverance more exemplified than in what may be called his *stationing or statu[a]ry*. He is not content with simple description, he must station,—thus here, we not only see how the Birds *"with clang despised the ground,"* but we see them *"under a cloud in prospect."* So we see Adam *"Fair indeed and tall—under a plantane"*—and so we see Satan *"disfigured—on the Assyrian Mount."* [3]

The union of the ideal of dynamic poise, of power kept in reserve, with the ideal of range of implication suggests one principal development in his own style throughout the next year and a half. The very triumph of this union—as triumphs often tend to do— could have proved an embarrassment to later ideals and interests had it become an exclusive stylistic aim. However magnificent the result in the great odes, in portions of *Hyperion*, or in what Keats called the "colouring" and "drapery" of *The Eve of St. Agnes*, it carried liabilities in both pace and variety that would have to be circumvented for successful narrative and, above all, dramatic poetry. But even at the moment, and throughout the next year, what he calls "intensity"—the "greeting of the Spirit" and its object —is by no means completely wedded to a massive centering of image through poise and "stationing." If his instinctive delight in fullness was strengthened in one direction by the Elgin Marbles —which he still made visits to see—other, more varied appeals to his ready empathy were being opened and reinforced by his reading of Shakespeare.

III

The second and longer of the crucial parts of the "Negative Capability" letter is preceded by some more remarks about what he has been doing since his brothers left, and the remarks provide a significant preface. He had dinner—"I have been out too much

3. Hampstead Keats, V.303–304. The comment is written next to the passage in *Paradise Lost*, VI.420–423:

> but feather'd soon and fledge
> They summ'd their pens, and, soaring
>   the air sublime,
> With clang despised the ground, under
>   a cloud
> In prospect.

lately"—with "Horace Smith & met his two Brothers with [Thomas] Hill & [John] Kingston & one [Edward] Du Bois."

Partly because he himself was so direct and—as Bailey said—"transparent," he was ordinarily tolerant of the more innocent affectations by which people hope to establish superiority. Moreover, such affectations appealed to his enormous relish for the idiosyncratic. As the next year passed, the very futility of such brief postures—the pointless intricacy of these doomed stratagems—against the vast backdrop of a universe of constantly unfolding "uncertainties, Mysteries, doubts," was also to take on a pathos for him. . . .

So at Horace Smith's dinner, which he describes to George and Tom, where he met five other men of literary interests. Their entire way of talking about literature fatigued him for the moment. The possible uses of literature seemed frozen into posture, into mannerism. Given his attempts to approach his new ideal of "disinterestedness," and the thoughts of "Humility" and of openness to amplitude that had become more specific, even more convinced, within the last few months, the gathering typified the exact opposite of what was wanted:

> They only served to convince me, how superior humour is to wit in respect to enjoyment—These men say things which make one start, without making one feel, they are all alike; their manners are alike; they all know fashionable; they have a mannerism in their very eating & drinking, in their mere handling a Decanter—They talked of Kean & his low company—Would I were with that company instead of yours said I to myself! I know such like acquaintance will never do for me.

But his humor was to return when he found himself again in Kingston's company at Haydon's a week and a half afterwards. The "mannerism" in the "mere handling a Decanter" had caught his fancy as a symbol of the entire evening. At Haydon's, as he gleefully told George and Tom, "I astonished Kingston at supper . . . keeping my two glasses at work in a knowing way."

Shortly after Smith's literary party, he went to the Christmas pantomime at Drury Lane with Charles Brown and Charles Dilke. Walking with them back, to Hampstead, he found himself having

> not a dispute but a disquisition with Dilke, on various subjects; several things dovetailed in my mind, & at once it struck me, what quality went to form a Man of Achievement especially in Literature & which Shakespeare possessed so enormously—I mean *Negative Capability*, that is when man is capable of being in uncertainties, Mysteries, doubts, without any irritable reaching after fact & reason—Coleridge, for instance, would let go by a

fine isolated verisimilitude caught from the Penetralium of mystery, from being incapable of remaining content with half knowledge. This pursued through Volumes would perhaps take us no further than this, that with a great poet the sense of Beauty overcomes every other consideration, or rather obliterates all consideration.

Using what we know of the background, we could paraphrase these famous sentences as follows. In our life of uncertainties, where no one system or formula can explain everything—where even a word is at best, in Bacon's phrase, a "wager of thought"—what is needed is an imaginative openness of mind and heightened receptivity to reality in its full and diverse concreteness. This, however, involves negating one's own ego. Keats's friend Dilke, as he said later, "was a Man who cannot feel he has a personal identity unless he has made up his Mind about every thing. The only means of strengthening one's intellect is to make up one's mind about nothing—to let the mind be a thoroughfare for all thoughts. . . . Dilke will never come at a truth as long as he lives; because he is always trying at it." To be dissatisfied with such insights as one may attain through this openness, to reject them unless they can be wrenched into a part of a systematic structure of one's own making, is an egoistic assertion of one's own identity. The remark, "without any irritable reaching after fact and reason," is often cited as though the pejorative words are "fact and reason," and as though uncertainities were being preferred for their own sake. But the significant word, of course, is "irritable." We should also stress "capable"—"capable of being in uncertainties, Mysteries, doubts" without the "irritable" need to extend our identities and rationalize our "half knowledge." For a "great poet" especially, a sympathetic absorption in the essential significance of his object (caught and relished in that active cooperation of the mind in which the emerging "Truth" is felt as "Beauty," and in which the harmony of the human imagination and its object is attained) "overcomes every other consideration" (considerations that an "irritable reaching after fact and reason" might otherwise itch to pursue). Indeed, it goes beyond and "obliterates" the act of "consideration"—of deliberating, analyzing, and piecing experience together through "consequitive reasoning."

<h2 style="text-align:center">IV</h2>

Such speculations could hardly be called more than a beginning. Taken by themselves they could lead almost anywhere. That, of course, was one of their principal assets. Even so, the need for at least some specific and positive procedures, helpful at any period of life, is particularly pressing at twenty-two. Keats understandably wavered throughout the next few months in trying to interpret whatever premises he had attained thus far—premises that were hardly more than the penumbra of the idea of "disinterestedness" as it touched his concrete experience. Such shadows at least involved extensions of a sort; and the thought of this was to give him some consolation as time passed.

But meanwhile he had moments when something close to mere passivity appealed strongly; and the image of the receptive flower, visited and fertilized by the bee, caught his fancy. The relentless labor of writing *Endymion* was producing a natural reaction. Insights, reconsiderations, "speculations" (to use his own word) overlooked during that huge scurry, were now presenting themselves more abundantly than ever before. Because the gains in having written the poem were becoming assimilated, they were at times almost forgotten. Slow development, maturity, rooted strength, leisure for growth, took on a further attraction. But in the very act of urging eloquently—and justly—the virtues of something not far from Wordsworth's "wise passiveness" the limitations would suddenly disclose themselves to him. He would begin to feel that this was not what he meant, or wanted, at all. At least it was not enough by itself. A letter to John Reynolds (February 19) finely illustrates the course of one "speculation." He starts with a now-favorite thought of his that any one point may serve as a fruitful beginning. A man could "pass a very pleasant life" if he sat down each day and

> read a certain Page of full Poesy or distilled Prose and let him wander with it, and muse upon it, and reflect from it and bring home to it, and prophesy upon it, and dream upon it—untill it becomes stale—but when will it do so? Never—When Man has arrived at a certain ripeness in intellect any one grand and spiritual passage serves him as a starting post towards all "the two-and-thirty Pallaces."

The result would be a genuine "voyage of conception." A doze on the sofa, a child's prattle, a strain of music, even "a nap upon Clover," could all engender "ethereal finger-pointings." It would have the impetus, the strength, of being self-directive. "Many have original Minds who do not think it—they are led away by Custom." The insight, substantiated by his own experience, leads him next to turn upside down the old fable of the spider and the bee, especially as Swift used it. The appeal of the spider as a symbol is that the points of leaves and twigs on which it begins its work can be very few, and yet it is able to fill the air with a "circuiting." "Now it appears to me that almost any Man may like the Spider spin from his own inwards his own airy Citadel," which will then be creatively meaningful—it will be "full of Symbols for his spiritual eye." Of course his starting-points, his "circuiting," and the achieved "space for his wandering," would all differ from that of others. If we wish to be militant, complications would result. Here Keats comes to the heart of his thought:

> The Minds of Mortals are so different and bent on such diverse Journeys that it may at first appear impossible for any common taste and fellowship to exist between two or three under these suppositions—It is however quite the contrary—Minds would leave each other in contrary directions, traverse each other in Numberless points, and all [at] last greet each other at the Journey's end—An old Man and a child would talk together and the old Man be led on his Path, and the child left thinking—Man should not dispute or assert but whisper results to his neighbour, and thus by every germ of Spirit sucking the Sap from mould ethereal every human might become great, and Humanity instead of being a wide heath of Furse and Briars with here and there a remote Oak or Pine, would become a grand democracy of Forest Trees.

At no later time would he have disagreed with what he has just said. But he carries the ideal of receptivity further in sentences that are sometimes separated from context and interpreted as a new, fundamental credo:

> It has been an old Comparison for our urging on—the Bee hive—however it seems to me that we should rather be the flower than the Bee . . . Now it is more noble to sit like Jove tha[n] to fly like Mercury—let us not therefore go hurrying about and collecting honey-bee like, buzzing here and there impatiently from a knowledge of what is to be arrived at: but let us open our leaves like a flower and be passive and receptive—budding patiently under the eye of Apollo and taking hints from every noble insect that favors us with a visit.

In this spirit he has just written the fine unrhymed sonnet, "What the Thrush Said," with its refrain "O fret not after knowledge." He had been "led into these thoughts . . . by the beauty of the morning operating on a sense of Idleness—I have not read any Books—the Morning said I was right—I had no Idea but of the Morning and the Thrush said I was right."

But as soon as he copies the poem for Reynolds, he becomes "sensible all this is a mere sophistication, however it may neighbour to any truths, to excuse my own indolence." There is not much chance of rivaling Jove anyway, and one can consider oneself "very well off as a sort of scullion-Mercury or even a humble Bee." Two days later he also tells his brothers that "The Thrushes are singing"; but he himself is now "reading Voltaire and Gibbon, although I wrote to Reynolds the other day to prove reading was of no use."

v

Wherever the more general implications might lead, he was clearer and more certain in his growing interest in the impersonality of genius, "especially in Literature." For here the ideal of "disinterestedness" directly touched an internal fund both of native gift and (considering his age) accumulated experience.

What strikes us most in his capacity for sympathetic identification, starting with the schooldays at Enfield, is its inclusiveness. This is not the volatile empathic range of even the rare actor. For the range is vertical as well as horizontal, and is distinguished more by an adhesive purchase of mind than by volubility. He might, in describing the bearbaiting to Clarke, instinctively begin to imitate not only the spectators but the bear, "dabbing his fore paws hither and thither," and, in diagnosing Clarke's stomach complaint and comparing the stomach to a brood of baby-birds "gaping for sustenance," automatically open his own "capacious mouth." But empathic expressions of this sort were mere side-effects—like the self-forgetful fights at Enfield—of an habitual capacity for identification that went deeper. When he picked up styles in the writing of poetry, it was not as a mimic or copyist but as a fellow participator identified even more with the other's aim and ideal than with the individual himself. If, when still a student at Guy's Hospital, he caught elements of Felton Mathew's style, he dignified them; and the result, poor as it is, transcends anything Mathew wrote. So later with Hunt. Except at the very start, and except for a few isolated passages afterwards, we have nothing of the routine mechanism of a copy. If anything, he brings Hunt more to life. Still later, in *Hyperion*, he was to write within little more than two or three months the only poem among all the Miltonic imitations in English that Milton himself might not have been ashamed to write.

Discussion of these larger manifestations would lead to a summary of his entire development as illustration. We can, however, linger for a moment on his delight in empathic imagery itself. For here, quickly and vividly, his ready sympathy appears long before anyone could have called his attention to such a thing or given him a vocabulary with which to describe it. We think back to Clarke's account of the lines and images that most caught Keats's imagination when they first read together at Enfield. Doubtless feeling the weight of the parting billows on his own shoulders, he "*hoisted* himself up, and looked burly and dominant, as he said, 'what an image that is—*sea-shouldering whales.*'" Much later there was the memorable introduction to Chapman's Homer, and the passage in the shipwreck of Ulysses that brought "one of his delighted stares": "Down he sank to death. / The sea had soak'd his heart through." His reading of Shakespeare, now that he was about to write with less sense of hurry, was beginning to encourage his gift for empathic concentration of image; and within two years this was to develop to a degree hardly rivaled since Shakespeare himself. Among the passages he excitedly copied out for Reynolds, a month before the "Negative Capability" letter, is the description of the trembling withdrawal of a snail into its shell:

> He has left nothing to say about nothing or any thing: for look at Snails, you know what he says about Snails, you know where he talks about "cockled snails"—well . . . this is in the Venus and Adonis: the Simile brought it to my Mind.

> Audi—As the snail, whose tender horns being hit,
> Shrinks back into his shelly cave with pain,
>   And there all smothered up in shade doth sit,
>   Long after fearing to put forth again.[4]

So with the comment he later wrote in his copy of *Paradise Lost* (IX. 179–191):

> Satan having entered the Serpent, and inform'd his brutal sense—might seem sufficient—but Milton goes on "*but his sleep disturb'd not.*" Whose spirit does not ache at the smothering and confinement—the unwilling stillness—the "*waiting close*"? Whose head is not dizzy at the possible speculations of satan in his serpent prison—no passage of poetry ever can give a greater pain of suffocation.[5]

Finally, before turning to the impact of Hazlitt, we may glance back a few months to Severn's account of his walks with Keats on Hampstead Heath during the preceding summer, while Keats was still working on Book II of *Endymion*. Nothing could bring him so quickly out of "one of his fits of seeming gloomful reverie" as his vivid identification with organic motion in what he called "the inland sea"—the movement of the wind across a field of grain. He "would stand, leaning forward," watching with a "serene look in his eyes and sometimes with a slight smile." At other times, "when 'a wave was billowing through a tree,' as he described the uplifting

4. In a letter to Bailey written the same day is the often-quoted remark, "If a Sparrow come before my Window I take part in its existence and pick about the Gravel"—later echoed in the little poem, "Where's the Poet–":

Tis the man who with a bird,
Wren or eagle, finds his way to
    All its instincts; he hath heard
The Lion's roaring, and can tell
    What his horny throat expresseth . . .

5. Hampstead Keats. V.305.

surge of air among swaying masses of chestnut or oak foliage," or when he could hear in the distance "the wind coming across woodlands,"

> "The tide! the tide!" he would cry delightedly, and spring on to some stile, or upon the low bough of a wayside tree, and watch the passage of the wind upon the meadow-grass or young corn, not stirring till the flow of air was all around him.

Severn, who tended rather toward revery and vagueness, was repeatedly "astonished" at the closeness with which Keats would notice details, until Severn himself began to catch a little of it:

> Nothing seemed to escape him, the song of a bird and the undertone of response from covert or hedge, the rustle of some animal, the changing of the green and brown lights and furtive shadows, the motions of the wind—just how it took certain tall flowers and plants—and the wayfaring of the clouds: even the features and gestures of passing tramps, the colour of one woman's hair, the smile on one child's face, the furtive animalism below the deceptive humanity in many of the vagrants, even the hats, clothes, shoes, wherever these conveyed the remotest hint as to the real self of the wearer.

Severn's notice of Keats's delight in whatever conveyed "the remotest hint as to the real self of the wearer" carries us forward to the Chaucerian relish of character that we find increasingly in the longer letters and even in the mere underlinings and marginal notes of Keats's reading. "Scenery is fine," he writes to Bailey (March 13, 1818), "but human nature is finer—The Sward is richer for the tread of a real, nervous [E]nglish foot." Reading a month or so later in an old copy (1634) of Mateo Aleman's *The Rogue: or, the Life of Guzman de Alfarache,* which James Rice had just given him, he underlines the words, "his voice lowd and shrill but not very cleere," and writes in the margin: "This puts me in mind of Fielding's Fanny 'whose teeth were white but uneven'; it is the same sort of personality. The great Man in this way is Chaucer."

VI

A fairly large internal fund was thus available to be tapped when Keats read, undoubtedly at Bailey's suggestion, Hazlitt's *Essay on the Principles of Human Action,* and bought a copy that was still in his library at his death.

Hazlitt's aim in this short book—his first published work—was to refute the contention of Thomas Hobbes and his eighteenth century followers that self-love, in one way or another, is the mainspring of all human action, and to prove instead, as the subtitle states, "the Natural Disinterestedness of the Human Mind." Since British philosophy for a century had devoted more speculation to this problem than to any other, Hazlitt's youthful aim was quite ambitious (he began the book in his early twenties, and was twenty-seven when it appeared). His procedure was ingenious, and to some extent original. Moralists trying to disprove Hobbes had for fifty years or more been stressing the sympathetic potentialities of the imagination. Adam Smith's influential *Theory of Moral Sentiments* (1759) is the best-known example. The interest spread to the critical theory of the arts; and well over a century before German psychology developed the theory of *Einfühlung*—for which the word "empathy" was later coined as a translation—English critical theory had anticipated many of the insights involved.[6] It was the peculiar fate of many psychological discoveries of the English eighteenth century to be forgotten from the 1830s until the hungry theorization of the German universities in the late nineteenth century led to a rediscovery and a more systematized and subjective interpretation.

In his *Principles of Human Action*, Hazlitt went much further than Adam Smith's *Theory of Moral Sentiments*. His hope was to show that imaginative sympathy was not a mere escape hatch from the prison of egocentricity, but something thoroughgoing, something indigenous and inseparable from all activities of the mind. Sympathetic identification takes place constantly—even if only with ourselves and our own desired future. Hazlitt's psychology, in effect, is a more dynamic version of Locke's. Instead of the image of the mind as a *tabula rasa* on which experience writes, we have an image of it as something more actively adhesive and projective: equally dependent on what is outside itself for its own coloration, so to speak, but actively uniting with its objects, growing, dwindling, even becoming poisoned, by what it assimilates. Hazlitt's argument turns on the nature of "identity." Suppose that I love myself in the thoroughgoing way that the Hobbists claim—that everything I do, or plan, or hope, is in order to help myself or avoid pain in the future: that even what we call generous acts are done solely (as the Hobbists maintained) because I wish to be praised,

6. A brief discussion of the subject as it applies to eighteenth-century literary criticism may be found in *From Classic to Romantic* (1946) by the present writer, pp. 131–147, 153–156. The theory of *Einfühlung*, developed by Lotze and later the school of Wundt, and treated most fully in the *Asthetik* (1903–1906) of Theodor Lipps, was more subjective in its premise: it signified less an actual participation in the object—less of an objective coloring of the mind by the object—than the attribution to it of qualities and responses peculiar to the imagination itself. The insight, in other words, though accompanied by the merging of the perceiving mind and the perceived object, is largely the by-product of the working of the imagination, projected upon the object. This restriction of *Einfühlung* is extended even more in the strict interpretation of "empathy"—the English equivalent popularized by Vernon Lee in 1912, and first supplied in 1909 by E. B. Titchener, a pupil of Wundt.

or because I wish to get along with others, or because I wish—at least—to be able to live with myself. But how can I know, how especially can I "love," this "identity" that I consider myself? If we look at the problem with empirical honesty, we have to admit that any feeling we have that we are one person, the same person, from one moment to the next (that we have, in short, an "identity") comes directly through two means only—"sensation" and "memory." A child who has burned his finger knows only through "sensation" that it is he and not someone else who has done so. In a similar way, he knows only through "memory" that it was he and not someone else who had this experience in the past. If our identities until now depend on sensation and memory, what can give me an interest in my future sensations? Sensation and memory are not enough. I can picture my future identity only through my *imagination*. The child who has been burned will dread the prospect of future pain from the fire because, through his imagination, he "projects himself forward into the future, and identifies himself with his future being." His imagination "creates" his own future to him.

In short, I can "abstract myself from my present being and take an interest in my future being [only] in the same sense and manner, in which I can go out of myself entirely and enter into the minds and feelings of others." The capacity for imaginative identification, in other words, is not instinctively or mechanically obliged to turn in one direction rather than another: the sole means by which "I can anticipate future objects, or be interested in them," throwing "me forward as it were into my future being" and anticipating events that do not yet exist, is equally able to "carry me out of myself into the feelings of others by one and the same process . . . I could not love myself, if I were not capable of loving others." If stronger ideas than those of one's own identity are present to the mind, the imagination can turn more easily to them. Hazlitt here develops the belief of the associationist psychologists of the time, in whom he was widely read, that the mind instinctively follows and "imitates" what is before it. . . .

The argument for "the natural disinterestedness of the mind" is not, of course, that most people are really disinterested, but that there is no mechanical determinism, such as Hobbes and his followers assumed, toward self-love. The disinterestedness exists as far as the *potential* development of the mind is concerned. Knowledge can direct and habituate the imagination to ideas other than that of our own identity. We commonly see that long acquaintance with another increases our sympathy, provided undesirable qualities in the other person, or sheer monotony, do not work against it. If the child is unsympathetic to others, it is not from automatic self-love but because of lack of knowledge—a lack that also prevents him

from identifying himself very successfully with his own future interests. Greatness in art, philosophy, moral action—the "heroic"
in any sense—involves losing the sense of "our personal identity in
some object dearer to us than ourselves." . . .

VII

Less than three weeks after Keats wrote the "Negative Capability" letter to his brothers around Christmastime, Hazlitt began a
course of lectures at the Surrey Institution, just south of Black-
friars Bridge, every Tuesday evening at seven o'clock. These were
the famous *Lectures on the English Poets*, the first of which was on
January 13 and the last on March 3. Keats looked forward to hearing them all, and, as far as we know, missed only one ("On Chaucer
and Spenser," January 20), when he arrived too late. A few sentences
at the start of the third lecture, "On Shakespeare and Milton"
(January 27), which Keats told Bailey he definitely planned to attend, may have especially struck him. Shakespeare, said Hazlitt,

> was the least of an egotist that it was possible to be. He was
> nothing in himself; but he was all that others were, or that they
> could become. He not only had in himself the germs of every
> faculty and feeling, but he could follow them by anticipation,
> intuitively, into all their conceivable ramifications, through every
> change of fortune, or conflict of passion, or turn of thought. . . .
> He had only to think of anything in order to become that thing,
> with all the circumstances belonging to it.

By contrast, much modern poetry seems to have become engaged in
a competition to "reduce" itself "to a mere effusion of natural sensibility," surrounding "the meanest objects with the morbid feelings and devouring egotism of the writers' own minds."

The immediate effect of Hazlitt's lectures was to open Keats's
eyes much sooner than would otherwise have happened to the limitations of the prevailing modes of poetry—limitations that were
far from obvious to most writers until a full century had run its
course. But the ideal of the "characterless" poet, touching as it did
qualities and habits of response intrinsic to himself, gradually took
a secure hold of his imagination throughout the months ahead,
though still later it was to appear to him as something of an over-
simplification. The extent to which it became domesticated in his
habitual thinking is shown by a letter the following autumn, at
the beginning of the astonishing year (October 1818 to October
1819) when his greatest poetry was written. He is writing to
Richard Woodhouse (October 27):

> As to the poetical Character itself (I mean that sort of which,
> if I am anything, I am a Member; that sort distinguished from

the wordworthian or egotistical sublime; which is a thing per se and stands alone) it is not itself—it has no self—it is everything and nothing—It has no character—it enjoys light and shade; it lives in gusto, be it foul or fair, high or low, rich or poor, mean or elevated—It has as much delight in conceiving an Iago as an Imogen. What shocks the virtuous philosop[h]er, delights the camelion Poet. It does no harm from its relish of the dark side of things any more than from its taste for the bright one; because they both end in speculation. A Poet is the most unpoetical of any thing in existence; because he has no Identity—he is continually in for—and filling some other Body—The Sun, the Moon, the Sea and Men and Women who are creatures of impulse are poetical and have about them an unchangeable attribute —the poet has none; no identity—he is certainly the most unpoetical of all God's Creatures. ⌣. . When I am in a room with People if I ever am free from speculating on creations of my own brain, then not myself goes home to myself: but the identity of every one in the room begins to press upon me [so] that I am in a very little time annihilated—not only among Men; it would be the same in a Nursery of children.

Woodhouse, who by now had acquired a close knowledge of Keats, found these remarks a good description of Keats's own bent of mind, and wrote to John Taylor,

> I believe him to be right with regard to his own Poetical Character—And I perceive clearly the distinction between himself & those of the Wordsworth School. . . . The highest order of Poet will not only possess all the above powers but will have [so] high an imag^n that he will be able to throw his own soul into any object he sees or imagines, so as to see feel be sensible of, & express, all that the object itself wo^d see feel be sensible or of express—& he will speak out of that object—so that his own self will with the Exception of the Mechanical part be "annihilated."—and it is [of] the excess of this power that I suppose Keats to speak, when he says he has no identity—As a poet, and when the fit is upon him, this is true. . . . Shakesp^r was a poet of the kind above ment^d—and he was perhaps the only one besides Keats who possessed this power in an extr^y degree.

Keats had talked with Woodhouse about the subject before, and had thrown himself into it with the fanciful exuberance he found irresistible when he was among serious people. For Woodhouse adds the comment noticed earlier: "He has affirmed that he can conceive of a billiard Ball that it may have a sense of delight from its own roundness, smoothness volubility & the rapidity of its motion." [7]

---

7. *Keats Circle,* I.57–60. When he was preparing to leave Margate for Canterbury, after beginning *Endymion,* he hoped "the Rememberance of Chaucer will set me forward like a Billiard-Ball" (I.147).

VIII

We have been anticipating, of course: the implications of the "Negative Capability" letter have encouraged us to look ahead a few months. Back in December, as ~~he~~ felt himself emerging onto this new plateau of thinking, the memory of *King Lear* kept recurring. When he had begun *Endymion* at the Isle of Wight, it was the sea—remembered from the cliff near Margate the summer before (1816)—that had led him to return to the play on this second venture: "the passage . . . 'Do you not hear the Sea?' has haunted me intensely." Now that *Endymion* was finished, and a third venture or transition lay ahead, he was remembering the play somewhat differently. It was probably in December, certainly by early January, that he bought a copy of Hazlitt's *Characters of Shakespear's Plays* (published late in 1817). With only one exception, all his underscorings and marginal comments are concentrated in the chapter on *Lear*.[8] They provide in their own way a further gloss to that "intensity" of conception—that identification and "greeting of the Spirit"—of which he had been thinking when he wrote to George and Tom ("Examine King Lear &you will find this exemplified throughout"): an identification especially prized when—as Hazlitt said in a passage Keats underlines—"the extremest resources of the imagination are called in to lay open the deepest movements of the heart." "The greatest strength of genius," said Hazlitt, "is shown in describing the strongest passions: for the power of the imagination, in works of invention, must be in proportion to the force of the natural impressions, which are the subject of them." Double-scoring this in the margin, Keats writes:

> If we compare the Passions to different tuns and hogsheads of wine in a vast cellar—thus it is—the poet by one cup should know the scope of any particular wine without getting intoxicated—this is the highest exertion of Power, and the next step is to paint from memory of gone self storms.

And beside another passage he draws a line, underscoring the italicized words, and writes "The passage has to a great degree hieroglyphic visioning":

> We see the ebb and flow of the feeling, its pauses and feverish starts, its impatience of opposition, its accumulating force when it has time to recollect itself, *the manner in which it avails itself of every passing word or gesture, its haste to repel insinuation, the alternate contradiction and dilatation of the soul.*

8. Harvard Keats Collection. Marked passages and comments are printed in Lowell, II.587–590, and Hampstead Keats, V.280–286.

Endymion, which he began to copy and correct for the press during the first week of January, seemed remote indeed from the thoughts that now preoccupied him. So in fact did romances generally, though he was to write two more (*Isabella* and *The Eve of St. Agnes*). On Thursday, January 22, he finished copying the first book of *Endymion;* and then, as he told his brothers the next day, "I sat down . . . to read King Lear once again the thing appeared to demand the prologue of a Sonnet, I wrote it & began to read." It is hardly one of his best sonnets—he never even bothered to publish it—but the occasion meant something to him. For he was approaching the play with a new understanding of how much lay beyond the "old oak Forest" of "Romance."

It was only another beginning, and it would have to proceed much more slowly than the other beginnings. But he was prepared, he thought, for "a very gradual ripening of the intellectual powers"; and all he can say now is that "I think a little change has taken place in my intellect lately." Then he turns to the sonnet, copies it out for George and Tom, and adds: "So you see I am getting at it, with a sort of determination & strength, though verily I do not feel it at this moment—this is my fourth letter this morning & I feel rather tired & my head rather swimming."

ALVIN B. KERNAN

Don Juan: The Perspective of Satire †

Lastly, I shall place the Cumbrous, which moves heavily under a Load of Metaphors, and draws after it a long Train of Words. And the Buskin, or *Stately,* frequently and with great Felicity mix'd with the Former. For as the first is the proper Engine to depress what is High, so is the second to raise what is Base and Low to a ridiculous Visibility: When both these can be done at once, then is the *Bathos* in Perfection; as when a Man is set with his Head downward, and his Breech upright, his Degradation is compleat: One End of him is as high as ever, only that End is the wrong one. (*Peri Bathous,* Ch. XII)

† From *The Plot of Satire* by Alvin B. Kernan. Copyright © 1965 by Yale University. Reprinted by permission of Yale University Press. Deletions made by the editor, with the author's permission.

This is Pope's statement, in ironic terms, of one of the critical problems of the author of satire. He must contrive to show in some manner that the mad world he constructs is truly mad, that it is the breech which is up not the head. The major actions of dullness —degrading, magnifying, and jumbling—are, after all, relative movements which can be seen for what they are only in relation to certain fixed points. . . .

I wish to turn now to a poem, Byron's *Don Juan*, which reveals this self-defeating, blind quality of dullness in an unusual and distinct way, and which, at the same time, will help us to place satire, and further define it, in relation to the other major literary genres.

I

> A rich confusion formed a disarray
>   In such sort, that the eye along it cast
> Could hardly carry anything away,
>   Object on object flashed so bright and fast;
> A dazzling mass of gems, and gold, and glitter,
> Magnificently mingled in a litter.
>
> (V, 93)[1]

This description of the Sultan's palace is also a perfect image of Byron's sprawling, wandering tale of the travels of Don Juan. The poem is like a new world seen for the first time in which the richness, plenitude, and variety of creation have not yet been named and catalogued. The events of the primary story, the adventures of Don Juan, take place over all Europe: Spain, Greece, Turkey, Russia, England. These countries are peopled by an enormous range of humanity: pirates, empresses, opera singers, grandees, slaves, lawyers, English peers, sailors, harem girls, poachers, educated women. This "ferment" is "in full activity," and the *dramatis personae* rush here and there into duels, love affairs, shipwrecks, slave trading, fox hunts, wars, commercial speculations, formal banquets, and divorce courts—only to come to rest at last in death, old age, or the tedium of daily life. Whatever of the fullness and variety of creation is not encountered by Don Juan in his wanderings is introduced from the side by a garrulous narrator who breaks in on the story at will to talk about such diverse matters as his own marriage, the fall of Troy, the latest styles of dress, idealist philosophy, contemporary politics, poetry ancient and modern, and the best cure for hangovers. The substance of the poem is, then, composed in part of the objective persons and events of the Don Juan

1. References to *Don Juan* give canto and stanza numbers. The text used is that in "Poetry," Volume 6 of *The Works of Lord Byron*, ed. E. H. Coleridge (London, 1903).

fable, in part of the narrator's personal memories, and in part of historical events and the memories of the race, which the narrator introduces in his digressions.

This crammed, various creation renders the Romantic view of a world too large in all directions and too complex in its workings to be captured and arranged in any neat system of thought or formal pattern. Throughout *Don Juan*, traditional forms and systems are reduced to nonsense by showing their inability to take the measure of man and his world. Plato's philosophy becomes no more than "confounded fantasies" which have paved the way to immoral conduct by deluding men into thinking that they can exercise some control over their "controlless core." The grave philosopher himself becomes a "bore, a charlatan, a coxcomb . . . a go-between." In dealing with the attack on Ismail, the narrator informs us that "History can only take things in the gross," and that the chronicle of the glories of conquest and the sweep of empire which makes up history is nothing but the childish sound of "Murder's rattles," which leaves out the infinite number of human actions and sufferings which are the truth of life. Science fares no better. Newton's "calculations" of the principles of nature—which the narrator begs leave to doubt—"I'll not answer above ground / For any sage's creed or calculation"—have led only to mechanical contrivances which balance one another out: rockets and vaccination, guillotines and surgery, artillery and artificial respiration. Religion, metaphysics, psychology, social custom, law, all received systems of thought, are sieves through which existence pours in the fluid, shifting world of *Don Juan*. Even poetry is mocked for its pretensions to tell the truth about the strange creature man. After testing many systems against the reality of life as his poem presents it, the narrator can only exclaim,

> Oh! ye immortal Gods! what is Theogony?
>   Oh! thou, too, mortal man! what is Philanthropy?
> Oh! World, which was and is, what is Cosmogony?
>
> (IX, 20)

Since all systems and forms are by their nature inadequate to life, than only by being unsystematic can the poet hope to describe things as they are, for

> if a writer should be quite consistent,
> How could he possibly show things existent?
>
> (XV, 87)

Don Juan, by and large, fulfills the implicit prescription for a poetry which wishes to "show things existent," and the result is a baffling

mixture of changes and shifting points of view.[2] Nothing, or almost nothing, remains constant: a love which at one moment seems
the source of the greatest good becomes a painful trap; spirit and
vitality which make their possessor in one incident attractive lead
him in the next to brutal and destructive actions; pleasure turns
pain and pain turns pleasure; what is now comic becomes in an instant tragic, and what was tragic with a sudden shift of perspective
becomes meaningless.

Yet, in this heterocosm, despite the poet's warnings about the
futility of systems, the parts are arranged and related to one another
in a loosely systematic manner. It will not do to call this arrangement "structure," for this metaphor suggests rigidity, a series of
modular units, of arrested, still *situations*. This is precisely not the
state of affairs in *Don Juan*, where nothing—man, woman, society,
nature, or poem—can "hold this visible shape" [3] for more than an
instant. Instead, the poem develops a recurring rhythm, flows again
and again through a particular movement, which imitates the essential movement of life as Byron sensed it. This central rhythm
comprehends and is made up of the movements of all the component parts, characters, events, metaphors, settings, stanza form,
rhythms, and rhymes.

We can begin our discussion of this rhythm on the most obvious
level of the poem, the Don Juan plot, which gives a loose continuity to the rambling collection of stories and digressions. The most
striking quality of this primary plot is its "but then" movement.
Juan's father and mother are apparently happily wed, but then Don
José begins to stray, the marriage is dissolved, and José dies. Donna
Inez plans to make of her son Juan a paragon of learning and virtue,
but then he falls in love with Donna Julia, is discovered by her
husband, fights and wounds him, and is forced to flee Spain. He sets
out for Italy, but then he is shipwrecked, cast ashore on a Greek
island, and falls in love with Haidée. Their love seems perfect and
enduring, but then Haidée's papa, the pirate Lambro, returns.
Juan is wounded and sold into slavery, and Haidée dies. Juan, unaware of Haidée's death (he never learns of it, nor does he ever seek
to return to her), is heartbroken and feels that he can never live or

2. Ernest J. Lovell, Jr., "Irony and
Image in *Don Juan*," in *The Major
English Romantic Poets*, eds. Thorpe,
Baker, and Weaver (Carbondale, Ill.,
1957), pp. 129–48, discusses the complexity of tone at verious levels of the
poem. Though my argument diverges
considerably from Lovell's, I am
greatly indebted to his insights, and
particularly to such statements as, "The
satire may merge so successfully with
comedy or at other times with tragedy
that it is often hardly recognizable as
'serious' satire."

3. *Antony and Cleopatra*, IV.10.14.
The sense of life as endless movement
and change which is central to *Don
Juan* is also the basic fact of existence
in *Antony and Cleopatra*, where Shakespeare catches it perfectly in such terms
as "the varying shore o' the world,"
and in the character of Cleopatra, the
woman of "infinite variety."

love again, but then he finds himself by strange accident in bed in a Turkish harem with the luscious Dudù, is thrown in the Bosporus, saved by some unmentioned good chance, and fights with the Russian army at the siege of Ismail. Bravery and fortune cause him to be chosen to carry dispatches to the Russian empress, Catherine, who is vastly pleased with the young man. They fall in "love"—at least Juan is flattered by the attentions of a Queen—but then he falls sick and is forced to leave Russia and travel as an emissary across Europe to England. Here he is accepted by the best society and accompanies the Amundevilles to their country estate. He seems destined to fall in love once more, with either Lady Adeline Amundeville or the young beauty Aurora Raby, but finds himself alone at night with "her frolic Grace," the Duchess of FitzFulke, dressed as a monk who haunts the castle. But then the poem ends, for Byron went to Greece to die there in the spring of 1824.

Don Juan is an unfinished poem, but then it seems doubtful that it ever could have been finished, for what conclusion could there have been to this sequence of events in which man settles for only a moment in one condition and identity, to be swept inevitably onward into further change? [4] In a curious way, the sudden transformation of the bored but resigned lover of the Countess Guiccioli into the martyr of liberty dying of fever at Missilonghi illustrates perfectly the vision of life his poem embodies—just as the death of the poet provides the final comment on the pilgrimage to Canterbury in the other most famous unfinished poem in English.

This particular rhythm of existence, eternally in movement like the ceaselessly changing waters of ocean, is the controlling concept of the poem, its basic action. It can be heard in the primary plot, and it remains audible in all the movements of the various world. It originates in that "indecent sun" which

> cannot leave alone our helpless clay,
> But will keep baking, broiling, burning on.
>
> (I, 63)

It sounds loudly and fiercely in the attack on Ismail:

> But on they marched, dead bodies trampling o'er,
> Firing, and thrusting, slashing, sweating, glowing.
>
> (VIII, 19)

It sounds softly, but just as insistently, in the description of poetry as the "shadow which the onward Soul behind throws," or in the

4. The accident of Byron's death was not the sole cause of the "unfinished" state of the poem. In I, 200, he states, though perhaps ironically, that *Don Juan* will have twelve books and three episodes. Considering his extension of the poem far beyond these limits, it seems certain that Byron himself felt or knew that an ending would be false to the action he was imitating.

sad description of the ladies in the harem who move "with stately march and slow, / Like water-lilies floating down a rill." It is present in the primeval forest where Daniel Boone and his men live as "fresh as is a torrent or a tree" with "motion . . . in their days"; and it is equally present in great cities "that boil over with their scum," where life is one great swirling movement,

> coaches, drays, choked turnpikes, and a whirl
> Of wheels, and roar of voices and confusion;
> Here taverns wooing to a pint of "purl,"
> There mails fast flying off like a delusion.

> (XI, 22)

The onward movement of life is not, however, uncomplicated. Like the waves to which it is frequently compared, the individual life and the life of civilizations sweep forward and upward to a crest, pause there for an illusory moment of certainty in love, identity, and glory, and then plunge downward and onward into the great sweep of eternity. We can hear this characteristic rhythm in the "but then" pattern of the Juan story, and it is compressed into a single line in which a young wife struggles not to give herself to a lover, "And whispering 'I will ne'er consent'—consented." It sounds again in the metamorphosis of the Greek pirate Lambro, who had once been an idealist and a patriot:

> His Country's wrongs and his despair to save her
> Had stung him from a slave to an enslaver.

> (III, 53)

It receives full orchestration in this description of the passing of life and empires:

> The eternal surge
> Of Time and Tide rolls on and bears afar
> Our bubbles; as the old burst, new emerge,
> Lashed from the foam of ages; while the graves
> Of Empires heave but like some passing waves.

> (XV, 99)

But this movement, upward to a pause, and then a sweep away, is most consistently present in the stanza form, *ottava rima*, which Byron found so suitable. The first six lines stagger forward, like the life they contain, toward the resting place of the concluding couplet and the security of its rhyme—and a very shaky resting place it most often is. Since the majority of these couplets are end-stopped, it is possible to pause for an instant, but only an instant, before pressing on to the inevitable next stanza, where the process is repeated once more. The length of the poem intensifies this onward effect, for there seems always another stanza or another canto to sweep forward and destroy every momentary conclusion.

However much the rising to pauses and falling away from them may complicate the rhythm of the poem, the over-all movement is one of change passing on to change. The pressure is in man's very blood which "flows on too fast . . . as the torrent widens toward the ocean," which "beats" in his heart, "moves" him to action, and "bursts forth" from his veins as "the Simoom sweeps the blasted plain" if his free movement is restrained. The same pressure is in nature: in the ever-present ocean which foams and surges ever onward, in the "showering grapes" which

> In Bacchanal profusion reel to earth,
> Purple and gushing.
>
> (I, 124)

It is the power which forces great poetry,

> As on the beach the waves at last are broke,
>   Thus to their extreme verge the passions brought
> Dash into poetry.
>
> (IV, 106)

It is the force of time which drives history onward and buries the past in oblivion:

> The very generations of the dead
>   Are swept away, and tomb inherits tomb,
> Until the memory of an Age is fled,
>   And, buried, sinks beneath its offspring's doom.
>
> (IV, 102)

No more can be done than to suggest the omnipresence of this onward rush in *Don Juan*, but it is quite obviously, whether Byron employed it consciously or unconsciously, the governing concept, the central action of life which the poem imitates. Even the slighter instances of imagery, conventional though they may appear to be, keep this idea of a vital, forceful onward movement playing through the poem. A family grows like a springing branch, the veins of a beautiful woman run lightning, the blood of a woman in love rushes to where her spirit's set, the blood pours on like a headlong torrent overpowering a river's rush, glances dart out, water ripples onto a beach as champagne brims over a glass, two lovers' senses dash on and their hearts beat against one another's bosom, revenge springs like the tiger, life is the current of years, fury is like the yeasty ocean, hair flows like an Alpine torrent, looks swim, two hearts pour into one another, blood runs like a brook, Fate puts from the shore, bosoms beat for love as a caged bird for free air, a girl in love expands into life, men are killed as gales sweep foam away.

Ultimately, all these various movements are included in the two master symbols of the poem, fire and ocean. Fire is the vital spirit, the Promethean flame, the mysterious, motivating energy which urges all life on to seek its full expression in love, war, pleasure, poetry. No explanation is offered for the sources of this fire, it simply is the vital power which "will keep baking, broiling, burning on." Ocean is the visible form of history, and is specifically identified as the, "Watery Outline of Eternity, / Or miniature, at least."

The poem reveals that Byron thought of "our nautical existence" as a process and that he consistently used a particular type of imagery to identify each stage of life. Early life is identified with the fresh-water stream flowing from high mountains, tumbling impetuously over rocks and down mountainsides; as youth passes and disillusionments come, the fresh stream is dammed up or flows into a lake, and then joins a river which broadens and deepens toward the sea; finally, when joy and illusion are gone, the waters flow into the salt "sea of ocean" to become mingled with and indistinguishable from all the other waters which have flowed there through all time. No reference is made in *Don Juan* to the other part of the natural cycle in which salt water is evaporated by the sun and returned sweet to the mountain tops once more.

II

Whene'er I have expressed
Opinions two, which at first sight may look
    Twin opposites, the second is the best.
Perhaps I have a third too, in a nook,
    Or none at all—which seems a sorry jest:
But if a writer should be quite consistent,
How could he possibly show things existent?

(XV, 87)

The constant flow of life leading on from change to change is the essential reality of the world of *Don Juan*, the basic action running through the poem and shaping life. The nominal hero, the young Spaniard Don Juan, lives this action but is not aware that he does so, for he is, as the narrator frequently reminds us, "thoughtless." He feels passionately, acts directly, moves with grace and ease through the flux of existence, but he does not know what he is or does.

Juan's lack of consciousness is constantly thrown into relief by the restless, probing, analytic quality of the narrator's mind; but though the two represent different aspects of being—Juan all body and passion, the narrator only a voice and mind—their different existences still follow the basic rhythm of life. If Juan lives change, the narrator thinks it. The stanza quoted above is an explicit recognition on his part that his thoughts on any subject are no more than opinions, and that these opinions shift as frequently and violently as do Juan's loves and fortunes. The instability of the narrator's thought has always been the most interesting part of the poem, and critics have long recognized that he makes startlingly contradictory statements about life and people. To take a simple example, in Stanza 31 of Canto V we are told that the enjoyment of food is piggish indulgence which always reminds us that we are gross animals, not pure spirits; but then in Stanza 47 food is cheerfully presented as man's restorer, an unalloyed benefit. To follow the narrator's views on food and drink through the entire poem is to be treated to a display of nearly every possible attitude toward this subject, and his position is further complicated by his endlessly ambiguous handling of the subject of food in such scenes as the feast on Haidée's island celebrating the marriage of Haidée and Juan, the cannibal feast in the open boat, and the elaborate formal banquet at Norman Abbey. The variety of opinions on food gives only a slight indication of the endless shifts of perspective on more complicated matters such as women, love, glory, society, or pleasure.

If, as is first suggested in the stanza quoted above, we could regard the narrator's second opinion as always better than the first, there would be little difficulty in following him on his journey toward wisdom. Since, as he frequently tells us, he was once a young man very like Juan who entered life with the same expectations and passed through the same experiences, we would account for his two opinions as a simple irony expressing the views of an old hand at life on the simplemindedness of youth and the ridiculous pretensions of the righteous. But one opinion never does cancel out its opposite in *Don Juan*, for the first opinion always comes back to haunt the second, and a third appears to qualify its predecessors. What we are faced with is not a simple irony, which involves only two points, what seems and what is, but an endlessly complicating ambiguity, a series of perspectives, each one of which is as true as any other. In the end, the narrator recognizes that all these opposites tend to cancel one another out, and we are left with the possibility that rather than having one, or two or three opinions, he actually may have "none at all."

But before we come to the nihilistic possibility, it is, I believe, possible to organize to some degree the variety of views expressed through the voice of the narrator and the events of the plot. Kenneth Burke in his *Attitudes Toward History* [5] has called the various literary categories, or genres, "strategies for living." Tragedy, epic, comedy, and satire cease in his view to be *merely* literary forms and

5. Rev. ed. (Los Altos, Cal., 1959).

become fundamental ways of thinking about, organizing, and managing the vast, confusing swirl of life. Thus, in Burke's view, a theology, a psychology, a form of government, a philosophical system, or a game, as well as a work of literature, may be termed comic or tragic—though Burke's literary orientation suggests that he still believes that literature provides the most complete and subtle statements of the different "strategies." Northrop Frye in *Anatomy of Criticism* supports Burke's position by designating the major genres as *mythoi* and arguing that they are not imitations of life but organizational forms imposed on experience which express man's deepest hopes and fears. The more cheerful literary kinds, comedy and romance, are described in the terms of William Blake, as "the forms of human desire," and the more somber kinds, tragedy and satire, "the world that desire totally rejects." No single genre, in the view of these critics, has any absolute validity as an image of the world; each is a fundamental pattern of thought which can be used to give shape and form to any group of experiences, historical events, or perceptions.

Don Juan puts this critical view in dramatic terms, for the bewildering number of contradictory opinions which the poem offers through the voice of the narrator and the actions of its *dramatis personae* resolve ultimately into three senses of life, comic, satiric, and tragic. The fact of life in the poem, the reality of the world, is the constant flux, the onward flow of all things under the pressure of the mysterious Promethean fire to their disappearance in the great sea of ocean. This is existence, and man willy-nilly participates in this flow, is one with it. He may swim on with it joyfully and vigorously, as Juan most often does, or he may resist it and seek to maintain the status quo, as the various political and social reactionaries in the poem do, but in the end everything is swept on in time to become as "indistinct as water is in water." [6] But man, as the poem often notes, is a curious creature who has a mind as well as a body and feelings; and while the body and feelings cannot escape being subject to mutability, the mind can reflect upon this experience and evaluate it in different ways. It is this aspect of man which is dramatized in the person of the narrator. As a result, we get a series of perspectives on the various, plentiful, turbulent world of the poem, and these perspectives, correspond, as I have said, to the major literary genres.

It is clear that the poet is also aware of the possibility of organizing life in an epic pattern, since he speaks regularly of the traditional devices of the heroic poem. There are even some remnants of true epic: the vast sweep of the world portrayed and the occasional serious uses of the grand style to describe some heroic act or the great

6. *Antony and Cleopatra,* IV.9.10–11.

powers that move through all being. But on the whole, the epic is invoked only for purposes of mockery. And while Byron occasionally uses the mock-epic technique as Pope and Dryden did to provide a standard of life and manners against which the shabbiness of the present can be measured, he ordinarily realizes a tendency always latent in the mock-epic to mock not only the unheroic present but the pretentiousness of the epic form itself. If its elevated view of man and its orderly view of the world define by contrast the self-seeking, stupidity, and confusion of the contemporary, then these latter-day realities raise inevitably the question of whether man and his world were not always so; and when the insights into reality are extended to cover the past in such a way that the ancient heroes and the gods become brutes and tyrants, then the epic form is itself discredited. . . .

Byron deliberately chose to narrate the youthful adventures of his hero before he arrived at the cynicism and hardened depravity which qualify his zest for life in the older legend and the versions of Tirso de Molina, Molière, and Mozart. Byron's Juan is the pure embodiment of all those virtues which comedy shows as the key to successful life. These virtues are in origin natural, innate in man, though they are refined and improved upon in some varieties of comedy—principally Shakespeare's—by the order, still natural in origin, of society. Juan is the very essence of the natural, as the Romantics understood that term. He is lively and vital,

> A little curly-headed, good-for-nothing,
> And mischief-making monkey from his birth.
>
> (I, 25)

As a youth he is tall, slim, lithe, and handsome—the human form of the beautiful and well-proportioned world of comedy. He possesses all the natural virtues—courage, quick wit, passionate feelings, uprightness, frankness, warmth—and all the natural appetites for love, food, and pleasure. These instincts are not destructive in him but lead to beneficient actions, to enjoyment, pity, love, concern for others.

Juan's heart is sound enough, and he does have sense enough to come in out of the rain, but by academic standards his mind is somewhat deficient. This is perfectly proper in the world of comedy where, since truth is obvious and value apparent, the analytic intellect can lead only to confusion and loss.[7] Occasionally, Juan does

---

7. There are comedies in which intelligence is one of the dominant qualities of the hero—Shaw's plays, for example, or Congreve's—but even in this kind of comedy the quality of mind celebrated is natural and immediate, an extended common sense, rather than the profound and brooding thought of tragedy.

attempt deep thought, but his nature always saves him, as in this effort to probe the cosmos and construct a metaphysic:

> He thought about himself, and the whole earth,
>   Of man the wonderful, and of the stars,
> And how the deuce they ever could have birth;
>   And then he thought of earthquakes, and of wars,
> How many miles the moon might have in girth,
>   Of air-balloons, and of the many bars
> To perfect knowledge of the boundless skies;—
> And then he thought of Donna Julia's eyes.
>
> (I. 92)

Juan's instincts are too clear and direct to allow him to lose himself in useless theoretical speculation and to forget the real and meaningful, a woman's beautiful eyes. The healthy limitations of his mind are realized by his speech, or more precisely, his failure to speak very often. His usual silence is emphasized by the loquaciousness of those around him, particularly the garrulous narrator who can never stop talking. Without question Juan is at his best when he neither tries to think or speak, for thinking always involves him in ludicrous tangles, and his few speeches are either commonplace or hopelessly romantic.

Nor does Juan learn very much from his experiences. By the end of the poem he has become a suave young diplomat, more courteous and formal than he was as a boy, but no more profound and still oblivious of those sad realities of life with which the narrator, who has traveled Juan's path before him, is forced to live. It is not only that Juan lacks the ability to organize and schematize life, but chiefly that he lacks that mental function which is the source of so much of the narrator's suffering: memory. Where the narrator cannot forget his loves, his youth, and his images of men who are not only dust and names, Juan's regrets for yesterday last only one intense moment and then are gone as yesterday ceases to be. He suffers horribly when first separated from Donna Julia and vows,

> Sooner shall Earth resolve itself to sea,
> Then I resign thine image, oh, my fair!
>
> (II, 19)

But the image fades quickly enough as he becomes sea-sick, struggles for survival in an open boat, and then finds another love. He never returns to Julia, and in fact never mentions her again. Even more curious is his relinquishment of his most intense love, the Greek girl, Haidée. Since Juan is wounded and carried off to slavery before Haidée dies, he never knows of her death. Yet despite his unusual grief for this loss—it lasts a week or so—he never tries to return to Lambro's island again, but drifts onward to further adventures and new loves.[8] Juan is a comic hero of the romantic variety, a Ferdinand rather than a Falstaff, but his virtues still enable him to live that life of immediacy which can always be described in somewhat cruder terms by a more earthy comic approach to life. When Juan and an Englishman named Acres are chained together in a Turkish slave market, Juan announces in his inflated style: not for the

> present doom
> I mourn, but for the past;—I loved a maid.
>
> (V, 18)

To which Acres replies that he understands, for he too cried when his first wife died, and again when the second ran away, but that he had run away from the third.

While Juan continues to take himself quite seriously, never quite seeing the wonderfully efficient way he manages to stay alive and happy in a constantly changing world, he is constantly being undercut by a comic sense of life more basic and honest than his own. The narrator and characters like Acres know that, since all things pass, there is no point in worrying or of taking yourself and your passions too seriously. At the same time, of course, Juan's delicacy and refinement in taking his pleasures call into question the lower comic values, and in this way the tone is complicated even within the comic portions of the poem. But whatever form the comic values may take—pure love or pure pleasure—the comic way of life remains a natural, unthinking instinct for what is good and a freedom in moving with the full stream of life.

For this way of life to be workable, it is necessary that the comic hero live in a world friendly to him and suitable to his virtues. The stream of life to which he commits himself cannot carry him to disaster but must cast him in the way of pleasure and joy. Viewed from one angle, Juan does live in a beneficent world. He often lands in temporary trouble, but bad luck is only momentary and usually turns out to be good luck in disguise. If he is wrecked at sea by a ferocious storm, he is thrown up on an island and into the arms of a beautiful princess. Sold into slavery, his good looks immediately attract the attention of the Sultan's wife, and in no time he finds himself in a harem with a multitude of beautiful women and in bed with a lovely harem girl. Tied in a sack and thrown into the Bosporus, he miraculously turns up in the Russian army and soon becomes the lover of Catherine the Great. While Juan's natural virtues, his courage and his physical attractiveness, contribute

---

8. In XV, 58, there is a comparison of Aurora Raby as a gem with Haidée as a flower, to the latter's advantage, but it is not clear whether the comparison is made in Juan's mind or that of the narrator. At any rate, we are not aware in reading the poem of Juan cherishing the memory of Haidée.

to his good fortune, such virtues would be of little use in a world which did not favor those who give themselves to it.

Furthermore, if lack of introspection, a poor memory, and a mind which has very limited analytical powers are to be valuable assets, they must be located in a world which is not only good enough to be trusted but of such a nature that any attempt to understand its operations through reason be futile and ludicrous. The relativism characteristic of *Don Juan* creates just such a world. Variety, plenitude, and mutability combine to make ridiculous all received philosophies and religions, to destroy any belief in history and progress, and to make laughable any attempts to speculate on and systematize the workings of the universe. And why worry about it, says comedy. Everything may change, but nothing can be done about it; and the world as immediately sensed is full of joy and pleasure. Women's eyes flash beauty, wine excites wonderfully, the pulse beats, torrents crash down mountainsides, and the whole spectacle of nature is a satisfying display of the richness, power, and springing vitality of the world. The over-all somberness of *Don Juan* often obscures this romantic and comic joy in life, man, and nature; but it is regularly present, and it validates both Juan's trust in the life known to his senses and feelings and his thoughtless commitment of himself to whatever chances the world offers.

But though the comic world is essentially good, it always allows for forces which attempt to pervert this good. The way of the world is inevitable, however, and these anti-life forces have no real chance of success. Foolishness, not evil, constitutes the opposition in comedy. Since in *Don Juan* the comic way is to give oneself to life and move with it through change, foolishness is necessarily any attempt to stay life, to deny its pleasures, and to cramp it into any rigid, permanent form, a philosophical system or a marriage bed. The poem is filled with characters who attempt to do just this: Donna Inez and her efforts to educate Juan by means of sermons and homilies which try to stifle his natural impulses and curb his passions; the stiff, placid, aristocratic ladies and gentlemen who gather at Norman Abbey, scarcely able to breathe within their stays and their rigid sense of propriety; the Turkish sultan who buys, locks away, and guards elaborately the numerous but unused beauties of his harem. The narrator, in his digressions, provides a host of parallels: the art of the Lake poets, which imposes ludicrous boundaries on human nature; Coleridge's metaphysics, which pretends to enfold the mysteries of the universe; Plato's philosophy of the ideal, which insists that the physical is unreal and that the passions can be controlled; the ridiculous attempts of tyranny through the ages to enslave men and contain their drive toward political freedom; the laughable pretensions of polite society to order and bottle up man's natural appetites. But restraint and enfolding are also treated as inescapable realities of life which takes such forms as physical ageing which stiffens and binds the once-free body, the tendency of the mind to remember what once was and therefore to suffer in the painful grasp of memory, the inevitable movement of time toward decay and death, that ultimate form of containment and stillness which contains all other forms of enslavement.

The attempts to impose bonds on life and the hero's successful escapes from each of the snares constitute the comic plot of *Don Juan*. Juan's pedantic tutors try to eradicate his passions, and Donna Julia's careful parents try to lock her into a marriage with a wealthy old man; but when the two young people meet, their love flares and destroys all barriers to pleasure. Caught in her bedroom, muffled under the bedclothes, his exit barred by an enraged husband, Juan, naked, nearly murders the old man and his servants to break free. Finding the garden gate, the last barrier to freedom, locked, Juan opens it and then relocks it from the outside, leaving the prisoners of society inside. Becalmed on the sea in an open boat, most of the survivors of a shipwreck turn cannibals and perish as a result, but Juan plunges into the sea and, aided by the current, swims to an island where he finds Haidée and the full enjoyment of natural love. But even on this Edenic island, restraints exist, and Haidée's papa, to give him his comic epithet, returns suddenly, has Juan bound, and ships him off to a Turkish slave market. From here on Juan's life is a continued series of escapes from a variety of bonds, political, physical, social, and amorous which the world attempts to impose upon him. . . .

If character makes plot in tragedy, the world often manages it in comedy, and the *deus ex machina*, coincidence, sudden reversals— a fortunate shift of the wind or the chance discovery of a lost will— are the devices by which its workings are manifested. To express this chancy working of nature in comedy, we often say that the comic hero is lucky, and certainly Juan is lucky in every way. Even his personal virtues are the unsought gifts of nature, and throughout the poem good chance plays a crucial part in his life. If his luck runs out in Spain, the sea carries him to a magical island; if he is sold to the Turks, he just happens to find his way into a harem. Perhaps nothing in the poem makes clearer the role that fortune plays in shaping Juan's plot than the absence of any explanation of how he gets out of trouble at the end of Canto VI. Gulbeyaz, the Sultan's favorite wife, has discovered that her pleasures with Juan have been anticipated by one of the ladies of the harem, Dudù, and wild with rage she calls all the guilty parties before her. The usual punishment, we are told, for such malefactors is to tie them in bags—another form of containment—and throw them into the Bosporus. But we are never told what actually happens. The narrator turns to a description of the siege of Ismail, "trusting Juan will escape the fishes." When next seen, however, Juan and his party are coming up to join the Russians. Good fortune has become such a commonplace in his life that the details of its workings no longer need to be described. . . .

The mere length of *Don Juan* and the multitude of adventures it contains create this long-range view. Juan rambles over all Europe, going from love to shipwreck to prison to war to court and back to love again. As he moves through his spacious world, time takes no toll of him. He grows less impulsive, but at the end of the poem he is still young and passionate and ready for further adventures. In himself, like a figure of myth rather than a mere man, he contains the timeless energy and appetite of the human race.[9] Byron suggests in several places that he plans to reduce Juan to marriage, disillusionment, and old age, but he can never bring himself to do it. Juan's ultimate escape from the poet's plans may be a result of the accident of Byron's death, but the adventure on which the poem ends is a climactic comic image of all the tests Juan has earlier endured, and once again his vitality and felt sense of life triumph. The scene is Norman Abbey, the country house of the Amundeville family, where Juan has gone as the member of a house party. Here, all is restraint and confinement. The water of the artificial lake is still, the skies overcast and gray, the landscape autumnal and dreary, the castle—a "Gothic Babel"—heavy and earthbound because its many dissimilar parts and styles lack any soaring quality and life-giving unity. The upper-class English men and women of the party are equally lifeless. Their clothes and manners are stiff and smooth, their vitality smothered in a fashionable ennui, their moral spots varnished over, and their only interests dinner and sleep. Beauty here is completely self-possessed, and Byron describes the great beauties of the party as locked in ice or buried deep within the polished surfaces of a gem. Whenever life does burst forth in this society it is destroyed by gossip and ostracism—as Byron had once been destroyed—or is brutally restrained. Two poachers are caught in huge steel traps and then imprisoned; a young unmarried girl with child, a "poacher upon Nature's manor," is made to wear a scarlet coat and hauled for sentencing before a Justice of the Peace.

This concentration of confinement and tyranny is further focused

9. The gap between the attributes necessary for the completely comic existence and those possessed by real men is stressed at the beginning of Canto I, where Byron finds real heroes living and dead, unable to stand the test of time. They live, fight, suffer, are disgraced and then forgotten; so the poet is forced to turn to romance for his hero and "take our ancient friend Don Juan."

in the ghost of a Monk who has haunted the castle since Henry VIII dissolved the monastery and gave the lands to the Amunde-villes. Juan and the ghostly Monk are worthy antagonists, and their combat raises to the mythic level the comic struggle which has heretofore been presented realistically. On one side we have the ultimate comic hero whose blazing vitality cannot weaken or be entrapped; on the other side the ultimate comic antagonist, the very spirit of the anti-vital. The ghostly form of the Monk makes him completely bodiless, and his monkishness is the absolute form of asceticism and a strict, religious ordering of life. His ceaseless search for revenge on those who have robbed him is the final extension of that perversion of life to a sterile emptiness which overtakes those characters in *Don Juan* who cramp their natural instincts too severely. He walks ordinarily in the portrait gallery where those other ghosts, the Amundeville ancestors, stiff and hypocritical enough in their own lifetimes, have been finally frozen in rigid, respectable, lifeless positions by the painter's art. The Monk haunts and curses the marriage beds of the Amundevilles, he attends their childbirths and tries to blight the children, he appears gloating at their deaths. He is, in short, the very spirit of death, and it is with death in some of its less obvious forms that Juan has struggled since childhood.

Juan's encounters with the Ghost are handled in the manner of a Gothic Tale, and it is impossible to consider the Ghost as a real threat to Juan's life. But on the symbolic level the struggle is to the death. The full force of the danger is carried by the language and imagery: when Juan sees the Ghost he is "petrified," and he gazes

> upon it with a stare,
> Yet could not speak or move; but, on its base
> As stands a statue, stood: he felt his hair
> Twine like a knot of snakes around his face.
>
> (XVI, 23)

After several appearances, the "sable Friar in his solemn hood" comes to fetch Juan from his bed. The door creaks on his entrance and seems to say, "Lasciate ogni speranza, voi, ch'entrate!" and the words over the entrance to Dante's Hell sum up all the many forms of damnation in *Don Juan*. Though terrified of this "darkening darkness," Juan moves to fight once more, and as he advances, the Monk retreats until pressed against a courtyard wall. Juan's hand reaches forward and presses a "hard but glowing bust." The sable frock and dreary cowl fall away to reveal,

> In full, voluptuous, but *not o'er*grown bulk,
> The phantom of her frolic Grace—Fitz-Fulke!

These are the last lines of the poem, though Byron may have written a few stanzas more, and while they have a realistic explanation—the Duchess of Fitz-Fulke is a rather forward beauty who has been eyeing Juan for some time and has taken advantage of the story of the ghost to get to his chamber unobserved—they are at the same time a climactic image of the comic triumph of life over death. The illusion of a pale, bloodless world moving toward sterility and death is transformed by courage, vitality, and good chance into a living, breathing, and satisfying immediacy.

Unfortunately, the majority of readers do not go past the Haidée episode or Juan's Turkish captivity, and for that reason overestimate the pessimistic qualities of the poem. But *Don Juan* as Byron left it ends on an affirmation of the goodness of life, and the entire poem is thus framed by a comic view of experience. . . .

Don Juan is not, of course, witless or amoral, but his wit is of the commonsense variety, and his morals, which have their source in his nature, are instinctive and uncodified. His life is spontaneous, and mind does not intervene between his perceptions of the world and his understanding of it. But the older, disillusioned narrator knows that the "sweetness" of life does not reside in life itself but in the spirit of the young man who perceives it.

> No more—no more—Oh! never more on me
>   The freshness of the heart can fall like dew,
> Which out of all the lovely things we see
>   Extracts emotions beautiful and new,
> Hived in our bosoms like the bag o' the bee.
>   Think'st thou the honey with those objects grew?
> Alas! 't was not in them, but in thy power
> To double even the sweetness of a flower.
>
> (I, 214)

The narrator's heart can no longer be his "sole world," his "universe"; and his head, his acquired "deal of judgment," reveals that the comic view of a world in which things always turn out for the best in the long run doesn't square with reality. Juan himself is not heavily attacked, but when he is viewed objectively and analytically, some most uncomic facts appear. He is often a ridiculous poseur, an ever-faithful lover who forgets the woman once she is out of sight, a fiery creature of spirit who cannot bear to miss a meal, and a lucky booby who has not the simple sense to see the dreadful realities around him or to realize that his life is saved again and again not by his own virtue but by the most miraculous, and ultimately ludicrous, chance. The criticism of Juan deepens when the narrator reminds us that greathearted and greatly loving though

Juan may be, he, without the slightest awareness that he does so, leaves a trail of bodies behind him in his comic adventures. Commenting on the carnage Juan's blazing spirit creates at the siege of Ismail, the narrator remarks wryly

> But Juan was quite "a broth of a boy,"
> A thing of impulse and a child of song;
> Now swimming in the sentiment of joy,
> Or the *sensation* (if that phrase seem wrong),
> And afterward, if he must needs destroy,
> In such good company as always throng
> To battles, sieges, and that kind of pleasure,
> No less delighted to employ his leisure.
>
> (VIII, 24)

The attacks on Juan are just heavy and frequent enough to call into question his way of life, but behind him the narrator opens up not the bubbling, racing, opportunity-filled world of comedy Juan thinks he lives in, but the heavy, hypocritical, confused world of satire where men seem determined to destroy themselves. Byron's contemporaries, shocked by his savage attacks on such living personalities as Lady Byron, Castlereagh, and the poet Southey, considered this "filthy and impious poem" nothing but a satire:

> Impiously railing against his God—madly and meanly disloyal to his Sovereign and his country—and abruptly outraging all the best feelings of female honour, affection, and confidence—how small a part of chivalry is that which remains to the descendant of the Byrons—a gloomy vizor and a deadly weapon! [1]

The *Blackwood's* reviewer goes on to put his finger on the immediate source of satire in the poem when he describes Byron as a "cool, unconcerned fiend, laughing with a detestable glee over the whole of the better and worse elements of which human life is composed —treating well nigh with equal derision the most pure of virtues, and the most odious of vices—dead alike to the beauty of the one, and the deformity of the other—a mere heartless despiser of that frail but noble humanity . . ." The impossibility of discriminating between what the world styles vice and what it styles virtue is Byron's immediate satiric subject, and the reviewer's impossible smugness, his calm assurance that, despite a few frailties, all legal governments are worthy respect, all religions religious, all ladies honest and chaste, all gentlemen honorable and noble, is a perfect instance of just what Byron was immediately attacking.

Byron admits in Canto II, Stanza 119, that "One should not rail without a decent cause," and in words which seem to recall the *Blackwood's* review he explicitly states his own decent cause:

---

1. "Remarks on *Don Juan*," *Blackwood's*, August 1819.

How differently the World would men behold!
How oft would Vice and Virtue places change!
  The new world would be nothing to the old,
If some Columbus of the moral seas
Would show mankind their Souls' antipodes.

What "antres vast and deserts idle" then,
  Would be discovered in the human soul!
What icebergs in the hearts of mighty men,
  With self-love in the centre as their Pole!
What Anthropophagi are nine of ten
  Of those who hold the kingdoms in control!
Were things but only called by their right name,
Caesar himself would be ashamed of Fame.

(XIV, 101–02)

Byron was, as satirist, that "Columbus of the moral seas" sailing to
the underside of his social world to reveal the shabby truths underlying the pretenses with which men cover themselves His rhetoric
and the events of the story are shaped to "call by their right name"
the perfect lovers who in fact seek only to control one another, the
learned doctors who practice only for their fees, the grave politicians
who rule for profit and because they fear those beneath them, the
eloquent poets who write out of confusion of mind and to increase
their sense of self-importance. Byron's keen sight sees that men who
profess to love one another will resort to cannibalism to live another day, and that the more beautiful ideals which man so prides
himself on yield always to such physical realities as seasickness, hunger, fear, and lust. Man is, after all,

a carnivorous production,
  And must have meals, at least one meal a day;
He cannot live, like woodcocks, upon suction,
  But, like the shark and tiger, must have prey.

(II, 67)

The point of these attacks is not that man is "a carnivorous
production," but that he tries so ridiculously to pretend that he is
not. In the Preface to Cantos VI, VII, and VIII, Byron quotes with
approval Voltaire's remark, "Plus les mœurs sont dépravés, plus
les expressions deviennent mesurées; on croit regagner en langage
ce qu'on a perdu en vertu." This compulsive hypocrisy is the most
evident quality of the world which satire constructs, and the first
activity of the satirist is exposing it. The rhetoric and events of
Don Juan, while they allow Byron to develop the comic progression
of his hero, are at the same time perfectly suited for revealing the
sham of civilized life. The staggering rhythms, the jingling rhymes,
the savage irony, the dreadful concluding couplet of the ottava-
rima stanza which so regularly deflates the pretenses built up in the

preceding six lines, the devices of mock epic and mock romance, all these open up the disguises of respectability and show men their "souls' antipodes." The events of the poem are constructed, as is usually the case in satire, to permit the satirist to reveal the truth not only about individual man but about his crucial institutions and social arrangements. We are given a close look at conventional marriage, at the activities of lawyers and the working of their law, at the education of a young man, at romantic love, at heroic war, at politics, and at upper-class social life. In every case the elaborate dressings are stripped away and revealed as only pretty covers for more basic and less attractive passions, lust, fear, hatred, envy, the desire for power.

But the perception, no matter how perfectly executed, that man and his institutions are shams is really so rudimentary that it would not by itself constitute that "decent cause" which Byron makes the condition for railing. Great satires have at their center not merely some observation about stupidity or pride, but some profound, through not necessarily complex, grasp of the nature of reality, things as they truly are. The dunces of satire are those who, knowingly or unknowingly, pervert this natural bent of life. We have already seen that at the center of *Don Juan* is a realized sense of life as constant flow and change in which all things, man, society, civilization, and nature are swept forward by their own pressure into new conditions of being and ultimately to oblivion. This is an unusual view of reality for a satirist to hold—Byron is one of the very few romantic satirists—but it is finally the key to his satire. In every case, what he holds up to ridicule is some attempt to restrain life, to bind and force it into some narrow, permanent form. This is the burden of the attack on the Lake Poets, who, however unjust the charge, are treated as dunces not because they traffic in mystifying metaphysics and seek jobs in the Excise, but because they are *lake* poets, because they are inlanders who try to contain man in their poems while knowing nothing of man's "fiery dust" and never having seen the "sea of ocean," that "vast, salt, dread, eternal deep." [2] Castlereagh and the legitimists who controlled Europe after the Congress of Vienna are attacked not just because they are self-seeking frauds, but because they try to restrain on the political level that urgent movement toward freedom which is natural to man. These politicians have

> just enough of talent, and no more,
> To lengthen fetters by another fixed,
> And offer poison long already mixed.
> (Dedication, 12)

2. Byron develops the limitations of the Lake Poets in III, 98 ff. and in VIII, 10.

Older forms of tyranny in the Sultan's Turkey and Catherine's Russia are attacked for the same reason. Beliefs in material progress, philosophy, all forms of poetry, theories of history, religions, and monumental statuary come in for their share of ridicule because they seek to contain the uncontainable, to give fixed shape and deadly order to what is always shifting and changing.

The kind of bondage which is ridiculed in these institutions and activities also appears in the lives of the characters of the story. Young women are bound into marriage with older men against their desires; children are forbidden the exercise of their natural instincts and interests by a religious and scholastic training which seeks to make them "still and steady" by means of instruction in the "dead languages"; females formed by nature for life and love are turned into narrow prudes and bluestockings; men are imprisoned and chained together in slave gangs and on galley benches; women are denied free choice and locked in carefully guarded harems; subjects are treated as personal possessions by rulers; and imperious lovers tyrannize over one another. Hypocrisy, the first object of attack, is but a special, though most virulent form of unnatural restraint which buries man's real nature under layers of pretense.

The action of binding is also woven deep into the poem's imagery and details. Wherever life flows men attempt to dam it up and control it: Juan as a young boy is forbidden to read anything "loose" which hints at the "continuation of the species"; a proud, aristocratic family achieves its lifelessness by breeding "in and in"; a handsome young woman's eye "supresses half its fire" and her soul is "chasten'd down"; when she struggles against illicit longings she vows she will never "disgrace the ring she wore"; a passive life leaves the blood "dull in motion"; an outraged husband finding a lover with his wife, grapples "to detain the foe." Byron had a genius for finding and effectively placing words closely associated with traditional social and ethical values which suggest restraint or stillness: lawful wedlock, conjugal love, self-control, calmness, polished manners, smooth management, and self-possession. He made good use too of common objects suggesting restraint: stays, wedding bands, rings, clasps, and chambers. The restraint carried by the language opens out into the scenes of the poem: overly elaborate and heavy banquets, stiff clothing, substantial wealth manifested in overly decorated and furnished rooms, becalmment on the ocean, prisons, harems. Nowhere does life seem more close and stifling than in England. The rich and well-born, stiff in their garments and manners, go dully through their daily routines trying to control "that awful yawn that sleep cannot abate," and longing only for dinner and retirement. All the rough, high spots of personality have been ground away, and now

> Society is smoothed to that excess,
> That manners hardly differ more than dress.
>
> (XIII, 94)

And though the English upper classes are still barbarians, their crudeness has become so homogenous that they can be described as

> one polished horde
> Formed of two mighty tribes, the *Bores* and *Bored.*
>
> (XIII, 95)

What I have said so far might suggest that Byron as satirist is championing libertinism, and this is, of course, how his contemporaries understood him, despite his protests that *Don Juan* was a moral poem.[3] But Byron had no illusions about the ultimate goodness of human nature or about the effects of the unlimited free exercise of instinct. Juan, for example, is praised for restraining his appetites and fears in the shipwreck scene in Canto II. But Byron did understand, however, that the human instincts are inescapable realities, dynamic forces surging toward satisfaction, and that to dam them up and deny them altogether is to intensify their explosive power when they inevitably detonate. He knew, furthermore, that when left free to realize themselves, these passions achieve a certain grandeur, but when restrained they corrupt and taint the character. The untrammeled love of Juan and Haidée has a quality of magnificence which is lacking in the covert liaison of Juan and Donna Julia; and when denied even illicit, hidden expression, the power of love sours to lust, sex hatred, and leering prudishness. What is true of love is equally true of the other passions. The courage of legitimists and tyrants like Castlereagh "stagnates to a vice," slavery turns the freedom-loving Lambro to an enslaver, social propriety makes walking dead of once vital men and women. The attempt to contain the passions and stop the flow of life always defeats itself in some manner. This is the particular form which the standard satiric plot takes in *Don Juan*.

The satiric elements of *Don Juan* are not arranged in so consistent a pattern as the comic plot built on the adventures of Don Juan. The satiric plot is made up of a great number of attenuated scenes, descriptions, and references which all show the same movement of life—in England, Spain, or Turkey, in the present or in the past— through containment to disaster. We can see this plot in little in the description of the textbooks given to young Juan. He is to be educated in the classics, of course, but the "filthy loves of gods and

3. "*Don Juan* will be known, *by and by,* for what it is intended—a *satire* on *abuses* in the present states of society, and not an eulogy of vice. It may be now and then voluptuous:—I can't help that. Ariosto is worse. Smollett ten times worse; and Fielding no better." Letter to John Murray, December 22, 1822, in *The Works of Lord Byron, Letters and Journals*, ed. R. E. Prothero (London, 1901), V, 242.

goddesses" and the "grosser parts" are removed from his texts, lest Juan "should grow vicious." The expurgation is done by pedants who are themselves such slaves to their training that, fearing "to deface . . . their modest bard," they cannot bring themselves to present an incomplete text. So they collect all the indecent passages in an appendix ("Which saves, in fact, the trouble of an index") where they stand like "garden gods—and not so decent either," easily accessible to "the ingenuous youth of future ages." These learned men no doubt congratulate themselves on their piety and their professional skill as educators, never knowing that they have achieved just the opposite of the intended effect. And this is the pattern of the satiric plot as we have seen it elsewhere, for dullness always manages to contrive the opposite of its intention, though it is always too stupid to realize what it has actually done.

But the satiric episodes do not always end so gaily in *Don Juan* as does the textbook incident. The city of Seville pictured in Canto I is a remarkably moral place, sternly dedicated to the control of those unruly passions which corrupt the young, create unpleasant scandal, and destroy sane and sensibly arranged marriages. But somehow it all works out contrarily. Donna Inez, Juan's mother, is learned, efficient, and virtuous, the perfect spouse; but her husband, Don José, "a mortal of the careless kind," does not appreciate this paragon sufficiently, and their marriage turns into a prison which intensifies and corrupts the very passions it is intended to control:

> Don José and the Donna Inez led
>   For some time an unhappy sort of life,
> Wishing each other, not divorced, but dead;
>   They lived respectably as man and wife,
> Their conduct was exceedingly well-bred,
>   And gave no outward signs of inward strife,
> Until at length the smothered fire broke out,
> And put the business past all kind of doubt.
>
> (I, 26)

Don José follows his fancy, takes a mistress or two, and soon the lawyers are busy for their fees, friends intrude with unwanted advice, and the city buzzes with gossip. The matter is at last settled amicably: Don José dies. It turns out, however, that Donna Inez herself probably had a lover, Don Alfonso, who for reasons of prudence had married a woman thirty years younger than himself, the Donna Julia. But she and Don Juan, who had been so carefully restrained by his mother and trained to the path of virtue by so moral an education, fall desperately in love and begin an affair which ends in a rousing bedroom scene where Juan and Alfonso nearly kill one another. Julia is buried in a convent for the remainder of her life, the families' names are on every tongue and in every paper, and Juan is forced to leave home. The result of too strict restraint and moral dishonesty has been two broken families, two deaths—one literal and one figurative—several ruined lives, and the advertisement of the fact that the best families of Seville are not what they are supposed to be. When last seen, Donna Inez, encouraged by "the great success of Juan's education," has set up "a Sunday school for naughty children," where she, according to a cancelled passage,

> Their manners helping and their morals curing
> Taught them to suppress their vice and urine.
>
> (II, 10)[4]

While Juan the comic hero always escapes this destructive pattern of restraint leading to explosion and perversion of what is best in man, the world he moves in does not. In Spain, in Greece, in Turkey, in Russia, and in England most of all, wherever Juan travels, the clothes and customs may differ, but the rich and powerful and virtuous are everywhere busily engaged in trying to dam up vitality, to bring social and political life to a standstill, to control the giddy fluctuations and powerful passions of their own and other natures by means of education, religion, philosophic systems, manners, and, if all else fails, brute force. The actions of the establishment are sometimes ludicrous, as in Seville, and sometimes deadly serious, as in England, but they always create the characteristic world of satire and produce the same plot. The world grows false and hypocritical; spirit is rejected for a gross, crammed materialism; the vital turns mechanical; direct, graceful bearing and style turn to heavy conglomerations. In this world the poorer spirits languish and corrupt, while the natural pressure of the bolder spirits is intensified until it rips apart the containing bonds. The narrator universalizes the pattern which his characters act out by tracing similar plots in history: tyranny leading again and again to bloody revolution, the search for reputation and fame leading to oblivion, the proud attempts to sum up the world in a single philosophy or to order life with a moral system making only more clear that life escapes any system and man any mortality, the technology intended to produce a better world providing more efficient means for killing and turning life into hell.

The most powerful statement of the corrupting effect of calm and restraint on man occurs in Canto II of *Don Juan*, where after their ship has been sunk in a great storm, Juan and a number of sailors are becalmed in a small boat without food or oars. The sun

---

4. This couplet is printed in *Byron's Don Juan, A Variorum Edition,* eds. Steffan and Pratt (Austin, Texas, 1957), 2, 162.

burns down, the sea is stagnant, the men lie like carcasses, and then
"the longings of the cannibal arise." Lots are made—from the
touching farewell letter Julia wrote to Juan, *"Elle vous suit partout"*
—the victim chosen and killed, the surgeon's fee paid by giving him
first choice of the parts, the body divided and eaten, and the offal
thrown to those sharks outside the boat. Juan, who as comic hero is
not subject to the effects of repression, does not join the feast, and
fortunately, for the results are ghastly. The cannibals

> Went raging mad—Lord! how they did blaspheme!
> And foam, and roll, with strange convulsions racked,
>   Drinking salt-water like a mountain stream,
> Tearing, and grinning, howling, screeching, swearing,
> And, with hyæna-laughter, died despairing.
>
> (II, 79)

The satiric plot which is presented in more conventional terms and
scenes elsewhere is offered here undisguised. When life is stilled,
the natural appetites unsatisfied, and free movement denied man,
then his powers take perverted forms, and he changes to a mad
animal and dies in despair. The food he seeks to sustain life drives
him insane, and he mistakes salt water for fresh. The perversions
of natural appetites and the movement toward self-destruction
are not so spectacular in a polite household in Seville, in an aristocratic English country house, in a Turkish court, or in the nations of
Europe controlled by the Holy Alliance, but they are of the same
order and they move to the completion of the same plot.

When viewed from the angle of the solitary man, the movement
of life which flows through *Don Juan* darkens to a tragic setting in
which while Life rolls on, the individual is fated to stillness and
obliteration. The life principle continues, but tragic man is unable
to maintain his oneness with the great energy which has briefly expressed itself in him. As the tragic situation begins to constrict, it
becomes clear that while the essence of life is movement and
change, every attempt to remain free and express the elemental
passions becomes in itself a trap. The narrator is painfully familiar
with this pattern, for his life as lover, romantic hero, sensualist,
and poet has continually brought him face to face with paradox.
Love, which begins so passionately and vitally, seeks marriage to express itself, but

> There's doubtless something in domestic doings
>   Which forms, in fact, true Love's antithesis.
>
> (III, 8)

Even when not consolidated in marriage, love wears itself out in
sameness and becomes a prison. Art which seeks to express the fullness and excitement of life's movement and variety deadens the

reality and reduces it to such icy forms as *The Laocoön* and *The Dying Gaul*, where

> energy like life forms all their fame,
> Yet looks not life, for they are still the same.
>
> (IV, 61)

The search for pleasure, the gusto for all that life has to offer through the senses, ends in surfeit and sameness as the distinguishing taste is lost. Man's body, the instrument of his vitality, ages and drags the spirit down with it. Joy in the objective world involves man in a deadening materialism. Even before man's great feeling for the free life entangles itself, it destroys the freedom in other great spirits: lover tyrannizes over lover, heroism feeds on the death of other heroes, passion extinguishes the passion which aroused it. All manifestations of vitality become the means of destroying the vital in individual man.

In words which suggest the essential quality of the tragic spirit large enough to meet the tragic situation, Wallace Stevens once defined imagination and nobility as a "violence from within that protects us from a violence without." [5] But very few people in the world of *Don Juan* have the violence necessary to resist the bondage which tragic life forces violently on them. They bend their knees to tyrants, stand submissively on slave blocks, go quietly off to convents, and grow old without protest. Only the pirate's daughter, Haidée, her human clay kindled from the sun and "full of power for good and evil," has the tragic strength and violence to know and maintain her kinship with the only god of Byron's universe, the onward surge of being. Like all tragic heroes, she is fated for her struggle. Life burns within her with more force than in other mortals, and her entire being is a flashing movement: her blood runs headlong like a torrent, her heart dashes on to beat against Juan's bosom, her spirit springs from her burning eyes, her hair flows downward like an Alpine stream, her kisses focus the rays of the sun, and her glances dart out like the swiftest arrow, or like

> the snake late coiled, who pours his length,
> And hurls at once his venom and his strength.
>
> (II, 117)

Haidée gives herself to love and life completely, and even as she does so, she encounters her fate. It comes in a number of forms. The narrator tells us that the act of love commits her to the loss of that love, for in time Juan can only grow weary of her and pass on to new loves:

---

5. "The Noble Rider and the Sound of Words," *The Necessary Angel* (New York, 1951), p. 36.

Oh, Love! what is it in this world of ours
   Which makes it fatal to be loved? Ah why
With cypress branches hast thou wreathed thy bowers,
   And made thy best interpreter a sigh?
As those who dote on odours pluck the flowers,
   And place them on their breast—but place to die—
Thus the frail beings we would fondly cherish
Are laid within our bosoms but to perish.

(III, 2)

While Haidée does not consciously know the dangers to which she has given herself, knowledge of her fate is deep within her, and it presents itself in a dream—"the mystical usurper of the mind"—in which she is bound immobile and forced to endure whatever the world, in the form of ocean, may do to her:

She dreamed of being alone on the sea-shore,
   Chained to a rock; she knew not how, but stir
She could not from the spot, and the loud roar
   Grew, and each wave rose roughly, threatening her;
And o'er her upper lip they seemed to pour,
   Until she sobbed for breath, and soon they were
Foaming o'er her lone head, so fierce and high—
Each broke to drown her, yet she could not die.

(IV, 31)

Here are all the elements of tragedy in little: the isolation of the hero, the Promethean chaining to a single spot, the necessity for enduring like Gloster who is "tied to th' stake and . . . must stand the course," the proud refusal to yield even while longing for death to escape the wheel of fire.

As is usual in the tragic world, the destructive forces are external as well as internal. The setting is a sea-surrounded Greek island, a Greece where the ancient spirit of freedom—recalled in the song, "The Isles of Greece"—has been destroyed by the savage, oppressive rule of the Turk. While Haidée's father, to give him his tragic epithet, the pirate Lambro, maintains his own island kingdom and rejects the Turkish rule and any law of man, he is in turn a tyrant who captures and sells men, an absolute ruler in his own small domain, and a loving but stern father who regards his daughter as a possession. The wealth Lambro has collected by piracy becomes a chain on Haidée's freedom in the form of the binding ornaments she wears: the "silken fillet" which "curbs" her flowing hair; the golden bracelet which "clasps" her arm, "clinging as if loath to lose its hold"; the rich, heavy garments which cover her and beneath which "her breasts heaved like a little billow."

Juan and Haidée further tighten the bonds around themselves in realizing their love, though unaware of what they are doing:

> that which destroys
> Most love—possession—unto them appeared
> A thing which each endearment more endeared.
>
> (IV, 16)

As their love ripens, its setting changes from the clear beach under the broad sky and in view of the pounding surf to an interior scene, heavy, ornate and grossly material. The rugs are crimson satin, the velvet cushions stiff with gold brocade; "crystal and marble, plate and porcelain" fill the room; heavy objects of ebony, mother of pearl, ivory, rare woods, gold, and silver cover the walls and press in on the lovers. Their entertainment and their service is provided by dwarfs and black slaves, who "gain their bread . . . by degradation." From the free, naked state in which they first loved, they have passed on to rich, intricate, confining clothing and circumstances.

Though they are tragically unable to escape the bondage they defy, the lovers do not ultimately chain themselves. But early death is the price that Haidée at least must pay for her escape— "whom the gods love die young." The final struggle comes with her father Lambro, who focuses all of the binding powers in the poem. He returns to find his daughter in a stranger's arms, has him bound, and ships him off to the slave market at Constantinople. The key words gathered around Lambro are "calm," "still," "fixed," and "hard." And, as always in *Don Juan*, a placid outer surface, a rigid control of feelings, guarantees that the fires within are dangerously compressed:

> High and inscrutable the old man stood,
>   Calm in his voice, and calm within his eye—
> Not always signs with him of calmest mood.
>
> (IV, 39)

Lambro, though a rebel himself against political and social authority, and though intensely fond of his daughter, in this moment acts like the most conventional father and invokes the sacred word "duty." Since his honor and his daughter's virtue have been marred, he feels that he must do his duty, and each of his duteous acts is identified as a binding. He *fixes* the lovers with a deadly look, he stands in the "fix'd ferocity" of relentless anger, he "compresses" his daughter "within his clasp," his followers wound Juan, bind him, carry him to a ship and chain him "so that he cannot move."

Juan is not fated to be a tragic hero, and he is carried away to new adventures, but Haidée is left with the tragic choice. Having asserted her freedom and then come against the inevitable countermovement, she can now either submit or die to maintain that freedom which in the tragic world can be asserted in no other way.

Earlier in the poem Donna Julia in a similar situation allowed herself to be buried alive in a convent, but life in Haidée is so powerful that it cannot be restrained. Caught within her father's arms, helpless against physical force,

> The fire burst forth from her Numidian veins,
> Even as the Simoom sweeps the blasted plains.
>
> (IV, 57)

Writhing and turning in confinement, she is unable to release her body, but a vein bursts and her free blood runs on. "She had so much of soul / Earth could not claim the whole." And though reduced now in body to a statue—"fixed as marble's unchanged aspect"—when she hears a poet sing of the freedom of "ancient days, ere tyranny grew strong," and then of love, that "fierce name," Haidée's tears break forth in a "gushing stream," and the "spirit from her passed." She was "One life could not hold, nor death destroy."

This is romantic tragedy. In its brief span it contains not only the isolation, the terror of death, and the narrowing movement which are characteristic of all tragedy, but also the fierce struggle of man with his paradoxical nature and world to win that freedom without which he feels he cannot truly live. And by her courage and tenacity, at enormous expense, Haidée achieves something like victory. But even as Byron writes of her, she and her lover fade back into some distant world:

> They were not made in the real world to fill
> A busy character in the dull scene,
> But like two beings born from out a rill,
> A Nymph and her beloved, all unseen
> To pass their lives in fountains and on flowers,
> And never know the weight of human hours.
>
> (IV, 15)

The narrator of *Don Juan*, who knows very well the weight of human hours, presses on beyond Haidée's tragedy to a darker tragic vision of an eternal ocean of time to which man, full and complete man, cannot possibly accommodate himself, and over which no victory, however qualified, is possible. In this vision men are born only to feed worms, the brazen head of the world tells no more than "Time is, Time was, Time's past," the only cry heard in the gray waste is the "solitary shriek . . . of some strong swimmer in his agony," "great names are nothing more than nominal," and the narrator who has "stood upon Achilles' tomb / And heard Troy doubted" knows that "time will doubt of Rome." This bleak view is fully revealed in the water imagery of one of the most moving stanzas of the poem:

Between two worlds Life hovers like a star,
  'Twixt Night and Morn, upon the horizon's verge.
How little do we know that which we are!
  How less what we may be! The eternal surge
Of Time and Tide rolls on and bears afar
  Our bubbles; as the old burst, new emerge,
Lashed from the foam of ages; while the graves
Of Empires heave but like some passing waves.

                         (XV, 99)

This "vast, salt, dread, eternal deep," is but one version of the world which always opens up to the tragic hero. It is the same mysterious darkness into which Hamlet peers beyond the battlements of Elsinore and sees in the skull of Yorick, it is the terror which Oedipus hears in the voice of the oracle at Delphi and in the riddle of the Sphinx outside Thebes, it is the malevolent waves breaking over Haidée in her dream. But the tragic situation of the narrator is more desperate than that of older tragic figures. He is completely disembodied, for while hs is the major character of the poem, we never see him. His reality is not material but entirely mental, and it is in his mind, endlessly reflecting on the scenes he creates before him, speculating on past and present, relating what he has seen to what he knows, and searching for meaning without finding any truth other than provisional, that we meet the tragic individual—late romantic or ironic type—and come to know the full loneliness of existence emptied of pure feeling and passion, estranged from nature, rejected by and rejecting society and history.

To this point the narrator's experience of his world is simply an intensification and self-conscious formulation of the situation in which Haidée and all tragic heroes find themselves. But where they in some manner validate their positive assertions about themselves and life, the narrator has no hope of meaningful action because he finds the universe itself ultimately meaningless. The rest is silence after Haidée's as well as Hamlet's death, but in *Don Juan* that silence no longer suggests a perfect though mysterious completeness in human life lived greatly. The poet's gaze travels over Lambro's island after the death of Haidée and the child she carried:

That isle is now all desolate and bare,
  Its dwellings down, it tenants passed away;
None but her own and Father's grave is there,
  And nothing outward tells of human clay;
Ye could not know where lies a thing so fair,
  No stone is there to show, no tongue to say,
What was; no dirge, except the hollow sea's,
Mourns o'er the beauty of the Cyclades.

                         (IV, 72)

Haidée gave her life to maintain the vital principle of her being, free movement in life. Having eluded stagnation and bondage, she achieves tragic stature and passes on to become an undiminished part of that ever-flowing power of the universe with which she identified herself. But the narrator has come to understand that movement and change, uncontrasted and infinite, become sameness: "Change grows too changeable, without being new." This being the case, tragic action, like comic and satiric, becomes meaningless, for in the end all things pass on to the *hollow* sea, where endless movement becomes only endless stasis, and the infinity of time and space become mere pinpoints. Man cannot accept such a world, nor can he deny it, so all action becomes equally meaningful and meaningless. "He who doubts all things nothing can deny."

Don Juan makes a crucial point about the nature and relationship of literary genres. The true subject of the poem, I take it, is freedom and the onward flow of all life. . . .

HAROLD BLOOM

The Unpastured Sea:
An Introduction to Shelley †

Mesdames, one might believe that Shelley lies
Less in the stars than in their earthy wake,
Since the radiant disclosures that you make
Are of an eternal vista, manqué and gold
And brown, an Italy of the mind, a place
Of fear before the disorder of the strange,
A time in which the poet's politics
Will rule in a poets' world.

—Wallace Stevens

I

Percy Bysshe Shelley, one of the greatest lyrical poets in Western tradition, has been dead for more than a hundred and forty years,

† From *The Selected Poetry of Shelley*, edited by Harold Bloom. Copyright © 1966 by Harold Bloom. Reprinted by permission of The New American Library, Inc.

and critics have abounded, from his own day to ours, to insist that his poetry died with him. Until recently, it was fashionable to apologize for Shelley's poetry, if one liked it at all. Each reader of poetry, however vain, can speak only for himself, and there will be only description and praise in this introduction, for after many years of reading Shelley's poems, I find nothing in them that needs apology. Shelley is a unique poet, one of the most original in the language, and he is in many ways *the* poet proper, as much so as any in the language. His poetry is autonomous, finely wrought, in the highest degree imaginative, and has the spiritual form of vision stripped of all veils and ideological coverings, the vision many readers justly seek in poetry, despite the admonitions of a multitude of churchwardenly critics.

The essential Shelley is so fine a poet that one can feel absurd in urging his claims upon a reader:

> I am the eye with which the Universe
>   Beholds itself and knows itself divine;
> All harmony of instrument or verse,
>   All prophecy, all medicine is mine,
> All light of art or nature;—to my song
> Victory and praise in its own right belong.

That is Apollo singing, in the "Hymn" that Shelley had the sublime audacity to write for him, with the realization that, like Keats, he was a rebirth of Apollo. When, in *The Triumph of Life*, Rousseau serves as Virgil to Shelley's Dante, he is made to speak lines as brilliantly and bitterly condensed as poetry in English affords:

> And if the spark with which Heaven lit my spirit
> Had been with purer nutriment supplied,
>
> Corruption would not now thus much inherit
> Of what was once Rousseau—nor this disguise
> Stain that which ought to have disdained to wear it.

The urbane lyricism of the "Hymn of Apollo," and the harshly self-conscious, internalized dramatic quality of *The Triumph of Life* are both central to Shelley. Most central is the prophetic intensity, as much a result of displaced Protestantism as it is in Blake or in Wordsworth, but seeming more an Orphic than Hebraic phenomenon when it appears in Shelley. Religious poet as he primarily was, what Shelley prophesied was one restored Man who transcended men, gods, the natural world, and even the poetic faculty. Shelley chants the apotheosis, not of the poet, but of desire itself:

> Man, oh, not men! a chain of linked thought,
> Of love and might to be divided not,

Compelling the elements with adamantine stress;
    As the sun rules, even with a tyrant's gaze,
    The unquiet republic of the maze
Of planets, struggling fierce towards heaven's free wilderness

    Man, one harmonious soul of many a soul,
    Whose nature is its own divine control,
Where all things flow to all, as rivers to the sea. . . .

The rhapsodic intensity, the cumulative drive and yet firm control of those last three lines in particular, as the high song of humanistic celebration approaches its goal—that seems to me what is crucial in Shelley, and its presence throughout much of his work constitutes his special excellence as a poet.

Lyrical poetry at its most intense frequently moves toward direct address between one human consciousness and another, in which the "I" of the poet directly invokes the personal "Thou" of the reader. Shelley is an intense lyricist as Alexander Pope is an intense satirist; even as Pope assimilates every literary form he touches to satire, so Shelley converts forms as diverse as drama, prose essay, romance, satire, epyllion, into lyric. To an extent he himself scarcely realized, Shelley's genius desired a transformation of all experience, natural and literary, into the condition of lyric. More than all other poets, Shelley's compulsion is to present life as a direct confrontation of equal realities. This compulsion seeks absolute intensity, and courts straining and breaking in consequence. When expressed as love, it must manifest itself as mutual destruction:

    In one another's substance finding food,
    Like flames too pure and light and unimbued
    To nourish their bright lives with baser prey,
    Which point to Heaven and cannot pass away:
    One Heaven, one Hell, one immortality,
    And one annihilation.

Shelley is the poet of these flames, and he is equally the poet of a particular shadow, which falls perpetually between all such flames, a shadow of ruin that tracks every imaginative flight of fire:

    O, Thou, who plumed with strong desire
        Wouldst float above the earth, beware!
    A Shadow tracks thy flight of fire—
        Night is coming!

By the time Shelley had reached his final phase, of which the great monuments are *Adonais* and *The Triumph of Life*, he had become altogether the poet of this shadow of ruin, and had ceased to celebrate the possibilities of imaginative relationship. In giving himself, at last, over to the dark side of his own vision, he resolved (or perhaps merely evaded, judgment being so difficult here) a conflict within his self and poetry that had been present from the start. Though it has become a commonplace of recent criticism and scholarship to affirm otherwise, I do not think that Shelley changed very much, as a poet, during the last (and most important) six years of his life, from the summer of 1816 until the summer of 1822. The two poems of self-discovery, of mature poetic incarnation, written in 1816, "Mont Blanc" and the "Hymn to Intellectual Beauty," reveal the two contrary aspects of Shelley's vision that his entire sequence of major poems reveals. The head and the heart, each totally honest in encountering reality, yield rival reports as to the name and nature of reality. The head, in "Mont Blanc," learns, like Blake, that there is no natural religion. There is a Power, a secret strength of things, but it hides its true shape or its shapelessness behind or beneath a dread mountain, and it shows itself only as an indifference, or even pragmatically a malevolence, towards the well-being of men. But the Power speaks forth, through a poet's act of confrontation with it which is the very act of writing his poem, and the Power, rightly interpreted, can be used to repeal the large code of fraud, institutional and historical Christianity, and the equally massive code of woe, the laws of the nation-states of Europe in the age of Castlereagh and Metternich. In the "Hymn to Intellectual Beauty" a very different Power is invoked, but with a deliberate and even austere tenuousness. A shadow, itself invisible, of an unseen Power, sweeps through our dull dense world, momentarily awakening both nature and man to a sense of love and beauty, a sense just beyond the normal range of apprehension. But the shadow departs, for all its benevolence, and despite the poet's prayers for its more habitual sway. The heart's responses have not failed, but the shadow that is antithetically a radiance will not come to stay. The mind, searching for what would suffice, encountered an icy remoteness, but dared to affirm the triumph of its imaginings over the solitude and vacancy of an inadvertent nature. The emotions, visited by delight, felt the desolation of powerlessness, but dared to hope for a fuller visitation. Both odes suffer from the evident straining of their creator to reach a finality, but both survive in their creator's tough honesty and gathering sense of form.

"Mont Blanc" is a poem of the age of Shelley's father-in-law, William Godwin, while the "Hymn to Intellectual Beauty" belongs to the age of Wordsworth, Shelley's lost leader in the realms of emotion. Godwin became a kind of lost leader for Shelley also, but less on the intellectual than on the personal level. The scholarly criticism of Shelley is full of sand traps, and one of the deepest is the prevalent notion that Shelley underwent an intellectual metamorphosis from being the disciple of Godwin and the French philosophical materialists to being a Platonist or Neoplatonist, an all but mystical idealist. The man Shelley may have undergone such a transformation, though the evidence for it is equivocal; the poet Shelley did not. He started as a split being, and ended as one, but his awareness of the division in his consciousness grew deeper, and produced finally the infernal vision of *The Triumph of Life*.

II

> But even supposing that a man should raise a dead body to life before our eyes, and on this fact rest his claim to being considered the son of God;—the Humane Society restores drowned persons, and because it makes no mystery of the method it employs, its members are not mistaken for the sons of God. All that we have a right to infer from our ignorance of the cause of any event is that we do not know it. . . .
>
> —Shelley, *Notes On Queen Mab*

The deepest characteristic of Shelley's poetic mind is its skepticism. Shelley's intellectual agnosticism was more fundamental than either his troubled materialism or his desperate idealism. Had the poet turned his doubt against all entities but his own poetry, while sparing that, he would have anticipated certain later developments in the history of literature, but his own work would have lost one of its most precious qualities, a unique sensitivity to its own limitations. This sensitivity can be traced from the very beginnings of Shelley's mature style, and may indeed have made possible the achievement of that style.

Shelley was anything but a born poet, as even a brief glance at his apprentice work will demonstrate. Blake at fourteen was a great lyric poet; Shelley at twenty-two was still a bad one. He found himself, as a stylist, in the autumn of 1815, when he composed the astonishing *Alastor*, a blank verse rhapsodic narrative of a destructive and subjective quest. *Alastor*, though it has been out of fashion for a long time, is nevertheless a great and appalling work, at once a dead end, and a prophecy that Shelley finally could not evade.

Shelley's starting point as a serious poet was Wordsworth, and *Alastor* is a stepchild of *The Excursion*, a poem frigid in itself, but profoundly influential, if only antithetically, on Shelley, Byron, Keats, and many later poets. The figure of the Solitary, in *The Excursion*, is the central instance of the most fundamental of Romantic archetypes, the man alienated from others and himself by excessive self-consciousness. Whatever its poetic lapses, *The Excursion* is our most extensive statement of the Romantic mythology of the Self, and the young Shelley quarried in it for imaginatively inescapable reasons, as Byron and Keats did also. Though the poet-hero of *Alastor* is not precisely an innocent sufferer, he shares the torment of Wordsworth's Solitary, and like him:

> sees
> Too clearly; feels too vividly; and longs
> To realize the vision, with intense
> And over-constant yearning;—there—there lies
> The excess, by which the balance is destroyed.

Alastor, whatever Shelley's intentions, is primarily a poem about the destructive power of the imagination. For Shelley, every increase in imagination ought to have been an increase in hope, but generally the strength of imagination in Shelley fosters an answering strength of despair. In the spring of 1815 Shelley, on mistaken medical advice, confidently expected a rapid death of consumption. By autumn this expectation was put by, but the recent imagining of his own death lingers on in *Alastor*, which on one level is the poet's elegy for himself.

Most critical accounts of *Alastor* concern themselves with the apparent problem of disparities between the poem's eloquent Preface and the poem itself, but I cannot see that such disparities exist. The poem is an extremely subtle internalization of the quest-theme of romance, and the price demanded for the internalization is first, the death-in-life of what Yeats called "enforced self-realization," and at last, death itself. The *Alastor* or avenging daemon of the title is the dark double of the poet-hero, the spirit of solitude that shadows him even as he quests after his emanative portion, the soul out of his soul that Shelley later called the epipsyche. Shelley's poet longs to realize a vision, and this intense and overconstant yearning destroys natural existence, for nature cannot contain the infinite energy demanded by the vision. Wordsworthian nature, and not the poet-hero, is the equivocal element in *Alastor*, the problem the reader needs to, but cannot, resolve. For this nature is a mirror-world, like that in Blake's "The Crystal Cabinet," or in much of Keats's *Endymion*. Its pyramids and domes are sepulchers for the imagination, and all its appearances are illusive, phantasmagoric, and serve only to thwart the poet's vision, and drive him on more fearfully upon his doomed and self-destructive quest. *Alastor* prophesies *The Triumph of Life*, and in the mocking light of the later poem the earlier work appears also to have been a dance of death.

The summer of 1816, with its wonderful products, "Mont Blanc" and the "Hymn to Intellectual Beauty," was for Shelley, as I have indicated, a rediscovery of the poetic self, a way out of the impasse of *Alastor*. The revolutionary epic, first called *Laon and Cynthia*, and then *The Revolt of Islam*, was Shelley's first major attempt to give his newly directed energies adequate scope, but the attempt proved abortive, and the poem's main distinction is that it is Shelley's longest. Shelley's gifts were neither for narrative nor for straightforward allegory, and the *terza rima* fragment, *Prince Athanase*, written late in 1817, a few months after *The Revolt of Islam* was finished, shows the poet back upon his true way, the study of the isolated imagination. Whatever the dangers of the subjective mode of *Alastor*, it remained always Shelley's genuine center, and his finest poems were to emerge from it. *Prince Athanase* is only a fragment, or fragments, but its first part at least retains something of the power for us that it held for the young Browning and the young Yeats. Athanase, from a Peacockian perspective, is quite like the delightfully absurd Scythrop of *Nightmare Abbey*, but if we will grant him his mask's validity we do find in him one of the archetypes of the imagination, the introspective, prematurely old poet, turning his vision outward to the world from his lonely tower of meditation:

> His soul had wedded Wisdom, and her dower
> Is love and justice, clothed in which he sate
> Apart from men, as in a lonely tower,
>
> Pitying the tumult of their dark estate.—

There is a touch of Byron's Manfred, and of Byron himself, in Athanase, and Byron is the dominant element in Shelley's next enduring poem, the conversational *Julian and Maddalo*, composed in Italy in the autumn of 1818, after the poets had been reunited. The middle portion of *Julian and Maddalo*, probably based upon legends of Tasso's madness, is an excrescence, but the earlier part of the poem, and its closing lines, introduce another Shelley, a master of the urbane, middle style, the poet of the "Letter to Maria Gisborne," the "Hymn to Mercury," of parts of *The Witch of Atlas* and *The Sensitive Plant*, and of such beautifully controlled love lyrics as "To Jane: The Invitation" and "Lines Written in the Bay of Lerici." Donald Davie, who as a critic is essentially an anti-Shelleyan of the school of Dr. Leavis, and is himself a poet in a mode antithetical to Shelley's, has written an impressive tribute to Shelley's achievement as a master of the urbane style. What I find most remarkable in this mastery is that Shelley carried it over into his major achievement, the great lyrical drama, *Prometheus Unbound*, a work written almost entirely in the high style, on the precarious level of the sublime, where urbanity traditionally has no place. The astonishingly original tone of *Prometheus Unbound* is not always successfully maintained, but for the most part it is, and one aspect of its triumph is that critics should find it so difficult a tone to characterize. The urbane conversationalist, the relentlessly direct and emotionally uninhibited lyricist, and the elevated prophet of a great age to come join together in the poet of *Prometheus Unbound*, a climactic work which is at once celebratory and ironic, profoundly idealistic and as profoundly skeptical, passionately knowing its truths and as passionately agnostic towards all truth. More than any other of Shelley's poems, *Prometheus Unbound* has been viewed as self-contradictory or at least as containing unresolved mental conflicts, so that a consideration of Shelley's ideology may be appropriate prior to a discussion of the poem.

The clue to the apparent contradictions in Shelley's thought is his profound skepticism, which has been ably expounded by C. E. Pulos in his study, *The Deep Truth.* There the poet's eclecticism is seen as centering on the point "where his empiricism terminates and his idealism begins." This point is the skeptic's position, and is where Shelley judged Montaigne, Hume, and his own older contemporary, the metaphysician Sir William Drummond, to have stood. From this position, Shelley was able to reject both the French materialistic philosophy he had embraced in his youth, and the Christianity that he had never ceased to call a despotism. Yet the skeptic's position, though it powerfully organized Shelley's revolutionary polemicism, gave no personal comfort, but took the poet to what he himself called "the verge where words abandon us, and what wonder if we grow dizzy to look down the dark abyss of how little we know." That abyss is Demogorgon's, in *Prometheus Unbound*, and its secrets are not revealed by him, for "a voice is wanting, the deep truth is imageless," and Demogorgon is a shapeless darkness. Yeats, sensing the imminence of his apocalypse, sees a vast image, a beast advancing before the gathering darkness. Shelley senses the great change that the Revolution has heralded, but confronts as apocalyptic harbinger only a fabulous and formless darkness, the only honest vision available to even the most apocalyptic of skeptics. Shelley is the most Humean poet in the language, oddly as his temperament accords with Hume's, and it is Hume, not Berkeley or Plato, whose view of reality informs *Prometheus Unbound* and the poems that came after it. Even Necessity, the dread and supposedly Godwinian governing demon of Shelley's early *Queen Mab*, is more of a Humean than a Holbachian notion, for Shelley's Necessity is "conditional, tentative and philosophically ironical," as Pulos points out. It is also a Necessity highly advantageous to a poet, for a power both sightless and unseen is a power removed from dogma and from philosophy, a power that only the poet's imagination can find the means to approach. Shelley is the unacknowledged ancestor of Wallace Stevens' conception of poetry as the Supreme Fiction, and *Prometheus Unbound* is the most capable imagining, outside of Blake and Wordsworth, that the Romantic quest for a Supreme Fiction has achieved.

The fatal aesthetic error, in reading *Prometheus Unbound* or any other substantial work by Shelley, is to start with the assumption that one is about to read Platonic poetry. I mean this in either sense, that is, either poetry deeply influenced by or expressing Platonic doctrine, or in John Crowe Ransom's special sense, a poetry discoursing in things that are at any point legitimately to be translated into ideas. Shelley's skeptical and provisional idealism is *not* Plato's, and Shelley's major poems are mythopoeic, and not translatable into any terms but their own highly original ones. Shelley has been much vicitimized in our time by two rival and equally pernicious critical fashions, one that seeks to "rescue" visionary poetry by reading it as versified Plotinus and Porphyry, and another that condemns visionary poetry from Spenser through Hart Crane as being a will-driven allegorization of an idealistic scientism vainly seeking to rival the whole of experimental science from Bacon to the present day. The first kind of criticism, from which Blake and Yeats have suffered as much as Shelley, simply misreads the entire argument against nature that visionary poetry complexly conducts. The second kind, as pervasively American as the first is British, merely underestimates the considerable powers of mind that Shelley and other poets of his tradition possessed.

Shelley admired Plato as a poet, a view he derived from Montaigne, as Pulos surmises, and he appears also to have followed Montaigne in considering Plato to be a kind of skeptic. Nothing is further from Shelley's mind and art than the Platonic view of knowledge, and nothing is further from Shelley's tentative myths than the dogmatic myths of Plato. It is one of the genuine oddities of critical history that a tough-minded Humean poet, though plagued also by an idealistic and psuedo-Platonic heart, should have acquired the reputation of having sought beauty or truth in any Platonic way or sense whatsoever. No Platonist would have doubted immortality as darkly as Shelley did, or indeed would have so recurrently doubted the very existence of anything transcendent.

The most obvious and absolute difference between Plato and Shelley is in their rival attitudes toward aesthetic experience. Shelley resembles Wordsworth or Ruskin in valuing so highly certain ecstatic moments of aesthetic contemplation precisely because the moments are fleeting, because they occupy, as Blake said, the pulsation of an artery. For Shelley these are not moments to be put aside when the enduring light of the Ideas is found; Shelley never encounters such a light, not even in *Adonais*, where Keats appears to have found a kindred light in death. There is no ladder to climb in Shelley's poetry, any more than there is in Blake's. There are more imaginative states-of-being and less imaginative ones, but no hierarchy to bridge the abyss between them.

III

It is no longer sufficient to say, like all poets, that mirrors resemble the water. Neither is it sufficient to consider that hypothesis as absolute and to suppose . . . that mirrors exhale a fresh wind or that thirsty birds drink them, leaving empty frames. We must go beyond such things. That capricious desire of a mind which becomes compulsory reality must be manifested—an individual must be shown who inserts himself into the glass and remains in its illusory land (where there are figurations and colors but these are impaired by immobile silence) and feels the shame of being nothing more than an image obliterated by nights and permitted existence by glimmers of light.

—Jorge Luis Borges

It has been my experience, as a teacher of Shelley, that few recent students enjoy *Prometheus Unbound* at a first reading, and few fail to admire it greatly at a second or later reading. *Prometheus Unbound* is a remarkably subtle and difficult poem. That a work of such length needs to be read with all the care and concentration a trained reader brings to a difficult and condensed lyric is perhaps unfortunate, yet Shelley himself affirmed that his major poem had been written only for highly adept readers, and that he hoped for only a few of these. *Prometheus Unbound* is not as obviously difficult as Blake's *The Four Zoas*, but it presents problems comparable to that work. Blake has the advantage of having made a commonplace understanding of his major poems impossible, while Shelley retains familiar (and largely misleading) mythological names like Prometheus and Jupiter. The problems of interpretation in Shelley's lyrical drama are as formidable as English poetry affords, and are perhaps finally quite unresolvable.

It seems clear that Shelley intended his poem to be a millennial rather than an apocalyptic work. The vision in Act III is of a redeemed nature, but not of an ultimate reality, whereas the vision in the great afterthought of Act IV does concern an uncovered universe. In Act IV the imagination of Shelley breaks away from the poet's apparent intention, and visualizes a world in which the veil of phenomenal reality has been rent, a world like that of the Revelation of St. John, or Night the Ninth of *The Four Zoas*. The audacity of Shelley gives us a vision of the last things without the sanction of religious or mythological tradition. Blake does the same, but Blake is systematic where Shelley risks everything on one sustained imagining.

I think that a fresh reader of *Prometheus Unbound* is best prepared if he starts with Milton in mind. This holds true also for *The Prelude*, for Blake's epics, for Keats's *Hyperion* fragments, and even for Byron's *Don Juan*, since Milton is both the Romantic starting point and the Romantic adversary. Shelley is as conscious of this as Blake or any of the others; the Preface to *Prometheus Unbound* refers to that demigod, "the sacred Milton," and commends him for having been "a bold inquirer into morals and religion." Searching out an archetype for his Prometheus, Shelley finds him in Milton's Satan, "the Hero of Paradise Lost," but a flawed, an imperfect hero, of whom Prometheus will be a more nearly perfect descendant. Shelley's poem is almost an echo chamber for *Paradise Lost*, but all the echoes are deliberate, and all of them are so stationed as to "correct" the imaginative errors of *Paradise Lost*. Almost as much as Blake's "brief epic," *Milton*, Shelley's *Prometheus Unbound* is a courageous attempt to save Milton from himself, and for the later poet. Most modern scholarly critics of Milton sneer at the Blakean or Shelleyan temerity, but no modern critic of Milton is as illuminating as Blake and Shelley are, and none knows better than they did how omnipotent an opponent they lovingly faced, or how ultimately hopeless the contest was.

Paraphrase is an ignoble mode of criticism, but it can be a surprisingly revealing one (of the critic as well as the work of course) and it is particularly appropriate to *Prometheus Unbound*, since the pattern of action in the lyrical drama is a puzzling one. A rapid survey of character and plot is hardly possible, since the poem in a strict (and maddening) sense has neither, but a few points can be risked as introduction. Shelley's source is Aeschylus, insofar as he has a source, but his genuine analogues are in his older contemporary Blake, whom he had never read, and of whom indeed he never seems to have heard. Prometheus has a resemblance both to Blake's Orc and to his Los; Jupiter is almost a double for Urizen, Asia approximates Blake's Jerusalem, while Demogorgon has nothing in common with any of Blake's "Giant Forms." But, despite this last, the shape of Shelley's myth is very like Blake's. A unitary Man fell, and split into torturing and tortured components, and into separated male and female forms as well. The torturer is not in himself a representative of comprehensive evil, because he is quite limited; indeed, he has been invented by his victim, and falls soon after his victim ceases to hate his own invention. Shelley's Jupiter, like Urizen in one of his aspects, is pretty clearly the Jehovah of institutional and historical Christianity. George Bernard Shaw, one of the most enthusiastic of Shelleyans, had some illuminating remarks on *Prometheus Unbound* in *The Perfect Wagnerite*. Jupiter, he said, "is the almighty fiend into whom the Englishman's God had degenerated during two centuries of ignorant Bible worship and shameless commercialism." Shaw rather understated the matter, since it seems indubitable that the Jupiter of Shelley's lyrical drama is one with the cheerfully abominable Jehovah of *Queen Mab*, and so had been degenerating for rather more than two centuries.

Prometheus in Shelley is both the archetypal imagination (Blake's Los) and the primordial energies of man (Blake's Orc). Jupiter, like Urizen again, is a limiter of imagination and of energy. He may masquerade as reason, but he is nothing of the kind, being a mere circumscriber and binder, like the God of *Paradise Lost*, Book III (as opposed to the very different, creative God of Milton's Book VII). Asia is certainly not the Universal Love that Shaw and most subsequent Shelleyans have taken her to be. Though she partly transcends nature she is still subject to it, and she is essentially a passive being, even though the apparently central dramatic action of the poem is assigned to her. Like the emanations in Blake, she may be taken as the total spiritual form or achieved aesthetic form quested after by her lover, Prometheus. She is less than the absolute vainly sought by the poet-hero of *Alastor*, though she is more presumably than the mortal Emilia of *Epipsychidion* can hope to represent. Her function is to hold the suffering natural world open to the transcendent love or Intellectual Beauty that hovers beyond it, but except in the brief and magnificent moment-of-moments of her transfiguration (end of Act II) she is certainly not one with the Intellectual Beauty.

That leaves us Demogorgon, the poem's finest and most frustrating invention, who has been disliked by the poem's greatest admirers, Shaw and Yeats. Had Shaw written the poem, Demogorgon would have been Creative Evolution, and had Yeats been the author, Demogorgon would have been the Thirteenth Cone of *A Vision*. But Shelley was a subtler dialectician than Shaw or Yeats; as a skeptic, he had to be. Shaw testily observed that "flatly, there is no such person as Demogorgon, and if Prometheus does not pull down Jupiter himself, no one else will." Demogorgon, Yeats insisted, was a ruinous invention for Shelley: "Demogorgon made his plot incoherent, its interpretation impossible; it was thrust there by that something which again and again forced him to balance the object of desire conceived as miraculous and superhuman, with nightmare."

Yet Demogorgon, in all his darkness, is a vital necessity in Shelley's mythopoeic quest for a humanized or displaced theodicy. The Demogorgon of Spenser and of Milton was the evil god of chaos, dread father of all the gentile divinities. Shelley's Demogorgon, like the unknown Power of *Mont Blanc*, is morally unallied; he is the god of skepticism, and thus the preceptor of our appalling freedom to imagine well or badly. His only clear attributes are dialectical; he is the god of all those at the turning, at the reversing of the cycles. Like the dialectic of the Marxists, Demogorgon is a necessitarian and materialistic entity, part of the nature of things as they are. But he resembles also the shadowy descent of the Holy Spirit in most Christian dialectics of history, though it would be more accurate to call him a demonic parody of the Spirit, just as the whole of *Prometheus Unbound* is a dark parody of Christian salvation myth. Back of Demogorgon is Shelley's difficult sense of divinity, an apocalyptic humanism like that of Blake's, and it is not possible therefore to characterize *Prometheus Unbound* as being either humanistic or theistic in its ultimate vision. Martin Price, writing of Blake's religion, observes that "Blake can hardly be identified as theist or humanist; the distinction becomes meaningless for him. God can only exist within man, but man must be raised to a perception of the infinite. Blake rejects both transcendental deity and natural man." The statement is equally true for the Shelley of *Prometheus Unbound*, if one modifies rejection of transcendental deity to a skeptical opening toward the possibility of such a Power. Though Demogorgon knows little more than does the Asia who questions him, that little concerns his relationship to a further Power, and the relationship is part of the imagelessness of ultimates, where poetry reaches its limit.

The events of *Prometheus Unbound* take place in the realm of mind, and despite his skepticism Shelley at this point in his career clung to a faith in the capacity of the human mind to renovate first itself, and then the outward world as well. The story of the lyrical drama is therefore an unfolding of renovation after renovation, until natural cycle itself is canceled in the rhapsodies of Act IV. Of actions in the traditional sense, I find only one, the act of pity that Prometheus extends towards Jupiter at line 53 of Act I. Frederick A. Pottle, in the most advanced essay yet written on the poem, insists that there ia a second and as crucial action, the descent of Asia, with her subsequent struggle to attain to a theology of love: "Asia's action is to give up her demand for an ultimate Personal Evil, to combine an unshakable faith that the universe is sound at the core with a realization that, as regards man, Time is radically and incurably evil." Behind Pottle's reading is a drastic but powerful allegorizing of the poem, in which Prometheus and Asia occupy respectively the positions of head and heart: "The head must sincerely forgive, must willingly eschew hatred on purely experimental grounds . . ." while the heart "must exorcize the demons of infancy." One can benefit from this provisional allegorizing even if one finds *Prometheus Unbound* to be less theistic in its implicatons than Pottle appears to do.

Further commentary on the complexities of the poem can be sought in works listed in the bibliography of this volume, but the aesthetic achievement needs to be considered here. Dr. Samuel Johnson still knew that invention was the essence of poetry, but this truth is mostly neglected in our contemporary criticism. It may be justly observed that Shelley had conquered the myth of Prometheus even as he had transformed it, and the conquest is the greatest glory of Shelley's poem. One power alone, Blake asserted, made a poet, the divine vision or imagination, by which he meant primarily the inventive faculty, the gift of making a myth or of so re-making a myth as to return it to the fully human truths of our original existence as unfallen men. If Johnson and Blake were right, then *Prometheus Unbound* is one of the greatest poems in the language, a judgment that will seem eccentric only to a kind of critic whose standards are centered in areas not in themselves imaginative.

IV

Nature has appointed us men to be no base or ignoble animals, but when she ushers us into the vast universe . . . she implants in our souls the unconquerable love of whatever is elevated and more divine than we. Wherefore not even the entire universe suffices for the thought and contemplation within the reach of the human mind.

—Longinus, *On the Sublime*

Published with *Prometheus Unbound* in 1820 were a group of Shelley's major odes, including "Ode to the West Wind," "To a Skylark," and "Ode to Liberty." These poems show Shelley as a lyricist deliberately seeking to extend the sublime mode, and are among his finest achievements.

Wallace Stevens, in one of the marvelous lyrics of his old age, hears the cry of the leaves and knows "it is the cry of leaves that do not transcend themselves," knows that the cry means no more than can be found "in the final finding of the ear, in the thing/ Itself." From this it follows, with massive but terrible dignity, that "at last, the cry concerns no one at all." This is Stevens' modern reality of *decreation*, and this is the fate that Shelley's magnificent "Ode to the West Wind" seeks to avert. Shelley hears a cry of leaves that do transcend themselves, and he deliberately seeks a further transcendence that will metamorphosize "the thing itself" into human form, so that at last the cry will concern all men. But in Shelley's "Ode," as in Stevens, "there is a conflict, there is a resistance involved;/ And being part is an exertion that declines." Shelley too feels the frightening strength of the *given*, "the life of that which gives life as it is," but here as elsewhere Shelley does not accept the merely "as it is." The function of his "Ode" is apocalyptic, and the controlled fury of his spirit is felt throughout this perfectly modulated "trumpet of a prophecy."

What is most crucial to an understanding of the "Ode" is the realization that its fourth and fifth stanzas bear a wholly antithetical relation to one another. The triple invocation to the elements of earth, air, and water occupies the first three stanzas of the poem, and the poet himself does not enter those stanzas; in them he is only a voice imploring the elements to hear. In the fourth stanza, the poet's ego enters the poem, but in the guise only of a battered Job, seeking to lose his own humanity. From this nadir, the extraordinary and poignantly "broken" music of the last stanza rises up, into the poet's own element of fire, to affirm again the human dignity of the prophet's vocation, and to suggest a mode of imaginative renovation that goes beyond the cyclic limitations of nature. Rarely in the history of poetry have seventy lines done so much so well.

Shelley's other major odes are out of critical favor in our time, but this is due as much to actual misinterpretations as to any qualities inherent in these poems. "To a Skylark" strikes readers as silly when they visualize the poet staring at the bird and hailing it as nonexistent, but these readers have begun with such gross inaccuracy that their experience of what they take to be the poem may simply be dismissed. The ode's whole point turns on the lark's being out of sight from the start; the poet *hears* an evanescent song, but can see nothing, even as Keats in the "Ode to a Nightingale" never actually sees the bird. Flying too high almost to be heard, the lark is crucially compared by Shelley to his central symbol, the morning star fading into the dawn of an unwelcome day. What can barely be heard, and not seen at all, is still discovered to be a basis upon which to rejoice, and indeed becomes an inescapable motive for metaphor, a dark justification for celebrating the light of uncommon day. In the great revolutionary "Ode to Liberty," Shelley successfully adapts the English Pindaric to an abstract political theme, mostly by means of making the poem radically its own subject, as he does on a larger scale in *The Witch of Atlas* and *Epipsychidion*.

In the last two years of his life, Shelley subtly modified his lyrical art, making the best of his shorter poems the means by which his experimental intellectual temper and his more traditional social urbanity could be reconciled. The best of these lyrics would include "Hymn of Apollo," "The Two Spirits: An Allegory," "To Night," "Lines . . . on . . . the Death of Napoleon," and the final group addressed to Jane Williams, or resulting from the poet's love for her, including "When the lamp is shattered," "To Jane: The Invitation," and "The Recollection," "With a Guitar, to Jane," and the last completed lyric, the immensely moving "Lines written in the Bay of Lerici." Here are nine lyrics as varied and masterful as the language affords. Take these together with Shelley's achievements in the sublime ode, with the best of his earlier lyrics, and with the double handful of magnificent interspersed lyrics contained in *Prometheus Unbound* and *Hellas,* and it will not seem as if Swinburne was excessive in claiming for Shelley a rank as one of the two or three major lyrical poets in English tradition down to Swinburne's own time.

The best admonition to address to a reader of Shelley's lyrics, as of his longer poems, is to slow down and read very closely, so as to learn what Wordsworth could have meant when he reluctantly conceded that "Shelley is one of the best *artists* of us all: I mean in workmanship of style":

> There is no dew on the dry grass tonight,
>   Nor damp within the shadow of the trees;
> The wind is intermitting, dry, and light;
>   And in the inconstant motion of the breeze
> The dust and straws are driven up and down,
> And whirled about the pavement of the town.
> —"Evening: Ponte Al Mare, Pisa"

This altogether characteristic example of Shelley's workmanship is taken from a minor and indeed unfinished lyric of 1821. I have undergone many unhappy conversations with university wits, poets, and critics, who have assured me that "Shelley had a tin ear," the assurance being given on one occasion by no less distinguished a prosodist than W. H. Auden, and I am always left wondering if my ears have heard correctly. The fashion of insisting that Shelley was a poor craftsman seems to have started with T. S. Eliot, spread from him to Dr. Leavis and the Fugitive group of Southern poets and critics, and then for a time became universal. It was a charming paradox that formalist and rhetorical critics should have become so affectively disposed against a poet as to be incapable of reading any of his verbal figures with even minimal accuracy, but the charm has worn off, and one hopes that the critical argument about Shelley can now move on into other (and more disputable) areas.

v

Cruelty has a Human Heart,
And Jealousy a Human Face;
Terror the Human Form Divine,
And Secrecy the Human Dress.

The Human Dress is forged Iron,
The Human Form a fiery Forge,
The Human Face a Furnace seal'd,
The Human Heart its hungry Gorge.
—Blake, "A Divine Image"

The Cenci occupies a curious place in Shelley's canon, one that is overtly apart from the sequence of his major works that goes from *Prometheus Unbound* to *The Triumph of Life*. Unlike the psuedo-Elizabethan tragedies of Shelley's disciple Beddoes, *The Cenci* is in no obvious way a visionary poem. Yet it is a tragedy only in a very peculiar sense, and has little in common with the stage-plays it ostensibly seeks to emulate. Its true companions, and descendants, are Browning's giant progression of dramatic monologues, *The Ring and the Book*, and certain works of Hardy that share its oddly effective quality of what might be termed dramatic solipsism, to have recourse to a desperate oxymoron. Giant incongruities clash in *Prometheus Unbound* as they do in Blake's major poems, but the clashes are resolved by both poets in the realms of a self-generated mythology. When parallel incongruities meet violently in *The Cenci*, in a context that excludes myth, the reader is asked to accept as human characters beings whose states of mind are too radically and intensely pure to be altogether human. Blake courts a similar problem whenever he is only at the borderline of his own mythical world, as in *Visions of the Daughters of Albion* and *The French Revolution*. Shelley's Beatrice and Blake's Oothoon are either too human or not human enough; the reader is uncomfortable in not knowing whether he encounters a Titaness or one of his own kind.

Yet this discomfort need not wreck the experience of reading *The Cenci*, which is clearly a work that excels in character rather than in plot, and more in the potential of character than in its realization. At the heart of *The Cenci* is Shelley's very original conception of tragedy. Tragedy is not a congenial form for apocalyptic writers, who tend to have a severe grudge against it, as Blake and D. H. Lawrence did. Shelley's morality was an apocalyptic one, and the implicit standard for *The Cenci* is set in *The Mask of Anarchy*, which advocates a nonviolent resistance to evil. Beatrice is tragic because she does *not* meet this high standard, though she is clearly superior to every other person in her world. Life triumphs over Beatrice because she does take violent revenge upon an intolerable oppressor. The tragedy Shelley develops is one of a heroic character "violently thwarted from her nature" by circumstances she ought to have defied. This allies Beatrice with a large group of Romantic heroes, ranging from the Cain of Byron's drama to the pathetic daemon of Mary Shelley's *Frankenstein* and, on the cosmic level, embracing Shelley's own Prometheus and the erring Zoas or demigods of Blake's myth.

To find tragedy in any of these, you must persuasively redefine tragedy, as Shelley implicitly did. Tragedy becomes the fall of the imagination, or rather the falling away from imaginative conduct on the part of a heroically imaginative individual.

Count Cenci is, as many critics have noted, a demonic parody of Jehovah, and has a certain resemblance therefore to Shelley's Jupiter and Blake's Tiriel and Urizen. The count is obsessively given to hatred, and is vengeful, anal-erotic in his hoarding tendencies, incestuous, tyrannical, and compelled throughout by a jealous possessiveness even toward those he abhors. He is also given to bursts of Tiriel-like cursing, and like Tiriel or Jupiter he has his dying-god aspect, for his death symbolizes the necessity of revolution, the breaking up of an old and hopeless order. Like all heavenly tyrants in his tradition, Cenci's quest for dominion is marked by a passion for uniformity, and it is inevitable that he seek to seduce the angelic Beatrice to his own perverse level. His success is an ironic one, since he does harden her into the only agent sufficiently strong and remorseless to cause his own destruction.

The aesthetic power of *The Cenci* lies in the perfection with which it both sets forth Beatrice's intolerable dilemma, and presents the reader with a parallel dilemma. The natural man in the reader exults at Beatrice's metamorphosis into a relentless avenger, and approves even her untruthful denial of responsibility for her father's murder. The imaginative man in the reader is appalled at the degeneration of an all-but-angelic intelligence into a skilled intriguer and murderess. This fundamental dichotomy *in the reader* is the theater where the true anguish of *The Cenci* is enacted. The overt theme becomes the universal triumph of life over integrity, which is to say of death-in-life over life.

The Cenci is necessarily a work conceived in the Shakespearean shadow, and it is obvious that Shelley did not succeed in forming a dramatic language for himself in his play. Dr. Leavis has seized upon this failure with an inquisitor's joy, saying that "it takes no great discernment to see that *The Cenci* is very bad and that its badness is characteristic." It takes a very little discernment to see that *The Cenci* survives its palpable flaws and that it gives us what Wordsworth's *The Borderers*, Byron's *Cain*, and Coleridge's *Remorse* give us also in their very different ways, a distinguished example of Romantic, experimental tragedy, in which a crime against nature both emancipates consciousness and painfully turns consciousness in upon itself, with an attendant loss of a higher and more innocent state of being. The Beatrice of Shelley's last scene has learned her full autonomy, her absolute alienation from nature and society, but at a frightful, and to Shelley, a tragic cost.

VI

> But were it not, that *Time* their troubler is,
>   All that in this delightfull Gardin growes,
>   Should happie be, and have immortall blis . . .
>
> —Spenser

In the spring of 1820, at Pisa, Shelley wrote *The Sensitive Plant*, a remarkably original poem, and a permanently valuable one, though it is little admired in recent years. As a parable of imaginative failure, the poem is another of the many Romantic versions of the Miltonic Eden's transformation into a wasteland, but the limitations it explores are not the Miltonic ones of human irresolution and disobedience. Like all of Shelley's major poems, *The Sensitive Plant* is a skeptical work, the skepticism here manifesting itself as a precariously poised suspension of judgment on the human capacity to perceive whether or not natural *or* imaginative values survive the cyclic necessities of change and decay.

The tone of *The Sensitive Plant* is a deliberate exquisitiveness, of a more-than-Spenserian kind. Close analogues to this tone can be found in major passages of Keats's *Endymion* and in Blake's *The Book of Thel*. The ancestor poet for all these visionary poems, including Shelley's *The Witch of Atlas* and the vision of Beulah in Blake's *Milton*, is of course Spenser, whose mythic version of the lower or earthly paradise is presented as the Garden of Adonis in *The Faerie Queene*, Book III, Canto VI, which is probably the most influential passage of poetry in English, if by "influential" we mean what influences other poets.

The dark melancholy of *The Sensitive Plant* is not Spenserian, but everything else in the poem to some extent is. Like many poems in this tradition, the lament is for mutability itself, for change seen as loss. What is lost is innocence, natural harmony, the mutual interpenetrations of a merely given condition that is nevertheless whole and beyond the need of justification. The new state, experiential life as seen in Part III of the poem, is the world without imagination, a tract of weeds. When Shelley, in the noblest quatrains he ever wrote, broods on this conclusion he offers no consolation beyond the most urbane of his skepticisms. The light that puts out our eyes is a darkness to us, yet remains light, and death may be a mockery of our inadequate imaginations. The myth of the poem—its garden, lady, and plant—may have prevailed, while we, the poem's readers, may be too decayed in our perceptions to know this. Implicit in Shelley's poem is a passionate refutation of time, but the passion is a desperation unless the mind's imaginings can cleanse perception of its obscurities. Nothing in the poem proper testifies to the mind's mastery of outward sense. The "Conclusion" hints at what Shelley beautifully calls "a modest creed," but the poet is too urbane and skeptical to urge it upon either us or himself. The creed appears again in *The Witch of Atlas*, but with a playful and amiable disinterestedness that removes it almost entirely from the anguish of human desire.

The Witch of Atlas is Shelley's most inventive poem, and is by any just standards a triumph. In kind, it goes back to the English Renaissance epyllion, the Ovidian erotic-mythological brief epic, but in tone and procedure it is a new departure, except that for Shelley it had been prophesied by his own rendition of the Homeric "Hymn to Mercury." Both poems are in *ottava rima*, both have a Byronic touch, and both have been characterized accurately as possessing a tone of visionary cynicism. Hermes and the Witch of Atlas qualify the divine grandeurs among which they move, and remind us that the imagination unconfined respects no orders of being, however traditional or natural.

G. Wilson Knight first pointed to the clear resemblance between the tone of *The Witch of Atlas* and Yeats's later style, and there is considerable evidence of the permanent effect of the poem's fantastic plot and properties upon Yeats. Shelley's *Witch* is Yeats's "Byzantium" writ large; both poems deal with Phase 15 of Yeats's *A Vision*, with the phase of poetic incarnation, and so with the state of the soul in which art is created. In a comparison of the two poems, the immediate contrast will be found in the extraordinary relaxation that Shelley allows himself. The nervous intensity that the theme demands is present in the *Witch*, but has been transmuted into an almost casual acceptance of intolerable realities that art cannot mitigate.

The Witch of Atlas, as Shelley says in the poem's highly ironic dedicatory stanzas to his wife, tells no story, false or true, but is "a visionary rhyme." If the Witch is to be translated at all into terms not her own, then she can only be the mythopoeic impulse or inventive faculty iteself, one of whose manifestations is the Hermaphrodite, which we can translate as a poem, or any work of art. The Witch's boat is the emblem of her creative desire, and like the Hermaphrodite it works against nature. The Hermaphrodite is both a convenience for the Witch, helping her to go beyond natural limitations, and a companion of sorts, but a highly inadequate one, being little more than a robot. The limitations of art are involved here, for the Witch has rejected the love of every mortal being, and has chosen instead an automaton of her own creation. In the poignant stanzas in which she rejects the suit of the nymphs, Shel-

ley attains one of the immese triumphs of his art, but the implications of the triumph, and of the entire poem, are as deliberately
chilling as the Byzantine vision of the aging Yeats.

Though the Witch turns her playful and antinomian spirit to
the labor of upsetting church and state, in the poem's final stanzas,
and subverts even the tired conventions of mortality as well as of
morality, the ultimate impression she makes upon us is one of remoteness. The fierce aspirations of *Prometheus Unbound* were
highly qualified by a consciously manipulated prophetic irony, yet
they retained their force, and aesthetic immediacy, as the substance
of what Shelley passionately desired. The ruin that shadows love in
Prometheus Unbound, the *amphisbaena* or two-headed serpent that
could move downward and outward to destruction again, the warning made explicit in the closing stanzas spoken by Demogorgon;
it is these antithetical hints that survived in Shelley longer than the
vehement hope of his lyrical drama. *The Sensitive Plant* and *The
Witch of Atlas* manifest a subtle movement away from that hope.
Epipsychidion, the most exalted of Shelley's poems, seeks desperately to renovate that hope by placing it in the context of hetero-
sexual love, and with the deliberate and thematic self-combustion
of the close of *Epipsychidion* Shelley appears to have put all hope
aside, and to have prepared himself for his magnificent but despairing last phase, of which the enduring monuments are *Adonais* and
The Triumph of Life.

VII

What man most passionately wants is his living wholeness and
his living unison, not his own isolate salvation of his "soul." Man
wants his physical fulfillment first and foremost, since now, once
and once only, he is in the flesh and potent. For man, as for
flower and beast and bird, the supreme triumph is to be most
vividly, most perfectly alive. Whatever the unborn and the dead
may know, they cannot know the beauty, the marvel of being alive
in the flesh. The dead may look after the afterwards. But the
magnificent here and now of life in the flesh is ours, and ours
alone, and ours only for a time.

D. H. Lawrence, *Apocalypse*

Except for Blake's *Visions of the Daughters of Albion*, which it
in some respects resembles, *Epipsychidion* is the most outspoken
and eloquent appeal for free love in the language. Though this
appeal is at the heart of the poem, and dominates its most famous
passage (lines 147–54), it is only one aspect of a bewilderingly
problematical work. *Epipsychidion* was intended by Shelley to be
his *Vita Nuova*, celebrating the discovery of his Beatrice in Emilia

Viviani. It proved however to be a climactic and not an initiatory poem, for in it Shelley culminates the quest begun in *Alastor*, only to find after culmination that the quest remains unfulfilled and unfulfillable. The desire of Shelley remains infinite, and the only emblem adequate to that desire is the morning and evening star, Venus, at whose sphere the shadow cast by earth into the heavens reaches its limits. After *Epipsychidion*, in *Adonais* and *The Triumph of Life*, only the star of Venus abides as an image of the good. It is not Emilia Viviani but her image that proves inadequate in *Epipsychidion*, a poem whose most turbulent and valuable element is its struggle to record the process of image-making. Of all Shelley's major poems, *Epipsychidion* most directly concerns itself with the mind in creation. "Mont Blanc" has the same position among Shelley's shorter poems, and has the advantage of its relative discursiveness, as the poet meditates upon the awesome spectacle before him. *Epipsychidion* is continuous rhapsody, and sustains its lyrical intensity of a lovers' confrontation for six hundred lines. The mind in creation, here and in *A Defense of Poetry*, is as a fading coal, and much of Shelley's art in the poem is devoted to the fading phenomenon, as image after image recedes and the poet-lover feels more fearfully the double burden of his love's inexpressibility and its necessary refusal to accept even natural, let alone societal limitations.

There is, in Shelley's development as a poet, a continuous effort to subvert the poetic image, so as to arrive at a more radical kind of verbal figure, which Shelley never altogether achieved. Tenor and vehicle are imported into one another, and the choice of natural images increasingly favors those already on the point of vanishing, just within the ken of eye and ear. The world is skeptically taken up into the mind, and there are suggestions and overtones that all of reality is a phantasmagoria. Shelley becomes an idealist totally skpetical of the metaphysical foundations of idealism, while he continues to entertain a skeptical materialism, or rather he becomes a fantasist pragmatically given to some materialist hypotheses that his imagination regards as absurd. This is not necessarily a self-contradiction, but it is a kind of psychic split, and it is exposed very powerfully in *Epipsychidion*. Who wins a triumph in the poem, the gambler with the limits of poetry and of human relationship, or the inexorable limits? Space, time, loneliness, mortality, wrong —all these are put aside by vision, yet vision darkens perpetually in the poem. "The world, unfortunately, is real; I, unfortunately, am Borges," is the ironic reflection of a great contemporary seer of phantasmagorias, as he brings his refutation of time to an unrefuting close. Shelley too is swept along by what destroys him and is inescapable, the reality that will not yield to the most relentless of imaginings. In that knowledge, he turns to elegy and away from celebration.

Adonais, Shelley's formal elegy for Keats, is a great monument in the history of the English elegy, and yet hardly an elegy at all. Nearly five hundred lines long, it exceeds in scope and imaginative ambition its major English ancestors, the *Astrophel* of Spenser and the *Lycidas* of Milton, as well as such major descendants as Arnold's *Thyrsis* and Swinburne's *Ave Atque Vale*. Only Tennyson's *In Memoriam* rivals it as an attempt to make the elegy a vehicle for not less than everything a particular poet has to say on the ultimates of human existence. Yet Tennyson, for all his ambition, stays within the bounds of elegy. *Adonais*, in the astonishing sequence of its last eighteen stanzas, is no more an elegy proper than Yeats's "Byzantium" poems are. Like the "Byzantium" poems (which bear a close relation to it), *Adonais* is a high song of poetic self-recognition in the presence of foreshadowing death, and also a description of poetic existence, even of a poem's state of being.

Whether Shelley holds together the elegiac and visionary aspects of his poem is disputable; it is difficult to see the full continuity that takes the poet from his hopeless opening to his more than triumphant close, from:

> I weep for Adonais—he is dead!
> O, weep for Adonais! though our tears
> Thaw not the frost which binds so dear a head!

to:

> I am borne darkly, fearfully, afar;
> Whilst, burning through the inmost veil of Heaven,
> The soul of Adonais, like a star,
> Beacons from the abode where the Eternal are.

From frost to fire as a mode of renewal for the self: that is an archetypal Romantic pattern, familiar to us from *The Ancient Mariner* and the *Intimations* Ode (see the contrast between the last line of stanza VIII and the first of stanza IX in that poem). But *Adonais* breaks this pattern, for the soul of Shelley's Keats burns through the final barrier to revelation only by means of an energy that is set against nature, and the frost that no poetic tears can thaw yields only to "the fire for which all thirst," but which no natural man can drink, for no living man can drink of the whole wine of the burning fountain. As much as Yeats's "All Souls' Night," *Adonais* reaches out to a reality of ghostly intensities, yet Shelley as well as Yeats is reluctant to leave behind the living man who blindly drinks his drop, and *Adonais* is finally a "Dialogue of Self and Soul," in which the Soul wins a costly victory, as costly as the Self's triumph in Yeats's "Dialogue." The Shelley who cries out, in rapture and dismay, "The massy earth and spherèd skies are riven!", is a poet who has given himself freely to the tempest of creative destruction, to a reality beyond the natural, yet who movingly looks back upon the shore and upon the throng he has forsaken. The close of *Adonais* is a triumph of character over personality, to use a Yeatsian dialectic, but the personality of the lyric poet is nevertheless the dominant aesthetic element in the poem's dark and fearful apotheosis.

"Apotheosis is not the origin of the major man," if we are to credit Stevens, but the qualified assertions of Shelley do proclaim such an imaginative humanism in the central poems that preceded *Adonais*. In *Adonais* the imagination forsakes humanism, even as it does in the "Byzantium" poems.

Though *Adonais* has been extensively Platonized and Neo-platonized by a troop of interpreters, it is in a clear sense a materialist's poem, written out of a materialist's despair at his own deepest convictions, and finally a poem soaring above those convictions into a mystery that leaves a pragmatic materialism quite undisturbed. Whatever supernal apprehension it is that Shelley attains in the final third of *Adonais*, it is not in any ordinary sense a religious faith, for the only attitude towards natural existence it fosters in the poet is one of unqualified rejection, and indeed its pragmatic postulate is simply suicide. Nothing could be more different in spirit from Demogorgon's closing lines in *Prometheus Unbound* than the final stanzas of *Adonais*, and the ruthlessly skeptical Shelley must have known this.

He knew also though that we do not judge poems by pragmatic tests, and the splendor of the resolution to *Adonais* is not impaired by its implications of human defeat. Whether Keats lives again is unknown to Shelley; poets are among "the enduring dead," and Keats "wakes *or* sleeps" with them. The endurance is not then necessarily a mode of survival, and what flows back to the burning fountain is not necessarily the *human* soul, though it is "pure spirit." Or if it is the soul of Keats as well as "the soul of Adonais," then the accidents of individual personality have abandoned it, making this cold comfort indeed. Still, Shelley is not offering us (or himself) comfort; his elegy has no parallel to Milton's consolation in *Lycidas*:

> There entertain him all the Saints above,
> In solemn troops, and sweet Societies
> That sing, and singing in their glory move,
> And wipe the tears forever from his eyes.

To Milton, as a Christian poet, death is somehow unnatural. To Shelley, for all his religious temperament, death is wholly natural, and if death is dead, then nature must be dead also. The final third of *Adonais* is desperately apocalyptic in a way that *Prometheus Unbound*, Act IV, was not. For *Prometheus Unbound* ends in a Saturnalia, though there are darker implications also, but *Adonais* soars beyond the shadow that the earth casts into the heavens. Shelley was ready for a purgatorial vision of earth, and no longer could sustain even an ironic hope.

VIII

> Mal dare, e mal tener lo mondo pulcro
> ha tolto loro, e posti a questa zuffa;
> qual ella sia, parole non ci appulcro.
>
> —*Inferno* 7:58–60

> That ill they gave,
> And ill they kept, hath of the beauteous world
> Deprived, and set them at this strife, which needs
> No labour'd phrase of mine to set it off.
>
> —Cary, *The Vision of Dante*

There are elements in *The Triumph of Life*, Shelley's last poem, that mark it as an advance over all the poetry he had written previously. The bitter eloquence and dramatic condensation of the style are new; so is a ruthless pruning of invention. The mythic figures are few, being confined to the "Shape all light," the charioteer, and Life itself, while the two principal figures, Shelley and Rousseau, appear in their proper persons, though in the perspective of eternity, as befits a vision of judgment. The tone of Shelley's last poem is derived from Dante's *Purgatorio*, even as much in *Epipsychidion* comes from Dante's *Vita Nuova*, but the events and atmosphere of *The Triumph of Life* have more in common with the *Inferno*. Still, the poem is a purgatorial work, for all the unrelieved horror of its vision, and perhaps Shelley might have found some gradations in his last vision, so as to climb out of the poem's impasse, if he had lived to finish it, though I incline to doubt this. As it stands, the poem is in hell, and Shelley is there, one of the apparently condemned, as all men are, he says, save for "the sacred few" of Athens and Jerusalem, martyrs to vision like Socrates, Jesus, and a chosen handful, with whom on the basis of *Adonais* we can place Keats, as he too had touched the world with his living flame, and then fled back up to his native noon.

The highest act of Shelley's imagination in the poem, perhaps in all of his poetry, is in the magnificent appropriateness of Rousseau's presence, from his first entrance to his last speech before the fragment breaks off. Rousseau is Virgil to Shelley's Dante, in the sense of being his imaginative ancestor, his guide in creation, and also in prophesying the dilemma the disciple would face at the point of crisis in his life. Shelley, sadly enough, was hardly in the middle of the journey, but at twenty-nine he had only days to live, and the imagination in him felt compelled to face the last things. Without Rousseau, Shelley would not have written the "Hymn to Intellectual Beauty", and perhaps not "Mont Blanc" either. Rousseau, more even than Wordsworth, was the prophet of natural man, and the celebrator of the state of nature. Even in 1816, writing his hymns and starting the process that would lead to the conception of *Prometheus Unbound*, Shelley fights against the natural man and natural religion, but he fights partly against his own desires, and the vision of Rousseau haunts him still in the "Ode to the West Wind" and in the greatest chant of the apocalyptic fourth act of the lyrical drama, the song of the Earth beginning "It interpenetrates my granite mass." Shelley knew that the spirit of Rousseau was what had moved him most in the spirit of the age, and temperamentally (which counts for most in a poet) it makes more sense to name Shelley the disciple and heir of Rousseau than of Godwin, or Wordsworth, or any of the later French theorists of Revolution. Rousseau and Hume make an odd formula of heart and head in Shelley, but they are the closest parallels to be found to him on the emotional and intellectual sides respectively.

Chastened and knowing, almost beyond knowledge, Rousseau enters the poem, speaking not to save his disciple, but to show him that he cannot be saved, and to teach him a style fit for his despair. The imaginative lesson of *The Triumph of Life* is wholly present in the poem's title: life always triumphs, for life, our life, is after all what the preface to *Alastor* called it, a "lasting misery and loneliness." One Power only, the Imagination, is capable of redeeming life, "but that Power which strikes the luminaries of the world with sudden darkness and extinction, by awakening them to too exquisite a perception of its influences, dooms to a slow and poisonous decay those meaner spirits that dare to abjure its dominion." In *The Triumph of Life*, the world's luminaries are still the poets, stars of evening and morning, "heaven's living eyes," but they fade into a double light, the light of nature or the sun, and the harsher and more blinding light of Life, the destructive chariot of the poem's vision. The chariot of Life, like the apocalyptic chariots of Act IV, *Prometheus Unbound*, goes back to the visions of Ezekiel and Revelation for its sources, as the chariots of Dante and Milton did, but now Shelley gives a demonic parody of his sources, possibly following the example of Spenser's chariot of Lucifera. Rousseau is betrayed to the light of life because he began by yielding his imagination's light to the lesser but seductive light of nature, represented in the poem by the "Shape all light" who offers him the waters of natural experience to drink. He drinks, he begins to forget everything in the mind's desire that had transcended nature, and so he falls victim to Life's destruction, and fails to become one of "the sacred few." There is small reason to doubt that Shelley, at the end, saw himself as having shared in Rousseau's fate. The poem, frag-ment as it is, survives its own despair, and stands with Keats's *The Fall of Hyperion* as a marvelously eloquent imaginative testament, fit relic of an achievement broken off too soon to rival Blake's or Wordsworth's, but superior to everything else in its own age.

IX

The great instrument of moral good is the imagination.
　　　　　　　　　　　　　　　　—*A Defence of Poetry*

Anti-Shelleyans have come in all intellectual shapes and sizes, and have included distinguished men of letters from Charles Lamb and De Quincey down to T. S. Eliot, Allen Tate, and their school in our day. To distinguish between the kinds of anti-Shelleyans is in-structive, though the following categories are by no means mutually exclusive. One can count six major varieties of anti-Shelleyans, whether one considers them historically or in contemporary terms:

(1) The school of "common sense"
(2) The Christian orthodox
(3) The school of "wit"
(4) Moralists, of most varieties
(5) The school of "classic" form
(6) Precisionists, or concretists.

It is evident that examples of (1), (2), and (4) need not be con-futed, as they are merely irrelevant. We may deal with (3), (5), and (6) in their own terms, rather than in Shelley's, and still find Shelley triumphant.

The "wit" of Shelley's poetry has little to do with that of seven-teenth-century verse, but has much in common with the dialectical vivacity of Shaw, and something of the prophetic irony of Blake. If irony is an awareness of the terrible gap between aspiration and fulfillment, then the skeptical Shelley is among the most ironical of poets. If it is something else, as it frequently is in the school of Donne, one can observe that there are many wings in the house of wit, and one ought not to live in all of them simultaneously.

Form is another matter, and too complex to be argued fully here. The late C. S. Lewis justly maintained against the school of Eliot that Shelley was more classical in his sense of form, his balance of harmony and design, than Dryden. One can go further: Shelley is almost always a poet of the highest decorum, a stylist who adjusts his form and tone to his subject, whether it be the hammer-beat low style of *The Mask of Anarchy*, the urbane middle style of the *Letter to Maria Gisborne*, or the sublime inventiveness of the high

style as it is renovated in *Prometheus Unbound*. Shelley was sometimes a hasty or careless artist, but he was always an artist, a poet
who neither could nor would stop being a poet. Dr. Samuel Johnson
would have disliked Shelley's poetry, indeed would have considered
Shelley to be dangerously mad, but he would have granted that it
was poetry of a high if to him outmoded order. Critics less classical
than Johnson will not grant as much, because their notions of classical form are not as deeply founded.

The precisionist or concretist is probably Shelley's most effective
enemy, since everything vital in Shelley's poetry deliberately strains
away from the minute particulars of experience. But this is oddly
true of Wordsworth as well, though Wordsworth usually insisted
upon the opposite. The poetry of renovation in the United States,
in our time, had its chief exemplars in William Carlos Williams and
in Wallace Stevens, and it is Stevens who is in the line of both
Wordsworth and of Shelley. Williams' famous adage, "no ideas but
in things," is the self-justified motto of one valid kind of poetic
procedure, but it will not allow for the always relevant grandeurs
of the sublime tradition, with its "great moments" of ecstasy and
recognition. Wordsworth on the mountainside looks out and finds
only a sea of mist, an emblem of the highest imaginative vision, in
which the edges of things have blurred and faded out. Stevens,
opening the door of his house upon the flames of the Northern
Lights, confronts an Arctic effulgence flaring upon the frame of
everything he is, but does not describe the flashing auroras.
Shelley, at his greatest, precisely chants an energetic becoming
that cannot be described in the concrete because its entire purpose
is to modify the concrete, to compel a greater reality to appear:

> . . . the one Spirit's plastic stress
> Sweeps through the dull dense world, compelling there,
> All new successions to the forms they wear;
> Torturing th' unwilling dross that checks its flight
> To its own likeness, as each mass may bear;
> And bursting in its beauty and its might
> From trees and beasts and men into the Heaven's light.

Had Shelley been able to accept any known faith, he would have
given us the name and nature of that "one Spirit." Unlike Keats,
he would not have agreed with Stevens that the great poems of
heaven and hell had been written, and that only the great poem of
earth remained to be composed. His own spirit was apocalyptic,
and the still unwritten poems of heaven and hell waited mute upon
the answering swiftness of his own imaginings, when he went on
to his early finalities:

> As if that frail and wasted human form,
> Had been an elemental god.

Bibliography

(A number of the titles have been shortened)

1. General

Abrams, M. H., ed. *English Romantic Poets*, New York, 1960.
Abrams, M. H., *The Mirror and the Lamp*, New York, 1953.
Auden, W. H., *The Enchafed Flood*, New York, 1950.
Barfield, Owen, *Romanticism Comes of Age*, London, 1965.
Bate, W. J., *From Classic to Romantic*, Cambridge, Mass., 1946.
Bate, W. J., *Criticism: The Major Texts*, New York, 1952.
Bloom, Harold, *The Visionary Company*, New York, 1961.
Bradley, A. C., *A Miscellany*, London, 1929.
Bush, Douglas, *Mythology and the Romantic Tradition in English Poetry*, Cambridge, Mass., 1937.
Cobban, Alfred, *Edmund Burke and the Revolt Against the Eighteenth Century*, London, 1929.
Eliot, T. S., *The Use of Poetry and the Use of Criticism*, Cambridge, Mass., 1933.
Frye, Northrop, *Anatomy of Criticism*, Princeton, 1957.
Frye, Northrop, *Fables of Identity*, New York, 1963.
Frye, Northrop, ed. *Romanticism Reconsidered*, New York, 1963.
Frye, Northrop, *A Study of English Romanticism*, New York, 1968.
Heath-Stubbs, John, *The Darkling Plain*, London, 1950.
Hilles, F. W., and Bloom, Harold, eds. *From Sensibility to Romanticism: Essays Presented to Frederick A. Pottle*, New York, 1965.
James, D. G., *Scepticism and Poetry*, London, 1937.
Kermode, Frank, *Romantic Image*, London, 1957.
Knight, G. Wilson, *The Starlit Dome*, London, 1943.
Langbaum, Robert, *The Poetry of Experience*, New York, 1957.
Lewis, C. S., *Rehabilitations*, London, 1939.
Miles, Josephine, *Eras and Modes in English Poetry*, Berkeley, 1957.
Perkins, David, *The Quest for Permanence*, Cambridge, Mass., 1959.
Wain, John, ed. *Contemporary Reviews of Romantic Poetry*, London, 1953.
Wimsatt, W. K., Jr., and Brooks, Cleanth, *Literary Criticism: A Short History*, New York, 1957.

2. William Blake

Texts:
Erdman, David V., ed. *The Poetry and Prose of William Blake*, [Commentary by Harold Bloom], New York, 1965.
Keynes, Geoffrey, ed. *Poetry and Prose of William Blake*, London, 1927.
Adams, Hazard, *William Blake: A Reading of the Shorter Poems*, Seattle, 1963.
Bloom, Harold, *Blake's Apocalypse*, New York, 1963.
Damon, S. Foster, *A Blake Dictionary*, Providence, 1965.
Damon, S. Foster, *William Blake: His Philosophy and Symbols*, Boston, 1924.
Erdman, David V., *Blake, Prophet against Empire*, Princeton, 1954.
Fisher, Peter F., *The Valley of Vision*, Toronto, 1961.
Frye, Northrop, ed. *Blake*, Englewood Cliffs, 1966.
Frye, Northrop, *Fearful Symmetry*, Princeton, 1947.
Gilchrist, Alexander, *Life of William Blake*, London, 1863; ed. Ruthven Todd, London, 1945.

Gleckner, Robert, *The Piper and the Bard,* Detroit, 1959.
Grant, J. E., ed. *Discussions of William Blake,* Boston, 1961.
Hagstrum, J. H., *William Blake, Poet and Painter,* Chicago, 1964.
Lowery, Margaret, *Windows of the Morning,* New Haven, 1940.
Margoliouth, H. M., *William Blake,* New York, 1951.
Murry, J. M., *William Blake,* London, 1933.
Percival, Milton, *Blake's Circle of Destiny,* New York, 1938.
Pinto, V. de S., ed. *The Divine Vision,* London, 1957.
Schorer, Mark, *Blake: The Politics of Vision,* New York, 1946.
Swinburne, A. C., *William Blake,* London, 1868.
Yeats, W. B., *Essays and Introductions,* New York, 1961.

3. William Wordsworth

Texts:
De Selincourt, Ernest, and Darbishire, Helen, eds. *The Poetical Works of William Wordsworth,* 5 vols., Oxford, 1940–1949.
George, Andrew J., *The Complete Poetical Works of Wordsworth,* Boston, 1904.
Hutchinson, Thomas, ed. *The Poetical Works of William Wordsworth,* London, 1936.
Abercrombie, Lascelles, *The Art of Wordsworth,* London, 1952.
Arnold, Matthew, *Essays in Criticism,* 2nd series, London, 1888.
Bradley A. C., *Oxford Lectures on Poetry,* Oxford, 1909.
Davis, Jack, ed. *William Wordsworth,* Boston, 1963.
Dunklin, G. T., ed. *Wordsworth,* Princeton, 1951.
Ferry, David, *The Limits of Mortality,* Middletown, 1959.
Hartman, Geoffrey, *The Unmediated Vision,* New Haven, 1954.
Hartman, Geoffrey, *Wordsworth's Poetry, 1787–1814,* New Haven, 1965.
Hirsch, E. D., Jr., *Wordsworth and Schelling,* New Haven, 1960.
Jones, John, *The Egotistical Sublime,* London, 1954.
Margoliouth, H. M., *Wordsworth and Coleridge, 1795–1834,* London, 1953.
Marsh, Florence, *Wordsworth's Imagery,* New Haven, 1952.
Moorman, Mary, *William Wordsworth: A Biography,* 2 vols., Oxford, 1957, 1965.
Sperry, W. L., *Wordsworth's Anti-Climax,* Cambridge, Mass., 1935.
Willey, Basil, *The Eighteenth Century Background,* London, 1941.
Williams, Charles, *The English Poetic Mind,* Oxford, 1932.
Woodring, Carl, *Wordsworth,* Boston, 1965.

4. Samuel Taylor Coleridge

Texts:
Coburn, Kathleen, ed. *The Notebooks,* New York, 1957–
Coleridge, E. H., ed. *The Complete Poetical Works,* Oxford, 1912.
Shawcross, J., ed. *Biographia Literaria,* 2 vols., London, 1907.
Bate, W. J., *Coleridge,* New York, 1967.
Beer, J B., *Coleridge, the Visionary,* London, 1959.
Boulger, James, *Coleridge, as Religious Thinker,* New Haven, 1961.
Coburn, Kathleen, ed. *Coleridge,* Englewood Cliffs, 1967.
Coburn, Kathleen, ed. *Inquiring Spirit,* New York, 1951.
House, Humphry, *Coleridge,* London, 1953.
Lowes, J. L., *The Road to Xanadu,* Boston, 1927.
Richards, I. A., *Coleridge on Imagination,* Bloomington, 1960.
Woodring, Carl, *Politics in the Poetry of Coleridge,* Madison, 1961.

5. George Gordon, Lord Byron

Text:
Coleridge, E. H., ed. *The Poetical Works,* London, 1905.
Cooke, M. G., *The Blind Man Traces the Circle,* Princeton, 1969.
Knight, G. Wilson, *The Burning Oracle,* New York, 1939.
Marchand, L. A., *Byron: A Biography,* 3 vols., New York 1957.
McGann, J. J., *Fiery Dust: Byron's Poetic Development,* Chicago, 1968.
Quennell, P. C., *Byron in Italy,* London, 1951.
Quennell, P. C., *Byron: The Years of Fame,* New York, 1935.
Ridenour, George, *The Style of "Don Juan,"* New Haven, 1960.
Rutherford, Andrew, *Byron,* Edinburgh, 1961.
West, Paul, ed. *Byron,* Englewood Cliffs, 1963.

6. Percy Bysshe Shelley

Texts:
Clark, D. L., ed. *Shelley's Prose*, Albuquerque, 1954.
Hutchinson, Thomas, ed. *Complete Poetical Works of Shelley*, London, 1904.
Reiman, D. H., ed. *Shelley's Triumph of Life*, Urbana, 1965.
Baker, Carlos, *Shelley's Major Poetry*, Princeton, 1948.
Bloom, Harold, *Shelley's Mythmaking*, New Haven, 1959.
Blunden, Edmund, *Shelley: A Life Story*, London, 1946.
Brailsford, H. N., *Shelley, Godwin and Their Circle*, New York, 1913.
Hughes, A. M. D., *The Nascent Mind of Shelley*, Oxford, 1947.
Pulos, C. E., *The Deep Truth*, Lincoln, 1954.
Ridenour, G. M., ed. *Shelley*, Englewood Cliffs, 1965.
Santayana, George, *Essays in Literary Criticisms*, New York, 1956.
Todhunter, John, *A Story of Shelley*, London, 1880.
Wasserman, Earl, *The Subtler Language*, Baltimore, 1959.
White, N. I., *Shelley*, 2 vols., New York, 1940.
Wilson, Milton, *Shelley's Later Poetry*, New York, 1959.
Yeats, W. B., *Essays and Introductions*, New York, 1961.
Yeats, W. B., *A Vision*, London, 1937.

7. John Keats

Texts:
Bush, Douglas, ed. *Selected Poems and Letters*, Boston, 1959.
Garrod, H. W., ed. *Poetical Works*, London, 1958.
Rollins, H. E., *The Letters of Keats*, 2 vols., Cambridge, Mass., 1958.
Bate, W. J., *Negative Capability*, Cambridge, Mass., 1939.
Bate, W. J., *John Keats*, Cambridge, Mass., 1963.
Bate, W. J., ed. *Keats, Engl*ewood, Cliffs, 1964.
Bate, W. J., *The Stylistic Development of Keats*, 1945.
Bush, Douglas, *John Keats*, New York, 1966.
Caldwell, J. R., *John Keats' Fancy*, Ithaca, 1945.
Muir, Kenneth, ed. *Keats: A Reassessment*, Liverpool, 1958.
Murry, J. M., *Keats*, 4th ed., New York, 1955.
Murry, J. M., *Keats and Shakespeare*, London, 1926.
Thorpe, C. D., *The Mind of Keats*, New York, 1926.
Wasserman, Earl, *The Finer Tone*, Baltimore, 1953.